ISBN 978-1-5279-1499-5
PIBN 10907467

FB &c Ltd, Dalton House, 60 Windsor Avenue, London, SW19 2RR.
Company number 08720141. Registered in England and Wales.

For support please visit www.forgottenbooks.com

A TREATISE

ON

RIMINAL LA

AND

PROCEDURE

By

T. W. HUGHES

Author of A TREATISE ON EVIDENCE

Dean School of Law

Washburn College

INDIANAPOLIS

THE BOBBS-MERRILL COMPANY

PREFACE

In writing this volume the design of the author has been to produce a book that would state systematically, concisely and with a reasonable measure of completeness, the rules and principles of both the substantive and the adjective law of crimes, and their application. He has taught both phases of the subject for many years and has given them much consideration.

The book is divided into three parts. Part one deals with certain preliminary topics pertaining to the substantive law of crimes. It consists of ten chapters, each of which contains a discussion of a preliminary topic. Part two deals with specific crimes. This part comprises, of course, a very large portion of the book. It contains sixty-three chapters. It divides crimes into seven general classes, as follows: Crimes against: 1, the person; 2, the habitation; 3, property; 4, public justice; 5, public peace; 6, public welfare, health, safety, morals and religion; 7, sovereignty. It then enumerates and discusses the various specific crimes that belong to these respective classes. Part three deals with criminal pleading and procedure. It discusses arrest and extradition, preliminary proceedings, including bail; modes of accusation, including indictment, arraignment and pleas; trial, and the various proceedings after verdict.

The cases supporting the text have been selected with discriminating care, and it is believed that they are sufficiently numerous and apt to serve the purpose intended.

In the preparation of this book, Mr. Aurelius Gale Pheasant has rendered much valuable assistance, and the author acknowledges a deep sense of his appreciation of the high character of these services. The author rests under a similar obligation to Professor Joseph Henry Beale, of Harvard Law School, for help received from his very complete book on Criminal Law. This case book has been used by the author in connection with his instruction in this subject for many years and he has found it exceedingly helpful in the preparation of this volume.

T. W. HUGHES.

Topeka, Kans., September, 1919.

TABLE OF CONTENTS

PART ONE.

PRELIMINARY TOPICS.

CHAPTER I. GENERAL NATURE OF CRIME.

CHAPTER II. SOURCES OF THE LAW OF CRIMES.

CHAPTER III. CONDITIONS OF CRIMINALITY.

CHAPTER IV. AGE LIMITS OF CRIMINAL CAPACITY.

CHAPTER V. MENTAL CAPACITY.

CHAPTER VI. ACT MUST BE VOLUNTARY.

CHAPTER VII. CRIMINAL INTENT.

CHAPTER VIII. THE OVERT ACT.

CHAPTER IX. MERGER OF CRIMES.

CHAPTER X. PARTIES TO CRIMES.

PART TWO.

SPECIFIC CRIMES.

Title One.

CLASSIFICATION OF CRIMES.

CHAPTER XI. CLASSIFICATION OF CRIMES.

Title Two.

CRIMES AGAINST THE PERSON.

CHAPTER XII. ABDUCTION.

CHAPTER XIII. ABORTION.

CHAPTER XIV. ASSAULTS.

PART TWO.

SPECIFIC CRIMES.

TITLE ONE.

CLASSIFICATION OF CRIMES.

CHAPTER XI. CLASSIFICATION OF CRIMES.

TITLE TWO.

CRIMES AGAINST THE PERSON.

CHAPTER XII. ABDUCTION.

CHAPTER XIII. ABORTION.

CHAPTER XIV. ASSAULTS.

CHAPTER XV. CONSPIRACY.

CHAPTER XVI. FALSE IMPRISONMENT.

CHAPTER XVII. HOMICIDE.

CHAPTER XVIII. KIDNAPPING.

CHAPTER XIX. MANSLAUGHTER.

CHAPTER XX. MAYHEM.

CHAPTER XXI. MURDER.

CHAPTER XXII. RAPE.

CHAPTER XXIII. SEDUCTION.

Title Three.

CRIMES AGAINST THE HABITATION.

CHAPTER XXIV. ARSON.

CHAPTER XXV. BURGLARY.

CHAPTER XXXI. MALICIOUS MISCHIEF.

CHAPTER XXXII. ROBBERY.

CHAPTER XXXIII. UTTERING A FORGED DOCUMENT.

TITLE FIVE.

CRIMES AGAINST PUBLIC JUSTICE.

CHAPTER XXXVI. BRIBERY AND EMBRACERY.

CHAPTER XXXV. COMPOUNDING AND MISPRISION OF FELONY.

CHAPTER XXXVI. CONTEMPT.

CHAPTER XXXVII. FRAUDULENT CONVEYANCES, AND CONCEALING PROPERTY.

CHAPTER XXXVIII. OFFICIAL MISCONDUCT.

CHAPTER XXXIX. PERJURY.

CHAPTER XL. RECEIVING STOLEN GOODS.

CHAPTER XLI. RESISTING AN OFFICER.

TITLE SIX.

CRIMES AGAINST PUBLIC PEACE.

CHAPTER XLII. AFFRAY.

CHAPTER XLIII. CARRYING CONCEALED WEAPONS.

CHAPTER XLIV. COMMON BARRATRY, MAINTENANCE AND CHAMPERTY.

CHAPTER XLV. DUELING AND PRIZE FIGHTING.

CHAPTER XLVI. ESCAPE, PRISON BREACH AND RESCUE.

CHAPTER XLVII. FORCIBLE ENTRY AND DETAINER.

CHAPTER XLVIII. LIBEL.

CHAPTER XLIX. UNLAWFUL ASSEMBLY, ROUT AND RIOT.

Title Seven.

CRIMES AGAINST PUBLIC WELFARE, HEALTH, SAFETY, MORALS AND RELIGION.

Article I. Nuisance and Like Offenses Against Morals and the Public Welfare.

CHAPTER L. GENERAL PRINCIPLES.

CHAPTER LI. NUISANCE.

CHAPTER LII. CRUELTY TO ANIMALS.

CHAPTER LIII. DISORDERLY HOUSE.

CHAPTER LIV. GAME.

CHAPTER LV. GAMES AND GAMING.

CHAPTER LVI. LOTTERIES.

CHAPTER LVII. OFFENSES AS TO HIGHWAYS.

CHAPTER LVIII. OFFENSES AGAINST RELIGION.

CHAPTER LIX. VIOLATION OF LIQUOR LAWS.

Article II. Sexual Crimes Against Decency and Morality.

CHAPTER LX. ADULTERY.

CHAPTER LXI. BIGAMY OR POLYGAMY.

CHAPTER LXII. FORNICATION.

CHAPTER LXIII. INCEST.

CHAPTER LXIV. INDECENT CONDUCT AND OBSCENITY.

CHAPTER LXV. MISCEGENATION.

CHAPTER LXVI. SODOMY.

Article III. Violation of the Elective Franchise.

CHAPTER LXVII. OFFENSES AGAINST THE ELECTIVE FRANCHISE.

Article IV. Postal Offenses and Other Federal Crimes.

CHAPTER LXVIII. OTHER FEDERAL CRIMES—POSTAL OFFENSES.

CHAPTER LXIX. COUNTERFEITING AND UTTERING COUNTERFEIT MONEY.

CHAPTER LXX. MISCELLANEOUS FEDERAL OFFENSES.

Article V. Admiralty Crimes.

CHAPTER LXXI. PARTICULAR CRIMES.

Article VI. Miscellaneous Statutory Offenses Under Police Regulations.

CHAPTER LXXII. PARTICULAR OFFENSES.

TITLE EIGHT.

CRIMES AGAINST THE SOVEREIGNTY.

CHAPTER LXXIII. CRIMES AGAINST THE SOVEREIGNTY.

PART THREE.

CRIMINAL PROCEDURE.

CHAPTER LXXIV. PRELIMINARY.

CHAPTER LXXV. ARREST AND EXTRADITION.

CHAPTER LXXVI. PREMIMINARY PROCEEDINGS AND BAIL.

CHAPTER LXXVII. MODES OF ACCUSATION AND INDICTMENT.

CHAPTER LXXVIII. ARRAIGNMENT AND DEFENDANT'S PLEAS.

CHAPTER LXXIX. TRIAL.

CHAPTER LXXX. PROCEEDINGS AFTER VERDICT.

PART ONE

PRELIMINARY TOPICS

CRIMINAL LAW

PART ONE

PRELIMINARY TOPICS

CHAPTER I.

GENERAL NATURE OF CRIME.

§ 1. **Definition of crime.**—A crime is an act injurious to the public, forbidden by law and punishable by the state through a judicial proceeding in its own name.

According to Bishop, "A crime is any wrong which the government deems injurious to the public at large, and punishes through a judicial proceeding in its own name."[1]

Blackstone says a crime is "An act committed or omitted in violation of a public law either forbidding or commanding it."[2] This definition, though often quoted, is faulty in several respects. It is not the act omitted which constitutes a crime, but the omission to act. Again, many acts which are not crimes are prohibited by public laws. Moreover, crimes are punishable only by the sovereign power.

§ 2. **Reasons for and purposes of punishment.**—It may be said that the purpose of punishment is the protection of society. Many theories have been put forth as the basis of punishment. Authorities have variously stated that its object is to prevent the offender from committing future wrongs, to provide for the public self-defense, to reform the offender, to terrify other offenders, to make public punishment an example to others, to bring about retribution for the

[1] 1 Bish. New Crim. L. (8th ed.), § 32.

[2] 4 Bl. Comm. 15.

moral wrong committed, to incite feelings of satisfied virtue among the people. Many of these elements do enter, or have entered, into the punishment of crime. The interests of society apart from the offender require that retribution shall be made for the wrong, and that future similar offenses by him or others shall be discouraged; the interests of society as a whole, including the offender, demand in addition his reformation into a law-abiding citizen. Some of these reasons for punishment are based on expediency, others on right. It is probable that most crimes have been punishable from the standpoint of expediency; but there have been times when the idea of retribution entered most largely into punishment.[8]

In early historical times, among the Anglo-Saxon as well as other peoples, it seems that the distinction between crime and tort did not exist; and the person injured by a murder, theft, or rape, was given the opportunity to avenge himself on the offender, or to compound the offense on the payment of compensation to him. In such times, also, the system of government being mainly tribal or patriarchal, the patriarch or head of the tribe, as its representative, was often the one to declare vengeance, and cause its infliction. A little later in history, when the units of government became larger, certain offenses, generally recognized as being morally wrong, were perceived to affect the security of the government and to defeat the purposes of government, and became the subjects of punishment by the state, first, conceivably, on the theory of retribution, which was the theory of the former private vengeance; next the theory of prevention came into being; and but recently has society become so far-seeing as to realize the general benefit, and so altruistic as to appreciate the benefit to the particular offender, if punishment

[8] Whart. Crim. L. (11th ed.), chaps. 1, 2; Kenny Outlines of Crim. L., ch. 1.

may be made a means of reformation. Historically speaking, it can not be said that the reformation of the offender has been often considered in fixing the punishment for crimes.

Usually there has been some method of proportioning punishment to the moral wrong committed, and moral guilt of the offender, as estimated by the spirit of the times. And naturally, with the passing of time, and changing conditions of life which have made economic conditions much more complex, many acts have been recognized as criminal, and made punishable by the state, which either were not considered criminal before, or could not have taken place at all under former conditions. An old example of this is embezzlement, made a crime by an old English statute, because not punishable under the common law. Late examples are the federal statutes punishing combinations and monopolies in business, or the giving of rebates on railway freights, and the White Slave Act prohibiting the taking of a woman from one state to another for immoral purposes.

§ 3. **Distinctions between a crime and a tort.**—A crime is a wrong which affects the community in its social aggregate capacity. A tort is a wrong, apart from contract, which affects persons in their individual capacity. The former is a public wrong, whereas the latter is a private wrong.

In the case of a crime the wrongdoer is liable to a criminal action by the state; whereas, in the case of a tort he is liable only to a civil action by the person injured. Again, in the former case, the person particularly injured may not condone the offense, whereas in the latter case he may. Moreover, in the case of the higher crimes, and also in the case of misdemeanors which are of a public rather than of a private nature, an agreement by him, in consideration of some reward, not to inform on the wrongdoer, renders himself guilty of a crime. Thus, when the owner of stolen property agrees not to prosecute the thief in consideration that the stolen property be returned to him, he commits the crime of compounding a felony.[4]

§ 4. **The same act both a crime and a tort.**—The same act may be both a crime and a tort. In such a case the wrongdoer is amenable both to a criminal action by the state and to a civil action by the party he has particularly injured. These two actions are separate and distinct. Neither of them is a bar to the other.[5] The object of the former is to punish as an example. The object of the latter is to compensate the injured party.[6] If the offense committed is a misdemeanor either action may precede the other; or both may be carried on at the same time.[7] And in the case of a felony the same rule obtains generally in this country; but in England and in a few of the states of this country the civil action may not precede the criminal action.[8] The basis of the English rule is the fact that holding the civil action in abeyance inspires activity on the part of the complaining witness in the criminal action.

§ 5. **Effect of condonation by party injured.**—Since the object sought in punishing the wrongdoer is the protection of the public and not to obtain redress for the party particularly injured, and since, as a rule, the latter party has no control over the criminal prosecution, the fact that such injured

[4] Commonwealth v. Pease, 16 Mass. 91.

[5] Knox County v. Hunolt, 110 Mo. 67, 19 S. W. 628.

[6] "The difference between crimes and civil injuries is not to be sought in a supposed difference between their tendencies, but in the difference between the mode wherein the sanction is applied in the two cases. An offense which is pursued at the discretion of the injured party, or his representative, is a civil injury. An offense which is pursued by the sovereign, or by a subordinate of the sovereign, is a crime." Aust. Jur., § 17.

[7] Shields v. Yonge, 15 Ga. 349, 60 Am. Dec. 698.

[8] Boody v. Keating, 4 Greenl. (Maine) 164.

party has condoned the offense, or effected a settlement with the wrongdoer, or recovered damages in a civil action, constitutes, ordinarily, no defense.[9] There are, however, some exceptions to this rule, both at common law and by statutory law. Assaults, for example, usually fall within these exceptions; but cases of larceny,[10] embezzlement, false pretenses,[11] forgery,[12] rape,[13] seduction,[14] etc., do not.

§ 6. **Effect of contributory negligence of party injured.**— In civil actions contributory negligence on the part of the plaintiff is usually a complete defense. In criminal actions, however, contributory negligence on the part of the complaining witness is no defense. This is owing to the fact that such actions are brought on behalf of the state to punish the wrong-doer for violating the law, and not to compensate the party particularly injured. In a criminal prosecution for involuntary manslaughter the fact that deceased was guilty of contributory negligence is no defense.[15] And in a criminal prosecution for false pretenses the fact that the victim was credulous and failed to exercise due care to avoid being cheated is no defense.[16]

[9] Commonwealth v. Slattery, 147 Mass. 423, 18 N. E. 399; State v. Noland, 111 Mo. 473, 19 S. W. 715; State v. Keep, 85 Ore. 265, 166 Pac. 936.

[10] Williams v. State, 105 Ga. 606, 31 S. E. 546; State v. Pratt, 98 Mo. 482, 11 S. W. 977.

[11] Commonwealth v. Brown, 167 Mass. 144, 45 N. E. 1.

[12] State v. Tull, 119 Mo. 421, 24 S. W. 1010.

[13] Commonwealth v. Slattery, 147 Mass. 423, 18 N. E. 399; State v. Newcomer, 59 Kans. 668, 54 Pac. 685, Derby's Cases 289.

[14] In re Lewis, 67 Kans. 562, 73 Pac. 77, 63 L. R. A. 281, 100 Am. St. 479.

[15] Belk v. People, 125 Ill. 584, 17 N. E. 744; State v. Moore, 129 Iowa 514, 106 N. W. 16, Derby's Cases 291; Reg. v. Longbottom, 3 Cox Cr. C. 439.

[16] Thomas v. People, 113 Ill. 531; Commonwealth v. Mulrey, 170 Mass. 103, 49 N. E. 91; Crawford v. State, 117 Ga. 247, 43 S. E. 762; Reg. v. Woolley, 4 Cox Cr. C. 193, 3 Car. & P. 98.

§ 7. Effect of contributory negligence of third party.— The contributory negligence of a third party is no defense. The negligence of one party is no excuse for the negligence or wrongful act of another party. Thus, in a criminal prosecution for involuntary manslaughter the fact that the physician who treated the deceased was guilty of gross negligence is no defense.[17] When, however, the intervening act is independent of that of the accused and constitutes the sole cause of the homicide, the accused is not liable for the death.[18] This principle is applicable even when the negligent act of the accused would have caused the death had no independent act intervened.

Again, when the death results from the negligent act of one of two or more parties acting independently of one another, and it is impossible to prove whose act causes the death, all must be acquitted.[19] When, however, all act in concert in a negligent enterprise, and the specific negligent act of one of them causes the death, all are criminally liable. In such a case it is immaterial that it is impossible to prove whose specific act causes the death. Thus, where three persons were culpably negligent in shooting across a public highway at a target, and the shot of one of them killed a boy who was in a tree in his father's garden about four hundred yards from the spot where the shot was fired, all were held guilty of involuntary manslaughter.[20]

§ 8. Effect of intentional wrong of the party injured.— The fact that the complaining witness was himself guilty of a crime or a tort growing out of the same transaction is no defense. Thus, in a case of false pretenses the fact that the complaining witness was also guilty of making false pre-

17 Commonwealth v. Hackett, 84 Mass. 136; Reg. v. Davis, 15 Cox Cr. C. 174.

18 Livingston v. Commonwealth, 14 Grat. (Va.) 592; State v. Scates, 50 N. Car. 420.

19 People v. Woody, 45 Cal. 289.

20 Reg. v. Salmon, 14 Cox Cr. C. 494; Derby's Cases 145.

tenses and thereby defrauded the accused is no defense.[21] However, if the complaining witness has also subjected himself to a prosecution for a like offense, he also may be punished.[22] In a case of uttering counterfeit money the fact that the complaining witness was a prostitute and received the counterfeit in payment of an illegal act is no defense.[23] And in a case of larceny or embezzlement the fact that the party from whom the property was stolen or embezzled had himself stolen or embezzled it is no defense.[24] A few courts, however, have held the contrary.[25] This contrary view, however, is wrong upon principle and not in accord with the weight of authority.

§ 9. **Effect of consent of person wronged.**—In a civil action, consent of the party injured is usually a defense. It was said in an English case that "whatever may be the effect of a consent in a suit between party and party, it is not in the power of any man to give an effectual consent to that which amounts to, or has a direct tendency to create a breach of the peace, so as to bar a criminal prosecution. Though a man may by his consent debar himself from his right to maintain a civil action, he can not thereby defeat proceedings instituted by the crown in the interests of the public for the maintenance of good order." So it was held that persons who had consented to fight each other, were each guilty of an assault on the other.[26] Where one was tried for manslaughter caused by a collision on a football field, it was

21 People v. Watson, 75 Mich. 582, 42 N. W. 1005; Gilmore v. People, 87 Ill. App. 128, Derby's Cases 292; Reg. v. Hudson, 8 Cox Cr. C. 305.

22 Commonwealth v. Morrill, 8 Cush. (Mass.) 571. See also In re Cummins, 16 Colo. 451, 27 Pac. 887, 13 L. R. A. 752, 25 Am. St. 291.

23 Reg. v. ——, 1 Cox Cr. C. 250.

24 Commonwealth v. Smith, 129 Mass. 104; Rex v. Beacall, 1 Car. & P. 454.

25 McCord v. People, 46 N. Y. 470 (in this case Justice Peckham gives an able dissenting opinion); State v. Crowley, 41 Wis. 271, 22 Am. Rep. 719.

26 Reg. v. Coney, 8 Q. B. Div. 534, Derby's Cases 267; Auge v. Woodmen, 173 N. Car. 33, 91 S. E. 586.

said that if accused was playing the game according to its rules, the jury might infer he was not guilty of a criminal intent, although no rules or practice of any game can make that lawful which is unlawful by the law of the land, and the law is that one shall not do that which is likely to cause another's death.[27]

Where a girl removed all her clothing to submit to a massage treatment, she did not thereby consent to indecent liberty taken with her by the healer.[28]

A married man suffering from a venereal disease who, without informing her of the disease, has intercourse with his wife, and infects her, is not criminally liable for the assault, notwithstanding the dastardly moral nature of the act.[29] The consent of the woman was sufficient to render the act not an assault.

A taking by voluntary consent does not constitute larceny; but mere exposing property with the expectation that the accused will take it is not a consent in law.[30]

§ 10. **Effect of entrapment.**—As a general rule, entrapment of the accused, either by the injured party or by the public authorities, is no defense; and in order to catch suspected persons, a complete opportunity to commit crime may be designedly given with the law's sanction.[31] Thus, the fact that a detective or other person buys intoxicating liquor with the view of prosecuting the vendor for selling it in violation of the law is no defense.[32] Nor the fact that a

27 Reg. v. Bradshaw, 14 Cox Cr. C. 83, Derby's Cases 269.

28 Bartell v. State, 106 Wis. 342, 82 N. W. 142, Derby's Cases 271.

29 Reg. v. Clarence, 16 Cox Cr. C. 511, Derby's Cases 272.

30 Lowe v. State, 44 Fla. 449, 32 So. 956, 103 Am. St. 171, Derby's Cases 279.

31 Williams v. State, 55 Ga. 391; Tones v. State, 48 Tex. Cr. 363, 88 S. W. 217, 1 L. R. A. (N. S.) 1024, 122 Am. St. 759, Derby's Cases 283; State v. Tibbs, 109 Minn. 247, 123 N. W. 54, 25 L. R. A. (N. S.) 449; Commonwealth v. Hollister, 157 Pa. St. 13, 27 Atl. 386, 25 L. R. A. 349; State v. Smith, 152 N. Car. 798, 67 S. E. 508, 30 L. R. A. (N. S.) 946n.

32 People v. Murphy, 93 Mich. 41, 52 N. W. 1042.

postal inspector by the use of decoy letters detects a person engaged in sending obscene matter, or letters the mailing of which is forbidden, through the mails;[33] nor the fact that a constable, with the view of arresting and prosecuting thieves, disguises himself, feigns drunkenness, lies down in an alley and remains passive while his pockets are being picked;[34] nor the fact that the occupant of a dwelling-house, who suspects a person of intention to commit burglary, leaves the door unlocked and watches with an officer with the view of arresting the expected intruder;[35] nor that an officer procures a key for another to take an impression and thereby enables him to break into a store room;[36] nor the fact that an officer, authorized to administer oaths, with the view of prosecuting the affiant for false swearing administers to him a false oath knowing at the time that the affiant's purpose is to obtain funds to which he knows he is not entitled;[37] nor that a woman represents she wants an abortion performed, in order merely to entrap a physician.[38]

It is to be observed, however, that the entrapment must not extend beyond passive participation. In other words the accused must not be solicited or actively encouraged to commit the offense.[39] In harmony with this view, the cases hold that acts, otherwise criminal, committed against property at the instigation and by the encouragement of a de-

33 Price v. United States, 165 U. S. 311, 41 L. ed. 727, 17 Sup. Ct. 360; Grimm v. United States, 156 U. S. 604, 39 L. ed. 550, 15 Sup. Ct. 470; Kemp v. United States, 41 App. D. C. 539, 51 L. R. A. (N. S.) 825, and note on instigation or consent to crime for purpose of detecting criminal as a defense to prosecution.

34 People v. Hanselman, 76 Cal. 460, 18 Pac. 425, 9 Am. St. 238.

35 State v. Jansen, 22 Kans. 498; People v. Laird, 102 Mich. 135, 60 N. W. 457; State v. Abley, 109 Iowa 61, 80 N. W. 225, 46 L. R. A. 862, 77 Am. St. 520, Derby's Cases 280.

36 State v. Abley, 109 Iowa 61, 80 N. W. 225, 46 L. R. A. 862, 77 Am. St. 220, Derby's Cases 280.

37 Thompson v. State, 120 Ga. 132, 47 S. E. 566.

38 People v. Conrad, 102 App. Div. 566, 92 N. Y. S. 606, 19 N. Y. Cr. 259, Derby's Cases 286.

39 Love v. People, 160 Ill. 501, 43 N. E. 710, 32 L. R. A. 139; Koscak v. State, 160 Wis. 255, 152 N. W. 181.

tective, who acts in pursuance of a plan previously arranged with the owner of the property, do not constitute a crime. Thus, where a person is employed by cattle owners to catch suspected thieves, and he, with their authority and consent, co-operates with the suspected parties in planning to take, and in taking, the cattle of such owners, no larceny is committed.[40] For to constitute larceny the property must be taken without the owner's voluntary consent.[41] The same is true of the crime of robbery.

But acquiescence on the part of railroad officials to the robbery of passengers on their trains, with the view of entrapping the guilty parties, is no defense.[42] This is owing to the fact that such officials are incapable of giving authoritative consent to such an act. For a like reason it is no defense to a charge of stealing public records that the officer intrusted with their custody delivered them to the accused with the view of entrapping him.[43] And where a person is charged with selling intoxicating liquor illegally it is no defense that the public authorities furnished the money to purchase it.[44] On the other hand, public sentiment does not favor the entrapment of would-be criminals by such detective methods. And some courts are decidedly inclined to take the same view.[45] As said in one case: "Human nature is frail enough at best, and requires no encouragement in wrongdoing. If we can not assist another and prevent him

[40] State v. Hull, 33 Ore. 56, 54 Pac. 159, 72 Am. St. 694; Connor v. People, 18 Colo. 373, 33 Pac. 159, 25 L. R. A. 341n, 36 Am. St. 295.

[41] State v. Waghalter, 177 Mo. 676, 76 S. W. 1028; State v. Adams, 115 N. Car. 775, 20 S. E. 722.

[42] State v. West, 157 Mo. 309, 57 S. W. 1071.

[43] People v. Mills, 178 N. Y. 274, 70 N. E. 786, 67 L. R. A. 131.

[44] Evanston v. Myers, 172 Ill. 266, 50 N. E. 204; State v. Smith, 152 N. Car. 798, 67 S. E. 508, 30 L. R. A. (N. S.) 946n.

[45] People v. McCord, 76 Mich. 200, 42 N. W. 1106; Love v. People, 160 Ill. 501, 43 N. E. 710, 32 L. R. A. 139; State v. Hayes, 105 Mo. 76, 16 S. W. 514, 24 Am. St. 360; Dalton v. State, 113 Ga. 1037, 39 S. E. 468; State v. Abley, 109 Iowa 61, 80 N. W. 225, 46 L. R. A. 862, 77 Am. St. 520, Derby's Cases 280; People v. Mills, 178 N. Y. 274, 70 N. E. 786, 67 L. R. A. 131.

from violating the laws of the land, we at least should abstain from any active efforts in the way of leading him into temptation."[46] Thus, where persons are desirous of prosecuting criminally a certain public official, and without any previous solicitation on his part they co-operate with the public authorities and lead him to accept a bribe, the accused should be acquitted.[47] This view, although the better one, is not supported by the weight of authority.[48] The adoption of devices to entrap criminals is legitimate and proper, provided they do not constitute active invitations to commit the acts.[49] It has been held that where a private detective incites another party to commit larceny that he himself is guilty of the crime.[50]

§ 11. **Effect of repentance and withdrawal from the act.**—Where two persons conspire to commit a crime and one of them repents and withdraws before the commission of the act he is not liable for the commission of the crime by the other, provided he informs the other beforehand of his intention to withdraw. This information may be conveyed to the other party either by words or acts. Moreover, if the party who withdraws does acts which naturally should inform the other party of his intention, but which do not, such acts are proper for the consideration of the jury in determining the relation of the party who withdraws to the crime subsequently committed.[51]

§ 12. **An act or omission to constitute a crime must be so declared by law and must be contrary to law when committed.**—The mere fact that an act or omission is sinful, or morally wrong, does not make it a crime. To be a crime it

[46] Saunders v. People, 38 Mich. 218; Sam Yick v. United States, 240 Fed. 60, 153 C. C. A. 96.

[47] State v. Dudoussat, 47 La. Ann. 977, 17 So. 685; People v. Liphardt, 105 Mich. 80, 62 N. W. 1022.

[48] People v. Liphardt, 105 Mich. 80, 62 N. W. 1022.

[49] Clark & M. Law of Crimes (2d ed.) 227.

[50] Slaughter v. State, 113 Ga. 284, 38 S. E. 854, 84 Am. St. 242.

[51] State v. Allen, 47 Conn. 121.

must be so declared by law. Moreover, to convict a person of a crime it must be punishable as such both at the time it is committed and at the time of conviction.[52]

The Constitution of the United States and most of the state constitutions forbid the passage of ex post facto laws; that is, laws prescribing a punishment for acts previously committed which were not then punishable, or which increase the punishment for past acts beyond that possible when they were committed.

And likewise, if a statute making an act a crime has been repealed, and later another statute is enacted covering the same offense, one can not be convicted for an act done in the interim between the repeal of the former act and the passage of the latter.[53] Nor can an act not an offense when committed become such by a subsequent independent act of the party with which it has no connection; that is, the criminal intent must exist when the act was done and can not be imputed from a subsequent independent transaction. So where one obtained goods upon false representations as to his business, which was not a crime, and later went into bankruptcy, he is not punishable under a federal statute which penalizes obtaining goods upon false credits by one within three months before the beginning of bankruptcy proceedings respecting him.[54]

§ 13. **When omission to act is a crime.**—There are many statutes which make the omission to do certain things misdemeanors; as for instance the failure to shovel snow off a sidewalk. Sometimes convictions of felony are sustained because of omission to act. A switch-tender who failed to adjust a switch and caused a passenger train to be thrown off the track and a passenger killed, was convicted of manslaughter, because the circumstances of his omission of duty

[52] Commonwealth v. Marshall, 11 Pick. (Mass.) 350, 22 Am. Dec. 377, Derby's Cases 47.

[53] Commonwealth v. Marshall, 28 Mass. 350, 22 Am. Dec. 377, Derby's Cases 47.

[54] United States v. Fox, 95 U. S. 670, 24 L. ed. 538, Derby's Cases 45.

were such as to make his negligence gross, culpable, and criminal.[55] A similar rule was applied where one in charge of the engine which hoisted or lowered men into a mine by baskets, left a fifteen-year-old boy in charge, and a miner was thrown out of the basket and killed because the boy did not understand how to work the machinery.[56]

But a conviction of manslaughter was set aside where one was living in adultery with a woman and they had been drinking intoxicating liquor steadily for two or three days and she took morphine without his knowledge, and was sent out of the house in the care of another into a basement room in a stupified condition, where she died. It was held in this case that he was not under any legal duty to take care for her protection.[57]

§ 14. **Acts mala in se and acts mala prohibita.**—Acts mala in se are acts which are inherently wrong, and not wrong merely owing to legislative enactment. They include all of the common-law crimes.

Acts mala prohibita are acts which are not inherently wrong but which are wrong merely because they are prohibited and made punishable by statutory law. They include those crimes which do not involve criminal intent.

The distinction between these two classes of crimes is sometimes of great importance. Thus, where a person, while driving at a speed prohibited by a city ordinance, but not recklessly, unintentionally runs over a person and seriously injures him he is not criminally liable for assault and battery;[58] nor would he be liable for involuntary manslaughter should the injured party die. On the other hand, if his driving is reckless, and therefore malum in se, he may be held criminally liable for the unintended result.

[55] State v. O'Brien, 32 N. J. L. 169, Derby's Cases 48.

[56] Reg. v. Lowe, 4 Cox Cr. C. 449, Derby's Cases 50.

[57] People v. Beardsley, 150 Mich. 206, 113 N. W. 1128, 121 Am. St. 617, Derby's Cases 51.

[58] Commonwealth v. Adams, 114 Mass. 323, 19 Am. Rep. 362, Derby's Cases 115.

§ 15. Police wrongs and criminal wrongs.—The distinction between police wrongs and criminal wrongs is often made. Mr. Wharton says, "By criminal wrongs the existence of the state is assailed; by police wrongs, only the administration of its economical structure: The first attack the fundamental institutes of society, the latter only its modes of operation; the first concern principle, the second concern procedure. It is true that the two classes melt undefinably into each other, as is the case with civil and criminal wrongs, and that an offense which in one aspect is a police wrong is a criminal wrong in another aspect. But that there is a distinction in ethics there can be no question, the one case involving, the other not involving, a moral taint. Nor can we refuse to admit a distinction in law. * * * Police offenses * * * are usually breaches of affirmative and not of negative commands. The police law says: 'You must do a particular thing.' The offender, either designedly or negligently omits to do this thing. A criminal offense on the other hand, is a breach of negative command; 'Thou shalt not steal.' "[59] However, not all police wrongs are concerned with administration. As said by McClain, "Aside from the crimes recognized at common law and resting on the general principles of protection to life, the person and property, new offenses are constantly being created by statute to prevent the commission of acts deemed by the legislature to be inimical to the public welfare, some of which are so analogous to common-law crimes that no other reason for their punishment need be suggested than the better protection of the public against classes of acts which have before been recognized as criminal, while others rest on doctrines of expediency not of such general recognition, and yet deemed sufficient by the legislature to warrant the infliction of a criminal punishment upon the violator."[60]

59 Whart. Crim. L. (11th ed.), § 29. See also Oshkosh v. Schwartz, 55 Wis. 483, 13 N. W. 552.

60 McClain Crim. L., § 23.

There are certain offenses recognized by the common law, such as being a common scold, or a common barrator, which are practically obsolete. There are many statutory offenses, such as the selling of intoxicating liquors without license, adulterating food, selling impure milk or imitation butter, practicing law or medicine without license, following certain occupations without license, taking usury, driving automobiles through cities at a rapid speed, quarantine regulations, traffic regulations, street, fire and market regulations, the protection of fish and game, regulation of sales, vagrancy, using false weights and measures, abandonment of a wife, mailing obscene matter, taking women from one state to another for immoral purposes, and others, many of which involve no moral turpitude and no common-law guilt. Most of these offenses would subject the offender to a common-law action for tort by the injured party.

As a general rule, in police offenses, it is not necessary that evil consequences result from the violation of law; it is enough that the law is violated.[61] The offenses are such that not every violation of the law would produce evil results. The prohibition is made because some violations produce such results.

The element of intent does not enter into many of these wrongs, but the person is punished irrespective of intent.[62] Attempts to commit police wrongs are not punishable.[63] Nor can accessories be involved in such offenses.[64]

[61] Commonwealth v. Starr, 144 Mass. 359, 11 N. E. 533; In re Ahart, 172 Cal. 762, 159 Pac. 160.

[62] State v. Ferry Line Auto Bus Co., 99 Wash. 64, 168 Pac. 893; Commonwealth v. New York C. & H. R. Ry. Co., 202 Mass. 394, 88 N. E. 764, 123 L. R. A. (N. S.) 350n, 132 Am. St. 507, 16 Am. Cas. 587; Commanwealth v. Closson, 229 Mass. 329, 118 N. E. 653.

[63] Hill v. State, 53 Ga. 125; Rex v. Upton, 2 Strange 816.

[64] Commonwealth v. Willard, 22 Pick. (Mass.) 476; Pulse v. State, 5 Humph. (Tenn.) 108.

CHAPTER II.

SOURCES OF THE LAW OF CRIMES.

§ 20. **The five sources of law.**—In the United States there are five sources of law. These five sources, in the order of superiority, are as follows: (1) The United States Constitution (2) acts of congress; (3) state constitutions; (4) acts of state and territorial legislatures; and (5) the common law If a provision of the United States Constitution conflicts with an act of congress the latter is void. If a valid act of congress conflicts with a provision of a state constitution the latter is void. If a provision of a state constitution conflicts with a statute of the same state the latter is void; and if an act of a state or territorial legislature conflicts with a provision of the common law the latter is void.

§ 21. **The United States Constitution.**—The United States Constitution, together with the treaties made in pursuance thereof, constitutes the supreme law of the land.

It provides that the trial of all crimes, except in cases of impeachment, shall be by jury; and that such trials shall be held in the state where the said crimes shall have been committed; but when not committed within any state, the trial shall be at such place or places as the congress may by law have directed.[1]

It also provides that treason against the United States shall consist only in levying war against them, or in adhering to their enemies, giving them aid and comfort; and that no person shall be convicted of treason, unless on the testimony of two witnesses to the same overt act, or on confession in open court.[2]

It further provides that a person charged in any state with treason, felony, or other crime, who shall flee from justice, and be found in another state, shall on demand of the executive authority of the state from which he fled, be delivered up to be removed to the state having jurisdiction of the crime.[3]

§ 22. **Acts of congress.**—Congress has no inherent power whatever. In this respect it differs widely from a state legislature. It has only such powers as are conferred upon it expressly or impliedly by the United States Constitution.[4] Moreover, this instrument contains some express restrictions upon its powers.[5] All legislative powers, however, granted by the United States Constitution, are conferred upon congress.[6] It has power to legislate not only for the United States as a whole but also for the territories and for the District of Columbia.[7]

§ 23. **State constitutions.**—State constitutions differ materially from the United States Constitution. The former constitute, for the most part, restrictions or limitations of powers; whereas the latter constitutes, for the most part, grants of powers.

The constitution of Illinois, which may be taken as typical,

1 U. S. Const., art. III, § 2.

2 U. S. Const., art. III, § 3.

3 U. S. Const., art. IV, § 2.

4 United States v. Arizona, 120 U. S. 479, 30 L. ed. 728.

5 U. S. Const., art. I, § 9.

6 U. S. Const., art. I § 1.

7 U. S. Const., art. I, § 8. See also Reynolds v. United States, 98 U. S. 244, 25 L. ed. 244.

in this respect, of most states, contains, among others, the following provisions:

"No person shall be deprived of life, liberty or property, without due process of law.[8]

"Every person may freely speak, write and publish on all subjects, being responsible for the abuse of that liberty; and in all trials for libel, both civil and criminal, the truth, when published with good motives and for justifiable ends, shall be a sufficient defense.[9]

"The right of trial by jury as heretofore enjoyed, shall remain inviolate; * * *[10]

"The right of the people to be secure in their persons, houses, papers and effects, against unreasonable searches and seizures, shall not be violated; and no warrant shall issue without probable cause, supported by affidavit, particularly describing the place to be searched, and the persons or things to be seized.[11]

"All persons shall be bailable by sufficient sureties, except for capital offenses, where the proof is evident or the presumption great; and the privilege or writ of habeas corpus shall not be suspended, unless when in cases of rebellion or invasion the public safety may require it.[12]

"No persons shall be held to answer for a criminal offense, unless on indictment of a grand jury, except in cases in which the punishment is by fine, or imprisonment otherwise than in the penitentiary, in cases of impeachment, and in cases arising in the army and navy, or in the militia, when in actual service in time of war or public danger: Provided, that the grand jury may be abolished by law in all cases.[13]

"In all criminal prosecutions the accused shall have the right to appear and defend in person and by counsel, to demand the nature and cause of the accusation and to have a copy thereof, to meet the witnesses face to face, and to have

[8] Ill. Const. (1870), art. II, § 2.

[9] Ill. Const (1870), art. II, § 4.

[10] Ill. Const. (1870), art. II, § 5.

[11] Ill. Const. (1870), art. II, § 6.

[12] Ill. Const. (1870), art. II, § 7.

[13] Ill. Const. (1870), art. II, § 8.

process to compel the attendance of witnesses in his behalf, and a speedy public trial by an impartial jury of the county or district in which the offense is alleged to have been committed.[14]

"No person shall be compelled in any criminal case to give evidence against himself, or be twice put in jeopardy for the same offense.[15]

"All penalties shall be proportioned to the nature of the offense, and no conviction shall work corruption of blood or forfeiture of estate; nor shall any person be transported out of the state for any offense committed within the same.[16]

"No person shall be imprisoned for debt, unless upon refusal to deliver up his estate for the benefit of his creditors, in such manner as shall be prescribed by law, or in cases where there is strong presumption of fraud.[17]

"No ex post facto law, * * * shall be passed."[18]

§ 24. **Acts of state legislatures.**—State legislatures, unlike congress, have inherent power to declare acts criminal and to impose penalties for their violation. Their power, however, in these respects, is not absolute. Their enactments must not conflict with any provision of the United States Constitution, or of the state constitution, or with any valid act of congress. Barring these limitations, however, their legislative authority is absolute; and their enactments, when they become law, must be enforced by the courts.[19] "It is the province of the legislature to determine in the interest of the public what shall be permitted or forbidden, and

[14] Ill. Const. (1870), art. II, § 9. See also Watt v. People, 126 Ill. 9, 18 N. E. 340, 1 L. R. A. 403.

[15] Ill. Const (1870), art. II, § 10.

[16] Ill. Const. (1870), art. II, § 11.

[17] Ill. Const. (1870), art. II, § 12. This provision has reference solely to debts arising ex contractu, and is not applicable to fines or penalties arising from criminal actions, or to obligations arising from tort actions. Kennedy v. People, 122 Ill. 649, 13 N. E. 213.

[18] Ill. Const. (1870) art. II, § 14.

[19] Powell v. Commonwealth, 114 Pa. St. 265, 7 Atl. 913, 60 Am. Rep. 350, 127 U. S. 678, 32 L. ed. 253, 8 Sup. Ct. 992, 1257; Commonwealth v. Evans, 132 Mass.. 11; State v. Addington, 77 Mo. 110.

the statutes contain very many instances of acts prohibited, the criminality of which consists solely in the fact that they are prohibited, and not at all in their intrinsic quality. The unnecessary multiplication of mere statutory offenses is undoubtedly an evil, and the general interests are best promoted by allowing the largest practical liberty of individual action, but nevertheless the justice and wisdom of penal legislation, and its extent within constitutional limits, is a matter resting in the judgment of the legislative branch of the government with which courts can not interfere."[20]

§ 25. **Acts of territorial legislatures.**—Territorial legislatures are created by congress, and their powers are limited to those conferred upon them by that body. Their legislative power "shall extend to all rightful subjects of legislation not inconsistent with the Constitution and laws of the United States."[21]

§ 26. **Acts of the British parliament.**—The British parliament, like state legislatures, has inherent power to declare acts criminal and to impose penalties for their violation. Unlike state legislatures, however, its hands are not tied by any written constitution. Its power to enact laws, therefore, is absolute.

§ 27. **The English common law.**—The basis of the English common law is immemorial usage and custom, and not legislative enactment. For this reason it is often called the "unwritten law." The generic term "common law" has been well defined as "those maxims, principles, and forms of judicial proceedings, which have no written law to prescribe or warrant them, but which, founded on the laws of nature and the dictates of reason, have, by usage and custom, become interwoven with the written laws; and, by such incor-

[20] People v. West, 106 N. Y. 293, 12 N. E. 610, 60 Am Rep. 452 As to acts which legislatures may or may not declare criminal, see note to 78 Am. St. 235-274. See also Booth v. People, 186 Ill. 43, 57 N. E. 798, 50 L. R. A. 762. 78 Am. St. 229.

[21] U. S. Comp. Stat. (1916), § 3438.

poration, form a part of the municipal code of each state or nation, which has emerged from the loose and erratic habits of savage life, to civilization, order, and government of laws."[22] "The authority of these maxims [and rules of the common law] rests entirely upon general reception and usage."[23]

§ 28. **The American common law.**—The American common law is similar in most respects to the English common law. In so far, however, as the latter is inapplicable to our conditions and surroundings it is not a part of our common law. On the other hand, it includes some usages adopted by the colonists, some English statutes in force when they settled in this country, and a few enacted afterward and before the Revolution. The Supreme Court of the United States has decided that English statutes which were enacted before the emigration of our ancestors, and which were in force at that time, and which are applicable to our conditions and surroundings, constitute a part of our common law.[24]

§ 29. **The common law as defined by legislature.**—The common law of many states is expressly defined by an act of the legislature. The Illinois act, which is practically the same as that of other states, provides "That the common law of England, so far as the same is applicable and of a general nature, and all statutes or acts of the British parliament made in aid of, and to supply the defects of the common law, prior to the fourth year of James the First, excepting the second section of the sixth chapter of 43d Elizabeth, the eighth chapter of 13th Elizabeth, and ninth chapter of 37th Henry Eighth, and which are of a general nature and not local to that kingdom, shall be the rule of decision, and shall

22 Ohio v. Lafferty, Tappan (Ohio) 81.

23 1 Bl. Comm. 68. See also, 6 Am. & Eng. Encyc. L. (2d ed.) 270, 271.

24 Patterson v. Winn, 5 Pet. (U. S.) 233, 241, 8 L. ed. 311. See also Nider v. Commonwealth, 140 Ky. 684, 131 S. W. 1024, Ann. Cas. 1913 E, 1246 and note on Adoption of Common Law in Relation to Crimes.

be considered as of full force until repealed by legislative authority."[25] The fourth year of James I began on March 24, 1606.

Criminal offenses, not defined in the Criminal Code of Illinois, are punishable under the common law.[26] In some states there are no criminal offenses except those expressly declared by statute.

In the absence of evidence of the contrary, the courts of any state presume that the common law prevails in the sister states.[27]

§ 30. **Mode of determining the common law.**—The common law of England may be found by reference to the decisions of the common law courts of that country.[28] "Judges are bound to resort to the best sources of instruction, such as the records of courts of justice, well authenticated histories of trials, and books of reports, digests, and brief statements of such decisions, prepared by suitable persons, and the treatises of sages of the profession, whose works have an established reputation for correctness."[29] Among the sages of the profession whose works have an established reputation for correctness are Coke, Hale, Hawkins, Foster and East. Stephens says, "Somehow, no one can say precisely how, * * * certain principles came to be accepted as the law of the land. The judges held themselves bound to decide the cases which came before them according to those principles, and, as new combinations of circumstances threw light on the way in which they operated, the principles were, in some cases, more and more fully developed and qualified, and in others evaded or practically set at naught and repealed. Thus, in order to ascertain what the

[25] Illinois: Hurd's Rev. Stat. (1916) ch. 28, § 1.

[26] Illinois: Jones & Add. Ann. Stat., ch. 38, div. II, § 20 (par. 3985).

[27] Van Ingen v. Brabrook, 27 Ill. App. 401.

[28] Kreitz v. Behrensmeyer, 149 Ill. 496, 36 N. E. 983, 24 L. R. A. 59.

[29] Chief Justice Shaw in Commonwealth v. Chapman, 13 Metc. (Mass.) 68.

principle is at any given moment, it is necessary to compare together a number of decided cases, and to deduce from them the principle which they establish."[80] It is to be observed that it is not essential that the facts of the case in question be "on all fours" with those of a decided case. The analogy between them may be sufficient to justify the application to the former of the principles established by the latter.[81]

§ 31. Importance of the common law.—The great importance of the common law is sometimes lost sight of. However, it constitutes the basis of instruction in all the leading law schools of the country. The reason is, that the common law is the foundation of our legal system. "To a very great extent, the unwritten law constitutes the basis of our jurisprudence, and furnishes the rules by which public and private rights are established and secured, the social relations of all persons regulated, their rights, duties, and obligations determined, and all violations of duty redressed and punished. Without its aid, the written law, embracing the constitution and statute laws, would constitute but a lame, partial, and impracticable system. Even in many cases where statutes have been made in respect to particular subjects, they could not be carried into effect, and must remain a dead letter, without the aid of the common law. In cases of murder and manslaughter, the statute declares the punishment; but what acts shall constitute murder, what manslaughter, or what justifiable or excusable homicide, are left to be decided by the rules and principles of the common law. If an act is made criminal, but no mode of prosecution is directed, or no punishment provided, the common law furnishes its ready aid, prescribing the mode of prosecution by indictment, the common-law punishment of fine and imprisonment. Indeed, it seems to be too obvious to require argument, that with-

80 Introduction to Steph. Dig. Crim. L., p. VIII.

81 Steph. Dig. Crim. L. (5th ed), art. 178. See also, Walsh v. People, 65 Ill. 58, 16 Am. Rep. 569; Commonwealth v. York, 9 Metc. (Mass.) 93.

out the common law, our legislation and jurisprudence would be impotent, and wholly deficient in completeness and symmetry, as a system of municipal law."[32]

§ 32. **Abolition of the common law.**—In some states, including Ohio, Oregon and Minnesota, all common-law crimes are abolished by statute.[33] In several other states, including Michigan, Iowa, Indiana, Kansas, Texas, Nebraska and Oregon no act is a crime unless so declared by statute; but in these states the principles of the common law are applied in construing the statute. In other words, the statute may limit the description of the crime to its common-law name, in which case the principles of the common law may be resorted to in determining what acts are essential to constitute the crime.[34]

In most of the states, however, common-law crimes have not been abolished. In a state which has a criminal code, but which has not expressly abolished common-law crimes, like Illinois, a common-law crime not covered by the code is still punishable.[35]

§ 33. **Federal courts have no common-law jurisdiction in criminal cases.**—Under the United States Constitution the

[32] Chief Justice Shaw in Commonwealth v. Chapman, 13 Metc. (Mass.) 68. See also State v. Lafferty, Tappan (Ohio C. P.) 81, Derby's Cases 3; State v. Pulle, 12 Minn. 164, Derby's Cases 6.

[33] Johnson v. State, 66 Ohio St. 59, 63 N. E. 607, 90 Am. St. 564; State v. Shaw, 39 Minn. 153, 39 N. W. 305; State v. Ayers, 49 Ore. 61, 88 Pac. 653, 10 L. R. A. (N. S.) 992, 124 Am. St. 1036.

[34] In re Lamphere, 61 Mich. 105, 27 N. W. 882; In re Lambrecht, 137 Mich. 450, 100 N. W. 606; State v. Twogood, 7 Iowa 252; Stephens v. State, 107 Ind. 185, 8 N. E. 94; Ledgerwood v. State, 134 Ind. 81, 33 N. E. 631; State v. Young, 55 Kans. 349, 40 Pac. 659; Prindle v. State, 31 Tex. Cr. 551, 21 S. W. 360, 37 Am. St. 833; State v. De Wolfe, 67 Nebr. 321, 93 N. W. 746; State v. Gaunt, 13 Ore. 115, 9 Pac. 55; State v. Clough (Ia.), 165 N. W. 59.

[35] Smith v. People, 25 Ill. 9, 76 Am. Dec. 780; Commonwealth v. McHale, 97 Pa. St. 397, 39 Am. Rep. 808. See also Nider v. Commonwealth, 140 Ky. 684, 131 S. W. 1024, Ann. Cas. 1913E, 1246, and note on Adoption of Common Law in Relation to Crimes.

federal courts have no jurisdiction except that conferred upon them by congress. To render an act punishable as a crime against the United States, congress must declare it a crime, affix a penalty, and declare the court which shall have jurisdiction of the offense.[36] It follows, therefore, that the federal courts have no common-law jurisdiction in criminal cases.[37]

[36] United States v. Hudson, 7 Cranch (U. S.) 32, 3 L. ed. 259; United States v. Eaton, 144 U. S. 677, 36 L. ed. 591, 12 Sup. Ct. 764, Derby's Cases 1; United States v. Stickrath, 242 Fed. 151.

[37] United States v. Miller, 236 Fed. 798.

CHAPTER III.

CONDITIONS OF CRIMINALITY.

§ 35. **Conditions of criminality.**—To render a person criminally responsible for the commission of a common-law crime, four conditions must exist. These four conditions of criminality are as follows: (1) The person must be of sufficient age; (2) he must have sufficient mental capacity; (3) he must act voluntarily; (4) he must have criminal intent.

These four conditions are next discussed in the order given, a chapter being devoted to each topic.

CHAPTER IV.

AGE LIMITS OF CRIMINAL CAPACITY.

§ 40. **Under seven years.**—At common law, a child under the age of seven years is conclusively presumed incapable of committing a crime. This is owing to the fact that such a child is conclusively presumed incapable of entertaining criminal intent, which is an essential element of every common-law crime.[1] This rule, however, is equally applicable to statutory crimes.[2] And it is immaterial whether the crime charged is a felony or a misdemeanor.[3]

In some states, including Illinois, the common-law age of conclusive incapacity has been raised by statute. In Illinois an infant under the age of ten years can not be found guilty of any crime or misdemeanor.[4] In Texas the age limit has been raised to nine years.[5]

§ 41. **Between seven and fourteen years.**—At common law, an infant between the ages of seven and fourteen years

[1] Angelo v. People, 96 Ill. 209, 36 Am. Rep. 132; State v. Fowler, 52 Iowa 103; State v. Adams, 76 Mo. 355; Reg. v. Smith, 1 Cox Cr. C. 260.

[2] Commonwealth v. Mead, 92 Mass. 398; State v. Goin, 9 Humph. (Tenn.) 175.

[3] Angelo v. People, 96 Ill. 209, 36 Am. Rep. 132.

[4] Illinois: Hurd's Rev. Stat. (1916) Div. 2, ch. 38, par. 283, § 11; Angelo v. People, 96 Ill. 209, 36 Am. Rep. 132.

[5] Texas: Vernon's Crim. Stat., (1916) ch. 3, art. 34.

is presumed incapable of committing a crime, but the presumption is rebuttable.[6] The proof of capacity, however, must be clear and convincing.[7] Proof that he knew the difference between good and evil, or that he was possessed of the intelligence of ordinary boys of his age, does not fill the requirements of the law. It must be shown that he had sufficient discretion to understand the nature and illegality of the particular act constituting the crime.[8] But, if the intelligence to apprehend the consequences of acts, to reason upon duty, to distinguish between right and wrong and if the consciousness of guilt and innocence be clearly manifested, then the capacity is shown.[9] And when capacity is shown, a child over seven years of age is as fully responsible as a person who has reached his majority.[10]

As a general rule, the question of capacity must be determined from the conduct of the accused and the circumstances which surrounded the commission of the act.[11] The mere naked confession of the accused is generally held insufficient to support a conviction.[12] Where, however, the corpus delicti is established by evidence aliunde, the confession may be sufficient.[13]

Both in England and in this country children of tender years have been convicted of the higher crimes and executed. Thus, in England, a boy of ten years of age was convicted of murder and hanged.[14] The fact that he hid the body of

[6] State v. Fowler, 52 Iowa 103, 12 N. W. 983; State v. Goin, 9 Humph. (Tenn.) 175; Hampton v. State, 1 Ala. App. 136, 55 So. 1018, Derby's Cases 199.

[7] Angelo v. People, 96 Ill. 209, 36 Am. Rep. 132; Rex v. Owen, 4 Car. & P. 236; State v. Tice, 90 Mo. 112, 2 S. W. 269.

[8] Carr v. State, 24 Tex. App. 562, 7 S. W. 328, 5 Am. St. 905. See also State v. Yeargan, 117 N. Car. 706, 23 S. E. 153, 36 L. R. A. 196n.

[9] State v. Aaron, 4 N. J. L. 231, 7 Am. Dec. 592; Angelo v. People, 96 Ill. 209, 36 Am. Rep. 132.

[10] State v. Aaron, 4 N. J. L. 231, 7 Am. Dec. 592.

[11] Carr v. State, 24 Tex. App. 562, 7 S. W. 328, 5 Am. St. 905.

[12] State v. Aaron, 4 N. J. L. 231, 7 Am. Dec. 592.

[13] State v. Guild, 10 N. J. L. 163, 18 Am. Dec. 404; State v. Bostick, 4 Har. (Del.) 563.

[14] York's Case, Fost. Cr. L. 70.

his little playmate whom he had killed was considered sufficient evidence of a consciousness of guilt, and knowledge of right and wrong. In another English case a child of only eight years of age was convicted of arson and hanged.[15] In New Jersey a boy twelve years of age was convicted of murder and hanged.[16] In Alabama a child only eleven years of age was convicted of murder and the conviction was sustained.[17] And in Louisiana a boy between ten and twelve years of age was convicted of arson and the conviction was sustained.[18] In Texas the death penalty can not be inflicted on an infant below seventeen years of age.

The burden of proving capacity is upon the state, and it must prove it beyond any reasonable doubt;[19] but the burden of proving nonage of the accused rests upon him.[20]

The presumption of incapacity decreases with the increase of years, and is much less in case of a child slightly under fourteen than in case of one but little over seven.[21]

§ 42. **Effect of command of parent to do the act.**—The command of a husband may constitute a complete defense to a criminal charge against his wife, but the command of a parent is no defense to a criminal charge against his child.[22]

§ 43. **Physical incapacity to commit rape.**—At common law, a boy under fourteen years of age is conclusively presumed to be physically incapable of committing rape, and testimony is inadmissible to rebut this presumption.[23] Some

15 Emlyn on 1 Hale, P. C. 25n.

16 State v. Guild, 10 N. J. L. 163, 18 Am. Dec. 404.

17 Godfrey v. State, 31 Ala. 323, 70 Am. Dec. 494.

18 State v. Nickleson, 45 La. Ann. 1172, 14 So. 134.

19 Godfrey v. State, 31 Ala. 323, 70 Am. Dec. 494; Angelo v. People, 96 Ill. 209, 36 Am. Rep. 132; State v. Tice, 90 Mo. 112, 2 S. W. 269.

20 State v. Arnold, 35 N. Car. 184.

21 Bish. New Crim. L. (8th ed.) § 370. See also McCormack v. State, 102 Ala. 156, 15 So. 438.

22 People v. Richmond, 29 Cal. 414, Derby's Cases 256; State v. Learnard, 41 Vt. 585. See also note to 36 L. R. A. 210.

23 Reg. v. Philips, 8 Car. & P. 736; Reg. v. Waite, 2 Q. B. Div. 600, 17 Cox Cr. C. 554. See also note to 36 L. R. A. 196.

of the courts of this country, however, treat the presumption as disputable,[24] while others follow the common-law rule.[25]

§ 44. **Over fourteen years of age.**—A child over fourteen years of age is presumed to have capacity to commit crimes, the same as an adult.[26] And a mere statement by him that he did not realize the act was wrong is entitled to little or no weight in rebuttal of this presumption.[27]

§ 45. **Infant's liability for counterfeiting, forgery, false pretenses and cheating.**—As a general rule an infant is not civilly liable on his contracts. He may be criminally liable, however, for counterfeiting, or forgery, or false pretenses, or cheating at common law.[28]

§ 46. **Infant's liability for bastardy.**—An infant may be held liable for his torts. And, since a charge of bastardy is in the nature of a civil charge rather than criminal, a plea of infancy to this charge is no defense.[29]

§ 47. **Infant's liability for acts of omission, such as non-support.**—Blackstone states: "The law of England does in some cases privilege an infant, under the age of twenty-one, as to common misdemeanors, so as to escape fine, imprisonment, and the like: and particularly in cases of omission, as not repairing a bridge, or a highway, and other similar offenses; for, not having command of his fortune till twenty-one, he wants the capacity to do those things which the law requires."[30] An emancipated minor without property is not liable for non-support,[31] nor vagrancy.[32]

24 Heilman v. Commonwealth, 84 Ky. 457, 1 S. W. 731, 4 Am. St. 207; Gordon v. State, 93 Ga. 531, 21 S. E. 54, 44 Am. St. 189; Williams v. State, 14 Ohio 222, 45 Am. Dec. 536. See also note to 36 L. R. A. 196.

25 Foster v. Commonwealth, 96 Va. 306, 31 S. E. 503, 42 L. R. A. 589, 70 Am. St. 846; Chism v. State, 42 Fla. 232, 28 So. 399.

26 Irby v. State, 32 Ga. 496.

27 State v. Kluseman, 53 Minn. 541, 55 N. W. 741.

28 People v. Kendall, 25 Wend. (N. Y.) 399, 37 Ann. Dec. 240.

29 Chandler v. Commonwealth, 61 Ky. 66.

30 4 Bl. Comm. 22.

31 People v. Todd, 61 Mich. 234, 28 N. W. 79.

32 Teasley v. State, 109 Ga. 282, 34 S. E. 577.

CHAPTER V.

MENTAL CAPACITY.

§ 55. **Insanity—Definition.**—Mental capacity is an important essential of criminal responsibility. This is owing to the fact that a mentally incapable person can not entertain a criminal intent. In the law of crimes this idea is involved in the definition of insanity. The books disclose great judicial efforts to reach up and grasp the definition of insanity; the results have been a discord.[1] It may, however, in its broadest sense, be defined as any defect or disease of the mind which renders it incapable of entertaining, or

[1] 1 Bish. New Crim. L. (8th ed.), § 381.

which prevents it entertaining in the particular instance, criminal intent. A statute, providing that insanity shall not be a defense to a charge of crime, is unconstitutional.[2]

§ 56. **Classification of insanity.**—Insanity, in the broad sense of the term, is divided into four general classes. These four classes are as follows: (1) Idiocy; (2) Imbecility; (3) Mania; (4) Dementia.[3]

Other classifications are total and partial insanity, and permanent and temporary insanity.

§ 57. **Idiocy.**—The term idiocy means the state of being an idiot. An idiot is a person having no mind, and therefore no reasoning power, and who has been a fool from his birth. A fool is not necessarily an idiot, but an idiot is always a fool. The former may intentionally violate common sense in his actions, whereas the latter is unable to do so. A buffoon is an artificial fool, whereas an idiot is a natural fool. Blackstone's definition is, "An idiot, or natural fool, is one that hath had no understanding from his nativity."[4]

§ 58. **Imbecility—Debility—Stupidity.**—Imbecility is the state of being an imbecile. An imbecile is a person who is mentally or physically weak.[5] Cases relating to imbecility often present very puzzling questions to a court and jury.

Imbecility differs from debility. Imbecility is always constitutional, and pertains more particularly to the mind. Debility may be otherwise than constitutional, and always pertains to the body.

Imbecility also differs from stupidity. An imbecile is very changeable in his views and very vacillating in his purposes; whereas a stupid person is very persistent in his views and in the resolutions he makes. Imbecility bears the same relation to stupidity that genius bears to talent. That which in

[2] State v. Strasburg, 60 Wash. 106, 110 Pac. 1020, Ann. Cas. 1912 B, 917.

[3] Ray on Insanity (3d ed.), § 104; Stew. Leg. Med., § 146.

[4] 1 Bl. Comm. 302.

[5] Ray on Insanity, (3d ed.), § 104. See also Pettigrew v. State, 12 Tex. App. 225, Derby's Cases 188.

its highest form is genius, in its lowest form is imbecility; and that which in its highest form is talent, in its lowest form is stupidity.

§ 59. **Mania—Intellect—Monomania.**—Mania, or madness, is a state or condition of the mind which renders the person a maniac. A maniac is a person who, owing to a diseased mind, has a disordered intellect which renders him insane.

Intellect is a generic term. A person may have intellect without talent or genius; but he can not have either talent or genius without intellect. A maniac has intellect, but an idiot has none. The former has a diseased mind, whereas the latter has no mind at all.

Monomania is a state of madness, or derangement of the mind, with respect to one subject only. Homicidal mania is an insane impulse to kill; pyromania is an insane impulse to burn buildings; and kleptomania is an insane impulse to steal. A person, therefore, may be insane and irresponsible as to one subject and at the same time sane and responsible as to others. He may be punished unless impelled to crime by his monomania.[6] But many courts hold that monomania, causing an irresistible impulse to crime is no defense when the offender knew the act was wrong.[7]

§ 60. **Dementia.**—The term dementia means loss or feebleness of the mental faculties. It ranges from mere failing memory to utter fatuity. Like mania, it is produced by lesion of the faculties subsequent to their development; whereas idiocy and imbecility result from defective development of the faculties. Senile dementia is loss or feebleness of the faculties produced by age.

§ 61. **Emotional insanity—Moral insanity**—The so-called emotional insanity is, in reality, no insanity at all.[8] It is

6 Commonwealth v. Mosler, 4 Pa. St. 264, 6 Pa. L. J. 90.

7 Lowe v. State, 44 Tex. Cr. 224, 70 S. W. 206, Derby's Cases 189.

8 People v. Mortimer, 48 Mich. 37, 11 N. W. 776; People v. Foy, 138 N. Y. 664, 34 N. E. 396; Garner v. State, 112 Miss. 317, 73 So. 50.

merely an excited condition of the mind produced by anger, jealousy or some other exciting cause, and constitutes no defense to a criminal charge.

Nor is the so-called moral insanity, which consists in a perverted condition of the moral system, produced by excessive and unrestrained indulgence in viciousness, any defense.[9] It has been held, however, that it may reduce a homicide from murder in the first degree to murder in the second degree.[10] This view is somewhat doubtful to say the least.[11]

§ 62. **Tests of criminal responsibility.**—To be held criminally responsible for his acts, a person must have intelligence and capacity enough to have a criminal intent and purpose. One not a responsible moral agent is not liable to punishment for criminal acts.[12] It is the conclusion, however, of many eminent authorities that no satisfactory test of criminal responsibility exists.[13]

The chief tests which have been recognized, at different times, are the following: (1) The child test; (2) the wild beast test; (3) the test of knowledge of right and wrong in the abstract; (4) the test of knowledge of right and wrong as to the particular act committed; and (5) the power of control test.

§ 63. **The child test.**—Since children under fourteen years of age are prima facie incapable of crime, the test was proposed that imbeciles or persons mentally deficient ought not to be held responsible criminally unless of capacity equal

[9] State v. Terry, 173 N. C. 761, 92 S. E. 154; Boswell v. State, 63 Ala. 307, 1 Ky. L. 285, 35 Am. Rep. 20; State v. Lawrence, 57 Maine 574; People v. Durfee, 62 Mich. 487, 29 N. W. 109; State v. Potts, 100 N. Car. 457, 6 S. E. 657.

[10] Andersen v. State, 43 Conn. 514, 21 Am. Rep. 669.

[11] United States v. Lee, 4 Mackey (15 D. C.) 489, 54 Am. Rep. 293.

[12] Commonwealth v. Rogers, 7 Metc. (Mass.) 500, 41 Am. Dec. 458.

[13] 1 Bish. New Crim. L. (8th ed.), § 381; Ray on Insanity (3rd ed.), § 24; Parsons v. State, 81 Ala. 577, 2 So. 854, 60 Am. Rep. 193; State v. Richards, 39 Conn. 591.

to that of an ordinary child of fourteen years.[14] The objection is that the workings of an insane mature mind and a sane immature one are very different.[15]

Owing to the vagueness and uncertainty of this test for practical application it has been abandoned.

§ 64. **The wild beast test.**—This test originated with Justice Tracy in 1724. He instructed the jury that a man, to be criminally irresponsible, "must be a man that is totally deprived of his reason and memory, and doth not know what he is doing, no more than an infant, than a brute, or a wild beast."[16] This test has never been recognized in this country, and long ago became obsolete in England.

§ 65. **Test of right and wrong in the abstract.**—This test originated with Lord Mansfield in 1812.[17] It became obsolete in England in 1843, and is obsolete in this country.

§ 66. **Test of right and wrong as to the particular act.**—This test had its origin in England in 1843, and is the only test recognized in that country today. It is also recognized in this country universally;[18] but it is not the sole test recognized here. This test grew out of the celebrated McNaghten case. McNaghten, intending to kill Sir Robert Peel, the

[14] 1 Hale P. C. 30; State v. Richards, 39 Conn. 591.

[15] 1 Bish. New Crim. L. (8th ed), § 376, par. 3. For the different workings referred to, see Ray on Insanity (3d ed.), § 8.

[16] Arnold's Case, 16 How. St. Tr. 764.

[17] Bellingham's Case, Coll. on Lun. 630.

[18] Guiteau's Case, 10 Fed. 161; Hornish v. People, 142 Ill. 620, 32 N. E. 677, 18 L. R. A. 237; Wilcox v. State, 94 Tenn. 106, 28 S. W. 312; State v. Hockett, 70 Iowa 442, 30 N. W. 742; Smith v. State, 95 Miss. 786, 49 So. 945, Ann. Cas. 1912A, 23n; State v. Riddle, 245 Mo. 451, 150 S. W. 1044, Ann. Cas. 1914A, 884; Flanagan v. People, 52 N. Y. 467, 11 Am. Rep. 731; Blackburn v. State, 23 Ohio St. 146; Alberty v. State, 10 Okla. Cr. 616, 140 Pac. 1025, 52 L. R. A. (N. S.) 248; Commonwealth v. Wireback, 190 Pa. St. 138, 42 Atl. 542, 70 Am. St. 625; State v. Levelle, 24 S. Car. 120, 13 S. E. 319, 27 Am. St. 799; Oborn v. State, 143 Wis. 249, 126 N. W. 737, 31 L. R. A. (N. S.) 966, Derby's Cases 185; Owen v. State, 13 Okla. Cr. 195, 163 Pac. 548; State v. Rose, 271 Mo. 17, 195 S. W. 1013.

premier of England, and mistaking the premier's private secretary for Sir Robert, killed the secretary. Upon a charge of murder his defense was insanity. His acquittal aroused much public discussion, and the question of insanity as a defense to a criminal charge was debated in the House of Lords. Growing out of this debate, the lords submitted certain questions to the judges. The judges replied that "to establish a defense on the ground of insanity, it must be clearly proved that, at the time of committing the act, the party accused was laboring under such a defect of reason, from disease of the mind, as not to know the nature and quality of the act he was doing, or, if he did know it, that he did not know he was doing what was wrong."[19]

This test, however, is an imperfect one, and it has been condemned by the great current of modern medical authorities, who believe it to be "founded on an ignorant and imperfect view of the disease;"[20] many of whom assert that the power of distinguishing right and wrong exists, at least to some extent, among most, if not all, lunatics.[21] "The memorials of our jurisprudence are written all over with cases in which those who are now understood to have been insane have been executed as criminals."[22]

As previously stated, however, this test is the only one recognized in England, and it is universally recognized in this country. The courts, unfortunately, have not kept abreast of scientific investigations; and the English courts have not been willing to consider insanity as a disease.[23] The existence of such a cerebral disease, however, is earn-

[19] McNaghten's Case, 10 Clark & F. 200, 1 Car. & K. 130, 8 Scott N. R. 595; Beale's Cases 231; Derby's Cases 172.

[20] Encyc. Brit., (9th ed.), title, Insanity.

[21] Judicial Aspects of Insanity (Ordrouaux, 1877) 427; Reynolds on "The Scientific Value of the Legal Tests of Insanity"; Bucknill Crim. Lun. 59; Sixteenth Annual Report Ala. Insane Hospital (1876), 22; Biennial Report (1886), 12-18; Guy & F. on Forensic Med. 220.

[22] 1 Bish. New Crim. L. (8th ed.), § 390.

[23] Parsons v. State, 81 Ala. 577, 2 So. 854, 60 Am. Rep. 193.

estly asserted by superintendents in insane hospitals, and other distinguished experts on insanity the world over. Practically all of these distinguished experts agree that the unconsciousness of right and wrong is one thing, and the powerlessness through cerebral defect or disease to do right quite another thing.

§ 67. **Power of control test.**—This test is also known as the irresistible impulse test. It is not recognized at all in England, and is rejected by many of the courts of this country. In one English case, however, decided before McNaghten's case, Lord Denman clearly recognized it, and said that if some controlling disease was in truth the acting power within the accused which he could not resist, then he would not be responsible.[24]

Experts on insanity, however, as previously stated, consider it a very important scientific test. Some medical experts state that the true test of insanity is not the knowledge of right and wrong, but whether, in consequence of congenital defect or acquired disease the power of self-control is absent altogether, or is so far wanting as to render the individual irresponsible.[25]

Some eminent jurists and law writers recognize this test, and hold one charged of crime blameless if by reason of insanity, he could not know he was doing wrong, or if he had not the power to resist the temptation to avoid doing wrong.[26]

§ 68. **Parsons v. State.**—Justice Somerville, in the lead-

[24] Reg. v. Oxford, 9 Car. & P. 525.

[25] Bucknill & Tuke on Psychological Med. (4th ed.) 269.

[26] Translation 22 Am. Jur. 311, 317, 1 Beck Med. Jur. (10th ed.) 765n; People v. Finley, 38 Mich. 482; State v. Jones, 50 N. H. 369, 9 Am. Rep. 242, Derby's Cases 176; Commonwealth v. Mosler, 4 Pa. St. 264, 6 Pa. L. J. 90. See also Coyle v. Commonwealth, 100 Pa. St. 573, 45 Am. Rep. 397. It has been held that a prior manifestation is not essential. Scott v. Commonwealth, 4 Metc. (Ky.) 227, 83 Am. Dec. 461; 1 Whart. Crim. L. (11th ed.), § 48; 1 Bish. New Crim. L. (8th ed.), § 383b.

ing case which emphatically supports the power of control test, states: "The inquiries to be submitted to the jury, then, in every criminal trial where the defense of insanity is interposed are these:

1. Was the defendant at the time of the commission of the alleged crime, as matter of fact, afflicted with a disease of the mind, so as to be either idiotic, or otherwise insane?

2. If such be the case, did he know right from wrong as applied to the particular act in question? If he did not have such knowledge, he is not legally responsible.

3. If he did have such knowledge, he may nevertheless not be legally responsible if the two following conditions concur:

a. If, by reason of the duress of such mental disease, he had so far lost the power to choose between the right and wrong, and to avoid doing the act in question, as that his free agency was at the time destroyed.

b. And if, at the same time, the alleged crime was so connected with such mental disease, in the relation of cause and effect, as to have been the product of it solely."[27]

§ 69. **The rule in Illinois.**—The Supreme Court of Illinois holds that "Whenever it should appear from the evidence that, at the time of doing the act charged, the prisoner was not of sound mind, but affected with insanity, and such affection was the efficient cause of the act, and that he would not have done the act but for that affection, he ought to be acquitted. But this unsoundness of mind, or affection of in-

27 Parsons v. State, 81 Ala. 577, 2 So. 854, 60 Am. Rep. 193. See also State v. Johnson, 40 Conn. 136; Flanagan v. State, 103 Ga. 619, 30 S. E. 550; Blake v. State, 121 Ind. 433, 23 N. E. 273, 16 Am. St. 408; State v. Felter, 25 Iowa 67; Scott v. Commonwealth, 4 Met. (Ky.) 227, 83 Am. Dec. 461; State v. Lyons, 113 La. 959, 996; 37 So. 890; State v. Peel, 23 Mont. 358, 59 Pac. 169, 75 Am. St. 529; and see note to Ann. Cas. 1912A, 37.

sanity, must be of such a degree as to create an uncontrollable impulse to do the act charged, by overriding the reason and judgment, and obliterating the sense of right and wrong as to the particular act done, and depriving the accused of the power of choosing between them."[28]

§ 70. **The New York rule.**—The penal code of New York, on the question of insanity, is in harmony with the English rule. It exempts a person only where "he was laboring under such a defect of reason as either (1) not to know the nature and quality of the act he was doing, or (2) not to know that the act was wrong."[29]

§ 71. **Insanity a question of fact.**—The existence or non-existence of insanity in a particular case is a question of fact for the jury to determine. It seems, therefore, that courts, in dogmatically denying that such a disease of the mind may exist as may preclude a person from doing what he knows is wrong, usurp the function of the jury. "If the tests of insanity are matters of law, the practice of allowing experts to testify what they are should be discontinued; if they are matters of fact, the judge should no longer testify without being sworn as a witness, and showing himself to be qualified to testify as an expert."[30]

§ 72. **Insane delusion—Monomania.**—A person may be insane as to one or more subjects and sane as to others. An insane delusion may constitute a complete defense to a criminal charge. To do so, it must be connected with the act committed in the relation of cause and effect.[31] According to the English rule, the delusion must be such that, if true,

[28] Hopps v. People, 31 Ill. 385, 83 Am. Dec. 231. See also Dacey v. People, 116 Ill. 555, 6 N. E. 165.

[29] Parker's N. Y. Crim. Code & Penal Law (1910), art. 104, § 1120. See also People v. Taylor, 138 N. Y. 398, 34 N. E. 275.

[30] State v. Pike, 49 N. H. 399, 6 Am. Rep. 533. See also People v. Scott, 195 N. Y. 224, 88 N. E. 35, 135 Am. St. 789.

[31] State v. Hockett, 70 Iowa 442, 30 N. W. 742; Wilcox v. State, 94 Tenn. 106, 28 S. W. 312. See also Smith v. State, 95 Miss. 786, 49 So. 945, 27 L. R. A. (N. S.) 461n.

it would constitute a defense to a sane person. As said by the judges, in McNaghten's case, "we think he must be considered in the same situation as to responsibility as if the facts with respect to which the delusion exists were real. For example, if under the influence of his delusion he supposes another man to be in the act of attempting to take away his life, and he kills that man, as he supposed, in self-defense, he would be exempt from punishment. If his delusion was that the deceased had inflicted a serious injury to his character and fortune, and he killed him in revenge for such supposed injury, he would be liable to punishment."[82] This rule has been followed since in England,[83] and is also followed by many of the courts of this country.[84] "If a man is under an insane delusion that another is attempting his life, and kills him in self-defense, he does not know that he is committing an unnecessary homicide. If a man insanely believes that he has a command from the Almighty to kill, it is difficult to understand how such a man can know it is wrong for him to do it."[85] Like reasoning is applicable to a somnambulist, who imagines, while laboring under his infirmity, that he is being attacked and that it is necessary to kill his adversary to save his own life or prevent great bodily harm. The homicide, in such a case, would not be felonious.[86]

On the other hand, where a person labors under the insane delusion that another is trying to marry his mother, and kills him in the belief that such act is necessary to prevent the consummation of the marriage, the slayer is criminally respon-

82 McNaghten's Case, 10 Clarke & F. 200, 1 Car. & K. 130, 8 Scott N. R. 595, Derby's Cases 172.

83 Reg. v. Burton, 3 Fost. & F. 772.

84 Taylor v. Commonwealth, 109 Pa. St. 262; State v. Lawrence, 57 Maine 574; Commonwealth v. Rogers, 7 Metc. (Mass.) 500, 41 Am. Dec. 458; Merritt v. State, 39 Tex. Cr. 70, 45 S. W. 21; Cunningham v. State, 56 Miss. 269, 21 Am. Rep. 360.

85 Guiteau's Case, 10 Fed. 161.

86 Fain v. Commonwealth, 78 Ky. 183, 39 Am. Rep. 213. See also Tibbs v. Commonwealth, 138 Ky. 558, 128 S. W. 871, 28 L. R. A. (N. S.) 665.

sible for his act;[37] and where a husband kills his wife, under the insane delusion that for several months she has been putting poison in his food, he is criminally responsible for her death.[38] Also where a convict, while laboring under the insane delusion that a fellow-convict has divulged a plan of escape and is spying upon him, kills him, his insane delusion is no defense.[39]

An insane delusion which constitutes a defense to a criminal charge is never the result of reasoning and reflection. A man may reason himself into absurd opinions or be persuaded into impracticable schemes or vicious resolutions;[40] but he can not be reasoned or persuaded into insanity or insane delusions.

§ 73. **Burden of proof.**—When a person is charged with the commission of a crime he is presumed innocent until proved guilty beyond a reasonable doubt. An essential element of guilt is sanity of the accused at the time of the commission of the alleged offense. It follows, therefore, that when insanity is pleaded in defense of a criminal charge the plea is a denial of an essential element of the crime, and not an affirmative defense in the nature of a plea of confession and avoidance. The burden, therefore, is upon the prosecution to prove the sanity of the accused, like all other facts in issue, beyond a reasonable doubt.[41]

Many courts erroneously treat the plea of insanity as an affirmative defense; and require the accused to prove his plea by a preponderance of the evidence, considering this defense as in the nature of a plea of confession and avoidance.[42]

37 Bolling v. State, 54 Ark. 588, 16 S. W. 658.

38 People v. Hubert, 119 Cal. 216, 51 Pac. 329, 63 Am. St. 72.

39 People v. Taylor, 138 N. Y. 398, 34 N. E. 275.

40 Guiteau's Case, 10 Fed. 161.

41 Dacey v. People, 116 Ill. 555, 6 N. E. 165; People v. Garbutt, 17 Mich. 9, 97 Am. Dec. 162; Plake v. State, 121 Ind. 433, 23 N. E. 273, 16 Am. St. 408; State v. Herring, 268 Mo. 514, 188 S. W. 169.

42 Parsons v. State, 81 Ala. 577, 2 So. 854, 60 Am. Rep. 193; State v. Potts, 100 N. Car. 457, 6 S. E. 657; Ortwein v. Commonwealth, 76 Pa. St. 414, 18 Am. Rep. 420;

The burden of proof in its true sense, that is, the duty of establishing one's case, never shifts. The presumption of innocence applies to the defendant, until it is established beyond a reasonable doubt that he not only committed the act, but also committed it with criminal intent.[43] The presumption of sanity, which, standing alone, is sufficient to make a prima facie case upon this point, has no effect whatever upon the question of burden of proof in its true sense. It merely takes the place of evidence, nothing more.

The true rule, therefore, as stated by Chief Justice Cooley, is, the prosecution "are at liberty to rest upon the presumption of sanity until proof of the contrary condition is given by the defense. But when any evidence is given which tends to overthrow that presumption, the jury are to examine, weigh, and pass upon it with the understanding that although the initiative in presenting the evidence is taken by the defense, the burden of proof upon this part of the case, as well as upon the other is upon the prosecution to establish the conditions of guilt."[44]

§ 74. **Somnambulism.**—Where one in his sleep shoots and kills one who attempts to awake him, and there is no motive or intention to injure, and the accused is not conscious of what he is doing, he is not guilty of murder.[45]

§ 75. **Intoxication.**—As a general rule, voluntary drunkenness is no defense to a criminal charge. A person can abstain from drunkenness, and if by drinking he brings upon

State v. Lawrence, 57 Maine 574; State v. Felter, 32 Iowa 49; Guiteau's Case, 10 Fed. 161; Boswell v. Commonwealth, 20 Grat. (Va.) 860; State v. Coleman, 27 La. Ann. 691; State v. Huting, 21 Mo. 464; Clark v. State, 12 Ohio 483, 495, 40 Ann. Dec. 481; Casat v. State, 40 Ark. 511; People v. Garbutt, 17 Mich. 9, 97 Am. Dec. 162.

43 People v. Garbutt, 17 Mich. 9, 97 Am. Dec. 162; State v. Wegener, 180 Ia. 102, 162 N. W. 1040.

44 People v. Garbutt, 17 Mich. 9, 97 Am. Dec. 162. See also Adair v. State, 6 Okla. Crim. 284, 118 Pac. 416, 44 L. R. A. (N. S.) 119, and cases cited in note; Knight v. State, 38 Nebr. 225, 78 N. W. 508, 76 Am. St. 78n.

45 Fain v. Commonwealth, 78 Ky. 183, 39 Am. Rep. 213, Derby's Cases 107.

himself a madness, it is held to be voluntary and he is not excused from crimes committed under the influence of such voluntary madness, if previously sane.[46]

§ 76. **Reasons for rule as to intoxication.**—The rule that voluntary drunkenness is no defense to a criminal charge is based upon principle and also policy. Its foundation pillars are justice and necessity. The justice of the rule grows out of the fact that every person owes to society, as to himself, the duty of preserving unclouded the priceless endowment of reason, while the necessity of the rule is owing to the fact that without it, life, liberty and property would be placed in serious jeopardy. There is no injustice in holding a person responsible for his acts committed when voluntarily intoxicated.[47]

§ 77. **Intoxication does not aggravate offense.**—According to Lord Coke, voluntary drunkenness aggravates the offense;[48] and other writers have sustained this view. From the ethical viewpoint the statement is correct. From the legal viewpoint it is not correct. A wilful murder, deliberately perpetrated with preconceived malice, can not be aggravated by drunkenness; nor is that which would be manslaughter in a sober man aggravated into murder if com-

[46] Rex v. Meakin, 7 Car. & P. 297; State v. Bobbst, 269 Mo. 214, 190 S. W. 257; Perryman v. State, 12 Okla. Cr. 500, 159 Pac. 937; State v. Cooley, 19 N. Mex. 91, 140 Pac. 1111, 52 L. R. A. (N. S.) 230n; O'Herrin v. State, 14 Ind. 420, Derby's Cases 191.

[47] People v. Rogers, 18 N. Y. 9, 72 Am. Dec. 484, Beale's Cases 264. See also Upstone v. People, 109 Ill. 169; Commonwealth v. Malone, 114 Mass. 295; Beasley v. State, 50 Ala. 149, 20 Am. Rep. 292; Flanigan v. People, 86 N. Y. 554, 40 Am. Rep. 556; Warner v. State, 56 N. J. L. 686, 29 Atl. 505, 44 Am. St. 415; Beck v. State, 76 Ga. 452; Goodwin v. State, 96 Ind. 550; State v. Kidwell, 62 W. Va. 466, 59 S. E. 494, 13 L. R. A. (N. S.) 1024; State v. Tatro, 50 Vt. 483, Derby's Cases 191; Harris v. United States, 8 App. D. C. 20, 36 L. R. A. 465 and note containing long list of cases.

[48] 3 Inst. 46; Beverley's Case, 4 Coke 125a; United States v. Cornell, 2 Mason (U. S.) 91; United States v. Claypool, 14 Fed. 127.

mitted by a drunken man.[49] That drunkenness aggravates the offense is not the law either in England or in this country. In some instances, however, it is held to lessen the degree of the offense.[50]

§ 78. **Exceptions to rule as to intoxication.**—In some cases voluntary drunkenness may be a complete defense to a criminal charge. If the drunkenness completely negatives the existence of an essential element of the crime it constitutes a defense. Thus, in the case of an aggravated assault, or larceny, or burglary, the drunkenness of the accused may completely negative the existence of the essential element of specific criminal intent, in which case the drunkenness will constitute a complete defense.[51] This principle is also applicable to the crimes of bribery,[52] perjury,[53] forgery,[54] and conspiracy,[55] in all of which a specific criminal intent to do the act is an essential element of the crime. It is also applicable to the crime of attempting to commit suicide; not as an excuse for the crime but as a material fact bearing on the question whether the accused intended to take his life.[56]

[49] McIntyre v. People, 38 Ill. 514.

[50] Atkins v. State, 118 Tenn. 458, 105 S. W. 353, 13 L. R. A. (N. S.) 1031.

[51] State v. Foster, 172 N. Car. 960, 90 S. E. 785; Reg. v. Doody, 6 Cox Cr. C. 463, Beale's Cases 261; Garner v. State, 28 Fla. 113, 9 So. 835, 29 Am. St. 232; Hill v. State, 42 Nebr. 503, 60 N. W. 916; State v. Phillips, 80 W. Va. 747, 93 S. E. 828; Chowning v. State, 91 Ark. 503, 121 S. W. 735, 18 Ann. Cas. 529. See also note 36 L. R. A. 467; State v. Rumble, 81 Kans. 16, 105 Pac. 1, 25 L. R. A. (N. S.) 376.

[52] White v. State, 103 Ala. 72, 16 So. 63.

[53] Lytle v. State, 31 Ohio St. 196; Lyle v. State, 31 Tex. Cr. 103, 19 S. W. 903.

[54] People v. Blake, 65 Cal. 275, 4 Pac. 1.

[55] Booher v. State, 156 Ind. 435, 60 N. E. 156, 54 L. R. A. 391.

[56] Reg. v. Doody, 6 Cox Cr. C. 463, Beale's Cases 261; United States v. Drew, 5 Mason (U. S.) 28, Fed. Cas. No. 14993. See also State v. Haab, 105 La. 230, 29 So. 725; (where Nicholls, C. J., comments approvingly on Judge Story's view); State v. Driggers, 84 S. Car. 526, 66 S. E. 1042, 19 Ann. Cas. 1166n; State v. O'Neil, 51 Kans. 651, 33 Pac. 287, 24 L. R. A. 555.

§ 79. **Effect of delirium tremens.**—Delirium tremens is an organic mental disease produced by excessive drinking of intoxicating liquor. Though caused by voluntary drunkenness, which is usually no defense to a criminal charge, delirium tremens may constitute a complete defense, even when the crime charged involves only a general criminal intent.[57] This is owing to the fact that the voluntary drunkenness which produces the delirium tremens is the remote, and not the proximate, cause of the crime. The mental aberration, to constitute a defense, must be of a permanent character; and separable from the intoxication which produces it. Mere temporary insanity, which immediately results from voluntary drunkenness, is no defense.[57a]

The question, whether a person, whose defense to a criminal charge is delirium tremens, was, at the time of the commission of the act, under the influence of a fixed insanity, or under a temporary one induced immediately by intoxication, is a fact for the jury to determine; and their verdict upon this point will not be disturbed by a higher court unless it is clearly against the evidence.[58]

§ 80. **Effect of insanity produced by excessive use of morphine or cocaine.**—When a person voluntarily uses morphine or cocaine, not as a medicine, but merely to gratify a passion, or to produce intoxication, his responsibility for crime while under its influence is precisely the same as that of a person who becomes drunk by the excessive use of intoxicating liquors. Ordinarily, temporary insanity produced by the excessive use of either or both of these drugs is no defense to a criminal charge. If the crime charged involves specific criminal intent, and the temporary insanity completely negatives the existence of this intent, the insanity necessarily constitutes a defense. If the temporary insanity is produced by the combined excessive use of cocaine, morphine

[57] People v. Goodrum, 31 Cal. App. 430, 160 Pac. 690.

[57a] Upstone v. People, 109 Ill. 169; State v. Kidwell, 62 W. Va. 466, 59 S. E. 494, 13 L. R. A. (N. S.) 1024; and note to 36 L. R. A. 479.

[58] Upstone v. People, 109 Ill. 169.

and intoxicating liquors, the criminal responsibility is the same as where the insanity is produced by the excessive use of the drugs alone.[59]

§ 81. Drunkenness may negative commission of the act. —When a person is upon trial for the commission of a crime, he may show, if he can, that, at the time the alleged offense was committed he was so drunk that he was physically incapable of committing the crime. "If a man by voluntary drunkenness renders himself incapable of walking for a limited time, it is just as competent evidence tending to show that he did not walk during the time he was so incapable as though he had been so rendered incapable by paralysis of his limbs from some cause over which he had no control."[60]

§ 82. Murder in first degree committed by intoxicated person—Manslaughter.—In many states, statutes exist which divide murder into degrees. Though voluntary drunkenness is no defense to murder at common law, so far as the element of criminal intent is concerned, it may reduce a homicide from murder in the first degree to murder in the second degree. The statutes usually provide that to constitute murder in the first degree there must exist an actual intent to kill, or deliberation and premeditation. The terms deliberation and premeditation are not synonymous. The former implies "reflection, however brief, upon the act before committing it; fixed and determined purpose as distinguished from sudden impulse;"[61] whereas, the latter implies merely "previous contrivance or formed design," irrespective of any question of sudden impulse.[62]

To constitute murder in the first degree, where deliberation and premeditation are essential, the intention must be

[59] Edwards v. State, 38 Tex. Cr. 386, 43 S. W. 112, 39 L. R. A. 262. See also Moss v. State, 57 Tex. Cr. 620, 124 S. W. 647, 136 Am. St. 1001.

[60] Ingalls v. State, 48 Wis. 647, 4 N. W. 785.

[61] Cent. Dict. & Cyc. "Deliberation."

[62] Cent. Dict. & Cyc. "Premeditation."

deliberated upon; but if the killing is not the instant effect of impulse, if there is hesitation or doubt to overcome, a choice made as the result of thought, however short the struggle between the intention and the act, it is sufficient to characterize the crime as deliberate and premeditated murder.[63] By the weight of authority, evidence of drunkenness of the accused is admissible to negative the existence of deliberation and premeditation and thus show that the homicide is not murder in the first degree.[64]

It is to be observed that while fixed insanity produced by habitual drunkenness excuses acts otherwise criminal, one who while sober deliberately resolves to kill another, and gets drunk for the purpose of nerving himself to perform the deed, and kills such person while he is so drunk as to be incapable of forming such design, and temporarily insane and unconscious of what he is doing, is still guilty of murder in the first degree.[65]

As a general rule, drunkenness will not reduce a homicide from murder to manslaughter, when the same offense, if committed by a sober man, would be murder.[66] A sufficient provocation in the case of a sober man, will reduce a homicide from murder to manslaughter; and exactly the same principle is applicable to a drunken man. Voluntary drunk-

[63] Leighton v. People, 88 N. Y. 117.

[64] Hopt v. People, 104 U. S. 631, 26 L. ed. 873; People v. Corey, 148 N. Y. 476, 42 N. E. 1066; State v. Johnson, 40 Conn. 136; Commonwealth v. Dorsey, 103 Mass. 412; Hopt v. People, 104 U. S. 631, 26 L. ed. 873; State v. Rumble, 81 Kans. 16, 105 Pac. 1, 25 L. R. A. (N. S.) 376. See also note to 36 L. R. A. 470.

[65] State v. Robinson, 20 W. Va. 713, 43 Am. Rep. 799. See also State v. Garvey, 11 Minn. 154; Marshall v. Commonwealth, 141 Ky. 222, 132 S. W. 139, 31 L. R. A. (N. S.) 379.

[66] Rafferty v. People, 66 Ill. 118. See also Rex v. Carroll, 7 Car. & P. 145; Keenan v. Commonwealth, 44 Pa. St. 55, 84 Am. Dec. 414; People v. Rogers, 18 N. Y. 9, 72 Am. Dec. 484; Commonwealth v. Hawkins, 3 Gray (Mass.) 463; McIntyre v. People, 38 Ill. 514; State v. Tatro, 50 Vt. 483; Shannahan v. Commonwealth, 8 Bush (Ky.) 463, 8 Am. Rep. 465; Malone v. State, 49 Ga. 210; Garner v. State, 28 Fla. 113, 9 So. 835, 29 Am. St. 232; State v. Morris, 83 Ore. 429, 163 Pac. 567.

enness which merely excites the passions of a man and stimulates him to the commission of a homicide, without any provocation, neither reduces the grade of the crime nor mitigates the punishment.

§ 83. **The rule as to intoxication in Illinois.**—The criminal code of Illinois provides that, "Drunkenness shall not be an excuse for any crime or misdemeanor, unless such drunkenness be occasioned by the fraud, contrivance or force of some other person, for the purpose of causing the perpetration of an offense."[67] Voluntary drunkenness in Illinois may be a complete defense to any crime an essential element of which is specific criminal intent.[68] It may be a complete defense to a charge of larceny, robbery, burglary or any aggravated assault, as each of these crimes involves a specific intent, and drunkenness may produce a state of mind such as to negative any positive or particular intent.[69]

On the other hand, when, without intoxication, the law imputes to an act a criminal intent, as in the case of wanton killing without provocation, drunkenness of the accused may not be shown to disprove such intent.[70]

Whether, in a given case, the intoxication of the accused was voluntary or involuntary is always a question of fact for the jury to determine; but the legal effect of voluntary intoxication upon a criminal act is a question of law.[71]

§ 84. **Intoxication of insane person.**—Voluntary drunkenness is no excuse for a criminal act. An insane person can become drunk as well as a sane person. His drunkenness however, will not withdraw from him his shield of insanity. "If a man is insane when sober, the fact that he increased the insanity, by the superadded excitement of liquor, makes no difference. An insane person is irresponsible, whether drunk

67 Illinois: Hurd's Rev. Stat. (1916) ch. 38, 291.

68 Schwabacher v. People, 165 Ill. 618, 46 N. E. 809.

69 Crosby v. People, 137 Ill. 325, 27 N. E. 49; Mooney v. State, 33 Ala. 419.

70 Rafferty v. People, 66 Ill. 118.

71 North v. People, 139 Ill. 81, 28 N. E. 966.

or sober."[72] It is to be observed that it is the original insanity which constitutes a defense, and not the drunkenness.[73]

§ 85. **Involuntary intoxication.**—Involuntary drunkenness, resulting from the fraud or stratagem of another, or the negligence of his physician, which renders the person unconscious of right and wrong as to the particular act, constitutes a defense.[74] But drunkenness, which results from satisfying an irresistible appetite which overcomes the will and amounts to a disease, is no excuse for a criminal act, nor is it material on the question of premeditation.[75]

It has been held that "if a person be subject to a tendency to insanity of which he is ignorant, which is liable to be excited by intoxication, and if, in consequence of intoxication, though voluntary, his mental faculties become excited to diseased action to such an extent that he does not know what he is doing nor why he is doing it, or if conscious of this, he is not conscious of any object in doing it, or if he does not know that what he is doing or the means he is using are adapted or likely to kill; or, though conscious of all these, yet, if the diseased action of his mind has so far overcome or perverted his reason that he does not know that what he is doing is wrong, then he will not be responsible for the intoxication, nor its consequences."[76] This is also Wharton's view.[77] The intoxication in such a case is regarded as involuntary.

§ 86. **Corporations.**—It was once doubted whether a corporation could be liable for a crime; but later decisions hold that a corporation is subject to common-law indictment.[78]

72 Choice v. State, 31 Ga. 424; Johnson v. State (Tex. Cr. App.), 193 S. W. 674.

73 State v. Kraemer, 49 La. Ann. 766, 22 So. 254, 62 Am. St. 664; Bailey v. State, 26 Ind. 422.

74 Pearson's Case, 2 Lew. Cr. C. 144, Beale's Cases 261.

75 Flanigan v. People, 86 N. Y. 554, 40 Ann. Rep. 556.

76 Roberts v. People, 19 Mich. 401.

77 1 Whart. Crim. L. (11th ed.), § 65.

78 Reg. v. Benningham, &c., R. Co., 9 Car. & P. 469; Commonwealth v. Lehigh Valley R. Co., 165 Pa. St. 162, 30 Atl. 836, 27 L. R. A. 231.

The difficulties about bringing a corporation into court for a crime because of the impossibility of its arrest, have been removed by statute.[79]

There are certain crimes involving personal malicious intent which can not be committed by corporations.[80] But a corporation may be indicted for a breach of duty, and for maintaining a nuisance,[81] keeping a disorderly house,[82] obstructing a highway,[83] libel,[84] violating Sunday laws,[85] selling intoxicating liquors,[86] or for public wrongs generally. Corporations may also be punished for criminal contempts.[87]

The method of punishment is by fine;[88] but there can be no punishment of the members unless proceeded against personally.[89] Stockholders are not criminally liable for offenses of officers.[90]

Under statutes defining homicide as the killing of one human being by another, a corporation can not be indicted for manslaughter or murder.[91]

79 State v. Western, &c. R. Co., 89 N. Car. 584.

80 Whart. Crim. L. (11th ed.), § 116.

81 Reg. v. Great North of England R. Co., 9 Q. B. 315, 2 Cox Cr. C. 70, 7 Eng. Rul. Cas. 466; People v. Albany, 11 Wend. (N. Y.) 539, 27 Am. Dec. 95.

82 State v. Passaic County Agr. Soc., 54 N. J. L. 260, 23 Atl. 680.

83 State v. Ohio, &c. R. Co., 23 Ind. 362; Commonwealth v. Vermont, &c. R. Co., 4 Gray (Mass.) 22; State v. Morris, &c. R. Co., 23 N. J. L. 360.

84 State v. Atchison, 3 Lea (Tenn.) 729, 31 Am. Rep. 663.

85 State v. Baltimore, &c. R. Co., 15 W. Va. 362, 36 Am. Rep. 803.

86 Stewart v. Waterloo Turnverein, 71 Iowa 226, 32 N. W. 275, 60 Am. Rep. 786.

87 State v. Baltimore, &c. R. Co., 15 W. Va. 362, 36 Am. Rep. 803; Telegram Newspaper Co. v. Commonwealth, 172 Mass. 294, 52 N. E. 445, 44 L. R. A. 159, 70 Am. St. 280.

88 Whart. Crim. L. (11th ed.), § 122; Reg. v. Birmingham &c. R. Co., 3 Q B. 223.

89 Whart. Crim. L. (11th ed.), § 116.

90 In re Greene, 52 Fed. 104; Union P. Cool Co. v. United States, 173 Fed. 737.

91 People v. Rochester R. & L. Co., 195 N. Y. 102, 88 N. E. 22, 21 L. R. A. (N. S.) 998, 133 Am. St. 770, 16 Ann. Cas. 837, Derby's Cases 207.

CHAPTER VI.

ACT MUST BE VOLUNTARY.

§ 90. **Classes of cases in which question of compulsion arises.**—The question of compulsion, as a defense to a criminal charge, arises in the following classes of cases: (1) Where a wife does a criminal act in her husband's presence; (2) where a subordinate does a criminal act by command of his superior; (3) where a person does a criminal act owing to actual duress by persons having no semblance of authority; (4) where a person does a criminal act for self-preservation in other cases; and (5) where a person does a criminal act owing to inability on his part to perform a legal duty

These various classes will be next discussed in the order given.

§ 91. **Coercion of husband.**—A married woman who commits a crime in the presence of her husband is presumed to act by his command and under the impulse of fear. For this reason the husband's coercion is usually a defense to a criminal charge against the wife for an act committed by her in his presence.[1] The presumption of coercion is not conclu-

1 Commonwealth v. Neal, 10 Mass. 152, 6 Am. Dec. 105; State v. Kelly, 74 Iowa 589, 38 N. W. 503; Davis v. State, 15 Ohio 72, 45 Am. Dec. 559; Commonwealth v. Daley, 148 Mass. 11, 18 N. E. 579; Reg. v. Dykes, 15 Cox Cr. C. 771; Commonwealth v. Adams, 186 Mass. 101, 71 N. E. 78.

sive. It may be disproved by proper evidence. On the other hand, it is sufficient, upon this point, to establish a prima facie case. It is said by Blackstone that this doctrine has been recognized in England for at least a thousand years.[2]

In order that coercion of the husband be available as a defense to a criminal charge against the wife, it is essential that the act be committed in the husband's presence. It is sufficient, however, if he be near enough to exercise a material influence over her. The ultimate question is whether she acted under his coercion or control, or of her own free will independently of any coercion or control by him.[3] It is not essential that he be in the same room with her, or even in the same house with her.[4] If he be on the premises and near at hand, a momentary absence from the house may still leave her under his influence.[5] On the other hand, if the wife commit a crime in her husband's absence, though by his direction, no presumption of coercion will arise.[6] Her coverture in such a case will be no defense; moreover, she may be prosecuted alone.[7]

The presumption of coercion is one of law and not fact. It is not a strong presumption, but one that may be overcome by slight circumstances.[8] It may be proved that she was the instigator of the crime and the more active party;[9] or that the husband was physically incapable of coercing her.[10] Even the nature of the offense may be sufficient to rebut the presumption.[11]

[2] 4 Bl. Comm. 28. See also State v. Ma Foo, 110 Mo. 7, 19 S. W. 222, 33 Am. St. 414.

[3] Commonwealth v. Daley, 148 Mass. 11, 18 N. E. 579, Derby's Cases, 203; State v. Fertig, 98 Iowa 139, 67 N. W. 87.

[4] Commonwealth v. Burk, 11 Gray (Mass.) 437.

[5] Commonwealth v. Welch, 97 Mass. 593; Commonwealth v. Flaherty, 140 Mass. 454, 5 N. E. 258, Derby's Cases 205.

[6] Commonwealth v. Munsey, 112 Mass. 287.

[7] Commonwealth v. Feeney, 13 Allen (Mass.) 560.

[8] State v. Cleaves, 59 Maine 298, 8 Am. Rep. 422.

[9] 1 Russ. on Crimes (6th ed.) 146 et seq.

[10] Reg. v. Cruse, 8 Car. & P. 553.

[11] State v. Williams, 65 N. Car. 398.

The rule, that a wife who commits a crime in the presence of her husband is presumed to be coerced by him, has some exceptions.[12] "A wife may be indicted together with her husband, and condemned to the pillory with him for keeping a bawdy-house; for this is an offense as to the government of the house, in which the wife has a principal share; and also such an offense as may generally be presumed to be managed by the intrigues of her sex."[13] The same principle has been applied to the crime of keeping a gaming house.[14] Nor does any presumption of coercion arise in the higher crimes of treason[15] and murder.[16] It has been held that where a wife at the trial of a criminal case is a witness for her husband, who is present in the prisoner's dock, and she commits perjury, there is no presumption of coercion.[17]

On the other hand, the presumption of coercion arises where a wife, in the presence of her husband, commits the crime of forgery,[18] larceny,[19] burglary,[20] robbery,[21] arson,[22] receiving stolen goods,[23] mayhem,[24] uttering counterfeit money,[25] assault and battery,[26] abortion,[27] or selling intoxicating liquors without a license.[28]

12 Bibb v. State, 94 Ala. 31, 10 So. 506, 33 Am. St. 88.

13 1 Hawk. P. C., ch. 1 § 12. See also, 4 Bl. Comm. 29; State v. Miller, 162 Mo. 233, 62 S. W. 692, 85 Am. St. 498.

14 King v. Dixon, 10 Mod. 335.

15 4 Bl. Comm. 29; 1 Hale P. C. 47.

16 State v. Ma Foo, 110 Mo. 7, 19 S. W. 222, 33 Am. St. 414; Bibb v. State, 94 Ala. 31, 10 So. 506, 33 Am. St. 88. See also, 4 Bl. Comm. 29.

17 Commonwealth v. Moore, 162 Mass. 441, 38 N. E. 1120. See also, Smith v. Meyers, 54 Nebr. 1, 74 N. W. 277.

18 People v. Ryland, 97 N. Y. 126, 2 N. Y. Cr. 441.

19 Seiler v. People, 77 N. Y. 411.

20 Anonymous, W. Kelyng 30, Beale's Cases 273.

21 People v. Wright, 38 Mich. 744, 31 Am. Rep. 331.

22 Davis v. State, 15 Ohio 72, 45 Am. Dec. 559.

23 Goldstein v. People, 82 N. Y. 231; State v. Houston, 29 S. Car. 108, 6 S. E. 943.

24 State v. Ma Foo, 110 Mo. 7, 19 S. W. 222, 33 Am. St. 414.

25 Rex v. Price, 8 Car. & P. 19; Rex v. Hughes, 2 Lew. Cr. C. 229.

26 Commonwealth v. Neal, 10 Mass. 152, 6 Am. Dec. 105; State v. Williams, 65 N. Car. 398, Derby's Cases 201; Commonwealth v. Gannon, 97 Mass. 547.

27 Tabler v. State, 34 Ohio St. 127.

28 State v. Cleaves, 59 Maine

The existence or nonexistence of coercion on the part of the husband is a question of fact for the jury. Either may be inferred from conduct. Where husband and wife are tried for robbery and the evidence shows that the wife choked the victim and told him to keep still, while her husband picked his pockets, the jury would be justified in finding that she was not acting under coercion, but independently.[29]

When a crime is committed by a husband and his wife jointly, and there is no coercion on his part, they may be jointly indicted and convicted. For in such a case the wife acts in her own capacity as one able to commit crime, of her own accord and intent, as much as an unmarried person.[30]

§ 92. Subordinate commits crime by command of superior.—An illegal act can not be justified by an order from superior authority, no matter how high the source from which such order emanates.[31] It follows that the command of a superior to his subordinate to do a criminal act is no defense. Both in civil and in military law this principle is fundamental. Not only is a soldier, or military officer, justified in refusing to obey an illegal order of his superior officer, but it is his duty to disobey such order.[32] Much more is it the duty of a subordinate to disobey the command of his superior when the command is to commit a crime.[33]

"In all cases in which force is used against the person of another, both the person who orders such force to be used and the person using that force are responsible for its use,

298, 8 Am. Rep. 422; Mulvey v. State, 43 Ala. 316, 94 Am. Dec. 684; Commonwealth v. Burk, 11 Gray (Mass.) 437.

29 People v. Wright, 38 Mich. 744, 31 Am. Rep. 331. See also, 3 Greenl. on Ev., § 7; 1 Russ. on Crimes (9th ed.) 32 et seq.; Roscoe's Crim. Ev. 911.

30 Goldstein v. People, 82 N. Y. 231. See also, State v. Bentz, 11 Mo. 27.

31 State v. Sparks, 27 Tex. 627; Reese v. State, 73 Ala. 18; State v. Sutton, 10 R. I. 159; People v. McLeod, 1 Hill (N. Y.) 377, 25 Wend. (N. Y.) 483, 37 Am. Dec. 328.

32 State v. Sparks, 27 Tex. 627.

33 United States v. Jones, 3 Wash. (C. C.) 209.

and neither of them is justified by the circumstance that he acts in obedience to orders given him by a civil or military superior; but the fact that he did so act, and the fact that the order was apparently lawful, are in all cases relevant to the question whether he believed, in good faith and on reasonable grounds, in the existence of a state of facts which would have justified what he did apart from such orders."[34] This principle is applicable to the case of a bartender who, by command of his employer, sells intoxicating liquors without a license.[35]

Where a child, who has capacity to commit a crime, is indicted for an offense, the fact that he committed the act by command of his parent is no defense.[36] The only case in which the command of one person is a defense to a criminal charge against another is where a wife, in the presence of her husband, commits a crime by his command.[36a]

But the criminal liability of a subordinate who does an act by command of his superior is never greater than that of the superior would have been had he done the act himself.[37] Thus, where a servant of the owner and occupant of a residence sets fire to it by command of his master, for the purpose of defrauding an insurance company, the servant is not liable for arson. This is owing to the fact that the master would not be liable were he to do the act himself.[38] And a soldier or militiaman on active duty, who, upon order from a superior which is in the line of his duty, apparently not illegal to a man of common understanding and reasonably justified, shoots and kills one who failed to halt on challenge, is not guilty of homicide.[39]

[34] Steph. Dig. Crim. L. (5th ed.), art. 223.

[35] Commonwealth v. Hadley, 11 Metc. (Mass.) 66, Beale's Case 372.

[36] People v. Richmond, 29 Cal. 414 (larceny); Carlisle v. State, 37 Tex. Cr. 108, 38 S. W. 991 (girl of sixteen poisoned her babe by command of her mother).

[36a] See ante § 91.

[37] Roberts v. State, 7 Cold. (Tenn.) 359; State v. Haynes, 66 Maine 307, 22 Am. Rep. 569.

[38] State v. Haynes, 66 Maine 307, 22 Am. Rep. 569; Roberts v. State, 7 Cold. (Tenn.) 359.

[39] Commonwealth v. Shortall, 206 Pa. St. 165, 55 Atl. 952, 65 L.

§ 93. Actual duress by persons without authority.—While the topic under discussion is somewhat difficult, and the views of such distinguished writers as Wharton,[40] Bishop,[41] Russell,[42] Lord Denman,[43] Blackstone,[44] Lord

R. A. 193, 98 Am. St. 759, Derby's Cases 257. See also, note to L. R. A. 1915A, 1173.

[40] "Compulsion may be viewed in two aspects: (1) When the immediate agent is physically forced to do the injury, as where his hand is seized by a person of superior strength, and is used, against his will, to strike a blow, in which case no guilt attaches to the person so coerced. (2) When the force applied is that of authority or fear. When a person not intending wrong, is swept along by a party of persons whom he can not resist, he is not responsible if he is compelled to do wrong by threats on the part of the offenders instantly to kill him, or to do him grievous bodily harm if he refuses." 1 Whart. Crim. L. (11th ed.) § 124. "No matter what may be the shape compulsion takes, if it affect the person and be yielded to bona fide, it is a legitimate defense." 3 Whart. Crim. L. (11th ed.) § 2150.

[41] "An act done from compulsion or necessity is not a crime. To this doctrine there can be and is no exception." 1 Bish. New Crim. L. (8th ed.), § 346. "In general, whatever it is necessary for a man to do to save his life is treated as compelled. If one, therefore, joins with rebels from fear of present death, he is not a traitor while the constraint remains." 1 Bish. New Crim. L. (8th ed), § 347, par. 3.

[42] The person committing the crime must be a free agent, and not subject to actual force at the time the act is done: Thus, if A by force take the arm of B, in which is a weapon, and therewith kill C, A is guilty of murder, but not B.: but if it be only a moral force put upon B, as by threatening him with duress or imprisonment, or even by an assault to the peril of his life, in order to compel him to kill C, it is no legal excuse. Russ. on Crimes (9th Am. ed.), 32.

[43] Lord Denman states, "that no man, from a fear of consequences to himself, has a right to make himself a party committing mischief on mankind." Reg. v. Tyler, 8 Car. & P. 616.

[44] "Though a man be violently assaulted, and has not other possible means of escaping death but by killing an innocent person, this fear and force shall not acquit him of murder, for he ought rather to die himself than escape by the murder of an innocent." 4 Bl. Comm., 30.

Hale,[45] Stephen,[46] and Hawkins[47] are more or less conflicting, it is believed that the following propositions state the law correctly:

(1) Actual duress, consisting of threats which reasonably produce a well-grounded fear of immediate death or grievous bodily harm, is usually a defense to a criminal charge.[47a]

(2) Actual duress, consisting of threats of future personal injury, even death, is no defense.[48] To constitute a defense, the duress must relate to a present impending injury.[49] Duress, consisting of threats to murder, is no defense to a charge of perjury.[50]

(3) Actual duress, consisting of threats of injury to property, or destruction thereof, is no defense.[51] "The only force that doth excuse, is a force upon the person, and present fear of death."[52]

[45] "A man can not even excuse the killing of another who is innocent, under a threat however urgent of losing his own life unless he comply." Opinion of Lord Hale in East's Crown L., 294.

[46] "An act which, if done willingly, would make a person a principal in the second degree and an aider and abettor in a crime, may be innocent if the crime is committed by a number of offenders, and if the act is done only because, during the whole of the time in which it is being done, the person who does it is compelled to do it by threats on the part of the offenders instantly to kill him, or to do him grievous bodily harm if he refuses; but threats of future injury or the command of any one not the husband of the offender, do not excuse any offense." Steph. Dig. Crim. L. (5th ed.), art 32. See also People v. Repke, 103 Mich. 459, 61 N. W. 861.

[47] "The question of the practicability of escape is to be considered, and that if the person thus acting under compulsion continued in the treasonable acts longer than was necessary, the defense pro timore mortis will not be available." Hawk. P. C., ch. 17, § 28n.

[47a] Seiler v. New York, 77 N. Y. 411.

[48] Steph. Dig. Crim. L. (5th ed.), art. 32.

[49] Bain v. State, 67 Miss. 557, 7 So. 408; Ross v. State, 169 Ind. 388, 82 N. E. 781, Derby's Cases, 253.

[50] People v. Repke, 103 Mich. 459, 61 N. W. 861.

[51] Respublica v. McCarty, 2 Dall. (Pa.) 86, 1 L. ed. 300, Beale's Cases 364; United States v. Vigol, 2 Dall. (U. S.) 346, 1 L. ed. 409, Fed. Cas. No. 16621.

[52] McGrowther's Case, Fost. C. C. 13, Beale's Cases 273.

§ 94. **Actual duress of necessity in other cases.**—"An act which would otherwise be a crime may in some cases be excused if the person accused can show that it was done only in order to avoid consequences which could not otherwise be avoided, and which, if they had followed, would have inflicted upon him, or upon others whom he was bound to protect, inevitable and irreparable evil, that no more was done than was reasonably necessary for that purpose, and that the evil inflicted by it was not disproportionate to the evil avoided."[53] Lord Mansfield states: "Wherever necessity forces a man to do an illegal act,—forces him to do it,—it justifies him, because no man can be guilty of a crime without the will and intention of his mind."[54] According to Lord Bacon, "If a man steal viands to satisfy his present hunger, this is no felony nor larceny. So if divers be in danger of drowning by the casting away of some boat or bark, and one of them get to some plank, or on the boat side to keep himself above water, and another, to save his life thrust him from it, whereby he is drowned, this is neither se defendendo nor by misadventure, but is justifiable."[55]

While it has been said by Lord Hale: "If a person, being under necessity for want of victuals, or clothes, shall upon that account clandestinely and animo furandi steal another man's goods, it is felony and a crime by the laws of England punishable with death."[56] Lord Chief Justice Coleridge thus disposes of the matter: "If Lord Bacon meant to lay down the broad proposition that a man may save his life by killing, if necessary, an innocent and unoffending neighbor, it certainly is not law at the present day."[57]

With respect to the foregoing views it is undoubtedly true

[53] Steph. Dig. Crim. L. (5th ed.), art. 33.

[54] Lord Mansfield in Rex v. Stratton, 21 How. St. Tr. 1045, 1223.

[55] Bacon's Maxims, reg. 5, Beale's Cases 356.

[56] 1 Hale P. C. 54.

[57] Lord Chief Justice Coleridge in Reg. v. Dudley, 14 Q. B. Div. 273, 15 Cox Cr. C. 624, Beale's Cases 357, Derby's Cases 261.

that Lord Bacon's, both as regards the stealing of the viands and also as regards the drowning of the castaway, is unsound; while Lord Hale's, as regards the guilt of the accused, and Lord Chief Justice Coleridge's, correctly state the law.[58] It has been held that a sailor on a vessel may not kill a passenger to save himself.[59] And where three persons were cast away on the high seas and two of them killed the third and fed on his body, believing it necessary to save their lives, they were held guilty of murder.[60]

Necessity is a defense where a person joins a rebellion to save his life;[61] or where owing to stress of weather the captain of a vessel is compelled to take refuge in a proscribed port;[62] or where the crew of a vessel are forced to depose her master.[63]

§ 95. **Inability to perform a legal duty.**—Inability to perform a legal duty may constitute a defense. Where a person is complained against for allowing his vehicle to stop in a street for a longer period than allowable under an ordinance, and the evidence shows that he was delayed unavoidably owing to the crowding of other vehicles in the street, the compulsion is a good defense;[64] and so where a person is unable to repair a highway owing to vis major, as where the materials for doing so are swept into the sea.[65] Again, circum-

58 Brewer v. State, 72 Ark. 145, 78 S. W. 773, Derby's Cases 254. In this case an instruction "that, though one may lawfully kill an assailant if it be necessary to save his own life, he can not lawfully slay an innocent third person, even to save his own life, but ought to die himself, rather than take the life of an innocent person," was sustained.

59 United States v. Holmes, Fed. Cas. No. 15383, 1 Wall. Jr. (U. S.) 1.

60 Reg. v. Dudley, (1884), 14 Q. B. Div. 273, 15 Cox Cr. C. 624, Derby's Cases 261, Beale's Cases 357.

61 McGrowther's Case. Fost. Cr. C. 13, Beale's Cases 273; Respublica v. McCarty, 2 Dall. (Pa.) 86, 1 L. ed. 300, Beale's Cases 364.

62 The Brig William Gray, 1 Paine (U. S.) 16, Fed. Cas. No. 17694.

63 United States v. Ashton, 2 Sumn. (U. S.) 13, Fed. Cas. No. 14470.

64 Commonwealth v. Brooks, 99 Mass. 434, Beale's Cases 364.

65 Reg. v. Bamber, 5 Q. B. 279, Beale's Cases 356.

stances may justify working on Sunday, though a statute prohibits labor on that day.[66] It is essential, however, that the necessity be actual. It has been held that the necessity was not actual in a case where a person cut his wheat on Sunday though it was overripe, and he was poor and had to depend upon his neighbor for the use of a cradle.[67]

[66] Commonwealth v. Knox, 6 Mass. 76.

[67] State v. Goff, 20 Ark. 289.

CHAPTER VII

CRIMINAL INTENT.

§ 100. **The general rule.**—As a general rule, criminal intent is an essential element of crime. The full definition of every crime contains expressly or by implication a proposition as to a state of mind. Therefore, if the mental element of any conduct alleged to be a crime is proved to have been absent in any given case, the crime so defined is not committed.[1] It is a sacred principle of criminal jurisprudence that the intention to commit the crime is of the essence of the crime.[2]

§ 101. **Exceptions to the general rule.**—The general rule, stated in the next preceding section, is applicable to all com-

[1] Reg. v. Tolson, L. R., 23 Q. B. Div. 168, Beale's Cases 286, Derby's Cases 133. See also Commonwealth v. Mixer, 207 Mass. 141, 93 N. E. 249, 20 Ann. Cas. 1152; People v. Connors, 253 Ill. 266, 97 N. E. 643, 39 L. R. A. (N. S.) 143n, Ann. Cas. 1913A, 196n.

[2] State v. Blacklock (N. Mex.), 167 Pac. 714.

mon-law crimes. There are, however, certain statutory crimes which are exceptions to it. No act is a crime unless so declared by positive law. A legislature may declare an act a crime irrespective of the element of criminal intent. Thus, where a statute imposes a penalty upon any person who shall keep, or offer for sale, naptha under any assumed name;[3] or shall wilfully place an obstruction on any railroad so as to endanger the safety of any train;[4] or shall fell any timber, brush, or any other obstruction into a certain river and allow the same to remain in said river for five days;[5] or shall permit a person under twenty-one to remain in his dance house;[6] or shall unite in wedlock persons whose marriage is declared invalid,[7] guilty knowledge is not an essential element of the crime. Where a statute in general terms makes an act indictable, criminal intent need not be shown unless, from the language of the statute, a purpose to require the existence of such intention is apparent.[8] If a statute makes criminal an act not malum in se, or infamous, without requiring the act to be knowingly done, a criminal intent need not be proved.[9]

§ 102. **Criminal negligence.**—Every person is presumed to intend the natural and probable consequences of his voluntary acts. And neglect in the discharge of a duty, or indifference to consequences, is, in many cases, equivalent to criminal intent.[10] Where a person recklessly discharges a gun, regardless of the lives of others, and kills or wounds a person,

[3] Commonwealth v. Wentworth, 118 Mass. 441.

[4] People v. Adams, 16 Hun (N. Y.) 549.

[5] State v. White Oak River Corp., 111 N. Car. 661, 16 S. E. 331.

[6] State v. Rosenfeld, 111 Minn. 301, 126 N. W. 1068, 29 L. R. A. (N. S.) 331, 137 Am. St. 557.

[7] Territory v. Harwood, 15 N. Mex. 424, 110 Pac. 556, 29 L. R. A. (N. S.) 504n.

[8] Halsted v. State, 41 N. J. L. 552, 32 Am. Rep. 247.

[9] Gardner v. People, 62 N. Y. 299; State v. Southern Express Co. (Ala.), 75 So. 343.

[10] 1 Bish. New Crim. L. (8th ed.) § 313; United States v. Thomson, 12 Fed. 245, 8 Sawy. 122; People v. Connors, 253 Ill. 266, 97 N. E. 643, 39 L. R. A. (N. S.) 143n, Ann. Cas. 1913A, 196; Belk v. People, 125 Ill. 584, 17 N. E. 744.

his acts will be construed as implying general malice, and render him criminally liable.[11] If a person negligently, but without criminal intent, delivers flour for export, without having the same inspected as required by a penal statute, his negligence may be so gross as to be equivalent to criminal intent.[12]

§ 103. **Criminal intent implied.**—Where a person voluntarily commits an unlawful act the law presumes a general criminal intent.[13] A person recklessly doing an act calculated to injure persons or property, is presumed to have intended to do what his act is calculated to accomplish.[14] One who does an act in violation of law is presumed to have done it wilfully; and the lack of intention to violate it will not release him from criminal liability.[15] It has been asserted by Lord Mansfield that, "Where an act in itself indifferent, if done with a particular intent becomes criminal; there the intent must be proved and found; but where the act is in itself unlawful, * * * the proof of justification or excuse lies on the defendant; and in failure thereof, the law implies a criminal intent."[16]

§ 104. **Criminal intent conclusively presumed.**—In some cases criminal intent is conclusively presumed. If a statute, for example, forbids the doing of an act under certain circumstances, and the statute is violated, criminal intent is conclusively presumed.[17] Where a common carrier, in direct violation of a statute, discriminates in the transportation of

[11] Vandermark v. People, 47 Ill. 122; State v. Tucker, 86 S. Car. 211, 68 S. E. 523, Derby's Cases 150.

[12] Sturges v. Maitland, Anth. N. P. (2d ed.) (N. Y.) 208.

[13] State v. Hall, 85 Mo. 669; State v. Jones, 70 Iowa 505, 30 N. W. 750.

[14] State v. Neville, 2 Ohio Dec. 358.

[15] Marmont v. State, 48 Ind. 21.

[16] Rex v. Woodfall, 5 Burr. 2667. See also Slattery v. People, 76 Ill. 217; State v. Goodenow, 65 Maine 30.

[17] Commonwealth v. New York Cent. &c. R. Co., 202 Mass. 394, 88 N. E. 764, 132 Am. St. 507; State v. Gilmore, 80 Vt. 514, 68 Atl. 658, 16 L. R. A. (N. S.) 786n, 13 Ann. Cas. 321.

goods or passengers, criminal intent is conclusively presumed.[18] Where a person, in direct violation of a statute, opens a grave for the purpose of removing a body interred therein, criminal intent is conclusively presumed.[19]

§ 105. **Specific criminal intent.**—Some crimes involve a specific, or particular, criminal intent. In larceny, robbery, burglary, and in all of the aggravated assaults, a specific criminal intent is an essential ingredient. And where a specific criminal intent is an essential ingredient of a crime such intent must be shown.[20] Moreover, such intent should be alleged in the indictment. But if the offense consists merely in doing an unlawful or criminal act and no particular intention is essential, an evil intention is presumed and need not be alleged or proved.[21]

§ 106. **Motive.**—A bad motive is not an essential element of any crime. The existence of a motive is a circumstance to be considered with all the other evidence by the jury in reaching a conclusion of guilt or innocence and the lack of proof of it may be a circumstance tending to show innocence; but proof of motive is not necessary to convict, nor is its absence ground for acquittal; for crimes may be thoroughly established and no motive appear.[22] Indeed, the very absence of known motive may aggravate the offense. On the other hand, a good motive is no defense. A wilful wrong inflicted on others, unwarranted by law, is malicious, though committed in pursuance of a general good purpose and sin-

18 State v. Southern R. Co., 122 N. Car. 1052, 30 S. E. 133, 41 L. R. A. 246.

19 State v. McLean, 121 N. Car. 589, 28 S. E. 140, 42 L. R. A. 721.

20 Ogletree v. State, 28 Ala. 693, Derby's Cases 126; State v. Meche, 42 La. Ann. 273, 7 So. 573, Derby's Cases 131.

21 Commonwealth v. Hersey, 2 Allen (Mass.) 173; State v. Thomas, 127 La. 576, 53 So. 868, Ann. Cas. 1912A, 1059; People v. Molineux, 168 N. Y. 264, 61 N. E. 286, 62 L. R. A. 193, Derby's Cases 101.

22 People v. Seppi, 221 N. Y. 62, 116 N. E. 793; People v. King, 276 Ill. 138, 114 N. E. 601; Stone v. State, 105 Ala. 60, 17 So. 114; People v. Zammuto, 280 Ill. 225, 117 N. E. 454.

cere design to bring about some altruistic end.[23] The fact that a person has conscientious scruples against being vaccinated is no defense in an action against him for refusing to be vaccinated where a penal statute requires it to be done.[24] Nor is the fact that a parent, who is financially capable, owing to conscientious religious scruples, wilfully fails to call a physician or supply proper medicines for his sick child, as a result of which the child dies, any defense.[25] The parent in such a case is guilty of involuntary manslaughter. The contrary doctrine has been held,[26] but such doctrine is not sound.[27] "The nature of one's legal duties, and the extent of his legal responsibilities, both civil and criminal, must be governed by general rules of law which will apply to all alike."[28] But evidence of motive is always admissible and frequently of great importance.

It matters little whether the motive be adequate, according to the standard of persons other than the defendant; but whether a motive is adequate to induce the commission of crime depends on the peculiar circumstances of each case, and the particular character of the defendant. Murders are often committed from motives comparatively trivial and slight, such as to obtain, by inheritance or otherwise, a small amount of property, or to remove some person who is an obstacle to a desired marriage.[29]

§ 107. Criminal intent usually transferable.—Many crimes involve only a general criminal intent, while others involve a

[23] Commonwealth v. Snelling, 15 Pick. (Mass.) 337; United States v. Harmon, 45 Fed. 414 (affd. 50 Fed. 921).

[24] Commonwealth v. Pear, 183 Mass. 242, 66 N. E. 719, 67 L. R. A. 935 (affd. 197 U. S. 11, 49 L. ed 643, 25 Sup. Ct. 358).

[25] State v. Chenoweth, 163 Ind. 94, 71 N. E. 197. See also Owens v. State, 6 Okla. Cr. 664, 116 Pac. 345, 36 L. R. A. (N. S.) 633n.

[26] Reg. v. Wagstaffe, 10 Cox Cr. C. 530.

[27] Reg. v. Downes, 13 Cox Cr. C. 111, Beale's Cases 195, Derby's Cases 97; State v. Chenoweth, 163 Ind. 94, 71 N. E. 197; Reg. v. Senior, 19 Cox Cr. C. 219.

[28] State v. Sandford, 99 Maine 441, 59 Atl. 597.

[29] State v. Lentz, 45 Minn. 177, 47 N. W. 720.

specific or particular criminal intent. A general criminal intent is always transferable.[29a] A particular criminal intent is sometimes transferable and sometimes not. It is transferable from person to person or from thing to thing; but not from person to thing or from thing to person. The latter part of this rule is wholly arbitrary, but it is recognized and enforced by the courts. Thus, where a person recklessly shoots at another's cattle in his corn field to frighten and run them out, and unintentionally kills his neighbor's mule, he is criminally liable for his act.[30] But a person who maliciously shoots at another person on horseback and kills his horse is not guilty of maliciously killing the horse, for malice implies intent and there is no intent to kill the horse.[31] And a person who maliciously throws a stone, intending to hit other persons, and the stone misses them and hits and breaks a large plate-glass window, is not guilty of malicious mischief, since he did not intend to break the window.[32] It has been held that one who, while assaulting another with intent to kill, injures unintentionally a third person, is not liable for assault with intent to kill such person.[33] But the weight of authority is to the contrary.[34]

§ 108. Criminal liability for unintended result.—Since criminal intent is generally transferable, a person may render himself criminally liable for an unintended result. To do so, however, two things are essential: (1) The act intended must be at least malum in se; and (2) the unintended result must be the natural and probable consequence of the act intended.

29a People v. Hodge, 196 Mich. 546, 162 N. W. 966.

30 State v. Barnard, 88 N. Car. 661.

31 Rex v. Scully, 1 Craw. & D. 186.

32 Reg. v. Pembliton, 12 Cox Cr. C. 607, Beale's Cases 210, Derby's Cases 127.

33 State v. Thomas, 127 La. 576, 37 L. R. A. (N. S.) 172n, Ann. Cas. 1912A, 1059, and cases cited; Scott v. State, 49 Ark. 156, 4 S. W. 750; Derby's Cases 129.

34 State v. Gilman, 69 Maine 163, 31 Ann. Rep. 257, Derby's Cases 123; Reg. v. Latimer, 16 Cox Cr. C. 70; Derby's Cases 120; State v. Mulhall, 199 Mo. 202, 97 S. W. 583, 7 L. R. A. (N. S.) 630, 8 Ann. Cas. 781.

If the act intended is merely malum prohibitum there is no criminal liability for an unintended result. Thus, where a person runs over a child unintentionally, while driving at a more rapid rate than allowable under a city ordinance, but not recklessly, the person is not criminally liable for assault and battery. Though the ordinance may have been wilfully violated, the offense consists not in the intent with which it was violated, but in the violation itself, an act prohibited but not otherwise wrong, and the intentional disregard of the ordinance does not in itself supply the intent to sustain the criminal charge of assault and battery.[35] The same principle is applicable where a person shoots out of season at what he believes to be a deer but which proves to be a man. Should he kill the man under such circumstances he would not be liable for felonious homicide.

Where the unintended result is not the natural and probable consequence of the act intended there is no criminal liability for the unintended result. Thus, where a person knocks another person down in a street and he is trampled upon by a horse passing by, as a result of which he dies, the person who knocks him down is not liable for felonious homicide, unless the act of the horse is the natural and probable consequence of the assault and battery.[36] But where one wantonly threw a box into the sea where there were bathers and struck one under water and killed him, he was guilty of manslaughter.[37]

Where a person intentionally commits a crime, and his act proves different from that which he intended, he is criminally liable for the consequences.[38] However, one who in seeking to steal rum, unintentionally set fire to a ship by means of

35 Commonwealth v. Adams, 114 Mass. 323, 19 Am. Rep. 362, Derby's Cases 115. See also, 1 Hale P. C. 39; Fost. C. L. 259.

36 People v. Rockwell, 39 Mich. 503.

37 Reg. v. Franklin, 15 Cox. Cr. C. 163, Derby's Cases, 113.

38 Commonwealth v. Murphy, 165 Mass. 66, 42 N. E. 504, 30 L. R. A. 734, 52 Am. St. 496; State v. Ruhl, 8 Iowa 447, Derby's Cases 112.

a lighted match, was held not criminally liable for the burning.[39]

Where a person is knowingly engaged in a criminal act and commits a greater offense than the one intended proof of an intent to commit the greater offense is not essential to a conviction for that offense. And it has been held that this rule is applicable not only to crimes which are mala in se, but also to those which are only mala prohibita.[40]

When several persons conspire to carry out a common design, and one of them commits a crime foreign to that design the others are not guilty of that crime.[41] This rule is applicable even when the crime is committed to aid all in making their escape, provided it is done without their knowledge or consent.[42] But when one of several persons associated in a criminal enterprise commits a crime in furtherance of their common object, all are equally liable for such crime.[43]

§ 109. **Malice — Definition — Classification.** —The term "malice" is used in a two-fold sense. It has a popular meaning and also a legal meaning. In its popular sense it means hatred or ill-will. In its legal sense it is synonymous with criminal intent. In the latter sense, "It comprehends not only a particular ill-will, but every case where there is wickedness of disposition, hardness of heart, cruelty, recklessness of consequences, and a mind regardless of social duty, although a particular person may not be intended to be injured."[44] In a legal sense, any act done wilfully and purposely to the prejudice and injury of another, which is unlawful, is, as against that person, malicious. It is not necessary, to render an act malicious, that the party be actuated by a feeling of hatred or ill-will toward the individual, or that

39 Reg. v. Faulkner, 13 Cox Cr. C. 550, Derby's Cases 117.

40 State v. Stanton, 37 Conn. 421.

41 Frank v. State, 27 Ala. 37.

42 Mercersmith v. State, 8 Tex. App. 211.

43 State v. Johnson, 7 Ore. 210.

44 Commonwealth v. Drum, 58 Pa. St. 9.

he entertain and pursue any general bad purpose or design. On the contrary, he may be actuated by a general good purpose, and have a real and sincere design to bring about a reformation of manners; but if in pursuing that design he wilfully inflicts a wrong on others, which is not warranted by law, such act is malicious.[45]

In some crimes, however, the terms "malice" and "malicious" are used in a more restricted sense than they are generally. Thus, in the crimes of malicious mischief, murder and arson, they have a more restricted meaning. In the crime of malicious mischief, Blackstone states that the mischief must be done "either out of a spirit of wanton cruelty or black and diabolical revenge."[46] The word "maliciously," relating to malicious mischief, is not sufficiently defined as "the wilfully doing of any act prohibited by law, and for which the defendant had no lawful excuse."[47]

§ 110. **Malice aforethought—Definition.**—Malice aforethought is the distinguishing feature of the crime of murder. Its absence renders a felonious homicide manslaughter. It does not imply ill-will or hatred, but, on the other hand, is something more than mere criminal intent. It does not, however, imply deliberation, nor does it imply intent to kill. It has been said that, "Reduced to its lowest terms, malice in murder means knowledge of such circumstances that according to common experience there is a plain and strong likelihood that death will follow the contemplated act, coupled perhaps with an implied negation of any excuse or justification."[48] The words "malice aforethought," in the description of murder, denote purpose and design in contra-

[45] Chief Justice Shaw in Commonwealth v. Snelling, 15 Pick. (Mass.) 337; Killian v. State, 19 Ga. App. 750, 92 S. E. 227.

[46] 4 Bl. Comm. 243.

[47] Commonwealth v. Walden, 57 Mass. (3 Cush.) 558.

[48] Commonwealth v. Chance, 174 Mass. 245, 54 N. E. 551, 75 Am. St. 306; People v. Venckus, 278 Ill. 124, 115 N. E. 880.

distinction to accident and mischance.[49] Malice aforethought is not so much malevolence to the individual in particular, as an evil design in general, the dictate of a wicked, depraved and malignant heart.[50]

§ 111. **Ignorance or mistake of law.**—Every person is presumed not only to intend the natural and probable consequences of his voluntary acts, but also to know the law. Ignorance or mistake of law, therefore, is no defense to a criminal charge.[51] Thus, where a person is indicted for violating a liquor law, an instruction by the trial court that, "if the defendant knew what he was doing and did what he intended to do, it was immaterial what his opinion was as to the legal effect of what he was doing, and it would be no defense that he did not know he was violating the law," is manifestly correct.[52]

It is to be observed, however, that the legal maxim, ignorantia legis neminem excusat, is not without limitations. "This rule, in its application to the law of crimes, is subject, as it is sometimes in respect to civil rights, to certain important exceptions. Where the act is malum in se, or where the law which has been infringed was settled and plain, the maxim, in its rigor, will be applied; but where the law is not settled, or is obscure, and where the guilty intention, being a necessary constituent of the particular offense, is dependent on a knowledge of the law, this rule, if enforced would be misapplied. To give it any force in such instances, would be to turn it aside from its rational and original purpose, and to convert it into an instrument of injustice. The

[49] Commonwealth v. Webster, 5 Cush. (Mass.) 295, 52 Am. Dec. 711.

[50] Ann v. State, 11 Humph. (Tenn.) 159.

[51] New York Cent. &c. R. Co. v. United States, 239 Fed. 130, 152 C. C. A. 172.

[52] State v. Carver, 69 N. H. 216, 39 Atl. 973, Knowlton's Cases 308. See also Reynolds v. United States, 98 U. S. 145, 25 L. ed. 224; 1 Bish. New Crim. L. (8th ed.), § 294.

judgments of the courts have confined it to its proper sphere."[53]

Moreover, the maxim is not applicable where a person relies upon a statute which subsequently is held by the court unconstitutional and void; but the rule is confined to presuming that all persons know the law exists, but not that they are presumed to know how the courts will construe it, and whether, if it be a statute, it will, or will not, be held to be constitutional. To extend the rule further would be to hold in effect that the legislature which passed, and the governor who approved, a statute, knew that it was unconstitutional and were thus guilty of bad faith.[54] So where a criminal statute is declared unconstitutional and afterward in another case, held to be constitutional, a prosecution under it can not be maintained for acts done intermediate the two decisions.[55]

The maxim is applicable even where it is physically impossible at the time the crime is committed for the perpetrator to have actual knowledge of the existence of the law violated. Thus, where a person is at sea when a criminal statute takes effect he is conclusively presumed to have knowledge of its contents; but his lack of knowledge is entitled to consideration in mitigation of the penalty.[56]

§ 112. **Advice of attorney.**—Generally speaking, the fact that a person receives and acts upon the advice of a lawyer, or a justice of the peace, is no defense. When a woman is indicted for voting illegally, the fact that she was advised by counsel that the statute in question was unconstitutional, and that she had the right to vote, is no defense. Such testimony is immaterial and inadmissible. That she believed she had a right to vote was immaterial, if in fact she had no

[53] Chief Justice Beasley in Cutter v. State, 36 N. J. L. 125.

[54] Brent v. State, 43 Ala. 297, 302.

[55] State v. O'Neil, 147 Iowa 513, 126 N. W. 454, 33 L. R. A. (N. S.) 788n, Ann. Cas. 1912 B, 691.

[56] Rex v. Bailey, Russ. & Ry. 1, Beale's Cases 280.

right.[57] If a married woman, whose husband is living and from whom she is not divorced, is advised by a justice of the peace that she has the legal right to marry another man, owing to the fact that her husband has gone through the marriage ceremony with another woman, and she goes through the marriage ceremony with the other man, in good faith, believing the advice to be true, and cohabits with him, the advice given her by the justice of the peace is no defense to the charge of adultery; and they having intentionally committed an act itself unlawful, the criminal intent is inferred from the criminality of the act, in spite of their ignorance of the law.[58]

§ 113. Religious belief.—The religious belief of a person is no defense to a criminal charge. Where parents, owing to conscientious religious scruples, refuse to provide necessary medical aid for their infant children, who are in the custody of their parents, and the children die in consequence, the parents' religious belief is no defense where a statute has imposed a positive duty on parents to provide medical aid for infant children in their custody.[59] If a man, having a living wife, from whom he is not divorced, marries another woman, owing to his religious belief in polygamy, such religious belief constitutes no defense.[60] And again, where a

[57] United States v. Anthony, Fed. Cas. No. 14459, 11 Blatch. (U. S.) 200.

[58] State v. Goodenow, 65 Maine 30, Beale's Cases 309; Weston v. Commonwealth, 111 Pa. St. 251, 2 Atl. 191. Same rule applies to bigamy. Staley v. State, 89 Nebr. 101, 131 N. W. 1028, 34 L. R. A. (N. S.) 613.

[59] Reg. v. Downes, 13 Cox Cr. C. 111, Derby's Cases 97.

[60] Reynolds v. United States, 98 U. S. 145, 25 L. ed. 244. "Laws are made for the government of actions, and while they can not interfere with mere religious belief and opinions, they may with practice. Suppose one believed that human sacrifices were a necessary part of religious worship, would it be seriously contended that the civil government under which he lived could not interfere to prevent a sacrifice? Of if a wife religiously believed it was her duty to burn herself upon the funeral pile of her dead husband, would it be beyond the power of the civil government to prevent her carrying her belief into practice? So here, as a law of the organization

person violates a statute which prohibits secular labor on Sunday, his religious belief in some other day of the week as a day of rest is no defense, the Sunday law being enacted to compel cessation of labor in order that those who wish to worship God then may not be interrupted.[61]

§ 114. **Mistake of fact.**—Blackstone says, "An unwarrantable act, without a vicious will is no crime at all."[62] He further states that, "Ignorance or mistake is another defect of will, when a man, intending to do a lawful act, does that which is unlawful. For here, the deed and the will acting separately, there is not that conjunction between them which is necessary to form a criminal act. But this must be an ignorance or mistake of fact and not an error in point of law."[63] Hale asserts that, "Where there is no will to commit an offense, there can be no transgression."[64] It is stated by Bishop that, "A mistake of fact, neither induced nor accompanied by any fault or omission of duty, excuses the otherwise criminal act which it prompts."[65] He also states that, "The wrongful intent being the essence of every crime, it necessarily follows that whenever one without fault or carelessness is misled concerning facts, and thereon acts as he would be justified in doing were they what he believes them to be, he is legally innocent."[66]

In some cases a mistake of fact is a defense to a criminal charge, and in others it is not. As a general rule, a bona fide and reasonable mistake of fact constitutes a complete defense. Such a mistake is said to be equivalent to a lack of

of society under exclusive dominion of the United States, it is provided that plural marriages shall not be allowed. Can a man excuse his practices to the contrary because of his religious belief? To permit this would be to make the professed doctrines of religious belief superior to the law of the land, and in effect to permit every citizen to become a law unto himself. Government could exist only in name under such circumstances."

[61] State v. Ambs, 20 Mo. 214.

[62] 4 Bl. Comm. 21.

[63] 4 Bl. Comm. 27.

[64] 1 Hale P. C. 15.

[65] 1 Bish. New Crim. L. (8th ed), § 303, par. 1.

[66] 1 Bish. New Crim. L. (8th ed.), § 303, par. 3.

perversion of the reasoning faculty, as exists in cases of infancy and insanity.[67] Thus, a street-car conductor who forcibly ejects a passenger under a bona fide but mistaken belief that he has not paid his fare, is not criminally liable for assault and battery.[68] And a policeman who arrests a person under a bona fide but mistaken belief upon reasonable and probable cause that he is drunk is not criminally liable for false arrest.[69]

Many other illustrations of the application of this principle are contained in the decisions. Where a person kills his assailant under a bona fide and reasonable belief that his act is necessary to save his life or protect him against grievous bodily harm, and he is mistaken, he is not criminally liable. To justify him, the killing need not have been done in necessary self-defense; it is sufficient if it appeared necessary to him as a reasonable man.[70] "What is absolute truth no man ordinarily knows. All act from what appears, not from what is. If persons were to delay their steps until made sure, beyond every possibility of mistake, that they were right, earthly affairs would cease to move; and stagnation, death, and universal decay would follow. All, therefore, must, and constantly do, perform what else they would not, through mistake of facts."[71]

In a leading English case, in which the defendant was on trial for felonious homicide, the proof showed that, believing a burglar was in his house, he thrust his sword in the dark where he thought the supposed burglar was in hiding, and killed a friend of his domestic, who had called upon the latter to assist her in performing her household duties; and it was held that the mistake of fact constituted a defense.[72]

[67] Reg. v. Tolson, L. R., 23 Q. B. Div. 168, Derby's Cases 133, Beale's Cases 286.

[68] State v. McDonald, 7 Mo. App. 510.

[69] Commonwealth v. Presby, 80 Mass. (14 Gray) 65.

[70] Steinmeyer v. People, 95 Ill. 383. See also Schmier v. People, 23 Ill. 17; Maher v. People, 24 Ill. 241; Roach v. People, 77 Ill. 25.

[71] 1 Bish. New Crim. L. (8th ed.), § 303, par. 2.

[72] Levett's Case, Cro. Car. 538, 1 Hale P. C. 474, Beale's Cases 279.

Where a person takes another's goods or chattels by mistake, believing they are his own or his master's, and appropriates them to his own or to his master's use, respectively, he is not guilty of larceny.[73] Nor is a person guilty of larceny who takes property by the direction or with the consent of another whom he erroneously believes to be the owner.[74]

When a specific criminal intent is an essential element of a crime, and this intent is negatived by a mistake of fact, the latter constitutes a defense. Thus, where a person signs another's name to a note or other instrument, under a bona fide but mistaken belief that he has authority so to do, he is not guilty of forgery.[75]

On the other hand, there are many cases in which a mistake of fact is no defense to a criminal charge, as where a person snaps a loaded pistol at another, believing that the cartridge in it is too old to explode, and it goes off and kills the party at whom it is aimed, he is criminally liable, since he used a dangerous and deadly weapon, in a careless and reckless manner.[76] And where a person is mistaken as to the identity of another, and shoots or strikes at him with intent to murder the person he believes him to be, his mistake of fact will constitute no defense.[77] He actually intends to kill the person at whom he shoots or strikes and his mistake of identity will not avail him.

§ 115. **Mistake in reference to statutory crimes.**—As a general rule, the effect of a mistake of fact in the case of a statutory crime is the same as it is in the case of a common-law crime. In every case, unless the legislature has made the act a crime, irrespective of criminal intent, a mistake of

[73] Phelps v. People, 55 Ill. 334, Derby's Cases 161; People v. Slayton, 123 Mich. 397, 82 N. W. 205, 81 Am. St. 211; Rex v. Hall, 3 Car. & P. 409, Beale's Cases 281.

[74] State v. Matthews, 20 Mo. 55. See also Mead v. State, 25 Nebr. 444, 41 N. W. 277.

[75] Kotter v. People, 150 Ill. 441, 37 N. E. 932.

[76] State v. Hardie, 47 Iowa 647, 26 Am. Rep. 496.

[77] McGehee v. State, 62 Miss. 772, 52 Am. Rep. 209.

fact has exactly the same effect as in the case of a common-law crime. But, as Bishop states, "One of the common forms of blundering on this subject consists of the assumption, contrary to established rule, that a statute in mere general terms is to be interpreted as excluding exceptions; so that if it says nothing of mistake of fact, the courts can not except a case of such mistake out of its operation."[78] It is to be observed, however, as stated by the same author, "All statutes are to be and constantly are interpreted with reference to the unwritten law, by the principles of which they are limited and extended, so as to preserve harmony in our juridical system and promote justice."[79]

A person who commits a criminal act under an insane delusion is not criminally responsible, provided the delusion is such that were it a fact it would be a defense to a sane person.[80]

The decisions, however, both in England and in this country, upon the question of the effect of mistake of fact in statutory crimes, are in hopeless conflict. Many of them hold that mistake of fact is no defense to a statutory criminal charge where the statute is silent upon the matter of criminal intent;[81] while many others hold exactly the con-

78 1 Bish. New Crim. L. (8th ed.), § 304.

79 1 Bish. New Crim. L. (8th ed.), § 304; New York Cent. etc. R. Co. v. United States, 239 Fed. 130, 152 C. C. A. 172.

80 Commonwealth v. Presby, 80 Mass. (14 Gray) 65.

81 Waterbury v. Newton, 50 N. J. L. 534, 14 Atl. 604; State v. Rogers, 95 Maine 94, 49 Atl. 564, 85 Am. St. 395; State v. Ryan, 70 N. H. 196, 46 Atl. 49, 85 Am. St. 629; State v. Kelly, 54 Ohio St. 166, 177, 43 N. E. 163; State v. Dorman, 9 S. Dak. 528, 70 N. W. 848; People v. Worden Grocer Co., 118 Mich. 604, 77 N. W. 315; Commonwealth v. Raymond, 97 Mass. 567; Commonwealth v. Wentworth, 118 Mass. 441; Farmer v. People, 77 Ill. 322; McCutcheon v. People, 69 Ill. 601; Commonwealth v. Smith, 103 Mass. 444; State v. Kinkead, 57 Conn. 173, 17 Atl. 855; State v. Probasco, 62 Iowa 400, 17 N. W. 607; People v. Dolan, 96 Cal. 315, 31 Pac. 107; Knight, &c., Co. v. Miller, 172 Ind. 27, 87 N. E. 823, 18 Ann. Cas. 1146; State v. Henzell, 17 Idaho 725, 107 Pac. 67, 27 L. R. A. (N. S.) 159; State v. Gilmore, 80 Vt. 514, 68 Atl. 658, 16 L. R. A. (N. S.) 786n, 13 Ann. Cas. 321; Reg. v. Prince, 13 Cox Cr. C. 138; Reg. v. Gibbons, 12 Cox Cr. C. 237;

trary.[82] In support of the former view which is based largely upon a public policy, it has been said: "In the earlier history of the common law only such acts were deemed criminal as had in them the vicious element of an unlawful intent, indicating a deviation from moral rectitude; but this quality has ceased to be essential, and now acts unobjectionable, in a moral view, except sc far as being prohibited by law makes them so, constitute a considerable portion of the criminal code. In such statutes the act is expressly prohibited, without reference to the intent or purpose of the party committing it, and is usually of the class in which the person committing it is under no obligation to act unless he knows he can do so lawfully. Under these statutes it is not a defense that the person acted honestly and in good faith, under a mistake of fact. He is bound to know the fact as well as the law, and he acts at his peril."[83] This statement is quoted approvingly.[84]

Where one was convicted of unlawfully taking a girl under sixteen out of the possession of her parents, and the girl appeared to be over eighteen, and the defendant believed her over eighteen, the conviction was upheld.[85] It is to be observed, however, that unless it is clear that the legislature intended that the act itself is to constitute a crime irrespective of any criminal intent the statute should be construed according to the principles of the common law.

Reg. v. Bennett, 14 Cox Cr. C. 45; Reg. v. Woodrow, 15 M. & W. 404.

82 Mulreed v. State, 107 Ind. 62, 7 N. E. 884; People v. Welch, 71 Mich. 548, 39 N. W. 747, 1 L. R. A. 385; Adler v. State, 55 Ala. 16; Farrell v. State, 32 Ohio St. 456, 30 Am. Rep. 614; Stern v. State, 53 Ga. 229, 21 Am. Rep. 266; Marshall v. State, 49 Ala. 21; Robinius v. State, 63 Ind. 235; Reg. v. Tolson, L. R., 23 Q. B. Div. 168, Derby's Cases 133, Beale's Cases 286; Reg. v. Turner, 9 Cox Cr. C. 145; Reg. v. Horton, 11 Cox Cr. C. 670; Reg. v. Moore, 13 Cox Cr. C. 544.

83 State v. Cornish, 66 N. H. 329, 21 Atl. 180, 11 L. R. A. 191n.

84 Chief Justice Blodgett in State v. Ryan, 70 N. H. 196, 46 Atl. 49, 85 Am. St. 629.

85 Reg. v. Prince, 13 Cox Cr. C. 138, Derby's Cases 102.

Many decisions, however, as heretofore stated, are in harmony with the view, last quoted above. Thus, based upon various statutes, the following propositions have been sustained. An hotel-keeper, who furnishes oleomargarine to a guest without first notifying him that the substance is not butter, is criminally liable although he acted without unlawful intent and under a mistake of fact.[86] A dealer in tobacco, who has in his possession adulterated tobacco, is criminally liable, although he purchased it as genuine and had no knowledge or cause to suspect that it was not.[87] A grocer who sells New Orleans molasses adulterated with glucose is criminally liable although he is ignorant of the adulteration.[88] In prosecuting a milk dealer for selling adulterated milk, or milk below a certain standard, it is not necessary to prove that he had knowledge of the adulteration.[89] In an indictment for selling intoxicating liquors to a minor, without the written order of his parents, guardian or family physician, it is not necessary to allege and prove that the defendant had knowledge that the purchaser was a minor.[90] He is bound to know, in such a case, whether he was a minor or not.[91] A person who keeps naphtha for sale under an assumed name is criminally liable irrespective of guilty knowledge.[92] A grocer, who sells vinegar below the standard prescribed, is criminally liable, even if he has no knowledge that it is not within the standard prescribed.[93] In an indictment charging a person with removing timber from school lands it is not necessary to allege or prove guilty

86 State v. Ryan, 70 N. H. 196, 46 Atl. 49, 85 Am. St. 629.

87 Reg. v. Woodrow, 15 M. & W. 404.

88 State v. Kelly, 54 Ohio St. 166, 43 N. E. 163.

89 Commonwealth v. Smith, 103 Mass. 444; Commonwealth v. Wheeler, 205 Mass. 384, 91 N. E. 415, 18 Ann. Cas. 319, 137 Am. St. 456.

90 McCutcheon v. People, 69 Ill. 601.

91 Farmer v. People, 77 Ill. 322.

92 Commonwealth v. Wentworth, 118 Mass. 441.

93 People v. Worden Grocer Co., 118 Mich. 604, 77 N. W. 315. See also People v. Snowberger, 113 Mich. 86, 67 Am. St. 449.

knowledge or criminal intent.[94] It is said by Wharton, "When a statute makes an act indictable irrespective of guilty knowledge, then ignorance of fact, no matter how sincere, is no defense."[95] In an indictment charging the defendant with selling oleomargarine colored with annatto it is not essential to allege that he had knowledge that the oleomargarine sold by him was so colored.[96] A carrier may be criminally liable for transporting intoxicating liquor in violation of statute, although it had no knowledge of the fact that intoxicating liquor was contained in packages carried by it.[97] "The object was, not to punish acts intrinsically wrong, but to prevent acts which in their results operated unjustly upon others."[98] To an indictment for bringing from another state a pauper having no settlement in the town to which the pauper it brought, it is no defense that the accused believed such settlement to exist.[99] In an indictment for killing, for the purpose of sale, a calf less than four weeks old, it is not necessary to allege or prove that the defendant knew that the calf was less than four weeks old. It has been said: "It was not necessary to allege in the indictment that he knew the calf to be less than four weeks old. Under this clause, as under the laws against the sale of intoxicating liquor or adulterated milk, and many other police, health and revenue regulations, the defendant is bound to know the facts and obey the law, at his peril. Such is the general rule where acts which are not mala in se are made mala prohibita from motives of public policy, and not because of their moral turpitude or the criminal intent with which they are committed."[1] A corporation

94 State v. Dorman, 9 S. Dak. 528, 70 N. W. 848.

95 1 Whart. Crim. L. (11th ed.), § 108.

96 State v. Welch, 145 Wis. 86, 129 N. W. 656, 32 L. R. A. (N. S.) 746.

97 Commonwealth v. Mixer, 207 Mass. 141, 93 N. E. 249, 31 L. R. A. (N. S.) 467n, 20 Ann. Cas. 1152, Derby's Cases 139.

98 Waterbury v. Newton, 50 N. J. L. 534, 14 Atl. 604.

99 State v. Cornish, 66 N. H. 329, 21 Atl. 180, 11 L. R. A. 191n.

1 Commonwealth v. Raymond, 97 Mass. 567.

which has failed to file a statement required by statute before doing business, can be fined, though its officers did not know of the existence of the statute and complied with it as soon as they learned of it.[2]

On the other hand, many courts hold, as heretofore stated, that a bona fide mistake of fact, not due to negligence, is a defense to a statutory criminal charge, unless the statute clearly shows that the legislature intended the act to constitute a crime irrespective of guilty knowledge or criminal intent. In harmony with this view the following propositions have been sustained. Under an indictment for receiving and carrying off a slave, guilty knowledge is essential to convict since it is said, the intention to commit the crime is of the essence of the crime, and to hold a man criminally responsible for an offense as to the commission of which he was ignorant at the time would be intolerable tyranny.[3] Under an indictment for selling intoxicating liquors to an habitual drunkard, or to a minor, guilty knowledge is essential to convict. And the questions of good faith and due care on the part of the accused, in seeking and obtaining information as to the habits or age of the party to whom the liquor was sold, are for the jury to determine.[4] When one honestly and with due care seeks information, such morally innocent person should not be condemned because a fact existed which he did not and could not know.[5] To relieve a party from the penalty provided by statute for selling intoxicating liquors to a minor, it is not enough that the seller believed in good faith from appearances that the minor was of legal age; it must also be shown that the accused exercised due care to ascertain his age.[6] A nonresident landowner may not be held criminally

[2] Jellico Coal Min. Co. v. Commonwealth, 96 Ky. 373, 29 S. W. 26; Derby's Cases 167.

[3] Duncan v. State, 7 Humph. (Tenn.) 148.

[4] Crabtree v. State, 30 Ohio St. 382.

[5] Bish. Stat. Crimes (3d ed.), §§ 1021, 1022; Crabtree v. State, 30 Ohio St. 382.

[6] Mulreed v. State, 107 Ind. 62, 7 N. E. 884.

liable because a stray thistle here and there growing on his land was overlooked and went to seed, when he had, in good faith, done all that could be reasonably expected of him to prevent it. A criminal offense consists in a violation of a public law, in the commission of which there is a union or joint operation of act and intention, or original negligence.[7] Under an indictment for "keeping a bowling alley, which was then and there resorted to for the purpose of gaming," the defendant is not guilty in the absence of guilty knowledge or criminal intent.[8] Under an indictment for selling intoxicating liquors to a minor, proof of such sale to the minor makes out a prima facie case for the people; but the defendant may overcome this prima facie case by showing that the minor's size and appearance, together with his statement that he was of age, led him honestly to believe him not a minor.[9] So a minor who votes illegally but who relies upon statements which gave him reasonable ground for believing himself of age, and has not been lacking in diligence to ascertain the real facts, should be excused from criminal intent.[10]

§ 116. **Mistake in bigamy and adultery.**—There is also much conflict in the decisions, both in England and in this country, as to the statutory criminal liability of a person, who, under a bona fide but mistaken belief that his or her spouse is dead, or divorced, marries again. Some courts hold

[7] Story v. People, 79 Ill. App. 562.

[8] State v. Currier, 23 Maine 43.

[9] People v. Welch, 71 Mich. 548, 39 N. W. 747, 1 L. R. A. 385. The same court, however, in People v. Roby, 52 Mich. 577, 18 N. W. 365, 50 Am. Rep. 270, holds that under an indictment for selling intoxicating liquors on Sunday the defendant may be convicted irrespective of criminal intent. In several states, including Illinois, a person may be convicted of selling intoxicating liquors to a minor irrespective of guilty knowledge or criminal intent. McCutcheon v. People, 69 Ill. 601; Farmer v. People, 77 Ill. 322.

[10] Gordon v. State, 52 Ala. 308, 23 Am. Rep. 575. See also 1 Bish. New Crim. L. (8th ed.), § 307. State v. Boyett, 32 N. Car. 336; Commonwealth v. Bradford, 9 Metc. (Mass.) 268; McGuire v. State, 7 Humph. (Tenn.) 54.

that such a mistake of fact constitutes a good defense,[11] while other courts hold the contrary.[12] In support of the latter view, it is said that the matter is of such importance to society that it is not the law's intention to make the legality of a second marriage while the former spouse is living, depend upon ignorance of such person's being alive or honest belief in his death,[13] unless the legal presumption of death has arisen from seven years' unexplained absence.[14]

In prosecutions for adultery there is also conflict in the decisions as to the effect of mistakes of fact. According to the Massachusetts rule a man may be convicted of adultery, who, in good faith, and in the belief that she is a widow, marries and cohabits with a woman who has left her husband and remains absent from him for more than seven years together without hearing of him, if in fact her husband is still living.[15] Some courts, however, hold the contrary. Thus, when a woman cohabits with a man after marriage to him she is not guilty of adultery, though he is already married to another woman, unless she knows that fact.[16]

11 Reg. v. Tolson, L. R., 23 Q. B. Div. 168, Derby's Cases 133, Beale's Cases 286; Reg. v. Turner, 9 Cox Cr. C. 145; Reg. v. Horton, 11 Cox Cr. C. 670; Reg. v. Moore, 13 Cox Cr. C. 554; Reg. v. Prince, L. R. 2 C. C. 154, 13 Cox Cr. C. 138; Squire v. State, 46 Ind. 459.

12 Reg. v. Gibbons, 12 Cox Cr. C. 237; Reg. v. Bennett, 14 Cox Cr. C. 45; Dotson v. State, 62 Ala. 141, 34 Am. Rep. 2, Derby's Cases 163.

13 Commonwealth v. Hayden, 163 Mass. 453, 40 N. E. 846, 28 L. R. A. 318, 47 Am. St. 468; State v. Goodenow, 65 Maine 30; Commonwealth v. Mash, 7 Metc. (Mass.) 472, Beale's Cases 304; State v. Zinchfeld, 23 Nev. 304, 46 Pac. 802, 34 L. R. A. 784, 62 Am. St. 800; State v. Goulden, 134 N. Car. 743, 47 S. E. 450. See also Reynolds v. State, 58 Nebr. 49, 78 N. W. 483; People v. Hartman, 130 Cal. 487, 62 Pac. 823 (accused believed first marriage illegal); State v. Sherwood, 68 Vt. 414, 35 Atl. 352; Commonwealth v. Munson, 127 Mass. 459, 34 Am. Rep. 411; Staley v. State, 89 Nebr. 701, 131 N. W. 1028, 34 L. R. A. (N. S.) 613.

14 Johnson v. Johnson, 114 Ill. 611, 3 N. E. 232, 55 Am. Rep. 883; Reynolds v. State, 58 Nebr. 49, 78 N. W. 483; Williams v. Williams, 63 Wis. 58, 23 N. W. 110, 53 Am. Rep. 253.

15 Commonwealth v. Thompson, 11 Allen (Mass.) 23, 87 Am. Dec. 685.

16 Banks v. State, 96 Ala. 78, 11 So. 404. See also Vaughan v. State, 83 Ala. 55.

§ 117. Bishop's view of mistake of fact.—Bishop says, "Suppose the first husband or wife is not directly shown to have been alive at the time of the solemnization of the second marriage, but at some point of time anterior thereto, under what circumstances is death to be presumed? If the absence had continued for seven years, the law, both by its common-law rules and by the statute, presumes death; but, even then, there is no presumption as to the particular time when it took place, especially there is none that life continued up to within a day of the expiration of the seven years. Now, under the combined operation of the polygamy statute and of the common law, if a man's wife abandons him, and a year afterward, having no information whether she is dead or alive, he marries another woman, he, in point of law, does not commit polygamy should it turn out that she is really dead; but, should it turn out that she is alive, he does. Then, suppose he is indicted for polygamy, and, at the trial, there is no evidence whether she is dead or alive, except that she was alive a year before the second marriage, what is the result? If, at the time of the trial, seven years have elapsed, and the woman has not been heard from, the law presumes that, now, she is dead, but it has no presumption as to the time of the death. The law, however, presumes the defendant to be innocent; and it would seem, on this state of the case, that, as there is no presumption of the life having continued even a year after the separation, the court should direct an acquittal. If, on the other hand, seven years have not elapsed at the time of the trial, then the presumption of life and innocence operate together, the one for the defendant and the other against him. They neutralize each other, and the jury must act on other presumptions and evidence, and decide, as matter of fact between them all. Perhaps there is not sufficient authority carrying the point in the former supposed instance to the full extent there intimated; but, at least, a verdict of acquittal in such a case would, on the authorities, and certainly in reason. be preferred."[17]

§ 118. **The better view of mistake as defense—The weight of authority.**—In a prosecution for bigamy, the state must prove beyond a reasonable doubt that the first spouse was living at the time of the second marriage. Upon principle, and according to the better view, when there is no direct evidence upon this point, and the only evidence is that the first spouse was alive within seven years previous to the second marriage, the presumption of the continuance of his or her life is neutralized by the presumption of the innocence of the defendant, and in such a case there should be no conviction.[18] If the evidence shows that the first spouse had not been heard of for seven years or more prior to the second marriage, there is a presumption of law that such spouse, at the time of the second marriage, was dead. Unless the state overcomes this presumption by evidence, the defendant must be acquitted.

In this country, however, the better view is not in accord with the weight of authority.[19] The former is based upon principle, while the latter is based upon public policy.[20]

In England, after much difference of opinion, the better view, as stated above, has become settled law, and an honest and reasonable belief in the death of the former spouse is a good defense to a charge of bigamy.[21]

§ 119. **Distinction between mistake of law and mistake of fact.**—Since a mistake of law is not a defense to a criminal charge, and a mistake of fact frequently is, the distinction between them is of vital importance. In discriminating between them, in a criminal prosecution for illegal voting, it is said: "If the voter believe himself to be twenty-one years

17 Bish. Stat. Crimes (1873), p. 403, § 611.

18 Squire v. State, 46 Ind. 459.

19 See ante, § 116, note 12.

20 Reynolds v. State, 58 Nebr. 49, 78 N. W. 483.

21 Reg. v. Tolson, L. R., 23 Q. B. Div. 168, Derby's Cases 133, Beale's Cases 286.

of age, when he is not, and vote, he does not know the existence of the disqualifying fact, and may, on that ground, be excused. But if he know that he is only twenty years of age, yet believes he is old enough, in point of law, to vote, such ignorance of the law will not excuse him. If the voter honestly believe that he has resided six months in the county before the election, and the fact turn out otherwise, he may be excused. But if he know that he has been only four months in the county before the election, yet he believes that to reside four months is, in point of law, residence enough, he shall not be excused. If a voter believe that he was born in the United States, and it turns out that he was born in a foreign country, he may be excused. But if he knows he is a foreigner, and has not taken the oath of allegiance to the United States, but has only made his declaration of renunciation, etc., and thinks the latter, in point of law, sufficient to entitle him to vote, this ignorance of the law shall not excuse him; for he voted knowing a state of facts to exist which, in point of law, disqualified him."[22]

When a person commits a criminal act as the result both of a mistake of fact and of a mistake of law, his mistake of fact will not excuse him. For example, when a private person, reasonably believing a man to have committed murder, shoots and kills him to prevent his escape, believing that he is justified in so doing, and it turns out that the man killed has not committed a crime, the mistake of fact, in believing that deceased had committed a murder, is no excuse. This is owing to the fact that his mistake of law, in believing that he is justified in killing the man if he reasonably believes he has committed murder, and that it is necessary to kill him to prevent his escape, is no excuse.

22 McGuire v. State, 7 Humph. (Tenn.) 54.

CHAPTER VIII.

THE OVERT ACT.

§ 125. **In general.**—A mere criminal intent does not of itself constitute a crime. There must be, in addition, an overt act.[1] The mere mental approval by a bystander of a murder committed in his presence does not make him an accomplice in the murder. "The words or approving of, have no place in legal phraseology to explain the meaning of the words to aid and abet. The fact itself is incapable of proof. Mental operations, not accompanied with any action, or language, are beyond the reach of testimony."[2] And where a person is indicted for assault and battery, an instruction "that if the jury believed, from the evidence, that defendant went to the meeting-house yard, and called Hughs out for the purpose of having a difficulty with him, they

[1] State v. Taylor, 47 Ore. 455, 84 Pac. 82, 4 L. R. A. (N. S.) 417, 8 Ann. Cas. 627.

[2] State v. Cox, 65 Mo. 29, 33.

should find defendant guilty, is prejudicially erroneous. The mere fact of going to a place with the intention of doing an unlawful act, will not of itself subject the party to the punishment denounced against such act, unless he also carries his intention into effect.[3] And if one intends to do something which he believes a crime, but is mistaken in the facts, and what he does is not a crime, he is not guilty because of his intent; as where a man votes, believing himself under age, when in fact he is of age.[4] If all one intends to do when done will constitute no crime, it can not be a crime for him with the same purpose to do part of what he intended.[5]

§ 126. **Mere possession.**—The mere possession of a thing is not, at common law, a sufficient overt act to constitute a crime. It is not a crime, at common law, knowingly to have in one's possession counterfeit money with intent to pass it as genuine;[6] or knowingly to have in one's possession indecent prints with intent to publish them;[7] or knowingly to have in one's possession forged bills with intent to pass them.[8] There are, however, upon this point, a few discordant decisions,[9] but these decisions do not represent the better view. An early English statute, however, makes possession, with criminal intent to pass, an indictable offense.[10]

§ 127. **Receiving with intent to pass or use.**—The act of receiving a thing with criminal intent is something more

3 Yoes v. State, 9 Ark. 42.

4 People v. Jaffe, 185 N. Y. 497, 78 N. E. 169, 9 L. R. A. (N. S.) 263, 7 Ann. Cas. 348; People v. Gardner, 144 N. Y. 119, 38 N. E. 1003, 28 L. R. A. 699, 43 Am. St. 741.

5 People v. Jaffe, 185 N. Y. 497, 78 N. E. 169, 9 L. R. A. (N. S.) 263; 7 Ann. Cas. 348.

6 Rex v. Heath, Russ. & Ry. 184; Rex v. Stewart, Russ. & Ry. 288.

7 Dugdale v. Reg., 1 El. & Bl. 435; Beale's Cases 221, Derby's Cases 43; Rex v. Rosenstein, 2 Car. & P. 414.

8 Commonwealth v. Morse, 2 Mass. 138.

9 Rex v. Sutton, 1 East. P. C. 172, Beale's Cases 125 (possession of tools for making counterfeit money, with intent to use them); Rex v. Parker, 1 Leach Cr. C. 48 (possession of counterfeit money with intent to utter it as good).

10 2 & 3 Wm. IV, ch. 34, § 8.

than merely having possession of it with criminal intent. The former constitutes an indictable offense. Thus, receiving counterfeit money with criminal intent to pass it;[11] or receiving dies with criminal intent to use them in making counterfeit money;[12] or receiving indecent prints with criminal intent to publish them,[13] constitutes a crime. On the other hand, receiving a thing innocently, and subsequently forming a criminal intent to pass or use it, is not a crime at common law.

§ 128. **Mere preparation to commit a crime.**—Mere preparation to commit a crime is not a crime. The act "must be sufficient in amount of evil to demand judicial notice."[14] It is sometimes difficult, however, to determine whether a particular act constitutes mere preparation or an indictable attempt. To constitute the latter it must be a cause of the thing contemplated rather than a mere condition which has been brought about as an aid in accomplishing the thing contemplated. Moreover, it must have proceeded far enough that the contemplated crime would have resulted had it not have been frustrated by extraneous circumstances. Between preparation for the attempt and the attempt itself, there is a wide difference. The preparation consists in devising or arranging the means or measures necessary for the commission of the offense; the attempt is the direct movement toward the commission after the preparations are made.[15] There may be acts done with some intent toward the commission of a crime which in themselves are not indictable attempts; such as purchasing a gun with a design to murder, or poison with the same intent. These preparations are considered mere conditions, not causes.[16] So if accused

[11] Rex v. Fuller, Russ. & Ry. 308.

[12] Reg. v. Roberts, 7 Cox Cr. C. 39.

[13] Dugdale v. Reg., 1 El. & Bl. 435, Beale's Cases 221, Derby's Cases 43

[14] 1 Bish. New Crim. L. (8th ed.), § 431.

[15] People v. Murray, 14 Cal. 159.

[16] Leverett v. State, 20 Ga. App. 748, 93 S. E. 232.

armed himself and went out intending to kill another, and met the other, who assaulted accused so that he had to kill him in self-defense, the previously formed intent of accused does not make him guilty of murder.[17]

It is plain that "if a man who has a wicked purpose in his heart does something entirely foreign in its nature from that purpose, he does not commit a criminal attempt to do the thing proposed. On the other hand, if he does what is exactly adapted to accomplish the evil meant, yet proceeds not far enough in the doing for the cognizance of the law, he still escapes punishment. Again, if he does a thing not completely, as the result discloses, adapted to accomplish the wrong, he may under some circumstances be punishable, while under other circumstances he may escape. And the difficulty is not a small one, to lay down rules readily applied, which shall guide the practitioner in respect of the circumstances in which the criminal attempt is sufficient."[18]

§ 129. **Solicitation to commit a crime—In general.**—Soliciting another to commit a crime is, in some cases at least, a sufficient overt act itself to constitute a crime.[19] There is, however, conflict of authority as to the question whether solicitations to commit crimes are independently indictable; and also as to the question what must be the nature of the act solicited in order that the solicitation constitute a crime.

§ 130. **Solicitation an independent offense.**—Some courts hold that solicitation to commit a crime is indictable as a criminal attempt, and it has been said that mere soliciting the servant to steal is an attempt or endeavor to commit a crime. It also has been held that to solicit another to commit arson, offering him at the same time a match with which

17 State v. Rider, 90 Mo. 54, 1 S. W. 825, Derby's Cases 43.

18 1 Bish. Crim. L. (5th ed.), 433, § 739. See also Whart. Crim. L. (11th ed.), § 219.

19 Rex v. Higgins, 2 East 5, Derby's Cases 58; United States v. Galleanni, 245 Fed. 977.

to commit the act, constitutes a criminal attempt.[20] There is some conflict of authority as to the question whether mere solicitation to commit a felony constitutes of itself an attempt to commit the felony, one of the leading text writers on criminal law, Wharton, denying the proposition, while another standard text writer, Bishop, supports it.[21]

The weight of authority, as well as the better opinion, sustains the view that solicitation to commit a crime may constitute an independent offense, but not a criminal attempt.[22] Thus, it has been held that the mere delivery of poison to a person, and soliciting him to place it in the spring of a certain party, is not "an attempt to administer poison."[23] It also has been held that a mere effort by solicitation to produce a condition of mind essential to the crime of incest does not constitute an attempt to commit the crime;[24] and that soliciting a female child under the age of consent, to submit to sexual intercourse, does not constitute an attempt to commit rape, as in such cases there must be an actual, not merely a constructive attempt in order to convict.[25]

§ 131. **Solicitation—Wharton's view.**—Wharton favors the view that solicitations to commit crimes are substantive offenses rather than criminal attempts. In discussing the question he says: "They certainly are (independent offenses) * * * when they in themselves involve a breach of the public peace, as is the case with challenges to fight and seditious addresses. They are also indictable when their object is interference with public justice, as where a resistance

20 People v. Bush, 4 Hill (N. Y.) 133. See also State v. Bowers, 35 S. Car. 262, 14 S. E. 488, 15 L. R. A. 199, 28 Am. St. 847.

21 State v. Bowers, 35 S. Car. 262, 264, 14 S. E. 488, 15 L. R. A. 199, 28 Am. St. 847.

22 State v. Butler, 8 Wash. 194, 35 Pac. 1093, 25 L. R. A. 434, 40 Am. St. 900.

23 Stabler v. Commonwealth, 95 Pa. St. 318, 40 Am. Rep. 653.

24 Cox v. People, 82 Ill. 191; People v. Murray, 14 Cal. 159, Derby's Cases 64.

25 State v. Harney, 101 Mo. 470, 14 S. W. 657; Stabler v. Commonwealth, 95 Pa. St. 318, 40 Am. Rep. 653.

to the execution of a judicial writ is counseled; or perjury is advised; or the escape of a prisoner is encouraged; or the corruption of a public officer or a witness is sought, or invited by the officer himself. They are indictable, also, when they are in themselves offenses against public decency, as is the case with solicitations to commit sodomy, and they are indictable also, when they constitute accessaryship before the fact. But * * * the better opinion is that, where the solicitation is not in itself a substantive offense, or where there has been no progress made toward the consummation of the independent offense attempted, the question whether the solicitation is by itself the subject of penal prosecution must be answered in the negative."[26] This view is not in harmony with Bishop's, but it is undoubtedly correct.

§ 132. **Solicitation to commit a felony.**—As a general rule, both in England and in this country, solicitations to commit felonies are indictable offenses. Therefore to solicit another to commit murder;[27] or arson;[28] or sodomy;[29] or adultery;[30] or embezzlement;[31] or to utter forged bank bills[32] has been held to be an indictable offense. It was held that the solicitation itself was an act done. In a leading English case, in which the defendant was charged with soliciting a servant to steal his master's goods, his counsel argued that since "a mere intent to commit evil is not indictable, without an act done," no crime was charged in the indictment. The case has been generally followed both in England and this country.[33]

[26] 1 Whart. Crim. L. (11th ed.), § 218.

[27] Commonwealth v. Randolph, 146 Pa. St. 83, 23 Atl. 388, 28 Am. St. 782, Beale's Cases 134.

[28] Commonwealth v. Flagg, 135 Mass. 545.

[29] Reg. v. Rowed, 2 G. & D. 518, 3 Q. B. 180; Rex v. Hickman, 1 Mood. Cr. C. 34.

[30] State v. Avery, 7 Conn. 266, 18 Am. Dec. 105. See also Cole v. State (Okla. Cr.), 166 Pac. 1115.

[31] Reg. v. Daniell, 6 Mod. 99; Reg. v. Quail, 4 Fost. & F. 1076.

[32] State v. Davis, Tappan (Ohio) 139.

[33] Rex v. Higgins, 2 East 5, Derby's Cases 58 See also Reg. v. Gregory, L. R., 1 C. C. 77, Derby's Cases 59.

In some states, however, including Illinois, it is held that solicitations to commit crimes are indictable, where their object is to provoke a breach of the public peace, or to interfere with public justice, or where perjury is advised, or the escape of a prisoner encouraged, or the corruption of a public officer is sought; but that, where the felony solicited to be done is not consummated, and its character is of such a nature that its solicitation does not tend to a breach of the peace, or the corruption of the body politic, the mere solicitation is not of itself indictable.[34] This is in harmony with Wharton's view.[35]

§ 133. **Solicitation to commit a misdemeanor.**—No precise line can be drawn between the cases in which the law holds it a misdemeanor to counsel, entice or induce another to commit a crime and where it does not. In general it is a misdemeanor to solicit one to commit a felony, though it has been held that it does not depend upon the mere legal and technical distinction between felony and misdemeanor.[36] The decisions, however, upon the question whether solicitation to commit a misdemeanor is an indictable offense or not are in hopeless conflict.[37] In a leading English case, frequently cited by text writers and courts, it is stated that, "All these cases prove that inciting another to commit a misdemeanor is itself a misdemeanor." This statement has been quoted approvingly many times; however, the cases to which the court referred were cases rather of attempts than of mere solicitations to commit misdemeanors.[38] Solicitation and attempt are separate and distinct acts; and this fact should not be lost sight of. Merely soliciting one to do an act is generally held not to be an attempt to do that act.[39]

[34] Cox v. People, 82 Ill. 191.

[35] Quoted in ante, § 131.

[36] Commonwealth v. Willard, 22 Pick. (Mass.) 476.

[37] Rex v. Higgins, 2 East 5, Derby's Cases 58.

[38] Smith v. Commonwealth, 54 Pa. St. 209, 93 Am. Dec. 686.

[39] Stabler v. Commonwealth, 95 Pa. St. 318, 40 Am. Rep. 653; Cole v. State (Okla. Cr.). 166 Pac. 1115.

Moreover, proof of one will not support an indictment for the other, as forms of indictments for solicitation to commit a crime are distinct and different from forms of indictments for attempts to commit felonies.[40] In Pierson's case[41] the distinction between solicitation and attempt is sharply drawn. It holds that keeping a bawdy house is an indictable offense, but that a mere solicitation of an immoral act is not.

Some decisions hold that soliciting another to commit a misdemeanor is not a crime. It is held that soliciting a woman to commit adultery, where adultery is a misdemeanor, is not a crime;[42] and also that soliciting another to sell intoxicating liquor in violation of law is not a crime.[43] On the other hand, other decisions hold that solicitations to commit misdemeanors may constitute crimes. Thus, it is held that, to solicit another to commit embracery;[44] or to solicit a witness for the state, in a criminal case, to absent himself from the trial;[45] or to solicit another to accept a bribe;[46] is a crime. It has also been held an indictable offense for an officer to solicit another person to pay him a bribe. "The distinction between an offer to bribe and a proposal to receive one is exceedingly nice. The difference is wholly ideal. If one man attempt to bribe an officer, and influence him, to his own degradation and to the detriment of the public, and fail in his purpose, is he more guilty than the officer, who is willing to make sale of his integrity, debase himself, and who solicits to be purchased, to induce a discharge of his duties? The prejudicial effects upon society are, at least, as great in the one case as in the other; the

40 State v. Bowers, 35 S. Car. 262, 14 S. E. 488, 15 L. R. A. 199, 28 Am. St. 847.

41 1 Salk. 382.

42 Smith v. Commonwealth, 54 Pa. St. 209, 93 Am. Dec. 686.

43 Commonwealth v. Willard, 22 Pick. (Mass.) 476, Derby's Cases 61.

44 State v. Bonds, 2 Nev. 265.

45 State v. Keyes, 8 Vt. 57, 30 Am. Dec. 450.

46 Rex v. Plympton, 2 Ld. Raym. 1377; United States v. Worrall, Fed. Cas. No. 16766, 2 Dall. (U. S.) 384, 1 L. ed. 426.

tendency to corruption is as potent; and when the officer makes the proposal, he is not only degraded, but the public service suffers thereby. According to the well-established principles of the common law, the proposal to receive the bribe was an act which tended to the prejudice of the community, greatly outraged public decency, was in the highest degree injurious to the public morals, was a gross breach of official duty, and must therefore be regarded as a misdemeanor, for which the party is liable to indictment."[47]

Of the two foregoing views, the latter is both correct upon principle and supported by the weight of authority. Clark and Marshall, in discussing the distinction made by some courts between solicitations to commit felonies and solicitations to commit misdemeanors assert, "There is no more reason, however, for such a distinction in the case of solicitation than there would be for holding an attempt to commit a misdemeanor not to be indictable; and there are many cases in which an indictment for solicitation to commit a misdemeanor has been sustained."[48]

Solicitation to commit either a felony or a misdemeanor, where the solicitation constitutes an indictable offense, is a misdemeanor.

§ 134. **Attempts to commit crimes—In general.**—As a general rule, attempts to commit crimes, whether felonies or misdemeanors, are indictable offenses. Some decisions, however, hold that attempts to commit misdemeanors which are merely mala prohibita are not indictable.[49]

§ 135. **Attempt—Definitions—Essential elements.** — An attempt to commit a crime has been defined as "an act done in part execution of a criminal design, amounting to more than mere preparation, but falling short of actual consum-

[47] Walsh v. People, 65 Ill. 58, 16 Am. Rep. 569, Beale's Cases 128.

[48] Clark & M. Law of Crimes, § 132.

[49] Commonwealth v. Willard, 22 Pick. (Mass.) 476, Derby's Cases 61; Dobkins v. State, 2 Humph. (Tenn.) 424.

mation, and possessing, except for failure to consummate, all the elements of the substantive crime,"[50] also as "An act done in part execution of a design to commit a crime."[51] It is also said that "An endeavor to commit a crime is defined to be an endeavor to accomplish it, carried beyond mere preparation, but falling short of the ultimate design."[52] Robinson says, "An attempt consists in the intent to commit a crime, combined with the doing of some act adapted to, but falling short of, its actual commission."[53] Burrill defines it as "An endeavor to commit an offense, carried beyond mere preparation, but falling short of actual commission."[54] Anderson defines it as "An act of endeavor to commit a particular offense, and an intent by that act alone, or in conjunction with other necessary acts, to commit it."[55] And Wharton defines it as "An intended apparent unfinished crime."[56]

An attempt to commit a crime embodies three essential elements. There must be a criminal intent to commit the particular crime; an act done in pursuance of such intent, which falls short of the actual commission of the particular crime; and an apparent ability, at least, to commit the particular crime.

§ 136. **Attempt—The intent.**—In many crimes a general criminal intent is sufficient. In every criminal attempt, however, a specific criminal intent is essential, and this intent must be to commit the particular crime attempted.[57] Thus, in a prosecution for an attempt to murder, an instruction that "the same facts and circumstances which would make the offense murder if death ensued, furnish sufficient evidence of the intention," is erroneous. "There are a number

50 3 Am. & Eng. Encyc. L. 250.

51 Cent. Dict., title Attempt, 4.

52 3 Am. & Eng. Encys. L. 251.

53 Robinson's Elem. L., § 472.

54 Burrill's Law Dict., 157.

55 Anderson's Law Dict., 90.

56 Whart. Crim. L. (11th ed.), § 212.

57 Wooldridge v. United States, 237 Fed. 775, 150 C. C. A. 529; Leverett v. State, 20 Ga. App. 748, 93 S. E. 232; Merritt v. State, 19 Ga. App. 616, 91 S. E. 885.

of cases, where a killing would amount to murder, and yet the party did not intend to kill."[58] In a like prosecution, an instruction that "if a man shoots another man with a deadly weapon the law presumes that by such shooting, he intended to take the life of the person shot," is also erroneous.[59] And an instruction which substantially charges that an intention to do such serious bodily injury as would probably end in death is sufficient to convict of an attempt to commit murder, is also erroneous.[60] On the other hand, where the accused is on trial for attempting to murder a child, and the evidence shows that he beat the child in such a manner as was likely to cause death, an instruction that "before you can find the prisoner guilty of this felony you must be satisfied that when he inflicted this violence on the child he had in his mind a positive intention of murdering that child," is correct.[61]

It is not essential, however, that the person actually injured be the person intended to be injured. This is owing to the fact that even a specific criminal intent is transferable from a person to a person. Where a person shoots at another with intent to murder him and hits a third person, he is liable for an attempt to murder the person hit.[62] There are, however, a few discordant decisions upon this proposition,[63] but they do not represent the correct view.

The rule that a specific criminal intent is essential to an attempt to commit a crime has been frequently applied. It

58 Moore v. State, 18 Ala. 532.

59 Simpson v. State, 59 Ala. 1, 31 Am. Rep. 1.

60 Pruitt v. State, 20 Tex. App. 129; Moore v. State, 26 Tex. App. 322, 9 S. W. 610.

61 Reg. v. Cruse, 8 Car. & P. 541, 34 E. C. L. 522.

62 Dunaway v. People, 110 Ill. 333, 51 Am. Rep. 686; State v. Gilman, 69 Maine 163, 31 Am. Rep. 257; State v. Montgomery, 91 Mo. 52, 3 S. W. 379; State v. Wansong, 271 Mo. 50, 195 S. W. 999.

63 Lacefield v. State, 34 Ark. 275, 36 Am. Rep. 8; Commonwealth v. Morgan, 11 Bush (Ky.) 601; Reg. v. Hewlett, 1 Frost, & F. 91; Scott v. State, 49 Ark. 156, 4 S. W. 750, Derby's Cases 129.

has been applied to attempts to commit robbery,[64] larceny,[65] rape,[66] bribery,[67] mayhem,[68] abortion,[69] etc.

It is not essential, however, that the specific criminal intent be established by direct evidence. It may be inferred from the conduct of the accused and other circumstances.[70]

§ 137. Attempt—The act done—A different question.—The act done in pursuance of the specific intent, to constitute a criminal attempt, must be distinct from mere solicitation, and something more than mere preparation. It must be "a step taken towards the actual commission of the offense, and not a mere effort, by persuasion, to produce the condition of mind essential to the commission of the offense."[71] "The act must reach far enough towards the accomplishment of the desired result to amount to the commencement of the consummation. It must not be merely preparatory. In other words, while it need not be the last proximate act to the consummation of the offense attempted to be perpetrated, it must approach sufficiently near to it to stand either as the first or some subsequent step in a direct movement towards the commission of the offense after the preparations are made."[72] There must be an actual, ineffectual deed done in pursuance and furtherance of the design to commit the offense.[73]

64 Hanson v. State, 43 Ohio St. 376, 1 N. E. 136.

65 Hall v. Commonwealth, 78 Va. 678.

66 State v. Kendall, 73 Iowa 255, 34 N. W. 843, 5 Am. St. 679; Lewis v. State, 35 Ala. 380; State v. Massey, 86 N. Car. 658, 41 Am. Rep. 478.

67 Barefield v. State, 14 Ala. 603; United States v. Worrall, Fed. Cas. No. 16766, 2 Dall. (U. S.) 384, 1 L. ed. 426.

68 Filkins v. People, 69 N. Y. 101, 25 Am. Rep. 143; Rex v. Boice, 1 Mood. Cr. C. 29, Beale's Cases 182.

69 State v. Moore, 25 Iowa 128, 95 Am. Dec. 776n.

70 Scott v. People, 141 Ill. 195, 30 N. E. 329; Commonwealth v. Hersey, 2 Allen (Mass.) 173, Beale's Cases 183; State v. Grossheim, 79 Iowa 75, 44 N. W. 541.

71 Cox v. People, 82 Ill. 191.

72 Hicks v. Commonwealth, 86 Va. 223, 227, 9 S. E. 1024, 19 Am. St. 891. See also McDade v. People, 29 Mich. 50.

73 Smith v. Commonwealth, 54 Pa. St. 209, 93 Am. Dec. 686; Shipp v. State (Tex. Cr. App.), 196 S. W. 840.

The border line between mere preparation and criminal attempt is often obscure and difficult to locate; and no general rule, which can be readily applied as a test to all cases, can be laid down. It has been truly said by a philosophical writer that "the subject of criminal attempt, though it presses itself upon the attention whenever we walk through the fields of the criminal law, is very obscure in the books, and apparently not well understood either by the text-writers or the judges." And it may be added that it is more intricate and difficult of comprehension than any other branch of the criminal law. Each case must, therefore, be determined upon its own facts, in the light of certain principles which appear to be well settled. The difficulty generally is in determining the proximity of the act in question to the offense in contemplation, and analogy is of very little help.[74]

§ 138. Attempt—Wharton's view criticised.—According to Wharton, "To make the act an indictable attempt, it must be a cause as distinguished from a condition. And it must go so far that it would result in the crime unless frustrated by extraneous circumstances."[75] The former of these two statements is correct. The latter has been frequently quoted approvingly by the courts, but it is not correct. As said by one court, in a comparatively recent case, "It is not necessary that the act should be such as inevitably to accomplish the crime by the operation of natural forces, but for some casual and unexpected interference. It is none the less an attempt to shoot a man that the pistol which is fired at his head is not aimed straight, and therefore in the course of nature can not hit him."[76]

In support of the above view expressed by the court, it has been held that, where a person is on trial for attempt to murder, and the evidence shows that the defendant shot

[74] Hicks v. Commonwealth, 86 Va. 223, 9 S. E. 1024, 19 Am. St. 891; Commonwealth v. Kennedy, 170 Mass. 18, 48 N. E. 770.

[75] 1 Whart. Crim. L. (11th ed.), § 220.

[76] Commonwealth v. Kennedy, 170 Mass. 18, 48 N. E. 770.

at the prosecuting witness twice, at a distance of some thirty paces, with a shotgun loaded with powder and shot; that one of the discharges, at least, was fired at the face and neck of the prosecuting witness, many of the shot taking effect and inflicting upon him great bodily harm, one of his eyes being destroyed and the other seriously wounded; assuming that the act was done with intent to murder the prosecuting witness, and that the defendant failed in his purpose only because the shot were incapable of producing death, owing to the distance between the parties and the manner in which the gun was loaded, the evidence justifies a conviction of the crime charged.[77] In this case the court substantially holds that, "where the object is not accomplished because of an impediment which is of such a nature as to be wholly unknown to the offender, who uses appropriate means, though not fully or only apparently adapted to the object, the criminal attempt is committed." This is also Bishop's view; and he adds that, "If we undertake to split hairs here, and say that, even to outward appearance, there must be, in all cases, a perfect adaptedness in the act performed, and in the circumstances surrounding the prisoner at the time, to accomplish what he meant to do, we shall do away with the doctrine of attempt, as a practical element in the law, almost entirely."[78]

Both in England and in this country the weight of authority supports the view that a reasonably apparent possibility to commit the crime attempted is sufficient to render the party liable for criminal attempt. It follows, therefore, that an actual impossibility of performance is not necessarily a defense. "Whenever the law makes one step toward the accomplishment of an unlawful object, with the intent or purpose of accomplishing it, criminal, a person taking that step, with that intent or purpose, and himself capable of doing every act on his part to accomplish that object, can not

[77] Kunkle v. State, 32 Ind. 220.

[78] 1 Bish. Crim. L. (7th ed.), § 750.

protect himself from responsibility by showing that, by reason of some fact unknown to him at the time of his criminal attempt, it could not be fully carried into effect in the particular instance."[79]

But as correctly stated by Wharton, "If the means are both absolutely and apparently inadequate, as where a man threatens another with magic, or aims at him a child's popgun, then it is plain that an attempt, in the sense of an apparent invasion of another's rights, does not exist. * * * When the means used are so preposterous that there is not even apparent danger, then an indictable attempt is not made out."[80]

§ 139. Attempt—Acts which have been held sufficient to constitute criminal attempts.—Since the subject of criminal attempts is especially difficult and obscure, the following examples, together with those in the next succeeding section, are given with the view of elucidating the subject more fully:

Putting one's hand in another's pocket, with intent to steal, constitutes an attempt to commit larceny, even when the pocket is empty.[81] The physical impossibility to accomplish the object sought is no defense. The earlier English decisions, however, hold the contrary,[82] but these decisions have been overruled.[83]

Performing an operation on a woman with the view of bringing about a miscarriage may constitute a criminal attempt, even when she is not pregnant.[84]

[79] Commonwealth v. Jacobs, 9 Allen (Mass.) 274.

[80] 1 Whart. Crim. L. (11th ed.), § 222.

[81] Commonwealth v. McDonald, 5 Cush. (Mass.) 365, Beale's Cases 141; People v. Jones, 46 Mich. 441, 9 N. W. 486; People v. Moran, 123 N. Y. 254, 25 N. E. 412, 10 L. R. A. 109, 20 Am. St. 732, Derby's Cases 68.

[82] Reg. v. McPherson, 7 Cox Cr. C. 281; Reg. v. Collins, 9 Cox Cr. C. 497, Beale's Cases 137.

[83] Reg. v. Brown, 24 Q. B. Div. 357; Reg. v. Ring, 66 L. T. (N. S.) 300.

[84] Reg. v. Goodchild, 2 Car. & K. 293; Reg. v. Goodall, 2 Cox Cr. C. 41. See also Commonwealth v. Tibbetts, 157 Mass. 519, 32 N. E. 910; Commonwealth v. Taylor, 132 Mass. 261.

Shooting at a knot hole with intent to murder a policeman who is believed to be spying through it, but who, in fact, is elsewhere at the time, but near enough to be within range of the gun, constitutes an attempt to commit murder.[85]

Setting a lighted candle under a stairway of another's dwelling-house, with malicious intent to burn the building, and close enough to the wood to accomplish, apparently, the object sought, constitutes an attempt to commit arson.[86]

Opening a vacant drawer, with intent to steal therefrom, constitutes an attempt to commit larceny.[87]

Using threats toward another with the intent to extort money from him by putting him in fear, and taking his money which is given up not through fear but with the view of prosecuting the offender, constitutes an attempt to extort money by putting in fear, notwithstanding the fact that the victim is not put in fear.[88]

Setting some of his employer's goods aside, with intent to steal them when an opportunity shall present itself to do so without detection, constitutes an attempt to commit larceny.[89]

Pointing a loaded gun at another within range, and pulling the trigger, with intent to murder him, and failing to discharge the gun owing to the fact that, without the offender's knowledge, there is no cap on the gun, constitutes an attempt to commit murder.[90]

Mixing poison with food and placing it on a table where a certain other person will be likely to eat it, with intent to

85 People v. Lee Kong, 95 Cal. 666, 30 Pac. 800, 17 L. R. A. 626, 29 Am. St. 165, Beale's Cases 142, Derby's Cases 76.

86 Rex v. Scofield, Cald. 397. See also State v. Taylor, 47 Ore. 455, 84 Pac. 82, 4 L. R. A. (N. S.) 417, 8 Ann. Cas. 627.

87 Clark v. State, 86 Tenn. 511, 8 S. W. 145.

88 People v. Gardner, 144 N. Y. 119, 38 N. E. 1003, 28 L. R. A. 699, 43 Am. St. 741.

89 Reg. v. Cheeseman, 9 Cox Cr. C. 100, Leigh & C. 140.

90 Mullen v. State, 45 Ala. 43, 6 Am. Rep. 691, Derby's Cases 74.

murder that person, constitutes an attempt to commit murder.[91]

Putting a teaspoonful of poisonous powder, known as "rough on rats," into an empty mustache cup, and causing the powder to adhere to the underside of the crossbar of the cup, and placing it where a certain other person will be likely to use it in drinking, with the malicious intent to cause that person's death by his drinking the poison, constitutes an attempt to commit murder.[92]

Using force on another, with the intent to compel him to give up money and other valuables he may have on his person, constitutes an attempt to commit robbery, even when the victim has no money or other valuables on his person.[93]

Giving a child a dose of poison, with intent to murder it, constitutes an attempt to commit murder, although the dose given is insufficient to accomplish the object sought.[94]

A man may be guilty of an attempt to commit rape, even where the woman immediately thereafter consents to sexual intercourse.[95]

Procuring dies with the intent to make counterfeit coin constitutes a criminal attempt. "If a man intends to commit murder, the walking to the place where he purposes to commit it would not be a sufficient act to evidence the intent to make it an indictable offense; but in this case no one can doubt that the procuring the dies and machinery was necessarily connected with the offense, and was for the express purpose of the offense, and could be used for no other purpose."[96]

[91] Reg. v. Bain, 9 Cox Cr. C. 98, Leigh & C. 129.

[92] Commonwealth v. Kennedy, 170 Mass. 18, 48 N. E. 770.

[93] Hamilton v. State, 36 Ind. 280, 10 Am. Rep. 741.

[94] State v. Glover, 27 S. Car. 602, 4 S. E. 564.

[95] State v. Cross, 12 Iowa 66, 79 Am. Dec. 519; People v. Marrs, 125 Mich. 376, 84 N. W. 284; State v. Hartigan, 32 Vt. 607, 78 Am. Dec. 609.

[96] Reg. v. Roberts, 33 Eng. L. & Eq. 553, 25 L. J. (N. S.) M. C. 17, Dears. 539.

Climbing onto a roof and making a hole in it, with criminal intent to enter the building, is an indictable attempt.[97]

Going to a house with intent to burglarize it, having in his possession a set of burglar's tools, and entering a shop to procure a crowbar with which to break into the house, renders the person liable for attempt to commit burglary.[98]

Burning one's own home, with the object in view of burning another's, constitutes an attempt to commit arson.[99]

Attempting to accomplish sexual intercourse with a sleeping woman, other than the offender's wife, without her knowledge or consent, constitutes an attempt to commit rape.[1] A few of the older decisions hold the contrary,[2] but they do not represent the better view.

Administering chloroform to a woman for the purpose of having sexual intercourse with her constitutes an attempt to commit rape.[3]

Attempting to accomplish sexual intercourse with another man's wife by inducing her to submit under the belief that the offender is her husband, constitutes an attempt to commit rape.[4]

A physician, who, under pretense of giving a woman patient medical treatment, attempts to have sexual intercourse with her, is guilty of attempt to commit rape.[5]

97 Reg. v. Bain, 9 Cox Cr. C. 98, Leigh & C. 129.

98 People v. Lawton, 56 Barb. (N. Y.) 126.

99 Reg. v. Young, 14 Cox Cr. C. 114; State v. Smith, 80 Mo. 516; Carter v. State, 35 Ga. 263.

1 Harvey v. State, 53 Ark. 425, 14 S. W. 645, 22 Am. St. 229 (overruling Sullivan v. State, 8 Ark. 400; and Charles v. State, 11 Ark. 389).

2 Commonwealth v. Fields, 4 Leigh (Va.) 648; King v. State, 22 Tex. App. 650, 3 S. W. 342.

3 Milton v. State, 23 Tex. App. 204, 4 S. W. 574, 24 Tex. App. 284, 6 S. W. 39.

4 State v. Shepard, 7 Conn. 54; Reg. v. Flattery, 2 Q. B. Div. 410. See also Reg. v. Dee, 15 Cox Cr. C. 579, in which all the leading English and Irish cases are reviewed, and in which the judges all agree. In the following year (1885), the English Parliament expressly enacted that sexual intercourse under such circumstances should constitute rape. 48 and 49 Vict., ch. 69, § 4.

5 Pomeroy v. State, 94 Ind. 96, 48 Am. Rep. 146; Reg. v. Case, Den. Cr. C. 580; Reg. v. Flattery, 2 Q. B. Div. 410.

§ 140. Attempt—Acts which have been held insufficient to constitute criminal attempts.—The following propositions are examples of acts which have been held insufficient to constitute criminal attempts:

A mere collection and preparation of materials in a room for the purpose of setting fire to it, without a present intent to set the fire, is not an attempt to commit arson.[6]

Sending an order from Alaska, where the sender resides, to a wholesale dealer in San Francisco, for one hundred gallons of whisky, to be shipped to him in Alaska, in violation of an act of congress, does not constitute an attempt to introduce the whisky into Alaska. It is merely a preparatory act.[7]

Eloping with one's niece, and requesting a third party to procure a magistrate to perform the marriage ceremony, does not constitute an attempt to commit incest. It is only mere preparation.[8]

Starting out with a loaded gun to hunt game during the close season does not constitute an attempt to kill game against the law. The act is merely preparatory.[9]

Soliciting a person to set fire to another's dwelling-house, and giving him matches and kerosene with which to do it, does not constitute an attempt to commit arson.[10]

Owing to the fact that a boy under fourteen years of age is conclusively presumed incompetent to commit rape, an attempt by him to have sexual intercourse with a girl by force and against her will does not constitute an attempt to commit rape. "The accused being under fourteen years of age, and conclusively presumed to be incapable of committing the crime of rape, it logically follows, as a plain, legal

6 Commonwealth v. Peaslee, 177 Mass. 267, 59 N. E. 55, Derby's Cases 65.

7 United States v. Stephens, 12 Fed. 52.

8 People v. Murray, 14 Cal. 159, Derby's Cases 64.

9 Cornwell v. Fraternal Acc. Assn., 6 N. Dak. 201, 69 N. W. 191, 40 L. R. A. 437n, 66 Am. St. 601.

10 McDade v. People, 29 Mich. 50.

deduction, that he was also incapable in law of an attempt to commit it. He could not be held to be guilty of an attempt to commit an offense which he was physically impotent to perpetrate."[11] The contra, however, has been held.[12]

The mere delivery of poison to a person, and soliciting him to place it in a spring on the premises of a certain party, does not constitute "an attempt to administer poison."[13]

One can not be convicted of subornation of perjury for attempting to secure false testimony which is so immaterial to the issue that the witness could not have been convicted of perjury had he given the testimony in the action.[14]

Pointing a loaded and cocked pistol at another person, the party so doing having his finger on the trigger at the time, does not constitute an attempt to discharge the weapon.[15] The correctness of this view, however, is somewhat doubtful.[16]

Nor can one be convicted of an attempt to receive stolen goods when he intended to receive goods which he believed were stolen, but in fact were not stolen.[17]

[11] Foster v. Commonwealth, 96 Va. 306, 31 S. E. 503, 42 L. R. A. 589, 70 Am. St. 846. See also Rex v. Eldershaw, 3 Car. & P. 366; Reg. v. Philips, 8 Car. & P. 736.

[12] Commonwealth v. Green, 2 Pick. (Mass.) 380.

[13] Stabler v. Commonwealth, 95 Pa. St. 318, 40 Am. Rep. 653; Hicks v. Commonwealth, 86 Va. 223, 9 S. E. 1024, 19 Am. St. 891.

[14] People v. Teal, 196 N. Y. 372, 89 N. E. 1086, 25 L. R. A. (N. S.) 120n.

[15] Reg. v. St. George, 9 Car. & P. 483.

[16] Whart. Crim. L. (11th ed.), § 221.

[17] People v. Jaffe, 185 N. Y. 497, 78 N. E. 169, 9 L. R. A. (N. S.) 263, 7 Ann. Cas. 348, Derby's Cases 70.

CHAPTER IX.

MERGER OF CRIMES.

§ 145. **Definition—Use of terms.**—Merger, in its comprehensive sense, consists in the absorption of one right or liability into another of higher legal degree, by operation of law, where the two rights or liabilities concur in the same person.[1] In this comprehensive sense, the term merger is applicable to contracts, estates, torts and crimes.

The phrase, "of higher legal degree," as used in the definition, has reference to technical legal classifications. A contract under seal is of higher degree than one resting in parol; a freehold estate is of higher degree than an estate for years; and a felony is of higher degree than a misdemeanor.

The phrase, "by operation of law," as used in the definition, means that merger takes place irrespective of the intention of the parties.

"Merger is the equivalent of confusion in the Roman law,"[2] and "Rights are said to be merged when the same person who is bound to pay is also entitled to receive. This is

1 20 Am. & Eng. Encyc. L. (2nd ed.) 588; Abbott's Law Dict.; Sweet's Law Dict.

2 2 Abbott's Law Dict., title, "Merger."

more properly called a confusion of rights, or extinguishment."[3]

§ 146. **Merger of tort in felony—English rule.**—In the ancient common law, where the same act constituted both a tort and a felony, the former merged in the latter so that the civil remedy was extinguished.[4] By the great weight of English authority, the tort does not merge in the felony. According to the English rule, however, the civil remedy is suspended until the criminal prosecution is terminated.[5] The reason assigned for this rule is that it tends to incite the victim to bring on a speedy criminal prosecution. And, growing out of this rule, it has been held that the plaintiff, in the tort action, must allege and prove due diligence on his part in the criminal prosecution.[6] This is not essential, however, where the plaintiff is not the felon's victim.[7] The reason for this latter rule is, no duty rests upon the plaintiff in such a case to prosecute the felon criminally.

§ 147. **Merger of tort in felony—American rule.**—In this country, as in England, the tort does not merge in the felony. In a few states, the English rule, that the civil remedy is held in abeyance until the criminal prosecution is terminated, was adopted; but in most states it was repudiated.[8] The reason assigned for its repudiation in the latter states was, that it was not adapted to our conditions and therefore was

[3] 2 Bouvier's Law Dict., title "Merger," head "Rights."

[4] Higgins v. Butcher, Yelv. 89. See also Cooper v. Witham, 1 Sid. 375; 1 Bish. New Crim. L. (8th ed.), § 267.

[5] Crosby v. Leng, 12 East 409; Chowne v. Baylis, 31 Beav. 351; Vincent v. Sprague, 3 U. C. Q. B. 283.

[6] Cox v. Paxton, 17 Ves. Jr. 329; Morton v. Bradley, 27 Ala. 640.

[7] Appleby v. Franklin, 17 Q. B. Div. 93; Osborn v. Gillett, L. R. 8 Ex. 88, 28 L. T. 197, 21 W. R. 409.

[8] Morton v. Bradley, 27 Ala. 640; Bell v. Troy, 35 Ala. 184; Weekes v. Cottingham, 58 Ga. 559; Nowlan v. Griffin, 68 Maine 235, 28 Am. Rep. 45n; Hutchinson v. Merchants' &c. Bank, 41 Pa. St. 42, 80 Am. Dec. 596.

of little or no importance.[9] In those states which adopted it statutes have been passed abolishing it, so that in this country to-day it is obsolete.[10]

§ 148. Merger of tort in felony—History of the doctrine—Judge Bigelow's view.—"The doctrine, that all civil remedies in favor of a party injured by a felony are, as it is said in the earlier authorities, merged in the higher offense against society and public justice, or, according to more recent cases, suspended until after the termination of a criminal prosecution against the offender, is the well settled rule of law in England at this day (1854), and seems to have had its origin there at a period long anterior to the settlement of this country by our English ancestors.

The source, whence the doctrine took its rise in England, is well known. By the ancient common law, felony was punished by the death of the criminal, and the forfeiture of all his lands and goods to the crown. Inasmuch as an action at law against a person, whose body could not be taken in execution and whose property and effects belong to the king, would be a useless and fruitless remedy, it was held to be merged in the public offense. Besides, no such remedy in favor of the citizens could be allowed without a direct interference with the royal prerogatives. Therefore a party injured by a felony could originally obtain no recompense out of the estate of a felon, nor even the restitution of his

[9] Boardman v. Gore, 15 Mass. 331; Hyatt v. Adams, 16 Mich. 180; Patton v. Freeman, 1 N. J. L. 134; Williams v. Dickenson, 28 Fla. 90, 9 So. 847; Lofton v. Vogles, 17 Ind. 105; Barton v. Faherty, 3 Greene (Iowa) 327, 54 Am. Dec. 503; Blassingame v. Glaves, 6 B. Mon. (Ky.) 38; Newell v. Cowan, 30. Miss. 492; Howk v. Minnick, 19 Ohio St. 462, 2 Am. Rep. 413; Allison v. Farmers' Bank, 6 Rand. (Va.) 204; Hoffman v. Carow, 22 Wend. (N. Y.) 285; Pettingill v. Rideout, 6 N. H. 454, 25 Am. Dec. 473; Gould v. Baker, 12 Tex. Civ. App. 669, 35 S. W. 708.

[10] Alabama: Civ. Code (1907), § 2481; California: Deering Code Civ. Proc. (1915), § 32; Maine: Rev. Stat. (1903), ch. 120, § 14; New York: Code Civ. Proc. (1902), § 1899; Pennsylvania: Stewart's Purd. Dig., p. 744, § 4.

own property, except after a conviction of the offender. * * * But these incidents of felony, if they ever existed in this state, were discontinued at a very early period in our colonial history. Forfeiture of lands or goods, on conviction of crime, was rarely, if ever, exacted here; and in many cases, deemed in England to be felonious and punishable with death, a much milder penalty was inflicted by our laws. Consequently the remedies, to which a party injured was entitled in cases of felony, were never introduced into our jurisprudence. * * * Without regard, however, to the causes which originated the doctrine, it has been urged with great force and by high authority, that the rule now rests on public policy; that the interests of society require, in order to secure the effectual prosecutions of offenders by persons injured, that they should not be permitted to redress their private wrongs, until public justice has been first satisfied by the conviction of felons; that in this way a strong incentive is furnished to the individual to discharge a public duty, by bringing his private interest in aid of its performance, which would be wholly lost, if he were allowed to pursue his remedy before the prosecution and termination of a criminal proceeding. The whole system of the administration of criminal justice in England is thus made to depend very much upon the vigilance and efforts of private individuals. There is no public officer, appointed by law in each county, as in this commonwealth, to act in behalf of the government in such cases and take charge of the prosecution, trial and conviction of offenders against the laws. It is quite obvious that, to render such a system efficacious, it is essential to use means to secure the aid and co-operation of those injured by the commission of crimes, which are not requisite with us. * * *

"On the other hand, in the absence of any reasons, founded on public policy, requiring the recognition of the rule, the expediency of its adoption may well be doubted. If a party is compelled to await the determination of a criminal prosecution before he is permitted to seek his private redress, he certainly has a strong motive to stifle the prosecution and compound with the felon. Nor can it contribute to the purity of the administration of justice, or tend to promote private morality, to suffer a party to set up and maintain in a court of law a defense founded solely upon his own criminal act. The right of every citizen under our Constitution, to obtain justice promptly and without delay, requires that no one should be delayed in obtaining a remedy for a private injury, except in a case of the plainest public necessity. There being no such necessity calling for the adoption of the rule under consideration, we are of the opinion that it ought not to be engrafted into our jurisprudence. We are strengthened in this conclusion by the weight of American authority, and by the fact that in some of the states, where the rule had been established by decisions of the courts, it has been abrogated by legislative enactments."[11]

§ 149. Felony versus misdemeanor—Doctrine of merger at common law.—At common law the distinctions between a felony and a misdemeanor were much greater than they are today. A misdemeanant was entitled at common law to certain privileges which were not allowed to a felon. Thus, the former was entitled to the full privilege of counsel, to a copy of the indictment against him and to a special jury; but a felon was not entitled to any of these privileges. Owing to these distinctions a person indicted for a felony might not be convicted of a misdemeanor which formed a constituent part of the felony.[12] His acquittal of the felony, however, was no bar to an indictment for the constituent

11 Boston & W. R. Corp. v. Dana, 1 Gray (Mass.) 83, Knowlton's Cases 20.

12 Rex v. Cross, 1 Ld. Raym. 711; Reg. v. Woodhall, 12 Cox Cr. C. 240; Black v. State, 2 Md. 376; Gillespie v. State, 9 Ind. 380, (overruling State v. Kennedy, 7 Blackf. (Ind.) 233); Commonwealth v. Roby, 12 Pick. (Mass.) 496, (overruling Commonwealth v. Cooper, 15 Mass. 187); Hunter v. Commonwealth, 79 Pa. St. 503, 21 Am. Rep. 83.

misdemeanor.[13] Where a person was indicted for a misdemeanor, and the proof showed that the crime committed was a felony, the court would order an acquittal. In which case, however, the defendant, subsequently, might be indicted and tried for the felony.[14] Again, where a misdemeanor at common law was made a felony by statute an indictment for the misdemeanor would not lie. "Unless the misdemeanor merges, the conviction therefor being no bar to a subsequent indictment for felony, one might be punished twice for the same offense. An ample sufficient reason is that the offense has been made a felony and a felony only, and therefore an indictment as for a misdemeanor will not lie."[15]

At common law, a constituent misdemeanor merged in the felony of which it formed a part. This doctrine of merger resulted from the marked differences which existed at common law between felonies and misdemeanors, not only in extent of punishment and consequences of conviction, but also in the methods of procedure as stated above. For if a misdemeanor formed a constituent of the felony, the prisoner would lose substantial advantages of the method of trying misdemeanors. And where one was indicted for misdemeanor and proof showed a felony he was acquitted of the misdemeanor in order to indict and try him for felony. Consequently it has been held in both England and America that where an indictment was for a conspiracy to commit a felony, though the conspiracy would be a misdemeanor, if the object of the conspiracy was completed and a felony was committed, then the misdemeanor would merge in the felony.[16]

13 Reg. v. Eaton, 8 Car. & P. 417; Reg. v. Woodhall, 12 Cox Cr. C. 240; Commonwealth v. Gable, 7 Serg. & R. (Pa.) 423.

14 Harmwood's Case, 1 East P. C. 411, 440; Reg. v. Nicholls, 2 Cox Cr. C. 182; Rex v. Evans, 5 Car. & P. 553, 24 E. C. L. 553.

15 Rex v. Cross, 1 Ld. Raym. 711. See also Reg. v. Button, 11 Q. B. 929, 63 E. C. L. 929, 3 Cox Cr. C. 229.

16 Graff v. People, 208 Ill. 312, 70 N. E. 299. See also Commonwealth v. Kingsbury, 5 Mass. 106; State v. Hattabough, 66 Ind. 223; People v. Mather, 4 Wend. (N. Y.) 230, 21 Am. Dec. 122.

Bishop says, "There is at common law a wide distinction between felony and misdemeanor. It affects alike the punishment, the procedure, and several rules governing the crime itself. Out of the distinction grows the doctrine that the same precise act, viewed with reference to the same consequences, can not be both a felony and a misdemeanor, —a doctrine which applies only when the identical act constitutes both offenses."[17]

§ 150. Felony versus misdemeanor—The modern doctrine—Common-law rule abrogated.—Modern legislation and judicial decisions have abrogated to a great extent the doctrine of merger as it existed at common law. The technical line of demarcation between felonies and misdemeanors still exists, but most of the distinctions which existed at common law have been swept away. In many states it is the law that a person charged with an atrocious offense may be convicted of any constituent offense of a lower degree, provided such minor offense is substantially included in the description in the indictment or accusation, and even without regard to the technical line of demarcation between felonies and misdemeanors.[18] Bishop, after discussing the rule that a conspiracy merges in a felony, says, "This doctrine, the reader perceives, is contrary to just principle; it has been rejected in England; and, though there may be states in which it is binding on the courts, it is not to be deemed general American law."[19] At common law it has been frequently held that if a misdemeanor (e. g. assault) turns out to be a felony (e. g. robbery) then, on the ground that the misdemeanor is extinguished by being merged in the felony, the defendant must be acquitted of the felony. A more rational doctrine, however, has been established by statutes, and in some jurisdictions by common

[17] 1 Bish. New Crim. L. (8th ed.), § 787.

[18] Graff v. People, 208 Ill. 312, 70 N. E. 299.

[19] 1 Bish. New Crim. L. (8th ed.), § 814.

law, to the effect that the prosecution may in such cases waive the felony, and prosecute only for the constituent misdemeanor, supposing the misdemeanor be proved.[20] According to Lord Denman, "A misdemeanor which is part of a felony may be prosecuted as a misdemeanor, though the felony has been completed."[21] And it is the opinion of Chief Justice Andrews that, "Upon the whole examination we are of opinion, upon principle as well as upon authority, that this conviction for a conspiracy to commit theft ought to be sustained, although the evidence by which it was proved, proved also that the theft had been actually committed."[22]

§ 151. **Crimes of equal grade do not merge.**—The doctrine of merger is not applicable to crimes of equal grade, even at common law. It follows, therefore, that where the two crimes are both misdemeanors, or both felonies, there is no merger. Thus where the indictment is a misdemeanor and the offense for the commission of which the conspiracy was formed is also a misdemeanor and is completed, there is no merger, and so if the conspiracy charged is a felony, and when completed the crime is a felony, there is no merger.[23]

§ 152. **Rule where one act includes two or more crimes.**—As a general rule, where the same act includes the requisite ingredients of two or more distinct crimes the offenses are not merged; and a prosecution for one will not bar a prosecution for the other, or others.[24] In some jurisdictions, how-

20 Whart. Crim. L. (11th ed.), § 33.

21 Reg. v. Button, 11 Q. B. 929, 63 E. C. L. 929, 3 Cox Cr. C. 229.

22 Chief Justice Andrews in State v. Setter, 57 Conn. 461, 18 Atl. 782, 14 Am. St. 121, Knowlton's Cases 109, 115.

23 Graff v. People, 208 Ill. 312 70 N. E. 229.

24 Hughes v. Commonwealth, 131 Ky. 502, 115 S. W. 744, 31 L. R. A. (N. S.) 693n; Morey v. Commonwealth, 108 Mass. 433; State v. Elder, 65 Ind. 282, 32 Am. Rep. 69; State v. Inness, 53 Maine 536; State v. Williams, 11 S. Car. 288.

ever, the contrary doctrine obtains.[25] In harmony with the general rule, it has been held that an acquittal or conviction under an indictment for the murder of one person will not bar an indictment for the murder of the other, where both were killed by the same act,[26] and that an acquittal, under an indictment charging the defendant with having mixed arsenic with flour and having caused it to be administered to a certain woman with intent to kill her, is no bar to a subsequent indictment charging him with the same act in mixing the arsenic with the flour and causing it to be administered to a certain man with intent to kill him.[27]

An assault and battery committed in the presence of a court is also a contempt; and the guilty party may be punished for both offenses.[28] So, an assault and battery may constitute an ingredient of a riot, in which case the offender may be convicted of both crimes.[29]

[25] Gunter v. State, 111 Ala. 23, 20 So. 632, 56 Am. St. 17; State v. Damon, 2 Tyler (Vt.) 387. See also note to 31 L. R. A. (N. S.) 693-736.

[26] People v. Majors, 65 Cal. 138, 3 Pac. 597, 52 Am. Rep. 295. But see Clem v. State, 42 Ind. 420, 13 Am. Rep. 369.

[27] People v. Warren, 1 Park. Cr. C. (N. Y.) 338.

[28] State v. Gardner, 72 N. Car. 379.

[29] Skidmore v. Bricker, 77 Ill. 164; State v. Inness 53 Maine 536

CHAPTER X.

PARTIES TO CRIMES.

§ 160. Classification.—At common law parties to crimes constituting felonies are classified as follows: (1) Principals in the first degree; (2) Principals in the second degree; (3) Accessories before the fact; (4) Accessories after the fact.

In treason[1] and in misdemeanors[2] there are no accessories. All who participate criminally in these offenses are guilty as principals.

§ 161. Principal in the first degree—Definition.—A principal in the first degree is a person who actually commits the crime himself, or commits it through an innocent agent. In the latter case, although absent, he is said to be constructively present.

The innocent agent may be animate or inanimate.

§ 162. Animate innocent agent as principal.—The agent who commits the act may be innocent because of ignorance, youthfulness or insanity. "If A procures B, an idiot or lunatic, to kill C, A is guilty of the murder as principal, and B is merely an instrument."[3] "The method of killing is immaterial. Thus * * * in some cases a man shall be said, in the judgment of the law, to kill one who is in truth actually killed by another, * * * as where one incites a madman to kill himself or another."[4] "A lets out a wild beast, or employs a madman to kill others, whereby any is killed, A is principal in this case, though absent, because the instrument can not be a principal."[5] Thus, where an officer is endeavoring to arrest an insane person, and a third person frees the lunatic's hand from the grasp of the officer, thereby

1 4 Bl. Comm. 35; 1 Hale P. C. 612, 613; 2 Hawk. P. C., ch. 29, § 2; Reg. v. Clayton, 1 Car. & K. 128, Beale's Cases, 388; United States v. Burr, 4 Cranch (8 U. S.) 470 appendix.

2 Bl. Comm. 36; 1 Hale P. C. 613; 2 Hawk. P. C., ch. 29, § 2; Stevens v. People, 67 Ill. 587; Wagner v. State, 43 Nebr. 1, 63 N. W. 95; State v. Stark, 63 Kans. 529, 66 Pac. 243, 54 L. R. A. 910, 88 Am. St. 251; Bracewell v. State (Ga. App.), 94 S. E. 91; State v. Gilbert, 107 S. Car. 443, 93 S. E. 125; McDaniels v. State, 185 Ind. 245, 113 N. E. 1004.

3 Russ. on Crimes 5.

4 2 Bish. New Crim. L. (8th ed.), § 635.

5 1 Hale P. C., ch. LV, Dalt. Cap. 108.

enabling the lunatic to shoot and kill the officer, the third party is criminally liable for the lunatic's act.[6]

§ 163. **Principle of constructive presence based upon necessity.**—The principle of constructive presence is said to be founded upon necessity. Since it is said that there could be no principal in a crime unless he is present when it is committed, in cases where the crime is committed through an innocent agent when personally absent, the presence of the agent is held to be constructive presence of the principal.[7]

§ 164. **Moral innocence of agent not the test in first degree.**—Whether the real instigator of the crime is an accessory before the fact or a principal in the first degree, does not depend upon the moral innocence or guilt of the agent, but upon the presence or absence of criminal liability on his part.[8] Thus, it has been held that one who procures an instrument for a woman, which he advises and directs her to use upon herself to produce a criminal abortion, may be convicted as principal, where the woman, pursuant to such advice and direction, uses the instrument for such purpose, though in the absence of the former, thereby causing her to miscarry and die.[9]

§ 165. **Principal and innocent agent in different jurisdictions.**—The fact that the principal and the innocent agent are in different jurisdictions at the time the crime is committed is immaterial. "Personal presence, at the place where a crime is perpetrated, is not indispensable to make one a principal offender in its commission. Thus, where a gun is fired from the land which kills a man at sea, the offense must be tried by the admiralty, and not by the common-law courts; for the crime is committed where the death occurs,

[6] Johnson v. State, 142 Ala. 70, 38 So. 182, 2 L. R. A. (N. S.) 897n.

[7] Seifert v. State, 160 Ind. 464, 67 N. E. 100, 98 Am. St. 340; State v. Bailey, 63 W. Va. 668, 60 S. E. 785; Derby's Cases 297; 1 Bish. New Crim. L. (8th ed.), § 651.

[8] Seifert v. State, 160 Ind. 464, 67 N. E. 100, 98 Am. St. 340.

[9] Seifert v. State, 160 Ind. 464, 67 N. E. 100, 98 Am. St. 340.

and not at the place from whence the cause of the death proceeds. And on the same principle an offense committed by firing a shot from one county which takes effect in another, must be tried in the latter, for there the crime was committed. In such cases the offender is an immediate actor, in the perpetration of the crime, although not personally present at the place where the law adjudges it to be committed. He is there, however, by the instrument used to effect his purpose, and which the law holds sufficient to make him personally responsible at that place for the act done there. But crimes may be perpetrated through the instrumentality of living agents in the absence of the principal, and our law books are full of such cases. Where poison is knowingly sent to be administered as medicine, by attendants who are ignorant that it is poison, and death ensues, the person who thus procures the poison to be taken is guilty of murder. So where a child without discretion, an idiot or a madman, is induced by a third person to do a felonious act, the instigator alone is guilty, and although not present at the perpetration of the crime, he is a principal felon."[10]

§ 166. Separate acts pursuant to common design as test of principal in first degree.—Where, pursuant to a common criminal design, separate acts are done by different persons in the absence of each other, all are guilty as principals.[11] The basis of this rule is necessity; for if the rule were otherwise none of the parties could be convicted. If several persons conspire to commit a forgery, and in pursuance of the conspiracy they make distinct parts of the forged instrument in the absence of some of their number, the forgery being completed by one of them adding the signature in the absence of all the rest, all are guilty as principals.[12] It is to be observed, however, that at common law forgery is only

10 People v. Adams, 3 Denio (N. Y.) 190, 45 Am. Dec. 468.

11 1 Bish. New Crim. L., § 650.

12 Rex v. Bingley, Russ. & Ry. 446, Beale's Cases 381; Rex v. Dade, 1 Moody 307. See also Hammack v. State, 52 Ga. 397.

a misdemeanor, and that in misdemeanors all accomplices are principals whether absent or present. By statute, however, forgery is made a felony, and the rule as stated is applicable to statutory forgery.

§ 167. Principal in the second degree—Definition.—A principal in the second degree is a person who is present, either actually or constructively, when a felony is committed by another, and who aids or abets in its commission.

Blackstone says, "A principal, in the first degree, is he that is the actor, or absolute perpetrator, of the crime; and, in the second degree, he who is present, aiding and abetting the fact to be done. Which presence need not always be an actual and immediate standing by, within sight or hearing of the fact; but there may be also a constructive presence, as when one commits a robbery or a murder, and another keeps watch or guard at some convenient distance."[13]

§ 168. Essential elements of principal in second degree.—To constitute a person a principal in the second degree the following conditions must exist: (1) There must be a guilty principal in the first degree; (2) the principal in the second degree must be present, either actually or constructively, when the felony is committed; (3) he must aid or abet in the commission of the felony to the knowledge of the former.

§ 169. The first condition of principal in second degree.—To have a principal in the second degree there must be a principal in the first degree, who actually commits the criminal act. It requires no aid from the act of the principal in the second degree to complete the guilt of the principal in the first degree; but the principal in the second degree can not be guilty of crime if the principal in the first degree fails to do his part, even though the principal in the second degree has performed his part.[14]

13 2 Bl. Comm. 34.

14 Mulligan v. Commonwealth, 84 Ky. 229, 232, 1 S. W. 417, 8 Ky. L. 211.

§ 170. The second condition of principal in second degree.—To constitute a person a principal in the second degree he must be present when the felony is committed. A constructive presence, however, is sufficient; but it is essential that he be near enough to render some assistance if needed.[15] It is also essential that his purpose in being present must be to render aid to the chief felon, and the latter must have knowledge of this fact.

It is to be observed, however, that it is possible for a person to be constructively present and at the same time be many miles away, and in a different county. Thus, where several persons conspired to commit a stage robbery, and pursuant to the conspiracy, one of them built a fire on a mountain forty miles away and in a different county, to give the others notice of the whereabouts of the stage at that time, he was held guilty as a principal in the second degree.[16] "If several unite in one common design, to do some unlawful act, and each takes the part assigned to him, though all are not actually present, yet, all are present in the eye of the law."[17] Thus, where several persons conspire to burglarize a store, and, to facilitate the burglary and lessen the danger of detection, they agree that one of them shall entice the proprietor away from the store in which he usually sleeps, to a party about a mile distant, and detain him there while the other confederates burglarize the store, and the conspiracy is carried out, the one who thus entices the proprietor away and detains him is constructively present, and guilty as principal in the second degree.[18] And where a person, pursuant to a preconcerted plan, devised by himself, remains downstairs in his own home while his confederate above

[15] Harris v. State, 19 Ga. App. 741, 92 S. E. 224; Whart. Crim. L. (11th ed.), § 256; Commonwealth v. Knapp, 9 Pick. (Mass.) 496, 20 Am. Dec. 491, Derby's Cases 299.

[16] State v. Hamilton, 13 Nev. 386; 1 Whart. Crim. L. (11th ed.), § 243.

[17] Hess v. State, 5 Ohio St. 5, 22 Am. Dec. 767n.

[18] Breese v. State, 12 Ohio St. 146, 80 Am. Dec. 340, Beale's Cases 386.

steals money from a lodger and brings it downstairs and delivers it to him, he may be convicted of the larceny as a principal.[19]

§ 171. The third condition of principal in second degree.—For a person to be a principal in the second degree he must aid or abet in the commission of the felony. One who by chance comes upon the commission of a crime and looks on but does not assist is not a principal in the second degree; some overt act is necessary. The law does not reach mental operations unaccompanied by any action or language.[20] Presence and mere mental approval are not sufficient to render a person guilty, as principal in the second degree.[21] On the other hand, actual physical aid is not essential to constitute a person a principal in the second degree.[22] It is enough that he was ready to assist if required.

§ 172. Practical distinction between principal in first degree and principal in second degree immaterial.—Practically speaking, there is no distinction between a principal in the first degree and a principal in the second degree; both are equally guilty. So if one be indicted as principal in the first degree, proof of his presence, aiding and abetting another in committing the offense, although not actually himself doing it will support the indictment; and if indicted as principal in the second degree, proof that he committed the crime will support the indictment.[23]

§ 173. Aider and abettor — Definition. — Technically speaking, the term aider and abettor is applicable only to a principal in the second degree. To constitute a person an aider and abettor he must be present, either actually or con-

19 Commonwealth v. Lucas, 84 Mass. 170.

20 1 Hale P. C. 439; Elmendorf v. Commonwealth, 171 Ky. 410, 188 S. W. 483.

21 Clem v. State, 33 Ind. 418; True v. Commonwealth, 90 Ky. 651, 654, 14 S. W. 684, 12 Ky. L. 594; State v. Cox, 65 Mo. 29.

22 Doan v. State, 26 Ind. 495.

23 1 Arch. Crim. Pl. & Ev., 13. See also Doan v. State, 26 Ind. 495.

structively, but he must not be the main actor in the commission of the crime. He is a person who watches to prevent his confederates from being taken by surprise; or stations himself at a convenient distance to aid them in escaping, if necessary; or is so situated as to be able readily to go to their assistance.[24] Thus, where one of several confederates leads a girl's escort away in order that his companions may rape her, and they commit the crime, he is constructively present and an aider and abettor.[25]

§ 174. **Accessory before the fact—Definition.**—An accessory before the fact is a person who counsels, commands or procures the commission of a felony by another, but who is not present, either actually or constructively, when the felony is committed.[26]

§ 175. **Essential elements of accessory before the fact.**—To constitute a person an accessory before the fact the following conditions are essential: (1) There must be a guilty principal in the first degree; (2) the accessory must not be present when the felony is committed, either actually or constructively; (3) the accessory must participate in the commission of the felony.

§ 176. **First condition of accessory before the fact.**—The felony must be committed by a guilty agent. This agent will constitute a principal in the first degree. Where a felony is committed through an innocent agent there is no accessory before the fact.[27]

To sustain an indictment against a person charged as an accessory before the fact to the commission of a felony, the prosecution must establish the guilt of the principal felon. This, however, can not be done by confessions of guilt of the

[24] Whart. Crim. L. (11th ed.), § 257.

[25] People v. Batterson, 50 Hun (N. Y.) 44, 2 N. Y. S. 376, 6 N. Y. Cr. 173, 18 N. Y. St. 845.

[26] 1 Hale P. C., ch. LV.

[27] Gregory v. State, 26 Ohio St. 510, 20 Am. Rep. 774; Commonwealth v. Hill, 11 Mass. 136.

latter, since as to the accessory, such confessions are mere hearsay. Such confessions might be used, however, against the principal himself.[28]

§ 177. Second condition of accessory before the fact.—To constitute a person an accessory before the fact he must be absent when the felony is committed. Presence on his part, either actual or constructive, renders him a principal if he participates in the crime.[29] One who procures another to take and carry away gold, but has no part in the taking or carrying away, is not a principal, but an accessory before the fact.[30]

§ 178. Third condition of accessory before the fact.—It is also essential, to constitute a person an accessory before the fact, that he participate in the commission of the crime, by counseling, commanding, advising or procuring it to be done. Mere mental approval, or bare permission, is not sufficient. As said by Sir Mathew Hale, "And therefore, words that sound in bare permission, make not an accessory, as, if A says he will kill JS, and B says, you may do your pleasure for me, this makes not B accessory."[31] Nor is mere knowledge that the crime is to be attempted, sufficient.[32]

It is not essential, however, that the procurement be direct. It may be through the agency of another. Moreover, the person employed by the agent to commit the crime may be wholly unknown to the accessory.[33] But if the accessory order or advise one crime and the principals intentionally commit another, as where he abets the robbery of a safe, but the principals rob a person, the accessory is not answerable.[34]

28 Ogden v. State, 12 Wis. 592, 78 Am. Dec. 754.

29 Williams v. State, 47 Ind. 568; Reg. v. Brown, 14 Cox Cr. C. 144, Derby's Cases 309.

30 Able v. Commonwealth, 5 Bush (Ky.) 698, Derby's Cases 310.

31 1 Hale P. C. 616.

32 Levering v. Commonwealth, 132 Ky. 666, 117 S. W. 253, 136 Am. St. 192, 19 Am. Cas. 140.

33 Rex v. Cooper, 5 Car. & P. 535.

34 State v. Lucas, 55 Iowa 321, 7 N. W. 583, Derby's Cases 312.

§ 179. Accessory after the fact—Definition.—An accessory after the fact is a person who receives, relieves, comforts or assists a felon personally, with knowledge that the latter has committed a felony.[85]

§ 180. Essential elements of accessory after the fact.—To constitute a person an accessory after the fact the following conditions must exist: (1) A completed felony must have been committed when the felon receives relief or assistance; (2) relief or assistance must, according to some decisions, be furnished to the felon personally; (3) the person who gives relief or assistance to the felon must have knowledge at the time he does so of the felon's guilt.

§ 181. First condition of accessory after the fact.—The person who receives the relief or assistance must have committed a felony and the felony must be completed at the time the relief or assistance is rendered. Thus, a person is not an accessory to the crime of murder where the victim dies after the felon receives the relief or assistance. Until such felony has been consummated, any aid or assistance rendered to a party, in order to enable him to escape the consequences of his crime, will not make the person affording such assistance guilty as an accessory after the fact.[86]

§ 182. Second condition of accessory after the fact.—Actual relief or assistance must be furnished, and it must be rendered to the felon personally. As a general rule, any assistance which may hinder his apprehension, trial or punishment, is sufficient. Thus, concealing him in the house, or shutting the door against his pursuers, to enable him to escape; taking money from him or supplying him with money, a horse, or other necessaries, for the same purpose; conveying to him instruments to enable him to break prison, or bribing the jailor to let him escape, is sufficient.[87]

85 1 Hale P. C., ch. LVI; Elmendorf v. Commonwealth, 171 Ky. 410, 188 S. W. 483.

86 Harrel v. State, 39 Miss. 702, 80 Am. Dec. 95n.

87 Wren v. Commonwealth, 67 Va. (26 Grat.) 952, Derby's Cases 313; 1 Bish. New Crim. L. (8th ed.), § 695.

On the other hand, merely suffering the principal to escape; or agreeing for money not to prosecute the felon; or having knowledge that a felony has been committed and failing to make it known, is not sufficient.[38]

The relief or assistance given must, as heretofore stated, be rendered to the felon personally. As said in an English case, "To substantiate the charge of harboring a felon, it most be shown that the party charged did some act to assist the felon personally."[39] It has been held, however, that where a person employs another to harbor the principal felon the employer may be convicted as accessory after the fact, though he himself did no act of relieving; and furthermore, that he may be convicted on the uncorroborated testimony of the party who actually did the harboring.[40] And some recent cases hold that one who destroys the incriminating evidence of a felony may be an accessory after the fact to such a felony.[41]

Where a person is charged as accessory after the fact to a murder, the question for the jury is, whether such person, with knowledge of the felony, either assisted the murderer to conceal the death, or in any way enabled him to evade the pursuit of justice.[42]

§ 183. Third condition of accessory after the fact.—Knowledge of the felony, at the time the relief or assistance is rendered is essential to constitute the aider an accessory after the fact.[43] Mere knowledge alone without giving information to authorities does not make one an accessory

38 Wren v. Commonwealth, 67 Va. (26 Grat.) 952, Derby's Cases 313; Villareal v. State, 80 Tex. Cr. 133, 189 S. W. 156; Garcia v. State (Tex. Cr. App.), 195 S. W. 196.

39 Reg. v. Chapple, 9 Car. & P. 355. See also Wren v. Commonwealth, 67 Va. (26 Grat.) 952, Derby's Cases 313; Arch. Crim. Pl. & Ev., 78, 79n.

40 Rex v. Jarvis, 2 M. & Rob. 40.

41 Rex v. Levy, L. R. (1912), 1 K. B. 158, Ann. Cas. 1912 B, 503n.

42 Rex v. Greenacre, 8 Car. & P. 35.

43 Wren v. Commonwealth, 67 Va. (26 Grat.) 952, Derby's Cases 313. Hale says, "There can be no accessory in receipt of a felon, unless he know him to have committed a felony. 1 Hale P. C. 622.

after the act.[44] It seems that actual knowledge is required, and implied knowledge from general notoriety will not be imputed.

Upon an indictment against a party as an accessory after the fact in robbery, proof of the prisoner's knowledge of the felony, together with proof of his aiding the principal in disposing of the fruits of the robbery, is sufficient evidence of comforting and assisting to support the indictment.[45]

§ 184. Basis of criminal liability of accessory after the fact.—An accessory after the fact is held criminally liable on the ground that the assistance he renders the felon constitutes an interference with public justice, in that it tends to facilitate the escape of the felon.[46]

§ 185. Parties incapable of being accessories after the fact.—At common law, a wife has capacity to be an accessory before the fact to her husband as principal, but not to be an accessory after the fact to her husband as principal. The husband, however, has capacity at common law, to be accessory either before or after the fact to his wife as principal. In some states, by statute, certain persons other than a wife are incapable of being accessories after the fact to certain other persons as principals. Thus in Illinois a husband, wife, parent, child, brother or sister to the offender can not be held as an accessory after the fact.[47]

At common law, however, as stated by Blackstone, "So strict is the law * * * that the nearest relations are not suffered to aid or receive one another. If the parent assists his child, or the child his parent, if the brother receives the brother, the master his servant, or the servant his master, or even if the husband relieves his wife, who have any of them

[44] Levering v. Commonwealth, 132 Ky. 666, 117 S. W. 253, 136 Am. St. 192, 19 Ann. Cas. 140.

[45] Reg. v. Butterfield, 1 Cox Cr. C. 39.

[46] Wren v. Commonwealth, 67 Va. (26 Grat.) 952, Derby's Cases 313.

[47] Illinois: Hurd's Rev. Stat. (1916), ch. 38, § 276.

committed a felony, the receivers become accessories.[48] * * * But a feme covert, however, can not become an accessory by concealing her husband, for she is presumed to act under his coercion, and therefore she is not bound neither ought she, to discover her lord."[49]

§ 186. Distinction between principals and accessories before the fact abolished.—In some states, among them Illinois, the distinction which existed at common law between principals and accessories before the fact has been abolished by statute. Thus, the Criminal Code of Illinois provides: "An accessory is he who stands by, and aids, abets or assists, or who, not being present, aiding, abetting or assisting, hath advised, encouraged, aided or abetted the perpetration of the crime. He who thus aids, abets, assists, advises or encourages, shall be considered as principal, and punished accordingly."[50]

§ 187. Mode of indictment of accessories before the fact.—At common law, a principal must be indicted as such, and an accessory as such. "If the participant is a principal, though of the second degree, he can not be charged in an indictment as accessory; if he is an accessory, he can not be held as principal."[51]

It is to be observed, however, that it is possible for a person to be both a principal and an accessory to the same felony;[52] or an accessory before the fact and an accessory after the fact to the same felony.[53]

48 4 Bl. Comm. 38. See also 1 Hale P. C. 621; 2 Hawk. P. C. 320; People v. Dunn, 53 Hun (N. Y.) 381, 6 N. Y. S. 805, 7 N. Y. Cr. 173, 25 N. Y. St. 460.

49 4 Bl. Comm. 39. See also 1 Hale P. C. 621.

50 Illinois: Hurd's Rev. Stat. (1916), ch. 38, § 274. See also State v. Burns, 82 Conn. 213, 72 Atl. 1083, 16 Ann. Cas. 465; State v. Whitman, 103 Minn. 92, 114 N. W. 363, 14 Ann. Cas. 309; State v. Eddy (Mo.), 199 S. W. 186; State v. Curtis, 30 Idaho 537, 165 Pac. 199.

51 1 Bish. New Crim. L. (8th ed.), § 663. See also State v. Buzzell, 58 N. H. 257, 42 Am. Rep. 586.

52 Reg. v. Hilton, 8 Cox Cr. C. 87.

53 Rex v. Blackson, 8 Car. & P. 43; State v. Butler, 17 Vt. 145.

Where the distinction between principals and accessories before the fact has been abolished by statute, as in Illinois and several other states, accessories before the fact are indicted as principals. In Illinois it is held that they must be so indicted.[54] Thus, where an indictment charges that three persons, named, with a stick of wood which each severally had and held in their several right hands, inflicted a mortal wound, causing death, proof that either one of them struck the fatal blow with the weapon described, and that the others were accessory to the fact, will be sufficient to sustain a conviction of all three as principals. There is no variance in such case between the allegations in the indictment and the proof.[55]

§ 188. Order of trial of accessory before the fact—Rule at common law—Rule by statute.—At common law, an accessory before the fact can not be put upon trial, without his consent, until after the conviction of the principal. This is owing to the fact that were the rule otherwise, as declared by Blackstone, "it might so happen that the accessory should be convicted one day, and the principal acquitted the next, which would be absurd."[56] Where, however, the accessory is indicted with the principal he may waive his right to have the principal tried first and be tried jointly with him.[57]

In England, as well as in some of the states of this country, the common-law rule relating to this matter has been changed by statute. The English statute provides that persons who shall counsel, procure or command any other person to commit a felony shall be deemed guilty of a felony, and may be indicted and convicted, either as accessory before the fact to the principal felony, together with the principal felon, or may be indicted and convicted of a substantive

[54] Coates v. People, 72 Ill. 303. See also Baxter v. People, 3 Gilm. (Ill.) 368; Usselton v. People, 149 Ill. 612, 36 N. E. 952; Fixmer v. People, 153 Ill. 123, 38 N. E. 667.

[55] Coates v. People, 72 Ill. 303.

[56] 2 Bl. Comm. 323.

[57] Usselton v. People, 149 Ill. 612, 36 N. E. 952.

felony, whether the principal felon shall have been convicted or not.[58]

§ 189. Accomplices—Definition—Criminal liability.—An accomplice is a person who participates in the commission of a crime, either as a principal or as an accessory, with criminal intent.

The participation requisite, however, must be something more than mere passive consent. As heretofore stated, consent which amounts only to mere mental approval is not sufficient.[59] On the other hand, an accomplice is criminally liable for all criminal acts in which he actively participates; and where several parties conspire or combine together to commit any unlawful act, each is criminally responsible for the acts of his associates or confederates committed in furtherance or in prosecution of the common design for which they combine.[60] When several persons conspire together to invade a man's home, and go there armed with deadly weapons for the purpose of attacking and beating him, and, in the furtherance of this common design, one of them gets into a difficulty with him and kills him, the others being present, or near at hand, they also are guilty of murder, although they did not intend to kill.[61] And if a third party espouses the cause of one of two parties to a fight, into which he enters to help whip the other party, he is criminally liable for the death of such party, whether caused by a blow given by himself, or by one given by the surviving party, or from both combined; and the criminal intent of such volunteer may be inferred from his conduct.[62]

[58] 7 Geo. IV, ch. 64, § 9. See also 11 and 12 Vic., ch. 46, § 1; Usselton v. People, 149 Ill. 612, 36 N. E. 952.

[59] White v. People, 139 Ill. 143, 28 N. E. 1083, 32 Am. St. 196. See also Lamb v. People, 96 Ill. 73; State v. Maloy, 44 Iowa 104; State v. Duff, 144 Iowa 142, 122 N. W. 829, 24 L. R. A. (N. S.) 625n, 138 Am. St. 269 and note on who is an accomplice.

[60] Williams v. State, 81 Ala. 1, 1 So. 179, 60 Am. Rep. 133.

[61] Williams v. State, 81 Ala. 1, 1 So. 179, 60 Am. Rep. 133.

[62] People v. Carter, 96 Mich. 583, 56 N. W. 79.

But, where one party, in an altercation with another party, knocks the former down, whereupon a mere bystander kicks the person knocked down, and the latter dies as a result of the kick, the party who knocks the victim down is not criminally liable for his death. The reason is he does not volunteer, in such case, in another's cause, while on the other hand, the bystander volunteers in his own behalf without request or expectation.[63]

§ 190. Accomplices—Act done must be the natural and probable consequence of the conspiracy.—If two persons conspire to commit a felony, and while they are engaged in prosecuting that common design one of them commits murder, the other also is guilty of murder. Thus, where a wife conspires with her husband to commit a robbery, and while both are so engaged he commits murder, the wife also is guilty of murder.[64]

The act done, however, must grow out of the conspiracy. In other words, it must be the natural consequence of it. Moreover, it must occur before the conspiracy is abandoned.[65] It is not necessary, however, that it be intended as a part of the original design if it be the ordinary and probable result of the wrongful act specifically agreed on, so that the connection between them may be reasonably apparent, and not a fresh and independent product of the mind of one of the confederates, outside of, or foreign to, the common design.[66] But a charge which requires proof of an express agreement to do an unlawful act before the defendants would be guilty of a conspiracy, ignoring the evidence which tended to prove that they were all present, or near at hand, when

63 People v. Elder, 100 Mich. 515, 59 N. W. 237.

64 Miller v. State, 25 Wis. 384. See also State v. Barrett, 40 Minn. 77, 41 N. W. 463, Derby's Cases 302; People v. Friedman, 205 N. Y. 161, 98 N. E. 471, 45 L. R. A. (N. S.) 55n.

65 State v. Allen, 47 Conn. 121, Derby's Cases 307.

66 Williams v. State, 81 Ala. 1, 1 So. 179, 60 Am. Rep. 133.

the homicide was committed, encouraging its perpetration, is misleading if not erroneous, and is properly refused.[67] Where several persons join in the commission of a crime, and, in attempting to escape, one of them commits a homicide, those who do not consent to the act, and who are not privy in fact, can not be held criminally liable by reason of the original combination. There can be no criminal liability on the part of one who is not himself engaged in the act of his associates, unless it is within the scope of the combination to which he was a party, and thus authorized as his joint act. The principle is analogous to that of agency where the liability is measured by the express or implied authority.[68] So where two steal property and are trying to dispose of it after carrying it away some distance, and an officer attempts to arrest them because they had stolen property in their possession, and one, in resisting arrest, shoots the officer, his companion can not be held for the shooting.[69] And where several men combine for the purpose of inducing a girl to go to a shop for the purpose of prostitution, and they induce her to go there, and all have sexual intercourse with her there, and, in order to avoid arrest or exposure, one of the conspirators, against the consent of the others, throws the girl out of a window, without any intention of killing her, but which causes injuries of which she dies, the others are not criminally liable for her death.[70]

§ 191. **Principal and agent.**—A principal is criminally liable for the criminal acts of his agent committed within the scope of the agency. In other words, a principal is criminally liable for criminal acts of his agent which the former ex-

67 Williams v. State, 81 Ala. 1, 1 So. 179, 60 Am. Rep. 133.

68 People v. Knapp, 26 Mich. 112.

69 White v. People, 139 Ill. 143, 28 N. E. 1083, 32 Am. St. 196, Derby's Cases 304.

70 People v. Knapp, 26 Mich. 112.

pressly or impliedly authorizes to be committed,[71] but not for an act which he has expressly forbidden.[72]

On the other hand, a principal is not criminally liable where he ratifies an unauthorized criminal act of his agent. "In the law of contracts, a posterior recognition, in many cases, is equivalent to a precedent command; but it is not so in respect to crimes. The defendant is responsible for his own acts, and for the acts of others done by his express or implied command, but to crimes the maxim, Omnis ratihabitio retrotrahibitur et mandato priori equiparatur, is inapplicable."[73] The agent himself is always liable for his criminal acts. The fact that he does the act for another will not excuse him.[74] And it is immaterial that he is a mere volunteer and receives no compensation for the act.[75]

The rules applicable to principal and agent are also applicable to master and servant.

[71] Commonwealth v. Stevens, 155 Mass. 291, 29 N. E. 508; State v. Mueller, 38 Minn. 497, 38 N. W. 691; Williams v. Hendricks, 115 Ala. 277, 22 So. 439, 41 L. R. A. 650, 67 Am. St. 32; Bryan v. Adler, 97 Wis. 124, 72 N. W. 368, 41 L. R. A. 658; State v. Cray, 85 Vt. 99, 81 Atl. 450, 36 L. R. A. (N. S.) 630; and note to 41 L. R. A. 650-677.

[72] Commonwealth v. Wachendorf, 141 Mass. 270, 4 N. E. 817, Derby's Cases 315.

[73] Morse v. State, 6 Conn. 9, Beale's Cases 223.

[74] State v. Chingren, 105 Iowa 169, 74 N. W. 946; Commonwealth v. Hadley, 11 Metc. (Mass.) 66, Beale's Cases 372; Abel v. State, 90 Ala. 631, 8 So. 760; Buchanan v. State, 4 Okla. Cr. 645, 112 Pac. 32, 36 L. R. A. (N. S.) 83; Alt v. State, 88 Nebr. 259, 129 N. W. 432, 35 L. R. A. (N. S.) 1212n.

[75] State v. Herselus, 86 Iowa 214, 53 N. W. 105.

PART TWO

SPECIFIC CRIMES

PART TWO

SPECIFIC CRIMES

Title

TITLE ONE.

Classification of Crimes.

Chapter

CHAPTER XI.

CLASSIFICATION OF CRIMES.

§ 195. Classification at common law.—Crimes at common law are divided into the following three classes: (1) Treason; (2) Felonies; (3) Misdemeanors.

§ 196. Treason—Definition—Requisites.—Treason consists in a criminal renunciation of one's allegiance to the sovereign power.

Treason against the United States, as defined in the Federal Constitution, "shall consist only in levying war against them, or in adhering to their enemies, giving them aid and comfort."[1] A similar definition of treason is contained in the constitutions of some of the states and in the statutes of other states.

To convict a person of treason against the United States it is essential that there be two witnesses to the same overt act, or confession of guilt in open court.[2] A similar rule obtains in the several states.

The Federal Constitution also provides that, "The Congress shall have power to declare the punishment of treason; but no attainder of treason shall work corruption of blood,

[1] U. S. Const., art. III, § 3, par. 1.
[2] U. S. Const., art, III, § 3, par. 1.

or forfeiture, except during the life of the person attainted."[3]

At common law, treason was divided into two classes, (1) High treason; (2) Petit treason. High treason consisted in compassing the king's death, aiding and comforting his enemies, forging or counterfeiting his coin, counterfeiting the privy seal, or killing the chancellor or either of the king's justices. Petit treason consisted of the murder of a superior by an inferior, as where a wife murdered her husband, a servant his master, or an ecclesiastic his lord or ordinary.[4]

§ 197. Felonies—Definition—Common-law felonies.—A felony at common law is a crime punishable by forfeiture of the felon's lands and goods, and generally death or other punishment, depending upon the degree of guilt. In this country a felony is a crime punishable by death, or imprisonment in a penitentiary. In a few states the imprisonment must be at hard labor.

At common law only eight or nine crimes constitute felonies. These are: murder, manslaughter, rape, sodomy, larceny, robbery, burglary, arson, and perhaps mayhem.

To constitute an offense a felony against the United States, it must be expressly so described by an act of congress.[5]

§ 198. Misdemeanor — Definition — The test.—A misdemeanor is any crime less than a felony.

The test by which a misdemeanor is distinguished from a felony is not wholly uniform in this country. For example, the New York rule makes the maximum punishment to which the offender is liable the test;[6] while in Illinois a crime punishable either by imprisonment in the state prison, or by a fine, is a misdemeanor.[7]

[3] U. S. Const., art. III, § 3, par. 2.

[4] 4 Bl. Comm. §§ 73 et seq. 93.

[5] United States v. Blevin, 46 Fed. 381; In re Acker, 66 Fed. 290.

[6] People v. Lyon, 99 N. Y. 210, 1 N. E. 673.

[7] Baits v. People, 123 Ill. 428, 16 N. E. 483; Lamkin v. People, 94 Ill. 501.

Where a person is convicted of a crime punishable by imprisonment in the state prison, but owing to his youth is sent to the state reformatory, he is convicted of a felony.[8]

§ 199. Another classification of crimes.—The more modern classification of crimes as outlined at the head of this chapter will be followed, and in the order given.

[8] People v. Park, 41 N. Y. 21.

TITLE TWO.

Crimes Against the Person.

CHAPTER XII.

ABDUCTION.

§ 205. **Definition.**—Abduction is the unlawful taking by force, fraud or enticement, of a woman or girl for the purpose of prostitution or marriage.[1]

Abduction has been also defined as the taking or carrying away of the child of a parent, or the wife of a husband, either by fraud, persuasion, or open violence; as "the unlawful seizure or detention of a female for the purpose of marriage, concubinage or prostitution";[2] as "the unlawful taking or detention, by force, fraud, or persuasion, of a person, as a wife, a child, or a ward, from the possession, custody, or control of the person legally entitled thereto";[3] as "the taking and carrying away of a child, a ward, a wife, etc.,

[1] 3 Bl. Comm. 139, 140; Webster's Dict.

[2] Brown's Law Dict. See also Russ. on Crimes (9th Am. ed.) 940; Head v. Commonwealth, 174 Ky. 841, 192 S. W. 861.

[3] Am. & Eng. Encyc. L. 163.

either by fraud, persuasion, or open violence";[4] and as "the taking of a female without her consent, or without the consent of her parents or guardian, for the purpose of marriage or prostitution."[5]

§ 206. A statutory crime.—At common law, abduction probably is not a crime, separate and distinct from that of kidnaping.[6] In England and in this country statutes have been enacted making abduction a distinct crime. These statutes, however, are not at all uniform.

§ 207. Early English statute.—As early as 1488 a statute was enacted in England making abduction a distinct crime. This statute forms the basis of most of the statutes in this country upon this subject.[7]

§ 208. Modern English statute.—Since the repeal of the statute of 3 Hen. VII, other statutes have been passed in England relating to abduction. The present one[8] enumerates the following five classes of cases in any one of which a person renders himself criminally liable for abduction:

(1) One who, from motives of lucre, shall take away or detain, against her will, any woman of any age, having certain property or expectancies, with intent to marry or carnally know her, or to cause her to be married or carnally known by any other person;

(2) One who, with such intent, shall fraudulently allure, take away, or detain such woman, being under the age of twenty-one years, out of the possession and against the will of her father or mother, or of any other person having the lawful care or charge of her;

(3) One who shall by force take away or detain against her will any woman of any age, with such intent;

[4] Justice Ashe, in State v. George, 93 N. Car. 567.

[5] Clark's Crim. Law 222.

[6] Anderson v. Commonwealth, 5 Rand. (Va.) 627, 16 Am. Dec. 776.

[7] 3 Hen. VII, ch. 2; 4 Bl. Comm. 208.

[8] 24 & 25 Vict., ch. 100, §§ 53-56; Clark & M. Law of Crimes 304.

(4) One who shall unlawfully take or cause to be taken any unmarried girl under the age of sixteen years, out of the possession and against the will of her father or mother, or of any person having the lawful care or charge of her;

(5) One who shall unlawfully, either by force or fraud, lead or take away, or decoy or entice away or detain, any child under the age of fourteen years, with intent to deprive any parent, guardian, or other person having the lawful care or charge of such child, of the possession of such child, or with intent to steal any article upon or about the person of such child, or any person who shall with such intent, and knowledge of the facts, receive or harbor any such child. Provided that, a person claiming to be the father of an illegitimate child shall be excepted from the operation of this section.

§ 209. Statutes in this country.—Statutes have been enacted in the various states of this country making abduction a distinct crime. These statutes, however, as heretofore stated, are not at all harmonious. Some of them contain substantially certain provisions of the present English statute, but, upon the whole, they vary greatly.[9]

§ 210. Abduction of wife—Civil remedy.—At common law any person who entices or takes away a man's wife by fraud, persuasion or violence, renders himself liable to her husband in a civil action.[10]

The enticement must be caused by the defendant knowingly, and by direct and active interference.[11] It is not essential, however, that the defendant's conduct be the sole cause of the wife's desertion; but it must be the controlling cause.[12]

The gist of the action in such case is the loss of the wife's

[9] 1 Am. & Eng. Encyc. L. (2 ed.) 173 et seq.

[10] 3 Bl. Comm. 139; 3 Steph. Comm. 536; 2 Inst. 434.

[11] 3 Bl. Comm. 139; 2 Inst. 434.

[12] Hadley v. Heywood, 121 Mass. 236.

society.[13] "The wife owes to the husband the duty of living with him, and seeking to promote his interests and happiness, and by preventing the performance of that duty a wrong is done him, involving a pecuniary loss as well as a loss of peace and comfort in the marriage relation. Whoever is the wrongdoer, whether the father of the wife or any other person, he should be subject to an action for damages by the husband."[14] The husband's remedy in such case is by writ of ravishment, or by an action of trespass vi et armis, de uxore rapta et abducta.[15]

Harboring another's wife is also actionable.[16] The ancient common law was so strict on this point that if one's wife missed her way upon the road it was not lawful for another to take her into his house unless she was benighted or in danger of being lost or drowned.[17] But under modern law the severity of the old rule is much lessened.[18]

§ 211. Consent of girl immaterial.—Under statutes which prohibit the taking away of any unmarried girl under a certain age, consent on her part is no defense.[19] Even when the taking is at her own suggestion, it is no defense.[20] Thus where a girl solicits her seducer to elope with her, and he does so, her solicitation is no defense.[21]

§ 212. Improper motive essential.—To constitute the crime of abduction the act must be done with an improper motive. Thus, where the proof shows that the accused

13 Perry v. Lovejoy, 49 Mich. 529, 14 N. W. 485.

14 Bennett v. Smith, 21 Barb. (N. Y.) 439, 441.

15 3 Bl. Comm. 139.

16 Barbee v. Armstead, 32 N. Car. 530, 51 Am. Dec. 404; Turner v. Estes, 3 Mass. 317.

17 3 Bl. Comm. 139.

18 Rabe v. Hanna, 5 Ohio 530 (father protected wife against drunken husband).

19 State v. Bussey, 58 Kans. 679, 50 Pac. 891; State v. Bobbst, 131 Mo. 328, 32 S. W. 1149. See also Ann. Cas. 1913A, 588n; Head v. Commonwealth, 174 Ky. 841, 192 S. W. 861.

20 People v. Cook, 61 Cal. 478; Reg. v. Robins, 1 Car. & K. 456.

21 Reg. v. Biswell, 2 Cox Cr. C. 279; Griffin v. State, 109 Tenn. 17, 70 S. W. 61.

honestly believed that he was entitled to the custody of the girl, although in fact not legally justified, he should be acquitted of the charge of abduction.[22]

§ 213. **For the purpose of prostitution.**—Where a person is prosecuted under a statute which prohibits the taking away of a girl for the purpose of prostitution, it is not sufficient to show that the wrongdoer's purpose was to have sexual intercourse with her himself. Thus, an indictment under a statute which makes it a crime to entice away an unmarried female for the purpose of prostitution is not sustained by proof that the accused, by false representations, procured her to go with him to a neighboring town, where, having induced partial intoxication, he had repeated sexual intercourse with her.[23]

A penal statute is to be construed strictly. And the word "prostitution" does not mean seduction, or sexual intercourse confined exclusively to one man, but a common indiscriminate illicit intercourse, or offering of the body for an indiscriminate commerce, with men.[24] "At least, she must be enticed away for the purpose of sexual intercourse by others than the party who thus enticed her; and that a mere enticing away of a female for a personal sexual intercourse, will not subject the offender to the penalties of the statute."[25]

A prostitute, as defined by Webster, is a "female given to indiscriminate lewdness; a strumpet." And prostitution, as defined by him, is "the act, or practice, of offering the body to an indiscriminate intercourse with men; common lewdness of a female."

22 Reg. v. Tinkler, 1 Fost. & F. 513, Beale's Cases, 285, 286.

23 State v. Stoyell, 54 Maine 24, 89 Am. Dec. 716. See also, Haygood v. State, 98 Ala. 61, 13 So. 325; State v. Rorebeck, 158 Mo. 130, 59 S. W. 67; Nichols v. State, 127 Ind. 406, 26 N. E. 839.

24 State v. Ruhl, 8 Iowa 447.

25 Commonwealth v. Cook, 12 Metc. (Mass.) 93; Head v. Commonwealth, 174 Ky. 841, 192 S. W. 861.

§ 214. **For the purpose of concubinage.**—When the indictment is under a statute which makes it a crime to take away a female for the purpose of concubinage, or prostitution, this particular purpose must be shown.[26]

As to the meaning of the terms "concubinage" and "prostitution," courts differ. Some give them a more liberal interpretation than others, and apply them to all cases of lewd intercourse. "The statute which names as illegal purposes of such enticement of females under the age of consent, includes marriage, concubinage, and prostitution. The last two were evidently intended to cover all cases of lewd intercourse. Neither of these words has any common-law meaning, but both are popular phrases, either of which might be made to cover the crime here shown without any change from general usage."[27] As a general rule, however, the enticing of a female from her parents' house solely for the purpose of having sexual intercourse with her by the party so enticing, is not a crime under the statute. Thus, where a young woman living with her parents is enticed by a man to leave home and meet him for a few hours, and have illicit intercourse with him, within a few rods of her home, after which she returns to her parents' house, as usual, the case is clearly not within the scope of the statute, as it lacks the necessary ingredient of the offense—an intention to induce the female to a condition of either common prostitution or concubinage.[28] Evidence of the enticing of a young woman to leave her parents' house and come to the defendant's, where he finally succeeded in overcoming her virtue, after which he had illicit intercourse with her two or three times a week, for about nine months, and solicited her

[26] State v. Gibson, 108 Mo. 575, 18 S. W. 1109.

[27] People v. Cummons, 56 Mich. 544, 23 N. W. 215. (In this case the defendant had invited the girl to visit his photographic rooms, showed her obscene pictures, gave her small sums of money and finally had illicit intercourse with her several times.)

[28] Slocum v. People, 90 Ill. 274.

to live with him, promising her money and clothes, and that he would treat her as well as his wife, is sufficient to convict the defendant under a count for enticing the young woman away from her home for the purpose of concubinage.[29]

§ 215. **Sexual intercourse not essential—Abduction committable by a woman.**—To constitute the crime of abduction, sexual intercourse is not essential. It is enough that the woman was taken for that purpose.[30]

Moreover, sexual intercourse is not essential to the crime of enticing away a female for the purpose of concubinage or prostitution. Nor is it essential to such crime that the wrongdoer succeed in reducing her to that condition. The gravamen of the offense is the purpose or intent with which the female is taken away from her parent or guardian, or person having legal charge of her person.[31]

§ 216. **Chastity of the female.**—Under the statutes of some states, the unchastity of the female, at and prior to the time of her alleged abduction, is immaterial; except in so far as it may affect her credibility as a witness.[32]

On the other hand, under the statutes of other states, including Illinois, chastity of the female is an essential element of this crime.[33]

It is to be observed, however, that the law presumes chastity; and notwithstanding the general presumption of innocence, in a prosecution for abduction the burden of proof, in its secondary sense of going forward with evidence, is upon the defendant, and he must overcome the

[29] Slocum v. People, 90 Ill. 274. See also Henderson v. People, 124 Ill. 607, 17 N. E. 68, 7 Am. St. 391.

[30] State v. Bobbst, 131 Mo. 328, 32 S. W. 1149.

[31] State v. Bobbst, 131 Mo. 328, 32 S. W. 1149.

[32] State v. Bobbst, 131 Mo. 328, 32 S. W. 1149. See also, South v. State, 97 Tenn. 496, 37 S. W. 210.

[33] Bradshaw v. People, 153 Ill. 156, 38 N. E. 652; People v. Flores, 160 Cal. 766, 118 Pac. 246, Ann. Cas. 1913A, 582.

presumption of chastity.[84] Moreover, an instruction that the presumption of chastity of an abducted female is "only a bare presumption, and does not continue after the production of any competent evidence to the contrary," is properly refused, since it ignores the probative force of such presumption.[85]

§ 217. Circumstances attending the taking.—The gist of the crime of abducting an unmarried female residing with her parents is the taking or enticing her away from her parents' house.[86]

The purpose of the taking or enticing must exist in the mind of the wrongdoer at the time of the act. On the other hand, the fact that such purpose is unknown to the girl is immaterial.[87]

The taking or enticing may be to a place distant or near, or for a long or a short space of time.[88] Moreover, it is not essential that the girl should be kept permanently away from the parental home, or that there should be any intention so to keep her, even where the charge is for the purpose of concubinage or prostitution.[89]

§ 218. Federal White Slave Traffic Act.—There is a federal statute which forbids the transportation from one state to another "of any woman or girl for the purpose of prostitution or the debauchery or for other immoral purpose, or with the intent and purpose to induce, entice or compel such woman or girl to become a prostitute or to give herself up to debauchery, or to engage in any other immoral prac-

84 Bradshaw v. People, 153 Ill. 156, 38 N. E. 652.

85 Bradshaw v. People, 153 Ill. 156, 38 N. E. 652. See also, Slocum v. People, 90 Ill. 274.

86 Slocum v. People, 90 Ill. 274; People v. Plath, 100 N. Y. 590, 3 N. E. 790, 53 Am. Rep. 236.

87 Slocum v. People, 90 Ill. 274.

88 Slocum v. People, 90 Ill. 274, 276.

89 Bish. Stat. Crimes (3d ed.) 637. See also Slocum v. People, 90 Ill. 274; Reg. v. Baillie, 8 Cox. Cr. C. 238.

tice."[40] This statute includes transportation for practically every form of sexual immorality, including mere fornication.[41]

[40] Act, June 25, 1910, 36 Stat. at L. 827, ch. 395; U. S. Comp. Stat. (1916) § 8819.

[41] Johnson v. United States, 215 Fed. 679, L. R. A. 1915A, 862n. See also Hoke v. United States, 227 U. S. 38, 57 L. ed. 23, 33 Sup. Ct. 281, 43 L. R. A. (N. S.) 906, Ann. Cas. 1913 E, 905, Suslak v. United States, 213 Fed. 913; Paulsen v. United States, 199 Fed. 423; Athanasaw v. United States, 227 U. S. 326, 57 L. ed. 528, Ann. Cas. 1913 E, 911; United States v. Rispoli, 189 Fed. 271; Bennett v. United States, 227 U. S. 333, 57 L. ed. 531.

CHAPTER XIII

ABORTION.

§ 220. Definition.—Abortion consists in the expulsion of a human foetus during utero gestation and before it has acquired power to sustain independent life.[1]

§ 221. Quickening of the child—Beginning of life.—A pregnant woman becomes "quick with child" the moment the foetus manifests life.

Life begins "in contemplation of law as soon as an infant is able to stir in the mother's womb."[2] "It is not material whether, speaking with physiological accuracy, life may be said to commence at the moment of quickening, or at the moment of conception, or at some intervening period. In contemplation of law life commences at the moment of quickening, at that moment when the embryo gives the first physical proof of life, no matter when it first received it."[3]

[1] Abrams v. Foshee, 3 Iowa 274, 66 Am. Dec. 77; Wells v. New England Mut. Life Ins. Co., 191 Pa. St. 207, 43 Atl. 126, 71 Am. St. 763, 53 L. R. A. 327.

[2] 1 Bl. Comm. 129.

[3] State v. Cooper, 22 N. J. L. 52, 54, 51 Am. Dec. 248.

§ 222. **Before and after quickening.**—Whether, at common law, abortion before quickening is a crime or not the courts do not agree.

Justice Tenney says, "At common law, it was no offense to perform an operation upon a pregnant woman by her consent, for the purpose of procuring an abortion, and thereby succeed in the intention, unless the woman was 'quick with child.'"[4] Chief Justice Green asserts, "We are of opinion that the procuring of an abortion by the mother, or by another with her assent, unless the mother be quick with child, is not an indictable offense at the common law, and consequently that the mere attempt to commit the act is not indictable. There is neither precedent nor authority to support it."[5]

On the other hand, it is said by Justice Coulter, "It is a flagrant crime at common law to attempt to procure the miscarriage or abortion of the woman, because it interferes with and violates the mysteries of nature in the process by which the human race is propagated and continued. It is a crime against nature which obstructs the fountains of life, and therefore it is punished. The next error assigned is, that it ought to have been charged in the count that the woman had become quick. But although it has been so held in Massachusetts and in some other states, it is not, I apprehend, the law in Pennsylvania, and never ought to have been the law anywhere. It is not the murder of a living child which constitutes the offense, but the destruction of gestation by wicked means and against nature. The

4 Smith v. State, 33 Maine 48, 54 Am. Dec. 607. See also, Commonwealth v. Parker, 9 Metc. (Mass.) 263, 43 Am. Dec. 396; Commonwealth v. Bangs, 9 Mass. 387. (In this case the court says: "if an abortion had been alleged and proved to have ensued, the averment that the woman was quick with child at the time is a necessary part of the indictment"); Mitchell v. Commonwealth, 78 Ky. 204, 39 Am. Rep. 227.

5 State v. Cooper, 22 N. J. L. 52, 58, 51 Am. Dec. 248. See also, State v. Alcorn, 7 Idaho 599, 64 Pac. 1014, 97 Am. St. 252.

moment the womb is instinct with embryo life and gestation has begun, the crime may be perpetrated."[6] And Chief Justice Smith, after quoting Justice Coulter's statement, says, "This enunciation of the law, so careful and distinct in expression, dispenses with the necessity for further discussion."[7]

While, upon principle, abortion before quickening should be punishable at common law, it is quite probable, to say the least, that the rule is to the contrary.

§ 223. **Lord Coke's view.**—"If a woman be quick with child, and by a potion or otherwise killeth it in her womb; or if a man beat her, whereby the child dieth in her body, and she is delivered of a dead child, this is a great misprision, and no murder."[8] The inference is that the child is not regarded as in being until it has quickened.

§ 224. **An anomaly in the law—Legislative enactments desirable.**—For certain civil purposes an unborn child is regarded in being from the time of conception. An illustration of this is the capacity to inherit property from that time. For certain other purposes it is not regarded in being, at common law, until it has quickened. Thus, when a woman is convicted of a capital offense, her pregnancy will not stay execution of the sentence of death unless the child has quickened.[9] And, as heretofore stated, abortion, prior to that time, is not a crime.

"In the interest of good morals and for the preservation of society, the law should punish abortions and miscarriages, wilfully produced, at any time during the period of gestation. That the child shall be considered in existence from the moment of conception for the protection of its rights of property, and yet not in existence, until four or

[6] Mills v. Commonwealth, 13 Pa. St. 631. See also, State v. Loomis, 90 N. J. L. 216, 100 Atl. 160; Munk v. Frink, 81 Nebr. 631, 116 N. W. 525, 17 L. R. A. (N. S.) 439.

[7] State v. Slagle, 83 N. Car. 630.

[8] 3 Inst. 50.

[9] 4 Bl. Comm. 395.

five months after the inception of its being, to the extent that it is a crime to destroy it, presents an anomaly in the law that ought to be provided against by the lawmaking department of the government."[10]

§ 225. Statutory modifications of the common law—Lord Ellenborough's Act.—Both in England and in this country there have been statutory modifications of the common law.

At common law, as heretofore stated, abortion before the child has quickened is no crime at all. Moreover, abortion after the child has quickened is only a misdemeanor.[11]

An early English statute, known as Lord Ellenborough's Act, provides that, to administer a drug to cause the miscarriage of any woman then being quick with child is a capital offense; and also that, to procure the miscarriage of a woman not being quick with child is a felony of a mitigated character.[12]

§ 226. Statutory modifications in this country.—Probably in all of the states of this country statutes have been passed defining, and fixing a penalty for the procuring of abortion. Most of these statutes make the offense a felony; and most of them make no distinction between committing the act before the child has quickened and committing it after the child has quickened.[13] In a few states, including Michigan, the statute provides that the child must have quickened.[14] A Kansas statute defines abortion as felon

10 Mitchell v. Commonwealth, 78 Ky. 204, 39 Am. Rep. 227.

11 Worthington v. State, 92 Md. 222, 48 Atl. 355, 84 Am. St. 506, 56 L. R. A. 352.

12 44 Geo. III, ch. 58.

13 Commonwealth v. Tibbetts, 157 Mass. 519, 32 N. E. 910; Eckhardt v. People, 83 N. Y. 462, 38 Am. Rep. 462; State v. Fitzgerald, 49 Iowa 260, 31 Am. Rep. 148n. State v. Alcorn, 7 Idaho 599, 64 Pac. 1014, 97 Am. St. 252; State v. Howard, 32 Vt. 380, 78 Am. Dec. 609.

14 People v. McDowell, 63 Mich. 229, 30 N. W. 68.

ious homicide; but this has been held a nullity, since there can be no homicide without a death.[15]

Under a statute which provides a penalty for doing acts "with intent to procure the miscarriage of any woman," it has been held that lack of pregnancy on the part of the woman is immaterial,[16] nor is it material whether the miscarriage is consummated.[17] And under a statute which provides a penalty for using an instrument or administering a drug "with intent to produce a miscarriage of any pregnant woman," it has been held that it is not necessary for the woman to be quick with child.[18] Moreover, it has been held that, under an indictment for attempting to commit an abortion by administering a drug it is no defense that the drug used was perfectly harmless.[19]

On the other hand, it has been held that, under a statute which makes it a crime to use an instrument "with intent to destroy the child of which a woman may be pregnant, and shall thereby destroy such child before its birth," the intent to destroy the child must be alleged and proved.[20] It also has been held that such a statute does not apply where the woman procures a miscarriage on herself.[21]

§ 227. **Intent necessary.**—It is said that the Illinois statute is evidently aimed at professional abortionists, and at those who, with the intent and design of producing abortion, shall use any means to that end, no matter what those

15 State v. Young, 55 Kans. 349, 40 Pac. 659.

16 Eggart v. State, 40 Fla. 527, 25 So. 144.

17 Smith v. State, 33 Maine 48, 54 Am. Dec. 607; State v. Longstreth, 19 N. Dak. 268, 121 N. W. 1114, Ann. Cas. 1912D, 1317.

18 State v. Fitzgerald, 49 Iowa 260, 31 Am. Rep. 148n; State v. Atwood, 54 Ore. 526, 102 Pac. 295, 104 Pac. 195, 21 Ann. Cas. 516n.

19 State v. Fitzgerald, 49 Iowa 260, 31 Am. Rep. 148n; Commonwealth v. Sinclair, 195 Mass. 100, 80 N. E. 799, 11 Ann. Cas. 217.

20 Smith v. State, 33 Maine 48, 54 Am. Dec. 607. See also, Lohman v. People, 1 N. Y. 379, 4 How. Prac. 445, 49 Am. Dec. 340.

21 State v. Prude, 76 Miss. 543, 24 So. 871; Thompson v. United States, 30 App. Cas. (D. C.) 352, 12 Ann. Cas. 1004.

means may be, but not at those who, with no such purpose in view, should, by a violent act, unfortunately produce such result. The intent to produce an abortion must exist when the means are used.[22]

Intent to commit abortion may be proved by acts done either before or after the particular act charged in the indictment.[23] And for the purpose of proving a motive for the crime, testimony showing sexual intercourse between the defendant and the prosecuting witness is admissible[24]

Under an indictment for murder by abortion the defendant may be convicted of manslaughter,[25] or of assault with intent to produce an abortion.[26]

An indictment which charges an attempt to produce an abortion, sufficiently charges intent. The term attempt includes intent.[27] "An attempt is an intent to do a particular thing, with an act toward it falling short of the thing intended."[28]

In a prosecution for administering drugs to a pregnant woman with intent to produce a miscarriage, if the jury find the defendant guilty, and fix his punishment at a term of imprisonment in the penitentiary, "together with a fine of one hundred dollars," the fine thus unlawfully imposed will not vitiate the verdict, since it will be rejected as surplusage.[29]

Where a physician, attending a woman sick with bilious fever, and who is five months advanced in pregnancy, gives her no strong medicines, or does any act to bring about a miscarriage, and she is taken in labor, which proves ineffectual until the fœtus is removed by force, and she

22 Slattery v. People, 76 Ill. 217; Austin v. State, 137 Tenn. 474, 194 S. W. 383.

23 Scott v. People, 141 Ill. 195, 30 N. E. 329.

24 Scott v. People, 141 Ill. 195, 30 N. E. 329.

25 Earll v. People, 73 Ill. 329.

26 Earll v. People, 99 Ill. 123.

27 Scott v. People, 141 Ill. 195, 30 N. E. 329.

28 1 Bish. New Crim. L. (8th ed.) § 728.

29 Armstrong v. People, 37 Ill. 459.

afterward dies of puerperal fever, not induced by anything done or omitted to be done by her physician, a conviction for manslaughter can not be sustained. "If physicians and surgeons can be convicted of manslaughter, and sent to the penitentiary, upon such evidence as this * * * there would soon be witnessed a frightful devastation of their ranks. * * * There is wanting in this case every element of the crime of manslaughter but that of the mere death of a human being."[80]

80 Honnard v. People, 77 Ill. 481. See also, People v. Hager, 181 App. Div. 153, 168 N. Y. S. 183; State v. Bolton (Vt.), 102 Atl. 489; Hunter v. State (Tex. Cr.), 196 S. W. 820; State v. Farnum, 82 Ore. 211, 161 Pac. 417; State v. Shapiro, 89 N. J. L. 319, 98 Atl. 437.

CHAPTER XIV.

ASSAULTS.

§ 230. Definition—Gist of the offense.—A criminal assault is an unlawful attempt to commit a physical injury upon another, or unlawfully putting another in fear of personal violence. In other words, it is an unlawful inchoate violence to the person of another with the present ability, either real or reasonably apparent, of carrying it into effect.

Among other definitions by standard authorities are the following: "Assault is an attempt or offer with force and violence to do a corporal hurt to another;"[1] it is an "attempt or offer to beat another without touching him;"[2] "an assault is an apparent attempt, by violence, to do corporal hurt to another;"[3] "an assault is an unlawful physical force, partly or fully put in motion, creating a reasonable apprehension of immediate physical injury to a human being."[4]

The essence or gist of assault is the intention to do harm.[5]

§ 231. An apparent intention sufficient.—Under the early English rule an actual intention to carry out the threatened harm was essential.[6] In this country some courts have followed this rule,[7] while others have repudiated it.[8] The true view is that a reasonably apparent intention is sufficient. Thus, when a person points an unloaded gun at another, or threatens him with a club or other weapon, and thereby puts him in fear and causes him to retreat, or act on the defensive, he commits an assault irrespective of his actual intent.[9] There is no assault if the intention

[1] Hawk. P. C. (6th ed.), ch. 62, § 1. See also 1 East P. C. 406; 1 Russ. on Crimes (7th ed.) 879.

[2] 3 Bl. Comm. 120; 4 Bl. Comm. 216.

[3] 1 Whart. Crim. L. (11th ed.), § 797.

[4] 2 Bish. New Crim. L. (8th ed.) § 23.

[5] Richels v. State, 1 Sneed (Tenn.) 606.

[6] 1 Russ. on Crimes (7th Eng. ed.) 880.

[7] Chapman v. State, 78 Ala. 463, 56 Am. Rep. 42; State v. Sears, 86 Mo. 169; White v. State, 29 Tex. App. 530, 16 S. W. 340; State v. Godfrey, 17 Ore. 300, 20 Pac. 625, 11 Am. St. 830.

[8] Commonwealth v. White, 110 Mass. 407, Beale's Cases 450; State v. Rawles, 65 N. Car. 334; State v. Triplett, 52 Kans. 678, 35 Pac. 815.

[9] Commonwealth v. White, 110 Mass. 407, Beale's Cases 450; Price v. United States, 156 Fed. 950, 15 L. R. A. (N. S.) 1272, 13 Ann. Cas. 483, Derby's Cases, 321; People v. Hopper (Colo.), 169 Pac. 152; State v. Cancelmo, 86 Ore. 379, 168 Pac. 721.

is to aid the person who is claimed to have been assaulted.[10] To constitute an indictable assault, however, the overt act must be accompanied with an intent, either express or implied, to do harm to another. But when the injury threatened would be the natural consequence of the overt act, the unlawful intent will be presumed.[11] In the aggravated assaults, however, in which the gist of the offense is the specific intent, the presumption is not conclusive.[12]

§ 232. **An apparent ability sufficient.**—It has been held, both in England and in this country, that an actual ability to carry out the threatened violence is an essential element of assault.[13] This view, however, has been repudiated by some courts, both in England and in this country.[14] The true view is that a reasonably apparent present ability is sufficient. The reason is that such a condition, accompanied by the threatened violence, tends directly to cause a breach of the public peace. It is well settled that any act, not excusable or justifiable, which tends directly to cause a breach of the public peace, is indictable.[15] In some states,

10 State v. Hemphill, 162 N. Car. 632, 78 S. E. 167, 45 L. R. A. (N. S.) 455n.

11 Conn v. People, 116 Ill. 458, 6 N. E. 463; People v. Jassino, 100 Mich. 536, 59 N. W. 230; Simpson v. State, 59 Ala. 1, 31 Am. Rep. 1n; Smith v. Commonwealth, 100 Pa. St. 324; Studstill v. State, 7 Ga. 2; Reg. v. Jones, 9 Car. & P. 258, 38 E. C. L. 159.

12 People v. Sweeney, 55 Mich. 586, 22 N. W. 50.

13 People v. Lilley, 43 Mich. 521, 5 N. W. 982; Tarver v. State, 43 Ala. 354; State v. Sears, 86 Mo. 169; State v. Godfrey, 17 Ore. 300, 20 Pac. 625, 11 Am. St. 830; State v. Napper, 6 Nev. 113; Chapman v. State, 78 Ala. 463, 56 Am. Rep. 42; Blake v. Barnard, 9 Car. & P. 626; Reg. v. James, 1 Car. & K. 530.

14 Commonwealth v. White, 110 Mass. 407, Beale's Cases 450; State v. Martin, 85 N. Car. 508, 39 Am. Rep. 711n; State v. Paxson (Del.), 99 Atl. 46; Crumbley v. State, 61 Ga. 582; People v. Lee Kong, 95 Cal. 666, 30 Pac. 800, 17 L. R. A. 626, 29 Am. St. 165, Beale's Cases 142, Reg. v. St. George, 9 Car. & P. 483.

15 Commonwealth v. Taylor, 5 Binn. (Pa.) 277; Commonwealth v. White, 110 Mass. 407, Beale's Cases 450

however, including Illinois, an actual present ability is required by statute.

§ 233. Mere words or gestures insufficient.—According to the ancient common law even words might constitute an assault. This view, however, long since passed away.[16] Nor can mere words, howsoever abusive, constitute a sufficient provocation to excuse an assault and battery.[17] It has been held that any threatening gesture, manifesting in itself, or by words accompanying it, an immediate intention coupled with ability to commit a battery, constitutes an assault.[18] There must be, however, violence actually offered, and within such distance that harm may follow it if the would-be assailant be not hindered.[19] When an act is done with intent to commit an assault, but the intent is voluntarily abandoned, or the would-be assailant is prevented from carrying it into effect, while the distance between the parties is too great to commit a battery, no assault is committed.[20] On the other hand, it has been held that where a person approaches another with gesticulations and menaces, but not with the intention of doing him harm, it is not an assault.[21] A mere insulting gesture does not constitute an assault. Thus where a man makes a kissing sign at a woman by puckering up his lips and smacking them, without manifesting any intent to lay hands on her or kiss her without her consent, he is not guilty of assault.[22]

[16] 1 Hawk. P. C., ch. 62, § 1.

[17] Goldsmith v. Joy, 61 Vt. 488, 17 Atl. 1010, 4 L. R. A. 500, 15 Am. St. 923; Willey v. Carpenter, 64 Vt. 212, 23 Atl. 630.

[18] People v. Lilley, 43 Mich. 521, 5 N. W. 982.

[19] People v. Lilley, 43 Mich. 521, 5 N. W. 982; Moreland v. State, 125 Ark. 24, 188 S. W. 1, L. R. A. 1917A, 140n.

[20] People v. Lilley, 43 Mich. 521, 5 N. W. 982; Lane v. State, 85 Ala. 11, 4 So. 730; 1 Russ. on Crimes (7th Eng. ed.) 882.

[21] Berkeley v. Commonwealth, 88 Va. 1017, 14 S. E. 916.

[22] Fuller v. State, 44 Tex. Cr. 463, 72 S. W. 184, 100 Am. St. 871. See also Flournoy v. State, 25 Tex. App. 244, 7 S. W. 865; Lee v. State, 34 Tex. Cr. 519, 31 S. W. 667.

§ 234. Mere preparation insufficient.—Mere preparation to commit a battery does not constitute an assault. Thus, picking up a stone twenty yards from the would-be victim, without offering or attempting to throw it, does not constitute an assault.[23] Nor does drawing a weapon without presenting it constitute an assault.[24] If, however, it be presented an assault will be committed.[25] Where several persons, with a gun, pitch-fork and other weapons, follow a person, who is where he has a right to be, and by using threatening and insulting language put him in fear and thereby cause him to go home sooner than he intended to go, and by a different route, they are guilty of assault.[26]

§ 235. Menacing acts accompanied by conditional threats.—To constitute an act an assault it must be accompanied by a reasonably apparent intention to injure. It follows, therefore, that menacing acts accompanied by words manifesting a contrary intent do not constitute an assault. Where a man angrily raises his cane within striking distance of another, shakes it at him and remarks that, "If you were not an old man I would knock you down," he is not guilty of assault.[27] And where a man angrily raises his hand within striking distance of another and says, "If it were not for your gray hairs I would tear your heart out," no assault is committed.[28] Again, where a man lays his hand on his sword and says to another, "If it were not assize time, I would not take such language from you," he does not commit an assault.[29]

23 Brown v. State, 95 Ga. 481, 20 S. E. 495.

24 Lawson v. State, 30 Ala. 14. See also People v. McMakin, 8 Cal. 547.

25 State v. Dooley, 121 Mo. 591, 26 S. W. 558; Hairston v. State, 54 Miss. 689, 28 Am. Rep. 392.

26 State v. Rawles, 65 N. Car. 334.

27 State v. Crow, 23 N. Car. 375.

28 Commonwealth v. Eyre, 1 Serg. & R. (Pa.) 347.

29 Tuberville v. Savage, 1 Mod. 3.

§ 236. Classification of assaults—Distinguishing feature. —Assaults are classified as simple assaults and aggravated assaults.

At common law, the distinguishing feature of these two classes of assault lies in the nature of the criminal intent involved. In a simple assault a general criminal intent is sufficient. This intent may be inferred from the act. Moreover, it is not essential that it be alleged in the pleadings. On the other hand, an aggravated assault involves a specific criminal intent. Moreover, it must be alleged in the pleadings and proved. And the penalty for an aggravated assault is, of course, greater than that for a simple assault.

At common law, however, both classes of assault are only misdemeanors; but in many states aggravated assaults are made felonies by statute.[80]

§ 237. The aggravated assaults.—The chief aggravated assaults are the following: (1) Assault with intent to murder; (2) Assault with intent to kill; (3) Assault with intent to rob; (4) Assault with intent to commit rape; (5) Assault with intent to do grievous bodily harm; and (6) Assault with a deadly weapon.

§ 238. Assault with intent to murder.—This offense involves the following two distinct elements: (1) A specific intent to murder; (2) an assault or attempt to carry the intent into execution.[81]

Since the gist of this offense is the specific intent to murder,[82] this intent must be alleged in the indictment. It is also essential that the malicious intent involved in this

[80] Simpson v. State, 59 Ala. 1, 31 Am. Rep. 1n.

[81] People v. Devine, 59 Cal. 630; Crosby v. People, 137 Ill. 325, 27 N. E. 49; State v. Fiske, 63 Conn. 388, 28 Atl. 572; Smith v. State, 83 Ala. 26, 3 So. 551.

[82] Hayes v. State, 14 Tex. App. 330. See also Long v. State, 46 Ind. 582.

crime be proved.[33] This may be done, nowever, by circumstantial evidence. Thus, it may be inferred from the use of a deadly weapon, or from the character of the assault and other attending circumstances.[34] Ordinarily, this offense is committed by the use of a deadly weapon. It may, however, be committed without the use of such a weapon.[35]

§ 239. Adaptation of act done and means employed to accomplish purpose.—To constitute an assault with intent to murder, the act done and the means employed must be adapted to accomplish the end sought. It is not essential that the adaptation be real.[36] It need only be apparent; because the evil to be corrected relates to apparent danger, rather than to actual injury sustained.[37] If it be evident to every reasonable mind that the means used are entirely inadequate to the consummation of the intent charged, that fact will rebut or disprove the felonious intent, and a conviction can not be justified. Where the object is not accomplished because of an impediment which is of such a nature as to be wholly unknown to the offender, who uses appropriate means, though not fully or only apparently adapted to the object, the criminal attempt is committed.[38] Hence, under an indictment for assault with intent to murder, if the proof show that the accused pointed a loaded gun at another and snapped it several times, but there was no cap on it, and the court charged the jury that the absence of the cap will not avail the accused if he believed at the time that it was on the gun, but the jury must be satisfied be-

[33] Simpson v. State, 59 Ala. 1, 31 Am. Rep. 1n; Hamilton v. People, 113 Ill. 34, 55 Am. Rep. 396; Slatterly v. People, 58 N. Y. 354; People v. Prague, 72 Mich. 178, 40 N. W. 243.

[34] People v. Lilley, 43 Mich. 521, 5 N. W. 982. See also Wright v. People, 33 Mich. 300.

[35] State v. Reed, 40 Vt. 603.

[36] Mullen v. State, 45 Ala. 43, 6 Am. Rep. 691; Kunkle v. State, 32 Ind. 220.

[37] 1 Bish. New Crim. L. (8th ed.), § 754.

[38] Kunkle v. State, 32 Ind. 220.

yond all reasonable doubt that he did not know there was no cap on the gun, a conviction will be sustained.[39] It has been often held that to constitute this offense, a specific intent to kill must be proved.[40] It also has been held that the means employed must be actually adapted to accomplish the end sought.[41] This view, however, is erroneous. It is not essential to constitute an assault, or an assault and battery, with intent to commit a felony, that the intent and the present ability to execute be conjoined.[42]

§ 240. **Proof that death of victim would have been murder essential, but not sufficient.**—To constitute assault with intent to murder, the proof must show that had the victim died the crime would have been murder.[43] On the other hand, proof that had the victim died the crime would have been murder is not of itself sufficient proof of assault with intent to murder. This is owing to the fact that murder involves only a general criminal intent and not necessarily a specific intent to kill.[44]

§ 241. **Assault with intent to commit manslaughter.**—Is there such a crime as assault with intent to commit manslaughter? Upon this point the decisions are not harmonious. In Iowa the question has been answered in the affirmative and it is held that if an unlawful assault was made upon reasonable provocation in the heat of blood, but without malice, and without legal excuse, and with in-

39 Mullen v. State, 45 Ala. 43, 6 Am. Rep. 691.

40 State v. Bennet, 128 Iowa 117, 5 Ann. Cas. 997; Chowning v. State, 91 Ark. 503, 121 S. W. 735, 18 Ann. Cas. 529.

41 State v. Swails, 8 Ind. 524, 65 Am. Dec. 772.

42 Kunkle v. State, 32 Ind. 220; 1 Bish. New Crim. L. (8th ed.), § 750.

43 Simpson v. State, 59 Ala. 1, 31 Am. Rep. 1n; State v. Conner, 59 Iowa 357, 13 N. W. 327, 44 Am. Rep. 686; People v. Prague, 72 Mich. 178, 40 N. W. 243; Hamilton v. People, 113 Ill. 34, 55 Am. Rep. 396; Elliott v. State, 46 Ga. 159; McCormack v. State, 102 Ala. 156, 15 So. 438.

44 Simpson v. State, 59 Ala. 1, 31 Am. Rep. 1a.

tent to kill, then the defendant would be guilty of an assault with intent to commit manslaughter.[45] On the other hand, the courts of some states, including those of Illinois and Michigan, hold the contrary view. It is said that if there was an intent to take life and the killing would not be excusable or justifiable, it would be assault with intent to commit murder;[46] that a specific intent can not be found to exist in the absence of reflection and deliberation.[47]

The latter view is correct upon principle and supported by the weight of authority.

§ 242. Assault with intent to kill.—This offense differs rom assault with intent to murder in the intent involved. In the case of intent to murder the proof must be such as shows that, if death had been caused by the assault, the assailant would have been guilty of murder; and in the case of assault with intent to kill the proof need only be such as that, had death ensued, the crime would have been manslaughter. In the former case the intent must be the result of malice aforethought, and in the latter, the result of sudden passion or emotion without time for deliberation or reflection.[48]

A conviction of assault with intent to kill may be proper though the wounds actually inflicted were not such as would be usually fatal.[49] On the other hand, the test whether a conviction of assault with intent to murder should be sustained is not whether the accused inflicted a wound likely to produce death, but whether the assault was of a character likely to be attended with dangerous consequences

45 State v. Connor, 59 Iowa 357, 13 N. W. 327, 44 Am. Rep. 686.

46 Moore v. People, 146 Ill. 600, 35 N. E. 166.

47 People v. Lilley, 43 Mich. 521, 5 N. W. 982. See also Wright v. People, 33 Mich. 300.

48 State v. Reed, 40 Vt. 603. See also State v. McGuire, 84 Conn. 470, 80 Atl. 761, 38 L. R. A. (N. S.) 1045.

49 Crosby v. People, 137 Ill. 325, 27 N. E. 49.

and of a nature to cause death, in which case malicious intent will be presumed.[50]

§ 243. **Assault with intent to rob.**—To constitute assault with intent to rob the act must be done with the specific intent to take from the person of another, or from his presence, his personal property, by violence or putting him in fear. If the intent be to take his property by stealth, and not by violence or putting in fear, the crime of assault with intent to rob will not be committed.

§ 244. **Assault with intent to commit rape.**—To constitute assault with intent to commit rape the act must be accompanied with a specific intent to have carnal knowledge of the woman without her consent and by the use of such force as should be sufficient to overcome such resistance as she should make.[51] On the other hand, if the proof show that the intent of the accused was to have carnal knowledge of the woman, but without force, and not against her consent, it will fall short of proving him guilty of assault with intent to commit rape.[52]

The foregoing propositions are not applicable, of course, when the female is under the age of consent. When the evidence shows that the accused intended forcibly to have carnal knowledge of the woman and his efforts failed owing to his inability to overcome her resistance, or from fear, a conviction will be sustained.[53] Some courts hold that actual violence is essential to constitute this offense.[54]

[50] Crowell v. People, 190 Ill. 508. 60 N. E. 872; People v. Connors, 253 Ill. 266, 97 N. E. 643, 39 L. R. A. (N. S.) 143n, Ann. Cas. 1913A, 196n.

[51] Shields v. State, 32 Tex. Cr. 498, 502, 23 S. W. 893; State v. Sanders, 92 S. Car. 427, 75 S. E. 702, 42 L. R. A. (N. S.) 424.

[52] State v. Canada, 68 Iowa 397, 27 N. W. 288; People v. Manchego, 80 Cal. 306, 22 Pac. 223; Douglas v. State, 105 Ark. 218, 150 S. W. 860, 42 L. R. A. (N. S.) 524n.

[53] Taylor v. State, 50 Ga. 79; Lewis v. State, 35 Ala. 380; People v. Stewart, 97 Cal. 238, 32 Pac. 8. See also Glover v. Commonwealth, 86 Va. 382, 10 S. E. 420.

[54] State v. Wells, 31 Conn. 210

Others hold the contrary. The latter hold that the specific intent to commit rape, preparations to carry out this intent and present ability to accomplish it, are sufficient.[55] It also has been held that impotency is not a defense to a charge of assault with intent to commit rape.[56]

§ 245. Transferability of the criminal intent.—It has been held that the specific criminal intent involved in an aggravated assault is not transferable. Thus, it has been held that where one aiming at A misses him and wounds B he can not be convicted of assault with intent to kill B.[57] This view, however, is not correct upon principle, nor is it in accord with the weight of authority.[58] Where a person deliberately shoots at A, and in the direction of B, and the ball misses A and strikes B, inflicting a wound, these facts will show sufficiently the intention of the person shooting to kill and murder B, although he has no actual malice or ill feeling toward B, and he may be convicted of an assault upon B with intent to murder him.[59] And where one, without provocation, discharges a gun directly at a group of persons, it is immaterial what person he intended to kill; or if, under such circumstances, he shoot a person other than the one intended, the act, from its recklessness and want of provocation, will be referred to no other cause than malice. Such recklessness implies malice.[60]

[55] State v. Shroyer, 104 Mo. 441, 16 S. W. 286, 24 Am. St. 344; People v. Carlsen, 160 Mich. 426, 125 N. W. 361, 136 Am. St. 447.

[56] Hunt v. State, 114 Ark. 498, 169 S. W. 773, L. R. A. 1915B, 131.

[57] Lacefield v. State, 34 Ark. 275, 36 Am. Rep. 8; Rex v. Holt, 7 Car. & P. 518; Reg. v. Stopford, 11 Cox Cr. C. 643; State v. Mulhall, 199 Mo. 202, 97 S. W. 583, 7 L. R. A. (N. S.) 630n, 8 Ann. Cas. 781.

[58] State v. Gilman, 69 Maine 163, 31 Am. Rep. 257; Callahan v. State, 21 Ohio St. 306; State v. Jump, 90 Mo. 171, 2 S. W. 279; Walker v. State, 8 Ind. 290.

[59] Dunaway v. People, 110 Ill. 333, 51 Am. Rep. 686; Vandermark v. People, 47 Ill. 122; State v. Thomas, 127 La. 576, 53 So. 868, 37 L. R. A. (N. S.) 172n, Ann. Cas. 1912A, 1059n.

[60] Dunaway v. People, 110 Ill. 333, 51 Am. Rep. 686.

The same principle is applicable where the offender is mistaken as to the identity of his victim. Thus, where A attacks B, believing him to be C, and tries to kill him, he will be guilty of assault with intent to kill.[61]

It is to be observed, however, that the courts refuse to recognize a transferability of specific criminal intent from a person to a thing, or vice versa. Thus, where one, who has been fighting, throws a stone at his adversary and it passes over the latter's head and shatters a large plate-glass window, the offender is not guilty of malicious mischief.[62] And where one shoots at another on horseback with intent to murder him, and misses the man but kills the horse, he is not guilty of maliciously killing the horse.[63]

It is also to be observed that a specific intent to commit one offense will not take the place of a specific intent to commit a different offense. Thus, where a burglar is convicted of assaulting a watchman with intent to commit murder, maim and disable him, and the proof shows that the burglar's intent was only to disable the watchman temporarily until the former could escape, the conviction will be set aside.[64]

§ 246. Assault with intent to do grievous bodily harm.— In some states statutes have been passed specifically punishing assault with intent to do grievous bodily harm. To constitute this offense the specific intent to do grievous bodily harm is essential. It has been held, however, that general malice is sufficient, that particular malice against the person wounded is not essential, and also that it is immaterial whether grievous bodily harm is committed or not.[65]

[61] McGehee v. State, 62 Miss. 772, 52 Am. Rep. 209, Knowlton's Cases 50.

[62] Reg. v. Pembliton, 12 Cox Cr. C. 607, Beale's Cases 210, L. R. 2 C. C. 119, Rood's Dig. Crim. L. 108.

[63] Rex v. Kelly, 1 Craw. & D. 186, Beale's Cases 182, Rood's Dig. Crim. L. 105.

[64] Rex v. Boyce, 1 Moody 29, Beale's Cases 182, Rood's Dig. Crim. L. 105.

[65] State v. Richardson, 179 Ia. 770, 162 N. W. 28, L. R. A. 1917D, 944; Rex. v. Hunt, 1 Moody 93.

§ 247. **Assault with a deadly weapon.**—In most states statutes have been passed creating this class of aggravated assault. The offense is made to depend, in part at least, upon the character of the weapon used. The statutes, however, are not uniform. Some require one specific criminal intent, others require a different one, while still others require none at all. Thus, the New York Penal Code requires that the act be done with a deadly or dangerous weapon, "with an intent to kill a human being, or to commit a felony upon the person or the property of the one assaulted."[66] The California Penal Code requires that it be "likely to produce great bodily injury."[67] Under these statutes the gist of the offense consists in the specific intent involved as well as in the dangerous nature of the weapon used.[67a] In Texas, if the assault be made with a deadly weapon it is ipso facto an aggravated assault irrespective of any specific criminal intent, and it is unnecessary to allege or prove the intent with which the assault was made.[68]

Upon an indictment for assault with a deadly weapon it has been held that, where it appears that the accused held a pistol in one hand and took hold of the prosecuting witness by the throat with the other hand, but did not present the pistol, or attempt to shoot, or even threaten to do so, the offense committed is false imprisonment but not assault with a deadly weapon.[69]

From the mere fact of the use of a deadly weapon, irrespective of the circumstances under which it was used, there is no necessary presumption of malicious intent.[70]

66 New York: Parker's Crim. Code (1910) § 240; Pen. Code, § 217.

67 California: Deering Pen. Code (1915), § 245; People v. Magri, 32 Cal. App. 536, 163 Pac. 503; People v. Grandi, 33 Cal. App. 637, 165 Pac. 1027.

67a State v. Lichter (Del.), 102 Atl. 529.

68 Texas: Vernon's Crim. Stat. (1916) arts. 1024a-1024b; Pinson v. State, 23 Tex. 579, Hunt v. State, 6 Tex. App. 663.

69 Tarpley v. People, 42 Ill. 340; People v. Stoyan, 280 Ill. 300, 117 N. E. 464.

70 Friederich v. People, 147 Ill. 310, 35 N. E. 472.

§ 248. **What is a deadly weapon?**—A deadly weapon is any instrument by which death may be produced, or would be likely to cause death, when used in the manner in which it may appear it was used in the particular case.[71] It is to be observed, however, that a weapon is not necessarily a deadly weapon merely because it is capable of causing death.[72]

In some cases courts take judicial notice that certain instruments are deadly weapons. Thus, courts have held that a loaded gun,[73] brass knuckles,[74] a hoe,[75] a sledge hammer,[76] an ax,[77] a club,[78] a rolling pin,[79] etc., are deadly weapons.

On the other hand, when the weapon is one not likely to cause death, either from its inherent nature or from the manner in which it is used, the question whether it is a deadly weapon or not is one for the jury to decide. Thus, where the assault is made with a stick,[80] a stone,[81] a glass tumbler,[82] a chain,[83] a horseshoe,[84] a pocket-knife[85] or a pistol used as a club,[86] the question is one of fact for the jury. Pointing an unloaded pistol at another is not an assault with a deadly weapon.[87]

71 Burgess v. Commonwealth, 176 Ky. 326, 195 S. W. 445; People v. Rodrigo, 69 Cal. 601, 11 Pac. 481.

72 Pittman v. State, 25 Fla. 648, 6 So. 437.

73 Hamilton v. People, 113 Ill. 34, 55 Am. Rep. 396.

74 Wilks v. State, 3 Tex. App. 34.

75 Hamilton v. People, 113 Ill. 34, 55 Am. Rep. 396.

76 Philpot v. Commonwealth, 86 Ky. 595, 6 S. W. 455, 9 Ky. L. 737.

77 State v. Shields, 110 N. Car. 497, 14 S. E. 779.

78 State v. Phillips, 104 N. Car. 786, 10 S. E. 463; Silgar v. People, 107 Ill. 563.

79 Greschia v. People, 53 Ill. 295.

80 State v. Dineen, 10 Minn. 407.

81 State v. Jarrott, 23 N. Car. 76.

82 Coney v. State, 2 Tex. App. 62.

83 Kouns v. State, 3 Tex. App. 13.

84 People v. Cavanagh, 62 How. Pr. (N. Y.) 187.

85 Sylvester v. State, 71 Ala. 17; Hilliard v. State, 17 Tex. App. 210.

86 Prior v. State, 41 Ga. 155.

87 Price v. United States, 156 Fed. 950, 15 L. R. A. (N. S.) 1272, 13 Ann. Cas. 483, Derby's Cases 321.

§ 249. **Assault and battery.**—Assault and battery is a separate and distinct offense from assault.[88] Every battery, however, includes an assault; and therefore, upon an indictment for assault and battery the accused may be convicted of assault only.[89]

A battery is any unlawful touching of the person of another, either by the offender himself, or by something put in motion by him. When done in an angry, rude, insolent or revengeful manner, any touching, however slight, will constitute a battery. The law does not discriminate between different degrees of force, and therefore the slightest force is sufficient.[90] Thus, spitting on another, in an angry, rude or insolent manner, constitutes an assault and battery.[91] To touch another in anger, though in the slightest degree, or under pretense of passing, is an assault and battery.[92] Even to snatch a paper from another is technically an assault and battery.[93] Shoving another with one's open hand,[94] upsetting a chair or carriage in which a person is sitting,[95] throwing oil of vitriol on the person of another,[96] or placing one's hand on another's head and pushing his hat back for the purpose of seeing his face, in order to identify him,[97] are all batteries.

[88] Moore v. People, 26 Ill. App. 137; Hunt v. People, 53 Ill. App. 111.

[89] 1 Hawk. P. C., ch. 62, Beale's Cases 420.

[90] 3 Bl. Comm. 120; Hunt v. People, 53 Ill. App. 111; State v. Philley, 67 Ind. 304; Engelhardt v. State, 88 Ala. 100, 7 So. 154; Norton v. State, 14 Tex. 387; Kirland v. State, 43 Ind. 146, 13 Am. Rep. 386.

[91] Reg. v. Cotesworth, 6 Mod. 172; Commonwealth v. Malone, 114 Mass. 295. See also State v. Baker, 65 N. Car. 332; Commonwealth v. McKie, 1 Gray (Mass.) 61, 61 Am. Dec. 410.

[92] Cole v. Turner, 6 Mod. 149; United States v. Ortega, Fed. Cas. No. 15971, 4 Wash. (C. C.) 531.

[93] Dyk v. De Young, 35 Ill. App. 138 (affirmed 133 Ill. 82, 24 N. E. 520).

[94] State v. Baker, 65 N. Car. 332.

[95] Clark v. Downing, 55 Vt. 259, 45 Am. Rep. 612.

[96] People v. Stanton, 106 Cal. 139, 39 Pac. 525; People v. Bracco, 69 Hun (N. Y.) 206, 23 N. Y. S. 505, 10 N. Y. Cr. 438, 53 N. Y. St. 227.

[97] Siegel v. Long, 169 Ala. 79, 53 So. 753, 33 L. R. A. (N. S.) 1070.

The following instruction is correct and has been sustained: "The court further instructs the jury that if they believed, beyond a reasonable doubt, from the evidence, that the defendant, in anger, laid his hand on Stephen Grant, or in any manner took hold of him in anger, then the defendant would be guilty of an assault and battery."[98]

§ 250. **Taking indecent liberties with women.**—When a man takes indecent liberties with a girl or woman, by handling or fondling her, without her consent and against her will, he is guilty of assault and battery.[99] Thus, when a man, without some innocent reason or excuse, puts his arm around the neck of another man's wife, without her consent and against her will, he is guilty of assault and battery.[1]

§ 251. **Mere familiarity not a crime.**—Mere familiarity between a male and female, even when the latter is under the age of consent, is not a crime. Thus, mere familiarity between a man and a girl under the age of consent, who have been intimate and frequently in each other's company, consisting of the man's putting his arm around the girl's waist with her consent, does not, in the absence of any offer or threat to take, or request to be allowed to take, any other liberties with her person, constitute an assault and battery.[2]

§ 252. **Consent obtained by fraud.**—Consent obtained by fraud is no defense.[3] The outrage upon the woman, and

98 Hunt v. People, 53 Ill. App. 111.

99 Ridout v. State, 6 Tex. App. 249; Moreland v. State, 125 Ark. 24, 188 S. W. 1, L. R. A. 1917A, 140n; Norris v. State, 87 Ala. 85, 6 So. 371; Commonwealth v. Bean, 111 Mass. 438; People v. Hicks, 98 Mich. 86, 56 N. W. 1102; Sample v. State, 52 Tex. Cr. 505, 108 S. W. 685, 124 Am. St. 1103.

1 Goodrum v. State, 60 Ga. 509; Rex v. Nichol, Russ. & Ry. 130; Reg. v. McGavaron, 3 Car. & K. 320.

2 People v. Sheffield, 105 Mich. 117, 63 N. W. 65.

3 Reg. v. Case, 4 Cox Cr. C. 220, Beale's Cases 435.

the injury to society, is as great as if actual force had been employed.[4] In this class of cases the courts discriminate between active consent and passive nonresistance

§ 253. Taking indecent liberties with children—Illinois statute.—The crime of assault and battery can be committed also by taking indecent liberties with children of either sex. And the fact that they consent to the act is no defense when ignorant of the offense committed.[5]

In some states, including Illinois, there are statutes which make the taking of indecent liberties with children a felony.[6]

§ 254. The force can be applied indirectly.—To constitute an assault and battery it is not essential that the force be applied directly. It also can be applied indirectly.

§ 255. Administering poison or other deleterious drugs.—When a person, knowing that a certain thing contains poison or other injurious drug, gives it to another to eat, and the person receiving it, being ignorant of its hurtful nature eats it and suffers injury, the giver is guilty of assault and battery. Thus, when a man gives a girl figs, he knowing at the time that they are medicated with cantharides, and she eats them, having no reason to suspect that they contain any foreign substance, and they make her sick, he is guilty of assault and battery. In this case the court said: "Although force and violence are included in all definitions of assault, or assault and battery, yet where there is physical injury to another person, it is sufficient that the cause is set in motion by the defendant, or that the person is subjected to its operation by means of any act or control which the defendant exerts. * * * If one should hand an explosive substance to another, and induce him to take it by misrepresenting or

[4] Reg. v. Stanton, 1 Car. & K. 415; People v. Crosswell, 13 Mich. 427, 437, 87 Am. Dec. 774.

[5] Reg. v. Lock, L. R. 2 C. C. 10. See also Cliver v. State, 45 N. J. L. 46.

[6] Illinois: Hurd's Rev. Stat. (1917), p. 950, § 42ha.

concealing its dangerous qualities, and the other, ignorant of its character, should receive it and cause it to explode in his pocket or hand, and should be injured by it, the offending party would be guilty of a battery, and that would necessarily include an assault; although he might not be guilty even of an assault, if the substance failed to explode or failed to cause any injury. It would be the same if it exploded in his mouth or stomach. If that which causes the injury is set in motion by the wrongful act of the defendant, it can not be material whether it acts upon the personal injury externally or internally, by mechanical or chemical force."[7]

In this class of cases, the deceit, by means of which the person is induced to take the drug, is a fraud upon his will equivalent to force in overpowering it.[8]

It has been held, however, both in England[9] and in this country,[10] that to administer poison or other deleterious drug to a person who takes it willingly, but in ignorance of its real nature, does not constitute an assault and battery. This view, however, is erroneous and not in accord with the weight of authority.[11]

§ 256. Striking a substance attached to a person.—When a person rudely or angrily strikes anything attached to an-

[7] Commonwealth v. Stratton, 114 Mass. 303, 19 Am. Rep. 350, Beale's Cases 451. See also, Derby's Cases, 318; Reg. v. Button, 8 Car. & P. 660. (This case has been overruled in England. See Reg. v. Hanson, 2 Car. & K. 912. It is, however, correct upon principle and in accord with the weight of authority.)

[8] Commonwealth v. Burke, 105 Mass. 376, 7 Am. Rep. 531, Derby's Cases 334; Reg. v. Sinclair, 13 Cox Cr. C. 28.

[9] Reg. v. Walkden, 1 Cox Cr. C. 282; Reg. v. Dilworth, 2 Mood. & Rob. 531, See also, Reg. v. Smith, 34 U. C. Q. B. 552.

[10] Garnet v. State, 1 Tex. App. 605, 28 Am. Rep. 425.

[11] Commonwealth v. Stratton, 114 Mass. 303, 19 Am. Rep. 350, Beale's Cases 451; Reg. v. Button, 8 Car. & P. 660; Treeve's Case, 2 East P. C. 821; Commonwealth v. Burke, 105 Mass. 376, 7 Am. Rep. 531, Derby's Cases 334.

other person he commits assault and battery. Thus when one rudely or angrily strikes a cane in another's hand the crime is committed.[12]

§ 257. **Setting a dog on a person.**—A person may be guilty of assault and battery in setting a dog on another and causing it to bite him.[13]

§ 258. **Striking another's horse.**—To strike another's horse attached to a carriage in which a person is riding may constitute an assault and battery.[14] To do so, however, it is essential that the person in the carriage receive some injury. This is owing to the fact that a battery consists in personal violence. On the other hand, merely to strike another's team, even angrily, which he is driving, does not, of itself, constitute assault and battery.[15]

§ 259. **Exposing a helpless person to the inclemency of the weather.**—Assault and battery can be committed by indirectly causing an injury to another by exposing him to the inclemency of the weather. Thus, where a person takes a helpless infant from its mother, even with her consent, telling her that he will take it to an institution to be cared for, but instead of doing so puts it in a bag and hangs it on a fence at the side of a public highway and leaves it there, and it suffers injury in consequence of inclement weather, the offender is guilty of assault and battery. Consent of the mother in such case is no defense, the court holding that since the mother gave that consent on the false pretext that the child was to be taken to some institution, and, as that

12 Respublica v. DeLongchamps, 1 Dall. (Pa.) 111, 1 L. ed. 60.

13 1 Russ. on Crimes; (7th ed.) 881.

14 Kirland v. State, 43 Ind. 146, 13 Am. Rep. 386; Knowlton's Cases 207.

15 Kirland v. State, 43 Ind. 146, 13 Am. Rep. 386; Knowlton's Cases 207.

pretext was false, it was really no consent.[16] To constitute an assault and battery, however, the infant must suffer an injury.[17]

Where a mother abandons her helpless babe in the public street at night, without clothes or covering, exposed to the elements and such other dangers as might beset it, with intent to accomplish its death, she is guilty of assault with intent to murder. And if the child die in consequence of such exposure the mother is guilty of murder.[18]

[16] Reg. v. March, 1 Car. & K. 496.

[17] Reg. v. Renshaw, 2 Cox. Cr. C. 285, Beale's Cases 434.

[18] Pallis v. State, 123 Ala. 12, 26 So. 339, 82 Am. St. 106.

CHAPTER XV.

CONSPIRACY.

§ 265. Definition.—It has been said that there is, perhaps, no crime, an exact definition of which it is more difficult to give than the offense of conspiracy.[1]

It may, however, be defined as a combination between two or more persons to accomplish an illegal purpose, either by legal or illegal means, or a legal purpose by illegal means. The purpose or means may be illegal either at common law

[1] State v. Donaldson, 32 N. J. L. 151, 90 Am. Dec. 649, Beale's Cases 828.

or by statute. Bouvier defines conspiracy as, "A combination of two or more persons by some concerted action to accomplish some criminal or unlawful purpose, or to accomplish some purpose, not in itself criminal or unlawful, by criminal or unlawful means."[2] Bishop states that "Conspiracy is the corrupt agreeing together of two or more persons to do, by concerted action, something unlawful either as a means or an end."[3] Desty observes, "A criminal conspiracy is (1) a corrupt combination (2) of two or more persons, (3) by concerted action, to commit (4) a criminal or an unlawful act; (a) or an act not in itself criminal or unlawful, by criminal or unlawful means; (b) or an act which would tend to prejudice the public in general, to subvert justice, disturb the peace, injure public trade, affect public health, or violate public policy; (5) or any act, however innocent, by means neither criminal nor unlawful, where the tendency of the object sought would be to wrongfully coerce or oppress either the public or an individual."[4] Chief Justice Shaw defines it as "a combination of two or more persons, by some concerted action, to accomplish some criminal or unlawful purpose, or to accomplish some purpose not in itself criminal or unlawful by criminal or unlawful means."[5] And as stated by Justice Gilchrist, "The authorities agree in stating that a conspiracy is a confederacy to do an unlawful act, or a lawful act by unlawful means, whether to the prejudice of an individual or of the public, and that it is not necessary that its object should be the commission of a crime."[6]

[2] Bouvier's Law Dict.

[3] 2 Bish. New Crim. L. (8th ed.) § 171.

[4] 4 Am. & Eng. Encyc. L. (1st ed.), 583.

[5] Commonwealth v. Hunt, 4 Metc. (Mass.) 111, 38 Am. Dec. 346, Beale's Cases 821.

[6] State v. Burnham, 15 N. H. 396, Knowlton's Cases 318. See also Ex parte Birdseye, 244 Fed. 972; Brewster v. State (Ind.), 115 N. E. 54; United States v. Rintelen, 233 Fed. 793; State v. Porter (Mo.), 199 S. W. 158

Judge Fitzgerald pertinently observes: "Conspiracy is aptly described as divisible under three heads—where the end to be attained is itself a crime; where the object is lawful but the means to be resorted to are unlawful; and where the object is to do injury to a third person or to a class, though if the wrong were effected by a single individual it would be a wrong, but not a crime."[7]

The trend of recent decisions is to hold, in many instances, that a combination to do an act, which would be lawful if done by an individual is indictable.[8]

It is not necessary either that the purpose should be criminal or the unlawful means criminal.[9]

§ 266. Gist of the offense.—The gist of the crime of conspiracy is the unlawful combination. As a general rule, no attempt to carry out the agreement is essential. The agreement itself constitutes a sufficient overt act.[10] In some states, however, by statute, a distinct overt act is essential in certain specified cases.[11]

[7] Reg. v. Parnell, 14 Cox Cr. C. 508, Derby's Cases, 79.

[8] State v. Huegin, 110 Wis. 189, 85 N. W. 1046, 62 L. R. A. 700; Franklin Union v. People, 220 Ill. 355, 77 N. E. 176, 4 L. R. A. (N. S.) 1001, 110 Am. St. 248.

[9] State v. Hardin, 144 Iowa 264, 120 N. W. 470, 138 Am. St. 292; State v. Davis, 88 S. Car. 229, 70 S. E. 811, 34 L. R. A. (N. S.) 295; Ware v. United States, 154 Fed. 577, 84 C. C. A. 503, 12 L. R. A. (N. S.) 1053, 12 Ann. Cas. 233.

[10] Ochs v. People, 124 Ill. 399, 423, 16 N. E. 662. See also Commonwealth v. Judd, 2 Mass. 329, 3 Am. Dec. 54; Garland v. State, 112 Md. 83, 75 Atl. 631, 21 Ann. Cas. 28n; People v. Richards, 1 Mich. 217, 51 Am. Dec. 75n, 80; State v. Ripley, 31 Maine 386; United States v. Galleanni, 245 Fed. 977 (conspiracy to prevent persons subject to registration for selective draft under Act May 18, 1917, § 5, from registering); Taylor v. United States, 244 Fed. 321, 156 C. C. A. 607; United States v. Bryant, 245 Fed. 682 (conspiracy to resist raising of army by conscription held conspiracy to resist authority of the United States, though Selective Draft Act had not then been passed).

[11] People v. Flack, 125 N. Y. 324, 26 N. E. 267, 11 L. R. A. 807n; Wood v. State, 47 N. J. L. 180; State v. Clary, 64 Maine 369; People v. Daniels, 105 Cal. 262, 38 Pac. 720; United States v. Barrett, 65 Fed. 62 (affirmed, 169 U. S. 218, 42 L. ed. 723, 18 Sup. Ct. 327).

§ 267. Contemplated crime one of which concert of conspirators is a constituent part.—When the contemplated crime is one of which concert of the conspirators is a constituent part, such as adultery, fornication, incest and bigamy, the courts hold that the mere agreement to commit it is not an indictable offense. The conspiracy in such a case is not treated as an integral offense, but rather as an integral part of another offense.[12]

But it has been held a woman may conspire to commit an offense against the United States, although the object of the conspiracy is her own transportation in interstate commerce for purposes of prostitution, in violation of the White Slave Act.[13]

§ 268. Third party implicated.—When a conspiracy to commit adultery, fornication and the like, implicates a third party, the conspiracy itself is indictable. It was said in one case, "The appellant contends there is no such crime as conspiracy to commit adultery. * * * This case is readily distinguishable from Shannon v. Commonwealth,[14] and Miles v. State.[15] In those decisions the agreement of a married woman to have intercourse with a man other than her husband was held not to amount to a conspiracy to commit adultery, for that the consent involved was a part of the offense itself. One may aid and abet in adultery without actually participating in the act. * * * And we can discover no ground for saying that a combination to commit the unlawful act, not an agreement between the immediate parties to the intended crime may not constitute a conspiracy."[16]

12 Shannon v. Commonwealth, 14 Pa. St. 226; Miles v. State, 58 Ala. 390.

13 United States v. Holte, 236 U. S. 140, 59 L. ed. 504, 35 Sup. Ct. 271, L. R. A. 1915 D, 281n.

14 14 Pa. St. 226

15 15 Ala. 390.

16 State v. Clemenson, 123 Iowa 524, 99 N. W. 139. See also, State v. Henderson, 84 Iowa 161, 50 N. W. 758.

The same principle is involved where the conspiracy is maliciously to injure another in his business and it is essential that both conspirators combine to effect the purpose contemplated.

§ 269. When the unlawful agreement is of itself a crime.—The doctrine that where concert of action is essential to a crime a charge of criminal conspiracy does not lie, does not apply when the unlawful agreement is of itself a crime, but applies only when the agreement and the consummation thereof are so closely connected that the two constitute really but one offense, as in the case of fornication, adultery, bigamy and the like. "The doctrine is invoked * * * that 'where concert of action is necessary to the offense, conspiracy does not lie.' That principle is familiar, but its application, as its language clearly indicates, is necessarily confined within very narrow limits. It does not reach a situation where mere combination to effect an object is itself criminal and not merged in a crime of higher degree, else the absurd result would follow that the offense of conspiracy would be impossible either at common law or under the statute. The rule applies where the immediate effect of the consummation of the act in view, which is the gist of the offense, reaches only the participants therein, and is in such close connection with a major wrong as to be inseparable from it, as for instance, in the offense of adultery, or bigamy, or incest, or dueling."[17]

§ 270. Wharton's view.—"When to the idea of an offense plurality of agents is logically necessary, conspiracy, which assumes the voluntary accession of a person to a crime of such a character that it is aggravated by a plurality of agents, can not be maintained. As crimes to which concert is neces-

17 State v. Huegin, 110 Wis. 189, 243, 85 N. W. 1046, 62 L. R. A. 700n.

sary (i. e., which can not take place without concert), we may mention dueling, bigamy, incest and adultery; to the last of which the limitation here expressed has been specifically applied by authoritative American courts. We have here the well-known distinction between concursus necessarius and concursus facultativus; in the latter of which the accession of a second agent the offense is an element added to its conception; in the former of which the participation of two agents is essential to its conception, and from this it follows that conspiracy, the gist of which is combination, added to crime, does not lie for concursus necessarius."[18]

§ 271. **Mode of making the agreement.**—It is not essential that the agreement be a formal one. Concurrence of sentiment, and co-operative conduct in an unlawful and criminal enterprise, and not formality of speech, are the essential ingredients of criminal conspiracy.[19] It is sufficient if two or more persons, in any manner or through any contrivance, positively or tacitly come to a mutual understanding to accomplish a common and unlawful design.[20]

§ 272. **Nature of the purpose involved.**—An agreement to perpetrate an unlawful act is indictable at common law. Just what is sufficient to constitute such an act, however, is difficult to determine. "To attempt to define the limit or extent of the law of conspiracy as deducible from the English decisions, would be a difficult if not an impracticable task. * * * We may safely assume that it is indictable to conspire to do an unlawful act by any means, and also that it

18 2 Whart. Crim. L. (11th ed.), § 1602.

19 McKee v. State, 111 Ind. 378, 12 N. E. 510.

20 United States v. Goldberg, 7 Biss. (U. S.) 175, 180 Fed. Cas. No. 15233. See also Gibson v. State, 89 Ala. 121, 8 So. 98, 18 Am. St. 96; Spies v. People, 122 Ill. 1, 12 N. E. 865, 17 N. E. 898, 3 Am. St. 320n; State v. Porter (Mo.), 199 S. W. 158; United States v. Bopp, 237 Fed. 283.

is indictable to conspire to do any act by unlawful means."[21] In a leading Maryland case, in which the early English cases upon the subject are exhaustively reviewed, Justice Buchanan enumerates the following classes of cases in which an indictment will lie:

For a conspiracy

(1) To do an act criminal per se.

(2) To do an act not illegal, nor punishable if done by an individual, but immoral only.

(3) To do an act neither illegal nor immoral in an individual, but to effect a purpose which has a tendency to prejudice the public.

(4) To extort money from another, or to injure his reputation by means not indictable if practiced by an individual.

(5) To cheat or defraud a third person, accomplished by means of an act which would not in law amount to an indictable cheat, if effected by an individual.

(6) To impoverish or ruin a third person in his trade or profession.

(7) To defraud a third person by means of an act not per se unlawful, and although no person be thereby injured.

(8) To cheat or defraud a third person, though the means of effecting it should not be determined on at the time.[22]

§ 273. **Historical development of the term.**—At the ancient common law, the term "conspiracy" had a much narrower meaning than it has today. "In very early times, the word had a completely different meaning from that which we attach to it."[23]

[21] Smith v. People, 25 Ill. 17, 76 Am. Dec. 780, Beale's Cases 811.

[22] State v. Buchanan, 5 Har. & J. (Md.) 317, 9 Am. Dec. 534.

[23] 2 Stephen's Hist. Crim. Law of England 227. See also 3 Chit. Crim. L. 1138; 3 Russ. on Crimes (9th Am. ed.) 116; Roscoe's Crim. Ev. (8th ed.) 423; 2 Bish. New Crim. L. (8th ed.), §§ 175, 176.

§ 274. Conspiracy to commit a crime.—A conspiracy to commit any act that is a crime is indictable at common law.[24] This is so self-evident that it can scarcely be necessary to offer any authority.[25] Moreover, whether the act be a felony or a misdemeanor, or a crime at common law or by statute, is immaterial.[26]

§ 275. Conspiracy to commit an immoral act.—A conspiracy to accomplish an immoral act is also indictable at common law.[27] It is not essential that the object of the conspiracy be indictable.[28] Thus, a conspiracy fraudulently to procure a girl to have sexual intercourse with a man is indictable although the object of the conspiracy is not.[29] In determining what sort of conspiracies may be entered into without committing an offense punishable by the common law, regard must be had to the influence which the act, if done, would actually have upon society.[30] So a conspiracy to procure a sham marriage is indictable,[31] and a conspiracy to procure a husband to desert his wife,[32] and

[24] People v. Richards, 67 Cal. 412, 7 Pac. 828, 56 Am. Rep. 716 (robbery); Miller v. Commonwealth, 78 Ky. 15, 39 Am. Rep. 194; People v. Katz, 209 N. Y. 311, 103 N. E. 305, Ann. Cas. 1915 A, 501n (larceny); Commonwealth v. Spink, 137 Pa. St. 255, 20 Atl. 680 (false imprisonment); People v. Butler, 111 Mich. 483, 69 N. W. 734; People v. Forster, 280 Ill. 486, 117 N. E. 761 (false pretenses).

[25] State v. Buchanan, 5 Har. & J. (Md.) 317, 351, 9 Am. Dec. 534.

[26] State v. Donaldson, 32 N. J. L. 151, 90 Am. Dec. 649, Beale's Cases 828; State v. Glidden, 55 Conn. 46, 8 Atl. 890, 3 Am. St. 23; Reg. v. Bunn, 12 Cox Cr. C. 316.

[27] 1 East P. C. 460; State v. Powell, 121 N. Car. 635, 28 S. E. 525; Smith v. People, 25 Ill. 17, 76 Am. Dec. 780, Beale's Cases 811; Rex v. Grey, 9 How. St. Tr. 127.

[28] Rex. v. Delaval, 3 Burr. 1434, 1 Wm. Bl. 410, 439, Beale's Cases 101 (conspiracy to put a girl, with her consent, in the hands of a man for the purpose of prostitution).

[29] Smith v. People, 25 Ill. 17, 76 Am. Dec. 780, Beale's Cases 811.

[30] Smith v. People, 25 Ill. 17, 76 Am. Dec. 780, Beale's Cases 811.

[31] State v. Murphy, 6 Ala. 765, 41 Am. Dec. 79. See also State v. Wilson, 121 N. Car. 650, 28 S. E. 416.

[32] Randall v. Lonstorf, 126 Wis. 147, 105 N. W. 663, 3 L. R. A. (N. S.) 470, 5 Ann. Cas. 371.

also a conspiracy to commit adultery, which implicates a third party;[83] otherwise not.[84]

§ 276. Conspiracy to commit a mere civil wrong—In general.—It has been held repeatedly that a conspiracy to accomplish an object which constitutes a mere civil wrong is not indictable.[85]

On the other hand, Hawkins observes, "There can be no doubt but that all confederacies whatsoever, wrongfully to prejudice a third person, are highly criminal at common law."[86] Chitty says, "All confederacies wrongfully to prejudice another, are misdemeanors at common law, whether the intention is to injure his property, his person, or his character."[87] This view is in accord with the great weight of authority.[88]

§ 277. Conspiracy to commit a civil trespass.—It also has been held that a conspiracy to commit a civil trespass is not indictable.[89] One text-book writer has said a conspiracy to commit a mere trespass on real estate is not criminal, because such an act by one person is not; for in this instance, differing from the last (conspiracy to cheat), combined numbers have no more power for harm, and do no

83 State v. Clemenson, 123 Iowa 524, 99 N. W. 139.

84 Miles v. State, 58 Ala. 390; Shannon v. Commonwealth, 14 Pa. St. 226.

85 Commonwealth v. Prius, 9 Gray (Mass.) 127, Beale's Cases 810, Rood's Dig. Crim. L. 190. See also State v. Straw, 42 N. H. 393; Alderman v. People, 4 Mich. 414, 69 Am. Dec. 321; Rex v. Turner, 13 East 228, Beale's Cases 805.

86 1 Hawk. P. C., ch. 72, § 2.

87 3 Chit. Crim. L., 1139.

88 People v. Donahoe, 279 Ill. 411, 117 N. E. 105; Wilson v. Commonwealth, 96 Pa. St. 56; State v. Norton, 23 N. J. L. 44; State v. Donaldson, 32 N. J. L. 151, 90 Am. Dec. 649, Beale's Cases 828; In re Sweitzer, 13 Okla. Cr. 154, 162 Pac. 1134.

89 Rex v. Turner, 13 East 228, Beale's Cases 805.

more harm, than if each proceeded with his part of the mischief alone.[40]

The foregoing view, however, is not in accord with the weight of authority.[41]

§ 278. Conspiracy to perpetrate a fraud.—A conspiracy to perpetrate a fraud upon another is indictable at common law. And whether the party to be defrauded be a natural or an artificial person is immaterial.

According to the great weight of authority, a conspiracy to defraud individuals or a corporation of their property, may constitute an indictable offense without regard to whether the act done or proposed to be done by the conspirators in pursuance of the conspiracy, be indictable or not.[42]

Thus: a conspiracy to charge another falsely with being the father of a bastard child;[43] a conspiracy to cheat another at cards after getting him drunk;[44] a conspiracy to marry paupers in order to charge one parish and exonerate another;[45] a conspiracy to induce another, by making false representations to him, to abandon a legal claim;[46] a conspiracy fraudulently to induce an illiterate person to sign a certain instrument by falsely representing to him that it

[40] 2 Bish. New Crim. L. (8th ed.) § 182; Rex v. Turner, 13 East 228, Beale's Cases 805.

[41] Reg. v. Rowlands, 5 Cox Cr. C. 436. See also Wilson v. Commonwealth, 96 Pa. St. 56; State v. Norton, 23 N. J. L. 33; State v. Donaldson, 32 N. J. L. 151, 90 Am. Dec. 649, Beale's Cases 828; Rex v. Edwards, 8 Mod. 320, Beale's Cases 804; State v. Huegin, 110 Wis. 189, 85 N. W. 1046, 62 L. R. A. 700; Franklin Union v. People, 220 Ill. 355, 77 N. E. 176, 4 L. R. A. (N. S.) 1001, 110 Am. St. 248; State v. Hardin, 144 Iowa 264, 120 N. W. 470, 138 Am. St. 292; State v. Davis, 88 S. Car. 229, 70 S. E. 811, 34 L. R. A. (N. S.) 295; Ware v. United States, 154 Fed. 577, 84 C. C. A. 503, 12 L. R. A. (N. S.) 1053n, 12 Ann. Cas. 233.

[42] State v. Norton, 3 Zab. (N. J.) 44; Preeman v. United States, 244 Fed. 1, 156 C. C. A. 429.

[43] Rex v. Armstrong, 1 Vent. 304; Rex v. Kimbertz, 1 Dev. 62; Rex v. Kimberly, 1 Sid. 68.

[44] State v. Younger, 1 Dev. (N. Car.) 357, 17 Am. Dec. 571.

[45] Rex v. Tarrant, 4 Burr. 2106.

[46] Reg. v. Carlisle, Dears. Cr. C. 337, 6 Cox Cr. C. 366.

is something different;[47] a conspiracy fraudulently to acquire from a county a certain sum of money;[48] a conspiracy to get possession of land by means of an extorted deed in favor of the lawful owner;[49] a conspiracy to obtain another's goods or money by false pretenses;[50] a conspiracy to stifle competition at an auction sale;[51] a conspiracy between a female servant and a man to perpetrate a fraud upon her master's relatives by the man personating her master and marrying her as such, with the view of defrauding the master's relatives out of part of his property;[52] a conspiracy to defraud another by inducing him to bet on a horse race which the conspirators know is to be fraudulently run;[53] a conspiracy to obtain money from a street car company by fraudulently representing that a certain person was a passenger on a car and injured by its derailment,[54] and a conspiracy to attempt to deceive the general public by conducting "materializing seances," and masquerading as spirits of the dead[55] have all been held indictable offenses.

§ 279.—Conspiracy to slander or extort money from another.—A conspiracy to injure another's reputation by slandering him is, as a general rule, at least, an indictable offense. Some authorities, however, hold that there are exceptions to this rule, and "that the mere conspiracy to slander a man will not be sufficient, but there must be, combined with it, the imputation of a crime cognizable either by the

[47] Reg. v. Skirret, 1 Sid. 312.

[48] People v. Butler, 111 Mich. 483, 69 N. W. 734. See also Commonwealth v. Warren, 6 Mass. 74; Reg. v. Hudson, 8 Cox Cr. C. 305, Beale's Cases 158.

[49] State v. Shooter, 8 Rich. (S. Car.) 72. See also People v. Richards, 1 Mich. 217, 51 Am. Dec. 75.

[50] Johnson v. People, 22 Ill. 314; Orr v. People, 63 Ill. App. 305.

[51] Reg. v. Lewis, 11 Cox Cr. C. 404; Levi v. Levi, 6 Car. & P. 239.

[52] Rex v. Robinson, 1 Leach Cr. C. 44, 2 East P. C. 1010.

[53] Reg. v. Orbell, 6 Mod. 42.

[54] State v. Bacon, 27 R. I. 253, 61 Atl. 653, Derby's Cases 87.

[55] People v. Gilman, 121 Mich. 187, 80 N. W. 4, 46 L. R. A. 218, 80 Am. St. 490.

temporal or ecclesiastical courts; or else an intent, by means of such false charges, to extort money from the party.[56]

All the authorities agree that a conspiracy falsely to charge another with the commission of a crime is an indictable offense.[57] Moreover, in an indictment for a conspiracy to accuse another of a crime it is not essential to allege that the defendants procured, or intended to procure, an indictment or other legal process.[58]

It is also well settled that a conspiracy to extort money from another is indictable. Thus, as heretofore stated, a conspiracy falsely to charge another with the paternity of a bastard child is a crime.[59]

§ 280. Conspiracy to obstruct or pervert public justice.— Since a wilful obstruction or perversion of public justice is indictable, a conspiracy to accomplish it is also indictable. Thus, it is an indictable offense to conspire to cause a marriage falsely to appear of record, and to obtain for that purpose from a justice of the peace a false certificate thereof, and from other parties false statements that they were witnesses of the ceremony, with intent to prevent a person from contracting another marriage;[60] or to conspire to induce a witness to suppress evidence, or give false evidence;[61] or to conspire to pack a jury;[62] or to conspire to commit an

[56] 1 Gabbett Crim. L. 252; State v. Hickling, 41 N. J. L. 208, 210, 32 Am. Rep. 198.

[57] People v. Dyer, 79 Mich. 480.

[58] Commonwealth v. Tibbetts, 2 Mass. 536.

[59] Rex v. Armstrong, 1 Vent. 304; Rex v. Kimbertz, 1 Lev. 62; Rex v. Timberly, 1 Sid. 68.

[60] Commonwealth v. Waterman, 122 Mass. 43.

[61] People v. Chase, 16 Barb. (N. Y.) 495; State v. DeWitt, 2 Hill (S. Car.) 282, 27 Am. Dec. 371.

[62] O'Donnell v. People, 41 Ill. App. 23. (For a forcible description of the character of the crime of packing juries, and the difficulty experienced in punishing the guilty parties, see Welch v. People, 30 Ill. App. 399.)

assault and battery upon a peace officer with the view of preventing him from making a legal arrest.[63]

§ 281. **Labor combinations.**—Labor unions are combinations of workmen whose object is the improvement of their industrial conditions.

The formation of labor unions for the purpose of mutual protection against unfairness or oppression is not unlawful unless it contemplates accomplishing the objects sought by unlawful means. Moreover, both in England and in this country workmen are encouraged to form associations for their mutual benefit.[64]

The real status of labor unions and strikes has been the subject of much discussion, both by political economists and by lawyers and jurists, and one upon which eminent jurists have rendered discordant opinions.

In a leading English case upon the subject certain journeymen tailors were indicted for conspiring to raise their wages. The proof showed that they had entered into a compact to refuse to work unless their wages were increased to a certain amount. It also showed, however, that the sum demanded was in excess of that allowable under a general act of parliament, and they were convicted on the ground that the object of the combination was unlawful.[65]

§ 282. **English statutes.**—Statutes have been enacted in England which make it a crime to molest and obstruct a workman with the view of coercing him to quit his employ-

[63] People v. Donahoe, 279 Ill. 411, 117 N. E. 105; State v. Noyes, 25 Vt. 415. See also, State v. McNally, 34 Maine 210, 56 Am. Dec. 650.

[64] People v. Fisher, 28 Am. Dec. 501, 508. See also Reg. v. Rowlands, 5 Cox Cr. C. 436; Carew v. Rutherford, 106 Mass. 1, 8 Am. Rep. 287; 2 Whart. Cr. L., § 1366; State v. Stockford, 77 Conn. 227, 58 Atl. 769, 107 Am. St. 28, Derby's Cases 91.

[65] Rex v. Journeymen Tailors of Cambridge, 8 Mod. 10, Beale's Cases 820. See also People v. Fisher, 14 Wend. (N. Y.) 9, 28 Am. Dec. 501n.

ment. They also make it a crime to molest and obstruct an employer with the view of coercing him to change his mode of carrying on business.[66]

The statute of 22 Vict. enacts, among other things, that "no workmen or other person, by reason merely of his entering into an agreement with any workman, or by reason merely of his endeavoring, peaceably and in a reasonable manner, and without threat or intimidation, direct or indirect, to persuade others to cease or abstain from work, shall be guilty of 'molestation' or 'obstruction,' within the meaning of the said act of 6 Geo. IV."[67]

The Conspiracy and Protection of Property Act of 1875 enacts that a combination of two or more persons to do or procure to be done any act in contemplation or furtherance of a trade dispute between employers and workmen shall not constitute an indictable conspiracy unless such act committed by one person shall constitute a crime.

§ 283. Combinations to force other employés to quit work.—Strikers may combine to persuade other workmen to leave the service of their employer. Their endeavors, however, must be peaceable and reasonable.[68] If, however, the purpose of the combination is to control the free agency, or overcome the free will, of the fellow workmen by force or intimidation, the combination is a crime. Actual violence, however, is not essential.[69] Thus, where employés of a railroad company that is in the hands of a receiver are dissatisfied with the wages paid them they may abandon

[66] 6 Geo. IV, ch. 129; 22 Vict., ch. 34; Criminal Law Amendment Act of 1875, and the Conspiracy and Protection of Property Act of 1875.

[67] 22 Vict., ch. 34; 6 Geo. IV, ch. 129.

[68] Richter v. Journeymen Tailors' Union, 24 Cin. L. Bul. 189, 11 Ohio Dec. (reprint) 49.

[69] State v. Glidden, 55 Conn. 46, 8 Atl. 890, 3 Am. St. 23; American Steel &c. Co. v. Wire Drawers' &c. Union, 90 Fed. 608; Newman v. Commonwealth, 8 Sad. (Pa.) 127, 7 Atl. 132. See also Elliott Contracts, § 2698.

the employment, and by persuasion or argument induce other employés to do the same; but if they resort to threats or violence to induce the others to leave, or accomplish their purpose, without actual violence, by overawing the others by preconcerted demonstrations of force, and thus prevent the receiver from operating the road, they may be punished for their unlawful acts.[70]

It has been held that where employés agree to quit work simultaneously, in large numbers and by preconcerted action, unless their employer discharge certain of their fellow workmen, the agreement constitutes an indictable offense.[71]

On the other hand, it has been recently held that, under the modern rule it is not unlawful for workmen, with the view of increasing their wages, to agree to quit work simultaneously and by preconcerted action.[72]

It is well settled that workmen may form themselves into a society and agree not to work for any person who shall employ a non-union workman, after notice given him to discharge such person.[73]

§ 284. Boycotting — Definition — Origin of term. — The meaning of the term "boycotting" is somewhat vague. The word is not easily defined. It is frequently spoken of as passive merely—a let-alone policy—a withdrawal of all business relations, intercourse and fellowship.[74] It may be defined, however, as a combination of persons whose purpose

70 United States v. Kane, 23 Fed. 748. See also Kemp v. Division, 255 Ill. 213, 99 N. E. 389, Ann. Cas. 1913 D, 347.

71 State v. Donaldson, 32 N. J. L. 151, 90 Am. Dec. 649, Beale's Cases 828. See also State v. Stewart, 59 Vt. 273, 9 Atl. 559, 59 Am. Rep. 710n.

72 Longshore Printing Co. v. Howell, 26 Ore. 527, 543, 38 Pac. 547, 28 L. R. A. 464, 46 Am. St. 640.

73 Commonwealth v. Hunt, 4 Metc. (Mass.) 111, 38 Am. Dec. 346, Beale's Cases 821; Bohn Mfg. Co. v. Hollis, 54 Minn. 223, 55 N. W. 1119, 21 L. R. A. 337, 40 Am. St. 319. See also Mogul Steamship Co. v. McGregor, 21 Q. B. Div. 544.

74 State v. Glidden, 55 Conn. 46, 76, 8 Atl. 890, 3 Am. St. 23. See also Elliott Contracts, § 2699.

is to injure another party by preventing other persons from doing business with him through fear of incurring the displeasure, persecution and vengeance of the conspirators.[75]

The term had its origin in Ireland during the premiership of William Ewart Gladstone. Captain Boycott, an Englishman, and agent of Lord Earne, who was owner of an estate in Ireland, was ostracized by his neighbors. "The population of the region for miles round resolved not to have anything to do with him, and as far as they could prevent it, not to allow any one else to have anything to do with him. His life appeared to be in danger—he had to claim police protection. His servants fled from him as servants flee from their masters in some plague-stricken city."[76]

It is to be observed, therefore, that the term originally signified violence. In many instances boycotts in our own country have been attended by violence and indeed it is a natural tendency when a boycott is instituted by ignorant or vicious persons to attempt by force to make it successful.[77]

§ 285. Legality of act depends upon means employed.— It is often said that, "What one man may lawfully do singly, two or more may lawfully agree to do jointly. The number who unite to do the act cannot change its character from lawful to unlawful."[78] A workman may refuse to trade with any party he chooses, absolutely or conditionally. It follows, therefore, that many may do likewise, and an agreement by them so to do is not unlawful.[79]

75 Bohn Mfg. Co. v. Hollis, 54 Minn. 223, 55 N. W. 1119, 21 L. R. A. 337, 40 Am. St. 319; State v. Glidden, 55 Conn. 46, 76, 8 Atl. 890, 3 Am. St. 23.

76 "England Under Gladstone," by Justin McCarthy. See also State v. Glidden, 55 Conn. 46, 8 Atl. 890, 3 Am. St. 23.

77 State v. Glidden, 55 Conn. 46, 76, 8 Atl. 890, 3 Am. St. 23.

78 Bohn Mfg. Co. v. Hollis, 54 Minn. 223, 55 N. W. 1119, 40 Am. St. 319.

79 Longshore Printing Co. v. Howell, 26 Ore. 527, 38 Pac. 547, 28 L. R. A. 464, 46 Am. St. 640; State v. Van Pelt, 136 N. Car. 633, 49 S. E. 177, 68 L. R. A. 760, 1 Ann. Cas. 495n.

Whether a combination to boycott a third party is lawful or not depends upon the means to be employed to carry it into effect. Peaceable persuasion in deterring others from dealing with that party and the withdrawal of their own patronage from him are lawful acts.[80] On the other hand, if violence is contemplated the combination is unlawful.[81]

When the act contemplated has a necessary tendency to prejudice the public or oppress individuals by unjustly subjecting them to the power of the confederates and giving effect to the purpose of the latter, whether of extortion or mischief, the combination is unlawful.[82] Thus, a combination by members of a typographical union to compel a firm of printers to make their office a "union office", and upon the refusal of the firm so to do, to boycott the firm, and send circulars to many of its customers notifying them that such firm is boycotted, and that the names of all persons who continue to patronize the firm will be published in a blacklist, and that such persons will be boycotted until they agree not to patronize such firm, is an unlawful combination.[83] And a combination of union workmen whose purpose is to intimidate and drive non-union workmen away from their employment by threatening that unless they quit the service of their employer their names will be published in the "scab list" in the journal of the union workmen, and that they will be shunned and not allowed to work with

[80] Dominion Steamship Co. v. M'Kenna, 30 Fed. 48; Elliott Contracts, § 2694, and cases there cited.

[81] State v. Stewart, 59 Vt. 273, 9 Atl. 559, 59 Am. Rep. 710n; State v. Stockford, 77 Conn. 227, 58 Atl. 769, 107 Am. St. 28, Derby's Cases 91; People v. McFarlin, 43 Misc. 591, 89 N. Y. S. 527, 18 N. Y. Cr. R. 412; State v. Eastern Coal Co., 29 R. I. 254, 70 Atl. 1, 132 Am. St. 817, 17 Ann. Cas. 96; Aikens v. Wisconsin, 195 U. S. 194, 49 L. ed. 154, 25 Sup. Ct. 3. See also Elliott Contracts, § 2695, and cases there cited.

[82] Hailey v. Brooks (Tex. Civ. App.), 191 S. W. 781; Crump v. Commonwealth, 84 Va. 927, 6 S. E. 620, 6 N. Y. Cr. 342, 10 Am. St. 895; State v. Huegin, 110 Wis. 189, 85 N. W. 1046, 62 L. R. A. 700.

[83] Crump v. Commonwealth, 84 Va. 927, 6 S. E. 620, 10 Am. St. 895.

union workmen engaged in a like occupation, is an unlawful combination.[84]

§ 286. **Picketing—Injunction.**—Picketing consists in detailing men by a labor union to watch an employer's place of business and speak to his workmen as they come and go with the view of inducing them to leave his service. It is not unlawful per se,[85] but when carried to such an extent as to amount to violence or intimidation it is unlawful.[86]

In some cases a court of equity will grant an injunction to prevent workmen from doing unlawful acts. Thus, a court of equity will restrain by injunction discharged employés, members of a union, from gathering about their former employer's place of business, from following the workmen whom he has employed in their places, and from interfering with them by threats, menaces, intimidation, opprobrious epithets, ridicule and annoyance on account of their working for the complainant.[87] It also will restrain by injunction the maintenance of banners displayed in front of a person's premises with inscriptions calculated to injure his business and to deter workmen from entering into or continuing in his employment.[88]

When, however, the party injured has an adequate remedy at law an injunction will be denied. Thus, in a complaint for an injunction to restrain a boycott on one's business, allegations that the officers and members of a certain trades union conspire to compel the plaintiff to submit to the dictation of the union upon pain of being boycotted in business; that the executive committee of the union entered his place of business without leave or license and ordered

84 Perkins v. Rogg, 28 Cin. L. Bul. 32, 11 Ohio Dec. (Reprint) 585.

85 Perkins v. Rogg, 28 Cin. L. Bul. 32, 11 Ohio Dec. (Reprint) 585.

86 Reg. v. Bauld, 13 Cox Cr. C. 282, 15 Moak 316. See also Elliott Contracts, § 2700.

87 Murdock, Kerr & Co. v. Walker, 152 Pa. St. 595, 25 Atl. 492, 34 Am. St. 678.

88 Sherry v. Perkins, 147 Mass. 212, 17 N. E. 307, 9 Am. St. 689.

the union men at work therein to cease work under penalty of being dealt with according to the laws and regulations of the union; that the defendants induced the city council, by threats of boycott at the polls, to reject the plaintiff's bid for the city printing, although it was the lowest made; that defendants threatened to boycott the plaintiff's customers if they patronized him, whereby he lost one customer and would lose another, and that defendants circulated a knowledge of such acts by the posting of notices, all of which acts were committed within a space of about ten months, to the past and future injury of the plaintiff's business, do not justify an injunction, as such acts do not show that the plaintiff is without an adequate remedy at law, or that the injury will be irreparable unless enjoined.[89]

Nor will an injunction be granted to restrain strikers from leaving the service of their employer. This is owing to the fact that a mandatory injunction will not be allowed in any case to compel the performance of personal service.[90] Moreover, to grant an injunction in such a case would place the parties enjoined in a condition of involuntary servitude, and, therefore, would be a violation of the United States Constitution.[91]

The fact that a threatened irreparable injury if committed would constitute a crime, is no bar to an injunction against the threatened injury.[92] It has been held, however that equity will not enjoin the publication of a libel.[93]

89 Longshore Printing Co. v. Howell, 26 Ore. 527, 38 Pac. 547, 28 L. R. A. 464, 46 Am. St. 640.

90 Toledo &c. R. Co. v. Pennsylvania Co., 54 Fed. 746.

91 Arthur v. Oaks, 63 Fed. 310.

92 Vegelahn v. Guntner, 167 Mass. 92, 44 N. E. 1077, 35 L. R. A. 722, 57 Am. St. 443; Hamilton-Brown Shoe Co. v. Saxey, 131 Mo. 212, 32 S. W. 1106, 52 Am. St. 622; Consolidated Steel &c. Co. v. Murray, 80 Fed. 811.

93 Mayer v. Journeymen Stone-Cutters' Assn., 47 N. J. Eq. 519, 20 Atl. 492; Richter v. Journeymen Tailors' Union, 24 Cin. L. Bul. 189, 11 Ohio Dec. (Reprint) 45.

§ 287. Combination to raise prices.—Lord Ellenborough has pertinently observed that every "corner", in the language of the day, whether it be to affect the price of articles of commerce, such as bread-stuffs, or the price of vendible stocks, when accomplished by confederation to raise or depress the price and operate on the markets, is a conspiracy; and that to combine to raise the price of the public funds on a particular day is an indictable offense.[94] It also has been held that an agreement by several coal corporations to divide the market for coal, from the two coal regions of which they had control, in certain proportions; to appoint a committee to take charge of the business of all the corporations and to appoint a general sales agent; to deliver coal at such times and to such parties as the committee should, from time to time, direct; that the committee should adjust the prices of coal in the different markets; that the general agent should direct a suspension of shipment or delivery of coal by any of the companies making sales or deliveries beyond its proportion, is against public policy and illegal, and by statute an indictable offense.[95] It is to be observed, however, that an agreement in unreasonable retraint of trade is not necessarily an indictable offense at common law. It has been said in a carefully considered opinion, "Contracts that were in unreasonable restraint of trade at common law were not unlawful in the sense of being criminal, or giving rise to a civil action for damages in favor of one prejudicially affected thereby, but were simply void, and not enforced by the courts."[96]

It has been held that a combination of insurance companies to fix insurance rates is not indictable, either at com-

[94] Rex v. De Berenger, 3 M. & S. 68.

[95] Morris Run Coal Co. v. Barclay Coal Co., 68 Pa. St. 173, 8 Am. Rep. 159.

[96] United States v. Addyston Pipe & Steel Co., 85 Fed. 271, 46 L. R. A. 122. See also Standard Oil Co. v. United States, 221 U. S. 1, 55 L. ed. 619, 31 Sup. Ct. 502, 34 L. R. A. (N. S.) 834, Ann. Cas. 1912 D, 734.

mon law or by statute.[97] In Kansas, however, such a combination has been held a misdemeanor by virtue of a statute.[98]

[97] Aetna Ins. Co. v. Commonwealth, 106 Ky. 864, 51 S. W. 624, 45 L. R. A. 355; Queen Ins. Co. v. State, 86 Tex. 250, 24 S. W. 397, 22 L. R. A. 483; Harris v. Commonwealth, 113 Va. 746, 73 S. E. 561, 38 L. R. A. (N. S.) 458, Ann. Cas. 1913 E, 597n.

[98] State v. Phipps, 50 Kans. 609, 31 Pac. 1097, 18 L. R. A. 657, 34 Am. St. 152.

Note. For a full historical account of the law of criminal conspiracy, see Wright's admirable little book upon the Law of Criminal Conspiracies. In commenting upon this book, Sir James Fitzjames Stephens says, "Mr. R. S. Wright, in a work of remarkable learning and ability, has laboriously collected every case bearing upon this subject * * * and having been decided since the Act of 1825." Stephens' History of the Criminal Law of England, ch. 30. For a discussion of the principles of the recent cases dealing with unlawfulness of combinations and conspiracy, see Elliott Contracts, ch. 56, §§ 2685-2703.

CHAPTER XVI.

FALSE IMPRISONMENT.

§ 290. Definition.—False imprisonment is the act of unlawfully detaining a person.

East says, "False imprisonment * * * is described to be every restraint of a man's liberty under the custody of another, either in a gaol house, stocks, or in the street, wherever it is done without a proper authority."[1] Bishop's definition is: "False imprisonment is any unlawful restraint of one's liberty whether in a place set apart for imprisonment generally or used only on the particular occasion, and whether between walls or not, effected either by physical forces actually applied or by words and an array of such forces."[2] By statute in Illinois it is defined as "an unlawful violation of the personal liberty of another, and consists in confinement or detention without sufficient legal authority."[3]

§ 291. A battery not essential.—As a general rule false imprisonment includes an assault and battery. A battery,

[1] East P. C., ch. ix.

[2] 2 Bish. New Crim. L. (8th ed.), § 748. See also Smith v. Clark, 37 Utah 116, 106 Pac. 653, Ann. Cas. 1912 B, 1366, 26 L. R. A. (N. S.) 953; Tryon v. Pingree, 112 Mich. 338, 70 N. W. 905, 37 L. R. A. 222, 67 Am. St. 398n.

[3] Illinois: Hurd's Rev. Stat. (1916), ch. 38, § 95.

however, is not essential.[4] On the other hand, there can not be false imprisonment without at least a technical assault.[5]

§ 292. Submission against the will essential.—The injured party must submit to the offender's will, and he must do so against his own will.[6] Where a person of his own free volition remains where he is, though at liberty to go if he desires, the offense is not committed.[7] And where a person is decoyed from his home by a mere ruse the fraud does not constitute false imprisonment.[8]

§ 293. Intent—Malice—Motive.—To constitute an act false imprisonment it is essential that the wrongdoer intends to detain the injured party, and also that the latter so understands his intent.[9]

Malice, however, is not an essential element of this crime. Moreover, the wrongdoer's motive is immaterial. Thus, where a peace officer arrests a person under a warrant that is void on its face, he is guilty of false imprisonment, although he acts in good faith in the belief that the warrant is valid.[10]

294. Place of imprisonment immaterial.—False imprisonment can be committed anywhere. Thus, it can be committed in the street, or in a field or woods, as well as in a jail or private house.[11]

4 Colter v. Lower, 35 Ind. 285, 9 Am. Rep. 735.

5 Bl. Comm. 137; Pike v. Hanson, 9 N. H. 491; State v. Lunsford, 81 N. Car. 528.

6 Floyd v. State, 12 Ark. 43, 54 Am. Dec. 250; State v. Lunsford, 81 N. Car. 528.

7 Kirk v. Garrett, 84 Md. 383, 35 Atl. 1089; Hill v. Taylor, 50 Mich. 549, 15 N. W. 899.

8 State v. Lunsford, 81 N. Car. 528.

9 Limbeck v. Gerry, 15 Misc. 663, 39 N. Y. S. 95.

10 Rich v. McInerny, 103 Ala. 345, 15 So. 663, 49 Am. St. 32; Comer v. Knowles, 17 Kans. 436; Holmes v. Blyler, 80 Iowa 365, 45 N. W. 756.

11 3 Bl. Comm. 127; People v. Wheeler, 73 Cal. 252, 14 Pac. 796; Floyd v. State, 12 Ark. 43, 54 Am. Dec. 250.

§ 295. Mode of detention immaterial.—No particular mode of detention is necessary. Actual force is not essential, nor even a touching of the person. Threats may be sufficient from a known officer.[12] Thus, where an officer, without legal authority, arrests a person by merely telling him he is under arrest the officer is guilty of false imprisonment.[13] False statements of the law may be sufficient.[14]

§ 296. Detention must be unlawful.—It is essential, however, that the detention be unlawful. No person can be guilty of false imprisonment who restricts another's liberty lawfully.[15]

§ 297. Restraint by parent or teacher.—To constitute false imprisonment, restraint of a child by its parent or teacher, or by a person in loco parentis, must be so immoderate and unreasonable as to be unlawful. The law gives parents a large discretion in the exercise of authority over their children. This is true, but this authority must be exercised within the bounds of reason and humanity. If the parent commits wanton and needless cruelty upon his child, either by imprisonment of this character or by inhuman beating, the law will punish him.[16]

[12] Hebrew v. Pulis, 73 N. J. L. 621, 64 Atl. 121, 7 L. R. A. (N. S.) 580, 118 Am. St. 716n.

[13] Smith v. State, 7 Humph. (Tenn.) 43; Pike v. Hanson, 9 N. H. 491; State v. Lunsford, 81 N. Car. 528.

[14] Whitman v. Atchison, etc., R. Co., 85 Kans. 150, 116 Pac. 234, 34 L. R. A. (N. S.) 1029, Ann. Cas. 1912 D, 722.

[15] State v. Hunter, 106 N. Car. 796, 11 S. E. 366, 8 L. R. A. 529n; Winchester v. Everett, 80 Maine 535, 15 Atl. 596, 1 L. R. A. 425, 6 Am. St. 228.

[16] Fletcher v. People, 52 Ill. 395. (Father indicted for the false imprisonment of his child, a blind and helpless boy, in a cold and damp cellar, without fire, during several days in mid-winter, the excuse given by the father for so doing being that the boy was covered with vermin. Held: Such treatment of a child by his parent is wanton, inhuman and needless cruelty, and renders the parent criminally liable for false imprisonment.)

§ 298. **Abuse of authority by officer.**—An officer may render himself criminally liable for false imprisonment by abusing his authority. Thus, where an officer makes an arrest without a warrant, or under a warrant void on its face, and a valid warrant is essential, he is criminally liable for false imprisonment.[17] Where an officer executes a valid warrant at a time prohibited by statute, as on Sunday, he is also criminally liable.[18] Moreover, an officer who unduly detains a prisoner, who has been lawfully arrested renders himself liable for false imprisonment;[19] or who unlawfully refuses to release a prisoner on bail,[20] or holds him an unreasonable time before taking him before a justice for examination or trial, is liable for false imprisonment.[21] A special officer in the employ of a corporation, may render the corporation liable for arrest beyond the extent of his authority.[22]

§ 299. **Nature of the offense.**— False imprisonment is both a tort and a crime. For the private injury an action lies for damages against the wrongdoer. For the public wrong he is subject to indictment.[23]

At common law false imprisonment is a misdemeanor; and usually by statute it is also a misdemeanor.[24]

17 State v. Hunter, 106 N. Car 796, 11 S. E. 366, 8 L. R. A. 529n; Winchester v. Everett, 80 Maine 535, 15 Atl. 596, 1 L. R. A. 425, 6 Am. St. 228. See also Rush v. Buckley, 100 Maine 322, 61 Atl. 774, 70 L. R. A. 464, 4 Ann. Cas. 318.

18 3 Bl. Comm. 127.

19 Bath v. Metcalf, 145 Mass. 274, 14 N. E. 133, 1 Am. St. 455; Price v. Tehan, 84 Conn. 164, 79 Atl. 68, 34 L. R. A. (N. S.) 1182n, Ann. Cas. 1912 B, 1183.

20 Manning v. Mitchell, 73 Ga. 660. See also Cargill v. State, 8 Tex. App. 431.

21 Twilley v. Perkins, 77 Md. 252, 26 Atl. 286, 19 L. R. A. 632n, 39 Am. St. 408; Blocker v. Clark, 126 Ga. 484, 54 S. E. 1022, 7 L. R. A. (N. S.) 268n, 8 Ann. Cas. 31.

22 Taylor v. New York, etc., R. Co., 80 N. J. L. 282, 78 Atl. 169, 39 L. R. A. (N. S.) 122.

23 4 Bl. Comm. 218; Commonwealth v. Blodgett, 12 Metc. (Mass.) 56; Campbell v. State, 48 Ga. 353.

24 Slomer v. People, 25 Ill. 70, 76 Am. Dec. 786; People v. Wheeler, 73 Cal. 252, 14 Pac. 796.

The offense includes two essentials: (1) Restraint of another's liberty; (2) act unlawful.

The magistrate who issues a void warrant or the person who procures it to be issued may under some circumstances be guilty of false imprisonment.[25]

[25] Rush v. Buckley, 100 Maine 322, 61 Atl. 774, 70 L. R. A. 464, 4 Ann. Cas. 318; Broom v. Douglass, 175 Ala. 268, 57 So. 860, 44 L. R. A. (N. S.) 164, Ann. Cas. 1914 C, 1155.

CHAPTER XVII.

HOMICIDE.

§ 305. Homicide in general—Definition.—Homicide is the killing of a human being by a person. The mode of doing it, and the circumstances attending it, do not enter into the definition, provided the killing be done by a person. Strictly speaking, when the killing is not done by a person it is not homicide. According to Bracton, "if it be done by an ox, a dog, or other thing, it is not properly termed homicide."[1]

[1] 2 Brac. F. 120b.

§ 306. Classification—Definition.—Homicide is divided into the following three classes: (1) Justifiable; (2) Excusable; (3) Felonious. Blackstone observes, "Now homicide, or the killing of any human creature, is of three kinds, justifiable, excusable, and felonious. The first has no share of guilt at all; the second very little; but the third is the highest crime against the law of nature that man is capable of committing."[2] It is to be observed, however, that treason is usually regarded the highest crime known to the law.

§ 307. Justifiable homicide—Definition.—Justifiable homicide is the killing of a human being in the discharge of a legal public duty.

§ 308. Justifiable homicide — Execution by sheriff. — Where a sheriff or his deputy, in the discharge of his public duty, executes a person who has been condemned to death by a judicial tribunal of competent jurisdiction, the homicide is justifiable. In such case the victim must have been given a legal trial, or confessed his guilt, and the execution must be in strict conformity with the sentence imposed. Thus, if the sentence is that the victim be hanged, and the sheriff execute him by shooting or electrocuting him, the sheriff would be guilty of murder. It is Blackstone's view that, "The law must require it, otherwise it is not justifiable; therefore, wantonly to kill the greatest of malefactors, a felon or a traitor, attainted or outlawed, deliberately uncompelled, and extrajudicially, is murder. * * * And farther, if judgment of death be given by a judge not authorized by lawful commission, and execution is done accordingly, the judge is guilty of murder. * * * Also, such judgment, when legal, must be executed by the proper officer, or his appointed deputy; for no one else is required by law to do

[2] 2 Bl. Comm., bk. 4, ch. 14, p. 177 (Cooley's 4th ed., p. 1347).

it, which requisition it is that justifies the homicide. If another person doth it of his own head, it is held to be murder; even though it be the judge himself. It must farther be executed servato juris ordine (according to the order of the court); it must pursue the sentence of the court. If an officer beheads one who is adjudged to be hanged, or vice versa, it is murder; for he is merely ministerial, and therefore only justified when he acts under the authority and compulsion of the law; but if a sheriff changes one kind of death for another, he then acts by his own authority, which extends not to the commission of homicide; and besides, this license might occasion a very gross abuse of his power."[3]

§ 309. Killing felon to effect arrest or prevent escape.— Where one necessarily kills a felon to effect his arrest, or prevent his escape, the homicide is justifiable. And in such case, the necessity is sufficient if reasonably apparent. Moreover, the homicide may be committed by a private person as well as by a police officer.

Stephen says, "The intentional infliction of death or bodily harm is not a crime when it is done by any person * * * in order to arrest a traitor, felon, or pirate, or retake or keep in lawful custody a traitor, felon, or pirate who has escaped, or is about to escape, from such custody, although such traitor, felon, or pirate offers no violence to any person; * * * provided * * * the object for which death or harm is inflicted can not be otherwise accomplished."[4] It is to be observed, however, that where even a police officer kills a misdemeanant to effect his arrest the homicide is not justifiable, the theory of the law being that it is better that a misdemeanant escape than that human

[3] 4 Bl. Comm. 178, 179.

[4] Steph. Dig. Crim. L. (5th ed), art. 220; Smith v. Commonwealth, 176 Ky. 466, 195 S. W. 811.

life be taken.[5] A few courts have held the contrary,[6] but they do not represent the better view.

On the other hand, where a peace officer, in attempting to arrest a misdemeanant, is threatened with death or great bodily harm, and he necessarily kills the latter to save himself, the homicide is justifiable.[7] Moreover, an officer, whose duty it is to preserve the peace, is not required to decline combat, when resisted in his duties, and to put himself out of danger, before he will be justified in killing his assailant.[8] But he will not be justified in taking human life to effect an arrest for a misdemeanor, or in preventing an escape or rescue from such arrest.[9] An officer making an arrest for misdemeanor may resist force by force, and when the resistance is violent and determined an officer is not bound to make nice calculations as to the degree of force necessary to accomplish the purpose, but may use such a reasonable degree of physical force in overcoming such resistance and effecting such arrest as may reasonably appear necessary therefor, and to prevent the escape of the party whom he is arresting. But he has no right to take the life of such person, or inflict on him great bodily harm, for the purpose of making such arrest, except when the officer has a reasonable apprehension of peril to his own life, or of suffering great bodily harm.[10]

§ 310. Killing to quell riot.—Where a person necessarily kills one or more persons to quell a riot the killing is justi-

[5] United States v. Clark, 31 Fed. 710, Beale's Cases, 319. See also Handley v. State, 96 Ala. 48, 11 So. 322, 38 Am. St. 81.

[6] State v. Garrett, 1 Win. L. (N. Car.) 144, 84 Am. Dec. 359.

[7] Lynn v. People, 170 Ill. 527, 48 N. E. 964, Derby's Cases 245; State v. Smith (Iowa), 101 N. W. 110.

[8] Lynn v. People, 170 Ill, 527, 48 N. E. 964, Derby's Cases, 245.

[9] State v. Smith (Iowa), 101 N. W. 110; Head v. Martin, 85 Ky. 480, 3 S. W. 622, 9 Ky. L. 45, Derby's Cases 246.

[10] State v. Smith (Iowa), 101 N. W. 110. See also Commonwealth v. Marcum, 135 Ky. 1, 122 S. W. 215, 24 L. R. A. (N. S.) 1194; Davis v. State (Tex. Cr.), 196 S. W. 520.

fiable. "The intentional infliction of death or bodily harm is not a crime when it is done either by justices of the peace, peace officers, or private persons, whether such persons are, and whether they act as, soldiers under military discipline or not for the purpose of suppressing a general and dangerous riot which can not otherwise be suppressed."[11] This constitutes the one exception to the rule that human life may not be taken to prevent a mere misdemeanor. The reason for this exception is the fact that while riot, at common law, is only a misdemeanor, its consequences may prove very disastrous, and therefore justify a killing where necessary to quell it.

It is to be observed, however, in this connection, that a homicide to quell an affray is never justifiable.[12] Nor is a homicide to prevent a mere trespass ever justifiable.[13]

§ 311. Killing to prevent felony.—Where any person necessarily kills another to prevent him from committing a felony attempted by force or surprise the homicide is justifiable. In such case it is not essential that the attempted felony be directed against the homicide himself, or against his habitation. It may be directed against the person or habitation of even a stranger. "Such homicide as is committed for the prevention of any forcible and atrocious crime, is justifiable by the law of nature, and also by the law of England, as it stood so early as the time of Bracton."[14] The "forcible and atrocious crime" may be murder, rape, robbery, burglary, arson or sodomy.[15] It does not include any secret felony like larceny.[16]

11 1 Steph. Dig. Crim. L. (5th ed.), art. 219. See also Pond v. People, 8 Mich. 150.

12 State v. Moore, 31 Conn. 479, 83 Am. Dec. 159n.

13 State v. Moore, 31 Conn. 479, 83 Am. Dec. 159n.

14 4 Bl. Comm. 180.

15 4 Bl. Comm. 180; 1 Steph. Dig. Crim. L. (5th ed.), art. 220; Pond v. People, 8 Mich. 150; Osborne v. State, 140 Ala. 84, 37 So. 105; State v. Moore, 31 Conn. 479, 83 Am. Dec. 159n; Ruloff v. People, 45 N. Y. 213.

16 Reg. v. Murphy, 1 Craw. & D. 20, Beale's Cases 318.

The basis of the justification in this class of homicide is necessity.[17] It is sufficient, however, if the necessity be reasonably apparent. One who is opposing and endeavoring to prevent the consummation of a felony by others may properly use all necessary force for that purpose, and resist all attempts to inflict bodily injury upon himself, and may lawfully detain the felons and hand them over to the officers of the law. Although the use of wanton violence and the infliction of unnecessary injury to the persons of the criminals is not permitted, yet the law will not be astute in searching for such line of demarcation in this respect as will take the innocent citizen, whose property and person are in danger, from its protection, and place his life at the mercy of the felon.[18]

§ 312. Excusable homicide—Definition—Classification.—Excusable homicide is the killing of a human being under circumstances which constitute an excuse for the act rather than a justification of it. This class of homicide is of two kinds: (1) Homicide by misadventure, (2) homicide in self-defense.

§ 313. Excusable homicide—Homicide by misadventure.—Homicide by misadventure is the killing of a human being by a person engaged in doing a lawful act with due care and without criminal intent. The decisions contain many examples of this class of homicide. Among them are the following:

1. One person accidentally kills another while playing football.[19]

[17] Storey v. State, 71 Ala. 329; Derby's Cases 240; State v. Moore, 31 Conn. 479, 83 Am. Dec. 159n; People v. Cook, 39 Mich. 236, 33 Am. Rep. 380, Beale's Cases 345. See also Scheuerman v. Scharfenberg, 163 Ala. 337, 50 So. 335, 24 L. R. A. (N. S.) 369n, 136 Am. St. 74.

[18] Ruloff v. People, 45 N. Y. 213.

[19] Reg. v. Bradshaw, 14 Cox Cr. C. 83, Beale's Cases 146.

2. A physician, in procuring an abortion where it is necessary, at least apparently, to save the mother's life, unintentionally kills the mother.[20]

3. A workman, after shouting warning, throws a piece of timber from a housetop and it strikes and kills a person.[21]

4. A steamboat, whose lookout is exercising due care, runs down another boat and lives are lost.[22]

5. A physician, in the exercise of due care, unintentionally causes death by administering a dangerous drug with the view of performing a surgical operation.[23]

6. A parent moderately punishes an offending child, or a teacher his pupil, and death ensues.[24]

7. A person is using a hatchet with due care and the head flies off and kills a bystander.[25]

8. A man, in the exercise of due care, shoots at a target and the ball glances off and kills a person.[26]

9. A watchman in a park, mistaking his master for a poacher, shoots and kills him.[27]

10. A person, while lawfully defending himself against the assaults of another, shoots and unintentionally kills a third party.[28]

On the other hand, if, in any of the foregoing examples, the perpetrator were guilty of negligence the homicide would be manslaughter; and if guilty of malice it would be murder.

§ 314. Homicide in self-defense—General requisites.—Homicide in self-defense is of two sorts, justifiable and ex-

20 State v. Moore, 25 Iowa 128, 95 Am. Dec. 776n.

21 Hull's Case, J. Kelyng, 40.

22 Rex v. Green, 7 Car. & P. 156; Rex v. Allen, 7 Car. & P. 153.

23 Reg. v. Chamberlain, 10 Cox Cr. C. 486, Beale's Cases 187; Reg. v. Macleod, 12 Cox Cr. C. 534; Commonwealth v. Thompson, 6 Mass. 134, 3 Wheeler Cr. Cases 312; Rice v. State, 8 Mo. 561.

24 4 Bl. Comm. 182; 1 East P. C. 260, 269; Fost, C. L. 258, Beale's Cases 185, 315.

25 4 Bl. Comm. 182.

26 4 Bl. Comm. 182; 1 East, P. C. 260, 269.

27 1 Hale, P. C. 40.

28 Plummer v. State, 4 Tex. App. 310, 30 Am. Rep. 165.

cusable. By statute, however, in some states all homicides in self-defense are justifiable. To render a homicide justifiable or excusable on the ground of self-defense the following conditions are essential:

1. Imminent danger of death or serious bodily harm to the slayer must be at least reasonably apparent.
2. When the danger is only apparent the slayer must believe, on reasonable grounds, that it is real.
3. When the killing grows out of a sudden affray the slayer, before killing his adversary, must retreat as far as possible with safety.
4. The slayer, as a general rule, must not be the aggressor.

§ 315. Homicide in justifiable self-defense.—This kind of homicide is committed when a person without fault, who is feloniously assaulted, necessarily kills his assailant to prevent him from committing a forcible felony. Where a woman kills a man necessarily to prevent him from committing rape upon her; or a man kills another person necessarily to prevent that person from killing him, or inflicting serious bodily injury upon him, or robbing him the homicide is justifiable.[29]

§ 316. Scope of the necessity for the killing.—The necessity for the killing is sufficient if reasonably apparent. The law does not require it to arise out of actual danger in order to excuse the slayer. He may act upon a belief arising from appearances, which give him reasonable grounds to believe that the danger is actual. His guilt must depend upon the circumstances as they appear to him, and he is not responsible for a knowledge of the facts, unless his ignorance

[29] 4 Bl. Comm. 180; Osborne v. State, 140 Ala. 84, 37 So. 105; State v. Moore, 31 Conn. 479, 83 Am. Dec. 159n; Pond v. People, 8 Mich. 150. See also State v. Larkins, 250 Mo. 218, 157 S. W. 600, 46 L. R. A. (N. S.) 13n.

arises from some fault on his part.[30] An instruction that "to justify a person in killing another in self-defense, it must appear that the danger was so urgent and pressing that in order to save his own life, or to prevent his receiving great bodily harm, the killing of the deceased was absolutely necessary," is erroneous.[31]

§ 317. Retreat unnecessary.—In this class of homicide the party assaulted is not bound to retreat at all. Since he is without fault he may stand his ground and, if necessary to save his own life or prevent serious bodily harm to himself, kill his assailant. "A true man, who is without fault, is not obliged to fly from an assailant, who, by violence or surprise, maliciously seeks to take his life or do him enormous bodily harm."[32]

§ 318. Homicide in excusable self-defense.—In this kind of homicide the slayer is not without fault. In this respect it differs from homicide in justifiable self-defense. It is committed when a person who is engaged in a sudden affray necessarily kills another person in it to save himself from death or serious bodily harm.[33] At common law it was punishable by forfeiture of goods.[34] According to Coke anciently it was punishable by death.[35] Later writers, how-

[30] Pond v. People, 8 Mich. 150; Hurd v. People, 25 Mich. 405; State v. Martin, 30 Wis. 216, 11 Am. Rep. 567; Beard v. State, 47 Tex. Cr. 50, 81 S. W. 33, 122 Am. St. 672.

[31] People v. Morine, 61 Cal. 367.

[32] Erwin v. State, 29 Ohio St. 186, 199, 23 Am. Rep. 733. See also Marshall v. United States, 45 App. (D. C.) 373; State v. Brooks, 79 S. Car. 144, 60 S. E. 518, 17 L. R. A. (N. S.) 483, 128 Am. St. 836; Miller v. State, 139 Wis. 57, 119 N. W. 850, Derby's Cases, 216; 4 Bl. Comm. 183, 184; 1 Hale P. C. 40.

[33] 4 Bl. Comm. 183. It has been held that the mere fact of being willing to enter into conflict with deadly weapons with another does not destroy right to rely on self-defense as justification if killing was done to protect life, not to harm adversary. State v. Pollard, 168 N. Car. 116, 83 S. E. 167, L. R. A. 1915 B, 529.

[34] 1 Hale P. C. 481, 482; Fost. C. L. 287; 1 East P. C. 279; 4 Bl. Comm. 188.

[35] 2 Co. Inst. 148, 315.

ever, deny this.[36] Blackstone says, "The penalty inflicted by our laws is said by Sir Edward Coke to have been anciently no less than death; which, however, is with reason denied by later and more accurate writers. It seems rather to have consisted in a forfeiture, some say of all the goods and chattels, others of only part of them."[37] At present, however, it is not punishable at all, either in England or in this country.[38]

The affray, from which this kind of homicide may spring, may arise in various ways, as from resenting and returning a blow, from resenting insulting words, from resisting a trespass on land or goods, or from resisting an unlawful arrest.[39] It is to be observed, however, that none of these provocations, of itself, excuses a homicide.

§ 319. The danger must be imminent.—To render the homicide excusable, the danger to the slayer must, at the time of the homicide, be at least apparently imminent and not merely prospective. The danger, or apparent danger, must be present, not prospective; not even in the near future. If it be prospective, it may, in most cases, be averted in various ways; as by taking shelter in one's own dwelling, having the would-be assailant arrested, etc. Human life must not be sacrificed under the apprehension of a prospective, probable danger, even in the near future.[40] When there is no necessity, real or apparent, to slay an adversary to save one's life or person from great harm, there can not, in the nature of things, be a right to kill in self-defense.[41]

36 1 Hale P. C. 425; 4 Bl. Comm. 188.

37 4 Bl. Comm. 188.

38 2 Bish. New Crim. L. (8th ed.) §§ 618, 622.

39 Bennett v. State, 19 Ga. App. 442, 91 S. E. 889.

40 Dolan v. State, 81 Ala. 11, 18, 1 So. 707. See also State v. Beckner, 194 Mo. 281, 91 S. W. 892, 3 L. R. A. (N. S.) 535n.

41 Kennedy v. Commonwealth, 77 Ky. (14 Bush) 340; United States v. Suterbridge, 5 Sawy. (U. S.) 620, Fed Cas. No. 15978, Derby's Cases 221.

§ 320. **Facts admissible to prove danger imminent.**—Any fact which tends to prove that the slayer was in imminent danger at the time he committed the homicide is admissible in evidence. Thus, it may be shown that deceased had made threats that he would shoot the slayer at sight; that he carried arms; that he attempted to draw from his pocket a weapon; that he lay in wait; that his character for violence or lawlessness was bad, etc.[42]

§ 321. **Evidence—Right of attack in self-defense.**—It is sometimes said that the right of self-defense does not imply the right of attack. This, however, is not strictly true. When a person has reasonable ground to believe that another person intends to do him immediate serious bodily harm, and that such design will be accomplished unless prevented, he need not wait until his adversary gets advantage over him, but, if necessary to avoid the danger, he may kill his would-be assailant immediately;[43] and the killing will be justifiable, although it may afterward turn out that the appearances were false, and there was, in fact, neither design to do him serious injury nor danger that it would be done.[44]

§ 322. **Evidence—Actual danger not essential.**—A few cases hold that actual danger of death or serious bodily injury to the slayer is essential to render his act excusable self-defense.[45] The better view, however, as well as the great

[42] Kennedy v. Commonwealth, 77 Ky. (14 Bush) 340.

[43] State v. Matthews, 148 Mo. 185, 49 S. W. 1085, 71 Am. St. 594. See also State v. Gardner, 96 Minn. 318, 104 N. W. 971, 2 L. R. A. (N. S.) 49n; and note to 109 Am. St. 805-820; McNeal v. State, 115 Miss. 678, 76 So. 625; Jones v. State, 147 Ga. 356, 94 S. E. 248; State v. Merk, 53 Mont. 454, 164 Pac. 655; State v. Goodwin, 271 Mo. 73, 195 S. W. 725; Tittle v. State (Ala. App.), 73 So. 142.

[44] Parker v. State, 24 Wyo. 491, 161 Pac. 552· State v. Towne (Iowa), 160 N. W. 10; State v. Bell, 38 S. Dak. 159, 160 N. W. 727; Commonwealth v. Digeso, 254 Pa. St. 291, 98 Atl. 882; Blacklock v. State (Tex. Cr.), 196 S. W. 822; State v. Dickens (N. Mex.), 165 Pac. 850; Mullins v. Commonwealth, 172 Ky. 92, 188 S. W. 1079; Barton v. State, 72 Fla. 408, 73 So. 230.

[45] Reg. v. Smith, 8 Car. & P. 160; Reg. v. Bull, 9 Car. & P. 22; State v. Vines, 1 Houst. Cr. C. (Del.) 424. See also State v. Benham, 23 Iowa, 154, 92 Am. Dec. 416.

weight of authority, is to the contrary.[46] The rule is that, a bona fide belief on the part of the slayer, founded upon reasonable grounds, that he will suffer death or great bodily harm unless he kills his assailant, will excuse him to the same extent as if the danger were real.[47] Thus, where a person has threatened to take another's life at sight, and upon meeting the latter makes a movement as if to draw a weapon to carry out the threat, and the other party, under a bona fide belief that it is necessary to kill him to save his own life or prevent great bodily harm, takes the life of his would-be assailant, the homicide is excusable, though it appear later that the deceased was unarmed.[48]

§ 323. Evidence—Grounds of apprehension must be reasonable.—It has been held that a homicide may be excusable where the slayer's apprehension of death or serious bodily harm results from cowardice on his part, rather than appearances.[49] This view, however, is erroneous, and not at all in harmony with the great weight of authority. The law makes no discrimination in favor of a coward, a drunkard, or any particular person. The circumstances must be such as to justify the fears of a reasonable man.[50]

A homicide is not excusable on the ground of self-defense unless the danger of death or serious bodily harm is actual,

[46] Shorter v. People, 2 N. Y. 193, 51 Am. Dec. 286, Beale's Cases 331; Logue v. Commonwealth, 38 Pa. St. 265, 80 Am. Dec. 481; Patten v. People, 18 Mich. 314, 100 Am. Dec. 173; People v. Morine, 61 Cal. 367; Keith v. State, 97 Ala. 32, 11 So. 914; Brown v. Commonwealth, 86 Va. 466, 10 S. E. 745; State v. Eaton, 75 Mo. 586; Steinmeyer v. People, 95 Ill. 383; Marts v. State, 26 Ohio St. 162.

[47] Enright v. People, 155 Ill. 32, 39 N. E. 561; Pond v. People, 8 Mich. 150; Brown v. Commonwealth, 86 Va. 466, 10 S. E. 745; Amos v. Commonwealth, 28 S. W. 152; 16 Ky. L. 358; State v. Dyer, 147 Iowa 217, 124 N. W. 629, 29 L. R. A. (N. S.) 459.

[48] Patillo v. State, 22 Tex. App. 586, 3 S. W. 766.

[49] Grainger v. State, 5 Yerg. (Tenn.) 459, 26 Am. Dec. 278.

[50] Golden v. State, 25 Ga. 527; Atkins v. State, 119 Tenn. 458, 105 S. W. 353, 13 L. R. A. (N. S.) 1031; State v. Stockman, 82 S. Car. 388, 64 S. E. 595, 129 Am. St. 888; State v. Goodwin, 271 Mo. 73, 195 S. W. 725.

present and urgent; or the slayer has reasonable ground to apprehend a design, on the part of the would-be assailant, to commit a felony, or do him some great bodily harm, and there is imminent danger of such design being accomplished. The mere fear, or belief, however sincerely entertained by one person, that another intends and designs to take his life will not justify the former in taking the life of the latter. Merely an attack with fists or mere threats of injury will not excuse killing another.[51]

Where the danger is neither real nor urgent, to render a homicide excusable or justifiable within the meaning of the law, there must, at the least, be some attempt to execute the apprehended design; or there must be reasonable ground for the apprehension that such design will be executed, and the danger of its accomplishment imminent.[52] "It is not essential that an actual felony should be about to be committed in order to justify the killing. If the circumstances are such as that, after all reasonable caution, the party suspects that the felony is about to be immediately committed, he will be justified."[53]

§ 324. Evidence—What constitutes reasonable caution—The correct standard.—The imminency of the danger and the necessity of the killing must, in the first instance, be determined by the slayer. In doing so, however, he acts at his peril; as the jury must pass upon his actions in the premises. The jury, however, must view those actions from the slayer's standpoint at the time of the killing; and if they believe, from all the facts and circumstances in the case, that the slayer had reasonable grounds to believe, and did believe, the danger imminent, and that the killing was

51 Shorter v. People, 2 N. Y. 193, 51 Am. Dec. 286, Beale's Cases 331; Derby's Cases 213; State v. Doherty, 52 Ore. 591, 98 Pac. 152; Derby's Cases 224; Newsom v. State (Ala. App.), 72 So. 579; Ex parte Newsom (Ala.), 73 So. 1001; Smith v. State, 80 Tex. Cr. 221, 189 S. W. 484.

52 Wesley v. State, 37 Miss. 327, 75 Am. Dec. 62; State v. Scott, 4 Ired. L. (N. Car.) 409, 42 Am. Dec. 148.

53 Roscoe's Crim. Ev. (8th ed.) 738.

at least apparently necessary to preserve his own life or to protect him from great bodily harm, they should acquit him.

It is important to remember, in this connection, that the question of apparent necessity for the killing must be determined from the slayer's standpoint. A reasonable apprehension in the mind of a man of ordinary intelligence and courage is not the standard.[54] The belief of the ideal reasonable man is not admissible to acquit, a fortiori, it is inadmissible to convict.[55]

In such a case the following instruction is correct: "As to the imminency of the danger, which threatened the prisoner and the necessity of the killing, in the first instance he is the judge, but he acts at his peril, as the jury must pass upon his actions in the premises, viewing said actions from the prisoner's standpoint at the time of the killing, and if the jury believe from all the facts and circumstances in the case, that the prisoner had reasonable grounds to believe, and did believe, the danger was imminent, and that the killing was necessary to preserve his own life, or to protect him from great bodily harm, he is excusable for using a deadly weapon in his defense; otherwise he is not."[56] For the purpose of showing that the defendant had reasonable grounds to believe that the danger was imminent and the killing necessary, "threats, menaces, assaults, lying in wait, carrying arms, the character of the deceased for violence or lawlessness, the circumstances of the meeting, and any other facts tending to show that the slayer was in peril at the time of the homicide," are admissible in evidence.[57]

[54] State v. Cain, 20 W. Va. 679.

[55] 1 Whart. Crim. L. (11th ed.), § 620.

[56] State v. Cain, 20 W. Va. 679. See also Beard v. State, 47 Tex. Cr. 50, 81 S. W. 33, 122 Am. St. 672; Andress v. State (Ala. App.), 72 So. 753.

[57] Kennedy v. Commonwealth, 77 Ky. (14 Bush) 340.

§ 325. Evidence—When duty to retreat exists—Distinction between excusable self-defense and justifiable self-defense.—Where two persons engage in a sudden affray, both being in fault, each is bound to retreat, if possible, before killing the other in self-defense. Blackstone thus states the rule: "The party assaulted must therefore flee as far as he conveniently can, either by reason of some wall, ditch, or other impediment; or as far as the fierceness of the assault will permit him."[58] On the other hand, where a party without fault is attacked by another he is not bound to retreat. He may stand his ground, and if necessary to save his life or prevent serious bodily harm he may kill his assailant.[59]

It is now well settled that the accused, when not in fault, is not compelled to flee from his adversary who assails him with a deadly weapon.[60] It is to be observed, however, that where both are in fault the accused must cease the combat and retreat as far as safety will permit before he is justified in taking a human life on the ground of self-defense.[61] Justice McIlvane says, "By observing the distinction between justifiable and excusable homicide se defendendo, as stated in the authorities above quoted, much of the discrepancy in the decisions of the courts where the common law prevails is

[58] 4 Bl. Comm. 185. See also Allen v. United States, 164 U. S. 492, 41 L. ed. 528, 17 Sup. Ct. 154, Derby's Cases 219; People v. Constantino, 153 N. Y. 24, 47 N. E. 37; Sullivan v. State, 102 Ala. 135, 15 So. 264, 48 Am. St. 22; Cole v. State (Ala. App.), 75 So. 261; McNeal v. State, 115 Miss. 678, 76 So. 625; State v. Albano (Vt.), 102 Atl. 333; State v. Di Maria, 88 N. J. L. 416, 97 Atl. 248.

[59] 1 Hale P. C., ch. 40; Marshall v. United States, 45 App. (D. C.) 373; State v. Merk, 53 Mont. 454, 164 Pac. 655; State v. Meyer, 96 Wash. 257, 164 Pac. 926; People v. McDonnell, 32 Cal. App. 694, 163 Pac. 1046; State v. Bell, 38 S. Dak. 159, 160 N. W. 727; State v. Donahue, 79 W. Va. 260, 90 S. E. 834; Page v. State, 141 Ind. 236, 40 N. E. 745; State v. Bartlett, 170 Mo. 658, 71 S. W. 148, 59 L. R. A. 756; Wallace v. United States, 162 U. S. 466, 40 L. ed. 1039, 16 Sup. Ct. 859.

[60] Tweedy v. State, 5 Iowa 433.

[61] State v. Cain, 20 W. Va. 679; People v. Filippelli, 173 N. Y. 509, 66 N. E. 402; Derby's Cases 225; State v. Donnelly, 69 Iowa 705, 27 N. W. 369, 58 Am. Rep. 234, Derby's Cases 220.

made to disappear; most of the cases upon the facts being such as would only excuse the killing.

"It is true, under our constitution, whether the killing in self-defense be justifiable or excusable, there must be an entire acquittal, for the reason that there is no forfeiture of goods in cases of excusable homicide. But this is no reason why the difference between the cases as to the duty of retreating to the wall should be ignored. The taking away of the forfeiture in cases of excusable homicide did not relieve the party in such case from the duty of retreating, nor did it impose such duty in cases where it was not before required.

"It is true, that all authorities agree that the taking of life in defense of one's person can not be either justified or excused, except on the ground of necessity, and that such necessity must be imminent at the time; and they also agree that no man can avail himself of such necessity if he brings it upon himself. The question, then, is simply this: Does the law hold a man who is violently and feloniously assaulted responsible for having brought such necessity upon himself, on the sole ground that he failed to fly from his assailant when he might have safely done so? The law, out of tenderness for human life and the frailties of human nature, will not permit the taking of it to repel a mere trespass, or even to save life, where the assault is provoked; but a true man, who is without fault, is not obliged to fly from an assailant, who, by violence or surprise, maliciously seeks to take his life or do him enormous bodily harm."[62]

The right of self-defense is the right to repel force by force unlawfully exerted. The repellent force is protective and not aggressive. When full protection is achieved, the legitimate end of this repellent force, which the law allows, is accomplished; and at this point it should cease.

[62] Erwin v. State, 29 Ohio St. 186, 23 Am. Rep. 733. See also State v. Cook, 78 S. Car. 253, 59 S. E. 862, 15 L. R. A. (N. S.) 1013n, 125 Am. St. 788; Young v. State, 53 Tex. Cr. 416, 110 S. W. 445, 126 Am. St. 792, and note to 109 Am. St. 805-820.

§ 326. Defense of third persons, dwelling, or property.—Homicide may be justifiable or excusable in the defense of third persons, as a wife, child or near relation, where the circumstances reasonably justify one in believing such person is in imminent danger of death or serious bodily harm.[63] This rule may be applied to the defense of persons not relatives.[64] But one defending a third person has no greater rights than such person would have in defending himself.[65]

Homicide may also be justifiable in defense of one's dwelling, where it reasonably appears necessary to kill in order to prevent the felonious destruction of one's property or habitation or the commission of a felony therein, or to defend one's self and family therein against a felonious assault upon life or person.[66]

§ 327. Felonious homicide—Definition—Classification.—Felonious homicide is the killing of a human being without justification or excuse.[66] In other words, it is the unlawful killing of a human being. This latter definition, however,

[63] Bailey v. People, 54 Colo. 337, 130 Pac. 832, 45 L. R. A. (N. S.) 145, Ann. Cas. 1914 C, 1142n; State v. Turner, 246 Mo. 598, 152 S. W. 313, Ann. Cas. 1914 B, 451; State v. Cook, 78 S. Car. 253, 59 S. E. 862, 15 L. R. A. (N. S.) 1013n, 125 Am. St. 788, 13 Ann. Cas. 1051; Mayhew v. State, 65 Tex. Cr. 290, 144 S. W. 229, 39 L. R. A. (N. S.) 671n; Yardley v. State, 50 Tex. Cr. 644, 100 S. W. 399, 123 Am. St. 869.

[64] State v. Hennesy, 29 Nev. 320, 90 Pac. 221, 13 Ann. Cas. 1122, Derby's Cases 230; Weaver v. State, 1 Ala. App. 48, 55 So. 956, Derby's Cases 232. But see Monson v. State (Tex.) 63 S. W. 647.

[65] State v. Taylor, 143 Mo. 150, 44 S. W. 785, Derby's Cases 234; Pryse v. State, 54 Tex. Cr. 523, 113 S. W. 938, Derby's Cases 237; State v. Gray, 162 N. Car. 608, 77 S. E. 833, 45 L. R. A. (N. S.) 71. See also note to 21 Ann. Cas. 721. So a grandmother is justified in killing her son-in-law to prevent his forcible entry into her dwelling to see his child, if her resistance is no greater than necessary nor earlier in time, especially where he is threatening to kill her. State v. Perkins, 88 Conn. 360, 91 Atl. 26, L. R. A. 1915 A, 73. And a brother-in-law is justified in killing his sister's husband who is trying to force his way in the house of the brother-in-law and mother-in-law to see his wife. Bailey v. People, 54 Colo. 37, 130 Pac. 832, 45 L. R. A. (N. S.) 145n, Ann. Cas. 1914 C, 1142.

[66] 4 Bl. Comm. 188, 189.

does not apply to conditions as they existed at common law, for the reason that excusable homicide was punishable by forfeiture of the slayer's estate. At present, however, both in England and in this country, the penalty of excusable homicide, which existed at common law, has been swept away.

In felonious homicide there are at common law, two degrees of guilt, which divide the offense into the following crimes: (1) Murder. (2) Manslaughter.

CHAPTER XVIII.

KIDNAPING.

§ 330 Definition.—Kidnaping, at common law, consists in unlawfully taking a person, against his will, from his own country to another.[1]

§ 331. Transportation to a foreign country not essential.—In this country, to constitute kidnaping, transportation to a foreign country is not essential.[2]

In many states statutes exist pertaining to the question of transportation, but they are not uniform. Thus, under the statutes of California it has been held that forcibly taking

[1] "The most aggravated species of false imprisonment is the stealing and carrying away, or secreting of any person, sometimes called kidnaping." East P. C. 429, ch. IX. Kidnaping is "the forcible abduction or stealing away of a man, woman, or child, from their own country and sending them to another." 4 Bl. Comm. 219; Furlong v. German-Amer. Press Assn. (Mo.), 189 S. W. 385. The most aggravated form of kipnaping is "the forcible abduction or stealing and carrying away of any person, by sending him from his own country into some other." 1 Russ. on Crimes (9 Am. ed.) 961.

two sailors from a certain county of the state and conveying them twenty miles across the channel to an island which formed part of the same county does not constitute kidnaping.[3] On the other hand, under the statutes of Louisiana, it has been held that an indictment for the forcible seizure and carrying a person from one part of the state to another part is supported by proof that the carrying was from one part of a city in the state to another part of that city.[4] And under a Maine statute it has been held that to incur the penalty for carrying or transporting "out of this state, any person under the age of twenty-one. * * * to any parts beyond the sea, without the consent of his parent, master, or guardian," the carrying must be to some foreign port or place, and not merely from one state to another;[5] while under a New York statute it has been held that where the intent and expectation is that the seaman kidnaped will be carried out of the state, the offense is complete, although the ship on which he is taken be not destined to leave the state.[6]

§ 332. **Physical force not essential.**—Actual force is not essential to constitute kidnaping. Intimidation may take the place of personal violence, and so may fraud. When the proof shows that the mind was operated upon by falsely exciting the fears, by the use of threats or undue influence, amounting substantially to a coercion of the will, it is sufficient.

In weighing the evidence, the jury should take into consideration the condition, education and mental capacity of the person kidnaped, and all the circumstances connected with the transaction.[8]

[3] Ex parte Keil, 85 Cal. 309, 24 Pac. 742.

[4] State v. Backarow, 38 La. Ann. 316.

[5] Campbell v. Rankins, 11 Maine 103.

[6] Hadden v. People, 25 N. Y. 373.

[7] Moody v. People, 20 Ill. 316.

[8] Moody v. People, 20 Ill. 316.

To constitute the crime of kidnaping, the removal of the party must be against his will; but where he is decoyed away fraudulently, his consent having been obtained by deception, the law regards such consent as a nullity, and the act is treated as against the will of the party decoyed away.[9]

On the other hand, when the person taken away is capable in law of giving consent, and, in the absence of fraud or deception, goes voluntarily, the taker is not guilty of kidnaping.[10] Thus, where a married man, somewhat intoxicated, induces a girl of his acquaintance, eighteen years old and unmarried, to go with him in his buggy to another state, where they commit adultery, and he subsequently takes her home at her request, he does not commit the crime of kidnaping.[11]

§ 333. **Age and consent of person taken.**—A child of tender years is incapable of giving a valid consent to be taken away by a person not entitled to his custody. Thus, a person who carries away a child eight years of age, or even eleven years of age, the latter manifesting a willingness to go, may be guilty of kidnaping the child.[12]

The consent of a girl to go, from her parent's home, to another county with a man, is no defense to the criminal charge of kidnaping.[13] But since in Georgia a girl of fourteen may be married without her parents' consent, it is not kidnaping where a man takes her away from her parents and marries her with her consent.[14]

A divorced father who forcibly takes a child four years old awarded to the custody of the mother and carries it out

9 John v. State, 6 Wyo. 203, 44 Pac. 51.

10 John v. State, 6 Wyo. 203, 44 Pac. 51.

11 Eberling v. State, 136 Ind. 117, 35 N. E. 1023.

12 Davenport v. Commonwealth, 1 Leigh (Va.) 588. See also note to 32 L. R. A. (N. S.) 845.

13 Thweatt v. State, 74 Ga. 821.

14 Cochran v. State, 91 Ga. 763, 18 S. E. 16.

of the state is guilty of kidnaping.[15] But where a father takes a child which is under a mother's custody by virtue of agreement of the parents, he is not criminally liable for kidnaping.[16]

§ 334. Specific intent essential.—To constitute the crime of kidnaping the person who commits the act must entertain a specific criminal intent.[17] Thus, a father, who honestly believes that his daughter is insane and institutes proceedings which culminates in her confinement in the state hospital for the insane, is not guilty of the crime of kidnaping, although he does not exercise that care and discretion which an ordinarily prudent man would exercise under the circumstances, since the malicious intent which is essential to the crime is lacking.[18]

Moreover, the indictment or information charging kidnaping must allege this specific intent. When it alleges the forcible confinement and imprisonment of a person within the particular state, against his will, and without lawful authority, but fails to allege any specific intent in such confinement, it charges merely the common-law offense of false imprisonment.[19]

§ 335. Intent to carry away from residence.—Where a statute provides that, "Whoever kidnaps, or forcibly or fraudulently carries off or decoys from his place of residence," etc., the term "residence" is given a liberal interpre-

[15] State v. Farrar, 41 N. H. 53. See also State v. Tillotson, 85 Kans. 577, 117 Pac. 1030, Ann. Cas. 1913A, 463; Hard v. Splain, 45 App. (D. C.) 1.

[16] State v. Powe, 107 Miss. 770, 66 So. 207, L. R. A. 1915 B, 189n.

[17] Smith v. State, 63 Wis. 453, 23 N. W. 879. But see State v. Holland, 120 La. 429, 45 So. 380, 14 Ann. Cas. 692.

[18] People v. Camp, 66 Hun 531, 21 N. Y. S. 741, 10 N. Y. Cr. 318, 51 N. Y. St. 30 (affd., 139 N. Y. 87, 34 N. E. 755).

[19] Smith v. State, 63 Wis. 453, 23 N. W. 879.

tation and is held to be used in the sense of any place where the child has a right to be.[20]

§ 336. Unlawful arrest.—When a peace officer, while acting in his official capacity, properly executes a warrant regularly issued by a court of competent jurisdiction, in no sense can he be guilty of the crime of kidnaping.[21]

On the other hand, when a peace officer acts unlawfully under a warrant which affords him no justification he may be guilty of this crime. Thus, where a constable, acting under a warrant regular on its face, arrests a woman in one county and takes her into another and there places her in a house of prostitution, instead of taking her before a magistrate as directed by his warrant, he is guilty of kidnaping.[22]

§ 337. Persons not liable.—One who is entitled to the legal custody of another can not be guilty of kidnaping him. Thus, a father, who has not parted with his parental right to the custody of his minor child can not be guilty of kidnaping the child.[23]

One who assists a wife in leaving her husband and taking away the infant child of herself and husband is not guilty of kidnaping, owing to the fact that she is as much entitled to the custody of the child as its father.[24]

But where a person harbors and conceals a child kidnaped by others he is guilty, under some statutes, as principal.[25]

§ 338. The indictment or information.—At common law, an indictment is not bad for duplicity or misjoinder because it charges assault, false imprisonment and kidnaping.[26]

20 Wallace v. State, 147 Ind. 621, 47 N. E. 13; Anderson's Law Dict.

21 Ex parte Sternes, 82 Cal. 245, 23 Pac. 38.

22 People v. Fick, 89 Cal. 144, 26 Pac. 759.

23 Hunt v. Hunt, 94 Ga. 257, 21 S. E. 515; John v. State, 6 Wyo. 203, 44 Pac. 51; State v. Dewey, 155 Iowa 469, 136 N. W. 533, 40 L. R. A. (N. S.) 478.

24 State v. Angel, 42 Kans. 216, 21 Pac. 1075.

25 Commonwealth v. Westervelt, 11 Phila. (Pa.) 461, 32 Leg. Int. 346.

26 State v. Rollins, 8 N. H. 550.

Nor is an information bad for duplicity or misjoinder where it charges a defendant with attempting to take and entice away two children under the age of twelve years, without intent to detain and conceal them from a person having their lawful custody.[27]

In an indictment for kidnaping a child, it is not essential to allege from what place the child was taken by the defendant, and by what means it was enticed away.[28] And where an indictment for kidnaping alleges that defendant forcibly took the prosecutrix "for the purpose and with the intent to wilfully and feloniously employ her * * * for the use, unlawfully," of certain named persons, the intent is surplusage and need not be proved.[29]

§ 339. A misdemeanor at common law.—At common law, kidnaping is only a misdemeanor;[30] but in some states, by statute is made a felony.[31]

27 People v. Milne, 60 Cal. 71.

28 Dowda v. State, 74 Ga. 12.

29 People v. Fick, 89 Cal. 144, 26 Pac. 759.

30 1 East P. C. 430; Furlong v. German-Amer. Press Assn. (Mo.), 189 S. W. 385.

31 Illinois: Hurd's Rev. Stat. (1916), ch. 38, §§ 166a, 166b. Where the proof shows that the defendant procured the intoxication of a sailor with the design of getting him on shipboard without his consent, and that he carried the sailor aboard in that condition, it establishes the crime of kidnaping. Hadden v. People, 25 N. Y. 373. Where a person, under the false and fraudulent pretense that he had secured employment for a certain girl as governess in the family of a certain person, induced her to take passage on a steamer for a foreign port for the purpose of engaging in that service, when, in fact, the person named by defendant to the girl kept a house of prostitution at that port, for which defendant acted as procurer, and defendant's object in inducing the girl to go to that port was that she should become an inmate of such house, he is guilty of inveiglement and kidnaping. People v. De Leon, 109 N. Y. 226, 16 N. E. 46, 4 Am. St. 444n. (The term "inveiglement" implies the acquiring of power over another by means of deceptive or evil practices, not accompanied by actual force.)

CHAPTER XIX.

MANSLAUGHTER.

§ 342. Definition—Classification.—Manslaughter is the unlawful killing of a human being, without malice aforethought, express or implied.

Manslaughter is divided into the following two classes: (1) Voluntary, and (2) Involuntary.

§ 343. Voluntary manslaughter.—Voluntary manslaughter is an intentional homicide committed in sudden passion caused by a reasonable provocation, and without malice aforethought.[1]

"If upon a sudden quarrel two persons fight, and one of them kills the other, this is manslaughter: and so it is, if they upon such an occasion go out and fight in a field; for this is one continued act of passion; and the law pays that regard to human frailty, as not to put a hasty and deliberate act upon the same footing with regard to guilt. So also if a man be greatly provoked, as by pulling his nose, or other great indignity, and immediately kills the aggressor, though this is not excusable se defendendo, since there is no absolute necessity for doing it to preserve himself; yet neither is it murder for there is no previous malice; but it is manslaughter."[2]

§ 344. Nature and requisites of voluntary manslaughter.—The basis of the mitigation in this crime is the fact that the

[1] 1 Hale P. C. 466; 1 Hawk. P. C., ch. 30, § 3; Brown v. Commonwealth, 86 Va. 466, 10 S. E. 745; Cavanaugh v. Commonwealth, 172 Ky. 799, 190 S. W. 123; State v. Schaeffer, 96 Ohio 215, 117 N. E. 220.

[2] 4 Bl. Comm. 191.

which are slight and trivial, ordinarily not followed by violence.[8]

Provocation to be adequate "should be real, or so apparent as to justify the assumption of its reality. It should also be sudden and sufficiently great. It should be calculated to exasperate both in its character, and in respect to the persons against whom it is directed."[9]

§ 348. Malice implied when acts barbarous.—When the punishment inflicted is far in excess of the provocation given, and under the circumstances outrageous, the law implies that it emanates from a malignant and cruel heart rather than from human frailty.[10] Thus, where a young man asked a crippled old man eighty years of age impertinent questions, to whom the latter replied, "None of your business," and the young man, whose feet were shod with heavy boots, knocked the old man down with his fist and brutally kicked him so that he died, it was implied that the slayer possessed a cruel and malignant heart.[11] An act which might constitute adequate provocation when done by one's equal in physical prowess, might fall short of being such when done by a cripple, a child or a woman.[12] "Violent acts of resentment, bearing no proportion to the provocation or insult, particularly where there is a decided preponderance of strength on the part of the party killing, are barbarous, proceeding rather from brutal malignity than human frailty; and barbarity will often imply malice."[13] "If, even upon a sudden provocation one beats another in a cruel and unusual manner, so that he

[8] State v. Ferguson, 2 Hill (S. Car.) 619, 27 Am. Dec. 412.

[9] Flanagan v. State, 46 Ala. 703, 707, 708.

[10] Keate's Case, 1 East P. C. 234; Johnson v. State, 129 Wis. 146, 108 N. W. 55, 5 L. R. A. (N. S.) 809; Commonwealth v. Paese, 220 Pa. 371, 69 Atl. 891, 17 L. R. A. (N. S.) 793n, 123 Am. St. 699, Derby's Cases 360; People v. Venckus, 278 Ill. 124, 115 N. E. 880; State v. Prettyman, 6 Boyce (29 Del.) 452, 100 Atl. 476.

[11] State v. Kloss, 117 Mo. 591, 23 S. W. 780.

[12] Commonwealth v. Mosler, 4 Pa. St. 264, 6 Pa. L. J. 90.

[13] Whart. Law of Homicide, § 425.

dies, though he did not intend his death, yet he is guilty of murder by express malice."[14]

§ 349. Nature and scope of the emotion engendered.—Strictly speaking, it is not the provocation which reduces a homicide from murder to manslaughter, but rather the state of mind produced by the provocation.[15] If the state of mind which caused the killing was not produced by the provocation but a cooling time intervened, then the killing is not manslaughter.[16] The passion, or state of mind, essential to render the homicide manslaughter must be sufficient to rebut the imputation of malice. But, to accomplish this end, it is not essential that the reason be dethroned and the power of volition destroyed.[17] The state of mind produced by the provocation must be such that the violence of the excitement impedes the exercise of judgment, and renders the slayer accountable as an infirm human being.[18] A transport of passion, which deprives of the power of self-control, is, in a modified or restricted sense, a dethronement of the reasoning faculty—a divestment of its sovereign power; but an entire dethronement is a deprivation of the intellect for the time being.[19] In the latter case the state of mind of the slayer would render him wholly innocent of crime.

§ 350. Co-existence of passion and malice.—Passion and malice may both exist in the mind of the slayer at the time of the act. In the eye of the law, however, they can not co-exist as the moving cause of the homicide.[20] In other words, the law presumes that the killing can not proceed

[14] 4 Bl. Comm. 199.

[15] State v. Ellis, 74 Mo. 207, 218; In re Fraleys, 3 Okla. Cr. 719, 109 Pac. 295, 139 Am. St. 988.

[16] Lindsey v. State, 125 Ark. 542, 189 S. W. 163; Marshbanks v. State, 80 Tex. Cr. 507, 192 S. W. 246; Hassell v. State, 80 Tex. Cr. 93, 188 S. W. 991.

[17] State v. Hill, 4 Dev. & B. (N. Car.) 491, 34 Am. Dec. 396.

[18] State v. Hill, 4 Dev. & B. (N. Car.) 491, 34 Am. Dec. 396.

[19] Smith v. State, 83 Ala. 26, 3 So. 551.

[20] State v. Johnson, 23 N. Car. 354, 35 Am. Dec. 742.

from both impulses. Either one or the other must be the dominant motive which characterizes the crime.

Malice is presumed from the act of killing; while, on the other hand, proof of adequate provocation neutralizes or overcomes this presumption. In other words, when the weight of the provocation is equal to, or greater than, that of the presumption of malice the provocation is adequate to reduce the killing from murder to manslaughter. Provocation, however great, never disproves malice. The most it can do in any case is to overcome the presumption of malice. A malicious killing, however, no matter how great the provocation, is always murder.[21]

§ 351. Passion, or state of mind, must emanate from the provocation.—The state of mind which the law recognizes as sufficient to reduce a voluntary homicide from murder to manslaughter must emanate from an adequate provocation. In other words, the provocation must be the direct and controlling cause of the excited condition of the mind at the time of the act. Passion which is not produced by provocation is insufficient;[22] and when produced by provocation the law requires it to be sufficient to render the slayer incapable of cool and deliberate reflection.[23]

§ 352. Provocation of illegal arrest.—A homicide, though unintentional, committed in resisting a lawful arrest is murder.[24] On the other hand, it is often said that even an intentional homicide committed in resisting an unlawful arrest is manslaughter. As a general rule this is true. It should be observed, however, that there are exceptions to it. But, or-

[21] State v. Johnson, 23 N. Car. 354, 35 Am. Dec. 742; State v. Lichter (Del.), 102 Atl. 529; Little v. Commonwealth, 177 Ky. 24, 197 S. W. 514.

[22] Rex v. Lynch, 5 Car. & P. 324, 24 E. C. L. (Reprint) 587; Reg. v. Welsh, 11 Cox Cr. C. 336.

[23] Crosby v. People, 137 Ill. 325, 27 N. E. 49. See also State v. Michael, 74 W. Va. 613, 82 S. E. 611, L. R. A. 1915 A, 533, where one was mistaken as to his assailant and shot another and killed him.

[24] Commonwealth v. Grether, 204 Pa. 203, 53 Atl. 753.

dinarily, when the attempted arrest is illegal, as where the warrant is void, or the person making the attempt to arrest does so without a warrant, or without the officer's jurisdiction, the killing of the officer in resisting the arrest, whether done intentionally or otherwise, is manslaughter. The unlawful attempt in such case is usually regarded by the law as a sufficient provocation to reduce the killing from murder to manslaughter.[25]

§ 353. Illegal arrest—Not a justification—An exception.—An attempted unlawful arrest will not, as a very general rule at least, justify a killing. "The attempt to take away one's liberty while it may be imposed by the imperfect defense, can not be resisted to the death. * * * Nothing short of an endeavor to destroy life or inflict great bodily harm will justify the taking of life, prevails in this case. * * * The reason why a man may not oppose an attempt on his liberty by the same extreme measures permissible in an attempt on his life, appears to be because liberty can be secured by a resort to the laws."[26] But there are cases where the party whose unlawful arrest is attempted may resist even to taking the wrongdoer's life, as where the attempt is to convey one by force beyond the reach of law, or to carry him out of the country.[27]

§ 354. Illegal arrest—When the killing constitutes murder.—Ordinarily, as heretofore stated, an attempted illegal arrest is a sufficient provocation to reduce a homicide from murder to manslaughter. It is to be observed, however, that the killing must be done in sudden anger, and by reason thereof. However great the provocation, if the killing re-

[25] Commonwealth v. Carey, 12 Cush. (Mass.) 246, 251; Creighton v. Commonwealth, 84 Ky. 103, 4 Am. St. 193, 7 Ky. L. 70, Beale's Cases 339. See also Roberts v. State, 14 Mo. 138, 55 Am. Dec. 97n; Drennan v. People, 10 Mich. 169.

[26] 1 Bish. Crim. L. (8th ed.), § 868. See also State v. Meyers, 57 Ore. 50, 110 Pac. 407, 33 L. R. A. (N. S.) 143.

[27] Creighton v. Commonwealth, 84 Ky. 103, 4 Am. St. 193, 7 Ky. L. 785, Beale's Cases 339.

sults from a malicious and cruel heart rather than from heat of blood, the homicide is murder. To render the homicide manslaughter, the proof must show that the killing, though intentional, was not the result of cool, deliberate judgment and previous malignity of heart, but, on the other hand. solely the result of sudden passion imputable to human frailty. In other words, it must be shown that the slayer was transported by ungovernable passion and deaf to the voice of reason, and that this state of mind was produced by an adequate provocation. Thus, where two men who had committed a crime killed the party who attempted to arrest them, not in sudden anger or heat of blood, but, conscious of their guilt, in order that they might escape just punishment, it was held that the homicide was murder and not manslaughter, even though the attempted arrest was illegal.[28]

§ 355. Illegal arrest—The slayer a felon.—Upon principle, it would seem that when a felon, conscious of his guilt, intentionally kills a person who attempts to arrest him, and the proof shows that the person attempting to make the arrest is without legal authority, the homicide is murder. A sense of guilt can not arouse honest indignation in the breast, and therefore can not extenuate a cruel and wilful murder to manslaughter.[29] In the case of a felon there is much less cause for his reason to be disturbed or obscured by passion than exists in the case of an innocent person. In the felon's case the homicide results from the exercise of judgment, whereas in the case of the innocent person it results from passion.

§ 356. Illegal arrest—The slayer a third party.—A third party may lawfully interfere to prevent an illegal arrest. In the eye of the law such an arrest is a provocation not only to the person arrested but also to bystanders. And if a by-

28 Brooks v. Commonwealth, 61 Pa. St. 352, 100 Am. Dec. 645.

29 Brooks v. Commonwealth, 61 Pa. St. 352, 100 Am. Dec. 645.

stander, without malice, kills another to prevent him from making an illegal arrest the homicide is manslaughter.[30]

§ 357. Homicide which results from mutual combat.—Ordinarily, a homicide which results from mutual combat is manslaughter and not murder.[31] This is owing to the fact that in such case the killing is regarded as done in the heat of blood rather than maliciously. When, however, the proof shows that the slayer began the affray with intent to kill his adversary, or do him grievous bodily harm, the homicide is murder. Where two persons meet, without any previous intention of quarreling, and, suddenly, angry words pass which lead to blows, and in the heat of blood one of them seizes a weapon and inflicts upon his adversary a mortal wound, the homicide is manslaughter and not murder. In such case, it is immaterial who strikes the first blow, and also whether the instrument which is used is a deadly weapon or not. If a quarrel ensue between two persons and one strikes the other, and the latter attacks the former with a knife and severely wounds him, and the wounded party immediately kills his adversary, the homicide is held manslaughter.[32]

Moreover, previous encounters between the parties, even when malicious, and threats by one against the other, do not raise a legal presumption of malice in the subsequent encounter. As said by Hawkins, "Certainly, where two persons have formerly fought on malice, and are apparently reconciled, and fight again on a fresh quarrel, it shall not be intended that they were moved by the old grudge, unless it so appears from the circumstances of the affair."[33]

30 Reg. v. Mawgridge, Kelyng 119. See also Hugget's Case, Kelyng 59; Reg. v. Phelps, Car. & M. 180; Reg. v. Tooley, 2 Ld. Raym. 1296; Steph. Dig. Crim. L., App. xv.

31 State v. Reeves (Mo.), 195 S. W. 1027.

32 State v. Hill, 4 Dev. & B. (N. Car.) 491, 34 Am. Dec. 396.

33 1 Hawk. P. C., ch. 13, § 30. See also Copeland v. State, 7 Humph. (Tenn.) 479; State v. Hildreth, 31 N. Car. 429, 51 Am. Dec. 364.

To constitute a mutual combat there must be mutual intent to fight and at least one blow struck.[34]

§ 358. Homicide which results from husband's knowledge of wife's adultery.—In an early English case it is said that "when a man is taken in adultery with another man's wife, if the husband shall stab the adulterer, or knock out his brains, this is bare manslaughter; for jealousy is the rage of a man, and adultery is the highest invasion of property."[35] Courts then hold that the husband must have discovered the adultery on the spot, or must have "ocular inspection of the act, and only then."[36] For the husband to kill his wife on suspicion that she had committed adultery, however well founded, or upon hearsay, was murder.

Modern decisions, however, upon this question, are in conflict. Some adhere to the old rule,[37] while others take a more liberal view.[38] Upon principle, the latter view is correct. The "law accepts human nature as God has made it, or as it manifests itself in the ordinary man, and every sort of conduct in others which commonly does in fact so excite the passions of the mass of men as practically to enthrall their reason the law holds to be adequate cause."[39]

[34] Tate v. State, 46 Ga. 148.

[35] Reg. v. Mawgridge, Kelyng 119.

[36] 4 Bl. Comm. 191. See also 3 Greenl. Ev. (16th ed.), § 122; Pearson's Case, 2 Lew. 216; 1 Hale P. C. 487.

[37] Reg. v. Fisher, 8 Car. & P. 182; Reg. v. Kelly, 2 Car & K. 814; State v. Neville, 51 N. Car. 423; State v. Samuel, 48 N. Car. 74, 64 Am. Dev. 596; State v. John, 30 N. Car. 330, 49 Am. Dec. 396. See also Jones v. People, 23 Colo. 276, 47 Pac. 275; Shufflin v. People, 62 N. Y. 229, 20 Am. Rep. 483; Bugg v. Commonwealth, 38 S. W. 684, 18 Ky. L. 844; State v. Young, 52 Ore. 227, 96 Pac. 1067, 18 L. R. A. (N. S.) 688n, 132 Am. St. 689n.

[38] Maher v. People, 10 Mich. 212, 81 Am. Dec. 781, Beale's Cases 482, Derby's Cases 355; State v. Grugin, 147 Mo. 39, 47 S. W. 1058, 42 L. R. A. 774, 71 Am. St. 553; Biggs v. State, 29 Ga. 723, 76 Am. Dec. 630; Hooks v. State, 99 Ala. 166, 13 So. 767. See also Stevens v. State, 137 Ga. 520, 73 S. E. 737, 38 L. R. A. (N. S.) 99.

[39] State v. Grugin, 147 Mo. 39, 47 S. W. 1058, 42 L. R. A. 774, 71 Am. St. 553. See also Rowland v. State, 83 Miss. 483, 35 So. 826, 1 Ann. Cas. 135.

In harmony with the better view, it has been well said that "since the law, as other sciences, makes progress, it is no longer accounted necessary that a husband should have 'ocular inspection,' etc. It suffices if the provocation be so recent and so strong that the husband could not be considered at the time master of his own understanding."[40] So where the evidence tended to show the commission of adultery by the deceased with the defendant's wife half an hour before the assault, the defendant seeing them go to the woods under circumstances tending strongly to impress an adulterous purpose on his mind, followed them, saw them come out together, and pursued the deceased toward a saloon and on the way was told that deceased and his wife committed adultery in the woods the day before, and defendant in great excitement entered the saloon and shot deceased, such evidence was proper to the issue of provocatio . and from it the jury might have found defendant guilty of manslaughter only.[41]

§ 359. Adultery—Reasonable belief of wife's guilt sufficient.—To reduce a homicide from murder to manslaughter actual guilt on the part of the wife is not essential. Apparent guilt may be sufficiently strong to constitute adequate provocation.[42] If the homicide is committed in a transport of passion upon discovering the decedent apparently in the act of adultery with the wife of the accused, under circumstances such as to induce and justify a reasonable belief on the part of the accused that such a crime was in progress, and there is no proof of actual malice, the offense is man-

40 State v. Grugin, 147 Mo. 39, 47 S. W. 1058, 42 L. R. A. 774, 71 Am. St. 553.

41 Maher v. People, 10 Mich. 212, 81 Am. Dec. 781, Beale's Cases 482, Derby's Cases 355.

42 State v. Yanz, 74 Conn. 177, 50 Atl. 37, 54 L. R. A. 780, 92 Am. St. 205n.

slaughter only, although it subsequently turns out that adultery was not in fact committed.[43]

§ 360. Illicit intercourse with slayer's sister or daughter.—Whether illicit intercourse with the slayer's sister or daughter constitutes sufficient provocation to reduce the homicide to manslaughter depends upon the circumstances of the particular case.[44] In England the court determines whether certain acts constitute adequate provocation and the jury determines whether the provocation caused heat of blood which resulted in the homicide.[45] And this view has been held in this county.[46] According to the better view, however, the existence or non-existence of adequate provocation in such a case is a question for the jury to decide.[47] Where a father slays a man who has ravished his daughter, the provocation may reduce the offense to manslaughter.[48]

§ 361. Insulting words and gestures.—As a general rule, insulting words, however opprobrious, and gestures, however contemptuous, do not constitute a sufficient provocation to reduce a homicide to manslaughter.[49] There are, however, exceptions to this rule. Special circumstances may render

43 State v. Yanz, 74 Conn. 177, 50 Atl. 37, 54 L. R. A. 780, 92 Am. St. 205n; State v. Will, 18 N. Car. 121. See also State v. Larkin, 250 Mo. 218, 157 S. W. 600, 46 L. R. A. (N. S.) 13.

44 Lynch v. Commonwealth, 77 Pa. St. 205; State v. Grugin, 147 Mo. 39, 47 S. W. 1058, 42 L. R. A. 774, 71 Am. St. 553.

45 Reg. v. Fisher, 8 Car. & P. 182; Reg. v. Kelly, 2 Car. & K. 814.

46 State v. John, 30 N. Car. 330, 49 Am. Dec. 396.

47 Maher v. People, 10 Mich. 212, 81 Am. Dec. 781, Beale's Cases 482, Derby's Cases 355; State v. Grugin, 147 Mo. 39, 47 S. W. 1058, 42 L. R. A. 774, 71 Am. St. 553.

48 State v. Grugin, 147 Mo. 39, 47 S. W. 1058, 42 L. R. A. 774, 71 Am. St. 553.

49 1 Hale P. C. 456; Reg. v. Rothwell, 12 Cox Cr. C. 145, Beale's Cases 481; State v. Carter, 76 N. Car. 20; Taylor v. State, 48 Ala. 180; Malone v. State, 49 Ga. 210; Keirsey v. State, 131 Ark. 487, 199 S. W. 532; State v. Fletcher (Mo.), 190 S. W. 317; State v. Buffington, 71 Kans. 804, 81 Pac. 465, 4 L. R. A. (N. S.) 154n; State v. Grugin, 147 Mo. 39, 47 S. W. 1058, 42 L. R. A. 774, 71 Am. St. 553.

words alone sufficient; for instance, "if a husband suddenly hearing from his wife that she had committed adultery, and he having had no idea of such a thing before, were thereupon to kill his wife, it might be manslaughter."[50] In some states, statutes have been passed expressly making insulting words, under certain conditions, adequate provocation.[51]

§ 362. **Trespass upon property insufficient provocation.**— A mere trespass upon property, other than the habitation, is not a sufficient provocation to reduce a homicide to manslaughter. Upon this point the decisions are in accord. "If one man be trespassing upon another, breaking his hedges or the like, and the owner, or his servant, shall upon sight thereof take up an hedge-stake and knock him on the head, that will be murder, because it was a violent act, beyond the provocation."[52] "It is a rule of law, that where the trespass is barely against the property of another, not his dwelling-house, it is not a provocation sufficient to warrant the owner in using a deadly weapon; and if he do, and with it kill the trespasser, this will be murder, because it is an act of violence beyond the degree of the provocation."[53]

It is to be observed, however, that when the killing is done by an instrument not a deadly weapon, and in a manner not likely to kill, the homicide is manslaughter.[54]

Moreover, when a trespasser is opposed by force barely sufficient to prevent him from committing a trespass, a deadly

[50] Reg. v. Rothwell, 12 Cox Cr. C. 145, Beale's Cases 481. See also Reg. v. Smith, 4 Fost. & F. 1066; Seals v. State, 3 Baxt. (Tenn.) 459; Wilson v. People, 4 Park. Cr. R. (N. Y.) 619; State v. Grugin, 147 Mo. 39, 47 S. W. 1058, 42 L. R. A. 774, 71 Am. St. 553.

[51] Hardcastle v. State, 36 Tex. Cr. 555, 38 S. W. 186; Brown v. State, 74 Ala. 42; Mitchell v. State, 41 Ga. 527.

[52] Reg. v. Mawgridge, Kelyng 119. See also State v. Vance, 17 Iowa 138.

[53] Chief Justice Parsons in Commonwealth v. Drew, 4 Mass. 391, 396. See also Simpson v. State, 59 Ala. 1, 31 Am. Rep. 1n; State v. Marfaudille, 48 Wash. 117, 92 Pac. 939, 14 L. R. A. (N. S.) 346.

[54] Commonwealth v. Drew, 4 Mass. 391; Simpson v. State, 59 Ala. 1, 31 Am. Rep. 1n.

weapon not being used, and during the encounter the trespasser is killed to save the other party from death or serious bodily harm, the homicide is excusable.[55] If, however, the killing is not to save the other party from death or grievous bodily harm, but results from passion caused by the other's blows, the homicide is manslaughter.[56] And if the killing is done maliciously it is murder.[57]

§ 363. Homicide resulting from a duel.—When two persons, pursuant to an agreement, fight a duel, each bent on killing the other, and death results, the homicide is murder, notwithstanding the fact that the combat was conducted fairly.[58]

§ 364. Reasonable cooling time.—An adequate provocation reduces a homicide to manslaughter, provided a reasonable cooling time does not intervene between the provocation and the killing. But if the blood has a reasonable time in which to cool, the killing, notwithstanding the provocation, is murder.[59] Actual cooling of the blood, however, is not the test. As a general rule, if, under all the circumstances attending the homicide, a reasonable length of time intervenes between the provocation and the act, within which under like circumstances an ordinarily reasonable man would cool, the homicide is murder. The law, in extending its indulgence to human frailty, does not look merely to the fact

55 4 Bl. Comm. 186, 187; 1 Hawk. P. C., ch. 28, § 24; Erwin v. State, 29 Ohio St. 186, 23 Am. Rep. 733; Pond v. People, 8 Mich. 149; Noles v. State, 26 Ala. 31, 62 Am. Dec. 711; State v. Ingold, 49 N. Car. 216, 67 Am. Dec. 283.

56 Commonwealth v. Drew, 4 Mass. 391; Claxton v. State, 2 Humph. (Tenn.) 181; Simpson v. State, 59 Ala. 1, 31 Am. Rep. 1n.

57 State v. Partlow, 90 Mo. 608, 4 S. W. 14, 59 Am. Rep. 31; Cates v. State, 50 Ala. 166; State v. Moore, 69 N. Car. 267; State v. Levigne, 17 Nev. 435, 30 Pac. 1084; Stiles v. State, 57 Ga. 183; State v. McDonnell, 32 Vt. 491.

58 State v. Hill, 4 Dev. & B. (N. Car.) 491, 34 Am. Dec. 396.

59 State v. McCants, 1 Speers L. (S. Car.) 384 (a most excellent case on this point); In re Fraley, 3 Okla. Cr. 719, 109 Pac. 295, 139 Am. St. 988.

that the act has proceeded from the violent impulse of anger, outstripping the tardier operations of reason, but asks whether the anger has been provoked by sufficient cause and whether it has been made to yield to reason within a reasonable time. It regards men as rational creatures and expects them to subject their passions to reasonable control.[60]

Many decisions hold that the question of reasonable cooling time is one of law for the court to decide.[61] Upon principle, however, the court should define to the jury the principles upon which the question is to be decided and leave it to them to determine whether the time was reasonable under all the circumstances of the particular case.[62]

§ 365. Involuntary manslaughter—Definition—Essentials.—Involuntary manslaughter is the unintentional killing of another person, without malice, but without excuse or justification.[62a]

Its general requisites are as follows: (1) The killing must be unintentional; (2) it must be without malice; (3) it must be unlawful.

Involuntary manslaughter may arise from an act of malfeasance or misfeasance, or from mere nonfeasance.

§ 366. Homicide arising from acts of malfeasance.—A homicide which arises unintentionally from the commission of another crime may be murder or manslaughter, depending upon the circumstances of the case.

When a homicide arises from the commission of, or an attempt to commit a felony, such as robbery, rape, burglary or arson, or an act which naturally tends to cause death or grievous bodily harm, the killing is murder. This is owing

60 State v. McCants, 1 Speers L. (S. Car.) 384.

61 Reg. v. Fisher, 8 Car. & P. 182; Rex v. Oneby, 2 Ld. Raym. 1485.

62 Maher v. People, 10 Mich. 212, 81 Am. Dec. 781, Beale's Cases 482, Derby's Cases 355.

62a Clouts v. State, 18 Ga. App. 707, 90 S. E. 373; Hunter v. Commonwealth, 171 Ky. 438, 188 S. W. 472; Maulding v. Commonwealth, 172 Ky. 370, 189 S. W. 251.

to the fact that in such cases malice is implied. On the other hand, when it arises from the commission of, or attempt to commit, a misdemeanor, or an act malum in se as distinguished from an act which is merely malum prohibitum, the killing is manslaughter.

§ 367. Homicide arising from assault and battery.—When a person commits an assault and battery which falls short of having a natural tendency to cause death or grievous bodily harm, and a homicide unintentionally arises therefrom, the killing is involuntary manslaughter.[63] This is true if the death is occasioned merely by fear or terror.[64]

§ 368. Homicide arising from a prize fight.—When two persons engage in a prize fight, which constitutes a breach of the peace, and one unintentionally kills the other, the homicide is manslaughter.[65]

In a state, however, in which prize fighting is lawful the unintentional killing of one of the contestants by the other would be excusable homicide.[66] While, on the other hand, where prize fighting is a felony, the homicide, according to the common-law rule, would be murder.[67] Moreover, under this principle, to constitute the killing murder it is not essential that the act intended be such as to endanger life or threaten grievous bodily harm. The mere fact that the kill-

63 People v. Steubenvoll, 62 Mich. 329, 28 N. W. 883; Reg. v. Towers, 12 Cox Cr. C. 530, Beale's Cases 425 (man assaulted a woman who was nursing a child, thereby causing the child to have convulsions and die); State v. Lockwood, 119 Mo. 463, 24 S. W. 1015, Derby's Cases 367; Fray's Case, 1 East P. C. 236, Beale's Cases 477; Wild's Case, 2 Lew. Cr. C. 214, Beale's Cases 347.

64 In re Heigho, 18 Idaho 566, 110 Pac. 256, 32 L. R. A. (N. S.) 877.

65 Reg. v. Knock, 14 Cox Cr. C. 1; Ward's Case, 1 East P. C. 270.

66 Reg. v. Bradshaw, 14 Cox Cr. C. 83, Beale's Cases 146, Derby's Cases 269 (football); Reg. v. Young, 10 Cox Cr. C. 371 (sparring); Reg. v. Bruce, 2 Cox Cr. C. 262. See also 4 Bl. Comm. 182; 1 Hale P. C. 473.

67 People v. Enoch, 13 Wend. (N. Y.) 159, 27 Am. Dec. 197n.

ing grows out of an act which constitutes a felony is sufficient.[68] It has been held that a homicide arising from the commission of a robbery where the killing is done in attempting to escape with the booty, is murder.[69]

§ 369. Homicide arising from playing football.—When several persons engage in a game of football, in a manner such as to be dangerous to life or limb, and one of the players unintentionally kills another, the homicide is manslaughter. Moreover, the fact that the game is played according to established rules is no excuse.[70] On the other hand, when the game is played in a lawful manner, and one of the players is killed unintentionally, the homicide is excusable.[71] For, in such case, "The act is lawful, and the effect is merely accidental."[72]

§ 370. Homicide arising from correction of a child, pupil or apprentice.—When a parent corrects his child, teacher his pupil or master his apprentice beyond the bounds of moderation, and death unintentionally arises from the undue chastisement, the homicide is manslaughter.[73] If, however, the chastisement is within the bounds of moderation, the homicide is excusable.[74]

[68] People v. Sullivan, 173 N. Y. 122, 65 N. E. 989, 63 L. R. A. 353n, 93 Am. St. 582; Adams v. People, 109 Ill. 444, 50 Am. Rep. 617; Kennedy v. State, 107 Ind. 144, 6 N. E. 305, 57 Am. Rep. 99; State v. Wagner, 78 Mo. 644, 47 Am. Rep. 131; Reg v. Serne, 16 Cox Cr. C. 311, Beale's Cases 465; Steph. Dig. Crim. L., art. 223.

[69] State v. Brown, 7 Ore. 186.

[70] Reg. v. Bradshaw, 14 Cox Cr. C. 83, Beale's Cases 146, Derby's Cases 269.

[71] Reg. v. Bradshaw, 14 Cox Cr. C. 83, Beale's Cases 146, Derby's Cases 269; Belk v. People, 125 Ill. 584, 17 N. E. 744.

[72] 4 Bl. Comm. 182. See also Reg. v. Bruce, 2 Cox Cr. C. 262, Beale's Cases 202.

[73] 1 Hale P. C. 455; State v. Fields, 70 Iowa 196, 30 N. W. 480; State v. Shaw, 64 S. Car. 566, 43 S. E. 14, 60 L. R. A. 801n, 92 Am. St. 817; Rex v. Cheeseman, 7 Car. & P. 455; Reg. v. Griffin, 11 Cox Cr. C. 402, Beale's Cases 315; Commonwealth v. Randall, 4 Gray (Mass.) 36.

[74] 1 East P. C. 260, 269; Fost. C. L. 262, Beale's Cases 185, 315; 4 Bl. Comm. 182.

§ 371. **Homicide arising from a riot.**—When a number of persons engage in the commission of a riot which results in an unintentional homicide, the killing is manslaughter and not murder. This is owing to the fact that riot, at common law, is only a misdemeanor.[75]

§ 372. **Homicide arising from an unlawful attempt to procure an abortion or from unlawful intercourse.**—When a person unlawfully attempts to procure an abortion, in a manner not to endanger life or inflict serious injury and the woman dies, the homicide is manslaughter,[76] When, however, the act is done under circumstances, or in a manner which endangers life or inflicts serious injury, and the woman dies, the homicide is murder.[77]

Where one raped a child and gave her venereal disease, from which she died, there may be conviction of either manslaughter or murder.[78]

§ 373. **Homicide arising from an act which is merely malum prohibitum.**—To render a person criminally liable for an unintended result, the act from which it arises must be at least malum in se. Hence, where it is merely malum prohibitum he is not criminally liable for such result. Thus, where a person, while driving at a speed prohibited by a city ordinance, but not recklessly, runs into another, he is not

[75] Brennan v. People, 15 Ill. 511; Patten v. People, 18 Mich. 314, 100 Am. Dec. 173; State v. Jenkins, 14 Rich. L. (S. Car.) 215, 94 Am. Dec. 132; Sloan v. State, 9 Ind. 565; Rex v. Murphy, 6 Car. & P. 103. See also 1 Whart. Crim. L. (11th ed.), §§ 451, 524, 527.

[76] Yundt v. People, 65 Ill. 372; Commonwealth v. Railing, 113 Pa. St. 37, 4 Atl. 459; People v. Olmstead, 30 Mich. 431; Worthington v. State, 92 Md. 222, 48 Atl. 355, 84 Am. St. 506, 56 L. R. A. 353; State v. Farnum, 82 Ore. 211, 161 Pac. 417, Ann. Cas. 1918A, 318.

[77] State v. Moore, 25 Iowa 128, 95 Am. Dec. 776n; 1 Hale P. C. 429, 430. See also Commonwealth v. Parker, 9 Metc. (Mass.) 263, 43 Am. Dec. 396; Peoples v. Commonwealth, 87 Ky. 487, 9 S. W. 509, 810, 10 Ky. L. 517; State v. Harris, 90 Kans. 807, 136 Pac. 264, 49 L. R. A. (N. S.) 580n.

[78] Reg. v. Greenwood, 7 Cox Cr. C. 404, Derby's Cases 343.

criminally liable for assault and battery.[79] Nor would he be liable for felonious homicide if the person run into were killed. And where a person, while carrying a concealed revolver in violation of law, accidentally discharges it and kills another, he is not liable for felonious homicide;[80] or where hunting game on another's land in violation of statute, he unintentionally without negligence kills another and such hunting is not in itself dangerous to life.[81]

§ 374. Homicide arising from a mere tort.—When an unintentional homicide arises from a mère tort the killing is excusable. As said in a leading English case, "The mere fact of a civil wrong committed by one person against another ought not to be used as an incident which is a necessary step in a criminal case."[82]

§ 375. Homicide arising from acts of misfeasance.—A homicide which arises unintentionally from the doing of a lawful act in a grossly negligent manner is involuntary manslaughter.[83]

There are many cases in which death is the result of an occurrence, in itself unexpected, but which arose from negligence or inattention. How far in such cases the agent of such misfortune is to be held responsible, as a general rule depends upon the inquiry, whether he was guilty of gross negligence at the time.[84] What constitutes gross negligence depends upon the circumstances attending the particular case. Thus, driving a team of horses, riding a bicycle or

[79] Commonwealth v. Adams, 114 Mass. 323, 19 Am. Rep. 362, Beale's Cases 204.

[80] Potter v. State, 162 Ind. 213, 70 N. E. 129, 64 L. R. A. 942, 102 Am. St. 198, 1 Ann. Cas. 32.

[81] State v. Horton, 139 N. Car. 588, 51 S. E. 945, 1 L. R. A. (N. S.) 991n, 4 Ann. Cas. 797.

[82] Reg. v. Franklin, 15 Cox Cr. C. 163, Beale's Cases 203.

[83] Fost. C. L. 262, Beale's Cases 185.

[84] 1 Whart. Crim. L. (11th ed.). §§ 454-495.

running an automobile at a certain speed, may be lawful and proper on a country road while grossly negligent on a city street.[85]

§ 376. Homicide arising from shooting at a target.—A homicide which arises from shooting at a target may be excusable or felonious. Its nature depends upon the circumstances attending the act. If, under the circumstances, proper precautions have not been taken and shooting at the target constitutes gross negligence, the unintended homicide resulting therefrom constitutes manslaughter. Thus, where several persons engage in shooting at a target, and the bullets cross several highways and go in the direction of a habitation, as a result of which a boy in his father's garden is unintentionally killed, the homicide is involuntary manslaughter. Moreover, since all engage in the common pursuit all are criminally liable.[86]

§ 377. Homicide arising from snapping a revolver at another merely to frighten.—A person who snaps a loaded revolver at another, honestly believing that it is not loaded, or, if possessing knowledge that it is loaded but honestly believing that it will not go off, and intending merely to frighten the other party, shoots and kills him, is guilty of gross negligence and liable for manslaughter.[87] Where one carelessly fires a pistol at the ground and the bullet glancing kills a bystander, he is not guilty of manslaughter unless the death was a natural and probable consequence of his act.[88]

[85] Belk v. People, 125 Ill. 584, 17 N. E. 744; Crum v. State, 64 Miss. 1, 1 So. 1, 60 Am. Rep. 44; White v. State, 84 Ala. 421, 4 So. 598.

[86] Reg. v. Salmon, 14 Cox Cr. C. 494, Beale's Cases 189.

[87] State v. Hardie, 47 Iowa 647, 29 Am. Rep. 496. See also State v. Emery, 78 Mo. 77, 47 Am. Rep. 92; State v. Vines, 93 N. Car. 493, 53 Am. Rep. 466; Sparks v. Commonwealth, 3 Bush (Ky.) 111, 96 Am. Dec. 196.

[88] Dixon v. State, 104 Miss. 410, 61 So. 423, 45 L. R. A. (N. S.) 219.

In such case, the following instruction correctly states the law: "If the defendant used a dangerous and deadly weapon, in a careless and reckless manner, by reason of which instrument so used he killed the deceased, then he is guilty of manslaughter, although no harm was in fact intended."[89]

§ 378. Homicide arising from turning a vicious animal where it may injure someone.—If a person has knowledge that a certain animal is vicious and dangerous, and turns it out where there is danger that it may injure some one, and it attacks and kills a person, he is guilty of manslaughter.[90]

§ 379. Homicide arising from negligent operation of automobile.—Where one wilfully drives an automobile in a public street at a speed or in a manner expressly forbidden by statute, and thereby causes the death of another, or with reckless disregard for the safety of others so negligently drives his automobile in a public street as to cause another's death, he is guilty of manslaughter.[91] This principle was also applied in a case where a passenger was thrown out by reckless driving and killed.[92]

§ 380. Homicide arising from treatment or operation by physician or surgeon.—When a physician or surgeon, in treating a patient or performing an operation upon him, causes his death by gross negligence he is guilty of manslaughter. Consent of the patient is no defense. Thus, where a practicing physician, on being called to attend a sick

[89] State v. Hardie, 47 Iowa 647, 29 Am. Rep. 496. But where one did not know a gun was loaded and merely intended to punch another with it and the gun was accidentally discharged, there is no presumption of an intent to kill. Delk v. State, 135 Ga. 312, 69 S. E. 541, Ann. Cas. 1912 A, 105.

[90] Reg. v. Dant, 10 Cox Cr. C. 102.

[91] State v. Campbell, 82 Conn. 671, 74 Atl. 927, 135 Am. St. 293, 18 Ann. Cas. 237; Commonwealth v. Horsfall, 213 Mass. 232, 100 N. E. 362, Ann. Cas. 1914 A, 682.

[92] State v. Block, 87 Conn. 573, 89 Atl. 167, 49 L. R. A. (N. S.) 913; State v. McIver, 175 N. Car. 761, 94 S. E. 682.

woman prescribed that her clothes should be kept saturated with kerosene, as a result of which treatment she died, he was guilty of manslaughter.[93]

It has been held, however, that when a licensed physician, or even a person who assumes the character of a physician whether licensed or not, through ignorance administers medicine which causes the death of the patient, with an honest intention and expectation of a cure, he is not guilty of felonious homicide. Such was the view of Lord Hale.[94] But, as said by Justice Holmes, "Lord Hale himself admitted that other persons might make themselves liable by wreckless conduct. We doubt if he meant to deny that a physician might do so, as well as any one else. He has not been so understood in later times."[95] And many modern English cases are in harmony with Justice Holmes' view.[96]

§ 381. Treatment or operation by physician—Bishop's view.—"From the relationship of physician and patient the death of the latter not unfrequently arises. On this subject the doctrine seemed to have been held that whenever one undertakes to cure another of disease, or to perform on him a surgical operation, he renders himself thereby liable to the criminal law, if he does not carry to this duty some degree of skill, though what degree may not be clear; consequently, if the patient dies through his ill treatment, he is indictable for manslaughter. On the other hand, a more humane doctrine is laid down, that, since it is lawful and commendable for one to cure another, if he undertakes this office in good faith, and adopts the treatment he deems best, he is not liable

93 Commonwealth v. Pierce, 138 Mass. 165, 52 Am. Rep. 264.

94 1 Hale P. C. 429; Commonwealth v. Thompson, 6 Mass. 134, 3 Wheeler Cr. Cases 312; State v. Schultz, 55 Iowa 628, 8 N. W. 469, 39 Am. Rep. 187.

95 Commonwealth v. Pierce, 138 Mass. 165, 52 Am. Rep. 264.

96 Reg. v. Whitehead, 3 Car. & K. 202; Reg. v. Markuss, 4 Fost. & F. 356; Reg. v. Spilling, 2 M. & Rob. 107; Reg. v. Chamberlain, 10 Cox Cr. C. 486; Reg. v. Macleod, 12 Cox Cr. C. 534.

to be adjudged a felon; though the treatment should be erroneous, and, in the eyes of those who assume to know all about this subject, which, in truth, is understood by no mortal, grossly wrong; and though he is a person called, by those who deem themselves wise, grossly ignorant of medicine and surgery. The former doctrine seems to be the English one; and so in England a person, whether a licensed medical practitioner or not, who undertakes to deal with the life or health of people, is bound to have competent skill, or suffer criminally for the defect. Now, if a man thinks he has competent skill, and makes no misrepresentation to his patients concerning the amount or kind of medical education actually received by himself, he seems in reason to stand on exactly the foundation occupied by every person who honestly undertakes medical practice after full advantages, so far as concerns his state of mind; and it is the mind to which we look in questions of legal guilt. Any person undertaking a cure, but being grossly careless, and thus producing death, is for a different reason liable to a charge of manslaughter, whether he is a licensed practitioner or not.[97]

§ 382. Homicide arising from nonfeasance.—A homicide which arises from a mere nonfeasance may constitute murder, manslaughter or excusable homicide. The nature of the killing depends upon the circumstances attending the particular case.

§ 383. The duty omitted must be a legal one.—To render a person criminally liable for a homicide which arose from nonfeasance, the proof must show that he neglected to perform a legal duty which he owed to the deceased. Omission to perform a merely moral duty is not criminal. Thus, where a mother omitted to procure the aid of a midwife for her emancipated daughter during child-birth, in consequence of

97 2 Bish. New Crim. L. (8th ed.), § 664; Feige v. State, 128 Ark. 465, 194 S. W. 865.

which neglect the daughter died, the mother was not criminally liable because the duty she omitted to perform was not a legal one.[98]

§ 384. Homicide arising from wilful omission to perform legal duty constitutes murder.—When a person owes to another a legal duty, and is wilfully and inexcusably negligent in failing to perform that duty, as a natural consequence of which the person to whom he owes the duty is killed, the homicide is murder. Parents are under a legal obligation to provide food, shelter and medical attendance for their children, and if they wilfully neglect so to do, and their children die as a result, the parents are guilty of murder.[99] The same principle is applicable to a switchman in the employ of a railroad company. If he wilfully omits to adjust a switch, thereby causing a collision of trains which results in the death of one or more passengers, he is guilty of murder.[1]

§ 385. Homicide arising from gross negligence.—When death is caused by gross negligence the homicide is manslaughter.[2] The principle involved has been recognized in a great variety of cases, including the following: Where, through gross negligence, a person discharges a revolver and kills another;[3] or a physician in treating a patient causes his death;[4] or a switchman causes a collision of trains resulting

[98] Reg. v. Shepherd, 1 Leigh & C. 147, 9 Cox Cr. C. 123.

[99] Reg. v. Conde, 10 Cox Cr. C. 547, Beale's Cases 424. See also Lewis v. State, 72 Ga. 164, 53 Am. Rep. 835; Territory v. Manton, 7 Mont. 162, 14 Pac. 637, 8 Mont. 95, 19 Pac. 387.

[1] State v. O'Brien, 32 N. J. L. 169. See also State v. Dorsey, 118 Ind. 167, 20 N. E. 777, 10 Am. St. 111.

[2] 1 Whart. Crim. L. (11th ed.), § 444. See also 124 Am. St. 322.

[3] State v. Emery, 78 Mo. 77, 47 Am. Rep. 92; State v. Vines, 93 N. Car. 493, 53 Am. Rep. 466; State v. Vance, 17 Iowa 138; Reg. v. Campbell, 11 Cox Cr. C. 323; State v. Hardie, 47 Iowa 647, 29 Am. Rep. 496.

[4] Commonwealth v. Pierce, 138 Mass. 165, 52 Am. Rep. 264, State v. Hardister, 38 Ark. 605, 42 Am. Rep. 5; Reg. v. Chamberlain, 10 Cox Cr. C. 486.

in the death of one or more passengers;[5] or the captain of a vessel fails to stop the boat to rescue a seaman who has fallen overboard and his omission results in the seaman's death;[6] or the motorman of a street-car fails to keep a proper lookout and his omission causes the death of a person;[7] or a person gives intoxicating liquor to a child, in a sufficient quantity, owing to its tender age, to cause its death;[8] or a person runs over another with an automobile, or vehicle of any kind, and causes his death;[9] or a druggist unintentionally gives another a poisonous drug which causes his death;[10] or a parent fails to provide food for his infant child;[11] or a husband to provide food and medicine for his sick and helpless wife.[12] It also applies in any other case where a person owes a legal duty to care for a helpless person. And whether he is to receive compensation for his services or not is immaterial.[13]

5 State v. O'Brien, 32 N. J. L. 169; State v. Dorsey, 118 Ind. 167, 20 N. E. 777, 10 Am. St. 111.

6 United States v. Knowles, 4 Sawy. (U. S.) 517, Fed. Cas. No. 15540.

7 Commonwealth v. Metropolitan R. Co., 107 Mass. 236.

8 Rex v. Martin, 3 Car. & P. 211.

9 Belk v. People, 125 Ill. 584, 17 N. E. 744; White v. State, 84 Ala. 421, 4 So. 598; State v. Campbell, 82 Conn. 671, 74 Atl. 927, 135 Am. St. 293, 18 Ann. Cas. 236; Lee v. State, 1 Cold. (Tenn.) 62.

10 Reg. v. Markuss, 4 Fost. & F. 356; State v. Center, 35 Vt. 378; Rice v. State, 8 Mo. 561.

11 Reg. v. Conde, 10 Cox Cr. C. 547, Beale's Cases 424; Gibson v. Commonwealth, 106 Ky. 360, 50 S. W. 532, 90 Am. St. 230, 20 Ky. L. 1908; Stehr v. State, 92 Nebr. 755, 139 N. W. 676, Ann. Cas. 1914 A, 573, 45 L. R. A. (N. S.) 559; Reg. v. Downes, 13 Cox Cr. C. 111, Beale's Cases 195, Derby's Cases 97. See also Reg. v. Nicholls, 13 Cox Cr. C. 75, Beale's Cases 193.

12 State v. Smith, 65 Maine, 257; Reg. v. Plummer, 1 Car. & K. 600. See also Westrup v. Commonwealth, 123 Ky. 95, 93 S. W. 646, 6 L. R. A. (N. S.) 685n, 124 Am. St. 316.

13 Reg. v. Instan (1893), 1 Q. B. Div. 450, 17 Cox Cr. C. 602, Beale's Cases 198; Reg. v. Marriott, 8 Car. & P. 425. See also Reg. v. Downes, 13 Cox Cr. C. 111, Beale's Cases 195, Derby's Cases 97; Steph. Dig. Crim. L., art. 213.

It is to be observed, however, that inability on the part of the accused constitutes a defense, provided he has reported the matter to the public authorities, where public aid to sick or helpless paupers is provided by law.[14] Moreover, if the neglected person could have saved himself from death the accused is not criminally liable.[15]

A person, engaged in operating a mine, who through gross negligence causes the death of another, is guilty of manslaughter. Thus, where an engineer, in charge of a steam-engine used to draw up miners from a coal pit, left his engine in charge of an ignorant boy, who was unable to stop it, as a result of which the skip was drawn over the pulley and one of the miners thrown down into the shaft and killed, the engineer was guilty of manslaughter.[16] The ground bailiff of a mine, whose duty it is to regulate the ventilation of the mine, and direct where air-headings should be placed, who is guilty of gross negligence in omitting to perform his duty, thereby causing an explosion of fire-damp which produces death, is guilty of manslaughter.[17]

§ 386. Homicide arising from omission to perform legal duty owing to religious scruples.—A good motive is no defense to a criminal charge. It follows, therefore, that a conscientious belief in the faith cure, or religious scruples against the use of drugs, is no excuse for omitting to perform a legal duty. Medical attendance and remedies are considered necessaries, both in England and in this country; and a person who owes a legal duty to another to provide him with such, and who is able to do so, is criminally responsible for

[14] Reg. v. Mabbett, 5 Cox Cr. C. 339; Reg. v. Philpott, 6 Cox Cr. C. 140; Reg. v. Hogan, 2 Den. Cr. C. 277, 5 Cox Cr. C. 255.

[15] Reg. v. Shepherd, Leigh & C. 147, 9 Cox Cr. C. 123.

[16] Reg. v. Lowe, 3 Car. & K. 123, Beale's Cases 192, Derby's Cases 50.

[17] Reg. v. Haines, 2 Car. & K. 368, Beale's Cases 170.

refusing because of conscientious religious scruples.[18] There are cases, however, holding the contrary.[19] The same principle is applicable where a person does not believe in the expediency of vaccination. His belief, in such case, will not exempt him from criminal liability for violating a statute which requires it to be done.[20]

§ 387. Homicide arising from negligence less than gross.—As heretofore stated, to render a person liable for involuntary manslaughter he must be guilty of gross negligence. Where, however, his negligence falls short of being gross, the killing constitutes excusable homicide.[21]

18 State v. Chenoweth, 163 Ind. 94, 71 N. E. 197; Reg. v. Senior, 1 Q. B. Div. 283, 19 Cox Cr. C. 219; Reg. v. Downes, 13 Cox Cr. C. 111, Beale's Cases 195, Derby's Cases 97; Rex v. Brooks, 9 Brit. Col. 13; People v. Pierson, 176 N. Y. 201, 68 N. E. 243, 63 L. R. A. 187, 98 Am. St. 666. See also Owens v. State, 6 Okla. Cr. 110, 116 Pac. 345, Ann. Cas. 1913 B, 1218n.

19 State v. Sanford 99 Maine 441, 59 Atl. 597; Justice v. State, 116 Ga. 605, 42 S. E. 1013, 59 L. R. A. 601.

20 Commonwealth v. Pear, 183 Mass. 242, 66 N. E. 719, 67 L. R. A. 935 (affd., 197 U. S. 11, 49 L. ed. 643, 25 Supp. Ct. 358).

21 4 Bl. Comm. 182; State v. Benham, 23 Iowa 154, 92 Am. Dec. 416; Pinder v. State, 27 Fla. 370, 8 So. 837, 26 Am. St. 75.

CHAPTER XX.

MAYHEM.

§ 390. Definition.—Mayhem consists in maliciously and wilfully causing an injury to some part of a person's body whereby he is rendered less able in fighting to defend himself or annoy his adversary.

Hawkins defines it as "a hurt of any part of a man's body whereby he is rendered less able, in fighting, either to defend himself or to annoy his adversary."[1] Blackstone defines it as "the violently depriving another of the use of such of his members as may render him the less able in fighting, either to defend himself or to annoy his adversary."[2] This definition, however, is faulty, as a person may be guilty of mayhem in causing an injury to himself. Thus, a person who maims himself to avoid impressment as a soldier or sailor,

[1] 1 Hawk. P. C. (Curw. ed.), p. 107, § 1. See also 1 East P. C. 393; Reg. v. Hagan, 8 Car. & P. 167, 171; Commonwealth v. Newell, 7 Mass. 245; State v. Johnson, 58 Ohio St. 417, 51 N. E. 40, 65 Am. St. 769n; Foster v. People, 50 N. Y. 598, Derby's Cases 325.

[2] 4 Bl. Comm. 205.

or to render himself more an object of pity for the purpose or obtaining alms, is guilty of the crime.[3]

§ 391. Nature of the crime at common law.—At the old common law, the part of the body injured, rather than the seriousness of the injury, determined the nature of the offense. The question was, did the injury impair the man's ability to fight or defend himself? "For," as said by Lord Coke, "the life and members of every subject are under the safeguard and protection of the law * * * to the end that they may serve the king and their country when occasion shall be offered."[4] To cut off, disable or weaken, a man's hand, finger or foot; or to knock out an eye or front tooth; or to castrate him; or break his skull, constituted mayhem at the old common law. But to bite off a man's ear, or nose, was not mayhem; for, as said by Hawkins, "they do not weaken, but only disfigure him."[5] It is to be observed, therefore, that, at the old common law, injuries which merely disfigured a person, no matter how seriously, did not constitute mayhem.

It is also to be observed that to constitute an act of mayhem the injury inflicted must result in a permanent disability. As said by Blackstone, the party injured must be "forever disabled from making so good a defense against future external injuries as he otherwise might have done."[6]

§ 392. Early English statutes.—The chief early English statutes on the subject of mayhem, and which form part of our common law, are the following: 5 Hen. IV, ch. 5; 37 Hen. VIII, ch. 6, and 22, 23 Charles II, ch. 1.

[3] Wright's Case, Beale's Cases 145; 1 Hawk. P. C. 108; 1 Russ. Law of Crimes (9th Am. ed) 852.

[4] Coke's Inst. 127a.

[5] 1 Hawk. P. C. 107. See also 1 East P. C. 393, 3 Bl. Comm. 121; 4 Bl. Comm. 205; Chick v. State, 7 Humph. (Tenn.) 161; State v. Johnson, 58 Ohio St. 417, 51 N. E. 40, 65 Am. St. 760n.

[6] 3 Bl. Comm. 121.

§ 393. The Coventry Act—The modern English statute.— The act of 22, 23 Charles II, is commonly known as the Coventry Act. This name was given to it owing to the fact that it was occasioned by an assault on Sir John Coventry in the street, and slitting his nose by persons who lay in wait for him for that purpose, in revenge, as was supposed, for some obnoxious words uttered by him in parliament, in which he had reflected upon the profligacy of the king.

This act provides "that if any person or persons shall, on purpose and of malice aforethought, by lying in wait, unlawfully cut out or disable the tongue, put out an eye, slit the nose, cut off a nose or lip, or cut off or disable any limb or member of any subject, with intention in so doing to maim or disfigure him in any of the manners before mentioned; that then the person or persons so offending, their counsellors, aiders, and abettors, knowing of and privy to the offense as aforesaid, shall be declared to be felons, and suffer death as in cases of felony without benefit of clergy."[7]

§ 394. American statutes.—In most of the states statutes have been enacted extending the scope of mayhem as it existed at the ancient common law. Many of these statutes are modeled, in a large measure at least, upon the Coventry Act. They provide, very generally, that mayhem shall include disfiguring a person, by putting out his eye,[8] biting off his ear,[9] slitting his nose,[10] etc., as well as to injure him in such a way as to render him less able to fight or defend himself. Breaking the skull is generally considered not mayhem under our statutes.[11]

[7] 1 East P. C. 394. For a definition of Mayhem as understood in England today, see the Offenses Against the Person Act, 24 & 25 Vict., ch. 100.

[8] Chick v. State, 7 Humph. (Tenn.) 161; State v. Ma Foo (Baker), 110 Mo. 7, 19 S. W. 222, 33 Am. St. 414. See also State v. Johnson, 58 Ohio St. 417, 51 N. E. 40, 65 Am. St. 769n.

[9] State v. Skidmore, 87 N. Car. 509; Godfrey v. People, 63 N. Y. 207; People v. Golden, 62 Cal. 542.

[10] State v. Mairs, 1 N. J. L. 518.

[11] Foster v. People, 50 N. Y. 598, Derby's Cases 374.

§ 395. Injury to genital organs.—Castration constitutes mayhem, even at common law,[12] and it has been held mayhem to commit this offense upon a slave.[13]

Malicious injury to the genital organs of a female was not mayhem at the old common law; but in some states it is made mayhem by statute.[14]

§ 396. Means used to inflict the injury.—Under most statutes the means employed to inflict the injury is immaterial. Thus, it may constitute mayhem to put out another's eye by throwing corrosive acid into it;[15] or to disable another's arm by shooting it;[16] or to bite off another's nose, where the statute makes it mayhem to "cut off the nose of another";[17] or to disable another by kicking him.[18] It has been held, however, under an English statute, that biting off the end of a person's nose, or biting off a joint from a person's finger, is not mayhem; that to constitute mayhem the injury must be done by means of an instrument.[19]

§ 397. Nature of the criminal intent involved—Presumption—Premeditation.—To constitute mayhem the injury must be inflicted wilfully and maliciously.[20] A general criminal intent is not sufficient. Under some statutes a specific

12 4 Bl. Comm. 206. See also People v. Schoedde, 126 Cal. 373, 58 Pac. 859; State v. Sheldon, 54 Mont. 185, 169 Pac. 37; Henry v. State, 125 Ark. 237, 188 S. W. 539.

13 Worley v. State, 11 Humph. (Tenn.) 172; Eskridge v. State, 25 Ala. 30.

14 Kitchens v. State, 80 Ga. 810, 812, 7 S. E. 209. See also Moore v. State, 3 Pin. (Wis.) 373, 4 Chand. 168; Rex v. Cox, Russ. & R. 362.

15 State v. Ma Foo (Baker), 110 Mo. 7, 19 S. W. 222, 33 Am. St. 414. See also Lee v. State (Tex. Cr.), 148 S. W. 567, 40 L. R. A. (N. S.) 1132.

16 Baker v. State, 4 Ark. 56; United States v. Scroggins, Hempst. (U. S.) 478.

17 State v. Mairs, 1 N. J. L. 518; State v. Enkhouse, 40 Nev. 1, 160 Pac. 23 (biting off portion of an ear sufficient).

18 Reg. v. Duffill, 1 Cox Cr. C. 49.

19 Rex v. Harris, 7 Car. & P. 446, 32 E. C. L. 700.

20 Molette v. State, 49 Ala. 18; Terrell v. State, 86 Tenn. 523, 8 S. W. 212; State v. Girkin, 23 N. Car. 121; State v. Ma Foo (Baker), 110 Mo. 7, 19 S. W. 222, 33 Am. St. 414; State v. Bloedow, 45 Wis. 279; State v. Cody, 18 Ore. 506, 23 Pac. 891, 24 Pac. 895.

intent to maim or disfigure is essential.[21] Under others a wilful and malicious intent is sufficient.[22] Moreover, under the latter statutes malice toward the injured person is not necessary; it may consist in an evil design in general, an intention to do evil, a wicked and corrupt motive.[23]

The requisite intent, however, may be presumed from the circumstances which surrounded the act.[24] This is owing to the fact that a person is presumed to have intended the natural and probable consequences of his voluntary act.[25] No presumption arises, however, where the result is not the natural and probable consequence of the act. Thus, where the defendant threw a stone at another and put out his eye the court held that the mere throwing of the stone did not raise a presumption of the requisite intent to constitute mayhem.[26] On the other hand, where the means used and the mode of using it would ordinarily result in mayhem, the law presumes the requisite intent, irrespective of the wrongdoer's lack of knowledge that the means used and the mode of using it were not calculated to maim.[27]

At common law, and under some statutes, premeditation is not an essential element of mayhem.[28] Under some stat-

21 State v. Jones, 70 Iowa 505, 30 N. W. 750; State v. Ma Foo (Baker), 110 Mo. 7, 19 S. W. 222, 33 Am. St. 414; State v. Mairs, 1 N. J. L. 518; State v. Cody, 18 Ore. 506, 23 Pac. 891, 24 Pac. 895.

22 Terrell v. State, 86 Tenn. 523, 8 S. W. 212; Bowers v. State, 24 Tex. App. 542, 7 S. W. 247, 5 Am. St. 901.

23 Terrell v. State, 86 Tenn. 523, 8 S. W. 212.

24 State v. Jones, 70 Iowa 505, 30 N. W. 750; State v. Ma Foo (Baker), 110 Mo. 7, 19 S. W. 222, 33 Am. St. 414; State v. Hair, 37 Minn. 351, 34 N. W. 893; State v. Mairs, 1 N. J. L. 518.

25 Ridenour v. State, 38 Ohio St. 272; United States v. Gunther, 5 Dak. 234, 38 N. W. 79.

26 State v. Bloedow, 45 Wis. 279.

27 Davis v. State, 22 Tex. App. 45, 2 S. W. 630. See also High v. State, 26 Tex. App. 545, 10 S. W. 235, 8 Am. St. 488.

28 1 East P. C. 393; State v. Jones, 70 Iowa 505, 30 N. W. 750; Terrell v. State, 86 Tenn. 523, 8 S. W. 212; State v. Bloedow, 45 Wis. 279; State v. Simmons, 3 Ala. 497.

utes, however, some act showing premeditation and deliberation, such as lying in wait, is essential.[29]

§ 398. Injury inflicted in self-defense.—When the injury is inflicted in necessary self-defense, to save one's life or prevent grievous bodily injury, the act is not mayhem.[30]

§ 399. Felony or misdemeanor—At common law—By statute.—Whether mayhem was a felony or a misdemeanor under the English common law is a question upon which the decisions are not harmonious. Some hold that it was a felony,[31] while others hold that it was only a misdemeanor.[32] This want of harmony probably has grown out of the fact that mayhem, under the English common law, passed through two stages, in the earlier one of which it was a felony and in the other a misdemeanor. Originally, according to the lex talionis, the penalty for mayhem was membrum pro membro.[33] But after the law of retaliation became obsolete, mayhem, perhaps barring castration, came to be looked upon as a crime in the nature of an aggravated trespass, and it became punishable as a misdemeanor.[34]

The Coventry Act made it a felony punishable with death. The penalty, however, did not include corruption of blood or forfeiture of estate.[35]

[29] Godfrey v. People, 63 N. Y. 207.

[30] State v. Danforth, 3 Conn. 112; State v. Skidmore, 87 N. Car. 509. See also State v. Abram, 10 Ala. 928; People v. Wright, 93 Cal. 564, 29 Pac. 240; Green v. State, 151 Ala. 14, 44 So. 194, 15 Ann. Cas. 81.

[31] 1 Hawk. P. C., ch. 44; 1 East P. C. 393; 4 Bl. Comm. 206; 1 Russ. L. of Crimes (9th Am. ed.) 971; Commonwealth v. Porter, 1 Pittsb. (Pa.) 502.

[32] Commonwealth v. Lester, 2 Va. Cas. 198; Commonwealth v. Newell, 7 Mass. 245.

[33] 1 Hawk. P. C., ch. 44; 4 Bl. Comm. 206; 1 East P. C. 393; Foster v. People, 50 N. Y. 598.

[34] 4 Bl. Comm. 206, 1 East P. C. 393, 1 Russ. L. of Crimes (9th Am. ed.) 971.

[35] 1 East P. C. 394.

The statutes of this country very generally make it a felony.[36] Under an early Massachusetts statute, however, it was held a misdemeanor.[37]

[36] Baker v. State, 4 Ark. 56; Molette v. State, 49 Ala. 18; State v. Brown, 60 Mo. 141; Clark v. State, 23 Miss. 261.

[37] Commonwealth v. Newell, 7 Mass. 245.

CHAPTER XXI.

MURDER.

§ 405. Definition—Coke's description—Requisites.—Murder is the killing of a human being without justification or excuse and with malice aforethought, express or implied. According to Sir Edward Coke murder is committed when a person of sound memory and discretion unlawfully kills any reasonable creature in being, and under the king's peace, with malice aforethought, either express or implied.[1]

To constitute murder the following conditions are essential:

[1] 3 Coke's Inst. 47; Hornsby v. State (Ala. App.), 75 So. 637; State v. McGarrity, 140 La. 436, 73 So. 259; Killian v. State, 19 Ga. App. 750, 92 S. E. 227; Little v. Commonwealth, 177 Ky. 24, 197 S. W. 514; State v. Lichter (Del.), 102 Atl. 529.

(1) The slayer must be of sound mind and discretion.

(2) The victim must be a reasonable creature in being, as distinguished from an unborn child.

(3) The slayer, at the time of the homicide, must entertain malice aforethought.

(4) The victim must die within a year and a day after the act.

§ 406. **Mental capacity of the slayer.**—The slayer, as heretofore stated, must be of sound mind and discretion at the time the act is committed. If his mind is diseased, so that he is incapable of distinguishing between right and wrong as to the act committed, or, according to some decisions, though he is capable of distinguishing between right and wrong as to that act, but, owing to want of power of control he is incapable of eschewing it, he lacks capacity to commit murder; or, if his mind is so immature that he lacks capacity to entertain legal malice, he can not be guilty of murder.

§ 407. **Victim must be a human being.**—It is not murder to terminate the life of an unborn child. It is Coke's view that "If a woman be quick with child, and by a potion or otherwise killeth it in her womb; or if a man beat her, whereby the child dieth in her body, and she is delivered of a dead child, this is a great misprision, and no murder."[2] And as said by Bishop, "A child within its mother's womb is not a being on whom a felonious homicide can be committed; it must be born."[3]

[2] 3 Coke's Inst. 50. See also 1 Hale P. C. 433.

[3] 2 Bish. New Crim. L. (8th ed.), § 632.

§ 408. Independent circulation.—To be fully born a child must have independent circulation.[4] It is possible, however, for a child to have a potential independence prior to its actual independence. An example of this is where a child is severed from its dead mother by the Cæsarean operation and survives. But even in this case an actual independence is essential to constitute the child a living human being.[5]

§ 409. Independent respiration.—Must a child have breathed independently of its mother to render it a living human being? Upon this question the authorities are not harmonious. It is Caspar's view that "In foro the term 'life' must be regarded as perfectly synonymous with 'respiration'. Life means respiration. Not to have breathed is not to have lived."[6] Bishop's opinion is that "neither need the child have breathed, if otherwise it had life and an independent circulation."[7] And according to Justice Park, "A child must be actually wholly in the world in a living state to be the subject of a charge of murder; but if it has been wholly born, and is alive, it is not essential that it should have breathed at the time it was killed; as many children are born alive, and yet do not breathe for sometime after their birth."[8] The latter view is in accord with the weight of modern authority.

§ 410. Severance of the umbilical cord.—Can a child be fully born before the severance of the umbilical cord? Upon this question, also, the authorities are not harmonious. Bishop answers it in the affirmative.[9] According to the

[4] State v. Winthrop, 43 Iowa 519, 22 Am. Rep. 257; Evans v. People, 49 N. Y. 86; Wallace v. State, 7 Tex. App. 570, 10 Tex. App. 255; State v. Prude, 76 Miss. 543, 24 So. 871; Rex v. Brain, 6 Car. & P. 349.

[5] State v. Winthrop, 43 Iowa 519, 22 Am. Rep. 257.

[6] 3 Casper Forensic Med. 33.

[7] 2 Bish. New Crim. L. (8th ed.), § 632. See also Rex v. Brain, 6 Car. & P. 349.

[8] Rex v. Brain, 6 Car. & P. 349.

[9] 2 Bish. New Crim. L. (8th ed.), § 632.

better view, however, as well as the weight of modern authority, a child is not fully born, and therefore not the subject of homicide, until the umbilical cord has been severed.[10]

§ 411. **Effect of premature birth.**—The fact that the child is born prematurely, that is, before the full period of gestation has elapsed, is immaterial. Hence, where a person unlawfully causes the premature delivery of a woman, and the child is born alive but subsequently succumbs owing to the fact of its premature birth, the person who thus causes its premature birth is guilty of murder.[11] "If the child be born alive, and dieth of the potion, battery, or other cause, this is murder."[12]

§ 412. **Malice aforethought—Express and implied.**—The distinguishing feature between murder and manslaughter is malice aforethought. Its presence is essential to make the crime murder.

In its ordinary sense, the term malice means hatred or ill-will. In the crime of murder, however, it has a technical meaning. In this sense it includes wicked and corrupt motives, as well as hatred or ill-will.

Malice is either express or implied. To constitute express malice there must be an actual intent to kill. "Express malice is when one, with a sedate, deliberate mind and formed design, doth kill another; which formed design is evidenced by external circumstances discovering that inward intention; as lying in wait, antecedent menaces, former grudges and concerted schemes."[13]

[10] Clark & M. Law of Crimes (2d ed.) 311, § 234. See also State v. Winthrop, 43 Iowa 519, 22 Am. Rep. 257.

[11] 2 Bish. New Crim. L. (8th ed.), § 633; Reg. & West, 2 Car. & K. 784. See also Rex v. Senior, 1 Moody 346.

[12] 2 Bish. New Crim. L. (8th ed.), § 633. See also 1 Hale P. C. 433.

[13] 4 Bl. Comm. 198. See also McWhirt's Case, 3 Grat. (Va.) 594, 46 Am. Dec. 196; McCoy v. State, 25 Tex. 33, 78 Am. Dec. 520; State v. Prettyman, 6 Boyce (29 Del.) 452, 100 Atl. 476.

Implied malice, on the other hand, is malice which is inferred from conduct on the part of the slayer which indicates an abandoned state of mind, fatally bent on mischief; and which is equivalent in the eye of the law to an actual intent to kill. Such malice may emanate from conduct which manifests cruelty of disposition and recklessness of consequences.[14] The law infers guilty intention from reckless conduct; and where the recklessness is of such a character as to justify this inference it is the same as if the accused had deliberately intended the act committed.[15]

§ 413. Actual intent to kill not essential.—To constitute a homicide murder an actual intent to kill is not essential. A sane person is presumed to have intended the natural and probable consequences of his voluntary acts. Hence, when he voluntarily does an act which has a direct tendency to destroy another's life the necessary conclusion is that he intended to so destroy such person's life.[16]

§ 414. Malice presumed from the act.—Upon principle, a legal presumption should not arise from the mere fact of homicide. As said by Judge Cooley, "As the majority of the homicides are not, in fact, malicious, but occur through misadventure, or under circumstances which would reduce the offense to manslaughter, a legal presumption of malice

[14] McClain v. Commonwealth, 110 Pa. St. 263, 1 Atl. 45. See also State v. Capps, 134 N. Car. 622, 46 S. E. 730; Commonwealth v. Cleary, 135 Pa. St. 64, 19 Atl. 1017, 8 L. R. A. 301, Derby's Cases 352; United States v. Outerbridge, 5 Sawy. (U. S.) 620, Fed. Cas. No. 15978, Derby's Cases 341; State v. Prettyman, 6 Boyce (29 Del.) 452, 100 Atl. 476.

[15] Pool v. State, 87 Ga. 526, 13 S. E. 556; Holt v. State, 89 Ga. 316, 15 S. E. 316; Commonwealth v. Chance, 174 Mass. 245, 54 N. E. 551, 75 Am. St. 306; People v. Huther, 184 N. Y. 237, 77 N. E. 6, Derby's Cases 347.

[16] Commonwealth v. Webster, 5 Cush. (Mass.) 295, 52 Am. Dec. 711n, Knowlton's Cases 140; Commonwealth v. York, 9 Metc. (Mass.) 93, 103, 43 Am. Dec. 373. See also State v. Levelle, 34 S. Car. 120, 13 S. E. 319, 27 Am. St. 799; Goodman v. State (Ala. App.), 72 So. 687.

seems inconsistent with the general doctrines of the criminal law, as well as with humanity."[17] Best takes an opposite view: "Although the law never presumes guilt or fraud in the first instance, yet it is held, that where a homicide has once been proved, the law will presume that it was done maliciously, and casts on the party accused the onus of proving either his complete justification or excuse, or such palliating circumstances as may reduce the offense to manslaughter."[18] This view is in accord with Foster's[19] and Blackstone's,[20] and is also supported by the great weight of authority. But, upon principle, as heretofore stated, no legal presumption of malice should arise from the mere fact of homicide. On the other hand, however, the surrounding circumstances may give rise to a presumption of facts.[21]

§ 415. Malice presumed from the use of a deadly weapon.—When a person, without justification, excuse or extenuating circumstances, commits homicide with a deadly weapon, malice is always presumed.[22] A deadly weapon is one likely to produce death or great bodily injury.[23] Some instruments are deadly weapons per se.[24]

As a general rule, when a homicide is committed by striking with the fists, or kicking with the feet, and the slayer has no actual intent to kill, or cause serious bodily harm, the necessary malice to render the offense murder is not

[17] Cooley's Bl. Comm. bk. 4, 201n.

[18] Best's Right to Begin and Reply, § 20.

[19] Foster C. L. 255.

[20] 4 Bl. Comm. 201.

[21] Dukes v. State, 14 Fla. 499; Maher v. People, 10 Mich. 212, 81 Am. Dec. 781; Farris v. Commonwealth, 14 Bush (Ky.) 362; State v. Swayze, 30 La. Ann. 1323; Clem v. State, 31 Ind. 480; Eiland v. State, 52 Ala. 322; 2 Bish. Crim. L. (8th ed.), § 673; 1 Whart. Crim. L. (11th ed.), §§ 437-439. See also Review of the trial of Prof. Webster, by Geo. Bemis, Esq., 72 North American Review 178.

[22] Grey's Case, Kelyng 64, Beale's Cases 463.

[23] McNary v. People, 32 Ill. App. 58.

[24] Hamilton v. People, 113 Ill. 34, 55 Am. Rep. 396; Greschia v. People, 53 Ill. 295; Silgar v. People, 107 Ill. 563.

implied.[25] On the other hand, when the circumstances surrounding a homicide manifest an abandoned and wicked heart, malice is implied.[26] It may be implied from setting fire to a building in which there are persons.[27]

§ 416. Wilful omission to perform a legal duty.—When death is caused by the negligent act of another the homicide, ordinarily, is manslaughter. But when it is caused by a wilful neglect to perform a legal duty it is murder. Thus, if a switchman of a railroad company is grossly negligent in failing to perform his duty in adjusting the tracks, thereby causing death, the homicide is manslaughter; but if his will concurred in his negligence he is guilty of murder.[28]

§ 417. Deliberation and premeditation.—Deliberation and premeditation are not essential elements of common-law murder. No specific time must necessarily elapse between the intent to kill and the overt act to render the homicide murder. It is sufficient if the malicious intention precedes and accompanies the overt act.[29]

§ 418. Deliberation and premeditation—Statutory degrees of murder.—At common law, murder is not divided

[25] Wellar v. People, 30 Mich. 16.

[26] Mayes v. People, 106 Ill. 306, 46 Am. Rep. 698. See also Whart. on Homicide (3rd ed.), 104; 2 Starkie Ev. 951; Adams v. People, 109 Ill. 444, 50 Am. Rep. 617; Maulding v. Commonwealth, 172 Ky. 370, 189 S. W. 251.

[27] Reg. v. Serne, 16 Cox Cr. C. 311, Derby's Cases 343.

[28] State v. O'Brien, 32 N. J. L. 169. See also Territory v. Manton, 7 Mont. 162, 14 Pac. 637.

[29] State v. Anderson, 2 Overt. (Tenn.) 6, 5 Am. Dec. 648. See also Commonwealth v. Webster, 5 Cush. (Mass.) 295, 52 Am. Dec. 711n, Knowlton's Cases 140; Commonwealth v. York, 9 Metc. (Mass.) 93, 43 Am. Dec. 373; Peri v. People, 65 Ill. 17; State v. Hockett, 70 Iowa 442, 30 N. W. 742; Nye v. People, 35 Mich. 16; Leighton v. People, 88 N. Y. 117, Beale's Cases 472; Cook v. State, 77 Ga. 96; State v. Moore, 69 N. Car. 267; Green v. State, 13 Mo. 382; State v. Ashley, 45 La. Ann. 1036; 13 So. 738; State v. Coffey, 174 N. Car. 814, 94 S. E. 416; State v. Walker, 173 N. Car. 780, 92 S. E. 327.

into degrees. In many states, however, there are statutes which divide murder into degrees. In most states it is divided into two degrees, but in a few states it is divided into three degrees.

Pennsylvania was the first state to divide murder into degrees. The statute was passed March 31, 1860, and provided that all murder which should be perpetrated by means of poison, or by lying in wait, or by any other kind of wilful, deliberate, and premeditated killing, or which should be committed in the perpetration of, or attempt to perpetrate, any arson, rape, robbery, or burglary, should be deemed murder of the first degree; and all other kinds of murder should be deemed murder of the second degree.[30]

The statutes of the various states in which murder is divided into degrees are not entirely harmonious,[31] but in most of them murder in the first degree consists in homicide in which there is actual intent to kill coupled with premeditation or deliberation, or, in homicide which is committed, though unintentionally, in the perpetration of certain felonies, such as rape, robbery, burglary, or arson.

§ 419. Meaning of terms "premeditation" and "deliberation."—The terms "premeditation" and "deliberation," as used in these statutes, are not synonymous. The former implies merely "previous contrivance or formed design," while the latter implies "reflection, however brief, upon the act before committing it; fixed and determined purpose, as distinguished from sudden impulse."[32] Thus, a homicide

[30] Penn. Pub. Stats., Act 1860, No. 374; P. L. 402, §§ 74, 75. See also Act 1893, P. L. 17; People v. Page (Mich.), 165 N. W. 755.

[31] Mass. Rev. Laws (1902), ch. 207, § 1; Penal Code of N. Y., §§ 183-187.

[32] Cent. Dict. and Cyc. "Premeditation" and "Deliberation." See also Copeland v. State, 7 Humph. (Tenn.) 479; Fahnestock v. State, 23 Ind. 231; Leighton v. People, 88 N. Y. 117, Beale's Cases 472; Harris v. State, 36 Ark. 127; Commonwealth v. Drum, 58 Pa. St. 9.

committed on a sudden impulse may be premeditated, owing to the intent to kill, and at the same time not deliberate. "An act co-existent with and inseparable from a sudden impulse, although premeditated, could not be deemed deliberate, as when under a sudden and great provocation one instantly, although intentionally, kills another. But the statute is not satisfied unless the intention was deliberated upon. If the impulse is followed by reflection, that is deliberation; hesitation, epen, may imply deliberation; so may threats against another, and selection of means with which to perpetrate the deed. If, therefore, the killing is not the instant effect of impulse, if there is hesitation or doubt to be overcome, a choice made as the result of thought, however short the struggle between the intention and the act, it is sufficient to characterize the crime as deliberate and premeditated murder."[83] "The deliberation and premeditation required by the statute are not upon the intent, but upon the killing. It is deliberation and premeditation enough to form the intent to kill, and not upon the intent after it has been formed. An intent distinctly formed, even 'for a moment' before it is carried into act, is enough."[84]

§ 420. Murder in the second degree.—In those states in which murder is divided into two degrees all murder which falls short of being murder in the first degree is, of course, murder in the second degree. And what was murder at common law is still murder under the statutes which divide it into degrees. In other words, these statutes have not changed the scope of murder as it existed at common law.[85]

[83] Leighton v. People, 88 N. Y. 117, Beale's Cases 472. See also State v. Williams, 69 Mo. 110; McDaniel v. Commonwealth, 77 Va. 281; Miller v. State, 54 Ala. 155; Wright v. Commonwealth, 33 Grat. (Va.) 880; People v. Kiernan, 101 N. Y. 618, 4 N. E. 130; Binns v. State, 66 Ind. 428; Atkinson v. State, 20 Tex. 522; Schlencker v. State, 9 Nebr. 241, 1 N. W. 857.

[84] Keenan v. Commonwealth, 44 Pa. St. 55, 56, 84 Am. Dec. 414; State v. Rodriguez (N. Mex.), 167 Pac. 420; State v. Coffey, 174 N. Car. 814, 94 S. E. 416.

[85] State v. Decklotts, 19 Iowa 447; Parker v. State, 24 Wyo. 491,

§ 421. **Suicide.**—At common law, suicide, or self-murder, was a crime punishable by forfeiture of the felon's estate and interment in the highway with a stake driven through his body.[36] These penalties, however, have been abolished.[37]

Where one person persuades another to kill himself, the former is guilty of murder. If present when the act is committed, he is a principal in the second degree; and if absent, he is an accessory before the fact.[38]

Where a person in attempting to commit suicide accidentally kills another, he is guilty of felonious homicide. But whether the offense is murder or manslaughter is a question upon which the courts express doubt.[39] Where two persons enter into a compact to kill themselves together and the means employed causes the death of only one of them the survivor is guilty of murder.[40]

At common law an attempt to commit suicide is a misdemeanor.[41] In some states, however, including Massachusetts, it is not punishable.[42]

161 Pac. 552; State v. Marino, 91 Vt. 237, 99 Atl. 882; State v. Prettyman, 6 Boyce (29 Del.) 452, 100 Atl. 476; State v. Burton, 172 N. Car. 939, 90 S. E. 561.

36 Commonwealth v. Mink, 123 Mass. 422, 25 Am. Rep. 109, Beale's Cases 206.

37 4 Geo. IV, ch. 52. See also 45 and 46 Vict., ch. 19.

38 Commonwealth v. Mink, 123 Mass. 422, 25 Am. Rep. 109, Beale's Cases 206; Commonwealth v. Bowen, 13 Mass 356, 7 Am. Dec. 154, Wheeler Cr. C. 226; 4 Bl. Comm. 189. See also Burnett v. People, 204 Ill. 208, 68 N. E. 505, 66 L. R. A. 304, 98 Am. St. 206.

39 Commonwealth v. Mink, 123 Mass. 422, 25 Am. Rep. 109, Beale's Cases 206; State v. Lindsey, 19 Nev. 47, 5 Pac. 822, 3 Am. St. 776; State v. Levelle, 34 S. Car. 120, 13 S. E. 319, 27 Am. St. 799.

40 Reg. v. Alison, 8 Car. & P. 418; Rex v. Tyson, Russ. & R. 523; Reg. v. Jessop, 16 Cox Cr. C. 204, 10 Crim. L. Mag. 862; Rex v. Abbott, 67 J. P. 151. See also Burnett v. People, 204 Ill. 208, 68 N. E. 505, 66 L. R. A. 304, 98 Am. St. 206.

41 Reg. v. Doody, 6 Cox Cr. C. 463, Beale's Cases 261; State v. Carney, 69 N. J. L. 478, 55 Atl. 44.

42 Commonwealth v. Dennis, 105 Mass. 162.

§ 422. **Proof of the corpus delicti.**—To convict a person of felonious homicide the law requires clear proof of the corpus delicti. The corpus delicti includes two things: (1) The fact of death; and (2) the fact that it was effected by means of human agency. Whether the corpus delicti can be established solely by circumstantial evidence or not is a question upon which the authorities are not agreed.[43] All agree, however, that the evidence upon this point must be clear and convincing to sustain a conviction.[44]

[43] 4 Bl. Comm. 358.

[44] People v. Videto, 1 Parker Cr. R. (N. Y.) 603; Tawell's Case, cited in Willis' Cir. Ev. (5th Am. ed.) 204; People v. Wilson, 3 Park. Cr. R. (N. Y.) 199, Starkie Ev. (10th Am. ed.) 862; 3 Greenl. Ev. (16th ed.), §§ 30, 131; Burr. Cir. Ev., § 682. See also Wills' Cir. Ev. 156-170; Whart. Crim. L (11th ed.), §§ 349-363; Best on Presump. 271-276; 3 Russ. on Crimes (6th ed.) 158; Ruloff v. People, 18 N. Y. 179, Knowlton's Cases 124.

CHAPTER XXII.

RAPE

§ 425. Definition.—Rape consists in the act of having carnal knowledge, by a man, of a woman other than his wife, forcibly and against her will, or without her conscious permission, or where her permission has been extorted by force or fear of immediate bodily injury.

Among other definitions by standard authorities are the following: "Rape is the unlawful carnal knowledge of a woman by force and against her will;"[1] "rape is when a man hath carnal knowledge of a woman by force and against her will;"[2] "rape is the carnal knowledge of any woman above the age of ten years against her will, and of a woman-child

[1] 1 East P. C. 434.

[2] 2 Coke's Inst. 180.

under the age of ten years with or against her will;"[3] "it seems that rape is an offense in having unlawful and carnal knowledge of a woman by force and against her will;"[4] "rape is the carnal knowledge of a woman forcibly and against her will;"[5] "rape has been defined to be the having unlawful and carnal knowledge of a woman by force and against her will;"[6] "rape is the having of unlawful carnal knowledge, by a man of a woman, forcibly and against her will.'"[7]

§ 426. "Against her will"—"Without her consent"—It has been suggested that the phrases "against her will" and "without her consent" are to be distinguished. "The question is, what is the real definition of the crime of rape, whether it is the ravishing of a woman against her will, or without her consent. If the former is the correct definition, the crime is not in this case proved; if the latter, it is proved."[8] It is to be observed, however, that this view, which has given rise to confusion upon this subject, is erroneous. The phrases are synonymous.[9]

§ 427. Scope of the resistance.—Must the woman resist "to the uttermost?" Upon this question the authorities are not harmonious. Many of the decisions hold that she must use all the resistance in her power under the circumstances up to the time of the intercourse; that is, until exhausted or overpowered.[10]

[3] 1 Hale P. C. 628. See also State v. Brooks (Iowa), 165 N. W. 194; State v. Shellman (Mo.), 192 S. W. 435; Gray v. State, 125 Ark. 272, 188 S. W. 820; State v. Volz, 269 Mo. 194, 190 S. W. 307.

[4] 1 Hawk P. C. (Curw. ed) 122.

[5] 4 Bl. Comm. 210.

[6] 1 Russ. on Crimes (9th Am. ed.) 904.

[7] 2 Bish. New Crim. L. (8th ed.), § 1113.

[8] Lord Chief Justice Campbell in Reg. v. Fletcher, Bell Cr. C. 63, 8 Cox Cr. C. 131.

[9] Commonwealth v. Burke, 105 Mass. 376, 7 Am. Rep. 531, Beale's Cases 457, Derby's Cases 334.

[10] O'Boyle v. State, 100 Wis. 296, 75 N. W. 989. See aso State v.

On the other hand, it has been held "that there was no rule of law requiring a jury to be satisfied that the woman, according to their measure of her strength, used all the physical force in opposition of which she was capable,"[11] and that it is enough that by word and act she showed her unwillingness.[12]

§ 428. Consent induced by fraud.—Upon this question, also, the authorities are not harmonious. By the weight of authority, however, when the woman understands the nature of the act, and her consent is obtained by fraud, the offense is not rape.[13]

§ 429. Fraudulently represents marriage ceremony legal.—When a man fraudulently represents to a woman that an illegal marriage to her is legal, and has carnal knowledge of her, induced by her belief in his fraudulent misrepresentation, he is not guilty of rape.[14]

§ 430. Man fraudulently personates the woman's husband.—At common law, when a man fraudulently personates a woman's husband and thereby has carnal knowledge of her he is not guilty of rape,[15] and it is held that fraud and

Ward, 73 Iowa 532, 35 N. W. 617; People v. Dohring, 59 N. Y. 374, 17 Am. Rep. 349; Brown v. State, 127 Wis. 193, 106 N. W. 536, 7 Ann. Cas. 258. See also State v. Cowing, 99 Minn. 123, 108 N. W. 851, 9 Ann. Cas. 566.

11 Commonwealth v. McDonald, 110 Mass. 405.

12 State v. Sudduth, 52 S. Car. 488, 30 S. E. 408; State v. Shields, 45 Conn. 256.

13 Reg. v. Barrow, L. R. 1 C. C. 156, 11 Cox Cr. C. 191, Beale's Cases 455; Wyatt v. State, 2 Swan (Tenn.) 394; Don Moran v. People, 25 Mich. 356, 12 Am. Rep. 283; Commonwealth v. Fields, 4 Leigh (Va.) 648; Bloodworth v. State, 6 Baxt. (Tenn.) 614, 32 Am. Rep. 546; Reg. v. Fletcher, L. R. I. C. C. 39, 10 Cox Cr. C. 248.

14 State v. Murphy, 6 Ala. 765, 41 Am. Dec. 79. See also Bloodworth v. State, 6 Baxt. (Tenn.) 614, 32 Am. Rep. 546. But see Wilkerson v. State, 60 Tex. Cr. 388, 131 S. W. 1108, Ann. Cas. 1912 C. 126n.

15 Reg. v. Barrow, L. R. 1 C. C. 156, 11 Cox Cr. C. 191, Beale's

stratagem can not be substituted for force, as an element of this offense.[16] On the other hand, there are decisions which hold the contrary view. Thus, in a leading Irish case, where a man personated a woman's husband and thereby had connection with her he was held guilty of rape.[17] In England, and in a few of the states of this country, statutes have been passed which make having carnal knowledge of a woman by falsely personating her husband rape.[18]

§ 431. **Woman insane or idiotic.**—When a woman is insane or idiotic, and does not know the nature of the act, carnal knowledge of her by a man other than her husband, who is charged with knowledge of her mental condition, constitutes rape.[19] If, however, she consents from passion, morbid desires or animal instincts, the offense is not rape.[20] Nor is it rape when the man does not know that the woman is incapable of giving consent and uses no actual force to compel her to submit to the act.[21] The mere fact that a woman is weak-minded does not show incapacity to give consent. A woman who lacks mental capacity to make a contract may have capacity to consent to sexual intercourse. But when a man has sexual intercourse with a woman, other than his wife, of such weak and disordered mind that she

Cases 455; Wyatt v. State, 2 Swan (Tenn.) 394; Don Moran v. People, 25 Mich. 356, 12 Am. Rep. 283; State v. Brooks, 76 N. Car. 1.

16 Wyatt v. State, 2 Swan (Tenn.) 394; Rex v. Jackson (1822) Russ. & R. 487 (earliest reported case); Reg. v. Barrow, L. R. 1 C. C. 156, 11 Cox Cr. C. 191, Beale's Cases 455.

17 Reg. v. Dee, L. R. 14 Ir. 468, 15 Cox Cr. C. 579.

18 48 & 49 Vict. ch. 69, § 4; State v. Wiliams, 128 N. Car. 573, 37 S. E. 952; Mooney v. State, 29 Tex. App. 257, 15 S. W. 724.

19 Gore v. State, 119 Ga. 418, 46 S. E. 671, 100 Am. St. 182 (an excellent case); People v. Crosswell (Cornwell), 13 Mich. 427, 87 Am. Dec. 774; Reg. v. Fletcher, Bell Cr. C. 63, 8 Cox Cr. C. 131; Reg. v. Mayers, 12 Cox Cr. C. 311; Bloodworth v. State, 6 Baxt. (Tenn.) 614, 32 Am. Rep. 546.

20 23 Am. & Eng. Encyc. L. (2d ed.) 856.

21 Roscoe's Crim. Ev. (8th ed.) 1118. See also State v. Cunningham, 100 Mo. 382, 12 S. W. 376; State v. Warren, 232 Mo. 185. 134 S. W. 522, Ann. Cas. 1912 B, 1043n.

cannot understand the nature and consequence of such act, he is guilty of rape.[22] There must be, however, some evidence that the act was without her consent.[23] But when she is incapable of expressing any intelligent assent or dissent, or of exercising any judgment in the matter, the offense is rape, though no more force be used than is necessary to accomplish the carnal act, and though the woman offer no resistance.[24]

§ 432. Clevenger's view.—Clevenger, in his work on Medical Jurisprudence of Insanity, gives the following comprehensive statement of the law upon this subject as applied by the American courts: "Sexual intercourse with a woman who is so destitute of mind as to be incapable of giving consent is rape, though she does not resist. The test of mental capacity under this rule is whether she was capable or incapable of giving consent or of exercising any judgment in the matter. And very slight proof of force is necessary where the woman lacks the intelligence to comprehend the nature and consequences of the act, and to distinguish morally and legally between right and wrong; and when the man does not suppose that he has her consent the force required and which is involved in the carnal act is sufficient. But where the will is active, though perverted, the act is not rape, when all idea of force or unwillingness is distinctly disproved. And the mere fact that a woman is weak-minded does not disable or debar her from giving consent to the act, and intercourse with her when she is capable of exercising her will sufficiently to control her personal actions is not rape; and if there is reasonable doubt whether force was used the jury should acquit though the woman was of weak mind. A woman with less intelligence than is requisite to

22 State v. Williams, 149 Mo. 496, 51 S. W. 88.

23 Reg. v. Connolly, 26 U. C. Q. B. 317.

24 Gore v. State, 119 Ga. 418, 46 S. E. 671, 100 Am. St. 182; State v.

make a contract may consent to sexual intercourse so that the act will not be rape upon the part of the man. And connection with a woman who is in a state of dementia, and not idiotic, but approaching toward it, having a predisposition to be with men and a morbid desire for sexual intercourse, is not rape when no circumstances of either force or fraud accompany the act; nor is intercourse without resistance with a woman subject to epileptic fits, where the evidence does not show that she was under the influence of a fit at the time. The burden of proof of insanity at the time of the act, and that the carnal knowledge was obtained by force and without consent, rests with the prosecution. There must be some evidence that she was incapable, from imbecility, of expressing assent or dissent, and when consent is given from mere animal passion or instinct, it is not rape, and a conviction can not be sustained in the absence of evidence as to her general character for chastity and decency, or anything else to raise a presumption that she did not consent. Evidence of the connection and the imbecility alone is insufficient. But evidence of habits of decency raises a presumption that she would not have consented."[25] The foregoing statement constitutes an epitome of the English and American decisions upon the questions involved.

§ 433. **Woman sane but insensible.**—When a woman is reduced to a state of insensibility by the use of drugs or intoxicating liquors, sexual intercourse with her while in

Warren, 232 Mo. 185, 134 S. W. 522, Ann. Cas. 1912 B, 1043.

[25] Clevenger's Med. Jur. of Insanity, 201-202; State v. Orth, 101 Kans. 183, 165 Pac. 652; State v. Ivy (Mo.), 192 S. W. 733; State v. Smith, 95 Wash. 271, 163 Pac. 759; State v. Bragdon, 136 Minn. 348, 162 N. W. 465. See also 2 Bish. New Crim L. (8th ed.), §§ 1121, 1123; 1 Whart. Crim. L. (11th ed.) §§ 694, 703; Russ. on Crimes (9th Am. ed.) 906; Clark & M. on Crimes, § 295; May's Crim. L., § 195; 2 Roscoe's Crim. Ev. (8th ed.) 1119; 13 Crim. L. Mag. 510; Clark's Crim L. 186.

such condition, by a man other than her husband, constitutes rape.[26] And whether her insensible condition has been produced by the man or not is immaterial.[27] This is the modern English rule as well as the American rule.[28]

§ 434. **Woman asleep.**—The rule applicable to the case where the woman is senselessly drunk is also applicable where she is asleep.[29] If she is asleep at the time of the act, so as to be unconscious of it, it is done without her consent and constitutes rape.[30]

§ 435. **Consent induced by intimidation.**—It has frequently been said that force is a necessary element in the crime of rape.[31] It is to be observed, however, that it may be constructive as well as actual; and furthermore, that fear may take its place. If, at the time a man has carnal knowledge of a woman, her mind is so overpowered by fear induced by him as to cause her to make no resistance, the offense is rape.[32] Where the woman is paralyzed from fear

26 Commonwealth v. Burke, 105 Mass. 376, 7 Am. Rep. 531, Beale's Cases 457, Derby's Cases 334; Reg. v. Fletcher, L. R. 1 C. C. 39, 10 Cox Cr. C. 248; Quinn v. State, 153 Wis. 573, 142 N. W. 510, 46 L. R. A. (N. S.) 422.

27 Commonwealth v. Burke, 105 Mass. 376, 7 Am. Rep. 531, Beale's Cases 457, Derby's Cases 334.

28 Commonweath v. Burke, 105 Mass. 376, 7 Am. Rep. 531, Beale's Cases 457, Derby's Cases 334; Reg. v. Fletcher, Bell Cr. C. 63, 8 Cox Cr. C. 131; Reg. v. Camplin, 1 Car. & K. 746, 1 Den. Cr. C. 89, 1 Cox Cr. C. 220.

29 Reg. v. Young, 14 Cox Cr. C. 114; State v. Shroyer, 104 Mo. 441, 16 S. W. 286, 24 Am. St. 344; Malone v. Commonwealth, 91 Ky. 307, 15 S. W. 856, 12 Ky. L. 895; Payne v. State, 40 Tex. Cr. 202, 49 S. W. 604, 76 Am. St. 712; State v. Welch, 191 Mo. 179, 89 S. W. 945, 4 Ann. Cas. 681, in which it is held that if offense is complete before the woman awakens, her consent afterward is no defense.

30 1 Whart. Crim. L. (11th ed.), §§704, 705; Malone v. Commonwealth, 91 Ky. 307, 15 S. W. 856, 12 Ky. L. 895.

31 State v. Murphy, 6 Ala. 765, 41 Am. Dec. 79n.

32 Rice v. State, 35 Fla. 236, 17 So. 286, 48 Am. St. 245; People v. Kincannon, 276 Ill. 251, 114 N. E. 508.

and terrified into submission her consent to the act is void.[33] The law does not require the doing of impossible or useless acts.[34] A reasonable apprehension of death, however, is not essential.[35] Fear of grievous bodily harm is sufficient. "An acquiescence obtained by duress, or fear of personal violence, will avail nothing, the law regarding such submission as no consent at all. If the mind of the woman is overpowered by a display of physical force, through threats, expressed or implied, or otherwise, or she ceases resistance through fear of great harm, the consummation of unlawful intercourse by the man would be rape."[36]

§ 436. Carnal knowledge of a child.—Carnal knowledge of a child, however young, with her consent, was not rape under the English common law.[37] The first statute of Westminster, passed in 1275, made the carnal knowledge of a child "within age" (12 years), even with her consent, a misdemeanor.[38] The second statute of Westminster, passed ten years later, made rape a felony, but it was silent as to the age of the victim.[39] The statute of 18 Elizabeth, passed some three centuries later, made the carnal knowledge of a child under ten years of age, with her consent, a felony.[40]

[33] 1 Hawk. P. C. 122, ch. 16, § 6; State v. Ruth, 21 Kans. 583; Austine v. People, 110 Ill. 248; Reg. v. Woodhurst, 12 Cox Cr. C. 443; Doyle v. State, 39 Fla. 155, 22 So. 272, 63 Am. St. 159.

[34] Austine v. People, 110 Ill. 248; 2 Bish. New Crim. L. (8th ed.), § 1125. See also Strang v. People, 24 Mich. 1. But see Whittaker v. State, 50 Wis. 518, 7 N. W. 431, 36 Am. Rep. 856n.

[35] Waller v. State, 40 Ala. 325; Crosswell v. People, 13 Mich. 427, 87 Am. Dec. 774.

[36] McQuirk v. State, 84 Ala. 435, 4 So. 775, 5 Am. St. 381. See also 2 Bish. Crim. L. (8th ed.), § 1125; 1 Whart. Crim. L. (11th ed.) § 700, 3 Greenl. Ev. (16th ed.), § 211; Huston v. People, 121 Ill. 497, 13 N. E. 538; State v. Ward, 73 Iowa 532, 35 N. W. 617; State v. Long, 72 Conn. 39, 43 Atl. 493; People v. Flynn, 96 Mich. 276, 55 N. W. 834.

[37] Reg. v. Johnson, 10 Cox Cr. C. 114; Moore v. State, 17 Ohio St. 521.

[38] Stat. Westm. I, ch. 13; 1 East P. C., ch. 10, § 1; 4 Bl. Comm. 212.

[39] Stat. Westm. II, ch. 34; 1 East P. C., ch. 10, § 1; 4 Bl. Comm. 212.

[40] Stat. 18 Eliz., ch. 7, § 4.

This statute, however, did not describe the felony as rape. All of these statutes form part of our American common law. And under this law the courts hold that carnal knowledge of a child under ten years of age, even with her consent, constitutes a felony.[41]

In this country statutes have been passed raising the age of consent, and making the crime rape within the age fixed, even when the child consents to the act. Under these statutes the age of consent varies greatly in the different states, in a few reaching as high as eighteen years.[42] In Illinois it is sixteen years.[43] In many of them it is fourteen years.

Ignorance of the accused as to the victim's age, and a bona fide belief on his part that she was above the age of consent at the time of the act, constitute no defense.[44]

The prosecution has the burden of showing, beyond a reasonable doubt, that the child was within the age of consent at the time of the act.[45] Testimony as to the child's age at

[41] Works v. State, 131 Ark. 593, 199 S. W. 531; State v. Kampert, 139 Minn. 132, 165 N. W. 972; Johnson v. Commonwealth, 7 Ky. L. (abstract) 47; Stephen v. State, 11 Ga. 225; Gosha v. State, 56 Ga. 36.

[42] State v. Newton, 44 Iowa 45; State v. Woods, 49 Kans. 237, 30 Pac. 520; State v. Wright, 25 Nebr. 38, 40 N. W. 596.

[43] Illinois: Hurd's Rev. Stat. (1916), ch. 38, § 237. The statute provides: "Every male person of the age of seventeen years and upwards, who shall have carnal knowledge of any female person under the age of sixteen years and not his wife, either with or without her consent shall be adjudged to be guilty of the crime of rape; provided, that in case the said parties shall be legally married to each other before conviction, any legal proceedings shall abate, and provided, that every male person of the age of 16 years and upwards who shall have carnal knowledge of a female forcibly and against her will shall be guilty of the crime of rape."

[44] State v. Baskett, 111 Mo. 271, 19 S. W. 1097; State v. Sherman, 106 Iowa 684, 77 N. W. 461; People v. Ratz, 115 Cal. 132, 46 Pac. 915; State v. Houx, 109 Mo. 654, 19 S. W. 35, 32 Am. St. 686; Heath v. State, 173 Ind. 296, 90 N. E. 310.

[45] State v. Houx, 109 Mo. 654, 19 S. W. 35, 32 Am. St. 686; Lawrence v. State, 35 Tex. Cr. 114, 32 S. W. 530.

the time of the act may be given by herself,[46] or by members of her family;[47] but declarations by her to others upon this point are inadmissible.[48] Medical expert opinion evidence is admissible,[49] and it is always proper for the jury to take into consideration the appearance of the child.[50] Whether the child was within the age of consent or not is a fact for the jury to decide;[51] but when the accused admits that she was, the question need not be submitted to the jury.[52] On the other hand, when the only evidence upon the point is that given by the child the trial court errs in assuming that the fact is established.[53] Some statutes make it essential to conviction that the child shall have been of previous chaste character;[54] but under these statutes the defendant can not take advantage of his own act in previously destroying her chastity.

§ 437. Consent obtained by fraudulent representation of physician.—When a medical practitioner falsely and fraudulently represents to a patient that coition is an essential part of the treatment in her case, and owing to her belief in the representation she consents to connection with him, he is not guilty of rape. The reason is she consents to the act.[55]

46 Commonwealth v. Hollis, 170 Mass. 433, 49 N. E. 632; People v. Bernor, 115 Mich. 692, 74 N. W. 184; Dodge v. State, 100 Wis. 294, 75 N. W. 954; State v. Lacey, 111 Mo. 513, 20 S. W. 238.

47 People v. Bernor, 115 Mich. 692, 74 N. W. 184; Lawrence v. State, 35 Tex. Cr. 114, 32 S. W. 530; George v. State, 61 Nebr. 669, 85 N. W. 840.

48 State v. Deputy, 3 Penn. (Del.) 19, 50 Atl. 176.

49 State v. Smith, 61 N. Car. 302; Lawrence v. State, 35 Tex. Cr. 114, 32 S. W. 530.

50 Commonweatlh v. Hollis, 170 Mass. 433, 49 N. E. 632; People v. Dickerson, 58 App. Div. (N. Y.) 202, 68 N. Y. S. 715, 15 N. Y. Cr. 365; State v. McNair, 93 N. Car. 628.

51 People v. Webster, 111 Cal. 381, 43 Pac. 1114.

52 People v. Baldwin, 117 Cal. 244, 49 Pac. 186.

53 People v. Webster, 111 Cal. 381, 43 Pac. 1114.

54 State v. Dacker, 59 Wash. 238, 109 Pac. 1050, 30 L. R. A. (N. S.) 173; State v. Sargent, 62 Wash. 692, 114 Pac. 868, 35 L. R. A. (N. S.) 173.

55 Don Moran v. People, 25 Mich. 356, 12 Am. Rep. 283n; Walter v. People, 50 Barb. (N. Y.) 144; State

On the other hand, when a medical practitioner, under pretense of making a professional examination of her person, or of performing a surgical operation, has connection with her, and she is ignorant of the nature of the act, he is guilty of rape. And the reason is she does not consent to the act.[56]

§ 438. The act itself—Penetration—Emission.—Carnal knowledge of the person of the female is an essential element of rape. And to have carnal knowledge there must be penetration.[57] The slightest penetration, however, is sufficient.[58] The fact of penetration does not have to be shown by the prosecutrix herself,[59] nor does it have to be established by direct evidence.[60]

Under the early common law, emission was not considered an essential element of rape.[61] Later, however, it was

v. Murphy, 6 Ala. 765, 41 Am. Dec. 79; Bloodworth v. State, 6 Baxt. (Tenn.) 614, 32 Am. Rep. 546; Reg. v. Barrow, L. R. 1 C. C. 156, 11 Cox Cr. C. 191, Beale's Cases, 455; Reg. v. Fletcher, L. R. 1 C. C. 39, 10 Cox Cr. C. 248.

56 Pomeroy v. State, 94 Ind. 96, 48 Am. Rep. 146; Eberhart v. State, 134 Ind. 651, 34 N. E. 637; Reg. v. Flattery, 13 Cox Cr. C. 388, 46 L. J. M. C. 130; Reg. v. Case, 1 Den. Cr. C. 580 (quoted in Pomeroy v. State, 94 Ind. 96, 48 Am. Rep. 146); Walter v. People, 50 Barb. (N. Y.) 144; People v. Crosswell, 13 Mich. 427, 87 Am. Dec. 774.

57 Galaviz v. State (Tex. Cr.), 198 S. W. 946; State v. Dalton, 106 Mo. 463, 17 S. W. 700. See also State v. Carnagy, 106 Iowa 483, 76 N W. 805; White v. Commonwealth, 96 Ky. 180, 28 S. W. 340, 16 Ky. L. 421; People v. Tench, 167 N. Y. 520, 60 N. E. 737; People v. Courier, 79 Mich. 366, 44 N. W. 571.

58 People v. Courier, 79 Mich. 366, 44 N. W. 571; State v. Grubb, 55 Kans. 678, 41 Pac. 951; White v. Commonwealth, 96 Ky. 180, 28 S. W. 340, 16 Ky. L. 421; 1 East P. C., ch. 10, § 3; 1 Hale P. C. 628; State v. Sullivan, Add. (Pa.) 143; Brauer v. State, 25 Wis. 413; Reg. v. Jordan, 9 Car. & P. 118.

59 State v. Tarr, 28 Iowa 397.

60 Taylor v. State, 111 Ind. 279, 12 N. E. 400; White v. Commonwealth, 96 Ky. 180, 28 S. W. 340, 16 Ky. L. 421; Commonwealth v. Hollis, 170 Mass. 433, 49 N. E. 632; State v. Carnagy, 106 Iowa 483, 76 N. W. 805; Bish. Stat. Crimes (3rd ed.), § 488.

61 1 Hale P. C. 628; Rex v. Sheridan, 1 East P. C. 438.

expressly adjudged essential.[62] The statute of Geo. IV provides that proof of emission is not necessary;[63] and this rule obtains in England to-day. In this country a few courts have held that proof of emission is essential;[64] but the great weight of authority is to the contrary.[65] In some of the states, including New York and Michigan, statutes have been passed expressly providing that proof of emission is not essential. And in a few cases it has been held that emission is presumed from the fact of penetration.[66]

§ 439. Incapacity of male—Boy under fourteen.—A male person who is impotent and incapable of copulation can not commit rape. To be capable of committing this crime a man must have physical capacity to perform the act of carnal knowledge. And evidence which tends to show that the accused at the time of the alleged offense was in a greatly debilitated condition from a previous debauch is admissible and constitutes a circumstance, however light, to be considered by the jury in ascertaining whether he was physically capable or not of committing the offense.[67] When, however, he is capable of penetration, though incapable of emission or procreation, he has capacity to commit rape.

At the early common law a boy under fourteen years of age was conclusively presumed incapable of committing rape; and testimony tending to show capacity was inadmissible.[68] This rule is followed by some of the courts of this

[62] Hill's Case (1781), 1 East P. C. 439. See also Rex v. Burrows, Russ. & R. 519.

[63] 9 Geo. IV, ch. 31, § 18.

[64] Brown v. State, 76 Ga. 623; Blackburn v. State, 22 Ohio St. 102; State v. Gray, 53 N. Car. 170.

[65] Harris v. State, 72 Fla. 128, 72 So. 520; Waller v. State, 40 Ala. 325; Taylor v. State, 111 Ind. 279, 12 N. E. 400; State v. Rollins, 80 Minn. 216, 83 N. W. 141; Barker v. State, 40 Fla. 178, 24 So. 69.

[66] Comstock v. State, 14 Nebr. 205, 15 N. W. 355; State v. Sullivan, Add. (Pa.) 143.

[67] Nugent v. State, 18 Ala. 521.

[68] 1 Hale P. C. 630; Step. Dig. Crim. L., art. 271; Rex v. Groombridge, 7 Car. & P. 582; Reg. v. Phillips, 8 Car. & P. 736; Reg. v. Waite (1892), 2 Q. B. Div. 600, 61 L. J. M. C. 187, 17 Cox Cr. C. 554.

CHAPTER XXIII.

SEDUCTION

§ 445. Definition.—Seduction consists in having sexual intercourse with a previously chaste unmarried woman, with her consent, obtained by means of adequate inducement, usually a promise of marriage.

Bouvier defines seduction as, "The act of a man in inducing a woman to commit unlawful sexual intercourse with him."[1] While this definition has been approved by some courts,[2] it is faulty, nevertheless, in that it omits the element of chastity of the female and also is too general as to the

[1] Bouvier's Law Dict.

[2] Patterson v. Hayden, 17 Ore. 238, 21 Pac. 129, 3 L. R. A. 529, 11 Am. St. 822; Robinson v. Powers, 129 Ind. 480, 28 N. E. 1112.

element of inducement. Seduction has been also defined as "the wrong or crime of inducing a woman to consent to unlawful sexual intercourse, by the use of some influence, promise, art, or enticement, which overcomes her scruples or reluctance."[3]

§ 446. Seduction not indictable at common law.—While offenses contra bonos mores are in general indictable at common law, fornication, adultery, seduction and the like are not. At common law an indictment or information will not lie either for simple incontinence or for incontinence produced by means of deception, inveiglement or enticement.[4] It is said that a case of slander may display as much baseness and malignity of purpose, as much falsehood in its perpetration, as ruinous effects in its consequences, and as pernicious an example in its dissemination, as a case of seduction. And yet none would think of prosecuting it criminally.[5]

§ 447. Statutes not harmonious.—In almost all of the states statutes have been enacted making seduction a criminal offense.

The phraseology of these statutes, however, varies so much that a uniform definition of the crime is impracticable. Most of them require that the female be chaste in fact, while others require that she be of "good repute." Most of them require that the inducement be a promise of marriage. Some, however, do not. While still others require some artifice or persuasion in addition to a promise of marriage. A few require that the female become pregnant. Nearly all of them, however, do not. Some require that the defendant be an unmarried man. Most of them, however, do

[3] 25 Am. & Eng. Encyc. L. 190.

[4] Rex v. Lord Grey, 9 State Trials (Cobbet's ed.) 127; Rex v. Sir Francis Blake Delaval, 3 Burr. 1434.

[5] Anderson v. Commonwealth, 5 Rand. (Va.) 627, 16 Am. Dec. 776.

not.[5a] It is to be observed, however, that a woman can not be seduced by means of a promise to marry when she has knowledge at the time that the man is legally the husband of another woman. Many statutes require that the female be under a certain specified age, usually twenty-one years. Many others, however, are silent upon this point.[6]

§ 448. Certain English statutes not applicable.—Certain English statutes, which relate to the taking, conveying and enticing away of females from persons having charge of them, for purposes of prostitution, do not apply to the crime of seduction.[7] Nor do similar statutes which obtain in this country.[8]

§ 449. Chastity of the female.—The statutes very generally provide that to constitute seduction the female must be of previously chaste character.[8a] When a statute is silent upon this point, the courts hold that the requisite of chastity is implied, the reasoning being that the legislature never intended to send a man to the penitentiary for having had illicit connection with a prostitute or a woman of easy virtue, where she had consented even under a promise of marriage.[9]

In a prosecution for adultery, or fornication, chastity of the female is not essential to a conviction; but in a prosecution for seduction the rule is otherwise.[10] Moreover, in a prosecution for seduction the statutory prerequisite in this regard must be alleged in the indictment.[11]

5a Smedley v. State, 130 Ark 149, 197 S. W. 275.

6 See note to 8 Am. St. 870, 872.

7 4 & 5 Wm. & M., ch. 8, § 2; 9 Geo. IV, ch. 31, § 20; 24 & 25 Vict., ch. 100, § 55.

8 People v. Roderigas, 49 Cal. 9.

8a Gaddis v. Commonweath, 175 Ky. 183, 193 S. W. 1052.

9 Polk v. State, 40 Ark. 482, 48 Am. Rep. 17. See also People v. Smith, 132 Mich. 58, 92 N. W. 776; People v. Clark, 33 Mich. 112; Wood v. State, 48 Ga. 192, 15 Am. Rep. 664; People v. Roderigas, 49 Cal. 9.

10 People v. Knapp, 42 Mich. 267, 3 N. W. 927, 36 Am. Rep. 438.

11 State v. Gates, 27 Minn. 52, 6 N. W. 404; State v. Stogdel, 13

§ 450. Meaning of the term "chaste character."—The term "chaste character" means more than reputation for chastity. It means actual personal virtue as a moral and physical fact.[12]

In the statutes the term "character" is used in its accurate sense and as signifying that which the person really is, in distinction from that which she may be reported to be.[13]

§ 451. Views conflicting as to meaning of term "personal virtue."—As regards the meaning of the term "personal virtue," however, the decisions are conflicting. Some restrict it to abstinence from sexual intercourse, while others do not.

Those which favor the former view hold that, although a female may, from ignorance or other causes, have so low a standard of delicacy and propriety as to commit or permit indelicate acts or familiarities, yet if she have enough of the womanly instinct or sense of virtue that she would not surrender her person, unless seduced to do so under promise of marriage, she can not be said to be a woman of unchaste character.[14]

"There are women in whose presence every evil thought stands abashed. They are guarded by their innocence and purity and need no other protection. They stand invulnerable in their own virtue. There are others whose dispositions are more easy and complaisant, but who would have perhaps escaped irretrievable ruin had not their confidence been secured, and their apprehensions put at rest, by a

Ind. 565; 3 Whart. Crim. L. (11th ed.), § 2109.

12 People v. Nelson, 153 N. Y. 90, 46 N. E. 1040, 60 Am. St. 592. See also Kenyon v. People, 26 N. Y. 203, 84 Am. Dec. 177; Andre v. State, 5 Iowa 389, 68 Am. Dec. 708; State v. Prizer, 49 Iowa 531, 31 Am. Rep. 155.

13 Andre v. State, 5 Iowa 389, 68 Am. Dec. 708. See also note to 76 Am. St. 678.

14 People v. Kehoe, 123 Cal. 224, 55 Pac. 911, 69 Am. St. 52; Thomas v. State, 19 Ga. App. 104, 91 S. E. 247.

promise of marriage. To shield and save them from the arts of the seducer was the object of the law. It would be but a mockery to extend its protecting care only to those who have no need of its assistance. It should be here and ever the refuge and support of those who need its protection."[15]

On the other hand, some decisions hold that the term "personal virtue" includes purity of mind and innocence of heart; and that a lascivious woman, who has been guilty of obscenity of language, indecency of conduct, undue familiarity with men, and the like, may not come within the meaning of the term. Under this construction of the statute, the manners and actions of the woman have more weight than under the other view. They serve to indicate the true character; they become exponents of it; and a defendant is not punished for an act with one whose conversation and manners may even have suggested the thought and opened the way to him, as he would be for the same act with one innocent in mind and manners.[16]

§ 452. Reformation of the female.—The fact that an unmarried female, at some time in the past, was guilty of sexual intercourse, does not prove conclusively that she is not of "previously chaste character." It may be that she has reformed. Moreover, when a reasonable time has elapsed after her unchaste act a presumption may arise in favor of her reformation.[17]

§ 453. Presumption of chastity—Burden of proof—Conflicting views.—Upon the questions of presumption and bur-

[15] Mills v. Commonwealth, 93 Va. 815, 22 S. E. 863.

[16] Andre v. State, 5 Iowa 389, 68 Am. Dec. 708n.

[17] People v. Clark, 33 Mich. 112. See also Wood v. State, 48 Ga. 192, 15 Am. Rep. 664; Kenyon v. People, 26 N. Y. 203, 84 Am. Dec. 177; State v. Brassfield, 81 Mo. 151, 51 Am. Rep. 234; State v. Carron, 18 Iowa 372, 87 Am. Dec. 401.

den of proof, as regards the chastity of the female, the decisions are conflicting. As a general rule, however, in prosecutions for seduction her chastity is presumed.[18]

Some decisions hold that the burden is upon the defendant to prove her unchastity.[19] Others hold that it is upon the prosecution to prove her chastity.[20] Upon principle, the latter view is correct. It is said that the latter view is the more logical because the legal presumption of innocence of the defendant overcomes the presumption of the chastity of the female.[21] It is to be observed, however, that presumptions never change the burden of proof in its true sense. The true reason why the latter of the two views stated above is correct is because chastity of the female is an essential element of the crime of seduction, and the prosecution, to secure a conviction, must prove all the requisites of the crime. It follows, therefore, that the burden is upon the prosecution to prove the chastity of the female as well as the act of intercourse and the requisite inducement.

§ 454. **Mode of proving chastity.**—The chastity of the female, as a general rule, is shown by evidence of her general reputation for chastity.[22]

It has been held, however, that testimony of the general reputation of the female for want of chastity is inadmissible. Thus, it has been said: "Nor can 'character,' as the term

[18] Smith v. State, 118 Ala. 117, 24 So. 55; Mills v. Commonwealth, 93 Va. 815, 22 S. E. 863; State v. Hemm, 82 Iowa 609, 48 N. W. 971; Andre v. State, 5 Iowa 389, 68 Am. Dec. 708; People v. Clark, 33 Mich. 112; Polk v. State, 40 Ark. 482, 48 Am. Rep. 17; Herbert v. State (Ala.), 77 So. 83, 78 So. 386.

[19] Smith v. State, 118 Ala. 117, 24 So. 55; State v. McClintic, 73 Iowa 663, 35 N. W. 696; Polk v. State, 40 Ark. 482, 48 Am. Rep. 17; State v. Turner, 82 S. Car. 278, 17 Ann. Cas. 88, 64 S. E. 424.

[20] State v. Horton, 100 N. Car. 443, 6 S. E. 238, 6 Am. St. 613; People v. Wallace, 109 Cal. 611, 42 Pac. 159; State v. Lockerby, 50 Minn. 363, 52 N. W. 958, 36 Am. St. 656.

[21] 25 Am. & Eng. Encyc. L. 240. See also, Herbert v. State (Ala.), 77 So. 83, 78 So. 386.

[22] Russell v. State, 77 Nebr. 519, 110 N. W. 380, 15 Ann. Cas. 222.

is used in the statute under which the prisoner was convicted, be proved by reputation. * * * Character, as here used, means actual personal virtue, and not reputation. The female must be unmarried and chaste in fact, when seduced. * * * It could not have been intended to substitute reputation for character in this, its primary and true sense. The accused may, by proof of specific acts of lewdness, on the part of the female, and not otherwise, show that she was in fact unchaste."[23] Some courts, however, hold the contrary.[24]

§ 455. Unchastity of female shown by particular acts.—The unchastity of the female may be established by evidence of specific acts. Thus, testimony is admissible to show, that she was a woman of a lewd or lascivious nature;[25] that she associated with men of bad character;[26] that often she was out late at night prior to the alleged seduction;[27] and that indecent remarks made in her presence caused no indignation on her part.[28] On the other hand, testimony that her mother, with whom she resided, kept a house of ill-fame at the time of the alleged seduction, is irrelevant and inadmissible.[29]

§ 456. Admissions of the prosecutrix.—Admissions of the prosecutrix, of misconduct on her part prior to the alleged seduction, are receivable in evidence against her.[30]

[23] Kenyon v. People, 26 N. Y. 203, 84 Am. Dec. 177. See also State v. Reinheimer, 109 Iowa 624, 80 N. W. 669. See also State v. Prizer, 49 Iowa 531, 31 Am. Rep. 155.

[24] Safford v. People, 1 Park. Cr. R. (N. Y.) 474.

[25] Keller v. State, 102 Ga. 506, 31 S. E. 92; O'Neill v. State, 85 Ga. 383, 11 S. E. 856. But see Russell v. State, 77 Nebr. 519, 110 N. W. 380, 15 Ann. Cas. 222.

[26] State v. Bige, 112 Iowa 433, 84 N. W. 518.

[27] State v. Clemons, 78 Iowa 123, 42 N. W. 562.

[28] State v. Bige, 112 Iowa 433, 84 N. W. 518.

[29] Kenyon v. People, 26 N. Y. 203, 84 Am. Dec. 177.

[30] State v. Eisenhour, 132 Mo. 140, 33 S. W. 785; State v. Clemons, 78 Iowa 123, 42 N. W. 562.

§ 457. Rule where chastity of prosecutrix is presumed.—In those states in which the chastity of the prosecutrix is presumed, the prosecution may not, in the first instance, introduce testimony of the general reputation of the prosecutrix for chastity. It may, however, introduce this class of testimony in rebuttal of the evidence of the defendant tending to show her unchastity.[81]

§ 458. The inducement must be adequate—Usually a promise of marriage.—Mere fornication is not seduction. To constitute the latter offense there must be an adequate inducement to influence the female to part with her virtue. And, as a general rule, the inducement must be a promise of marriage. Under statutes which require such inducement, the evidence must show that the intercourse took place subsequently to the promise of marriage, and that such promise was the inducement to the intercourse.[82]

§ 459. Female under age of consent—Same act both rape and seduction.—One of the requisites of seduction is consent of the female founded upon an adequate inducement—usually a promise of marriage. When the girl is under the age of consent, but old enough to contract to marry, and submits to sexual intercourse induced by a promise of marriage, is the man guilty of seduction? Can

[81] State v. Reinheimer, 109 Iowa 624, 80 N. W. 669; Smith v. State, 118 Ala. 117, 24 So. 55; Lewis v. State, 89 Ga. 396, 15 S. E. 489; State v. Prizer, 49 Iowa 531, 31 Am. Rep. 155.

[82] State v. Adams, 25 Ore. 172, 35 Pac. 36, 22 L. R. A. 840, 42 Am. St. 790. See also note to 76 Am. St. 670; Durrence v. State, 20 Ga. App. 192, 92 S. E. 962. It was held in the case of State v. Mitchell, 229 Mo. 683, 129 S. W. 917, 138 Am. St. 425, that illicit intercourse permitted by a woman as a mere barter and trade for a promise of marriage is not seduction; there must be the exercise of certain influences upon her affections by reason of the promise, and to some extent the bringing into play of certain arts and blandishments, reasonably sufficient, aided by the promise to marry to have her yield to the desires of the defendant.

the same act constitute rape and also seduction? Seduction is a statutory crime; and penal statutes must be strictly construed. Because a girl is under the age of consent under a statute relating to rape, it does not follow that she is under the age of consent under a statute relating to seduction.

An essential element in the crime of seduction is the consent of the female, founded upon a contract to marry. If she is old enough to make the contract, she may be held old enough to consent to seduction.[33] It follows, therefore, that a man who has sexual intercourse with a girl under the age of consent, induced by a promise of marriage, may be guilty not only of rape but also of seduction.

§ 460. Effect of subsequent marriage.—As a general rule, a person can not purge himself of a criminal offense by a subsequent act. In the case of seduction, however, the statutes usually provide that the subsequent intermarriage of the parties is a bar to a prosecution.[34] Where the statutes are silent upon this point, however, the rule does not obtain.[35]

§ 461. Effect of subsequent offer of marriage and refusal.—Upon this point the decisions are conflicting. Some courts hold that proof of such facts does not constitute a bar to the prosecution;[36] while other courts hold the contrary,[37] especially if the woman has in the meantime married another.[38] All courts, however, hold that testimony of such facts is ad-

[33] People v. Nelson, 153 N. Y. 90, 46 N. E. 1040, 60 Am. St. 592.

[34] People v. Gould, 70 Mich. 240, 38 N. W. 232, 14 Am. St. 493; People v. Frost, 198 N. Y. 110, 91 N. E. 376, 139 Am. St. 801.

[35] Commonwealth v. Slattery, 147 Mass. 423, 18 N. E. 399, Beale's Cases 151; In re Lewis, 67 Kans. 562, 73 Pac. 77, 63 L. R. A. 281, 100 Am. St. 479.

[36] State v. Thompson, 79 Iowa 703, 45 N. W. 293; Bolline v. State, 127 Ark. 271, 192 S. W. 196.

[37] Commonwealth v. Wright, 27 S. W. 815, 16 Ky. L. 251.

[38] Thorp v. State, 59 Tex. Cr. 517, 129 S. W. 607, 29 L. R. A (N. S.) 421n.

missible upon the question whether or not the alleged seduction was induced by a promise of marriage.[39]

§ 462. Effect of promise of marriage conditioned on pregnancy.—A promise of marriage conditioned on pregnancy is not an adequate inducement to constitute the act of intercourse seduction.[40] "It was never intended to protect a woman who was willing to speculate upon the results of her intercourse with a man and who only exacted as the price of her consent a promise on his part to marry her in case the intercourse resulted in her pregnancy."[41] The promise of marriage must be absolute.

§ 463. Effect when the seducer is a married man.—When the seducer is a married man, his criminal liability depends upon the woman's belief. If she thinks he is unmarried that is sufficient; but if she has knowledge to the contrary he is not liable for seduction.[42] It is held that a woman who has been married and divorced is not an "unmarried female," within the meaning of the Virginia statute.[43]

§ 464. Corroboration essential.—In a criminal prosecution for seduction testimony of the prosecutrix must be corroborated both as to the promise of marriage and the sexual intercourse.[44]

39 State v. Thompson, 79 Iowa 703, 45 N. W. 293.

40 People v. Smith, 132 Mich. 58, 92 N. W. 776; State v. Adams, 25 Ore. 172, 35 Pac. 36, 22 L. R. A. 840, 42 Am. St. 790; Russell v. State, 77 Nebr. 519, 110 N. W. 380, 15 Ann. Cas. 222; Hamilton v. United States, 41 App. D. C. 359, 51 L. R. A. (N. S.) 809n.

41 People v. Van Alstyne, 144 N. Y. 361, 39 N. E. 343.

42 Callahan v. State, 63 Ind. 198, 30 Am. Rep. 211; Wood v. State, 48 Ga. 192, 15 Am. Rep. 664.

43 Jennings v. Commonwealth, 109 Va. 821, 63 S. E. 1080, 21 L. R. A. (N. S.) 265n, 132 Am. St. 946, 17 Ann. Cas. 64.

44 Brooks v. State, 126 Ark. 98, 189 S. W. 669. See also, Smedley v. State, 130 Ark. 149, 197 S. W. 275; State v. Griffin, 106 S. Car. 283, 91 S. E. 318; State v. Stoker (Mo.). 190 S. W. 294; State v. Moody, 172 N. Car. 967, 90 S. E. 900; Tindel v. State (Tex. Cr.), 189 S. W. 948.

TITLE THREE.

Crimes Against the Habitation.

CHAPTER XXIV.

ARSON.

§ 465. List of crimes.—The two crimes against the habitation are arson and burglary.

§ 466. Definition.—Arson is the wilful and malicious burning of the dwelling-house of another.

§ 467. Essentials.—To constitute the crime of arson, at common law, the following elements are essential: (1) The building must be a dwelling-house. (2) It must be occupied by some other person. (3) There must be a charring of the wood. (4) The act must be done wilfully and maliciously.

§ 468. **Character of the building.**—At common law, the building must be a dwelling-house, or an outhouse within the curtilage used in connection therewith. A barn or stable, which is within the curtilage, is within the definition,[1] but a building which is separated from the dwelling-house by a highway is not.[2] It is not essential, however, that the outhouse adjoin the dwelling-house.[3] Nor is it essential that it be enclosed with the dwelling-house by a fence.[4]

An essential element of arson is occupancy of the house. A building designed for a dwelling-house and constructed in the usual manner, but which has not been occupied as such, does not come within the definition.[5] It is to be observed, however, that temporary absence of the occupant is immaterial.[6] It is not essential that the whole of the building be occupied for residence purposes. Thus, part of it may be used as a store,[7] or as a jail.[8]

§ 469. **Ownership.**—According to the definition the building must be the dwelling-house of another. Ownership, however, in this connection is used in the sense of occupancy.[8a] It is not essential that the occupant be the legal owner. He may be only a tenant. And, at common law, since arson is a crime against the home rather than against the property as such, a lessee can not be guilty of arson in

[1] People v. Aplin, 86 Mich. 393, 49 N. W. 148; Commonwealth v. Barney, 10 Cush. (Mass.) 480; Washington v. State, 82 Ala. 31, 2 So. 356. See also 101 Am. St. 22n, 71 Am. St. 66n.

[2] Luke v. State, 49 Ala. 30, 20 Am. Rep. 269; Curkendall v. People, 36 Mich. 309.

[3] Reg. v. James, 1 Car. & K. 303; Mary v. State, 24 Ark. 44, 81 Am. Dec. 60.

[4] Pond v. People, 8 Mich. 150.

[5] State v. McGowan, 20 Conn. 245, 52 Am. Dec. 336, Derby's Cases 549; Davis v. State, 153 Ala. 48, 44 So. 1018, 127 Am. St. 17, 15 Ann. Cas. 547.

[6] Meeks v. State, 102 Ga. 572, 27 S. E. 679; State v. Meerchouse, 34 Mo. 344, 86 Am. Dec. 109.

[7] People v. Orcutt, 1 Park. Cr. R. (N. Y.) 252; Spears v. State, 92 Miss. 613, 46 So. 166, 16 L. R. A. (N. S.) 285.

[8] Luke v. State, 49 Ala. 30, 20 Am. Rep. 269.

[8a] State v. Hanna, 131 Ark. 129, 198 S. W. 881.

burning the house he lives in,[9] whereas the landlord can be.[10] However, the statutes have extended the crime of arson to include offenses against property as well as against the habitation and by statute in most of the states a person can be guilty of arson in burning his own dwelling-house.[11] At common law, a man can not commit arson in burning his wife's house which they jointly occupy. Nor can the wife commit arson in burning her husband's house which they jointly occupy. In the former case, the house, in legal contemplation, as regards the crime of arson, is the dwelling house of the husband.[12] And in the latter case the wife's legal identity is blended with that of her husband.[13] But under some statutes one spouse is liable for burning the house of the other.[14]

§ 470. **The burning.**—To constitute arson there must be an actual burning of at least some part of the house. It is not essential, however, that any part of it be wholly consumed.[15] Nor is it essential that the wood be in a blaze, for some species of wood will burn and entirely consume without blazing at all.[16] On the other hand, some part of it must be at least charred.[17]

[9] State v. Lyon, 12 Conn. 487; 2 Russ. on Crimes 550; State v. Martin, 87 Nebr. 529, 127 N. W. 896, Ann. Cas. 1912A, 1125n.

[10] 2 East P. C. 1023, 1024.

[11] State v. Hurd, 51 N. H. 176; Shepherd v. People, 19 N. Y. 537. See also note to Ann. Cas. 1912 B, 1126; Lipschitz v. People, 25 Colo. 261, 53 Pac. 1111, Derby's Cases 551; People v. Abrams, 174 Cal. 172, 162 Pac. 395.

[12] Snyder v. People, 26 Mich. 106, 72 Am. Rep. 202; State v. Young, 139 Ala. 136, 36 So. 19, 101 Am. St. 21; Kopcyznski v. State, 137 Wis. 358, 118 N. W. 863, 16 Ann. Cas. 865. See also State v. Shaw, 79 Kans. 396, 100 Pac. 78, 21 L. R. A. (N. S.) 27, 131 Am. St. 298.

[13] Snyder v. People, 26 Mich. 106, 12 Am. Rep. 302.

[14] Williams v. State, 177 Ala. 34, 58 So. 921, Ann. as. 1915 A, 584.

[15] Woolsey v. State, 30 Tex. App. 346, 17 S. W. 546.

[16] Reg. v. Parker, 9 Car. & P. 45.

[17] Woolsey v. State, 30 Tex. App. 346, 17 S. W. 546.

Where personal property in a dwelling-house is set on fire and wholly consumed, with intent to burn the house, the offense is not arson, even although the wood of the house is scorched black, provided no part of it is charred.[18]

§ 471. The intent.—The act of setting fire to the house must be done with wilful and malicious intent.[19] It is not essential, however, that it be done with the specific intent to consume the building. The intent may be to accomplish some other offense; and where the firing is done with the intention to commit any felony, it is arson.[20] But whether it is arson or not where the burning is done with the intention of committing a misdemeanor the authorities are in conflict. Some authorities say that in such case the doctrine of constructive intent does not apply.[21]

It is observed, however, that the motive is immaterial. The criminal intent is inferred from the act.[22] Suppose, for example, that the accused is indicted for arson, and the proof shows that he attempted to break jail by burning a hole through the jail floor. At common law, breaking jail is a felony or a misdemeanor, according as the cause of imprisonment belongs to the one grade or the other.[23] Why should the cause of his imprisonment affect the question of his guilt on the indictment for arson? The answer is, it should not. The causeless setting fire to a house, by a person of responsible mind, is arson, because the necessary intention is presumed from the act. The same act, done with the

18 Reg. v. Parker, 9 Car. & P. 45.

19 State v. Pienick, 46 Wash. 522, 90 Pac. 645, 11 L. R. A. (N. S.) 987, 13 Ann. Cas. 800; Spears v. State, 92 Miss. 613, 46 So. 166, 16 L. R. A. (N. S.) 285; Crow v. State, 136 Tenn. 333, 189 S. W. 687; Carr v. State (Ala. App.), 76 So. 413; State v. Sieff, 54 Mont. 165, 168 Pas. 524.

20 Luke v. State, 49 Ala. 30, 20 Am. Rep. 269.

21 1 Bish. New Crim. L. (8th ed.), Bish. New Crim. L. (8th ed.), § 14; Clark's Crim. L. 229.

22 Clark's Crim. L. 230.

23 2 Bish. New Crim. L. (8th ed.) § 155.

intention of committing a crime, whether felony or misdemeanor, must also be held to be arson, because the very recklessness of the deed supplies the wilful intention. The guilt or innocence of the defendant is not dependent upon whether he was in commission of a different felony or not. If he intentionally and designedly sets fire to the jail, in order to accomplish an unlawful purpose, the burning is wilfully done.[24] This is in accord with the better view, as well as the weight of authority.

§ 472. **Statutory changes.**—The common law relative to arson has been materially changed by statutes. The general effect of these statutes is to enlarge the scope of the crime. They differ a good deal, however, in the various states. Some make it arson to burn various kinds of buildings other than dwelling-houses; and some make it arson to burn cars, boats, or even hay, lumber, etc., while others make it arson, or criminally punishable, for the owner of house which he occupies to burn it with the fraudulent intent to obtain the insurance thereon.[25]

At common law, as well as by statute, arson is a felony.

§ 473. **Proof of corpus delicti.**—It is the modern doctrine that before there can be a lawful conviction of arson, there must be satisfactory evidence that the burning was effected by a criminal agency.[26]

[24] Luke v. State, 49 Ala. 30, 20 Am. Rep. 269.

[25] Heard v. State, 81 Ala. 55, 1 So. 640, Derby's Cases 553. See also State v. Greer, 243 Mo. 599, 147 S. W. 968, Ann. Cas. 1913C, 1163n; Allen v. Commonwealth, 176 Ky. 475, 196 S. W. 160.

[26] People v. Hannibal, 259 Ill. 512, 102 N. E. 1042, Ann. Cas. 1914C, 329n.

CHAPTER XXV.

BURGLARY.

§ 475. Definition.—Burglary is the breaking and entering of the dwelling-house of another in the nighttime with intent to commit a felony therein. Possession of burglar's tools is also indictable under some statutes.[1]

§ 476. Essentials.—To constitute burglary, at common law, the following elements are essential: (1) There must be a breaking of the house. (2) There must be an entry of the house. (3) The house must be the dwelling-house of another. (4) The breaking and entry must be in the nighttime. (5) The breaking and entry must be done with intent to commit a felony inside the house.

§ 477. The breaking.—The term breaking, in the definition of burglary, has a technical meaning. It is not essential that any part of the house be actually broken. Merely opening a closed door, or raising a closed window, is sufficient.[2] It is not essential that the door or window be even fastened. Thus, a refusal by the trial court to charge the

[1] State v. Boliski, 156 Wis. 78, 145 N. W. 368, 50 L. R. A. (N. S.) 825n. State v. Dotson, 97 Wash. 607, 166 Pac. 769; Black v. Commonwealth, 171 Ky. 280, 188 S. W. 362.

[2] Ferguson v. State, 52 Nebr. 432, 72 N. W. 590, 66 Am. St. 512; Commonwealth v. Mackey, 171 Ky. 473, 188 S. W. 676. See generally on breaking, State v. Vierck, 23 S.

jury that if the window was not fastened on the night in question the entry was not burglarious, was held on appeal not erroneous. In this case the court said: "There must be a breaking, removing, or putting aside of something material, which constitutes a part of the dwelling-house, and is relied on as a security against intrusion. Leaving a door or window open shows such a negligence and want of proper care, as to forfeit all claim to the peculiar protection extended to dwelling-houses. But if the door or window be shut, it is not necessary to resort to locks, bolts, or nails, because a latch to the door, and the weight of the window, may well be relied on as a sufficient security."[3] Digging under the wall of an unfloored building,[4] or breaking a mosquito netting fastened over an open window,[5] or opening an area gate by means of a skeleton key and thereby effecting an entrance to the house through the kitchen door,[6] or rolling back the closed door of a freight house,[7] or pushing open an unfastened transom,[8] is sufficient breaking. Burglary can be committed even where the entry is made through an open chimney.[9] This is owing to the fact that the house is closed in such case as much as the nature of the thing will permit. It is not burglary, however, where the entry is made through an opening already in the wall or roof.[10] The breaking must be such as will afford the burg-

Dak. 166, 120 N. W. 1098, 139 Am. St. 1040, and note.

[3] State v. Boon, 35 N. Car. 244, 57 Am. Dec. 555. See also Cox v. State (Tex. Cr.), 194 S. W. 138; People v. Kelley, 274 Ill. 556, 113 N. E. 926.

[4] Pressley v. State, 111 Ala. 34, 20 So. 647.

[5] Commonwealth v. Stephenson, 8 Pick. (Mass.) 354; People v. Nolan, 22 Mich. 229.

[6] Rex v. Davis, Russ & R. 322.

[7] State v. Richmond, 138 Iowa 494, 116 N. W. 609, 16 Ann. Cas. 457.

[8] Timmons v. State, 34 Ohio St. 426, 32 Am. Rep. 376, Derby's Cases 541.

[9] Olds v. State, 97 Ala. 81, 12 So. 409; State v. Willis, 52 N. Car. 190, 4 Bl. Comm. 226.

[10] Rex v. Spriggs, 1 M. & Rob. 357.

lar an opportunity to enter so as to commit the intended felony.[11] One author, however, states that the slightest actual breaking of any part of the house is sufficient.[12] This view, however, is erroneous. To open a door or window which is already partially open, but not sufficiently so as to permit a person to enter, is not sufficient.[13] But for the burglar to raise the window slightly in the daytime, with a view of preventing the bolt from fastening it, is immaterial.[14] It is a sufficient breaking if one open an unlocked screen door fitted so closely into the frame as to require strength to open it.[15]

Where the intruder enters the house through an open door, and breaks an inner door with intent to commit a felony in the room broken into, and enters the room with such intent, he is guilty of burglary.[16] But, at common law, where he enters a house without making a breaking, and breaks out after committing a felony therein, he is not guilty of burglary.[17] By an early English statute, however, this is made burglary.[18] This statute, however, is not generally regarded as part of the American common law, but similar statutes obtain in many of the states.[19] Merely breaking

11 Clark's Crim. L. 262.

12 Rex v. Hughes, 2 East P. C. 491, 1 Leach 452.

13 Commonwealth v. Strupney, 105 Mass. 588, 7 Am. Rep. 556; Rex v. Hyams, 7 Car. & P. 441. See also People v. White, 153 Mich. 617, 117 N. W. 161, 17 L. R. A. (N. S.) 1102, 15 Ann. Cas. 927. But see State v Lapoint, 87 Vt. 115, 88 Atl. 523, 47 L. R. A. (N. S.) 717.

14 People v. Dupree, 98 Mich. 26, 56 N. W. 1046.

15 Collins v. Commonwealth, 146 Ky. 698, 143 S. W. 35, 38 L. R. A. (N. S.) 769; State v. Henderson, 212 Mo. 208, 110 S. W. 1078, 17 L. R. A. (N. S.) 1100, 15 Ann. Cas. 930.

16 Rex v. Johnson, 2 East P. C. 488; State v. Wilson, 1 N. J. L. 439, 1 Am. Dec. 216; State v. Scripture, 42 N. H. 485.

17 Brown v. State, 55 Ala. 123, 28 Am. Rep. 693; State v. McPherson, 70 N. Car. 239, 16 Am. Rep. 769.

18 12 Anne, ch. 7, § 1 (1713).

19 Lawson v. Commonwealth, 160 Ky. 180, 169 S. W. 587, L. R. A. 1915D, 972.

open a trunk, cupboard, chest or box, within the house is not sufficient to make the offense burglary.[20]

The mere fact that the accused might have entered the house without opening a door or window is immaterial. Thus, where the door was double, being cut across the middle, and the upper half was open, and the accused lifted the hook that fastened the lower half and opened this part and walked in, the breaking was sufficient, the court holding that the fact that the accused could have jumped over the lower part of the door was no defense.[21] Merely going upon a piazza with felonious intent is not burglary.[22]

The breaking may be constructive as well as actual. This may be accomplished in various ways. Thus, the intruder may be admitted by an accomplice already within the house. This accomplice may be a servant, an apprentice, or some other person.[23] Again, the intruder may gain admittance by fraudulently concealing himself in a trunk, wardrobe, chest or box, which is taken into the house,[24] or by false representing that he desires to interview the occupant on business,[25] or by knocking on the door and rushing into the house without an invitation, after the door has been opened.[26] And one who has authority to enter a house or place of business for certain purposes may be held guilty of burglary if he abuses such authority and makes use of it to gain admission to commit a felony, as where an employé

[20] State v. Wilson, 1 N. J. L. 439, 1 Am. Dec. 216; State v. Scripture, 42 N. H. 485.

[21] Ferguson v. State, 52 Nebr. 432, 72 N. W. 590, 66 Am. St. 512; State v. Rowe, 98 N. Car. 629, 4 S. E. 506. See also Collins v. Commonwealth, 146 Ky. 698, 143 S. W. 35, 38 L. R. A. (N. S.) 769.

[22] State v. Puckett, 95 S. Car. 114, 78 S. E. 737, 46 L. R. A. (N. S.) 999.

[23] Walker v. State, 63 Ala. 49, 35 Am. Rep. 1; Commonwealth v. Lowrey, 158 Mass. 18, 32 N. E. 940.

[24] Nicholls v. State, 68 Wis. 416, 32 N. W. 543, 60 Am. Rep. 870; State v. Johnson, 61 N. Car. 186, 93 Am. Dec. 587.

[25] Young v. Commonwealth, 126 Ky. 474, 104 S. W. 266, 128 Am. St. 326, 15 Ann. Cas. 1022.

[26] State v. Henry, 31 N. Car. 463; 4 Bl. Comm. 226, 227.

who had a key to his employer's building opened it when his duties did not require him to do so and took property intending to convert it to his own use.[27] In all of the foregoing instances the breaking is sufficient.

§ 478. **The entry.**—To constitute burglary, it is essential that some part of the body, or some part of the instrument used to commit the felony, enter the house.[28] An entry of some part of the instrument used solely to make the breaking is not sufficient.[29] Thus, where the burglar bored a hole with a center-bit through the panel of the house door, near one of the bolts by which it was fastened, and some pieces of the broken panel were found within the threshold of the door, the court held that since the entry of the center-bit was not made for the purpose of committing a felony it was not sufficient.[30] On the other hand, when the instrument used is employed not only to make the breaking, but also to effect the only entry contemplated and necessary to the consummation of the felonious intent, the offense is complete. Thus, where the accused bored a hole through the floor of a granary, using a large auger, and then held a sack under the hole to catch the corn that came through the hole, the entry was sufficient, for the auger was the instrument employed not only to make the entrance but also to effect the larceny.[31]

Any entry, however slight, is sufficient. Thus, where the accused cut a hole in the window shutters of the prosecutor's shop, which was part of his dwelling-house, and put his hand

[27] State v. Corcoran, 82 Wash. 44, 143 Pac. 453, L. R. A. 1915D, 1015n.

[28] Commonwealth v. Glover, 111 Mass. 395; Harrison v. State, 20 Tex. App. 387, 54 Am. Rep. 529; State v. McCall, 4 Ala. 643, 39 Am. Dec. 314; Evans v. State, 19 Ga. App. 68, 90 S. E. 1025; Gilford v. State, 115 Miss. 300, 76 So. 279.

[29] Rex v. Rust, 1 Moody Cr. C. 183.

[30] Rex v. Hughes, 2 East P. C. 491, 1 Leach 452.

[31] Walker v. State, 63 Ala. 49, 35 Am. Rep. 1, Derby's Cases 544.

through the hole with intent to steal watches and other things within his reach, the entry was sufficient.[82] And again, where the accused broke a pane of glass in the upper sash of a window and introduced his hand between the glass and the inside shutters of the window, which were fastened, all the judges were of the opinion that the entry was sufficient.[83] On the other hand, where the accused raised a window and introduced a crowbar to force open the inside shutters, the judges held that the conviction was wrong because it did not appear that any part of his hand was inside the window although the aperture was large enough to admit it.[84] And again, where the accused broke open outside window shutters, and in attempting to raise the window sash put his hands in the space between the shutters when closed and the sash, the entry was not sufficient. The court observed in this particular case, "To constitute burglary, an entry must be made into the house with the hand, foot, or an instrument with which it is intended to commit a felony. In the present case there was nothing but a breach of the blinds, and no entry beyond the sash window. The threshold of the window had not been passed, so as to have enabled the defendant to have consummated a felonious intention."[85]

The breaking and the entry may be on different nights, but each must be done with intent to commit a felony.[86]

§ 479. **Dwelling-houses.**—At common law, as in case of arson, the building must be the dwelling-house of another, or an outhouse within the curtilage. The only exceptions to the rule were as to breaking and entering into a church or through the walls or gates of a town.[87]

[82] Gibbon's Case, 2 East P. C. 490, Foster C. L. 107.

[83] Rex v. Bailey, Russ. & Ry. 341.

[84] Rex v. Rust, 1 Mood. Cr. C. 183.

[85] State v. McCall, 4 Ala. 643, 39 Am. Dec. 314.

[86] Commonwealth v. Glover, 111 Mass. 395.

[87] People v. Richards, 108 N. Y. 137, 15 N. E. 371, 2 Am. St. 373.

Outbuildings closely and intimately connected with the habitation, the use of which is essential to its enjoyment, are protected as is the dwelling-house itself.[38] Where a shop is part of a dwelling-house, breaking and entering into the shop may be burglary.[39]

A room in a hotel in which a man resides with his family, has been held a dwelling-house.[40]

Statutes in many states have extended the offense of burglary to include breaking and entering into buildings other than a dwelling-house.[40a]

§ 480. Nighttime.—To constitute burglary, at common law, both the breaking and the entering must be in the nighttime; but, as previously stated, they may occur on different nights. The term nighttime, like the terms breaking and entering, has a technical meaning. At common law, it begins when daylight ceases and ceases when daylight begins again. In other words it exists during the time that a person's countenance is not reasonably discernible by sunlight. Moonlight and artificial lights, such as gas and electric lights, do not enter into the definition.[41] Hence the ability to distinguish objects at the time is not the test. And if daylight has ceased or not begun the offense is burglary, no matter how bright the moonlight or artificial light.[42]

"It is now generally agreed, that if there be daylight enough begun or left either by the light of the sun or twilight, whereby the countenance of a person may be reasonably discerned, it is no burglary; but that this does not extend to moonlight; for then many midnight burglaries would

[38] Unseld v. Commonwealth, 140 Ky. 529, 131 S. W. 263, 140 Am. St. 393.

[39] Quinn v. People, 71 N. Y. 561, 27 Am. Rep. 787, Derby's Cases 536.

[40] People v. Carr, 255 Ill. 203, 99 N. E. 357, Ann. Cas. 1913D, 864n, 41 L. R. A. (N. S.) 1209n.

[40a] State v. Dotson, 97 Wash. 607, 166 Pac. 769 (garage).

[41] State v. Morris, 47 Conn. 179; People v. Griffin, 19 Cal. 578; 4 Bl. Comm. 224.

[42] State v. Bancroft, 10 N. H. 105; State v. McKnight, 111 N. Car. 690, 16 S. E. 319, Derby's Cases 540.

go unpunished."[43] In some of the states what constitutes nighttime is fixed by statute.[44] In a few of them it extends from one hour after sundown to one hour before sunrise.[45]

§ 481. The intent.—The breaking and the entering must be done with intent to commit a felony within the house.[46] If done with the intent to commit a misdemeanor, and the intruder commits a felony, he is not guilty of burglary. On the other hand, if he breaks and enters with intent to steal all the money in the house that he can find, and he finds only two dollars, which he carries away, and stealing two dollars is only a misdemeanor, he is guilty of burglary.[47] As a general rule, the intent is to commit larceny: but it may be to commit any other felony.[48] It is not burglary at common law, to break and enter with intent to commit fornication, incest or adultery; for neither of these crimes is a felony at common law.[49] Nor is it burglary where the intent is to recapture goods which the intruder believes he has a right to take, although he is wholly mistaken.[50] Where the intent is to get intercourse with a woman by fraudulently impersonating her husband, the breaking and entering is burglary, provided the intercourse under such circumstances amounts to rape. Whether such intercourse amounts to rape is a question upon which the decisions are in conflict. In an

43 2 East P. C. 509; 1 Hale P. C. 550.

44 See the statutes and codes of the various states.

45 Mass. Rev. Laws (1902), ch. 219, p. 1853, § 10.

46 Vickery v. State, 62 Tex. Cr. 311, 137 S. W. 687, Ann. Cas. 1913C, 517n; Cox v. State (Tex. Cr.), 194 S. W. 138; State v. Phillips, 80 W. Va. 748, 93 S. E. 828 (intoxication a defense); People v. Kelley, 274 Ill. 556, 113 N. E. 926; Howard v. People, 62 Colo. 131, 160 Pac. 1060; State v. Bricker, 178 Iowa 297, 159 N. W. 873; Meadows v. State, 128 Ark. 639, 193 S. W. 264.

47 Harvick v. State, 49 Ark. 514, 6 S. W. 19.

48 Walton v. State, 29 Tex. App. 163, 15 S. W. 646; Harvey v. State, 53 Ark. 425, 14 S. W. 645, 22 Am. St. 229.

49 State v. Cooper, 16 Vt. 551; Robinson v. State, 53 Md. 151, 36 Am. Rep. 399, Derby's Cases 547.

50 Rex v. Knight, 2 East P. C. 510.

English case upon this point, eight of the judges thought that having carnal knowledge of a woman under such circumstances was rape and four thought it was not.[51] The fact that the intruder changes his intent after entering the house is immaterial.[52] And the fact that it proves physically impossible to carry out his intent is also immaterial.[53]

[51] Rex v. Jackson, Russ. & Ry. 487, 2 B. & H. Lead. Cas. 254n.

[52] Lanier v. State, 76 Ga. 304; Hunter v. State, 29 Ind. 80.

[53] State v. Beal, 37 Ohio St. 108, 41 Am. Rep. 490; State v. McDaniel, 60 N. Car. 245. See also State v. Simpson, 32 Nev. 138, 104 Pac. 244, Ann. Cas. 1912 C, 115; Schultz v. State, 88 Nebr. 613, 130 N. W. 105, 34 L. R. A. (N. S.) 243n.

TITLE FOUR.

Crimes Against Property.

CHAPTER XXVI.

BLACKMAIL OR THREATENING LETTERS.

§ 485. Definition.—In practically all jurisdictions it is now an offense to obtain money or property from another by threatening injury to person, property or character. This is ordinarily known as blackmail.

It is possible that such offenses were punishable at common law,[1] but today the offense is entirely statutory, and

[1] Rex v. Southerton, 6 East. 126; 3 Russ. Crimes h Am. ed.) 177.

it is necessary in any jurisdiction to go to the statute in order to find just what acts are indictable thereunder. The earliest English statutes related to the sending of anonymous letters demanding money or property, and threatening injury for noncompliance.[2]

§ 486. **What kind of threats are indictable.**—Generally speaking, threats to accuse one of crime[3] or of committing gross misconduct not criminal,[4] to set fire to property,[5] to do personal violence,[6] to injure one's business,[7] to begin a criminal prosecution,[8] to accuse one of something which would bring him disgrace or contempt[9] are indictable.

§ 487. **Purpose of threats.**—In order to convict under almost any blackmail statute, it is necessary to show that the threats were made for the purpose of obtaining money or something of value, or the inducing of another to do something against his will,[10] that they were communicated to and intended to be communicated to, the person against whom they were directed,[11] and that the threats were of a

2 4 Bl. Comm. 144; Robinson's Case, 2 East. P. C. 1110. See also note to 116 Am. St. 457, 475; Commonwealth v. Swartz, 65 Pa. Sup. Ct. 159.

3 Rex v. Pickford, 4 Car. & P. 227; Reg. v. Chalmers, 16 L. T. 363; State v. Louanis, 79 Vt. 463, 65 Atl. 532, 9 Ann. Cas. 194n.

4 Reg. v. Tomlinson, L. R. (1895) 1 Q. B. Div. 706; Reg. v. Redman, L. R. 1 C. C. 12; Reg. v. Miard, 1 Cox Cr. C. 22.

5 Reg. v. Taylor, 1 Fost. & F. 511.

6 State v. Hollyway, 41 Iowa 200, 20 Am. Rep. 586; Reg. v. Murphy, 6 Cox Cr. C. 340.

7 People v. Hughes, 137 N. Y. 29, 32 N. E. 1105.

8 People v. Whittemore, 102 Mich. 519, 61 N. W. 13; Commonwealth v. Buckley, 148 Mass. 27, 18 N. E. 577, 1 L. R. A. 624; Elliott v. State, 36 Ohio St. 318.

9 Motsinger v. State, 123 Ind. 498, 24 N. E. 342, 8 Am. Cr. R. 110n; People v. Tonielli, 81 Cal. 275, 22 Pac. 678. See also State v. Coleman, 99 Minn. 487, 110 N. W. 5, 116 Am. St. 441, and note where subject of blackmail is fully discussed.

10 Elliott v. State, 36 Ohio St. 318. See also cases cited in preceding note.

11 State v. Brownlee, 84 Iowa 473, 51 N. W. 25; Castle v. State, 23 Tex. Cr. 286, 4 S. W. 892.

character such as to produce in a reasonable mind alarm or bodily fear, and of a nature to take away the voluntary action which constitutes consent.[12] It is immaterial whether any advantage be actually gained by the threats.[13] Under most statutes conviction may be had for oral threats as well as written. Threats by gestures are insufficient.[14]

It is immaterial whether the thing threatened was to be done by the accused or another.[15] The venue of the prosecution, where the threats were made by a mailed letter, may be laid where the letter was received.[16]

12 Reg. v. Walton, Leigh. & C. 288; Reg. v. Smith, 1 Den. Cr. C. 510.

13 State v. Bruce, 24 Maine 71; People v. Tonielli, 81 Cal. 275, 22 Pac. 678; State v. Young, 26 Iowa 122.

14 Robinson v. Commonwealth, 101 Mass. 27.

15 State v. Brownlee, 84 Iowa 473, 51 N. W. 25.

16 Rex v. Esser, 2 East. P. C. 1125.

CHAPTER XXVII.

CHEATING AND FALSE PRETENSES.

§ 490. Cheating at common law.—The common-law crime of cheat consists in fraudulently obtaining a pecuniary interest in another's property by means of some false symbol or token of such a nature that common prudence can not guard against it. It is essential that the means of perpetrating the fraud be a false symbol or token, such as a false measure, a false weight, a false stamp, etc., or a conspiracy to cheat. A false statement is not sufficient. Where the defendant delivered sixteen gallons of beer to the prosecutor, falsely representing the quantity to be eighteen gallons, and for which he received pay, the conviction was quashed because the fraud was not perpetrated by means of a false measure.[1] In the case cited Lord Mansfield observed: "The of-

[1] Rex v. Wheatley, 2 Burr. 1125, 1 Wm. Bl. 273. See also, Commonwealth v. Warren, 6 Mass. 72; People v. Babcock, 7 Johns. (N.

fense that is indictable must be such a one as affects the public. As if a man uses false weights and measures, and sells by them to all or to many of his customers, or uses them in the general course of his dealing; so, if a man defrauds another, under false tokens. For these are deceptions that common care and prudence are not sufficient to guard against. So, if there be a conspiracy to cheat; for ordinary care and caution is no guard against this. Those cases are much more than mere private injuries; they are public offenses. But here, it is a mere private imposition or deception; no false weights or measures are used; no false tokens given; no conspiracy; only an imposition upon the person he was dealing with, in delivering him a less quantity instead of a greater, which the other carelessly accepted. It is only a nonperformance of his contract, for which nonperformance he may bring his action. The selling an unsound horse, as and for a sound one, is not indictable, the buyer should be more upon his guard." In the same case Justice Wilmot held, "The true distinction that ought to be attended to in all cases of this kind, and which will solve them all, is this—that in such impositions or deceits, where common prudence may guard persons against the suffering from them, the offense is not indictable, but the party is left to his civil remedy for the redress of the injury that has been done him; but where false weights and measures are used, or false tokens produced, or such methods taken to cheat and deceive, as people can not, by any ordinary care or prudence be guarded against, there it is an offense indictable." Again, where the defendant was convicted of knowingly exposing for sale and selling a gold chain, under the sterling alloy, as and for gold of the true standard weight, a motion in arrest of judgment was sustained.[2] In this case Lord Mansfield, C. J. said: "The

Y.) 201, 5 Am. Dec. 256; note, 25 Am. St. 378.

[2] Rex v. Bower, 1 Cowper 323.

question is, whether the exposing wrought gold to sale under the standard is indictable at common law? * * * It is certainly an imposition, but I incline to think it is one of those frauds only which a man's own common prudence ought to be sufficient to guard him against, and which, therefore, is not indictable, but the party injured is left to his civil remedy." Notwithstanding the earlier rule that a false statement alone is not sufficient, in some recent cases in this country one has been convicted of false pretense who sold as sound a horse which he knew to be unsound.[3]

Wharton states broadly that this crime can be committed by means of deceitful and illegal practices and devices,[4] and this view is supported by Stephen;[5] but Bishop's view is that the devices used must be symbols and tokens.[6] Again, the former states that the device used must be such as might deceive the public generally,[7] while the latter states that this is not essential.[8] By an old English statute,[9] the token used may be a privy one, and this statute is part of our common law.

§ 491. What constitutes a false token.—A false token, at common law, is anything which has the semblance of public authority, as false weights, measures, seals and marks of produce and manufacture, false dice, marked cards, and things of a similar kind, false and deceptive.[10] A privy token has been defined as something false and purporting to come from one not the bearer, and having in itself some private

[3] State v. Stone, 95 S. Car. 390, 79 S. E. 108, 49 L. R. A. (N. S.) 574, and note, reviewing generally American cases on false pretense.

[4] Whart. Crim. L. (11th ed.), §§ 1378-1389.

[5] Steph. Dig. Crim. L., art. 338.

[6] 2 Bish. New Crim. L. (8th ed.), § 143.

[7] 2 Whart. Crim. L. (11th ed.), § 1385.

[8] 2 Bish. New Crim. L. (8th ed.), § 157.

[9] 33 Hen. VIII, ch. 1, § 2.

[10] 2 Russ. on Crimes (9th Am. ed.), 609, 610. See also State v. Hammelsly, 52 Ore. 156, 96 Pac. 865, 132 Am. St. 686, 17 L. R. A. (N. S.) 244n.

mark or sign, calculated to induce the belief that it is real, and thus to cause the person to whom it is delivered to part with his money or goods to the bearer or person delivering it.[11] In the case cited the defendant was convicted of cheating by passing to the prosecutors a promissory note for $10, pretending that it was of that value, and that the makers were in law liable to pay, and would pay the same, when she in fact knew that they were not liable to pay, and would not pay the same. The court held that the offense was a mere civil injury and a motion in arrest of judgment was granted. Similarly, where the defendant was convicted of cheating by passing to another a fictitious order on a banker, knowing that he had no authority to draw it, by means of which he got possession of certain lottery tickets, the judgment was arrested.[12] Again, where the defendant was convicted of cheating at common law, and the proof showed that he obtained a letter from the judgment creditor to the magistrate who rendered the judgment against defendant, to discharge it on receipt of costs; and that he obtained the letter owing to his statement that he had come to settle, and would pay $10 down and give his note for the balance, but that, on receiving the letter went away without giving either the $10 or the note, the court arrested the judgment, and in doing so, said: "We search in vain for the false token. * * * There was not even the production of either note or money; and common prudence would have dictated the withholding of the receipt until the money was paid and the note drawn. To support this indictment would be to overset established principles."[13] On the other hand, where the defendant, a baker employed by the United States army, was indicted for a cheat, in baking two hundred nineteen barrels of bread, and marking them as weighing eighty-eight pounds

[11] Middleton v. State, Dudley (S. Car.) 275.

[12] Rex v. Lara, 6 Term Rep. 565.

[13] People v. Babcock, 7 Johns. (N. Y.) 201, 5 Am. Dec. 256.

each, whereas they severally weighed only sixty-eight pounds, the indictment was sustained, the court saying, "that this was clearly an injury to the public, and the fraud the more easily perpetrated, since it was the custom to take the barrels of bread at the marked weight, without weighing them again. The public, indeed, could not by common prudence prevent the fraud, as the defendant himself was the officer of the public pro hac vice."[14] Under some statutes there must be more than mere false words to constitute the offense.[15] The delivery of short weight for full price is held false pretense.[16]

§ 492. **Cheating by false pretenses.**—Obtaining anotner's property by means of false and fraudulent representations is not a crime at common law. To overcome this defect of the common law, statutes have been passed both in England and in this country. The original English statute provides as follows: "Whereas divers evil-disposed persons, to support their profligate way of life, have by various subtle stratagems, threats and devices, fraudulently obtained divers sums of money, goods, wares, and merchandises, to the great injury of industrious families, and to the manifest prejudice of trade and credit; therefore for the punishing all such offenders, be it enacted by the king's most excellent majesty, by and with the advice and consent of the lords spiritual and temporal and commons in this present parliament assembled, and by the authority of the same, that from and after the twenty-ninth day of September, one thousand seven hundred and fifty-seven, all persons who knowingly and designedly, by false pretense or pretenses, shall obtain from any person or persons, money, goods, wares or merchandises, with in-

[14] Respublica v. Powell, 1 Dall. (Pa.) 47, 1 L. ed. 155, 1 Am. Dec. 246.

[15] Wheeler v. People, 49 Colo. 402, 113 Pac. 312, Ann. Cas. 1912 A, 755; State v. Phifer, 65 N. Car. 321, Derby's Cases 496.

[16] State v. Ice & Fuel Co., 166 N. Car. 366, 81 S. E. 737, 52 L. R. A. (N. S.) 216.

tent to cheat or defraud any person or persons of the same; or shall knowingly send or deliver any letter or writing, with or without a name or names subscribed thereto, or signed with a fictitious name or names, letter or letters, threatening to accuse any person of any crime punishable by law with death, transportation, pillory, or any other infamous punishment, with a view or intent to extort or gain money, goods, wares or merchandises from the person or persons so threatened to be accused, shall be deemed offenders against law and the public peace; and the court before whom such offender or offenders shall be tried, shall, in case he, she or they shall be convicted of any of the said offenses, order such offender or offenders to be fined and imprisoned, or to be put in the pillory, or publicly whipped, or to be transported, as soon as conveniently may be (according to the laws made for the transportation of felons) to some of his majesty's colonies or plantations in America, for the term of seven years, as the court in which any such offender or offenders shall be convicted shall think fit and order."[17] Somewhat similar statutes have been enacted in the various states of this country.

§ 493. **Definition and essentials.**—The crime of false pretenses is the act of knowingly and designedly obtaining the property of another by means of a false and fraudulent representation.

The representation must relate to a past or existing fact, and not be a mere promise or expression of opinion. It must be knowingly false and be made with intent to obtain another's property fraudulently. It must be calculated to deceive and defraud, and actually induce another to part with his property by reason of the deceit and fraud.

§ 494. **The representation must relate to a past or existing fact.**—The representation must be more than a mere

17 30 Geo. II, ch. 24, § 1.

promise to perform some future act. It must relate to a past or existing fact.[18]

Thus where proof showed that the defendant procured the prosecutor's indorsement of the defendant's promissory note by falsely and fraudulently representing to the prosecutor that he would use the note so indorsed to take up and cancel another note of the same amount then about to mature, and upon which the prosecutor was liable as indorser; that instead of so doing he procured it to be discounted and used a portion of the proceeds for other purposes; on appeal, the order arresting the judgment of conviction for cheating by means of false pretenses was affirmed, for the reason that, "A false pretense to be within the statute, must be the assertion of an existing fact, not a promise to perform some act in the future."[18a] A statement that a horse is sound made knowingly that he is not, may constitute the basis of an indictment for false pretenses.[19] In another case,[20] where the defendant was convicted of this crime, the proof showed that he falsely and fraudulently promised the prosecutor that he would employ him and pay him fifty dollars a month for his services; that the prosecutor, believing the representation and relying on the promise, deposited one

[18] Commonwealth v. Moore, 99 Pa. St. 570. See also Scarlett v. State, 25 Fla. 717, 6 So. 767; Commonwealth v. Wallace, 114 Pa. St. 405, 6 Atl. 685, 60 Am. Rep. 353; Commonwealth v. Schwartz, 92 Ky. 510, 18 S. W. 775, 36 Am. St. 609; Thomas v. State, 90 Ga. 437, 16 S. E. 94; Commonwealth v. Warren, 94 Ky. 615, 23 S. W. 193; State v. Kube, 20 Wis. 217, 91 Am. Dec. 390; State v. Kingsley, 108 Mo. 135, 18 S. W. 994; Morgan v. State, 42 Ark. 131, 48 Am. Rep. 55; State v. Fcoks, 65 Iowa 196, 21 N. W. 561; People v. Wasservogle, 77 Cal. 173, 19 Pac. 270; Commonwealth v. Althause, 207 Mass. 32, 93 N. E. 202, 31 L. R. A. (N. S.) 999; State v. Hammelsly, 52 Ore. 156, 96 Pac. 865, 132 Am. St. 686, 17 L. R. A. (N. S.) 244; State v. Eudaly (Mo.), 188 S. W. 110; State v. Selleck (Mo.), 199 S. W. 129; State v. Tanner, 22 N. Mex. 493, 164 Pac. 821; People v. Cerrato, 165 N. Y. S. 694, 99 Misc. 256; Spriggs v. Craig, 36 N. Dak. 160, 161 N. W. 1007.

[18a] Commonwealth v. Moore, 99 Pa. St. 570.

[19] Commonwealth v. Watson, 146 Ky. 83, 142 S. W. 200, Ann. Cas. 1913 C, 272n.

[20] Ranney v. People, 22 N. Y. 413.

hundred dollars as security for the faithful performance of the contract. On appeal, the conviction was reversed on the ground that the transaction was simply a private cheat. that in morals, the imposition was gross and detestable. But, in logic and law, the offense consisted in making a false and delusive promise, with no intention of performing it, which is not indictable. Again, where the defendant went to prosecutor's stall to purchase some meat, the prosecutor informed him that he would not trust him, the defendant promised that he would pay for the meat when delivered and by the subterfuge got the meat, intending all the time not to pay for it. The judges held the conviction wrong; that the false pretense was merely a promise for future conduct, and common prudence and caution would have prevented any injury resulting from its breach.[21]

Where the false pretense consists of a statement of fact and promise combined, it is sufficient to make the offense indictable. Thus, where the defendant was convicted of obtaining £8 from the prosecutrix by falsely and fraudulently representing to her that he was a single man, and that he would use the money in furnishing a house for them to reside in, and that he would then marry her, the conviction was affirmed.[22]

False statements as to the power to communicate with spirits may constitute false pretenses.[23]

[21] Rex v. Goodhall, Russ. & Ry. 461. See also, Reg. v. Walne, 11 Cox Cr. C. 647; State v. Dowe, 27 Iowa 273, 1 Am. Rep. 271; Glackan v. Commonwealth, 3 Metc. (Ky.) 233.

[22] Reg. v. Jennison, 9 Cox Cr. C. 158, Leigh & C. 157, 6 L. T. 256, 10 W. R. 488. See also, Jules v. State, 85 Md. 305, 36 Atl. 1027; Commonwealth v. Wallace, 114 Pa. St. 405, 6 Atl. 685, 60 Am. Rep. 353; State v. Thaden, 43 Minn. 325, 45 N. W. 614; Boscow v. State, 33 Tex. Cr. 390, 26 S. W. 625; State v. Briggs, 74 Kans. 377, 86 Pac. 447, 7 L. R. A. (N. S.) 278, 10 Ann. Cas. 904.

[23] 1 Bish. New Cr. L. (8th ed.), § 593. See also People v. Orris, 53 Colo. 244, 121 Pac. 163, 41 L. R. A. (N. S.) 170; State v. Ferris, 171 Ind. 562, 86 N. E. 993, 41 L. R. A. (N. S.) 173.

§ 495. Representation must be more than an expression of opinion.—Where the false representation is a mere expression of opinion as to value, quality, etc., or a mere puffing of one's property, it is not an indictable false pretense. Thus, where the defendant was convicted of obtaining money by false pretenses, and the proof showed that he obtained a loan secured by mortgage on his wife's land by stating to the lender that the lots were near the city limits, on a street leading directly to the business district, "nicely located, and would sell any day for twelve hundred dollars to fifteen hundred dollars cash," the conviction was set aside, because the representation that the lots were "nicely located, and would sell any day for twelve hundred dollars to fifteen hundred dollars cash," was a mere expression of opinion.[24]

On the other hand, where the false representation is something more than a mere expression of opinion, amounting substantially to a statement of fact, the false pretense is indictable.[25] Where the defendant was convicted of false pretenses, and the proof showed that he defrauded the prosecuting witness by inducing him to purchase a horse which had long been afflicted with swinney, by falsely stating to him that the horse's lameness was the result of recent shoeing, and was merely temporary, a refusal by the trial court to instruct the jury that, if the purchaser could perceive the lameness the principle of caveat emptor was applicable and the defendant was not guilty, was held proper and the conviction was affirmed.[26] Again, where the defendant was convicted of this crime, and the proof showed that he fraud-

[24] People v. Jacobs, 35 Mich. 36. See also, People v. Morphy, 100 Cal. 84, 34 Pac. 623; People v. Gibbs, 98 Cal. 661, 33 Pac. 630.

[25] Williams v. State, 77 Ohio St. 468, 83 N. E. 802, 14 L. R. A. (N. S.) 1197, Derby's Cases 504; State v. Chambers, 179 Iowa 436, 161 N. W. 470.

[26] State v. Wilkerson, 103 N. Car. 337, 9 S. E. 415. See also, State v. Burke, 108 N. Car. 750, 12 S. E. 1000; State v. Stanley, 64 Maine 157; Watson v. People, 87 N. Y. 561, 41 Am. Rep. 397n; People v. Crissie, 4 Denio (N. Y.) 525.

ulently induced the prosecuting witness to purchase a diseased horse that was almost worthless by stating that the horse in question was a real nice driving-horse, was a good one and very fast, that it belonged to a lady, but that it had always worked for him, all of which statements were false, the conviction was sustained.[27]

It is sometimes difficult, to discriminate between fact and mere opinion. Thus, where the defendant was convicted of obtaining money by false and fraudulently representing to a pawnbroker that certain spoons he pawned were plated equal to Elkington's A, and on the best foundation material, the conviction was set aside by a divided court, the majority reasoning that it was not the intention of the legislature to make it an indictable offense for the seller to exaggerate the quality of that which he was selling, any more than it would be an indictable offense for the purchaser, during the bargain, to depreciate the quality of the goods and to say that they were not equal to that which they really were; while the minority held that there was a false pretense, namely, that the goods had as much silver on them as Elkington's A, and as to the foundation, that these were matters of fact, not opinion, as to matters of quantity and quality.[28]

The dissenting opinion in this case, it is submitted, is, upon principle, correct. Moreover, statements relative to quality and value can be statements of fact, as well as statements relative to quantity and weight; and such statements, knowingly false, and which fraudulently induce another to part with his property, may be sufficient to make the offense criminal.[29]

27 Jackson v. People, 126 Ill. 139, 18 N. E. 286.

28 Reg. v. Bryan, 7 Cox Cr. C. 312, 26 L. J. M. C. 84, 5 W. R. 598, Dears. & B. 265, 3 Jur. (N. S.) 620. See also Reg. v. Ardley, L. R. 1 C. C. 301, Derby's Cases 502, where conviction was sustained on representation that chain was 15 carat gold.

29 People v. Peckens, 153 N. Y.

§ 496. The representation must be knowingly false and made with fraudulent intent.—The representation must be actually false and made with intent to obtain another's property fraudulently. To obtain goods with the intent to defraud is not enough. It must be accomplished by a pretense which is false. If the party who makes it believes it to be false, when as a matter of fact it is true, the act is not indictable.[80] So, where the defendant was convicted of obtaining goods by falsely and fraudulently representing that a certain crop to be raised was not under mortgage, and the proof showed that a mortgage, which the indictment alleged covered the crop in question, did not specify the land on which it was to be raised, the conviction, on appeal, was reversed, because the trial court erred in admitting parol evidence to supply the omission, and therefore there was no false representation.[81]

The representation must also be known to be false. To give it a criminal character there must be scienter. Thus, where the defendant was convicted of procuring money from a bank by false pretenses and with intent to defraud, and the proof showed that he obtained the money by presenting two checks which were overdrafts, on appeal the verdict was set aside and a new trial granted on the ground that the proof did not establish the element of scienter. "If the checks in question had been passed to a third person, it could not be said that the defendant knew that they would not be paid. On the contrary, he had an open account with the bank, and although he knew there was nothing due to him, yet he might suppose that they would be paid. And the fact that he presented them himself, shows that he did not know that they would be refused. * * * They were mere requests to pay to

576, 47 N. E. 883; Williams v. State, 77 Ohio St. 468, 83 N. E. 802, 14 L. R. A. (N. S.) 1197.

80 State v. Asher, 50 Ark. 427, 8 S. W. 177.

81 State v. Garris, 98 N. Car. 733, 4 S. E. 633; Rand v. Commonwealth, 176 Ky. 343, 195 S. W. 802 (statement made recklessly).

him the amount named in them, couched in the appropriate and only language known there; and addressed to the person whose peculiar province and duty it was to know whether they ought to be paid or not. He complied with the requests, and charged the sums paid, to the defendant, and thus created a contract between the parties. Upon this contract the bank must rely for redress."[32] It is to be observed, however, that the drawing and passing a check on a banker with whom the drawer has no account, and which he knows will not be paid, is a false pretense within the statute.[33] This doctrine is approved by all the text writers.

Moreover, the representation must be made with fraudulent intent. The defendant was convicted of obtaining a pair of shoes by means of false pretenses, and the proof showed that he and his family received relief from the parish; that the overseers of the parish ordered him to go to work and help maintain his family; that he replied that he could not because he had no shoes; that the overseer thereupon supplied him with a pair of shoes; that at the time he had, in fact, two pairs of new shoes which he had previously received from the parish. On the case reserved the conviction was set aside on the ground that the representation made by the defendant was rather a false excuse for not working than a false pretense to obtain goods.[34] Again, where the defendant was convicted of obtaining money by false pretenses, and the proof showed that he intended to buy a lot; that he told R that he was the owner of it and sold it to him for two hundred dollars; that he then made a contract with the true owner for the purchase of it, paying part of the pur-

[32] Commonwealth v. Drew, 19 Pick. (Mass.) 179. See also State v. Hicks, 77 S. Car. 289, 57 S. E. 842, Derby's Cases 510; State v. Pilling, 53 Wash. 464, 102 Pac. 230, 132 Am. St. 1080; State v. Miller, 47 Ore. 562, 85 Pac. 81, 6 L. R. A. (N. S.) 365.

[33] Rex v. Jackson, 3 Camp. 370; Williams v. Territory, 13 Ariz. 27, 108 Pac. 243, 27 L. R. A. (N. S.) 1032; State v. Crockett, 127 Tenn. 679, 195 S. W. 583.

[34] Rex v. Wakeling, Russ. & Ry. 504.

chase-price; that he went into bankruptcy and never paid the full price of the lot nor acquired title to it, but that after his discharge in bankruptcy from liability on his land contract he revived this liability by making a new promise to pay it; the conviction, on appeal, was reversed on the ground that when he made the false representation to R, gave him the deed to the lot and obtained the two hundred dollars, he did not entertain a fraudulent intent.[35] So where a congregation invited one not a minister to preach and paid him for his services he was not guilty of false pretenses in obtaining the money, when, beyond representing himself a minister he took no steps to obtain employment.[36]

The fact that the other party to the transaction is also guilty of false pretenses is no defense. Where the defendants were convicted of obtaining watches by false pretenses, and the proof showed that in the trade the prosecuting witness also overstated the value of his watches, the conviction, on appeal, was affirmed, the court holding that, "If the other party has also subjected himself to a prosecution for a like offense, he also may be punished. This would be much better than that both should escape punishment because each deserved it equally."[37] Some courts have erroneously held the contrary.[38] Again, where the defendant was convicted of procuring by false pretenses another's indorsement upon a promissory note and the proof showed that the party who indorsed the note knew that his indorsement was to be used dishonestly, this fact was held to be no defense.[39] The pro-

[35] Fay v. Commonwealth, 28 Grat. (Va.) 912.

[36] Bowler v. State, 41 Miss. 576, Derby's Cases 508.

[37] Commonwealth v. Morrill, 8 Cush. (Mass.) 571. See also Reg. v. Hudson, 8 Cox Cr. C. 305; People v. Watson, 75 Mich. 582, 42 N. W. 1005; In re Cummins, 16 Colo. 451, 27 Pac. 887, 25 Am. St. 291, 13 L. R. A. 752; Commonwealth v. O'Brien, 172 Mass. 248, 52 N. E. 77.

[38] McCord v. People, 46 N. Y. 470; Commonwealth v. Henry, 22 Pa. St. 253.

[39] People v. Henseler, 48 Mich. 49, 11 N. W. 804.

curing of the payment of a just debt, already due by false pretenses, is not indictable.[40]

§ 497. The representation must be calculated to deceive and defraud and actually do so.—Where the representation is plainly irrational or absurd, and the victim is defrauded owing to his own gross carelessness, the crime of false pretenses is not committed. Thus, where the defendant was convicted of false pretenses, and the proof showed that he obtained money by representing to his victim that he was a witch doctor, and could kill and destroy witches; that the person to whom the representations were made was the victim of witches; that unless this person employed him to destroy the witches they would kill him and his family, the conviction, on appeal, was set aside on the ground that the representations were mere expressions of opinion and not calculated to deceive a man of ordinary understanding.[41] On the other hand, where the defendant was indicted for obtaining money under false pretenses, and the indictment alleged that he obtained two hundred dollars by falsely pretending to sell and deliver two thousand dollars in a box for two hundred dollars well knowing that the box contained only one dollar, a writ of certiorari to review a refusal of the trial court to quash the indictment was dismissed, the court saying, "The third alleged infirmity in the indictment is that the false pretense charged is such that a person of ordinary prudence and caution would not be deceived by it. To this, it is a sufficient answer that it is of common knowledge that many persons have been deluded by a like artifice. Laws are made to protect weak-minded and credulous, as well as sagacious, per-

[40] State v. Williams, 68 W. Va. 86, 69 S. E. 474, 32 L. R. A. (N. S.) 420.

[41] State v. Burnett, 119 Ind. 392, 21 N. E. 972. See also, Commonwealth v. Grady, 13 Bush (Ky.) 285, 26 Am. Rep. 192. But compare Lefler v. State, 153 Ind. 82, 54 N. E. 439, 45 L. R. A. 424, 74 Am. St. 300, Derby's Cases 509; People v. McAllister, 49 Mich. 12, 12 N. W. 891; State v. Young, 76 N. Car. 258; State v. Estes, 46 Maine 150.

sons. The wise and wary can protect themselves."[42] As a rule, gross carelessness is a defense, but not mere credulity.[43] Whether the representation is calculated to deceive or not is to be determined by giving consideration to the surrounding circumstances and the intelligence of the victim.[44] And it has been held that even where the proof shows that the exercise of ordinary care on the part of the defrauded party would have prevented him from being misled, it is still for the jury to determine whether he relied on the false representation and was thereby defrauded.[45] However, it is not necessary that the deceived party should ultimately suffer loss.[46]

§ 498. **Nature of the property obtained.**—As a rule, the property obtained by means of the false pretenses must be such as to be capable of being stolen. Hence it can not be land.[47] It is to be observed, however, that there are exceptions to this rule. Thus, the statutes of Wisconsin provide that obtaining by false pretenses a signature to a written instrument, the false making whereof would be punishable as forgery, is indictable.[48] Under these statutes, however, which make "money, goods, wares, merchandise or other property" the subject of false pretenses, it has been held that

42 Oxx v. State, 59 N. J. L. 99, 35 Atl. 646; People v. Rosenberg, 200 Ill. App. 13.

43 State v. Fooks, 65 Iowa 196, 21 N. W. 561; People v. Cole, 137 N. Y. 530, 33 N. E. 336.

44 Smith v. State, 55 Miss. 513; People v. Summers, 115 Mich. 537, 73 N. W. 818; State v. Davis, 56 Iowa 202, 9 N. W. 123; Cowen v. People, 14 Ill. 348; Bowen v. State, 9 Baxt. (Tenn.) 45, 40 Am. Rep. 71n.

45 State v. Knowlton, 11 Wash. 512, 39 Pac. 966.

46 Commonwealth v. Ferguson, 135 Ky. 32, 121 S. W. 967, 24 L. R. A. (N. S.) 1101, 21 Ann. Cas. 434.

47 People v. Cummings, 114 Cal. 437, 46 Pac. 284; Hayes v. Commonwealth, 173 Ky. 188, 190 S. W. 700; People v. Miller, 278 Ill. 490, 116 N. E. 131, L. R. A. 1917 E, 797n (cashier's check); State v. Ball (Miss.), 75 So 373 (physician's services a "valuable thing"); State v. Freeman, 172 N. Car. 925, 90 S. E 507.

48 Wisconsin Statutes (1913), § 4423. See also, State v. Black, 75 Wis. 490, 44 N. W. 635.

they do not include boarding and lodging.[49] And, at common law, obtaining dogs by means of false pretenses is not a crime. Real property does not fall within the statute.[50]

§ 499. **Property versus mere possession.**—In the crime of larceny the thief acquires only possession of the property. In the crime of false pretenses, however, the wrongdoer acquires, under most of the statutes, the property itself.[51] It has been held, however, that it is not essential that title to the property pass. It has been held that where the wrongdoer obtains the goods by falsely and fraudulently representing that he was sent for them by a customer for whom they are intended, he is guilty of the crime of false pretenses, notwithstanding the fact that the title to the goods does not pass.[52]

§ 500. **The false pretenses can be by acts as well as words.**—It has been held that the false pretenses must be either oral or written.[53] This view, however, is erroneous. Words are merely signs of ideas. If the ideas are conveyed, the channel of communication, or the garb in which they are clothed, is immaterial.[54] In this case the distinctive dress worn by the wrongdoer constituted, in part, the false pretenses. He was convicted of obtaining a pair of boot-

[49] State v. Black, 75 Wis. 490, 44 N. W. 635. See also, Reg. v. Gardner, 7 Cox Cr. C. 136.

[50] State v. Klinkenberg, 76 Wash. 466, 136 Pac. 692, Ann. Cas. 1915 D, 468.

[51] Reg. v. Kilham, L. R. 1 C. C. 261. See also, Cline v. State, 43 Tex. 494; Kellogg v. State, 26 Ohio St. 15, Derby's Cases 499; 2 Bish. New Crim. L. (8th ed.), § 477.

[52] Rex v. Adams, Russ. & Ry. 225; People v. Johnson, 12 Johns. (N. Y.) 292; Whart. Crim. L. (11th ed.), §§ 1405, 1443. See also, Commonwealth v. Langley, 169 Mass. 89, 47 N. E. 511. (In this case the court holds that it is not essential that title to the property pass to the wrongdoer.)

[53] People v. Conger, 1 Wheeler's Cr. C. (N. Y.) 448; People v. Dalton, 2 Wheeler Cr. C. (N. Y.) 161.

[54] Rex v. Barnard, 7 Car. & P. 784. See also, Reg. v. Goss, 8 Cox. Cr. C. 262 (displaying false sample); Rex v. Story, Russ. & Ry. 81; Rex v. Freth, Russ. & Ry. 127; Commonwealth v. Drew, 19 Pick. (Mass.) 179.

straps of one V by falsely representing that he was a student at Oxford University and a commoner of Magdalen College. The conviction was sustained upon proof that at the time he obtained the goods he wore a commoner's cap and gown, and falsely stated that he belonged to Magdalen College. So convictions of false pretense have been sustained where there was a mere drawing of a check on a bank where the drawer had no funds, though there was no representation that the check was good, except that implied from offering it.[55] But one who merely goes in an eating house and orders food with no money to pay for it is not guilty of false pretense.[56]

It also has been held that the false pretense must be the sole inducement that causes the party to part with his property.[57] This view is contrary to the weight of authority.[58] The false pretense must play a material part, however, in defrauding the party, and must have such an influence upon the owner, that, had it not been for the false pretenses, he would not have parted with his property.[59]

§ 501. The statutes applicable to donations for charitable purposes.—It has been held that the statutes relating to false pretenses are restricted in their application to commercial transactions.[60] This view, however, is wrong on principle and contrary to the great weight of authority. They are also applicable where the wrongdoer by false and fraudulent

[55] State v. Foxton, 166 Iowa 181, 147 N. W. 347, 52 L. R. A. (N. S.) 919.

[56] Reg. v. Jones, L. R. (1898) 1 Q. B. Div. 119, Derby's Cases 501.

[57] People v. Conger, 1 Wheeler Cr. C. (N. Y.) 448; People v. Dalton, 2 Wheeler Cr. C. (N. Y.) 161.

[58] Woodbury v. State, 69 Ala. 242, 44 Am. Rep. 515; State v. Metsch, 37 Kans. 222, 15 Pac. 251; People v. McAllister, 49 Mich. 12, 12 N. W. 891; State v. Thatcher, 35 N. J. L. 445; State v. Stone, 75 Iowa 215, 39 N. W. 275; People v. Haynes, 11 Wend. (N. Y.) 557.

[59] Commonwealth v. Drew, 19 Pick. (Mass.) 179; Whitehead v. State (Tex. Cr.), 196 S. W. 851.

[60] People v. Clough, 17 Wend. (N. Y.) 351, 31 Am. Dec. 303.

representations induces another to donate money for charitable purposes.[61]

§ 502. **Confidence games.**—In some states there are statutes which make it a crime to obtain money or property "by any means, instrument or device commonly called confidence games." This is in fact a species of false pretense. Confidence games have been defined as "a swindling operation in which advantage is taken of the confidence reposed by the victim in the swindler."[62] It seems that the employment of false tokens is unnecessary to conviction for this crime, and that it is sufficient to prove the obtaining of property by false verbal representations.[63]

It is immaterial that the scheme by which the accused took advantage of the confidence of the one swindled, was in form a business transaction.[64]

[61] Baker v. State, 120 Wis. 135, 97 N. W. 566. See also, Commonwealth v. Whitcomb, 107 Mass. 486; State v. Mathews, 91 N. Car. 635; State v. Carter, 112 Iowa 15, 83 N. W. 715; Strong v. State, 86 Ind. 208, 44 Am. Rep. 292n; State v. Styner, 154 Ind. 131, 56 N. E. 98; Reg. v. Jones, 1 Den. Cr. C. 551; 2 Whart. Crim. L. (11th ed.), § 1416; 2 Bish. New Crim. L. (8th ed.), § 467; State v. Swan, 55 Wash. 97, 104 Pac. 145, 24 L. R. A. (N. S.), 575, 133 Am. St. 1024, 19 Ann. Cas. 1129.

[62] Powers v. People, 53 Colo. 43, 123 Pac. 642; Elliott v. People, 56 Colo. 236, 138 Pac. 39; People v. Warfield, 261 Ill. 293, 103 N. E. 979; People v. Donaldson, 255 Ill. 19, 99 N. E. 62, Ann. Cas. 1913 D, 90. See also Wheeler v. People, 49 Colo. 402, 113 Pac. 312, and note to Ann. Cas. 1912 A, 758; People v. Weil, 243 Ill. 208, 90 N. E. 731, 134 Am. St. 364; People v. Crawford, 278 Ill. 134, 115 N. E. 901.

[63] People v. Bertsche, 265 Ill. 272, 106 N. E. 823, Ann. Cas. 1916 A, 729; People v. Miller, 278 Ill. 490, 116 N. E. 131, L. R. A. 1917 E, 797n.

[64] Hughes v. People, 223 Ill. 417, 79 N. E. 137; People v. Bertsche, 265 Ill. 272, 106 N. E. 823, Ann. Cas. 1916 A, 729.

CHAPTER XXVIII.

EMBEZZLEMENT.

§ 505. **Definition.**—Embezzlement is the wrongful appropriation, animo furandi, of the personal property of another by one to whom the possession has been entrusted by the owner. The gist of the offense is breach of trust.[1]

§ 506. **A statutory offense.**—Embezzlement is not a crime at common law.[2] The original English statute making this offense a crime was passed the last year of the eighteenth century. This statute provides as follows: "Whereas, bankers, merchants and others, are, in the course of their dealings and transactions, frequently obliged to entrust their servants, clerks, and persons employed by them in the like capacity, with receiving, paying, negotiating, exchanging or transferring, money, goods, bonds, bills, notes, banker's

1 State v. Burgess, 268 Mo. 407, 188 S. W. 135; People v. Knox, 32 Cal. App. 158, 162 Pac. 407; Ambrose v. United States, 45 App. D. C. 112; People v. Scudder, 163 N. Y. S. 739, 177 App. Div. 225; McCoy v. State, 9 Ga. App. 32, 90 S. E. 737.

2 State v. Burgess, 268 Mo. 407, 188 S. W. 135.

drafts and other valuable effects and securities; and, whereas, doubts have been entertained whether the embezzling of the same by such servants, clerks and others, so employed by their masters, amounts to felony by the law of England, and it is expedient that such offenses should be punished in the same manner in both parts of the united kingdom; be it enacted and declared by the king's most excellent majesty, by and with the advice and consent of the lords spiritual and temporal, and commons, in this present parliament assembled, and by the authority of the same, that if any servant or clerk, or any person employed for the purpose in the capacity of a servant or clerk, to any person or persons whomsoever, or to any body corporate or politic, shall, by virtue of such employment, receive or take into his possession any money, goods, bond, bill, note, banker's draft, or other valuable security, or effects, for or in the name or on the account of his master or masters, or employer or employers, and shall fraudulently embezzle, secrete, or make away with the same, or any part thereof, every such offender shall be deemed to have feloniously stolen the same from his master or masters, employer or employers, for whose use or in whose name or names, or on whose account the same was or were delivered to, or taken into the possession of such servant, clerk, or other person so employed, although such money, goods, bond, bill, note, banker's draft, or other valuable security, was or were not otherwise received into the possession of his or their servant, clerk, or other person so employed; and every such offender, his adviser, procurer, aider, or abettor, being thereof lawfully convicted or attainted, shall be liable to be transported to such parts beyond the seas of his majesty, by and with the advice of his privy council, shall appoint, for any term not exceeding fourteen years, in the discretion of the court before whom such offender shall be convicted or adjudged."[2a]

[2a] 39 Geo. III, ch. 85. See generally note to 87 Am. St. 21.

§ 507. **Origin of the English statute.**—The statute quoted in the preceding section was enacted in consequence of the decision in Bazeley's Case.[8] In that case the chief teller of a bank received from a customer one hundred thirty-seven pounds for deposit to his credit. The teller gave the customer credit for the amount in his passbook, put one hundred pounds of the money in his own pocket and deposited the balance in the money drawer of the bank. All the judges agreed that it was not felony for the reason that the one hundred pounds was never in the possession of the bank, distinct from the possession of the defendant.

§ 508. **American statutes.**—Statutes have been enacted in this country similar to the English statute. They vary more or less, however, and as penal statutes are strictly construed the one involved in the particular case should be carefully studied. As a rule, these statutes are aimed at servants, clerks and agents who wrongfully appropriate to their own use property which they have received in the course of their employment for their master or principal, and also as trustees, who violate their trust by wrongfully appropriating property in their possession belonging to another. In several states a public officer who does not pay over to his successor all public moneys in his hands at the end of his term, is guilty of embezzlement.[8a]

§ 509. **Scope of the statutes.**—The purpose of the embezzlement statutes is to supply a defect of the common law. In a Massachusetts case the court remarks: "The statutes relating to embezzlement, both in this country and in England, had their origin in a design to supply a defect which

[8] East P. C. 571, 2 Leach 973.

[8a] State v. Ensley, 177 Ind. 483, 97 N. E. 113, Ann. Cas. 1914 D, 1306; United States v. Davis, 243 U. S. 570, 37 Sup. Ct. 442, 61 L. Ed. 906; Cowart v. State (Ala. App.), 75 So. 711; Commonwealth v. Sitler, 67 Pa. Sup. Ct. 1; Parker v. State, 130 Ark. 234, 197 S. W. 283.

was found to exist in the criminal law. By reason of nice and subtle distinctions, which the courts of law had recognized and sanctioned, it was difficult to reach and punish the fraudulent taking and appropriation of money and chattels by persons exercising certain trades and occupations, by virtue of which they held a relation of confidence or trust toward their employers or principals, and thereby became possessed of their property. In such cases the moral guilt was the same as if the offender had been guilty of an actual felonious taking; but in many cases he could not be convicted of larceny, because the property which had been fraudulently converted was lawfully in his possession by virtue of his employment, and there was not that technical taking or asportation which is essential to the proof of the crime of larceny."[4] It follows, therefore, that common-law larceny and statutory embezzlement do not overlap. In other words, the former can not be the latter. This is Wharton's view,[5] and it is also supported by the great weight of authority.[6] Bishop, however, takes the contrary view.[7]

§ 510. Receiving the property by virtue of the employment.—The original English statute provided that the property fraudulently appropriated by the wrongdoer must have been received by him "by virtue of his employment." Owing to confusion caused by this phrase, however, a later statute omits it, and provides instead that the "chattel, money or valuable security * * * shall be delivered to or received or

[4] Commonwealth v. Hays, 14 Gray (Mass.) 62, 74 Am. Dec. 662, Derby's Cases 488.

[5] Whart. Crim. L. (11th ed.), §§ 1256, 1275, 1276, 1294. See also, Colip v. State, 153 Ind. 584, 55 N. E. 739, 74 Am. St. 322, Derby's Cases 491.

[6] Rex v. Headge, Russ. & Ry. 160; Rex v. Sullens, 1 Mood. Cr. C. 129; Commonwealth v. Davis, 104 Mass. 548; Lowenthal v. State, 32 Ala. 589, Quinn v. People, 123 Ill. 333, 15 N. E. 46; Cody v. State, 31 Tex. Cr. 183, 20 S. W. 398; People v. Perini, 94 Cal. 573, 29 Pac. 1027; State v. Sias, 17 N. H. 558; Ennis v. State, 30 Okla. Cr. 675, 167 Pac. 229.

[7] 2 Bish. New Crim. L. 8th ed.), §§ 328, 329.

taken into possession by him, for or in the name or on account of his master or employer." Thus the operator of a barge under the direction of its owner who hauled a load against the owner's express orders and kept the money was not guilty of embezzlement, because the money was not received by the defendant "for or in the name or on account of his master or employer," as provided by statute.[8] Nor was a miller in a county jail so guilty, whose duty was to grind grain when ordered to do so by the governor of the jail, receive the money for so doing and account for the same, and who ground grain without being ordered to do so, received the money for so doing and appropriated it to his own use.[9]

In this country, however, the courts very generally hold that the property must be received by the wrongdoer by virtue of his employment. "The term, agent. or servant, as used in the statute, imports the correlative idea of a principal, or master, and 'implies employment, service, delegated authority, to do something in the name or stead of the principal—an employment by virtue of which the money or property came into his possession.' "[10] In this case the defendant was convicted of embezzling money which the indictment alleged came into his possession by virtue of his employment as servant or agent of one Rainer. The proof showed that the defendant, while acting in the capacity of mail carrier, fraudulently appropriated three hundred ninety-five dollars

8 Reg. v. Cullum, 12 Cox Cr. C. 469, L. R. 2 C. C. 28, 42 L. J. M. C. 64, 28 L. T. 571, 21 W. R. 687, Derby's Cases 486.

9 Reg. v. Harris, 6 Cox Cr. C. 363, 23 L. J. M. C. 110. But see, Hartnett v. State, 56 Tex. Cr. 281, 119 S. W. 855, 23 L. R. A. (N. S.) 761, 133 Am. St. 971.

10 Brewer v. State, 83 Ala. 113, 3 So. 816, 3 Am. St. 693. See also, Commonwealth v. Williams, 3 Gray (Mass.) 461; Rex v. Snowley, 4 Car. & P. 390; Rex v. Hawtin, 7 Car. & P. 281; State v. Goode, 68 Iowa 593, 27 N. W. 772; Brady v. State, 21 Tex. App. 659, 1 S. W. 462; State v. Casey, 207 Mo. 1, 123 Am. St. 367, 13 Ann. Cas. 878; Smith v. State, 53 Tex. Cr. 117, 109 S. W. 118, 15 Ann. Cas. 435, 17 L. R. A. (N. S.) 531.

which Rainer had sent by registered letter. The conviction was quashed because the defendant was not in the employ of Rainer, but in the employ of the United States government. Again, where a clerk collects money for his employer without authority, and fraudulently appropriates it he is not guilty of embezzlement.[11] Nor is a person, not a public officer, who receives public money by representing that he is entitled to receive it, guilty of embezzlement.[12] It has been held, however, that an agent, who, after the expiration of his term, receives money belonging to his former employer and fraudulently converts it to his own use, is guilty of embezzlement.[13]

§ 511. **The fraudulent intent.**—To constitute embezzlement the property must be appropriated with fraudulent intent.[14] Mere breach of contract is not sufficient. Thus where a lawyer, who also acted in the capacity of a loan and land agent, was convicted of embezzling two hundred seventy-five dollars from a client, and the proof showed that the latter had given him four hundred dollars to loan for her; that he had loaned this for her and also seven hundred dollars more which she gave him to loan for her; that he showed her a letter from a man who had forty acres of land for sale, and requested her to let him have the money to buy the land, stating that he knew of a purchaser who would buy it at an advance; that she let him have four hundred dollars more to buy the land, saying that he might have the profit; that a month or so later she asked him for her money, and that he

11 Brady v. State, 21 Tex. App. 659, 1 S. W. 462.

12 State v. Bolin, 110 Mo. 209, 19 S. W. 650.

13 State v. Jennings, 98 Mo. 493, 11 S. W. 980.

14 State v. Moyer, 58 W. Va. 146, 6 Ann. Cas. 344; State v. Sage, 22 Idaho 489, 126 Pac. 403, Ann. Cas. 1914 B, 251; Ambrose v. United States, 45 App. D. C. 112; State v. Burgess, 268 Mo. 407, 188 S. W. 135; State v. Gulledge, 173 N. Car. 746, 91 S. E. 362 (bank president); State v. McAvoy, 40 R. I. 437, 101 Atl.. 109; People v. Scudder, 163 N. Y. S. 739, 177 App. Div. 225; State v. Ward, 96 Wash. 550, 165 Pac. 794.

gave her one hundred dollars and a chattel mortgage for twenty-five dollars which he owned; that several months later he conveyed to her forty acres of land as security until he could pay her the balance. The conviction on appeal was quashed on the ground that the defendant did not entertain a fraudulent intent.[15] Again where a person retains property, under a bona fide claim of right, however untenable or frivolous his claim may be, he is not guilty of embezzlement for the reason that he does not entertain felonious intent.[16] And mere neglect to turn over funds belonging to another does not constitute embezzlement for the same reason.[17] Where the funds are feloniously retained, however, demand that they be turned over is not essential.[18]

§ 512. **Intent or offer to return property.**—The fact that one who intentionally and wrongfully appropriates the property of another lawfully in his possession, intends to subsequently return it, or make restitution to the owner, does not make his offense any the less embezzlement.[19]

After the crime of embezzlement has been consummated, an offer by the defendant to turn over the property to the owner will not purge him of the offense. Nor will a settlement with the owner have this effect.[20]

§ 513. **Ownership of the property in another.**—To constitute common-law larceny, ownership of the property appro-

15 People v. Hurst, 62 Mich. 276, 28 N. W. 838.

16 Reg. v. Norman, Car. & M. 501.

17 Kribs v. People, 82 Ill. 425; Etheridge v. State, 78 Ga. 340; Penny v. State, 88 Ala. 105, 7 So. 50; Fitzgerald v. State, 50 N. J. L. 475, 14 Atl. 746; People v. Galland, 55 Mich. 628, 22 N. W. 81.

18 Hollingsworth v. State, 111 Ind. 289, 12 N. E. 490; State v. Comings, 54 Minn. 359, 56 N. W. 50; Wallis v. State, 54 Ark. 611, 16 S. W. 821.

19 State v. Duerksen, 8 Okla. Cr. 601, 129 Pac. 881, 52 L. R. A. (N. S.) 1013n.

20 State v. Pratt, 98 Mo. 482, 11 S. W. 977; Robson v. State, 83 Ga. 166, 9 S. E. 610; People v. De Lay, 80 Cal. 52, 22 Pac. 90; Fleener v. State, 58 Ark. 98, 23 S. W. 1; State v. Baxter, 89 Ohio St. 1019, 104 N. E. 331, 52 L. R. A. (N. S.) 1019.

priated must be in another. And the embezzlement statutes of nearly all the states which undertake to define the crime provide that the subject of the offense must be the property of another. Moreover, this has been almost universally construed to mean that it must be wholly the property of another. As a result, a member of an ordinary partnership can not, as a rule, be guilty of embezzling partnership property.[21]

It is to be observed, however, that where the statute is silent as to ownership of the property, and simply provides that an agent, etc., who embezzles or converts to his own use "anything of value which shall come into his possession by virtue of his employment" shall be guilty of embezzlement, this constitutes the test of the crime.[22] Thus the cashier of an unincorporated banking association who was also a stockholder therein, who by virtue of his employment fraudulently converted to his own use assets of the association was held guilty of embezzlement.[23]

It has been well observed that considering the statutes are numerous, and in some respects diverse in their provisions, the practitioner should be cautious about coming to conclusions upon a question under the law of embezzlement, unless, when he examines a decision relied upon, he first sees whether the statute on which it was rendered is, in its terms, similar to the one of his own state.[24]

21 McCrary v. State, 51 Tex. Cr. 502, 103 S. W. 924, 123 Am. St. 905, 14 Ann. Cas. 722; State v. Hogg, 126 La. 1053, 53 So. 225, 29 L. R. A. (N. S.) 830, 21 Ann. Cas. 124; People v. Dettmering, 278 Ill. 580, 116 N. E. 205. See People v. Maljan, 34 Cal. App. 384, 167 Pac. 547.

22 State v. Kusnick, 45 Ohio St. 535, 15 N. E. 481, 4 Am. St. 564. See also State v. Moyer, 58 W. Va. 146, 6 Ann. Cas. 344; Commonwealth v. Jacobs, 126 Ky. 536, 104 S. W. 345, 13 L. R. A. (N. S.) 511, 15 Ann. Cas. 1226; People v. Birnbaum, 114 App. Div. 480, 100 N. Y. S. 160, Derby's Cases 493; State v. McAvoy, 40 R. I. 437, 101 Atl. 109; State v. Klingman, 172 N. Car. 947, 90 S. E. 690; Smith v. State (Fla.), 76 So. 334.

23 State v. Kusnick, 45 Ohio St. 535, 15 N. E. 481, 4 Am. St. 564.

24 2 Bish. New Crim. L. (8th ed.), § 326; Mehaffey v. State (Ala. App.), 75 So. 647.

§ 514. Money paid or property delivered by mistake.— As previously stated, the essential element of embezzlement is breach of trust. It follows, therefore, that where money is paid or property delivered by mistake, and the receiver of it wrongfully converts it to his own use, he is not guilty of this crime. In such case there is no breach of a trust or violation of a confidence intentionally reposed by one party and voluntarily assumed by another.[25] A bank depositor, who was paid by mistake of the treasurer two hundred thirty dollars, instead of one hundred thirty dollars, the amount he had on deposit, and who, knowing of the mistake and knowing he was not entitled to the money which the treasurer afterward demanded of him, was not liable for embezzlement even though he appropriated the money to his own use with an intent to deprive the bank of its property.[26]

[25] Commonwealth v. Hays, 14 Gray (Mass.) 62, 74 Am. Dec. 662, Derby's Cases 488. See also, Neal v. State, 55 Fla. 140, 46 So. 845, 19 L. R. A. (N. S.) 371.

[26] Commonwealth v. Hays, 14 Gray (Mass.) 62, 74 Am. Dec. 662, Derby's Cases 488.

CHAPTER XXIX.

FORGERY.

§ 516. **Definition and essentials.**—Forgery, at common law, as defined by Blackstone, is the fraudulent making or altering of a writing to the prejudice of another's right.[1] In its broadest sense it includes the making or altering of any writing or record with the intent to prejudice the interest

[1] 4 Bl. Comm. 247. Bishop defines it as the false making or materially altering, with intent to defraud, of any writing which, if genuine, might apparently be of some legal efficacy, or the foundation of a legal liability. 2 Bish. New Crim. L. (8th ed.), § 572. See also, Reg. v. Closs, 7 Cox Cr. C. 494, Derby's Cases 523.

or right of another.[2] It is essential that the making or altering be false and be done with intent to deceive.[3]

§ 517. Nature of the instrument.—The document must possess at least apparent legal efficacy.[4] It is not forgery to make or alter a void instrument. Hence it is not forgery to alter a will that is not signed. Any instrument which may be the basis of a suit against another can be the object of forgery at common law.[5] Thus, deeds,[6] wills,[7] invoices,[8] bank checks,[9] money orders,[10] deposit slips,[11] receipts,[12] records,[13] book entries,[14] orders for the delivery of goods,[15] railway and other tickets,[16] certificates of character,[17] affidavits,[18] acceptance of service and waiver of citation in petition

[2] Jones v. State, 50 Ala. 161, 163; Moore v. Commonwealth, 92 Ky. 630, 18 S. W. 833; State v. Murphy, 17 R. I. 698, 24 Atl. 473, 16 L. R. A 550; State v. Gavigan, 36 Kans. 322, 13 Pac. 554, 556; State v. Wheeler, 20 Ore. 192, 25 Pac. 394, 10 L. R. A. 779, 23 Am. St. 119.

[3] People v. Pfeiffer, 243 Ill. 200, 90 N. E. 680, 26 L. R. A. (N. S.) 138, 17 Ann. Cas. 703; People v. Warner, 104 Mich. 337, 62 N. W. 405.

[4] Commonwealth v. Baldwin, 11 Gray (Mass.) 197, 71 Am. Dec. 703, Derby's Cases 529; State v. Darrance, 86 Iowa 428, 53 N. W. 281, Derby's Cases 532; State v. Sisson, 270 Mo. 59, 192 S. W. 454 (trading stamps); State v. Walton, 107 S. Car. 353, 93 S. E. 5 (cotton ticket reciting sale and giving weights, held subject to forgery).

[5] Dixon v. State, 81 Ala. 61, 1 So. 69; Wheeler v. State, 62 Tex. Cr. 370, 137 S. W. 124.

[6] State v. Sharpless, 212 Mo. 176, 111 S. W. 69.

[7] State v. Ready, 77 N. J. L. 329, 72 Atl. 445.

[8] Ex parte Fischl, 51 Tex. Cr. 63, 100 S. W. 773.

[9] State v. Coyle, 41 Wis. 267, 2 Am. Cr. Rep. 149.

[10] Rose v. State, 80 Ark. 222, 96 S. W. 996.

[11] State v. Jackson, 221 Mo. 478, 120 S. W. 66, 133 Am. St. 477.

[12] Sims v. State, 155 Ala. 96, 46 So. 493.

[13] State v. Tompkins, 71 Mo. 613.

[14] Commonwealth v. Boutwell, 129 Mass. 124, Ann. Cas. 1914 C, 466.

[15] People v. Rising, 207 N. Y. 195, 100 N. E. 694.

[16] Roberts v. State, 92 Ga. 451, 17 S. E. 262.

[17] Waterman v. People, 67 Ill. 91, 1 Am. Cr. Rep. 225; People v. Abeel, 182 N. Y. 415, 1 L. R. A. (N. S.) 730n.

[18] State v. Hilton, 35 Kans. 338, 11 Pac. 164, 8 Am. Cr. Rep. 261; Territory v. Gutierrez, 13 N. Mex. 312, 78 Pac. 139, 5 L. R. A. (N. S.) 375.

for divorce,[19] chattel mortgages,[20] indorsements on notes,[21] subscription lists,[22] seals of corporations,[23] orders for credit,[24] due bills,[25] warrants on county treasury,[26] and bills of lading,[27] have been held capable of being forged. Making a false indorsement on an instrument is a forgery.[28] On the other hand, agreements to pay for advertisements,[29] applications for insurance policies,[30] invalid affidavits[31] and mere complimentary letters of introduction,[32] have been held not capable of being forged.

§ 518. Imitating another's trade-mark or label.—Whether to imitate another's trade-mark or label is forgery or not depends upon whether it can be made the basis of a suit against the imitator or not in an action for deceit or warranty. Thus, in an English case,[33] where the proof showed that the defendant obtained from a printer ten thousand labels resembling those used on Borwick's baking and egg powders and put them on packages resembling Borwick's and sold many of them, the conviction of forgery was quashed by the higher court. The defendant was found guilty of fraud, but the fraud consisted in selling spurious powders as real ones. To constitute forgery the document itself must be the instru-

19 State v. Stringfellow, 126 La. 720, 52 So. 1002.

20 People v. Cotton, 250 Ill. 338, 95 N. E. 283.

21 State v. Carragin, 210 Mo. 351, 109 S. W. 553, 16 L. R. A. (N. S.) 561n.

22 State v. Hazzard, 168 Ind. 163, 80 N. E. 149.

23 United States v. Andem, 158 Fed. 996.

24 Forcy v. State, 60 Tex. Cr. 206, 131 S. W. 585, 32 L. R. A. (N. S.) 327.

25 Rembert v. State, 53 Ala. 467, 25 Am. Rep. 639, 2 Am. Cr. Rep. 141.

26 Saucier v. State, 102 Miss. 647, 59 So. 858, Ann. Cas. 1915 A, 1044.

27 State v. Bierbauer, 111 Minn. 129, 126 N. W. 406; Fischl v. State, 54 Tex. Cr. 55, 111 S. W. 410.

28 Saucier v. State, 102 Miss. 647, 59 So. 858, Ann. Cas. 1915 A, 1044.

29 People v. Parker, 114 Mich. 442, 72 N. W. 250.

30 Commonwealth v. Dunleay, 157 Mass. 386, 32 N. E. 356.

31 Commonwealth v. Cochran, 143 Ky. 807, 137 S. W. 521.

32 Mitchell v. State, 56 Ga. 171.

33 Reg. v. Smith, 8 Cox Cr. C. 32, Dears. & B. Cr. C. 566, 27 L. J. M. C. (N. S.) 225, 4 Jur. (N. S.) 1003, 6 W. R. 495.

ment of the fraud. As said by the court, "The fraud consists in putting inside the wrappers powder which is not genuine, and selling that. If the prisoner had had one hundred genuine wrappers and one hundred not genuine, and had put genuine powder in the spurious wrappers and spurious powder into the genuine wrappers, he would not have been guilty of forgery."

§ 519. Fraudulently assuming authority to sign another's name.—It is not forgery for a person fraudulently to assume authority to sign another's name to a document. Where the defendant fraudulently represented that he was a member of "Schouler, Baldwin & Co." and assumed authority to sign this firm name to a promissory note which he gave in payment of his own overdue note, his conviction of forgery was set aside by the higher court.[84] In this case the court states, "The writing alleged to be forged in the case at bar was the handwriting of the defendant, known to be such, and intended to be received as such. It binds the defendant. Its falsity consists in the implication that he was a partner of Schouler and authorized to bind him by his act. This, though a fraud, is not, we think, a forgery." And in another case where the defendant fraudulently assumed authority to indorse a bill of exchange "per procuration, Thomas Tomlinson, Emanuel White," the twelve judges were unanimously of the opinion that the offense was not forgery.[85]

§ 520. Fraudulently obtaining another's signature to a document.—It has been held that it is not forgery fraudulently to obtain another's signature to a document,[86] where the defendant was convicted of forging a promissory note,

84 Commonwealth v. Baldwin, 11 Gray (Mass.) 197, 71 Am. Dec. 703.

85 Reg. v. White, 2 Cox Cr. C. 210, 2 Car. & K. 404, 1 Den. Cr. C. 208.

86 Commonwealth v. Sankey, 22 Pa. St. 390, 60 Am. Dec. 91. See also, People v. Pfeiffer, 243 Ill. 200, 90 N. E. 680, 26 L. R. A. (N. S.) 138, 19 Ann. Cas. 703.

and the proof showed that he induced an illiterate man to sign the note, payable to himself for one hundred forty-one dollars by fraudulently pretending that it was for only forty-one dollars. On appeal, the conviction was set aside. In the opinion, the court says: "Forgery is the fraudulent making or altering of a writing to the prejudice of another's right. The defendant was guilty of the fraud, but not of the making. The paper was made by the other person himself, in prejudice of his own right. To complete the offense, according to the definition, it requires a fraudulent intent and a making both. The latter is innocent without the former, and the former, if carried into effect without the latter, is merely a cheat."

§ 521. **Fraudulently filling in blanks.**—Where an agent is authorized by his principal to fill in the amount of a check signed by the latter in blank, and the agent fraudulently fills in a greater amount with intent to appropriate the excess, he is guilty of forgery.[37] But an agent who has general authority to insert the amounts in checks signed in blank, who fraudulently fills in greater amounts than required and appropriates the excess, is guilty of embezzlement and not forgery.[38]

§ 522. **Fraudulently signing a false name.**—Forgery is committed where a person, with intent to defraud another, signs a false name to a check or bill of exchange. In such case it is immaterial whether the name signed is fictitious or not. Thus, where the defendant was convicted of forging a bill of exchange, and the proof showed that he purchased goods of the prosecutor and presented in payment therefor a bill of exchange signed in the name of a fictitious person,

[37] Rex v. Hart, 7 Car. & P. 652; People v. Dickie, 62 Hun (N. Y.) 400, 17 N. Y. S. 51; Hooper v. State, 30 Tex. App. 412, 17 S. W. 1066, 28 Am. St. 926.

[38] Reg. v. Richardson, 2 Fost. & F. 343; People v. Reinitz, 7 N. Y. Cr. 71, 6 N. Y. S. 672.

the conviction was affirmed.[39] Moreover, it is immaterial that the fictitious name signed is unnecessary. Thus, where the defendant was convicted of forging a bill of exchange, and the proof showed that he picked it out of the pocket of the owner and presented it at a bank for payment; that the clerk requested him to indorse it, which he did in the fictitious name of "John Williams"; that the clerk thereupon paid him the cash for it, the higher court affirmed the conviction.[40] In this case the judges were unanimously of the opinion that although the fictitious indorsement was unnecessary to get the money, yet the offense was forgery, since the owner thereby lost the opportunity of tracing his property and the bank its indorser. Again, where the defendant signed the fictitious name "John Williams" to a promissory note and thereby fraudulently secured a loan of eighty-five dollars and fifty cents, having previously offered to give a mortgage on a team of horses in his charge, his conviction for forgery was affirmed.[41]

§ 523. Fraudulently signing name of a deceased person.— Forgery is also committed where the name of a deceased person is signed to an instrument with intent to defraud. "It is contended, inasmuch as Hathaway was dead at the time his name was signed to the check, that therefore the making of the false instrument can not constitute the crime of forgery. The authorities do not sustain this position. On the other hand, so far as we have been able to ascertain, the contrary doctrine has been held to be the correct one, and adhered to wherever the question has been adjudicated."[42]

39 Rex v. Lockett, 2 East P. C. 940; Maloney v. State, 91 Ark. 485, 121 S. W. 728, 134 Am. St. 83, 18 Ann. Cas. 480; State v. Larson, 39 S. Dak. 120, 163 N. W. 566.

40 Rex v. Tuft, 1 Leach C. C. (3d ed.) 206.

41 State v. Wheeler, 20 Ore. 192, 25 Pac. 394, 10 L. R. A. 779n, 23 Am. St. 119. See also, People v. Campbell, 160 Mich. 108, 125 N. W. 42, 34 L. R. A. (N. S.) 58, 136 Am. St. 417.

42 Brewer v. State, 32 Tex. Cr. 74, 22 S. W. 41, 40 Am. St. 760. See also, Henderson v. State, 14 Tex. 503; Billings v. State, 107 Ind. 54, 6 N. E. 914, 57 Am. Rep. 77; 2 Bish. New Crim. L. (8th ed.), § 543n.

§ 524. **Legal efficacy of document.**—To constitute forgery the document must be of legal efficacy, either real or apparent. Hence it is not forgery to make or alter a will which is not subscribed by the required number of witnesses;[43] nor is it forgery to add names of witnesses to a document which the law does not require to be witnessed;[44] nor to imitate a bank note which is declared void by statute.[45]

Some courts hold that a letter of recommendation is capable of being forged.[46] Other courts, however, hold the contrary.[47]

A note barred by the statute of limitations is capable of being forged since the statute to be effectual must be pleaded.[48] And for a similar reason a note purporting to be signed by a minor is capable of being forged.

Where an instrument is prohibited by statute under a penalty, but which is not rendered void, it is capable of being forged.[49] But a city warrant which is void,[50] or an invalid contract owing to want of consideration,[51] or a married woman's deed which is void for want of acknowledgment,[52] or an affidavit not required by law,[53] is not capable of being forged.

43 Rex v. Wall, 2 East P. C. 953; State v. Smith, 8 Yerg. (Tenn.) 150. See also, State v. Cordray, 200 Mo. 29, 98 S. W. 1, 9 Ann. Cas. 1110; Pelton v. State, 60 Tex. Cr. 412, 132 S. W. 480, Ann. Cas. 1912 C, 86.

44 State v. Gherkin, 29 N. Car. 206.

45 Cunningham v. People, 4 Hun (N. Y.) 455 (bond not executed according to the provisions of the statute). See also, 2 Bish. New Crim. L. (8th ed.), § 538.

46 Reg. v. Sharman, Dears. Cr. C. 285; Commonwealth v. Coe, 115 Mass. 481.

47 Waterman v. People, 67 Ill. 91.

48 State v. Dunn, 23 Ore. 562, 32 Pac. 621, 37 Am. St. 704.

49 Nelson v. State, 82 Ala. 44, 2 So. 463. See also, Butler v. Commonwealth, 12 Serg. & R. (Pa.) 237, 14 Am. Dec. 679; Thompson v. State, 9 Ohio St. 354. But see, Gutchins v. People, 21 Ill. 642.

50 Raymond v. People, 2 Colo. App. 329, 30 Pac. 504.

51 People v. Shall, 9 Cow. (N. Y.) 778.

52 Roode v. State, 5 Nebr. 174, 25 Am. Rep. 475.

53 United States v. Barhart, 33 Fed. 459, 13 Sawy. (U. S.) 126.

Where a person fraudulently makes or alters a document, which on its face is apparently without legal efficacy, but which in fact, if genuine, would have legal efficacy, he is guilty of forgery.[54] Where a document is valid on its face, but invalid owing to some extrinsic fact, it is capable of being forged.[55] For example an insurance premium note which is to become valid when the policy is issued is capable of being forged although the policy is not issued.[56] The same principle is applicable to a usurious note or bill of exchange.[57] Mere misspelling of the signature attached to a note and intended to be regarded as that of another person does not prevent the offense from being forgery.[58]

§ 525. **The document may be printed or engraved.**—It is not essential that the document be written. It may be printed or engraved. Thus, a railway ticket can be the subject of forgery.[59] In the case cited, the defendant was convicted of forgery and the proof showed that he fraudulently procured innocent engravers and printers, in his absence, to engrave and print facsimiles of the tickets used on a railroad and disposed of the same. "The definition of forgery at common law is quite sufficient to embrace the present case. * * * It is then objected that the crime of forgery can not be committed by counterfeiting an instrument wholly printed or engraved, and on which there is no written signature personally made by those to be bound. * * * In the opinion of the court, such an instrument may be the subject

[54] Rembert v. State, 53 Ala. 467, 25 Am. Rep. 639; State v. Wheeler, 19 Minn. 98; Commonwealth v. Ray, 3 Gray (Mass.) 441.

[55] State v. Johnson, 26 Iowa 407, 96 Am. Dec. 158; State v. Hilton, 35 Kans. 338, 11 Pac. 164.

[56] State v. McMackin, 70 Iowa 281, 30 N. W. 635.

[57] People v. Wheeler, 47 Hun (N. Y.) 484.

[58] State v. Chance, 82 Kans. 388, 108 Pac. 789, 27 L. R. A. (N. S.) 1003, 20 Ann. Cas. 164.

[59] Commonwealth v. Ray, 3 Gray (Mass.) 441. See also, Baysinger v. State, 77 Ala. 63, 54 Am. Rep. 46n. But see, under Texas Statute, Heath v. State, 49 Tex. Cr. 49, 89 S. W. 1063, 122 Am. St. 783.

of forgery, when the entire contract, including the signature of the party, has been printed or engraved." Forgery may be committed with a typewriting machine.[60]

§ 526. **Signing own name with intent to cheat.**—A person can commit forgery by signing his own name so as to make the document purport to be that of another. "If the note is prepared for the purpose of being fraudulently used as the note of another person, it is falsely made. The question of forgery does not depend upon the presence upon the note itself of the indicia of falsity. If extrinsic circumstances are such as to facilitate the accomplishment of the cheat without the aid of any device in the note itself, the preparation of a note with intent to take advantage of those circumstances and use it falsely is 'making a false instrument.' "[61]

§ 527. **Alterations and erasures.**—An erasure can constitute forgery as well as an interlineation. In either case, however, it must be material. It is forgery to erase a condition in a negotiable promissory note so as to render it non-negotiable.[62] The maker of a note, in doing this to his own note after it is delivered, commits forgery,[63] It is not forgery to add to a document words already implied by law.[64] Thus, where a note is payable "with interest" it is not forgery to add words stating the legal rate, because they do not prejudice the maker's rights. On the other hand, changing the middle initial of a person's name has been held a material change, and therefore forgery.[65]

[60] State v. Bradley, 116 Tenn. 711, 94 S. W. 605, 115 Am. St. 836, 8 Ann. Cas. 86.

[61] Commonwealth v. Foster, 114 Mass. 311, 19 Am. Rep. 353. See also, State v. Farrell, 82 Iowa 553, 48 N. W. 940; People v. Rushing, 130 Cal. 449, 62 Pac. 742, 80 Am. St. 141; Barfield v. State, 29 Ga. 127, 74 Am. Dec. 49.

[62] State v. Stratton, 27 Iowa 420, 1 Am. Rep. 282.

[63] State v. Young, 46 N. H. 266, 88 Am. Dec. 212; Commonwealth v. Mycall, 2 Mass. 136.

[64] Hunt v. Adams, 6 Mass. 519.

[65] State v. Higgins, 60 Minn. 1, 61 N. W. 816, 27 L. R. A. 74, 51 Am. St. 490. For other changes held to be material, see Powell v.

§ 528. The intent.—To constitute forgery the act must be done with fraudulent intent.[66] And in England it has been held that the intent must be to defraud an individual.[67] In the case cited the defendant was convicted of forging and uttering a college diploma. The proof showed that he procured a diploma that had been granted by a college of surgeons to another person; that he substituted his own name, changed the date, etc., announced that he was a member of the college, applied for the position of vaccinator at the poorhouse and offered to produce the diploma to establish his qualifications for the position. The conviction was quashed, however, on the ground that no particular intent to defraud any individual was proved. But it has been held in England that where the intent is to defraud one party and the act defrauds another it constitutes forgery.[68] In this country the courts hold that a general intent to defraud is sufficient.[69]

§ 529. Doctrine of lucri causa not applicable.—As in the crime of larceny, the doctrine of lucri causa is not applicable to forgery. It is not essential that the accused entertains any intent to benefit by the act. It is sufficient if he does the act for the benefit of another.[70] Moreover, it is not essential that any one benefit by the act. Thus, the fact that a forged

Commonwealth, 11 Grat. (Va.) 822 (indorsement on a note); State v. Davis, 53 Iowa 252, 5 N. W. 149; State v. Robinson, 16 N. J. L. 507; People v. Lewinger, 252 Ill. 332, 96 N. E. 837, Ann. Cas. 1912 D, 239n.

66 Kotter v. People, 150 Ill. 441, 37 N. E. 932; Pauli v. Commonwealth, 89 Pa. St. 432.

67 Reg. v. Hodgson, 7 Cox Cr. C. 122, Dears. & B. Cr. C. 3, 36 Eng. L. & Eq. 626, 25 L. J. M. C. 78, 4 W. R. 509, 2 Jur. (N. S.) 453.

68 Rex v. Sheppard, 2 East P. C. 967, Russ. & Ry. 169.

69 Commonwealth v. Ladd, 15 Mass. 526; Barnes v. Commonwealth, 101 Ky. 556, 41 S. W. 772; Arnold v. Cost, 3 Gill & J. (Md.) 219, 22 Am. Dec. 302n; United States v. Long, 30 Fed. 678.

70 State v. White, 101 N. Car. 770, 7 S. E. 715, 9 Am. St. 53.

check is not accepted is immaterial.[71] Or that the person whose name is signed to it has no account with the bank.[72]

§ 530. Injury from forgery.—To render a person guilty of forgery it is not essential that the party whose name is forged has suffered any actual damage.[73]

§ 531. Similitude of false instrument to genuine.—The mere fact that the forgery was so crude that it ought not to have deceived any one is no defense.[74] Nor is the fact that the party whose name is forged has, in a few instances. paid checks where the accused had wrongfully signed the former's name.[75]

71 Crawford v. State, 31 Tex. Cr. 51, 19 S. W. 766. See also, State v. Cross, 101 N. Car. 770, 7 S. E. 715, 9 Am. St. 53; Hawkins v. State, 28 Fla. 363, 9 So. 652.

72 Commonwealth v. Russell, 156 Mass. 196, 30 N. E. 763. See also, State v. McMackin, 70 Iowa 281, 30 N. W. 635.

73 People v. Kuhn, 33 Cal. App. 319, 165 Pac. 26.

74 Commonwealth v. Fenwick, 177 Ky. 685, 198 S. W. 32.

75 Tongs v. State, 130 Ark. 344, 197 S. W. 573.

CHAPTER XXX.

LARCENY.

§ 533. **Definition.**—Larceny is the taking and removing of personal property of another by trespass with knowledge that neither the general nor special ownership of the property is in the taker, and with felonious intent to deprive the owner of his ownership therein.[1]

[1] Baron Parke, in speaking of the early definitions of larceny, says that none of them are complete. He also says that the most nearly complete one among them is East's, which defines the offense as the wrongful or fraudulent taking and carrying away by any person of the mere personal goods of another, from any place, with a felonious intent to convert them to his (the taker's) own use, and

§ 354. **Essentials.**—The essential elements of larceny are as follows: (1) The thing taken must be personal property. (2) The taking must be by trespass. (3) The general or special ownership of the property must be in another. (4) The property must be removed. (5) The taking and removing must be done with felonious intent to deprive the owner of his property. (6) The property must have some value.

§ 535. **Nature of the subject-matter.**—The thing taken must be of such a nature that the law regards it as property, and thus capable of being owned. Hence animals ferae naturae which have not been reclaimed, or which, though reclaimed, are unfit for food or valuable for their fur, can not, at common law, be the subject of larceny. It has been held, therefore, that dogs, cats, bears, foxes, apes, monkeys, polecats, ferrets, squirrels, parrots, singing birds, martins and coons are incapable of being the subject of larceny. While on the other hand it has been held that deer, hares, conies, pigeons, doves, pheasants, partridges, cranes, swans, wild boars, wild turkeys, wild geese, wild ducks, oysters, and certain kinds of fish, when reclaimed, are capable of being the subject of larceny.[2] Yet in many places squirrels, coons and bears are used as food, and a better distinction might be, not whether the animals were capable of use for food, but whether they were kept for food purposes.[3]

make them his own property without the consent of the owner. Reg. v. Holloway, 2 Car. & K. 942. See also, Holly v. State, 54 Ala. 238; Brown v. United States, 35 App. D. C. 548, Ann. Cas. 1912 A, 388; and extended note on larceny in 88 Am. St. 559; State v. White, 29 Del. 86, 97 Atl. 231.

[2] Haywood v. State, 41 Ark. 479.

[3] Haywood v. State, 41 Ark. 479; Miller v. United States, 242 Fed. 907, L. R. A. 1918 A, 545 (live fish).

§ 536. **Dogs.**—Some courts hold that dogs can be the subject of larceny.[4] Other courts, however, hold the contrary.[5] The two reasons assigned for the latter view are (1) the baseness of their nature, and (2) the fact that they are kept for the mere whim and pleasure of their owners. This reasoning is scarcely sound. There are many chattels protected which are used only for pleasure. Dogs have a commercial value, large in some instances and in many ways render useful services.[6] It is also held that dogs are subject of larceny for the reason that they are made taxable by statute and therefore are deemed property.[7]

§ 537. **Killing animals.**—When a hunter kills a wild animal on another's premises and removes it under circumstances which render the killing and the asportation parts of the same transaction, so that in the eye of the law there is continuity of possession in the trespasser, he is not guilty of larceny.[8] If he abandons it after killing it and subsequently returns and removes it animo furandi he is guilty of larceny.[9] In the latter case possession is transferred from the owner of the premises to the trespasser; while in the former case possession is continuous in the trespasser. The question of abandonment in this class of cases involves the question of intention. If the trespasser, at the time he goes away, intends to return for the animal within a reasonable time he does not abandon it. Thus, where hunters killed and concealed one hundred twenty-six rabbits on another's prem-

4 Mullaly v. People, 86 N. Y. 365; Commonwealth v. Hazelwood, 84 Ky. 681, 2 S. W. 489.

5 State v. Holder, 81 N. Car. 527, 31 Am. Rep. 517; Ward v. State, 48 Ala. 161, 17 Am. Rep. 31; State v. Lymus, 26 Ohio St. 400, 20 Am. Rep. 772; Findlay v. Bear, 8 Serg. & R. (Pa.) 571.

6 Mullaly v. People, 86 N. Y. 365.

7 Commonwealth v. Hazelwood, 84 Ky. 681, 2 S. W. 489; State v. Brown, 9 Baxt. (Tenn.) 53, 40 Am. Rep. 81; Hurley v. State, 30 Tex. App. 333, 17 S. W. 455, 28 Am. St. 916.

8 Reg. v. Townley, 12 Cox Cr. C. 59; Reg. v. Petch, 14 Cox Cr. C. 116.

9 Reg. v. Townley, 12 Cox Cr. C. 59.

ises, and returned after several hours and carried them away, the court held that there was a continuity of possession in the trespassers and that for this reason they were not guilty of larceny.[10] It has been held that where domestic animals were killed and their flesh or hides taken away and sold, it was larceny.[11]

§ 538. **Fruit trees, fixtures, etc.**—The principles involved where a hunter kills a wild animal on another's premises and removes it are also applicable where fruit is severed from a tree and carried away, where natural grass or standing trees are cut and removed and where fixtures are severed from the realty and taken away. "If a man enters my orchard and fills a wheelbarrow with apples, which he has gathered from my trees, he is not guilty of larceny, though he has certainly possessed himself of my property; and the same principle is applicable to wild animals."[12]

The common law distinguished between things that are connected with or savor of the real estate, and those that are personal goods. An apple growing upon a tree was connected with the land by means of the tree that bore it, and so held to partake of the nature of the land and to be real estate. One who plucked it from the tree and at once ate or carried it away was therefore a trespasser; but if he laid it down, and afterward carried it away, so that the taking and the asportation were not one and the same act, then, if the carrying away was done animo furandi, the elements of larceny were present.[13]

At common law the gas and water pipes of a house, its doors, window shutters, mantels, etc., can not be stolen, unless they are severed from the house under circumstances

10 Reg. v. Foley, 26 L. R. (Ireland) 299.

11 Flowers v. State, 69 Fla. 620, 68 So. 754, L. R. A. 1915 E, 848n.

12 Reg. v. Townley, 12 Cox Cr. C. 59. See also note, 49 L. R. A. (N. S.) 966.

13 Commonwealth v. Steimling, 156 Pa. St. 400, 27 Atl. 297.

which render them personal property.[14] Similarly, ore which has not been mined and natural ice which has not been cut are incapable of being stolen. Ore which has been mined, and ice which has been cut and stored, or cut and merely placed ready for hauling away, are personal property and therefore capable of being stolen.[15] It has been held, however, that where a person takes coal which has been deposited by a stream on another's land, sifts it, loads it on a flatboat and carries it away animo furandi, he is guilty of larceny.[16] There have been attempts to connect one who defrauded the owner of land and obtained title to it, of larceny, but this can not be done.[17]

§ 539. Chandeliers, keys, etc.—Chandeliers, though attached to a house, are deemed furniture, and therefore capable of being stolen.[18] And the keys of a house, though they would pass with the inheritance, have been held the subject of larceny. Thus, a refusal by the trial court to instruct the jury "that the key in the lock of a door of a house, and belonging thereto, is part of the realty, and not the subject of larceny, unless the same is first severed from the realty by one act, and then stolen by another and distinct act," was held not erroneous for the reason that the keys of a house, though they follow the inheritance, are nevertheless personal property.[19] It has also been held that the valves attached to a pump and boiler which were used for irrigating purposes, and which constituted permanent improvements to the real estate, were capable of being stolen, since they were easily removable. The court held, however, that where they were

14 Rex v. Westbeer, 1 Leach 14, 2 East P. C. 596.

15 State v. Burt, 64 N. Car. 619; People v. Williams, 35 Cal. 671; State v. Berryman, 8 Nev. 262, Derby's Cases 374.

16 Commonwealth v. Steimling, 156 Pa. St. 400, 27 Atl. 297.

17 State v. Klinkenberg, 76 Wash. 466, 136 Pac. 692, 49 L. R. A. (N. S.) 965.

18 Smith v. Commonwealth, 14 Bush (Ky.) 31, 29 Am. Rep. 402.

19 Hoskins v. Tarrence, 5 Blackf. (Ind.) 417, 35 Am. Dec. 129.

screwed to pipes which were fastened to the building they were not capable of being stolen.[20]

§ 540. **Choses in action.**—A chose in action, strictly speaking, is an incorporeal right, which can not, of course, be the subject of larceny. At common law the written instrument, which is evidence of the chose in action, is also incapable of being the subject of larceny. This is owing to the fact that its character as paper is regarded as merged in its character as a chose in action.[21] It is otherwise, however, where the instrument is void. Where the accused was charged with stealing a check, which was described in one of the counts of the indictment as a piece of paper, and the proof showed that the check was void, a conviction of larceny of the paper was affirmed.[22] It is to be observed that where the instrument has a potentiality of being rendered available, it is not the subject of larceny, even as a mere piece of paper. Thus, where the accused was charged with the larceny of a piece of paper, which consisted of an unstamped agreement for the building of two cottages, which agreement was not available as such, because it was not stamped as provided by statute, the conviction was reversed because the writing had a potentiality of being rendered available as a valid contract and was admissible in evidence to prove a right. "There is a very clear distinction between instruments, which without a stamp are wholly void, and those which may be rendered available at any moment, by having a stamp impressed upon them. There are many cases in which an unstamped agreement is considered evidence of a right. * * * I agree that we must look at the state of the instrument at the time of

[20] Langston v. State, 96 Ala. 44, 11 So. 334.

[21] Bl. Comm. 234; Culp v. State, 1 Port. (Ala.) 33, 26 Am. Dec. 357; United States v. Davis, Fed. Cas. No. 14930, 5 Mason (U. S.) 356; People v. Griffin, 38 How. Pr. (N. Y.) 475, Derby's Cases 371, holding that under the New York statute stock certificates are subject of larceny.

[22] Reg. v. Perry, 1 Car. & K. 725, 1 Cox Cr. C. 222.

the larceny committed; but it then had a potentiality of being rendered available, and it was evidence of an agreement; it was therefore evidence of a chose in action, and not the subject of larceny."[23] Railroad tickets, though not stamped or delivered to a passenger, have been held the subject of larceny.[24]

§ 541. **Manure.**—Manure which is piled in a heap for subsequent disposal is personal property and therefore capable of being stolen; but manure which has been spread upon the land is real estate and therefore incapable of being stolen.[25]

§ 542. **Gas, water, etc.**—Illuminating gas[26] and water[27] supplied in pipes to consumers are personal property and capable of being stolen. Electricity, however, is not, at common law, but in some states it is made the subject of larceny by statute.

§ 543. **Gambling devices—Liquor illegally kept for sale.**—The fact that intoxicating liquor is illegally kept for sale does not render it incapable of being stolen.[28] But whether devices used for gambling are the subject of larceny or not is a question upon which the decisions are in conflict.[29]

§ 544. **Abandoned property.**—Property which has been wholly abandoned by the owner is not the subject of larceny.[30] But pigs, which had been bitten by a mad dog and shot and buried on the owner's land, were held not aban-

[23] Lord Campbell in Reg. v. Watts, 6 Cox Cr. C. 304.

[24] State v. Wilson, 63 Ore. 344, 127 Pac. 980, Ann. Cas. 1914 D, 646.

[25] Carver v. Pierce, K. B. 1648. Style 66.

[26] Reg. v. White, 6 Cox Cr. C. 213; Woods v. People, 222 Ill. 293, 78 N. E. 607, 113 Am. St. 415, 7 L. R. A. (N. S.) 520n; Commonwealth v. Shaw, 4 Allen (Mass.) 308, 81 Am. Dec. 706, Derby's Cases 373.

[27] Ferens v. O'Brien, 15 Cox Cr. C. 332, L. R. 11 Q. B. Div. 21.

[28] State v. May, 20 Iowa 305; Commonwealth v. Coffee, 9 Gray (Mass.) 139.

[29] Bales v. State, 3 W. Va. 685 (yes); State v. Wilmore, 9 Ohio Dec. (Reprint) 61 (no).

[30] People v. Hoban, 240 Ill. 303, 88 N. E. 806, 22 L. R. A. (N. S.) 1132, 16 Ann. Cas. 226.

doned property, and the defendants who had dug them up and sold them, animo furandi, were held guilty of larceny.[31]

§ 545. **Body of dead person, grave clothes, etc.**—The body of a dead person is not the subject of larceny at common law but the coffin containing the body, and the grave clothes, are.[32] The clothes on the body of a dead person who has been drowned and driven ashore from a wreck are likewise the subject of larceny.[33]

§ 546. **Value of the property.**—To be the subject of larceny, the thing taken must be of some value.[34] The slightest value, however, is sufficient. Even a piece of paper can be the subject of larceny.[35] But, as heretofore stated, a paper which constitutes evidence of a chose in action can not be the subject of larceny because the paper becomes evidence of a right, and ceases to have any existence as anything else.[36] The same principle is applicable to title deeds, for they are evidence of title to lands.[37]

Dead infected animals which have been buried still retain sufficient value to be the subject of larceny.[38]

§ 547. **Mode of taking—Trespass.**—One of the essentials of larceny at common law is that the taking must be by trespass. It must be done under such circumstances that the taker would be liable in an action for damages for trespass to goods.[39] To constitute trespass the taking must be unlawful and without the owner's consent. Ownership, however, may

[31] Reg. v. Edwards, 13 Cox Cr. C. 384.

[32] State v. Doepke, 68 Mo. 208, 30 Am. Rep. 785.

[33] Wonson v. Sayward, 13 Pick. (Mass.) 402, 23 Am. Dec. 691.

[34] Hope v. Commonwealth, 9 Metc. (Mass.) 134; People v. Wiley, 3 Hill (N. Y.) 194; Gates v. State, 20 Ga. App. 171, 92 S. E. 974.

[35] Reg. v. Perry, 1 Car. & K. 725, 1 Cox Cr. C. 222.

[36] Reg. v. Watts, 6 Cox Cr. C. 304.

[37] Reg. v. Watts, 6 Cox Cr. C. 304.

[38] Reg. v. Edwards, 13 Cox Cr. C. 384.

[39] Reg. v. Smith, 2 Den. Cr. C. 449; State v. Casey, 207 Mo. 1, 105 S. W. 645, 123 Am. St. 367, 13 Ann.

be special as well as general. Moreover, the general owner can commit larceny by feloniously taking the property from the possession of the special owner. Thus, a pledgee has a special property in the thing pledged; and if the pledgor, who has a general property in it, takes it from him without his consent, and with the fraudulent design of depriving him of his security, he commits larceny. Furthermore, even where the pledgee consents to the taking for a particular purpose the pledgor is guilty of larceny, if the taking is with the fraudulent design of depriving the pledgee of his security.[40]

§ 548. Possession versus custody.—Possession may be either actual or constructive. Where goods are in the bare charge or custody of a mere servant the constructive possession of them is in the master. In such case the servant has no special property in them, and for this reason if he fraudulently converts them to his own use he is guilty of trespass and larceny. So a servant who had charge of his master's mule and took it from the plow while in his custody, was nevertheless guilty of larceny.[41] The custody of a servant is distinguishable from the possession of a bailee by reason of the fact that the bailee is under a special contract with respect to the goods which gives him a special property in them; whereas a mere servant has no such special property. Hence a bailee who converts them to his own use does not commit a trespass, and therefore is not guilty of larceny, unless at the time he receives them he has a felonious intent

Cas. 878; People v. Csontos, 275 Ill. 402, 114 N. E. 123; People v. Brenneauer, 166 N. Y. S. 801, 101 Misc. 156.

40 Bruley v. Rose, 57 Iowa 651, 11 N. W. 629. See also Vaught v. State, 135 Wis. 6, 114 N. W. 518, 646, 32 L. R. A. (N. S.) 234, 128 Am. St. 1008.

41 Crocheron v. State, 86 Ala. 64, 5 So. 649, 11 Am. St. 18, Derby's Cases 441; People v. Brenneauer, 166 N. Y. S. 801, 101 Misc. 156; Hatcher v. State (Fla.), 76 So. 694; King v. State (Ala. App.), 72 So. 552.

to wrongfully convert them.[42] But if such intent exists at the time he receives the goods his possession is unlawful and he is guilty of trespass, and a subsequent conversion of them to his own use is larceny. So, one who hires a horse from a livery stable with an intent at the time to steal it, is guilty of larceny.[43]

And where a bailee of goods breaks the package in which they are contained and takes out some of the articles, animo furandi, he has terminated the bailment, and may be convicted of larceny.[44]

On the other hand, where the owner of a horse gave the defendant permission to ride it to a certain place, with instructions to turn it loose there, and while on the way the defendant exchanged the horse for an overcoat, and the proof did not show that possession of the horse was obtained by any false pretext, or with intent to deprive the owner of his property, the court held that he was guilty of larceny.[45] And where a bailee of clothes to be repaired took money from the pockets, a conviction of larceny was sustained.[46]

Also a conviction may be had for taking a box of matches placed on a store counter for the use of customers or the public.[47]

Where a third party hands money or other personal property to a servant with instructions to take it to his master,

[42] Watson v. State, 70 Ala. 13, 45 Am. Rep. 70; Reg. v. Thristle, 3 Cox Cr. C. 573, Derby's Cases 399; People v. Cruger, 102 N. Y. 510, 7 N. E. 555, 55 Am. Rep. 830, Derby's Cases 402; Johnson v. People, 113 Ill. 99, Derby's Cases 410; 2 Whart. Crim. L. (11th ed.), §§ 1177, 1178. But see State v. Levine, 79 Conn. 714, 66 Atl. 529, 10 L. R. A. (N. S.) 286.

[43] People v. Smith, 23 Cal. 280; Hill v. State, 57 Wis. 377, 15 N. W. 445, Derby's Cases 405.

[44] State v. Fairclough, 29 Conn. 47, 76 Am. Dec. 590, Derby's Cases 451.

[45] Stokely v. State, 24 Tex. App. 509, 6 S. W. 538. See also State v. Coombs, 55 Maine 577, 92 Am. Dec. 610, Derby's Cases 407; State v. Ruffin, 164 N. Car. 416, 79 S. E. 417, 47 L. R. A. (N. S.) 852; and note to 43 L. R. A. (N. S.) 1179.

[46] Rose v. State, 52 Tex. Cr. 154, 106 S. W. 143, Derby's Cases 404.

[47] Mitchum v. State, 45 Ala. 29, Derby's Cases 414.

and instead of so doing the servant wrongfully converts the property to his own use he is not guilty of larceny. This is owing to the fact that in such case the master has neither the actual nor constructive possession of the property.[48] One who receives money to change or count, in the presence of the owner, and appropriates it, is guilty of larceny.[49]

§ 549. **Finding lost property.**—Whether the finder of lost goods is guilty of larceny or not depends upon the circumstances of the particular case. If at the time he finds them he knows who the owner is, or has reasonable means of gaining such knowledge, and at the time of the finding appropriates them animo furandi, he is guilty of larceny.[50] If, however, the felonious intent is formed afterward, the finder is not guilty of larceny, even where he has knowledge at the time of the finding of the true ownership of the goods.[51]

§ 550. **Property merely mislaid.**—There is a clear distinction between property lost and property mislaid, put down, and left by mistake, under circumstances which would enable the owner to know the place where he had left it, and to which he would naturally return for it.[52] Where the property

[48] Rex v. Sullens, 1 Mood. C. C. 129, Derby's Cases 444; Reg. v. Reed, 6 Cox Cr. C. 284, Derby's Cases 445; Commonwealth v. Ryan, 155 Mass. 523, 30 N. E. 364, 15 L. R. A. 317, 31 Am. St. 560, Derby's Cases 447.

[49] Commonwealth v. O'Malley, 97 Mass. 584, Derby's Cases 429; State v. Walker, 65 Kans. 92, 68 Pac. 1095, Derby's Cases 434; Hildebrand v. People, 56 N. Y. 394, 15 Am. Rep. 435, Derby's Cases 436; Justices v. People, 90 N. Y. 12, 1 N. Y. Cr. 83, 43 Am. Rep. 135n, Derby's Cases 439. But see Reg. v. Reynolds, 2 Cox Cr. C. 170, Derby's Cases 438.

[50] Merry v. Green, 7 M. & W. 623; State v. Courtsol, 89 Conn. 564, 94 Atl. 973, L. R. A. 1916 A, 465n; People v. Csontos, 275 Ill. 402, 114 N. E. 123.

[51] Commonwealth v. Titus, 116 Mass. 42, 17 Am. Rep. 138n. See also Williams v. State, 165 Ind. 472, 75 N. E. 875, 2 L. R. A. (N. S.) 248; Reg. v. Thurborn, 1 Den. Cr. C. 387, Derby's Cases 454; People v. Anderson, 14 Johns. (N. Y.) 294, 7 Am. Dec. 462; People v. Csontos, 275 Ill. 402, 114 N. E. 123.

[52] Reg. v. West, 6 Cox Cr. C. 415; Dears. Cr. C. 402, 24 L. J. M. C. 4.

taken is merely mislaid, the fact that the wrongful intent is subsequently formed is immaterial. Where a person bought at public auction a piece of furniture and some time after the delivery of the same he discovered money in a secret drawer and appropriated it animo furandi he was held guilty of larceny.[53] Again, where a bureau was delivered to the defendant to repair, and subsequently he discovered nine hundred guineas in a secret drawer and appropriated the money animo furandi, he was held guilty of larceny. As said by Lord Eldon, in this case, "To constitute felony there must of necessity be a felonious taking. Breach of trust will not do. But from all the cases in Hawkins there is no doubt, this bureau being delivered to the defendant for no other purpose than repair, if he broke open any part, which it was not necessary to touch for the purpose of repair, but with an intention to take and appropriate to his own use what he should find, that is a felonious taking within the principle of all the modern cases, as not being warranted by the purpose for which it was delivered. If a pocketbook containing banknotes was left in the pocket of a coat sent to be mended, and the tailor took the pocketbook out of the pocket, and the notes out of the pocketbook, there is not the least doubt that is a felony. So, if the pocketbook was left in a hackney coach, if ten people were in the coach in the course of the day, and the coachman did not know to which of them it belonged, he acquires it by finding it certainly, but not being intrusted with it for the purpose of opening it, that is a felony according to the modern cases."[54] The defendant, a hackman, took the prosecuting witness to meet a train and upon arriving at the station the latter left with him a quilt and requested him to return it to the owner's home, which the defendant agreed to do, but instead of so doing took it to a store and sold it,

53 Merry v. Green, 7 M. & W. 623.

54 Cartwright v. Green, 8 Ves. (Jr.) 405; People v. Csontos, 275 Ill. 402, 114 N. E. 123.

a request by the defendant that the court charge the jury that if the quilt was received with intent to deliver it as requested and the intent to sell it was subsequently formed they must acquit, was held properly refused since the defendant had mere custody of the quilt rather than possession of it.[55]

§ 551. **Property delivered by mistake.**—If property of one person is delivered to another by mistake and he appropriates it, he is guilty of larceny if at the time of the taking he knew it was not his, and then had the intent to keep it; but if he acquires it believing it his and afterward forms the intent of keeping it, it is not larceny. These rules are applied where money and checks have been mistakenly delivered to one other than the owner.[56]

§ 552. **Possession or custody obtained by fraudulent trick.**—Where possession or custody of the chattel is obtained by means of a fraudulent trick the taker commits trespass; and if he converts it to his own use, animo furandi, he is guilty of larceny.[57] It is to be observed, however, that if he obtains title to the property he is not guilty of larceny. It is sometimes difficult to discriminate between these two classes of cases. The following examples will help to elucidate the distinction:

1. Defendants obtained cigarettes from a slot machine by fraudulently putting into it metal discs about the size of a penny, and appropriated the cigarettes to their own use

[55] Holbrook v. State, 107 Ala. 154, 18 So. 109, 54 Am. St. 65.

[56] Reg. v. Middleton, L. R. 2 C. C. 38, Derby's Cases 458; Reg. v. Flowers, 16 Cox Cr. C. 33, Derby's Cases 462; Reg. v. Hehir, 18 Cox Cr. C. 267, Derby's Cases 466; Rex v. Mucklow, 1 Mood. Cr. C. 160, Derby's Cases 398.

[57] State v. Dobbins, 152 Iowa 632, 132 N. W. 805, 42 L. R. A. (N. S.)735; Commonwealth v. Althause, 207 Mass. 32, 93 N. E. 202, 31 L. R. A. (N. S.) 999; Aldrich v. People, 224 Ill. 622, 79 N. E. 964, 7 L. R. A. (N. S.) 1149, 115 Am. St. 166, 8 Ann. Cas. 284; State v. Ryan, 47 Ore. 338, 82 Pac. 703, 1 L. R. A. (N. S.) 862; State v. Donaldson, 35 Utah 96, 99 Pac. 447, 136 Am. St. 1041, 20 L. R. A. (N. S.) 1164.

animo furandi. In doing so they acquired mere possession and not title and therefore were guilty of larceny.[58] Similarly, they would have been guilty of larceny of the cigarettes had they fraudulently used a penny with a hole in it with a string attached. In withdrawing the penny after it had accomplished its purpose they would not have been guilty of the larceny of the penny for the reason that they would not have parted with possession of it.

2. Defendant hired a mare with intent to steal her and subsequently converted her to his own use by selling her. Judge Ashurst instructed the jury that if the prisoner hired the mare to take the journey mentioned, and afterward changed his mind and sold her while the privity of contract subsisted they should acquit him; but if they found that the journey was a mere pretense to get possession, and he hired her to steal her, they ought to convict him. The jury found him guilty, and on appeal ten of the eleven justices were of the opinion that so obtaining the mare by fraud and falsehood, intending then to steal her, was larceny at common law.[59]

3. Defendant's pal pretended that he had found a purse containing a receipt for two hundred ten pounds for a diamond ring and also the ring; and the prosecutor, who was with the pal at the time, was fraudulently induced by the confederates to give the pal twenty guineas and four doubloons and take the ring and keep it until the next day when the three were to meet again, at which time the prosecutor was to receive the money back and also one hundred guineas additional as his share of the find, and return the ring to the defendant's pal. Instead of so doing, however, the latter kept the money given him by the prosecutor, and the jury

[58] Reg. v. Hands, 16 Cox Cr. C. 188, 56 L. T. 370; Jarvis v. State (Fla.), 74 So. 796; Glaze v. State, 13 Okla. Cr. 431, 165 Pac. 211; People v. Howard, 31 Cal. App. 358, 160 Pac. 697; People v. Deinhardt, 179 App. Div. 228, 166 N. Y. S. 502.

[59] Rex v. Pear, 1 Leach 253, 2 East P. C. 685, 3 R. R. 703. See also Rex v. Semple, 2 Leach 469, Derby's Cases 415.

convicted him of larceny. On appeal, nine of the eleven justices affirmed the conviction, the other two dissenting on the ground that the money paid by the prosecutor was a loan on the security of the ring, which the prosecutor believed to be of much greater value than the money advanced on it, and therefore that he had voluntarily parted with the possession of the money. All the judges agreed, however, that in considering the nature of larceny it was necessary to discriminate between the parting with the possession only and the parting with the property; that in the former case it was larceny and in the latter not.[60]

4. Defendant was convicted of the larceny of a quantity of bacon and hams. The proof showed that he went to A's shop and told A that B had asked him to call there and get some bacon and hams for him; that he produced a writing which purported to be signed by B, and which requested A to send him the meat by the defendant and which stated that B would pay for it the next time he went to town; that A, believing the writing to be genuine, delivered the meat to the defendant, and that subsequently he learned that the writing was a forgery. On appeal, all the justices held that the conviction was wrong for the reason that the prosecutor parted with the property and not merely the possession of it.[61]

5. Defendant was convicted of the larceny of certain goods. The proof showed that by falsely and fraudulently representing himself as the agent of another he obtained the goods of the prosecutor. On appeal, the conviction was affirmed on the ground that the defendant acquired only the mere custody of the goods. In this case Justice Simmons, speaking for the court, says: "Harris fraudulently represented to High and Ryan's sons that he was the agent of Moore & Marsh. They did not sell him the goods, nor did they intend

60 Rex v. Moore, 1 Leach 354, 2 East P. C. 679.

61 Reg. v. Adams, 1 Den. Cr. C. 38. See also, Rex v. Coleman, 2 East P. C. 672.

the title to go into Harris; but they simply delivered him the custody of the goods, to be delivered by him to Moore & Marsh. He having converted the proceeds of the sale of the boxes to his own use, he was guilty of larceny. The title still remained in the vendor. Harris got the custody of the goods wrongfully and fraudulently."[62]

6. Defendant was convicted of the larceny of five quarters of wheat. The proof showed that he obtained the wheat from the servant in charge of the storehouse where it was stored by falsely and fraudulently representing to him that he had been sent for it by another superior servant in charge of another storehouse. On appeal, the conviction was affirmed.[63]

7. Defendant was convicted of the larceny of two dollars in money, a watch and some jewels. The proof showed that he falsely and fraudulently represented to prosecutor's wife that her husband had been arrested for striking a man on the head with a chair, and that he would be put in jail if he could not produce twelve dollars, for which he had sent defendant to her; that the wife had only two dollars, but, at defendant's suggestion, she gave him this, together with a watch and some jewels to pawn, and directed him to take the money and the pawn ticket to her husband; but that, instead of so doing, he appropriated the two dollars and the chattels to his own use. The trial court instructed the jury that if they found that defendant, when he obtained the property, had a felonious intent to keep it he was guilty of larceny. On appeal, the conviction was affirmed. In this case, Justice Allen, speaking for the court, says: "The accused obtained the custody of the chattels and money of the prosecutor from his wife by a fraudulent device and trick, and for a special purpose, connected with the falsely represented necessities of the owner, with the felonious intent to appropriate the same to his own use. He did not pawn or pledge the goods,

[62] Harris v. State, 81 Ga. 758, 7 S. E. 689, 12 Am. St. 355.

[63] Reg. v. Robins, Dears. Cr. C. 418, 6 Cox Cr. C. 420.

as he proposed to do, but did appropriate the same to his own use, in pursuance of the felonious intent with which he received them. This constitutes the crime of larceny. The owner did not part with the property in the chattels, or transfer the legal possession. The accused had merely the custody; the possession and ownership remaining in the original proprietor. * * * The conviction was right and the judgment must be affirmed.[64]

8. Defendant was convicted of the larceny of two hundred eighty dollars in currency. The testimony of the prosecuting witness was: "The defendant asked me if I was going to take that train; I said, 'Yes.' He said he thought he would go on that train, too. Then a man came up to us and said to the defendant, 'If you want to go on that train, you had better get your baggage and pay your freight bill.' The defendant then said, 'Confound those fellows, they won't pay me any premium on my gold, and I have no other money to pay this freight bill, and I don't want to give them two hundred and eighty dollars in gold and get no premium.' He then said to me, 'Will you let me have two hundred eighty dollars in currency, and I will give you this gold to hold as security until I can go to the bank.'" And furthermore, that the prosecuting witness took the pieces offered, believing them to be gold, gave the defendant the two hundred eighty dollars in currency and soon afterward discovered that he had been buncoed with bogus coin. On appeal, the conviction was set aside on the ground that title to the currency passed to the defendant. In this case, Chief Justice McIlvaine, speaking for the court, says: "The testimony of the witness was that he voluntarily delivered the money to the defendant and never expected to get the same money again. It is true he was induced to make the loan through the fraud and false pretenses of the defendant. No doubt a crime was thus committed by the defendant, but it was the crime of false pretenses, and not larceny. To constitute lar-

[64] Smith v. People, 53 N. Y. 111, 13 Am. Rep. 474.

ceny in a case where the owner voluntarily parts with the possession of his property, two other conditions are essential: (1) The owner, at the time of parting with the possession, must expect and intend that the thing delivered will be returned to him or disposed of under his direction for his benefit. (2) The person taking the possession must, at the time, intend to deprive the owner of his property in the thing delivered. But where the owner intends to transfer, not the possession merely, but also the title to the property, although induced thereto by the fraud and fraudulent pretenses of the taker, the taking and carrying away do not constitute larceny."[65]

9. Defendant was convicted of the larceny of five shillings. The proof showed that he had a stand at certain races and took bets; that he took five shillings of prosecutor on a bet by the latter that a certain horse, "Bird of Freedom", would win; that this horse won and prosecutor went for his money but found that defendant had absconded with it. On appeal, the conviction was affirmed. In this case Justice Smith says: "I think that it is clear the prosecutor never intended to part with the property in the five shillings except on condition that a bona fide bet was made. I think also that there is evidence that at the time the prosecutor handed the five shillings to the prisoner, the prisoner intended to keep possession of the money, whether 'Bird of Freedom' lost or won. He therefore obtained the possession of the prosecutor's money by means of a preconcerted and premeditated fraud; in other words, by a trick. There was, therefore, abundant evidence of larceny, and, in my opinion the conviction should be affirmed." The other justices rendered similar opinions.[66]

10. Defendants were convicted of the larceny of one thousand dollars in money and a promissory note for four thousand dollars. The proof showed that they induced the prosecuting witness to give them the money by falsely and fraudulently representing that they would transfer to him within

65 Kellogg v. State, 26 Ohio St. 15.

66 Reg. v. Buckmaster, 16 Cox Cr. C. 339, L. R., 20 Q. B. Div. 182.

thirty days counterfeit bank bills of the face value of twenty-five thousand dollars, which they failed to do. On appeal, the conviction was affirmed on the ground that the prosecuting witness parted with possession only and not title to the property.[67]

11. One, who with intent to convert the proceeds to his own use, secured from his fiancé a conveyance of property upon the representation that he would sell it and could sell it, to better advantage than she could, and would turn the proceeds over to her and then sold the property and appropriated the proceeds, was held guilty of larceny, since, though she conveyed the title to the property, she did not part with the right to the proceeds.[68]

12. One who represented that he had inside information of the operations of the New York Stock Exchange, and organized a "Franklin Syndicate" and promised to pay ten per cent. weekly on money deposited, was held guilty of larceny.[69]

§ 553. **Ownership must be in another.**—To constitute the crime of larceny ownership of the property must be in another. It may be special, however, as well as general. It is not essential that the person from whom the property is taken, have the legal title. In fact, he may have absolutely no title at all, as where the taker steals from a person who himself has stolen it. In such case ownership may be laid in the indictment in the thief from whom the property is taken, or in the general owner.[70] A bailee has special owner-

[67] Crum v. State, 148 Ind. 401, 47 N. E. 833.

[68] Morton v. Commonwealth, 159 Ky. 231, 166 S. W. 974, 52 L. R. A. (N. S.) 1222.

[69] People v. Miller, 169 N. Y. 339, 62 N. E. 418, 88 Am. St. 546n, Derby's Cases 418.

[70] Commonwealth v. Finn, 108 Mass. 466; Ward v. People, 3 Hill (N. Y.) 395 (affd. 6 Hill (N. Y.) 144). See also State v. Pigg, 80 Kans. 481, 18 Ann. Cas. 521; Rex v. Beboning, 17 Ont. L. R. 23, 13 Ann. Cas. 491.

ship in the chattel,[71] and even the general owner is guilty of larceny in appropriating it animo furandi.[72] And where the general owner clandestinely removes property from the rightful possession of another who has a valid lien on it he is guilty of larceny.[73] Similarly, the general owner of chattels which have been levied on under execution is guilty of larceny if he takes them animo furandi. "There is no doubt a man may be guilty of larceny in stealing his own property, when done with intent to charge another person with the value of it."[74] Again, one is guilty of larceny where he takes property animo furandi which is in the possession of his co-owner as bailee.[75]

At common law husband and wife are regarded as one person, and for this reason one spouse can not steal from the other.[76] But in those jurisdictions where the husband's interests in his wife's personal property is abolished by statute he can be guilty of larceny in appropriating them.[77] Where a third person assists the wife in appropriating her husband's

71 Barnes v. People, 18 Ill. 52, 65 Am. Dec. 699, Derby's Cases 378; Kasle v. United States, 233 Fed. 878; Ward v. State (Tex. Cr.), 197 S. W. 1102; Jackson v. State (Ga. App.), 94 S. E. 55 (in indictment for larceny ownership of the property stolen may not be laid in a servant having the mere custody of the property).

72 Commonwealth v. Greene, 111 Mass. 392; People v. Thompson, 34 Cal. 671; Henry v. State, 110 Ga. 750, 36 S. E. 55, 78 Am. St. 137, Derby's Cases 380; Atchison, &c. R. Co. v. Hinsdell, 76 Kans. 74, 90 Pac. 800, 12 L. R. A. (N. S.) 94n, 13 Ann. Cas. 981.

73 People v. Long, 50 Mich. 249, 15 N. W. 105.

74 Chief Justice Savage in Palmer v. People, 10 Wend. (N. Y.) 165, 25 Am. Dec. 551. See also, Adams v. State, 45 N. J. L. 448.

75 Reg. v. Webster, 9 Cox Cr. C. 13.

76 Reg. v. Kenny, 13 Cox Cr. C. 397; Lamphier v. State, 70 Ind. 317; State v. Parker, 3 Ohio Dec. 551, Derby's Cases 382.

77 Beasley v. State, 138 Ind. 552, 38 N. E. 35, 46 Am. St. 418; Hunt v. State, 72 Ark. 241, 65 L. R. A. 71, 105 Am. St. 34, 2 Ann. Cas. 33. But see, State v. Philips, 85 Ohio St. 317, 97 N. E. 976, 40 L. R. A. (N. S.) 142, Ann. Cas. 1913 B, 250.

property he is not guilty of larceny, unless she has committed, or intends to commit, adultery with him.[78]

Where clothing or other chattels are stolen from the body of a dead person ownership may be laid in his executors.[79]

§ 554. Asportation of the property.—One of the essentials of larceny is removal of the property. The slightest removal, however, is sufficient, provided the taker has absolute control of it even for only an instant.[80] Where, in a case, the proof showed that the accused went behind the prosecutor's counter, opened the money drawer, took the money contained therein in his hand and disarranged the bills, but upon being discovered left the money in the drawer, the conviction was affirmed. In another case the proof showed that the accused opened a money drawer, lifted six dollars, but upon being discovered dropped it, and his conviction of the larceny of the entire contents of the drawer, fifty-one dollars, was affirmed.[81] Where the thief snatches an earring from a lady's ear and drops it in her hair;[82] or lifts money an appreciable distance in another's pocket;[83] or takes clothes from a bedroom into a hall adjoining;[84] or lifts a sword partly out of its scabbard;[85] or removes a chattel from one end of a wagon

[78] Reg. v. Flatman, 14 Cox Cr. C. 396; People v. Swalm, 80 Cal. 46, 22 Pac. 67, 13 Am. St. 96.

[79] Hayne's Case, 12 Coke 113.

[80] State v. Jones, 65 N. Car. 395, Derby's Cases 386; Eckels v. State, 20 Ohio St. 508. See also, Harrison v. People, 50 N. Y. 518, 10 Am. Rep. 517, Derby's Cases 388; State v. Higgins, 88 Mo. 354, Derby's Cases 389; Thomas v. State (Ala. App.), 72 So. 686; Looney v. State, 80 Tex. Cr. 317, 189 S. W. 954; People v. Ostrosky, 95 Misc. 104, 160 N. Y. S. 493 (chickens); McKenzie v. State, 111 Miss. 780, 72 So. 198 (hog); Starnes v. State, 128 Ark. 302, 194 S. W. 506; State v. Maddaus, 137 Minn. 249, 163 N. W. 507.

[81] Harris v. State, 29 Tex. App. 101, 14 S. W. 390, 25 Am. St. 717.

[82] Lapier's Case, 1 Leach 360.

[83] Commonwealth v. Luckis, 90 Mass. 431, 96 Am. Dec. 769; State v. Chambers, 22 W. Va. 779, 46 Am. Rep. 550.

[84] 3 Inst. 108, 1 Hale P. C. 507, 508.

[85] 2 Russ. on Crimes (9th Am. ed.) 153.

to the other;[86] or removes grain from the owner's garner in a mill to the thief's garner adjoining;[87] or removes a money drawer from a safe to the floor;[88] or rolls tubs of butter from one end of a car to another and changes the address tags, so that the carrier will transport them as his agent,[89] the asportation is sufficient to render the offense larceny. On the other hand, merely setting a bale,[90] or barrel, [91] upon end; or killing or trapping an animal;[92] or shooting and wounding an animal; [93] or unfastening a dress on a display model in order to remove it,[94] has been held insufficient.

§ 555. **Asportation by enticement.**—The asportation may be effected by means of enticement. Thus, an animal may be stolen by enticing it away by means of food. It is essential, however, that the thief acquire dominion over it. "If one entice a horse, hog, or other animal, by placing food in such a situation as to operate on the volition of the animal, and he assumes the dominion over it, and has it once under his control, the deed is complete; but if we suppose him detected before he has the animal under his control, yet after he has operated on its volition, the offense would not be consummated."[95] It is to be observed, therefore, that "It would seem there can be no asportation, within the legal acceptation of the word, without a previously acquired dominion."[96]

[86] Coslet's Case, 1 Leach 271.

[87] State v. Craige, 89 N. Car. 475, 45 Am. Rep. 698.

[88] State v. Green, 81 N. Car. 560.

[89] State v. Rozeboom, 145 Iowa 620, 124 N. W. 783, 29 L. R. A. (N. S.) 37, Derby's Cases 395.

[90] Cherry's Case, 2 East P. C. 556.

[91] State v. Jones, 65 N. Car. 395, Derby's Cases 386.

[92] Ward v. State, 48 Ala. 161, 17 Am. Rep. 31; Williams v. State, 63 Miss. 58; State v. Alexander, 74 N. Car. 232, Derby's Cases 387.

[93] Minter v. State, 26 Tex. App. 217, 9 S. W. 561; Molton v. State, 105 Ala. 18, 16 So. 795, 53 Am. St. 97.

[94] Clark v. State, 59 Tex. Cr. 246, 128 S. W. 131, 29 L. R. A. (N. S.) 323, Derby's Cases 392.

[95] State v. Wisdom, 8 Port. (Ala.) 511.

[96] Edmonds v. State, 70 Ala. 8, 45 Am. Rep. 67.

But, as said in the same opinion, "Where a person takes an animal into an enclosure, with intent to steal it, and is apprehended before he can get it out, he is guilty of larceny." In this case the defendant was convicted of the larceny of a hog. The proof showed that his confederate got some corn and an ax; that the confederate, having given defendant the ax, tolled the hog some twenty yards by dropping some of the corn on the ground; that the defendant then struck the hog with the ax which caused the animal to squeal, whereupon both men ran away leaving the hog where it fell. The conviction was set aside on the ground that there was not a sufficient caption and asportation to constitute larceny.

§ 556. **Asportation by innocent agent.**—The asportation may also be effected by means of an innocent agent. "There is no occasion that the carrying away be by the hand of the party accused, for if he procured an innocent agent, as a child or a lunatic, to take the property, * * * he will himself be a principal offender."[97] "An asportation may be effected by means of innocent human agency. as well as by mechanical agency; or by the offender's own hand."[98] In the case from which the quotation is taken the proof showed that one Kerr, owner of a trunk, checked it at Worcester for Hartford; that one Briggs, defendant's confederate, checked his valise at Worcester for New York; that defendant surreptitiously interchanged the checks on the trunk and valise, in consequence of which the trunk went to New York, where Briggs took it from the station. The defendant was convicted of the larceny of the trunk and its contents, and appealed the case to the Supreme Court. In the opinion, Justice Lord observes: "The real question was, whether the defendant, at that time, feloniously and with intent to steal, set

97 3 Chit. Crim. L. 925.

98 Commonwealth v. Barry, 125 Mass. 390. See also, Aldrich v. People, 224 Ill. 622, 79 N. E. 964, 7 L. R. A. (N. S.) 1149, 115 Am. St. 166, 8 Ann. Cas. 284.

in motion an innocent agency, by which the trunk and contents were to be removed from the possession of the true owner, and put into the defendant's possession, and whether such purpose was actually accomplished," and the conviction is affirmed.

§ 557. **The caption and asportation must be felonious.**—The taking and removal must be done animo furandi. The intent must be to deprive the owner permanently of his property, and it must concur with the caption and asportation. Thus, where one borrows or hires a horse intending to return it, but subsequently changes his mind and converts it by selling it, he is not guilty of larceny.[99] Nor is the taker guilty of larceny where his intent is merely to deprive the owner of his property temporarily. Thus, where he takes another's horse to go a short distance, intending to return it, he is not guilty of larceny.[1] It has been held, however, that where a person takes another's horse, without his consent, to ride a short distance, intending to turn it loose to stray back, that he is guilty of larceny;[2] but this view is not sustained by the weight of authority.[3] Where one takes another's property with intent to return it to its owner upon receiving a reward for so doing he is guilty of larceny.[4] And where his intent is to sell it back to the owner, or to apply it on a debt owing to the owner by the thief, or to induce the owner to sell it at a reduced price, it is sufficient to render the offense larceny.[5] Where the property is taken with intent to

99 Gooch v. State, 60 Ark. 5, 28 S. W. 510.

1 State v. South, 28 N. J. L. 28, 75 Am. Dec. 250; Schultz v. State, 30 Tex. App. 94, 16 S. W. 756. See also, Wilson v. State, 18 Tex. App. 270, 51 Am. Rep. 309n, Derby's Cases 477.

2 State v. Ward, 19 Nev. 297, 10 Pac. 133.

3 Rex v. Crump, 1 Car. & P. 658; Umphrey v. State, 63 Ind. 223; Dove v. State, 37 Ark. 261; State v. York, 5 Harr. (Del.) 493.

4 Berry v. State, 31 Ohio St. 219, 27 Am. Rep. 506; Commonwealth v. Mason, 105 Mass. 163, 7 Am. Rep. 507.

5 Reg. v. Hall, 3 Cox Cr. C. 245, 2 Car. & K. 947; Commonwealth v. Stebbins, 8 Gray (Mass.) 492; Fort v. State, 82 Ala. 50, 2 So. 477.

pledge it and subsequently to redeem and return it to the owner, the act constitutes larceny.[6] Some decisions are to the contrary.[7] According to the better view the taker's intent to redeem and return the property to the owner, and his ability to do so, are immaterial.[8]

It is to be observed, therefore, that the term "permanently," as used in the definition of larceny, has a restricted meaning. It does not mean precisely keeping the specific property from the owner's possession. So a conviction of larceny was upheld where the defendant and two others took from the owner, without his consent, two geldings which they secreted in the woods, some three miles distant, for the purpose of securing a reward which the parties to the transaction expected would be offered for their return and the result contemplated was accomplished by their return and a receipt of the reward offered.[9]

§ 558. Asportation need not be for benefit of taker.— Some authorities hold that to constitute larceny the caption and asportation must be done lucri causa.[10] These authorities, however, are not in accord with the better view, or weight of authority.[11] It has been declared not to be larceny, but malicious mischief, to take the horse of another, not

[6] Reg. v. Beecham, 5 Cox Cr. C. 181; Reg. v. Trebilcock, 7 Cox Cr. C. 408.

[7] Rex v. Wright, 9 Car. & P. 554n.

[8] Reg. v. Phetheon, 9 Car. & P. 552.

[9] Berry v. State, 31 Ohio St. 219, 27 Am. Rep. 506.

[10] McDaniel v. State, 8 Smedes & M. (Miss.) 401, 47 Am. Dec. 93; State v. Brown, 3 Strob. (S. Car.) 508; Pence v. State, 110 Ind. 95, 10 N. E. 919; Respublica v. Teischer, 1 Dall. (Pa.) 335, 1 L. ed. 163; United States v. Durkee, Fed. Cas. No. 15009, 1 McAll (U. S.) 196; Reg. v. Bailey, L. R. 1 C. C. 347, Derby's Cases 475.

[11] Williams v. State, 52 Ala. 411 (overruling State v. Hawkins, 8 Port. (Ala.) 461, 33 Am. Dec. 294); State v. Davis, 38 N. J. L. 176, 20 Am. Dec. 367; Warden v. State, 60 Miss. 638; Delk v. State, 64 Miss. 77, 1 So. 9, 60 Am. Rep. 46; State v. Wellman, 34 Minn. 221, 25 N. W. 395; State v. Caddle, 35 W. Va. 73, 12 S. E. 1098; Dignowitty v. State, 17 Tex. 521, 67 Am. Dec. 670; Best v. State, 155 Ind. 46, 57 N. E. 534; State v. Slingerland, 19

lucri causa, but in order to destroy him.[12] Bishop's view is in accord with the weight of authority.[13] The gist of the criminal intent is the purpose to deprive the owner of his property rather than to benefit by the act.[14]

"The rule is now well settled, that it is not necessary to constitute larceny, that the taking should be in order to convert the thing stolen to the pecuniary advantage or gain of the taker; and that it is sufficient if the taking is fraudulent, and with an intent wholly to deprive the owner of the property. * * * The reason of the law is to secure a man's property to him, and that is to be carried out, rather by punishing the thief for feloniously depriving him of it, than for the wrongful gain he has made by the theft. The moral wrong is founded in the wrongful and felonious deprivation."[15] It is immaterial whether the motive of the taker was to benefit himself or injure another. Thus, where one took two horses, saddles and spurs, and removed them about three miles, his object being to put the owner to all the expense and trouble possible in order to find the property, and he had no idea of benefiting himself in any way, his only object having been to get revenge a conviction was sustained.[16]

The term "lucri causa," it may be well to observe, is not restricted in its meaning to some pecuniary advantage. It includes benefits of every kind. Thus, where the defendant had applied for a position as cook for a certain person, and,

Nev. 135, 7 Pac. 280; People v. Juarez, 28 Cal. 380; Hamilton v. State, 35 Miss. 214; Reg. v. Richards, 1 Car. & K. 532, Derby's Cases 474; Reg. v. Beecham, 5 Cox Cr. C. 181, Derby's Cases 473.

12 Rex v. Cabbage, Russ. & Ry. 292, Derby's Cases 471 (five judges dissenting).

13 2 Bish. New Crim. L. (8th ed.), § 842 et seq.; Canton Nat. Bank v. American Bonding &c. Co., 111 Md. 41, 73 Atl. 684, 18 Ann. Cas. 820, Derby's Cases 476.

14 Williams v. State, 52 Ala. 411.

15 Hamilton v. State, 35 Miss. 214. See also, Canton Nat. Bank v. American Bonding &c. Co., 111 Md. 41, 73 Atl. 684, 18 Ann. Cas. 820, Derby's Cases 476.

16 State v. Slingerland, 19 Nev. 135, 7 Pac. 280.

knowing that a former employer had written to this party an unfavorable letter relative to her character, she called at the post office and by means of false representations was given the letter, which she subsequently burned, the court held that supposing lucri causa to be an essential element of larceny (which was not admitted) the benefit she gained by destroying the letter was sufficient to supply this ingredient.[17]

§ 559. Not larceny where taken under claim of right.—Where the property is taken under a bona fide claim of right, however unfounded the claim may be, the offense is not larceny.[18] This is owing to the fact that the element of felonious intent is lacking. It is immaterial whether the unfounded claim results from a mistake of law or a mistake of fact.[19] Thus, where the defendant had sold an organ, and a dispute arose as to the amount due on it, took it from the prosecutor's home owing to his refusal to pay what the defendant claimed was due on it, informing the prosecutor's wife at the time where he was going to leave it, and that her husband could come there and get it upon paying the balance due, the court held that the element of felonious intent was lacking to make the offense larceny.[20] Again, where the defendant was convicted of the larceny of a sewing machine, and the proof showed that he had once owned it; that when a judgment creditor seized and sold it on execution he

[17] Reg. v. Jones, 2 Cox Cr. C. 6, 1 Den. Cr. C. 188, 2 Car. & K. 236. See also Reg. v. Wynn, 3 Cox Cr. C. 271, 1 Den. Cr. C. 365, 2 Car. & K. 859.

[18] Hall v. State, 34 Ga. 208; State v. Fisher, 70 N. Car. 78; McGowan v. State, 27 Tex. App. 183, 11 S. W. 112; People v. Devine, 95 Cal. 227, 30 Pac. 378; Causey v. State, 79 Ga. 564, 5 S. E. 121, 11 Am. St. 447; People v. Slayton, 123 Mich. 397, 82 N. W. 205, 81 Am. St. 211; Dean v. State, 41 Fla. 291, 26 So. 638, 79 Am. St. 186; State v. Main, 75 Conn. 55, 52 Atl. 257; Wilson v. State, 96 Ark. 148, 131 S. W. 336, 41 L. R. A. (N. S.) 549n, Ann. Cas. 1912 B, 339n, Derby's Cases 409.

[19] Rex v. Hall, 3 Car. & P. 409; Commonwealth v. Stebbins, 8 Gray (Mass.) 492.

[20] People v. Walburn, 132 Mich. 24, 92 N. W. 494.

claimed that it was exempt from seizure; that the judgment creditor obtained it from the purchaser at the execution sale and left it with another person who desired to purchase it on trial; that defendant, acting under the advice of his attorney, peaceably took it from this person, explaining to him under what right he claimed it and giving him a receipt therefor, and stating his name and place of residence, the higher court set aside the conviction and dismissed the case.[21]

Where the property is taken with the intent to get false credit for work done relative to it, the intent is felonious.[22] In this case the defendants were convicted of burglary. The proof showed that they broke into a cotton-house where seed cotton was stored and carried a quantity of the cotton to a field with the view of getting paid for picking it. On appeal, the conviction was affirmed. The court said, "We think deprivation of the ownership of property is one of the essentials of larceny. But, is it necessary that the intent shall be to deprive the owner of the whole property taken? Is not the animus furandi as manifestly shown, when the intent is simply to deprive him of a partial, though unsevered interest in the property? * * * The taking and asportation were with the intent of depriving the owner of property, which was absolutely his and in his possession, and fraudulently placing it where the taker could assert a lien, or claim to hold it, until certain charges were paid him by the owner." The contrary, however, has been erroneously held in a case where the defendant was employed to tan hides and was paid by the piece, and he secretly entered the house where dressed hides were kept, and removed one hundred twenty hides, which he was charged with having stolen with intent to add them to those which he had dressed, with the view of getting credit for the work done on them. On appeal the five judges who heard the case held unanimously that the

21 People v. Schultz, 71 Mich. 315, 38 N. W. 868.

22 Fort v. State, 82 Ala. 50, 2 So. 477.

conviction should be set aside because the defendant had no intention of depriving the owner of the hides permanently, nor of taking them entirely from the owner's possession.[23]

§ 560. The property must have some value.—It is essential to the crime of larceny that the property taken have some value. Thus, a void check is not the subject of larceny, except to the extent of the value of the paper upon which it is written.[24]

At common law, choses in action are not the subject of larceny; nor is the paper upon which they are written, for the reason that it merges in the choses in action. And even where the chose in action is unenforcible because not properly stamped, the paper upon which it is written is not the subject of larceny because the former is still capable of being rendered available as evidence.[25] Upon this point Lord Chief Justice Campbell says: "By the common law, larceny can not be committed of a chose in action. Strictly speaking, the instrument of course is not a chose in action, but evidence of it, and the reason of the common-law rule seems to be that stealing the evidence of the right does not interfere with the right itself; jus non in tabulis; the evidence may be taken but the right still remains. * * * I agree that we must look at the state of the instrument at the time of the larceny committed; but it then had a potentiality of being rendered available, and it was evidence of an agreement; it was therefore evidence of a chose in action, and not a subject of larceny."[26] In another English case the defendant was indicted for robbing the prosecutor of a promissory note for two thousand pounds. The proof showed that by putting him in fear she

[23] Chief Justice Stone in Reg. v. Holloway, 3 Cox Cr. C. 241, 2 Car. & K. 942, T. & M. 40.

[24] Reg. v. Perry, 1 Cox Cr. C. 222, 1 Car. & K. 725, 1 Den. Cr. C. 69.

[25] Reg. v. Watts, 6 Cox Cr. C. 304.

[26] Reg. v. Watts, 6 Cox Cr. C. 304.

compelled him to sign the note which was written on a piece of stamped paper which she had furnished. The court held that it was essential to the crime of larceny that the property stolen be of some value; that the note in question did not import, on the face of it, either a general or special property in the prosecutor, and that it was so far from being of any the least value to him that he had not even the property of the paper on which it was written.[27]

Dogs, at common law, as heretofore stated, were not the subjects of larceny.[28] This rule, however, was changed in England by act of Parliament,[29] and in this country similar statutes obtain in some of the states.

§ 561. **Forms of larceny.**—Larceny, at common law, was divided into grand larceny and petit larceny, depending upon the value of the property stolen. Where the value was twelve pence or more the offense was grand larceny, and where it was less than that amount the offense was petit larceny.

Larceny, both at common law and by statute, is divided into simple larceny and compound larceny. In both classes the property taken must have some value, but the amount is immaterial so far as classification is concerned. Compound larceny is committed where the circumstances are aggravating. Where the property is taken from the person of another,[30] or from a building, [31] the offense is compound larceny. Some courts hold that it must be taken without the owner's knowledge.[32] Other courts, however, hold the con-

[27] Rex v. Phipoe, 2 East P. C. 599, 2 Leach 774; 2 Roscoe's Crim. Ev. (8th ed.), 684.

[28] Mullaly v. People, 86 N. Y. 365. See also 4 Bl. Comm. 235, 236; 1 Hale P. C. 510-512.

[29] 10 Geo. III, ch. 18.

[30] Flynn v. State, 42 Tex. 301; State v. Chambers, 22 W. Va. 779, 46 Am. Rep. 550, Derby's Cases 481.

[31] Commonwealth v. Hartnett, 3 Gray (Mass.) 450, Derby's Cases 483.

[32] Moye v. State, 65 Ga. 754.

trary.[33] The latter is the better view and the weight of authority.

[33] Green v. State, 28 Tex. App. 493, 13 S. W. 784; Brown v. State (Tex.), 22 S. W. 24; Hall v. People, 39 Mich. 717. (In this case the victim was asleep and the court holds that the offense was compound larceny.)

CHAPTER XXXI.

MALICIOUS MISCHIEF.

§ 563. Definition.—As regards the definition of malicious mischief, at common law, the authorities are in hopeless conflict. As generally understood at present, the offense may be defined as the wilful, physical injury to, or destruction of, the property of another, either personal or real, from ill will toward the owner or possessor thereof, or, as held by some courts, from wantonness.

§ 564. The offense at common law.—According to Blackstone, malicious mischief, at the English common law, was only a trespass. He states, however, that "it is now by a multitude of statutes made penal in the highest degree."[1] A few decisions in this country are in accord with Blackstone's view that malicious mischief was not indictable at common law;[2] but by the great weight of authority this view is not sustained.[3]

[1] 4 Bl. Comm. 244. See also, note to State v. Robinson, 32 Am. Dec. 661.

[2] State v. Wheeler, 3 Vt. 344, 23 Am. Dec. 212; State v. Beekman, 27 N. J. L. 124, 72 Am. Dec. 352; State v. Burroughs, 7 N. J. L. 426; Brown's Case, 3 Greenl. (Maine) 177.

[3] State v. Enslow, 10 Iowa 115;

§ 565. Statutory enactments.—As previously stated, numerous statutes have been passed in England declaring malicious mischief, in specific cases, a penal offense. Many similar statutes have been enacted in this country.

§ 566. Malice against the owner.—Many decisions hold that the element of malice, which is an essential of malicious mischief, must be against the owner or possessor of the thing injured.[4] Mr. Freeman says "That the malice called for in a charge of malicious mischief, is malice against the owner or possessor of the property, and not toward the property itself or toward any other person, is no doubt the established rule relative to this crime, as it existed at common law at least, and as it has been expounded and determined by a long and uniform line of judicial decisions."[5] It has been held, however, that malice against the owner or possessor is not essential.[6]

§ 567. Origin of the rule requiring malice against the owner.—The origin of the discordant rule requiring malice

note to State v. Robinson, 32 Am. Dec. 661; People v. Smith, 5 Cow. (N. Y.) 258; People v. Moody, 5 Parker (N. Y.) 568; State v. Latham, 35 N. Car. 33. See also, Nehr v. State, 35 Nebr. 638, 53 N. W. 589, 17 L. R. A. 771. See note to 128 Am. St. 163.

[4] State v. Pierce, 7 Ala. 728; Northcot v. State, 43 Ala. 330; Hobson v. State, 44 Ala. 380; Wright v. State, 30 Ga. 325, 76 Am. Dec. 656; State v. Churchill, 15 Idaho 645, 98 Pac. 853, 19 L. R. A. (N. S.) 835; Dawson v. State, 52 Ind. 478; State v. Enslow, 10 Iowa 115; State v. Williamson, 68 Iowa 351, 27 N. W. 259; Duncan v. State, 49 Miss. 331; State v. Hill, 79 N. Car. 656; State v. Jackson, 34 N. Car. 329; State v. Minor, 17 N. Dak. 454, 117 N. W. 528, 19 L. R. A. (N. S.) 273; Goforth v. State, 8 Humph. (Tenn.) 37; Stone v. State, 3 Heisk. (Tenn.) 457.

[5] Note to State v. Robinson, 32 Am. Dec. 661. See also, State v. Leslie, 138 Iowa 104, 115 N. W. 897, 128 Am. St. 160; State v. Johnson, 7 Wyo. 512, 54 Pac. 502, 11 Am. Cr. Rep. 598.

[6] Funderburk v. State, 75 Miss. 20, 21 So. 658. See also, State v. Gilligan, 23 R. I. 400, 50 Atl. 844; State v. Boies, 68 Kans. 167, 74 Pac. 630, 1 Ann. Cas. 491; Bish. Stat. Crim. (3d ed.), §§ 435, 436; note to State v. Robinson, 32 Am. Dec. 661.

against the owner or possessor of the property was the general reluctance on the part of the courts to recognize this offense as a crime at all, preferring to treat it merely as a civil trespass. In consequence of this reluctance they required that a vindictive and malevolent motive actuated by malice toward the owner of the property, and intended to annoy and injure him, be shown.[7]

§ 568. **Mode of proving malice.**—It has been held that positive proof of actual malice against the owner or possessor of the property is essential.[8] This view, however, is not in accord with the great weight of authority. It may be inferred from declarations, prior acts, or the nature of the injury.[9] Moreover, personal ill will against the owner is not essential. The element of malice may be inferred from wanton and reckless acts showing a mind disposed to mischief.[10] And in an Ohio case,[11] where the accused was indicted for unlawfully, wilfully and maliciously injuring a horse, the court holds, after an exhaustive examination of the English cases, that where the incentive for the act is general malevolence, cruelty or depravity, it is sufficient.

§ 569. **Acts within the scope of this offense.**—The following acts, when done maliciously, have been held by the courts to constitute malicious mischief: To kill a cow, or other domestic animal;[12] to break up a boat;[13] to deface tombs or

7 Note to State v. Robinson, 32 Am. Dec. 661.

8 State v. Newby, 64 N. Car. 23.

9 State v. Williamson, 68 Iowa 351, 27 N. W. 259; People v. Keeley, 81 Cal. 210, 22 Pac. 593; State v. Blacklock (N. Mex.), 167 Pac. 714.

10 People v. Keeley, 81 Cal. 210, 22 Pac. 593; People v. Burkhardt, 73 Mich. 172, 40 N. W. 240; State v. Davis, 88 S. Car. 229, 70 S. E. 811, 34 L. R. A. (N. S.) 295; People v. Olsen, 6 Utah 284, 22 Pac. 163.

11 Brown v. State, 26 Ohio St. 176.

12 Commonwealth v. Leach, 1 Mass. 59; State v. Scott, 19 N. Car. 35; State v. Hambleton, 22 Mo. 452; State v. Clifton, 24 Mo. 376.

13 Loomis v. Edgerton, 19 Wend. (N. Y.) 419.

monuments;[14] to shave a horse's tail;[15] to set fire to barrels of turpentine;[16] to break and tear down telephone wires;[17] to injure a harness;[18] to injure fruit and ornamental trees;[19] to cut the guy-posts of a lighting plant;[20] to place obstructions on railway tracks,[21] and to discharge a gun with intent to annoy and injure a sick person who is near.[22]

§ 570. Justification of the act.—The plea of justification may constitute a good defense. For example, where the accused is indicted for maliciously killing an animal, he is entitled to introduce evidence to show that his purpose in doing the act was to protect his crop; and it is error for the court to refuse to permit him to show that the animal was habitually inclined to commit mischief, and that it was restrained with difficulty from doing so.[23] Again, the accused may justify his act by showing that it was done under legal advice, and that he entertained the belief that he was authorized to do it under a claim of right.[24] The fact, however, that the holder of the property was wrongfully in possession of the same is no defense.[25]

§ 571. Injury to the property.—However malicious the act may be, it is not criminal unless the property is materially

14 3 Co. Inst. 202.

15 Boyd v. State, 2 Humph. (Tenn.) 39.

16 State v. Simpson, 9 N. Car. 460.

17 State v. Watts, 48 Ark. 56, 2 S. W. 342, 3 Am. St. 216.

18 People v. Moody, 5 Parker (N. Y.) 568.

19 Daily v. State, 51 Ohio St. 348, 37 N. E. 710, 24 L. R. A. 724, 46 Am. St. 578.

20 Ross v. Leggett, 61 Mich. 445, 28 N. W. 695, 1 Am. St. 608.

21 State v. Johns, 124 Mo. 379, 27 S. W. 1115; Barton v. State, 28 Tex. App. 483, 13 S. W. 783; Allison v. State, 42 Ind. 354.

22 Commonwealth v. Wing, 9 Pick. (Mass.) 1, 19 Am. Dec. 347.

23 Wright v. State, 30 Ga. 325, 76 Am. Dec. 656; State v. Waters, 6 Jones L. (N. Car.) 276. See also, People v. Ratcliffe, 204 Ill. App. 584.

24 Lossen v. State, 62 Ind. 437; Sattler v. People, 59 Ill. 68; State v. Flynn, 28 Iowa 26; Goforth v State, 8 Humph. (Tenn.) 37.

25 State v. Pike, 33 Maine 361.

injured or destroyed.[26] And where the property is an animal, it has been held that the act must amount to a killing.[27] This view, however, is not the better one.[28]

§ 572. **The indictment.**—The nature and character of the injury should be alleged with sufficient certainty to identify the transaction and accurately describe it in detail.[29] The malice of the accused should be alleged and the name of the owner of the property stated.[30] Where the property belongs to an unincorporated company the names of the members should be stated.[31] But it is not necessary to allege the value of the property unless it is material as to the penalty.[32]

26 Wait v. Green, 5 Parker (N. Y.) 185; Davis v. Chesapeake & O. Ry. Co., 61 W. Va. 246, 56 S. E. 400, 9 L. R. A. (N. S.) 993.

27 State v. Manuel, 72 N. Car. 201, 21 Am. Rep. 455.

28 Oviatt v. State, 19 Ohio St. 573.

29 Nicholson v. State, 3 Tex. App. 31.

30 3 Bish. New Crim. Proc. (2d ed.), § 839; Lunsford v. State (Ga. App.), 94 S. E. 80.

31 Staaden v. People, 82 Ill. 432, 25 Am. Rep. 333.

32 Caldwell v. State, 49 Ala. 34; State v. Heath, 41 Tex. 426.

CHAPTER XXXII.

ROBBERY.

§ 575. Definition and essentials.—Robbery is the felonious taking of personal property of another from his person, or in his presence, against his will, by violence or intimidation. It is an aggravated form of larceny, and is a crime, both against the person and against property.

The essentials of this crime are as follows: (1) The taking must be done with intent to steal the property. (2) The property taken must be capable of being stolen. (3) There must be a caption and asportation of the property the same as in larceny. (4) The property must be taken from another's person, or in his presence. (5) The taking must be by violence or intimidation.

The first three essentials of robbery enumerated above, are also requisites of larceny; and as they are fully discussed heretofore in the treatment of that subject a further discussion of them here is unnecessary.[1]

§ 576. Taking from another's person, or in his presence.—To constitute robbery, the taking must be from another's person, or in his presence.[2] In an English case the defendants

[1] See ante, §§ 533, 534, 560.

[2] United States v. Jones, Fed. Cas. No. 15494, 3 Wash. (C. C.) 209; Clary v. State, 33 Ark. 561, Derby's Cases 328; People v. Anderson, 80 Cal. 205, 22 Pac. 139; Crawford v.

were convicted of robbing another of nine pounds. The proof showed that the prosecutor while riding on horseback passed the accused on the highway and was asked by one of them to change a half crown; that he took from his pocket several pieces of coin; that one of the accused thereupon struck his hand gently and caused the money to fall to the ground; that the prosecutor thereupon dismounted to pick it up, but was prevented from so doing by threats of the accused that they would knock his brains out if he did so; that the accused thereupon picked up the money, got on their horses and rode away.[8] In another case, the defendants were convicted of robbing the prosecutor of a chest and several hundred dollars contained therein. The proof showed that while the prosecutor was in the smoke-house, fifteen feet back of his residence, one of the defendants, holding a gun in his hands, stepped up and said that the first man who put his head out would get it shot off; that while the prosecutor was in the smoke-house no one touched him or said anything about his money, but that, by peeping through the cracks he saw a rather stout man standing just outside facing toward him, with a gun in his hand ready to shoot; that in the meantime the other defendant went to the prosecutor's residence and took and carried away a chest and several hundred dollars

State, 90 Ga. 701, 17 S. E. 628, 35 Am. St. 242; Clements v. State, 84 Ga. 660, 11 S. E. 505, 20 Am. St. 385; Bussey v. State, 71 Ga. 100, 51 Am. Rep. 256; State v. Miller, 83 Iowa 291, 49 N. W. 90; State v. Calhoun, 72 Iowa 432, 34 N. W. 194, 2 Am. St. 252; State v. Miller, 53 Kans. 324, 36 Pac. 751; State v. Jenkins, 36 Mo. 372; Hill v. State, 42 Nebr. 503, 60 N. W. 916; Hope v. People, 83 N. Y. 418, 38 Am. Rep. 460; Crews v. State, 3 Cold. (Tenn.) 350; Williams v. State, 12 Tex. App. 240; Reges v. State, 51 Tex. Cr. 420, 102 S. W. 421; State v. McAllister, 65 W. Va. 97, 63 S. E. 758, 131 Am. St. 955; Rex v. Francis, 2 Strange 1015, 2 East P. C. 708; Reg. v. Selway, 8 Cox Cr. C. 235; 2 Russ. on Crimes (9th Am. ed.) 106, 107; 2 Roscoe's Crim. Ev. (8th ed.), 935, 936. See also note to 135 Am. St. 474.

8 Rex v. Francis, 2 Strange 1015, 2 East P. C. 708.

contained therein, from under a bed a few feet from the front door. On appeal, the conviction was affirmed.[4]

The test, as to whether the property is taken "in his presence," or not, is whether, at the time of the caption, it is virtually under the protection of his person or not. Actual presence in the narrow sense of the term, is not essential. Thus, where the defendants were convicted of assault with intent to rob a station and the proof showed that they entered a car and attacked the watchman and intended to blow open a safe and take property therefrom, the conviction, on appeal, was affirmed, on the ground that at the time the property was attempted to be taken it was virtually under the protection of the agent's person.[5]

§ 577. The caption must be by violence or intimidation.—The property must be taken by violence or by putting the other party in fear.[6] Where a thief abstracts money from another's pocket by stealth he is not guilty of robbery. His offense is compound larceny. Even where the taking is more forcible, as where the thief snatches money from another's open hand, or snatches a shawl from a woman's shoulders without tearing it or injuring the woman, he is not guilty of robbery.[7] As stated by Baron Garrow, "The mere act of

[4] Clements v. State, 84 Ga. 660, 20 Am. St. 385; State v. Kennedy, 154 Mo. 268, 55 S. W. 293; People v. Madas, 201 N. Y. 349, 94 N. E. 857, Ann. Cas. 1912 B, 229; note to 46 L. R. A. (N. S.) 1149; 2 Bish. Crim. L. (8th ed.), §§ 1177, 1178; Whart. Crim. L. (11th ed.), § 1082.

[5] O'Donnell v. People, 224 Ill. 218, 79 N. E. 639, 8 Ann. Cas. 123, Derby's Cases 331.

[6] Brown v. Commonwealth, 135 Ky. 635, 117 S. W. 281, 135 Am. St. 471, 21 Ann. Cas. 672; People v. Nolan, 90 N. E. 140, 34 L. R. A. (N. S.) 301n, Ann. Cas. 1912 B, 401n. See also note to 44 L. R. A. (N. S.) 637; State v. McDonald, 89 N. J. L. 421, 99 Atl. 128; People v. Pasqueria, 30 Cal. App. 625, 159 Pac. 173; Gordon v. State, 125 Ark. 111, 187 S. W. 913, Ann. Cas. 1918 A, 419; People v. Ferrara, 31 Cal. App. 1, 159 Pac. 621.

[7] Fanning v. State, 66 Ga. 167; Spencer v. State, 106 Ga. 692, 32 S. E. 849; Territory v. McKern, 3 Idaho 15, 26 Pac. 123; Shinn v. State, 64 Ind. 13, 31 Am. Rep. 110; State v. Miller, 83 Iowa 291, 49 N. W. 90.

taking, being forcible, will not make this offense highway robbery. To constitute the crime of highway robbery, the force used must be either before, or at the time of the taking, and must be of such a nature, as to show that it was intended to overpower the party robbed, and prevent his resisting, and not merely to get possession of the property stolen. "If a man, walking after a woman in the street, were by violence to pull her shawl from her shoulders, though he might use considerable violence, it would not, in my opinion, be highway robbery, because the violence was not for the purpose of overpowering the party robbed; but only to get possession of the property."[8] In this case the defendant snatched the prosecutor's watch-chain, as he was going along the street, and with considerable force jerked it from his pocket, and was convicted of larceny. This case was decided in 1824, and is in harmony with the very early view, as well as the modern view. After Foster's day, however, the doctrine was extended so as to make snatching a thing out of a person's hand sufficient violence to constitute the act robbery. Later, in Plunkett Horner's case,[9] it was held that snatching an umbrella out of a lady's hand as she was walking along the street was not robbery. In this case the court says: "It had been ruled about eighty years before, by very high authority, that snatching anything from a person unawares constituted robbery; but the law was now settled, that unless there was some struggle to keep it, and it were forced from the hand of the owner, it was not so. This species of larceny seemed to form a middle case between stealing privately from the person, and taking by force and violence." In Lapier's case[10] the defendant snatched an earring from a lady's ear with such violence as to draw blood from her ear and to otherwise hurt it considerably, and the offense was held robbery. In Davis' case[11] the defendant took hold of a gen-

8 Rex v. Gnosil, 1 Car. & P. 304.

9 2 East P. C. 703.

10 1 Leach 320; 2 East P. C. 557, 708.

11 2 East P. C. 709.

tleman's sword, who, perceiving it, laid hold of it at the same time and struggled for it, and this was held robbery. In Mason's case[12] the defendant took a watch out of a gentleman's pocket, but it was fastened by a steel chain which was around his neck. The defendant made two or three jerks and succeeded in breaking the chain, and his offense was held robbery.

In a leading American case,[13] decided in 1857, a negro slave was convicted of robbing a white man of two hundred twenty-seven dollars. The proof showed that the prosecuting witness had sold a load of tobacco and was driving along a country road, about dark, with the proceeds in his pocket, when he overtook the negro going the same way; that the negro said to the white man that he had found a bill and requested the latter to examine it and tell him how much it was; that the white man objected at first, owing to the darkness, but that he finally consented to do so; that he lighted a torch and began to examine the bill when suddenly he felt the negro's hand in his pocket on his pocketbook; that he immediately seized his arm, the negro at the same time snatching the bill; that a scuffle ensued in which the white man was thrown out of the wagon under the tongue; that when he got up he observed the negro running away, having taken the pocketbook from his pocket and also the bill he was examining; that the pocketbook contained two hundred twenty-seven dollars. On appeal, the judgment was set aside and a venire de novo awarded, the court assigning as the reason for so doing that, "There was no violence—no circumstance of terror resorted to for the purpose of inducing the prosecutor to part with his property for the sake of his person * * * The prosecutor did not have hold of the pocketbook; there was no struggle for it; but he had hold of the prisoner's arm. So he could not, by letting go the pocket-

12 Rex v. Mason, Russ. & Ry. 419.

13 State v. John, 50 N. Car. 163, 69 Am. Dec. 777.

book, have avoided the necessity for violence, and the struggle in which the prosecutor fell under the tongue of the wagon, is fairly imputable to an effort on the part of the prisoner to get loose from his grasp and make his escape. * * * After much consideration, I am convinced that the facts set out in this record do not constitute highway robbery." Justice Battle, the only other member of the court who heard the case, entertained a different view, but for certain incidental reasons consented to a new trial.

It should be observed, in this connection, that violence can be used for different purposes; and that in some cases it falls within the scope of robbery, while in others it does not. Thus, it can be used to prevent resistance; or to overcome the other party; or to obtain possession of the property; or to effect an escape. In the first two cases it falls within the scope of robbery. In the third case it depends upon the nature and extent of the violence. In the last case it falls without the scope of robbery. Russell observes, "The rule appears to be well established, that no sudden taking or snatching of property from a person unawares, is sufficient to constitute robbery, unless some injury be done to the person, or there be some previous struggle for the possession of the property, or some force used in order to obtain it."[14] Chitty pertinently observes, "there must be a struggle, or at least a personal outrage."[15] And in his notes to Blackstone's Commentaries, he states, "To constitute a robbery where an actual violence is relied on, and no putting in fear can be expressly shown there must be a struggle, or at least a personal outrage."[16] There are, however, many cases holding that the snatching of money out of another's hand may be force enough to constitute robbery.[17]

14 2 Russ. on Crimes (9 Am. ed.) 110. See also, People v. Campbell, 234 Ill. 391, 84 N. E. 1035, 123 Am. St. 107, 14 Ann. Cas. 186; Roscoe's Crim. Ev. (8th ed.) 1161; 2 East P. C. 708.

15 Chit. Crim. L. 804.

16 Chit. Bl. bk. 4, 197.

17 Stockton v. Commonwealth, 125 Ky. 268, 101 S. W. 298, Derby's Cases 330.

It also may be well to observe that the violence used need not intimidate.[18] And furthermore, that where one person forcibly holds another while the former's confederate rifles his pockets, both are guilty of robbery.[19] Again, where one uses violence to obtain property from another under a bona fide belief that it belongs to him he is not guilty of robbery, for the reason that the caption is not animo furandi.[20] The same principle is applicable where a person by threats compels another to pay him money which he honestly believes the other party owes him.[21] Again, where money is illegally acquired at gaming, and the receiver of it is not entitled even to possession, the loser who forcibly takes it from him is not guilty of robbery.[22] This is owing to the fact that he takes his own property. In robbery, as well as in larceny, the property taken must belong to another.[23] Officers who arrest a person, forcibly search him and take from him valuables intending to keep them are guilty of robbery.[24]

18 People v. Glynn, 54 Hun (N. Y.) 332, 7 N. Y. S. 555, 20 N. Y. St. 27 (affd. 123 N. Y. 631, 25 N. E. 953.

19 Wheeler v. Commonwealth, 86 Va. 658, 10 S. E. 924; People v. Madas, 201 N. Y. 349, 94 N. E. 857, Ann. Cas. 1912 B, 229.

20 Rex v. Hall, 3 Car. & P. 409; People v. Hughes, 11 Utah 100, 39 Pac. 492.

21 State v. Hollyway, 41 Iowa 200, 20 Am. Rep. 586. See also, State v. Brown, 104 Mo. 365, 16 S. W. 406; Crawford v. State, 90 Ga. 701, 17 S. E. 628, 35 Am. St. 242; Fanin v. State, 51 Tex. Cr. 41, 100 S. W. 916, 123 Am. St. 874, 10 L. R. A. (N. S.) 744.

22 Thompson v. Commonwealth (Ky.), 18 S. W. 1022; Sikes v. Commonwealth (Ky.), 34 S. W. 902.

23 Barnes v. State, 9 Tex. App. 128.

24 Tones v. State, 48 Tex. Cr. 363, 88 S. W. 217, 1 L. R. A. (N. S.) 1024, 13 Ann. Cas. 455; State v. Parsons, 44 Wash. 299, 87 Pac. 349, 7 L. R. A. (N. S.) 566, 12 Ann. Cas. 61.

CHAPTER XXXIII.

UTTERING A FORGED DOCUMENT.

§ 580. Definition and essentials.—The crime of uttering a forged document is offering a forged instrument as genuine with knowledge of its falsity and with intent to defraud.

The instrument offered must be a forgery. It must be offered as genuine. The person offering it must have knowledge of its falsity. And he must intend to defraud.

At common law, uttering a forged document is a distinct misdemeanor.

§ 581. What constitutes an uttering.—To constitute an uttering it is not essential that the forged document be actually received as genuine by the party upon whom the attempt to defraud is made.[1] Exhibiting a forged receipt for inspection is sufficient.[2] In such a case the defendant, who was a stone mason, had purchased stone to the amount of some five pounds, and payment had been frequently demanded and promised. Finally he claimed that he had paid the bill to the former manager of the quarry and produced a receipt for the same purporting to be signed by him. He was requested to deliver the receipt but refused to do so. Subsequently he was convicted of uttering forged paper, and

[1] Rex v. Welch, 2 Den. Cr. C. 78, 15 Jur. 136; Maloney v. State, 91 Ark. 485, 121 S. W. 728, 134 Am. St. 83, 18 Ann. Cas. 480; State v. Weaver, 149 Iowa 403, 128 N. W. 559, Ann. Cas. 1912 C, 1137. See also, note to 119 Am. St. 317.

[2] Reg. v. Radford, 1 Den. Cr. C. 59, 1 Cox Cr. C. 168, 1 Car. & K. 707.

on the question being reserved the eleven judges were of opinion that proof established an uttering.

To utter a forged instrument is to declare or assert, directly or indirectly, by words or actions, that it is good.[3] It is not only a sale or paying away a counterfeit note or indorsement, but obtaining credit on it in any form, as by leaving it in pledge,[4] or indeed offering it in dealing, though it be refused,[5] amounts to an uttering and publishing.[6] Presenting a forged deed for record,[7] aiding to get a forged will probated,[8] recording a forged discharge of a mortgage,[9] exhibiting a forged receipt by a proposed surety to establish his credit,[10] pledging a forged document,[11] offering a forged check,[12] have all been held to come within the scope of this crime. And it has also been held that to offer a check, payable to the order of a third person and not indorsed, constitutes the crime.[13]

Having in one's possession forged notes "with intent falsely, fraudulently, and deceitfully to utter and pass the same for and as true and genuine notes" is not a crime. "The allegations amount only to an intention to cheat, which at com-

[3] Commonwealth v. Searle, 2 Binn. (Pa.) 332, 4 Am. Dec. 446; Graham v. Commonwealth, 174 Ky. 645, 192 S. W. 683; Martin v. State (Tex. Cr.), 194 S. W. 1105; May v. State, 115 Miss. 708, 76 So. 636.

[4] Rex v. Birkett, Russ. & Ry. 86.

[5] Rex v. Arscott, 6 Car. & P. 408; Rex v. Shukard, Russ. & Ry. 200; Rex v. Palmer, 2 Leach 782.

[6] People v. Rathbun, 21 Wend. (N. Y.) 509. See also, People v. Caton, 25 Mich. 388 (uttering a forged mortgage).

[7] Espalla v. State, 108 Ala. 38, 19 So. 82.

[8] Corbett v. State, 3 Ohio Cir. Dec. 79, 5 Ohio Cir. Ct. 155.

[9] People v. Swetland, 77 Mich. 53, 43 N. W. 779.

[10] Reg. v. Ion, 2 Den. Cr. C. 475.

[11] Thurmond v. State, 25 Tex. App. 366, 8 S. W. 473.

[12] Walker v. State, 127 Ga. 48, 56 S. E. 113, 8 L. R. A. (N. S.) 1175, 119 Am. St. 314, Derby's Cases 534.

[13] Smith v. State, 20 Nebr. 284, 29 N. W. 923, 57 Am. Rep. 832; Maloney v. State, 91 Ark. 485, 12 S. W. 728, 134 Am. St. 83, 18 Ann. Cas. 480; Walker v. State, 127 Ga. 48, 56 S. E. 113, 8 L. R. A. (N. S.) 1175, 119 Am. St. 314, Derby's Cases 534.

mon law is not indictable."[14] It has been held that knowingly having in one's possession a box containing counterfeit coins, and the delivery of the same to a common carrier, consigned to a man in another city, is not a crime.[15] In the case cited, the defendant delivered a box containing two thousand eight hundred counterfeit shillings and one thousand counterfeit sixpences to a coach officer for carriage to a man in Glasgow. The box was stopped, however, at the place where it was received, and the court held that the act was not a sufficient uttering to make it a crime. But a mere silent offer to pass a document which is known to be a forgery is sufficient,[16] So is mailing a forged document for delivery in another jurisdiction.[17]

In England,[18] and also in this country,[19] statutes have been passed which make having in one's possession a forged document, with intent to pass it, a crime. Scienter may be proved by evidence of other crimes of a similar nature.[20]

14 Commonwealth v. Morse, 2 Mass. 138.

15 Rex v. Heath, Russ. & Ry. 184.

16 State v. Calkins, 73 Iowa 128, 34 N. W. 777; United States v. Long, 30 Fed. 678.

17 Reg. v. Finkelstein, 16 Cox Cr. C. 107.

18 8 & 9 Wm. III, ch. 26.

19 U. S. Comp. Stat. (1916), § 10321, and statutes of the particular states; Martin v. State (Tex. Cr.), 194 S. W. 1105.

20 Anson v. People, 148 Ill. 494, 35 N. E. 145; Commonwealth v. Russell, 156 Mass. 196, 30 N. E. 763; People v. Kemp, 76 Mich. 410, 43 N. W. 439.

TITLE FIVE.

Crimes Against Public Justice.

CHAPTER XXXIV.

Bribery and Embracery.

§ 585. Definition of bribery.—Bribery is the act of voluntarily giving or receiving something of value in corrupt payment of an official act.[1]

§ 586. Another view.—According to Blackstone, the official act must be one connected with the administration of jus-

[1] People v. Peters, 265 Ill. 122, 106 N. E. 513, Ann. Cas. 1916 A, 813n; People v. Halpin, 276 Ill. 363, 114 N. E. 932; State v. Williams, 22 N. Mex. 337, 161 Pac. 334; Sims v. State, 131 Ark. 185, 198 S. W. 883; Colson v. State, 71 Fla. 267, 71 So. 277.

tice.[2] This was also Lord Coke's view.[3] As understood in this country, however, the official act may be judicial, legislative or administrative.[4] The gist of the crime of bribery is the tendency of the bribe to pervert justice and thereby injuriously affect the public; and since this tendency is applicable to official acts of all three of the governmental departments Blackstone's definition of the crime is too narrow. As declared by Justice Dalrimple, "It is said that the common-law offense of bribery can only be predicated on a reward given to a judge or other official concerned in the administration of justice. * * * The later commentators, supported as I think, by the adjudged cases, however, maintain the broader doctrine, that any attempt to influence an officer in his official conduct, whether in the executive, legislative, or judicial department of the government, by the offer of a reward on pecuniary consideration, is an indictable common-law misdemeanor. * * * Indeed, the authorities seem to be all one way. Neither upon principle nor authority can the crime of bribery be confined to acts done to corrupt officers concerned in the administration of justice."[5]

§ 587. **Official acts.**—Voting for a candidate for a public office in any of the three governmental departments is an official act, and bribing a voter is indictable at common law.[6] It is bribery to pay a state legislator money to vote for a certain candidate for United States senator.[7] And it has been held bribery for a candidate for a county office to offer to

[2] 4 Bl. Comm. 139.

[3] 3 Co. Inst. 145. See also, 1 Russ. on Crimes (9th Am. ed.) 223 et seq.

[4] 2 Bish. New Crim. Law (8th ed.), § 85.

[5] State v. Ellis, 33 N. J. L. 102, 97 Am. Dec. 707n. See also, State v. Potts, 78 Iowa 656, 43 N. W. 534, 5 L. R. A. 814; note to 116 Am. St. 38.

[6] Reg. v. Lancaster, 16 Cox Cr. C. 737; State v. Jackson, 73 Maine 91, 40 Am. Rep. 342; Commonwealth v. Bell, 145 Pa. St. 374, 22 Atl. 641, 644; Commonwealth v. McHale, 97 Pa. St. 397, 39 Am. Rep. 808; State v. Humphreys, 74 Tex. 466, 12 S. W. 99, 5 L. R. A. 217n.

[7] State v. Davis, 2 Pennew. (Del.) 139, 45 Atl. 394.

return into the county treasury part of his salary if elected.[8] A promise by a candidate for county judge to draw papers in settlement of estates free of charge if elected, is not bribery.[9] On the other hand it has been held not bribery to give a note as an inducement to vote for the removal of the county seat.[10] It is not bribery to offer money to a public official to induce him to refrain from performing acts for which there is no legal or constitutional warrant.[11] Nor is it bribery to give a present to an official, after the performance by him of an official act, provided there was no understanding between him and the donor relative thereto prior to the doing of the official act, since the gift is not made in corrupt payment thereof.[12]

An offer to give or receive a bribe, in corrupt payment of an official act, is indictable at common law.[13] Strictly speaking, however, it is an attempt to commit bribery rather than bribery.

Where one party knowingly carries a bribe from another party to a third party who receives it in corrupt payment for an official act all three are guilty of bribery.[14]

Bribery at common law is a misdemeanor. The fact that one who holds himself out as an officer has no legal right to the office, and has no power to do the act for which bribe was taken or offered, is not a defense to a charge of bribery.[15] It is generally held not to be bribery to offer a gift to the public to secure the passage of a law, or ordinance, as a promise

8 State v. Purdy, 36 Wis. 213, 17 Am. Rep. 485.

9 State v. Bunnell, 131 Wis. 198, 110 N. W. 177, 11 Ann. Cas. 561.

10 Herman v. Edson, 9 Nebr. 152, 2 N. W. 368.

11 United States v. Boyer, 85 Fed. 425.

12 Hutchinson v. State, 36 Tex. 293.

13 Walsh v. People, 65 Ill. 58, 16 Am. Rep. 569; State v. Ellis, 33 N. J. L. 102, 97 Am. Dec. 707n; Rudolph v. State, 128 Wis. 222, 107 N. W. 466, 116 Am. St. 32n.

14 People v. Northey, 77 Cal. 618, 19 Pac. 865, 20 Pac. 129; People v. Kerr, 6 N. Y. S. 674, 6 N. Y. Cr. 406.

15 People v. Jackson, 191 N. Y. 293, 84 N. E. 65, 15 L. R. A. (N. S.) 1173, 14 Ann. Cas. 243; Ex parte Winters, 10 Okla. Cr. 592, 140 Pac. 164, 51 L. R. A. (N. S.) 1087.

by a citizen to pay part of the expense of opening a street;[16] but the contrary has been held as to a bonus offered by a city, which is a candidate for a county seat.[17]

§ 588. **Definition of embracery.**—Embracery is a corrupt attempt to influence a jury to render their verdict in favor of a particular party.[18]

§ 589. **Nature of the influence.**—The influence may consist of promises, entreaties, persuasions, gifts, treating, and the like. It does not, of course, include legitimate arguments of counsel. On the other hand, where counsel unduly take advantage of the opportunity afforded and corruptly influence the jury they are guilty of embracery.[19]

§ 590. **Who can commit embracery.**—The crime of embracery can be committed by a party to the suit, a witness, counsel, a stranger, or even by one of the jurymen.

§ 591. **Attempt to commit the crime.**—Since embracery itself is only an attempt, an attempt to commit it is not indictable. As said by Chief Justice Lewis, "As the crime itself consists of a mere attempt to do an act or to accomplish a result, it is difficult to comprehend how there can be an attempt to commit such crime. Any attempt or effort corruptly to influence a juror, whether it be successful or not, is itself embracery."[20] In this case the defendant, a juror in a civil action, was charged with "the crime of attempt to commit the crime of embracery," and a demurrer to the indictment was sustained on the ground that no crime was charged.

It is to be observed that the fact that the jury disagree, or that they render a true verdict in the case, is no defense to a subsequent prosecution for embracery.

Embracery at common law is a misdemeanor.

16 State v. Orange, 5 N. J. L. 111, 22 Atl. 1004, 14 L. R. A. 62.

17 Ayres v. Moan, 34 Nebr. 210, 51 N. W. 830, 15 L. R. A. 501.

18 State v. Brown, 95 N. Car. 685; State v. Sales, 2 Nev. 268; Gibbs v. Dewey, 5 Cow. (N. Y.) 503; 4 Bl. Comm. 140.

19 1 Hawk. P. C. 548, ch. 85.

20 State v. Sales, 2 Nev. 268.

CHAPTER XXXV.

COMPOUNDING AND MISPRISION OF FELONY.

§ 595. **Definition of compounding a felony.**—Compounding a felony consists of knowing that a felony has been committed and forbearing to prosecute the felon in consideration of some reward.

§ 596. **Requisites of the crime.**—The three essentials of this crime are the following: (1) Knowledge that a felony has been committed; (2) agreement not to prosecute; (3) the receiving of some reward.

§ 597. **Scope of the crime.**—A common illustration of compounding a felony is where the owner of stolen goods agrees to forbear prosecuting the thief in consideration that the goods be returned.[1] It is to be observed, however, that anyone, who has knowledge of the felony and who agrees not to prosecute in consideration of a reward, is guilty of this crime. The crime is not committed, however, where the owner of the stolen goods merely takes the goods back without any inducement made to the thief, for the gist of the offense is the agreement to take compensation for forbearing

1 Commonwealth v. Pease, 16 Mass. 91.

to prosecute. Receiving a promissory note constitutes a sufficient consideration for forbearing to prosecute although the note is never paid.[2] The fact that the defendant subsequently prosecuted the felon is no defense to the prosecution for compounding the felony.[3] Nor the fact that the felon was acquitted.[4] Nor the fact that the consideration for forbearing to prosecute was received by the defendant for the benefit of a third party.[5] Nor the fact that the defendant corruptly acted under the instructions of a superior officer.[6] It is said that there can be no conviction unless it is charged and proved that a felony was committed.[7]

§ 598. **Compounding a misdemeanor.**—Compounding a misdemeanor of a private nature, as an assault or private cheat, is not a crime at common law. On the other hand, compounding a misdemeanor of a public nature is a crime at common law. Thus, where the defendant informed a liquor dealer that he had a case against him for illegally selling liquor; that he would forbear prosecuting him if the latter would pay him thirty dollars, which amount was so paid, the defendant was convicted of compounding a misdemeanor and the conviction was sustained.[8] In this case the court stated: "The bargain and acceptance of the reward makes the crime. And in such a case, the party may be convicted though no offense liable to a penalty has been committed by the person from whom the reward is taken."[9]

2 Commonwealth v. Pease, 16 Mass. 91.

3 State v. Duhammel, 2 Har. (Del.) 532; State v. Ash, 33 Ore. 86, 54 Pac. 184.

4 People v. Buckland, 13 Wend. (N. Y.) 592.

5 State v. Ruthven, 58 Iowa 121, 12 N. W. 235; State v. Ash, 30 Ore. 86, 54 Pac. 184.

6 State v. Ash, 30 Ore. 86, 54 Pac. 184 (defendant in this case was a police officer).

7 State v. Hodge, 142 N. Car. 665, 55 S. E. 626, 7 L. R. A. (N. S.) 709n, 9 Ann. Cas. 563.

8 State v. Carver, 69 N. H. 216, 39 Atl. 973.

9 State v. Carver, 69 N. H. 216, 39 Atl. 973. See also People v. Buckland, 13 Wend. (N. Y.) 592; Reg. v. Best, 9 Car. & P. 368, 38 E. C. L. 368; Rex v. Gotley, Russ. & Ry. 84; 1 Russ. Crimes (9th Am. ed.) 195; Arch. Crim. Pr. & Pl. 623.

§ 599. Definition of misprision of felony.—Misprison of felony is a criminal neglect either to prevent a felony from being committed, or to bring to justice the offender after its commission.[10]

§ 600. Offender distinguished from an accessory or principal.—One who merely neglects either to prevent a felony or to bring the offender to justice is not an accessory to the felony. On the other hand, if he encourages or aids the felon he is either an accessory or a principal. "As to the receiving, relieving, and assisting one known to be a felon, it may be said in general terms, that any assistance given to one known to be a felon in order to hinder his apprehension, trial or punishment, is sufficient to make a man accessory after the fact; as that he concealed him in the house, or shut the door against his pursuers, until he should have an opportunity to escape; * * * or supplied him with money, a horse or other necessaries in order to enable him to escape; or that the principal was in prison, and the jailor was bribed to let him escape; or conveyed instruments to him to enable him to break prison and escape. This and such like assistance to one known to be a felon, would constitute a man accessory after the fact. * * * But merely suffering the principal to escape, will not make the party accessory after the fact; for it amounts at most but to a mere omission. * * * Or if he agree for money not to prosecute the felon; or if knowing of a felony, fails to make it known to the proper authorities; none of these acts would be sufficient to make the party an accessory after the fact. If the thing done amounts to no more than the compounding a felony, or the misprision of it, the doer will not be an accessory. * * * If, knowing that a felony had been committed, he (the defendant) concealed it, then he is guilty of misprision of felony. If, knowing a felony to

10 Wren v. Commonwealth, 26 Grat. (Va.) 952; 1 Bish. New Crim. L. (8th ed.), § 717.

be committed, he concealed it or forbore to arrest and prosecute the felon, for fee or reward, then he is guilty of compounding a felony. Both of these are grave offenses, but they do not constitute a party an accessory after the fact."[11]

Misprision of felony at common law is a misdemeanor.

[11] Wren v. Commonwealth, 26 Grat. (Va.) 952.

CHAPTER XXXVI.

CONTEMPT.

§ 605. **Definition.**—Contempt of court is said to be a despising of the authority, justice or dignity of the court, and one is guilty of contempt whose acts tend to bring the authority and administration of the law into disrespect or disregard, or to interfere with or prejudice parties or witnesses during litigation.[1] The power to punish persons guilty of contempt is essential to judicial authority, and inherent in courts.[2]

Criminal proceedings in contempts are those prosecuted to preserve the power and vindicate the dignity of the courts and to punish for disobedience of their orders, as distinguished from civil proceedings instituted to preserve and enforce rights of private litigants.[3] Direct contempts are those

[1] Dahnke v. People, 168 Ill. 102, 48 N. E. 137, 39 L. R. A. 197; People v. Samuel, 199 Ill. App. 294; People v. Friedlander, 199 Ill. App. 300; Adams v. Gardner, 176 Ky. 252, 195 S. W. 412.

[2] Ex parte Beville, 58 Fla. 170, 50 So. 685, 27 L. R. A. (N. S.) 273n, 19 Ann. Cas. 48; People v. Wilson, 64 Ill. 195, 16 Am. Rep. 528; Ex parte Adams, 25 Miss. 883, 59 Am. Dec. 234; Burnett v. State, 8 Okla. Cr. 639, 129 Pac. 1110, 47 L. R. A. (N. S.) 1175n; People v. Samuel, 199 Ill. App. 294; In re Anderson, 97 Wash. 683, 167 Pac. 70; People v. Seymour, 272 Ill. 295, 111 N. E. 1008; People v. Hoyne, 195 Ill. App. 272; Platnauer v. Superior Court, 32 Cal. App. 463, 163 Pac. 237.

[3] Clay v. Waters, 178 Fed. 385, 21 Ann. Cas. 897n; Rothchild &c. Co. v. Steger &c. Co., 256 Ill. 196,

offered in the presence of the court, when sitting judicially; indirect contempts, are acts committed outside of court which tend to embarrass the administration of justice.[4]

§ 606. What acts have been held contempts.—Among acts which have been punished criminally as contempts are a false pretense that a party to a civil action is too ill to attend court,[5] a failure to turn over property according to the court's order,[6] to proceed with a sale,[7] or persist in a boycott,[8] in defiance of the court's orders, or violate an injunction against interfering with another's employés,[9] though in the latter case the contrary has also been held.[10] Concealment of assets by a bankrupt is a criminal contempt.[11] Among direct criminal contempts are language used in presence of court intimating the judge is unfair and ignorant,[12] profanity in the court's presence,[13] fighting in the court room,[14] assaulting the judge as he leaves the room,[15] appearing in court so

99 N. E. 920, 42 L. R. A. (N. S.) 793n, Ann. Cas. 1913 E, 276; O'Brien v. People, 216 Ill. 354, 75 N. E. 108, 108 Am. St. 219, 3 Ann. Cas. 966; People v. Court, 101 N. Y. 245, 4 N. E. 259, 54 Am. Rep. 691; In re Merrill, 88 N. J. L. 261, 102 Atl. 400.

4 People v. Wilson, 64 Ill. 195, 16 Am. Rep. 528; In re Clark, 208 Mo. 121, 106 S. W. 990, 15 L. R. A. (N. S.) 389n. See also In re Glenn, 103 S. Car. 501, 88 S. E. 294 (juror assaulted out of court after verdict not contempt); People v. Samuel, 199 Ill. App. 294.

5 Welch v. Barber, 52 Conn. 147, 52 Am. Rep. 567.

6 Carnahan v. Carnahan, 143 Mich. 390, 107 N. W. 73, 114 Am. St. 660, 8 Ann. Cas. 53.

7 State v. Knight, 3 S. Dak. 509, 54 N. W. 412, 44 Am. St. 809.

8 Gompers v. Buck Stove & Range Co., 221 U. S. 418, 55 L. ed. 797, 34 L. R. A. (N. S.) 874n.

9 Garrigan v. United States, 163 Fed. 16, 23 L. R. A. (N. S.) 1295n; Stewart v. United States, 236 Fed. 838.

10 Franklin Union No. 4 v. People, 220 Ill. 355, 77 N. E. 176, 4 L. R. A. (N. S.) 1001, 110 Am. St. 248.

11 Clay v. Waters, 178 Fed. 385, 21 Ann. Cas. 897.

12 Mahoney v. State, 33 Ind. App. 655, 72 N. E. 151, 104 Am. St. 276; In re Hanson, 99 Kans. 23, 160 Pac. 1141; In re Willis, 94 Wash. 180, 162 Pac. 38.

13 22 L. R. A. 353.

14 State v. Woodfin, 27 N. Car. 199, 42 Am. Dec. 161.

15 Ex parte McCown, 139 N. Car. 95, 51 S. E. 957, 2 L. R. A. (N. S.) 603.

intoxicated as to disturb order,[16] failing to produce a prisoner,[17] attempting to influence a judge's decision,[18] or bribe or influence a juror.[19]

§ 607. **Newspaper articles.**—Certain newspaper publications pending a suit, reflecting on the court, jury, parties, attorneys, or others, tending to influence the action of the court or prejudice jurors, are criminal contempts.[20] Divulging secrets of the jury room is a contempt.[21] A newspaper article commenting on past conduct of a judge, without relation to a pending case, is not contemptuous.[22] It is criminal contempt for a judge of a trial court to write a newspaper article reflecting on the decision of the court of appeals in reversing a case tried by him, scandalizing the judicial action of the reviewing court and casting reflections upon the character of the judges in their judicial capacity.[23] Direct contempts are punished summarily, upon view, and without trial; there is a trial of indirect contempts similar to other criminal trials.

§ 608. **Burden of proof.**—In cases involving criminal contempts the accused is presumed to be innocent, and the burden of proving his guilt rests upon his accuser.[24]

16 Neely v. State, 98 Miss. 816, 54 So. 315, 33 L. R. A. (N. S.) 138n, Ann. Cas. 1913 B, 281n.

17 Ex parte Sternes, 77 Cal. 156, 19 Pac. 275, 11 Am. St. 251.

18 State v. Johnson, 77 Ohio St. 461, 83 N. E. 702, 21 L. R. A. (N. S.) 905n.

19 Poindexter v. State, 109 Ark. 179, 159 S. W. 197, 46 L. R. A. (N. S.) 517; Little v. State, 90 Ind. 3 :, 46 Am. Rep. 224; State v. District Court, 37 Mont. 191, 95 Pac. 593, 15 Ann. Cas. 743n, 747; In re Oldham, 89 N. Car. 23, 45 Am. Rep. 673; United States v. Toledo Newspaper Co., 220 Fed. 457, 488; State v. Howell, 80 Conn. 668, 69 Atl. 1057, 125 Am. St. 141, 13 Ann. Cas. 501; People v. Wilson, 64 Ill. 195, 16 Am. Rep. 528.

20 Myers v. State, 46 Ohio St. 473, 22 N. E. 43, 15 Am. St. 638; notes to 2 Am. Dec. 391 and 97 Am. Dec. 629; People v. Gilbert, 281 Ill. 619, 118 N. E. 196; United States v. Toledo Newspaper Co., 220 Fed. 458.

21 Burns v. State, 145 Wis. 373, 128 N. W. 987, 140 Am. St. 1081.

22 Cheadle v. State, 110 Ind. 301, 11 N. E. 426, 59 Am. Rep. 199; State v. Young, 113 Minn. 96, 129 N. W. 148, Ann. Cas. 1912 A, 163.

23 In re Fite, 11 Ga. App. 665, 76 S. E. 397.

24 State v. Daugherty, 137 Tenn. 125, 191 S. W. 974; People v. Gilbert, 281 Ill. 619, 118 N. E. 196.

CHAPTER XXXVII.

FRAUDULENT CONVEYANCES, AND CONCEALING PROPERTY.

§ 610. **Fraudulent conveyances.**—Under an old English statute of 13 Eliz. which makes void conveyances of property with intent to defraud creditors, a criminal penalty for such an act is added, and there are similar statutes in many of our states. The intent to defraud creditors is the essential criminal element.[1] Among acts indictable under such statutes are the fraudulent alienation of real estate,[2] making a second deed without disclosing a prior one to the same property,[3] or knowingly conveying incumbered land with intent to defraud.[4] However, today the records usually furnish protection against such conveyances.

§ 611. **Concealing property.**—Concealing or secreting goods with intent to defraud creditors is indictable under statutes in many states. The two essential elements of the offense are an actual fraudulent secreting, assigning, or reception of the goods, and an intention to prevent the property being made liable for the payment of debts, and both these elements must be shown before conviction can be had.[5] It is not necessary that the concealment be from every one, if

[1] State v. Leslie, 16 N. H. 93.

[2] Reg. v. Smith, 6 Cox Cr. C. 31.

[3] State v. Jones, 68 Mo. 197.

[4] State v. Hunkins, 90 Wis. 264, 62 N. W. 1047, 63 N. W. 167.

[5] Whart. Crim. Law (11th ed.), §§ 1505, 1506, 1507.

it be from the officer entitled to the property.[6] It is not secreting to refuse to give up property to an officer levying execution from one's person.[7]

Many statutes provide penalties for the removal from the state of property covered by chattel mortgage, or subject to lien, without the mortgagee's or lienholder's consent.

[6] State v. Williams, 30 Maine 484.

[7] People v. Morrison, 13 Wend. (N. Y.) 399.

§ 615. In general.—Official misconduct which is indictable at common law may consist of malfeasance or nonfeasance. Malfeasance by a public officer consists of the performance of an illegal act, or the abuse of a discretionary power, from an improper motive. Nonfeasance consists in wilful neglect by a public officer to perform an official duty which he is legally bound to perform, provided the discharge of such duty does not entail greater danger than a person of ordinary firmness and activity may be expected to encounter.[1] In malfeasance, the illegal act may consist in extortion, oppression, fraud or breach of trust. Extortion consists in taking from a person, under color of office, something of value which is not due.[2] It is separate and distinct from the crime of bribery.[3] Oppression consists in inflicting upon a person bodily injury, imprisonment or other harm not amounting to extortion.[4] Fraud or breach of trust affecting the public, committed by a public officer in the discharge of

[1] State v. Kern, 51 N. J. L. 259, 17 Atl. 114.

[2] State v. Pritchard, 107 N. Car. 921, 12 S. E. 50; 2 Bishop's New Crim. L. (8th ed.), §§ 390-408.

[3] Williams v. United States, 168 U. S. 382, 42 L. ed. 509; Levar v. State, 103 Ga. 42, 29 S. E. 467; People v. McLaughlin, 2 App. Div. 419, 37 N. Y. S. 1005, 73 N. Y. St. 496, 11 N. Y. Cr. 97.

[4] Steph. Dig. Crim. L., art. 119.

his official duties, may be indictable although the same act when affecting only a private party would not be indictable.[5]

§ 616. Partial, malicious and corrupt acts by magistrates.—Where magistrates in the exercise of their official duties act partially, maliciously or corruptly, they are criminally liable.[6] Where a justice of the peace refused a license to a man because of the latter's refusal to vote as the justice desired him to do he committed a nisdemeanor.[7] And where two justices of the peace, whose duty it was to vote for certain candidates for office, entered into a corrupt bargain whereby each agreed to vote for a certain candidate, and the nefarious bargain was carried out, their offense was held indictable at common law. "The defendants were justices of the peace, and as such held an office of high trust and confidence. In that character they were called upon to vote for others, for offices, also implying trust and confidence. Their duty required them to vote in reference only to the merit and qualifications of the officers; and yet, upon the pleadings in this case, it appears that they wickedly and corruptly violated their duty, and betrayed the confidence reposed in them, by voting under the influence of a corrupt bargain, or reciprocal promise, by which they had come under a reciprocal obligation to vote respectively for a particular person, no matter how inferior the qualifications to their competitors. It would seem, then, upon these general principles (previously stated), that the offense in the information is indictable at common law."[8] A de facto officer is criminally liable for misfeasance.[9]

§ 617. Other misconduct of officials which is indictable.—Where a commissary of public stores contracts with a party

5 State v. Glasgow, 1 N. Car. 264, 2 Am. Dec. 629.

6 Rex v. Holland, 1 Term. R. 692; Rex v. Young, 1 Burr. 556; Rex v. Davis, 3 Burr. 1317; Rex v. Hann, 3 Burr. 1786.

7 Rex v. Williams, 3 Burr. 1317.

8 Commonwealth v. Callaghan, 2 Va. Cas. 460.

9 People v. McCann, 247 Ill. 130, 93 N. E. 100, 20 Ann. Cas. 496n.

for supplies on condition that the latter divide with him the profits the former is criminally liable.[10] And where an accountant in a public office fraudulently omits to make entries in his accounts, whereby the cashier is enabled to retain money and appropriate the interest thereon, the accountant is guilty of a criminal offense.[11] It also has been held that a public officer who gets drunk while engaged in discharging his official duties commits a misdemeanor.[12]

§ 618. Refusal to accept public office.—At common law it is a misdemeanor for any person unlawfully to refuse or omit to take upon himself and serve in any public office which he is by law required to accept if duly appointed, provided no other penalty is imposed by law for such refusal or neglect, or the law or custom does not permit composition in place of serving.[13]

§ 619. Extortion.—This, as previously defined, is the taking under color of office, something of value which is not due.[14] It is often considered by text-writers as a distinct crime under a separate heading. To be guilty of the offense one must be an officer, and if no such officer is known to the law, as defendant was claimed to be, then he can not be guilty of extortion.[15] But a de facto officer may commit the offense,[16] or one who after his term has expired, collects illegal fees.[17] The fees must have been exacted by the officer, not paid to him voluntarily,[18] and must have been received in an

10 Rex v. Jones, 31 How. St. Tr. 251.

11 Rex v. Bembridge, 3 Doug. 327.

12 Commonwealth v. Alexander, 4 Hen. & M. (Va.) 522.

13 Rex v. Bower, 1 Barn. & C. 585; Steph. Dig. Crim. L., art. 123; 1 Russ. on Crimes (9th Am. ed.) 212.

14 Walsh v. People, 65 Ill. 58, 16 Am. Rep. 569; Commonwealth v. Mitchell, 3 Bush (Ky.) 25, 96 Am. Dec. 192; State v. Pritchard, 107 N. Car. 921, 12 S. E. 50; note 116 Am. St. 448.

15 Herrington v. State, 103 Ga. 318, 29 S. E. 931, 68 Am. St. 95.

16 Kirby v. State, 57 N. J. L. 320, 31 Atl. 213.

17 Jackman v. Bentley, 10 Mo. 293.

18 United States v. Harned, 43 Fed. 376. See also, Leggatt v. Prideaux, 16 Mont. 205, 40 Pac. 377, 50 Am. St. 498.

official capacity.[19] The taking of fees on the ground of extra work is prohibited and such fees are illegal.[20] A corrupt intent was essential at common law,[21] but is not under some statutes.[22] An honest belief the fees were due is no defense.[23] Demanding fees before due is extortion at common law.[24] Threatening prosecution to collect a debt or claim is not extortion.[25]

[19] Collier v. State, 55 Ala. 125; Shattuck v. Woods, 1 Pick. (Mass.) 171.

[20] Shattuck v. Woods, 1 Pick. (Mass.) 171.

[21] Leeman v. State, 35 Ark. 438, 37 Am. Rep. 44; Cobbey v. Burks, 11 Nebr. 157, 8 N. W. 386, 38 Am. Rep. 364.

[22] Leeman v. State, 35 Ark. 438, 37 Am. Rep. 44; Cobbey v. Burks, 11 Nebr. 157, 8 N. W. 386, 38 Am. Rep. 364.

[23] Levar v. State, 103 Ga. 42, 29 S. E. 467; Commonwealth v. Bagley, 7 Pick. (Mass.) 279. But see Hirshfield v. Ft. Worth Bank, 83 Tex. 452, 18 S. W. 74? .5 L. R. A. 639, 29 Am. St. 660n.

[24] State v. Burton, 3 Ind. 93; Lane v. State, 49 N. J. L. 673, 10 Atl. 360.

[25] Slater v. Taylor, 31 App. (D. C.) 100, 18 L. R. A. (N. S.) 77; State v. Ricks, 108 Miss. 7, 66 So. 281, L. R. A. 1915 B, 1140.

CHAPTER XXXIX.

PERJURY.

§ 625. **Definition.**—Perjury, as generally understood today, is the wilful and corrupt assertion of a falsehood, material to the matter of inquiry, made under oath or affirmation in a judicial proceeding or course of justice.[1] False swearing may, at common law, fall short of being perjury and still be indictable as an independent misdemeanor. In such case, however, the oath must be taken to affect a judicial right.[2] At common law perjury is only a misdemeanor, but generally by statute it is a felony.[2a]

§ 626. **Requisites.**—The essential elements of perjury are as follows: (1) The act must be wilful and corrupt. (2) The oath or affirmation must be a lawful one. (3) The proceed-

1 United States v. Bailey, 9 Pet. (U. S.) 238, 9 L. ed. 113; People v. Collier, 1 Mich. 137, 48 Am. Dec. 699; Moore v. State, 91 Miss. 250, 44 So. 817, 124 Am. St. 652n; People v. Martin, 175 N. Y. 315, 67 N. E. 589, 96 Am. St. 628, 15 Am. Crim. 591; People v. Osborne, 158 N. Y. S. 330; Commonwealth v. Hinkle, 177 Ky. 22, 197 S. W. 455.

2 State v. Coleman, 117 Ga. 973, 42 So. 471, 8 Ann. Cas. 881n; Reg. v. Chapman, 1 Den. Cr. C. 432, Temp. & M. 90, 2 Car. & K. 846, 3 Cox. Cr. C. 467; United States v. Morehead, 243 U. S. 607, 61 L. ed. 926.

2a People v. Ashbrook, 276 Ill. 382, 114 N. E. 922.

ing which is the occasion of the act must be judicial, or one which occurs in the course of justice. (4) The testimony must be either false, or believed to be false and corruptly given. (5) It must be material to the matter of inquiry.

§ 627. **Act wilful and corrupt.**—To render the act perjury the testimony must be given wilfully and corruptly. If given inadvertently by mistake, but honestly, the act is not perjury.[3] But when a witness wilfully and corruptly swears to the existence of a fact which he has no probable cause to believe true he commits perjury.[4] And when he swears that he thinks or believes so and so when he really thinks and believes the contrary he commits perjury.[5] Again, when he wilfully and corruptly swears to the existence of a certain fact which he really believes does not exist, but which in fact does exist, he commits perjury.[6] Where one wilfully and corruptly swears that a certain person revoked his will in his presence, and the witness has no knowledge of the revocation, the fact that the will had been revoked is no defense to an indictment for perjury.[7] But when a person honestly swears to an assertion upon advice of counsel he does not commit perjury. If a witness honestly but erroneously swears to a written statement which he is advised by his counsel is substantially correct he does not commit perjury.[8] And where a bankrupt, who has submitted to his counsel a fair statement relative to his property, and who, acting upon

[3] Martin v. Miller, 4 Mo. 47, 28 Am. Dec. 342; Lambert v. People, 76 N. Y. 220, 6 Abb. N. Cas. 181, 32 Am. Rep. 293; Steinman v. McWilliams, 6 Pa. St. 170; McDonough v. State, 47 Tex. Cr. 227, 84 S. W. 594, 122 Am. St. 684; People v. Osborne, 158 N. Y. S. 330; State v. Lazarus (Iowa), 164 N. W. 1037.

[4] Becherer v. Stock, 49 Ill. App. 270; Gilson v. State (Tex. App.), 15 S. W. 118; Rex v. Edwards, 1 Rus. C. & M. 293; People v. Grout, 161 N. Y. S. 718, 174 App. Div. 608.

[5] Rex v. Pedley, 1 Leach Cr. C. 325; Reg. v. Schlesinger, 10 Q. B. 670, 2 Cox Cr. C. 200.

[6] 1 Hawk. P. C., ch. 69, § 6.

[7] Allen v. Westley, Heb. 97.

[8] United States v. Stanley, Fed. Cas. No. 16375, 6 McLean (U. S.) 409; Commonwealth v. Clark, 157 Pa. St. 257, 27 Atl. 723.

the advice of his counsel, withholds some items from his schedule, he is not guilty of perjury.[9]

It has been held that drunkenness is no defense to the crime of perjury.[10] But according to the better view, as well as the weight of authority, when the drunkenness is such as to negative the existence of such a state of mind as to render the witness capable of giving wilfully corrupt false testimony it is a defense.[11]

§ 628. Lawful oath or affirmation.—The oath or affirmation must be lawful. The form of it, however, is immaterial, provided it is authorized by law.[12] It is essential, however, that it be solemnly administered by a duly authorized officer. And when a statute directs a certain form of swearing the statute must be substantially followed.[13] But merely technical variations do not affect the validity of the oath;[14] nor does a mere irregularity in the administration of the oath.[15] Thus, where the words "so help me God" are omitted from the form prescribed by statute the omission is no defense to an indictment for perjury.[16] There is an abundance of authority that a substantial compliance with the statute in administering the oath is sufficient, and where the oath is taken on a book believed by the witness to be a Bible, but which is not, false testimony by the witness may constitute perjury.[17]

9 United States v. Stanley, Fed. Cas. No. 16375, 6 McLean (U. S.) 409.

10 People v. Willey, 2 Park. Cr. (N. Y.) 19.

11 Lytle v. State, 31 Ohio St. 196.

12 Van Dusen v. People, 78 Ill. 645; Campbell v. People, 8 Wend. (N. Y.) 636; State v. Whisenhurst, 9 N. Car. 458; Wheeler v. People (Colo.), 165 Pac. 257; State v. Thornhill, 99 Kans. 808, 163 Pac. 145.

13 Ashburn v. State, 15 Ga. 246; Maher v. State, 3 Minn. 444; State v. Davis, 69 N. Car. 383.

14 Ashburn v. State, 15 Ga. 246; Edwards v. State, 49 Ala. 334; State v. Owen, 72 N. Car. 605.

15 Walker v. State, 107 Ala. 5, 18 So. 393; People v. Rodley, 113 Cal. 240, 63 Pac. 351; Burk v. Clark, 8 Fla. 9.

16 People v. Parent, 139 Cal. 600, 73 Pac. 423.

17 People v. Cook, 8 N. Y. 67, 59 Am. Dec. 451.

§ 629. Judicial proceeding or in course of justice.—At common law the false testimony must be given in a valid judicial proceeding or in the course of justice.[18] It is not essential, however, that it be given before a court.[19] It may be contained in an affidavit required by law.[20] It is not perjury to swear falsely to an affidavit not required by law,[21] nor in a court without jurisdiction.[22] Nor is it perjury to swear falsely to a bill in equity not required to be sworn to, or to an answer to a bill in equity where an oath is not required.[23] Nor is it perjury to swear falsely to an oath of office for in such case the oath is merely promissory.[24] But to swear falsely in a proceeding that is authorized or required by law to establish a legal right is usually held to constitute perjury.[25]

In some states "false swearing" is made a statutory crime. To constitute this offense the false oath must be taken knowingly and wilfully before a duly authorized person, but not in the course of a judicial proceeding.[26] This offense, as previously stated, is also indictable at common law.

§ 630. Falsity of testimony and knowledge thereof.—To constitute perjury the testimony must be either wilfully false,

18 State v. Dayton, 23 N. J. L. 49, 53 Am. Dec. 270; State v. Chandler, 42 Vt. 446; State v. Shupe, 16 Iowa 36, 85 Am. Dec. 485; Manning v. State, 46 Tex. Cr. 326, 81 S. W. 957, 3 Ann. Cas. 867n; State v. Thornhill, 99 Kan. 808, 163 Pac. 145 (a de facto title to the office of justice of the peace is sufficient to authorize the administration of the oath); Garrett v. State, 18 Ga. App. 360, 89 S. E. 380; People v. Osborne, 158 N. Y. S. 330.

19 Arden v. State, 11 Conn. 408.

20 State v. Dayton, 23 N. J. L. 49, 53 Am. Dec. 270; Shipp v. State (Tex. Cr.), 196 S. W. 840; People v. McLeod, 30 Cal. App. 435, 158 Pac. 506.

21 State v. McCarthy, 41 Minn. 59, 42 N. W. 599; Davidson v. State, 22 Tex. App. 372, 3 S. W. 662.

22 Moss v. State, 47 Tex. Cr. 459, 83 S. W. 829, 11 Ann. Cas. 710; People v. Hebberd, 162 N. Y. S. 80, 96 Misc. 617.

23 People v. Gaige, 26 Mich. 30.

24 State v. Dayton, 23 N. J. L. 49, 53 Am. Dec. 270.

25 State v. Estabrooks, 70 Vt. 412, 41 Atl. 499; Ray v. State (Ind.), 114 N. E. 866.

26 Langford v. State, 9 Tex. App. 283; State v. Smith, 63 Vt. 201, 22 Atl. 604.

or, if true, believed to be false and corruptly given.[27] To swear rashly to one's belief of a matter of which he does not profess to have personal knowledge is not perjury. But when a person swears to a material matter, whether it be a statement of knowledge, or of information or belief, or a simple statement of a fact, if he knows it is false, or that he has no such information or belief, he is guilty of perjury.[28] To swear to the existence of a certain fact of which the witness is wholly ignorant,[29] or to swear that one's belief is so and so when it is exactly the contrary,[30] constitutes perjury. A witness may be guilty of perjury in falsely testifying to his opinion as to a material matter of fact.[31] In such case, however, it must clearly appear that there is a wilful failure and refusal on his part to exercise an honest judgment.[32] On the other hand, a witness does not commit perjury in falsely testifying to his opinion as to a conclusion of law.[33] Thus, an indictment charging that the defendant wilfully and knowingly swore falsely that he never "made any trade" with a certain person was held demurrable as not charging that the defendant swore falsely to a fact as distinguished from a conclusion.[34] In the case last cited the court held that where the statement which is the basis of the accusation is a matter of construction, or a deduction from given facts, the fact that it is erroneous, or is not a correct construction, or is not

27 State v. Hascall, 6 N. H. 352; Flowers v. State, 13 Okla. Cr. 221, 163 Pac. 558; State v. Jones, 185 Ind. 234, 113 N. E. 755.

28 United States v. Moore, Fed. Cas. No. 15803, 2 Lowell (U. S.) 232.

29 State v. Gates, 17 N. H. 373; Miller v. State, 15 Fla. 577.

30 Rex v. Pedley, 1 Leach Cr. C. 325.

31 In re Howell, 114 Cal. 250, 46 Pac. 159; Commonwealth v. Edison, (Ky.), 9 S. W. 161.

32 In re Howell, 114 Cal. 250, 46 Pac. 159; Smith v. Hubbell, 142 Mich. 637, 106 N. W. 547; State v. Fannon, 158 Mo. 149, 59 S. W. 75.

33 Harp v. State, 59 Ark. 113, 26 S. W. 714; State v. Henderson, 90 Ind. 406.

34 Commonwealth v. Bray, 123 Ky. 336, 96 S. W. 522.

a logical deduction from all the facts, can not constitute it perjury or false swearing.

The terms "wilful" and "corrupt," as applied to perjury, mean merely that the false testimony was given with some deliberation and from some improper and corrupt motive.[35] Moreover, the term "knowingly" does not necessarily imply actual knowledge. That with which the defendant is chargeable owing to his association with the transaction which constitutes the subject of investigation is sufficient.[36]

§ 631. Materiality of the testimony.—To constitute perjury the testimony must be material.[37] It is not essential, however, that it be material to the main issue. It is sufficient if it is material to a collateral matter brought into the case.[38] It may relate to facts affecting the credibility of the witness himself or that of other witnesses.[39]

The fact that the witness is incompetent;[40] or that he might have refused to testify;[41] or that the testimony given has no influence upon the court or jury;[42] or is not legally relevant,[43] is immaterial. Testimony which tends to prove

[35] People v. Von Tiedeman, 120 Cal. 128, 52 Pac. 155.

[36] State v. Faulkner, 185 Mo. 673, 84 S. W. 967; State v. Smith, 47 Ore. 485, 83 Pac. 865.

[37] State v. Smith, 40 Kans. 631, 20 Pac. 529; Shevalier v. State, 85 Nebr. 366, 123 N. W. 424, 19 Ann. Cas. 361; State v. Whittemore, 50 N. H. 245, 9 Am. Rep. 196; Wood v. People, 59 N. Y. 117; State v. Miller, 26 R. I. 282, 58 Atl. 882, 3 Ann. Cas. 943; Huffine v. State, 13 Okla. 239, 163 Pac. 557.

[38] State v. Shupe, 16 Iowa 36, 85 Am. Dec. 485; Herndon v. State, 72 Fla. 108, 72 So. 833; People v. Hebberd, 162 N. Y. S. 80, 96 Misc. 617; People v. Howland (Colo), 167 Pac. 961; Commonwealth v. Bobanic, 62 Pa. Sup. Ct. 40; Wheeler v. People (Colo.), 165 Pac. 257; Beavers v. State, 124 Ark. 38, 186 S. W. 300.

[39] Commonwealth v. Grant, 116 Mass. 17; Wood v. People, 59 N. Y. 117; State v. Brown, 79 N. Car. 642.

[40] Chamberlain v. People, 23 N. Y. 85, 80 Am. Dec. 255.

[41] Mackin v. People, 115 Ill. 312, 3 N. E. 222, 56 Am. Rep. 167.

[42] Pollard v. People, 69 Ill. 148; Hoch v. People, 3 Mich. 552.

[43] 2 Whart. Crim. L. (11th ed.), §§ 1579, 1580.

an alibi;[44] or which tends to mitigate or aggravate the damages,[45] is material, and when wilfully and corruptly false constitutes perjury. It is not essential that the false testimony be sufficient in itself to establish the issue.[46] It is sufficient if it be circumstantially material.[47]

§ 632. **By whom punishable.**—Perjury is committed against the sovereign whose law is violated by the making of the false oath, and is punishable by that sovereign. No state executes the penal laws of another state. Nor does a state court execute the penal laws of the United States. Hence a false oath taken under the homestead act of congress and administered by an officer acting under authority of that act, to be used before a United States land officer to procure a homestead entry, is not punishable by a state court, for it is not in violation of a state law, nor against the sovereignty of the state.[48]

§ 633. **Attempt to commit perjury.**—Where the accused swears falsely and corruptly before an incompetent official, believing him to be competent, the offense may be indictable at common law.[49] But a mere attempt to induce another to swear falsely as to a given matter is not, of itself, sufficient to constitute an indictable offense.[50]

§ 634. **Subornation of perjury.**—Subornation of perjury consists in corruptly instigating or procuring another to com-

44 Masterson v. State, 144 Ind. 240, 43 N. E. 138; State v. Gibbs, 10 Mont. 213, 25 Pac. 289, 10 L. R. A. 749.

45 State v. Swafford, 98 Iowa, 362, 67 N. W. 284; State v. Blize, 111 Mo. 464, 20 S. W. 210.

46 Robinson v. State, 18 Fla. 898; State v. Norris, 9 N. H. 96.

47 State v. Brown, 128 Iowa 24, 102 N. W. 799; Commonwealth v. Grant, 116 Mass. 17; State v. Faulkner, 175 Mo. 546, 75 S. W. 116.

48 State v. Kirkpatrick, 32 Ark. 117.

49 Reg. v. Stone, 6 Cox Cr. C. 235, Dears. Cr. C. 251; Shipp v. State (Tex. Cr.), 196 S. W. 840.

50 Nicholson v. State, 97 Ga. 672, 25 S. E. 360; Commonwealth v. Douglass, 5 Metc. (Mass.) 241.

mit perjury. At common law it is an accessorial offense, but in many states it has been made by statute a separate and distinct crime.[51] To sustain an indictment for subornation of perjury it must be averred and proved that the witness alleged to have been suborned actually committed perjury,[52] that the defendant induced or procured him to do so,[53] and that the defendant believed he would do so.[54]

[51] Stone v. State, 118 Ga. 705, 45 S. E. 630, 98 Am. St. 145. (In this case Justice Lamar says: "In perjury and subornation of perjury the act of the two offenders is concurrent, parallel, and closely related in point of time and conduct. The two crimes both culminate in the delivery of false testimony. Still the offenses are dual, each having in it elements not common to the other. There is sufficient inherent difference between the two to warrant the law-making power in separating the act into its component parts, making that of the suborner a new and independent offense, punishable with greater or less severity than that inflicted on the perjurer." See also, People v. Teal, 196 N. Y. 372, 89 N. E. 1086, 25 L. R. A. (N. S.) 120n, 17 Ann. Cas. 1175n.

[52] Smith v. State, 125 Ind. 440, 25 N. E. 598; Garrett v. State, 18 Ga. App. 360, 89 S. E. 380.

[53] Smith v. State, 125 Ind. 440, 25 N. E. 598; Commonwealth v. Douglass, 5 Metc. (Mass.) 241.

[54] Coyne v. People, 124 Ill. 17, 14 N. E. 668, 7 Am. St. 324; Stewart v. State, 22 Ohio St. 477.

CHAPTER XL.

RECEIVING STOLEN GOODS.

§ 640. Definition and essentials.—The crime of receiving stolen goods is the act of taking into one's possession, animo furandi, personal property of another with actual or constructive knowledge that it is stolen property.

It is essential not only that the property has been stolen, but also that it possess the character of stolen property at the time it is received into the possession of the accused. He must have actual or constructive knowledge when he acquires possession of it that it is stolen property, and must receive it animo furandi and with the consent of the other party.

§ 641. A statutory offense.—At common law, receiving stolen goods is probably not even a substantive misdemeanor. In 1691 a statute was passed in England which provided "That if any person or persons shall buy or receive any goods or chattel that shall be feloniously taken or stolen from any other person, knowing the same to be stolen, he or they shall be taken and deemed an accessory or accessories to such felony after the fact, and shall incur the same punishment, as an accessory or accessories to the felony after the felony committed."[1]

[1] 3 Wm. & M., ch. 9, § 4.

In 1827 another statute was passed which provided "That if any person shall receive any chattel, money, valuable security or other property whatsoever, the stealing or taking whereof will amount to a felony either at common law, or by virtue of this act, such person knowing the same to have been feloniously stolen or taken, every such receiver shall be guilty of felony, and may be indicted and convicted as an accessory after the fact, or for a substantive felony."[2]

It will be observed that under the former of these statutes the offense was only an accessorial crime, whereas under the latter it was also a substantive crime. Hence under the former statute it was essential that the property be received from the thief while under the latter it was not.

In this country, statutes have been enacted in probably all the states making the offense a substantive crime. Under these statutes it is not essential that the property be received from the thief. The contrary, however, has been held,[3] but this view is not correct upon principle, nor in harmony with the great weight of authority.[4] Some statutes make it a crime to receive goods animo furandi which have been embezzled or obtained by false pretenses.[5] These statutes are separate and distinct from those which make it a crime to receive stolen goods. It has been held that one who participates in the larceny may not be convicted also of the offense of receiving stolen goods.[6] On the other hand however, it has been held that a verdict for receiving stolen goods will

[2] 7 & 8 Geo. IV, ch. 29, § 54.

[3] State v. Ives, 35 N. Car. 338; United States v. De Bare, Fed. Cas. No. 14935, 6 Biss. (U. S.) 358.

[4] Levi v. State, 14 Nebr. 1, 14 N. W. 543; Smith v. State, 59 Ohio St. 350, 52 N. E. 826; Kirby v. United States, 174 U. S. 47, 43 L. ed. 890; Anderson v. State, 38 Fla. 3, 20 So. 765; Curran v. State, 12 Wyo. 553, 76 Pac. 577; Campbell v. State (Miss.), 17 So. 441; 2 Bish. New Crim. L. (8th ed.), § 1140.

[5] Commonwealth v. Leonard, 140 Mass. 473, 4 N. E. 96, 54 Am. Rep. 485.

[6] Adams v. State, 60 Fla. 1, 53 So. 451, Ann. Cas. 1912 B, 1209; Bloch v. State (Tex. Cr.), 193 S. W. 303.

not be set aside because the evidence would have justified a verdict for the separate offense of larceny.[6a]

§ 642. **The act must be felonious.**—The act of receiving the property must be felonious. It is essential, therefore, that the thing received be stolen property. This attribute must exist at the time the property is received. Thus, where the defendant was convicted of receiving stolen goods, and the proof showed that they had been found in the pockets of the thief by the owner; that with the view of catching the receiver of such goods (brass castings) the owner returned them to the thief and directed him to sell them to the defendant, which was accordingly done, the conviction was set aside because the goods, when received by the defendant, had ceased to be stolen property, and were sold to the defendant with the consent of the owner.[7] Again, in another case, the defendant was convicted of receiving a parcel of postage stamps, of the value of one hundred fifty dollars which had been stolen. The proof showed that the stamps were stolen at Unionville, Mo., and sent by the thief, by express, to Milwaukee, Wis., addressed to the defendant; that the thief was arrested at Quincy, Ill., and that he gave an order to the postmaster there on the express agent at Milwaukee by which that postmaster acquired possession of the parcel; that the United States authorities ordered the postmaster to enclose them in the same wrapper and forward them as first directed; that this order was carried out and that the parcel was received at Milwaukee by the defendant. On appeal, the conviction was set aside and a new trial granted on the ground that the stamps when received by the defendant had lost their character as stolen property. "The ownership of these stamps was in the United States. The

6a People v. Thompson, 274 Ill. 214, 113 N. E. 322.

7 Reg. v. Dolan, 6 Cox Cr. C. 449, Dears. Cr. C. 436. See also People v. Jaffe, 185 N. Y. 497, 78 N. E. 169, 9 L. R. A. 263, 7 Ann. Cas. 348, Derby's Cases 70.

Quincy postmaster was the agent of the owner. When Crawford (the thief) surrendered them to this agent they were reclaimed property that had been stolen, but their character as stolen property ceased in the hands of the postmaster, so far as the subsequent receiver was concerned. The moral turpitude of a receiver under such circumstances may be as great as in case the property comes directly from the hands of the thief, because the criminal intent on his part exists equally in both cases. But to create the offense which the law punishes, the property when received, must, in fact, and in a legal sense, be stolen property. If these stamps were received by the defendant, they did not, when received, upon the proof made, bear this character. They had been captured from the thief by the owner, and the act of forwarding them to the alleged receiver was the act of the owner."[8]

§ 643. Consent of the other party essential.—Possession of the property must be obtained with the consent of the party from whom it is received. If acquired by trespass the offense is larceny.[9]

§ 644. Guilty knowledge of the recipient.—It is also essential that the recipient possess guilty knowledge as to the character of the property. And this guilty knowledge must exist at the time he receives it. It can be constructive, however, as well as actual; and, it has been held, may be implied from the receipt of goods under circumstances sufficient to satisfy a man of ordinary intelligence and caution that they were stolen.[10] Other jurisdictions hold that knowl-

[8] United States v. De Bare, Fed. Cas. No. 16935, 6 Biss. (U. S.) 358. See also Reg. v. Schmidt, 10 Cox Cr. C. 172, L. R. 1 C. C. 15, 35 L. J. M. C. 94, 12 Jur. (N. S.) 149.

[9] Reg. v. Wade, 1 Car. & K. 739.

[10] Huggins v. People, 135 Ill. 243, 25 N. E. 1002, 25 Am. St. 357; State v. Feuerhaken, 96 Iowa 299, 65 N. W. 299; Luery v. State, 116 Md. 284, 81 Atl. 681, Ann. Cas. 1913D, 161; State v. D'Adame, 84 N. J. L. 386, 86 Atl. 414, Ann. Cas. 1914B, 1109; Murio v. State, 31 Tex. Cr.

edge must be actual.[11] But if one after obtaining knowledge undertakes to deprive the owner of the rightful use of the property, he may be convicted of receiving stolen goods.[12] And a lawyer who aided the thieves who had stolen securities in getting a reward for their return and had the securities in his possession while the reward was being paid, was convicted of receiving stolen goods.[13]

§ 645. Doctrine of lucri causa.—As in the case of larceny, the doctrine of lucri causa is not applicable, as a rule, to the crime of receiving stolen goods. It is not essential that the recipient gain any benefit therefrom, or expect to do so.[14] It is sufficient if he aids the thief to conceal the property.[15] Guilty knowledge that the goods were stolen has been held sufficient.[16] But where a statute expressly provides that the property must be received for "gain" of the recipient the foregoing rule does not apply.[17]

§ 646. Manual possession not essential.—It is not essential that the accused have manual possession of the stolen

210, 20 S. W. 356; Reg. v. White, 1 Fost. & F. 665; and note to 4 L. R. A. (N. S.) 31 on statutes by which failure to inquire as to possessor's right is made equivalent to guilty knowledge. See also Frank v. State, 67 Miss. 125, 6 So. 842; People v. Zimmer, 160 N. Y. S. 459, 174 App. Div. 470. See also Kasle v. United States, 233 Fed. 878, 147 C. C. A. 552.

11 First Nat. Bank v. Gilbert, 123 La. 845, 49 So. 593, 25 L. R. A. (N. S.) 631n, 131 Am. St. 382; State v. Rountree, 80 S. Car. 387, 61 S. E. 1072, 22 L. R. A. (N. S.) 833; James v. State (Ala. App.), 74 So. 395.

12 Commonwealth v. Kronick, 196 Mass. 286, 82 N. E. 39, Derby's Cases 515.

13 People v. O'Reilly, 153 App. Div. 854, 138 N. Y. S. 776, Derby's Cases 519.

14 State v. Rushing, 69 N. Car. 29, 12 Am. Rep. 641; Commonwealth v. Beam, 117 Mass. 141; Rex v. Richardson, 6 Car. & P. 335. See also State v. Pirkey, 22 S. Dak. 550, 118 N. W. 1042, 18 Ann. Cas. 192.

15 People v. Reynolds, 2 Mich. 422.

16 State v. Smith, 88 Iowa 1, 55 N. W. 16.

17 Aldrich v. People, 101 Ill. 16.

property.[18] In one of the cases the defendant was convicted of knowingly receiving a stolen watch. His contention was that there was no proof that he had possession of it. The judge instructed the jury that if the defendant knew that the watch was stolen, that H had it, that the defendant could make him deliver it, and had absolute control over him, they would be justified in finding him guilty. On appeal, the conviction was affirmed. Again, where C stole goods and took them to the defendant's store, and the defendant ordered her servant to take them to a pawnshop and bring back the money received for them and give it to C, which order was carried out, the conviction, on appeal, was sustained,[19] since it was virtually as much a receiving of stolen goods by the defendant as if her own hand, and not that of her servant, had received them. It is enough to aid in the concealment of the goods, knowing them to be stolen.[20]

§ 647. Subsequent adoption of wife's act.—Where the thief leaves the stolen goods with the wife of the accused, and she pays him part of the price, and her husband subsequently meets him, agrees on the price and pays him the balance, the husband is guilty of receiving stolen goods.[21] The act of receiving the goods is incomplete until the husband meets the thief and they agree to the terms.

§ 648. Depriving the owner permanently of possession.—The term "permanently," in its application to the crime of receiving stolen goods, has the same restricted meaning that it has in its application to the crime of larceny. Where the defendant was convicted of receiving stolen goods, and he contended that the conviction should be quashed because the

[18] Reg. v. Smith, Dears. Cr. C. 494, 6 Cox Cr. C. 554, 3 W. R. 484, 33 Eng. L. & Eq. 531.

[19] Reg. v. Miller, 6 Cox Cr. C. 353.

[20] State v. Conklin, 153 Iowa 216, 133 N. W. 119, Derby's Cases 518.

[21] Reg. v. Woodward, 9 Cox Cr. C. 95, Leigh & C. 122, 31 L. J. M. C. 91, 5 L. T. 686, 10 W. R. 298, 8 Jur. (N. S.) 104, Derby's Cases 513.

proof showed that he did not intend to deprive the owner of the property of his ownership in it; that he intended to return it upon receiving a reward for so doing, the court held that if the jury believed from the evidence, as they well might, that the defendant concealed from the owner the fact that he had the property, intending to defraud him into paying a reward for it, the crime was established.[22]

§ 649. Recent possession of stolen goods.—The recent possession of stolen goods, unexplained, is a circumstance from which the jury may infer the possessor's guilt.[23] But it does not raise a presumption of guilt as a matter of law.[24]

22 Baker v. State, 58 Ark. 513, 25 S. W. 603. See also, Commonwealth v. Mason, 105 Mass. 163, 7 Am. Rep. 507; Berry v. State, 37 Ohio St. 227; Reg. v. O'Donnell, 7 Cox Cr. C. 337.

23 Kinard v. State, 19 Ga. App. 624, 91 S. E. 941.

24 Kinard v. State, 19 Ga. App. 624, 91 S. E. 941.

CHAPTER XLI.

RESISTING AN OFFICER.

§ 650. Obstructing justice.—Wilfully obstructing the administration of justice is a crime at common law.[1] It has been held criminal to destroy a dead body to prevent an inquest,[2] to wilfully destroy public records,[3] to cause another to be falsely convicted of a crime,[4] to refuse as a jailer to deliver over prisoners on proper order,[5] or generally, to obstruct an officer in the execution of his office.[6] The crime must be committed with knowledge that justice is being administered.[7] Tampering with witnesses is a crime.[8]

§ 651. Resisting an officer.—One who resists the acts of an officer in making a legal arrest,[9] or who prevents or hin-

[1] 1 Bish. New Crim. L. (8th ed.), §§ 465, 467. See also, United States v. Tinklepaugh, Federal Case No. 16525, 3 Blatch. (U. S.) 425; Bosselman v. United States, 239 Fed. 82, 152 C. C. A. 132.

[2] Reg. v. Stephenson, 13 Q. B. Div. 331.

[3] United States v. De Groat, 30 Fed. 764.

[4] United States v. Kindred, 5 Fed. 43, 4 Hughes (U. S.) 493.

[5] United States v. Martin, 17 Fed. 150, 2 Sawy. (U. S.) 90.

[6] Brooker v. Commonwealth, 12 Serg. & R. (Pa.) 175; State v. Bradshaw, 53 Mont. 96, 161 Pac. 710.

[7] Pettibone v. United States, 148 U. S. 197, 37 L. ed. 419; State v. Bradshaw, 53 Mont. 96, 161 Pac. 710.

[8] People v. Brown, 74 Cal. 306, 16 Pac. 1; Commonwealth v. Reynolds, 14 Gray (Mass.) 87, 74 Am. Dec. 665; State v. Ames, 64 Maine 386; State v. Cole, 107 S. Car. 285, 92 S. E. 624; State v. Wingard, 92 Wash. 219, 158 Pac. 725.

[9] State v. Scott, 123 La. 1085, 49 So. 715, 24 L. R. A. (N. S.) 199n; Commonwealth v. Foster, 1 Mass. 488; People v. Haley, 48 Mich. 495, 12 N. W. 671; Bryant v. State, 16 Nebr. 651, 21 N. W. 406; State v. Scammon, 22 N. H. 44; State v. Bradshaw, 53 Mont. 96; 161 Pac. 710.

ders the execution of a lawful civil process,[10] may be con victed of crime. The officer resisted must have been within his jurisdiction, acting under a lawful warrant.[11]

Resistance to an officer serving civil process, who is acting unlawfully and without authority, is not a crime,[12] for wrongful intent is necessary to the crime. One who prevents an officer from taking exempt property of his wife on an exemption issued against him, is not guilty.[13] One who has no knowledge of the official character of the person resisted is not guilty.[14] Mere threats,[15] or refusal to give information to an officer,[16] are insufficient to support conviction. But threats coupled with present ability and apparent intent to execute them, thus preventing service of process, may constitute the offense.[17]

10 State v. Morrison, 46 Kans. 679, 27 Pac. 133; Commonwealth v. McHugh, 157 Mass. 457, 32 N. E. 650; Braddy v. Hodges, 99 N. Car. 319, 5 S. E. 17.

11 See § 811.

12 Agee v. State, 64 Ind. 340; People v. Hopson, 1 Denio (N. Y.) 574.

13 People v. Clements, 68 Mich. 655, 36 N. W. 792, 13 Am. St. 373.

14 State v. Garrett, 80 Iowa 589, 46 N. W. 748; People v. Durfee, 62 Mich. 487, 29 N. W. 109.

15 State v. Welch, 37 Wis. 196.

16 Reg. v. Green, 8 Cox Cr. C. 441.

17 Reed v. State, 103 Ark. 391, 147 S. W. 76, Ann. Cas. 1914B, 811n; Slim and Shorty v. State, 123 Ark. 583, 186 S. W. 308.

TITLE SIX.

Crimes Against Public Peace

CHAPTER XLII

AFFRAY.

§ 655. Definition.—Affray consists in the public fighting of two or more persons to the terror of the people.[1]

§ 656. Mere words not sufficient.—A mere dispute, accompanied by loud and angry words, does not constitute an affray. There must be a fight. It is not essential, however,

[1] 4 Bl. Comm. 145; State v. Sumner, 5 Strob. (S. Car.) 53; Haverebakken v. State (Tex. Cr.), 194 S. W. 1114; Commonwealth v. Merrick, 65 Pa. Super. Ct. 482, 499; Commonwealth v. Blum, 65 Pa. Super. Ct., 493, 498; Commonwealth v. Tepsick, 65 Pa. Super. Ct., 493; Commonwealth v. Detwiler, 65 Pa. Super. Ct. 494; Commonwealth v. Weston, 65 Pa. Super. Ct., 497; Commonwealth v. Zerber, 65 Pa. Super. Ct., 497; Commonwealth v. Esick, 65 Pa. Super. Ct. 498.

that each party receive a blow. Where an altercation arose between two persons in a public place and one drew his knife and cut at the other, whereupon the latter drew his knife from his pocket but was prevented from using it by bystanders, they were held guilty of affray. As said by Justice Warner, "The words alone of the parties, independent of their acts, would not have constituted an affray; but their words, accompanied by their acts respectively, in drawing their knives and attempting to use them, was calculated to terrify the good citizens of Milledgeville, and disturb the public tranquility."[2]

§ 657. **The fighting must be by agreement.**—To re .der a person guilty of affray he must unlawfully fight by agreement. If a person merely defends himself against an attack he is not guilty of affray.[3]

[2] Hawkins v. State, 13 Ga. 322, 58 Am. Dec. 517.

[3] Klum v. State, 1 Blackf. (Ind.) 377; State v. Harrell, 107 N. Car. 944, 12 S. E. 439.

CHAPTER XLIII

CARRYING CONCEALED WEAPONS.

§ 659. **Carrying concealed weapons.**—The English statute of 1328 making it a crime for any one except the king or his servants to go armed, was held merely declaratory of the common law.[1] Now the crime in this country is entirely governed by statutes, which usually prohibit the wearing of concealed weapons in public places. These statutes are constitutional.[2] Under most of them the open wearing of weapons is not punishable,[3] but the concealment even for a moment is within the statute.[4] Nor does it matter how the weapon is hidden, concealment in a basket,[5] satchel,[6] or even wearing a pistol in a holster,[7] being indictable. But it was held that carrying in one's hands saddlebags with the lid down, in which a pistol was hidden, was not indictable.[8] It is enough that the weapon was worn in one's own house, if

[1] Knight's Case, 3 Mod. 117; Statutes 2 Edw. III, ch. 3.

[2] Salina v. Blaksley, 72 Kans. 230, 83 Pac. 619, 3 L. R. A. (N. S.) 168, 115 Am. St. 196, 7 Ann. Cas. 925; 3 Whart. Crim. Law (11th ed.), § 1875.

[3] Shields v. State, 104 Ala. 35, 16 So. 85, 53 Am. St. 17, 9 Am. Cr. 149; State v. Swope, 20 Ind. 106.

[4] Brinson v. State, 75 Ga. 882.

[5] Boles v. State, 86 Ga. 255, 12 S. E. 361, 8 Am. Cr. 126.

[6] Warren v. State, 94 Ala. 79, 10 So. 838.

[7] Barton v. State, 7 Baxt. (Tenn.) 105; Lewis v. State, 2 Tex. App. 26.

[8] Southerland v. Commonwealth, 109 Va. 834, 65 S.E. 15, 23 L. R. A. (N. S.) 172.

the statute makes no exception,[9] and it does not matter that a gun was unloaded,[10] or was carried for hunting,[11] or was so defective that it could not be fired.[12] But criminal intent may be negatived by showing that the weapon was being carried merely as property, to a repair shop,[13] or to return it to its owner,[14] or as merchandise for sale.[15]

Under most statutes the weapons must be worn in a public place, and under many, travelers are excepted from the penalty. To fall within this exception, one must be absent from home on an occasional business trip,[16] and the exemption covers the period of such journey. Making a daily trip from one's house to his place of business,[17] or a trip from the outlying townships to a county seat in the usual manner,[18] is not travel.

Where persons threatened with or apprehending personal danger are excepted, reasonable ground for apprehension must be shown.[19]

Officers in discharge of their duties are usually excepted;[20] the exemption applying only when actually in discharge of official duty, and affording no protection when the officer is outside of his district.[21]

9 State v. Workman, 35 W. Va. 367, 14 S. E. 9, 14 L. R. A. 600.

10 Ridenour v. State, 65 Ind. 411.

11 Sanderson v. State, 23 Tex. App. 520, 5 S. W. 138.

12 Mitchell v. State, 99 Miss. 579, 55 So. 354, 34 L. R. A. (N. S.) 1174, Ann. Cas. 1913E, 512.

13 Pressler v. State, 19 Tex. App. 52, 53 Am. Rep. 383; State v. Gilbert, 87 N. Car. 527, 42 Am. Rep. 518.

14 State v. Brodnax, 91 N. Car. 543.

15 Foster v. State, 59 Tex. Cr. 44, 126 S. W. 1155, Ann. Cas. 1912A, 1206.

16 Lott v. State, 122 Ind. 393, 24 N. E. 156; Chaplin v. State, 7 Tex. App. 87.

17 Eslava v. State, 49 Ala. 355.

18 Carr v. State, 34 Ark. 448, 36 Am. Rep. 15.

19 Smith v. State, 69 Ind. 140; State v. Wilburn, 7 Baxt. (Tenn.) 57, 32 Am. Rep. 551; Reach v. State, 94 Ala. 113, 11 So. 414; Suddith v. State, 70 Miss. 250, 11 So. 680; Chatteaux v. State, 52 Ala. 388.

20 Bell v. State, 100 Ala. 78, 14 So. 763; Love v. State, 32 Tex. Cr. 85, 22 S. W. 140.

21 Shirley v. State, 100 Miss. 799, 57 So. 221, 38 L. R. A. (N. S.) 998, Ann. Cas. 1914A, 252 and note.

CHAPTER XLIV

COMMON BARRATRY, MAINTENANCE AND CHAMPERTY.

§ 661. Common barratry.—Common barratry consists in frequently exciting and stirring up suits and quarrels either at law or otherwise.[1] There must be a series of at least three distinct acts to constitute this offense.[2] Moreover, the acts must be more than merely unsuccessful suits. If the suits are brought, however, merely to annoy the adversary, and are unfounded, the offense is committed.[3] It has been held that a justice of the peace who stirs up criminal prosecutions for the purpose of obtaining fees is guilty of this crime.[4]

§ 662. Maintenance.—Maintenance consists in the officious intermeddling in a suit by one who has no interest therein by maintaining or assisting either party with money or otherwise, to prosecute or defend it.[5] Thus, it has been held that where a stranger to a suit induces the plaintiff to sue by promising to pay the costs in case he loses, the promisor is guilty of maintenance.[6] As a rule, however, this of-

[1] 4 Bl. Comm. 134; 1 Hawk. P. C. 524, ch. 81; Commonwealth v. Davis, 11 Pick. (Mass.) 432.

[2] Commonwealth v. Davis, 11 Pick. (Mass.) 432; Commonwealth v. McCulloch, 15 Mass. 227.

[3] Commonwealth v. McCulloch, 15 Mass. 227.

[4] State v. Chitty, 1 Bailey (S. Car.) 379

[5] 1 Hawk. P. C. 535, ch. 83; 4 Bl. Comm. 134.

[6] Hutley v. Hutley, L. R. 8 Q. B. Div. 112.

fense "is confined to cases where a man improperly, and for the purpose of stirring up litigation and strife, encourages others either to bring actions or to make defenses which they have no right to make."[7] In some jurisdictions this offense is not recognized at all. And in no jurisdiction is it held an offense for a man to maintain the suit of his near kinsman, servant or poor neighbor, out of charity and compassion.[8] But the assistance must be because of the interest or relationship.[9] Where several persons have a common interest in a suit brought by one of them it is not maintenance for the others to contribute to the expense of the suit.[10]

§ 663. **Champerty.**—Champerty, according to Blackstone, consists in an agreement to divide the land or other matter sued for between the parties if they prevail at law, whereupon the champertor is to carry on the party's suit at his own expense.[11] It has been held, however, that it is not essential for the champertor to carry on the suit at his own expense; that champerty is committed by an attorney, for example, where he agrees to conduct the suit for a contingent compensation.[12] This view, however, is very generally repudiated.[13]

In many states the courts have repudiated the common-law doctrine relative to maintenance and champerty;[14] and in many of them statutes have virtually repealed the common

[7] Findon v. Parker, 11 M. & W. 682; Employers' Liability Assur. Corp. v. Kelly-Atkinson Const. Co., 195 Ill. App. 620.

[8] 4 Bl. Comm. 134; Walker v. Perryman, 23 Ga. 309, 316.

[9] Dunn v. Herrick, 37 Ill. App. 180.

[10] Davies v. Stowell, 78 Wis. 334, 47 N. W. 370, 10 L. R. A. 190.

[11] 4 Bl. Comm. 135. See also Huston v. Scott, 20 Okla. 142, 94 Pac. 512, 35 L. R. A. (N. S.) 721, and note.

[12] Lathrop v. Amherst Bank, 9 Metc. (Mass.) 489.

[13] Phillips v. South Park Commissioners, 119 Ill. 626, 10 N. E. 230; Aultman v. Waddle, 40 Kans. 195, 19 Pac. 730.

[14] Lewis v. Broun, 36 W. Va. 1, 14 S. E. 444; Sedgwick v. Stanton, 14 N. Y. 289; Winslow v. Central Iowa R. Co., 71 Iowa 197, 32 N. W. 330; Gilman v. Jones, 87 Ala. 691, 5 So. 785, 7 So. 48, 4 L. R. A. 113. See also, note to 83 Am. St. 167.

law pertaining to them. At the old common law both of these offenses, as well as common barratry, were misdemeanors.[15]

§ 664. **Modern rule.**—According to the modern rule the mere fact that an agreement between an attorney and his client provides for contingent compensation for the former's services, thereby giving the attorney an interest in the subject-matter of the suit, does not render the contract void.[16] But where the attorney agrees to conduct the litigation, pay the costs and expenses of the suit, or advance money therefor, in consideration of a portion of the sum or property to be recovered, the agreement is champertous, and void as against public policy[17] and where an attorney is so interested in the result of the suit as to pay the entire expense, control the settlement and take joint interest in the property, the contract will be void.[18] An assignment of a claim to an attorney for a sum much less than he considers the claim worth, is champertous and void.[19] The gist of champerty, according to a recent decision,[20] is the malicious or officious intermeddling in a suit in which the intermeddler has no interest. This, however, is the gist of maintenance rather than the gist of champerty.

Where the facts justify it, the defense of champerty is tenable whether pleaded or not.[21]

15 Wildey v. Crane, 63 Mich. 720, 30 N. W. 327.

16 Holloway v. Dickinson, 137 Minn. 410, 163 N. W. 791 (attorney took a personal injury case for one-third of the amount to be obtained either by settlement or suit); Rohan v. Johnson, 33 N. Dak. 179, 156 N. W. 936, L. R. A. 1916 E. 64n, Ann. Cas. 1918A, 794; Bennett v. Tighe, 224 Mass. 159, 112 N. E. 629; Dennin v. Powers, 160 N. Y. S. 636, 96 Misc. 252.

17 Young v. Young, 196 Mich. 316, 162 N. W. 993. See also, Jones v. Pettingill, 245 Fed. 269, 157 C. C. A. 461, certiorari denied; Pettingill v. Jones, 245 U. S. 663, 38 Sup. Ct. 61, 62 L. ed. 519; Chreste v. Louisville R. Co., 173 Ky. 486, 191 S. W. 265.

18 Jones v. Pettingill, 245 Fed. 269, 157 C. C. A. 461.

19 Sampliner v. Motion Picture Patents Co., 243 Fed. 277.

20 Rohan v. Johnson, 33 N. Dak. 179, 156 N. W. 936, L. R. A. 1916E, 64n, Ann. Cas. 1918A, 794.

21 Reynolds v. Binion, 177 Ky. 189, 197 S. W. 641.

CHAPTER XLV

DUELING AND PRIZE FIGHTING.

§ 665. Dueling.—Dueling is the fighting of two persons against each other, at an appointed place, founded upon a precedent quarrel. It results from design, whereas affray results from a sudden quarrel.

If one of the fighters kills the other the crime is murder. Moreover, all who are present and abet the crime are also guilty of murder as principals in the second degree.[1]

To challenge another to fight a duel is a misdemeanor at common law.[2] It is also a misdemeanor to provoke another to send a challenge or to be the bearer of it.

The fact that the duel is to occur in another state is immaterial.[3]

§ 666. Prize fighting.—Consent to an assault and battery is a good defense provided the act does not amount to a breach of the public peace.[4] Manly sports, such as wrestling, boxing, playing at cudgels or foils, and the like, where there

[1] Cullen v. Commonwealth, 24 Grat. (Va.) 624; Reg. v. Young, 8 Car. & P. 644.

[2] State v. Farrier, 8 N. Car. 487; note to 25 L. R. A. 437; 1 East P. C. 242; 1 Hawk. P. C., ch. 31, § 21.

[3] Harris v. State, 58 Ga. 332; State v. Farrier, 8 N. Car. 487.

[4] People v. Bransby, 32 N. Y. 525; Champer v. State, 14 Ohio St. 437.

is no motive or intent to do bodily harm, are not crimes. But prize fighting, which amounts to a breach of the public peace, or which tends to cause such, is a misdemeanor, and the consent of the parties is no defense.[5]

§ 667. Importation of prize fight picture films.—By an act of congress, which became effective July 31, 1912, the importation of pictorial representations of prize fights is made a penal offense.[6] And, in construing this act, it has been held that where a picture film, of a prize fight on the Canadian side, was made by means of photographic apparatus on the American side, opposite apparatus on the Canadian side, the two being connected, it constituted a violation of the statute, since the parties, by the means employed, caused the picture to be brought into the United States in violation of the statute.[7]

5 Commonwealth v. Collberg, 119 Mass. 350, 20 Am. Rep. 328; Seville v. State, 49 Ohio 117, 30 N. E. 621, 15 L. R. A. 516 and note.

6 United States v. Johnston, 232 Fed. 970.

7 Pantomimic Corp. v. Malone, 238 Fed. 135, 151 C. C. A. 211.

CHAPTER XLVI

ESCAPE, PRISON BREACH AND RESCUE.

§ 668. In general.—Escape, prison breach and rescue are various modes of liberating a prisoner unlawfully. Escape is accomplished without violence; prison breach by means of violence, and rescue by the aid of a third party, either with or without violence.

§ 669. Escape.—Escape, at common law, is a misdemeanor. As said by Justice Peters, in a case frequently cited, "The escape of a person lawfully arrested, by eluding the vigilance of his keepers, before he is put in hold or in prison, is an offense against public justice; and the party himself is punishable by fine and imprisonment. For however strong the natural desire of liberty may be, yet every man is bound to submit himself to the restraints of the law."[1]

This offense can be committed by the officer or other person who has the prisoner in custody as well as by the prisoner himself.

Where the custodian either negligently or voluntarily allows a prisoner to go under circumstances which do not constitute due course of law he commits a misdemeanor.[2] To render the custodian criminally liable, however, the prisoner

1 State v. Doud, 7 Conn. 384.

2 Houpt v. State, 100 Ark. 409, 140 S. W. 494, Ann. Cas. 1913C, 690 and note. See also, note to 95 Am. St. 115.

must be lawfully under arrest for a criminal offense.[3] The guilt or innocence of the prisoner, however, is immaterial.[4]

§ 670. Prison breach.—Under the old common law, prison breach was a felony irrespective of the cause of the imprisonment. As said by Justice Peters, "By the ancient common law, prison breaches were felonies, if the party were lawfully imprisoned, for any cause whatever, whether civil or criminal, and whether he were actually within the walls of a prison, or in the stocks, or in the custody of a person who had lawfully arrested him."[5] By an early English statute,[6] however, prison breaches were made misdemeanors in those cases where the prisoners were under arrest for misdemeanors; and this statute is part of our common law.

As stated by Justice Peters, the imprisonment must be lawful. Hence, if the warrant was void and the prisoner uses no more force than is necessary to acquire his liberty the offense is not committed.[7] It is also essential that there be a breaking, but it is sufficient if only slight. Where the prisoner merely climbs over the prison wall he is not guilty of prison breach; but if in doing so he causes a loose stone in the wall to fall he is.[8] In the former case the offense is merely escape. It has been held that a forcible breaking from an officer anywhere constitutes this offense.[9] It seems, however, that this constitutes escape rather than prison breach.

The fact that the jail or other place of imprisonment is

[3] Hitchcock v. Baker, 2 Allen (Mass.) 431. See also, State v. Owens (Mo.), 187 S. W. 1189; Maggard v. Commonwealth, 173 Ky. 97, 190 S. W. 666.

[4] State v. Leach, 7 Conn. 452, 18 Am. Dec. 113; State v. Lewis, 19 Kans. 260, 27 Am. Rep. 113.

[5] State v. Doud, 7 Conn. 384.

[6] 1 Edw. II, Stat. 2.

[7] People v. Ah Teung, 92 Cal. 425, 28 Pac. 577, 15 L. R. A. 190; State v. Leach, 7 Conn. 452, 18 Am. Dec. 113; State v. Clark, 32 Nev. 145, 104 Pac. 593, Ann. Cas. 1912C, 754 and note.

[8] Rex v. Haswell, Russ. & Ry. 458.

[9] State v. Beebe, 13 Kans. 589, 19 Am. Rep. 93; Commonwealth v. Filburn, 119 Mass. 297; Rex v. Stokes, 5 Car. & P. 148.

unhealthy or in a filthy state is no defense to this crime.[10] And, as in the case of escape, the guilt or innocence of the prisoner is also no defense.

§ 671. Rescue.—Rescue, like prison breach, is a felony or a misdemeanor according to the crime charged against the prisoner. To constitute this offense the act of the rescuer must result in an actual exit by the prisoner. A mere breaking of the prison is not sufficient. Where the prisoner is unlawfully imprisoned and he breaks out, using no more force than is necessary, and other prisoners escape in consequence, he is not guilty of this offense.[11]

[10] State v. Davis, 14 Nev. 439, 33 Am. Rep. 563.

[11] State v. Leach, 7 Conn. 452, 18 Am. Dec. 113.

CHAPTER XLVII

FORCIBLE ENTRY AND DETAINER.

§ 673. Forcible entry.—Forcible entry consists in violently entering upon real property which is in the occupation of another, without legal authority, and with threats, menaces or force and arms.[1]

To constitute forcible entry the act must be accompanied by violence, either real or apparent. Actual force, however, is not essential. Where a number of people so terrorize the occupants of the premises by menaces and threats that they give up possession, it is sufficient. On the other hand, actual force which is merely enough to make the entry a mere trespass is not sufficient. As said by Justice Dewey, "To sustain an indictment for a forcible entry, the entry must be accompanied with circumstances tending to excite terror in the owner, and to prevent him from maintaining his right. There must at least be some apparent violence; or some unusual weapons; or the parties attended with an unusual number of people; some menaces, or other acts giving reasonable cause to fear that the party making the forcible entry will do some bodily hurt to those in possession if they do not give up the same. It is the existence of such facts and circumstances, connected with the entry, that removes it from the class of cases of civil injury, to be redressed in actions of trespass or other civil proceedings, and holds the party thus making an unlawful entry amenable to the public as for

[1] State v. Lawson, 123 N. Car. 740, 31 S. E. 667, 68 Am. St. 844; 4 Bl. Comm. 148.

a public wrong."[2] Where the entry is accomplished by mere artifice or trick it is not sufficient to render the act indictable.

The fact that statutes provide other remedies for the parties aggrieved does not prevent the offense from being punishable criminally at common law.[3] The preservation of the public peace still requires that the offense be indictable.[4]

The term "force and arms" does not imply sufficient force to sustain an indictment for this offense; but the additional words, "and with a strong hand," would render the allegation sufficient.[5]

§ 674. Forcible detainer.—Forcible detainer consists in violently keeping possession of lands or tenements, without legal authority, and by means of threats, menaces or force and arms.[6]

Forcible entry and detainer are both misdemeanors at common law. Though usually referred to conjunctively they are distinct offenses. The offender, however, may be prosecuted for either or both.[7]

To sustain a criminal prosecution, at common law, for forcible entry and detainer, it has been held that both the entry and detainer must be forcible.[8] On the other hand, it has been held that a forcible detainer will relate back to the entry, and if the latter was unlawful, though peaceable, it is sufficient.[9]

By statute, the possessory action of forcible entry and detainer has been extended to certain cases of constructive force, as where a tenant holds over after his term.

2 Commonwealth v. Shattuck, 4 Cush. (Mass.) 141.

3 Rex v. Wilson, 8 Term. R. 357, 362; 3 Chitty Crim. L. 1135 et seq.; 2 Roscoe's Crim. Ev. (8th ed.), 535 et seq.

4 Commonwealth v. Shattuck, 4 Cush. (Mass.) 141.

5 Commonwealth v. Shattuck, 4 Cush. (Mass.) 141; Kilpatrick v. People, 5 Denio (N. Y.) 277; Rex v. Bake, 3 Burr. 1731.

6 Fults v. Munro, 202 N. Y. 34, 95 N. E. 23, 37 L. R. A. (N. S.) 600; note to 120 Am. St. 33, 34, 56, 66.

7 McMinn v. Bliss, 31 Cal. 122.

8 Vess v. State, 93 Ind. 211.

9 Conroy v. Duane, 45 Cal. 597.

CHAPTER XLVIII

LIBEL.

§ 676. Definition.—Libel is a malicious defamation, expressed either in printing or writing, or by signs or pictures, and tending either to blacken the memory of one who is dead, or the reputation of one who is alive, and expose him to public hatred, contempt, or ridicule.[1] It also has been defined as a censorious or ridiculous printing, writing, picture or sign, made with a malicious or mischievous intent toward government, magistrates or individuals.[2] Odgers says that any publication not oral, which exposes a person to hatred, contempt, ridicule or obloquy, or tends to injure him in his business or calling, impair his standing in society or cause him to be shunned or avoided by his neighbors, constitutes a libel.[3]

§ 677. Gist, requisites.—The gist of this offense is its tendency to provoke retaliation and a breach of the peace.[4]

[1] 1 Hawk. P. C., ch. 73, § 1; 4 Bl. Comm. 150; 2 Kent. Comm. 13.

[2] People v. Croswell, 3 Johns. Cas. (N. Y.) 354; Steele v. Southwick, 9 Johns. (N. Y.) 215.

[3] Odgers, Libel and Slander (1st Am. ed.) 21; State v. Kollar, 93 Ohio St. 89, 112 N. E. 196; Crane v. State (Okla. Cr.), 166 Pac. 1110; Nicholson v. State, 24 Wyo. 347, 157 Pac. 1013; State v. Haffer, 94 Wash. 136, 162 Pac. 45, L. R. A. 1917C, 610n, Ann. Cas. 1917E, 133.

[4] Commonwealth v. Clap, 4 Mass. 163, 3 Am. Dec. 212; State v.

Hence, at common law, the truth of the matter constituting the alleged libel is no defense. Statutory enactments, however, have modified this rule.[5]

To render matter defamatory it must tend, either directly or indirectly, to expose a person to contempt, hatred or ridicule.[6] It is also essential that it be published. This may be done by reading it, delivering it, sending it by mail, or by communicating its purport in any other way.[7] Some courts hold that publication be made to a third person.[8] Other courts hold that it is sufficient if made to the person injured by it.[9] Upon this point, "it is said that the letter in question is not a libel, because it was not published, by the defendant. But it is well settled, that the sending of a letter to the party, filled with abusive language, is an indictable offense, because it tends to a breach of the peace. It has, indeed, been a matter of doubt whether the sending of such a letter to another would support an action for a libel, because there is no publication. But the sending of such a letter, without other publication, is clearly an offense of a public nature, and punishable as such, as it tends to create ill-blood, and cause a disturbance of the public peace."[10] This is the better view and the one which is supported by the weight of authority. It may be well to observe, however, that the rule is otherwise in civil libel.[11]

Burnham, 9 N. H. 34, 31 Am. Dec. 217.

5 State v. Hinson, 103 N. Car. 374, 9 S. E. 552; Commonwealth v. Morris, 1 Va. Cas. 176, 4 Wheeler Cr. C. 464, 5 Am. Dec. 515. See also, State v. Fosburgh, 32 S. Dak. 370, 143 N. W. 279, Ann. Cas. 1916A, 424; note to 91 Am. St. 290; note to 21 Ann. Cas. 832; note to 21 L. R. A. 509; People v. Taylor, 279 Ill. 481, 117 N. E. 62, affirming judgment in 201 Ill. App. 541.

6 State v. Smily, 37 Ohio St. 30, 41 Am. Rep. 487.

7 Swindle v. State, 2 Yerg. (Tenn.) 581, 24 Am. Dec. 515.

8 State v. Syphrett, 27 S. Car. 29, 2 S. E. 624, 13 Am. St. 616.

9 Reg. v. Brooke, 7 Cox Cr. C. 251.

10 State v. Avery, 7 Conn. 266, 18 Am. Dec. 105.

11 Sheffill v. Van Deusen, 13 Gray (Mass.) 304, 74 Am. Dec. 632.

Malice is an essential element of libel, but actual hatred or ill-will toward the person libelled is not essential. In the eye of the law, to publish intentionally defamatory matter is malicious.[12] And the malicious intent may be inferred from the fact of publication.[13] Moreover, actual knowledge of the publication is not essential. Where the defendant was convicted of publishing a libel in a magazine, which purported to be printed by him, and which was sold at his store by his clerk, the higher court held that "bare proof of sale in Mr. Almon's (the defendant's) shop, without any proof of privity, knowledge, consent, approbation, or malus animus, in Mr. Almon himself, was sufficient in law to convict him criminally of publishing a libel.[14] Circulating a libelous and untruthful article was held a criminal offense, irrespective of the motives of the accused.[14a] And a false, printed article, circulated among voters, charging a member of the grand jury with malfeasance in such public office by protecting the biggest swindler that ever struck the county, was held criminally libelous.[14b] It also has been held that a statement in a newspaper charging a county clerk with dishonesty in office, is libelous per se.[14c] In New York, however, to establish a criminal libel a malicious intent must be shown.[14d]

§ 678. Jurisdiction.—Where a libel is written in one jurisdiction and published in another the author may be prosecuted in the latter jurisdiction. The fact that at the time of the publication he is still in the former jurisdiction is imma-

12 Benton v. State, 59 N. J. L. 551, 36 Atl. 1041; State v. Mason, 26 Ore. 273, 38 Pac. 130, 26 L. R. A. 779, 46 Am. St. 629; Rex v. Harvey, 2 Barn. & C. 257.

13 Pledger v. State, 77 Ga. 242, 3 S. E. 320; Commonwealth v. Blanding, 3 Pick. (Mass.) 304, 15 Am. Dec. 214; Commonwealth v. Graffius, 67 Pa. Super. Ct. 281.

14 Rex v. Almon, 5 Burr. 2686, 20 St. Tr. 803. See also, Reg. v. Clayton, 1 Car. & K. 128.

14a State v. Fish, 90 N. J. L. 17, 100 Atl. 181.

14b State v. Fish, 90 N. J. L. 17, 100 Atl. 181.

14c People v. Talbot, 196 Mich. 520, 162 N. W. 1017.

14d People v. Hebberd, 162 N. Y. S. 80, 96 Misc. 617.

terial. Where the defendant was indicted in Middlesex in England, for procuring a libel to be published in that county, the court held that the fact that he was in Ireland when it was published, as well as when he wrote it, was immaterial.[15] And where a libel was contained in a newspaper that circulated in Massachusetts, but which was published in a different state, the court held that the author of the libel was subject to criminal prosecution in Massachusetts.[16]

The federal courts have no common-law criminal jurisdiction of this offense. As said in an early case, "The legislative authority of the Union must first make an act a crime, affix a punishment to it, and declare the court that shall have jurisdiction of the offense."[17] In this case the defendant was indicted for libel in publishing that the President and Congress of the United States had secretly voted tribute to Napoleon, and a demurrer to the indictment was sustained.

§ 679. Miscellaneous libels.—There are various classes of libels which are indictable on grounds other than that of having a tendency to cause a breach of the public peace. Among these are seditious libels, obscene libels and blasphemous libels. Seditious libels are publications which tend to bring the government into contempt, or which tend to expose to hatred, contempt, or ridicule, foreign potentates, ambassadors, etc. Obscene libels consist in the publication of obscene books and pictures. As they tend to shock and corrupt the public morals they are indictable as common nuisances.[18] Blasphemous libels are publications which maliciously revile Christianity. They are looked upon as an insult to the

[15] State v. Piver, 74 Wash. 96, 132 Pac. 858, Ann. Cas. 1915A, 695; State v. Huston, 19 S. Dak. 644, 104 N. W. 451, 117 Am. St. 970, 9 Ann. Cas. 381; Rex v. Johnson, 6 East 583, 7 East 65.

[16] Commonwealth v. Blanding, 3 Pick. (Mass.) 304, 15 Am. Dec. 214.

[17] United States v. Hudson, 7 Cranch (U. S.) 32, 3 L. ed. 259.

[18] Commonwealth v. Dejardin, 126 Mass. 46, 30 Am. Rep. 652; People v. Muller, 96 N. Y. 408, 2 N. Y. Cr. 297, 48 Am. Rep. 635;

religious convictions of the public in general and for this reason they are punishable criminally as common nuisances.[19]

§ 680. Privileged communications.—A publication may be defamatory and still not be libelous. As said by Bishop, "Rights and privileges which one doctrine establishes another qualifies, and thus the process goes on through the entire field of our jurisprudence."[20] Circumstances may arise where a duty devolves upon a person to make derogatory statements relative to the character of another. This duty may be a legal, moral or social one. In these cases the derogatory statements are not indictable, provided they do not exceed the duty and no express malice is involved. Where a member of a school district, honestly believes that a certain candidate for the position of teacher is incompetent, and, in good faith, writes a letter to the board of trustees remonstrating against his appointment, he is not guilty of criminal libel.[21] And where a former employer of a servant or agent is asked for information relative to the employe's character, by a person who contemplates employing him, a derogatory reply, made in good faith, is not indictable.[22] Again, where information derogatory to the character of another is given in good faith to a relative who is about to marry the party whose character is thus assailed the communication is privileged.[23]

Honest and fair public criticisms of literary productions, works of art, dramatic performances, etc., that are publicly set forth, are also allowable. In this class of cases the criticisms are not libelous even though they contain statements

Commonwealth v. Sharpless, 2 Serg. & R. (Pa.) 91, 7 Am. Dec. 632; Reg. v. Grey, 4 Fost. & F. 73.

19 State v. Appling, 25 Mo. 315, 69 Am. Dec. 469; State v. Toole. 106 N. Car. 736, 11 S. E. 168; Commonwealth v. Linn, 158 Pa. St. 22, 27 Atl. 843, 22 L. R. A. 353.

20 2 Bish. New Crim. L. (8th ed.), § 913. See also, note to 104 Am. St. 112 et seq.

21 Bodwell v. Osgood, 3 Pick. (Mass.) 379, 15 Am. Dec. 228.

22 Todd v. Hawkins, 2 Mood & R. 20, 8 Car. & P. 88.

23 Note to 4 L. R. A. (N. S.) 1104.

which are false in fact, and of a nature injurious to another.[24] It is otherwise, however, if the criticisms are actuated by malice.

The above doctrine is also applicable to public speeches and legislative and judicial proceedings. It is to be observed, however, that an abuse of the privilege may render the offender liable. Thus, an attorney who inserts in a pleading libelous matter that is irrelevant, merely to subject the party defamed to ridicule and contempt, may be convicted of libel.[25]

And lastly, the law of this country sanctions and upholds the just liberty of the press; and in the administration of the law of libel the courts see to it that this freedom is not impaired.[26] Proper and open discussion in the newspapers of matters which concern the public is encouraged; and, as said by Bishop, "though a particular publication is such on its face as the general law of libel prohibits, yet if a suppression of it would be a restraint upon that open discussion of proper subjects which is essential to the liberty of the people, or to any other public or even private right, it can not be punished criminally."[27]

§ 681. Excitement or anger of accused.—Excitement or anger of the accused, at the time of making the libelous statement, has been held not a defense unless so great as to amount to temporary insanity.[28]

[24] Commonwealth v. Clap, 4 Mass. 163, 3 Am. Dec. 212; State v. Burnham, 9 N. H. 34, 31 Am. Dec. 217; Commonwealth v. Morris, 1 Va. Cas. 176, 2 Wheeler Cr. C. 464, 5 Am. Dec. 515; Green v. Chapman, 4 Bing. N. Cas. 92, 5 Scott 340; Carr v. Hood, 1 Camp. 355 (literary criticism); Thompson v. Shackell, Mood. & M. 187.

[25] Gilbert v. People, 1 Denio (N. Y.) 41, 43 Am. Dec. 646.

[26] State v. Balch, 31 Kans. 465, 2 Pac. 609; Morton v. State, 3 Tex. App. 510; Rex v. Burdett, 4 B. & Ald. 95, 132. See also, note to 104 Am. St. 128.

[27] 2 Bish. New Crim. L. (8th ed.) 913.

[28] Pickerell v. State (Tex. Cr.), 198 S. W. 303.

CHAPTER XLIX

UNLAWFUL ASSEMBLY, ROUT AND RIOT.

§ 682. In general.—Blackstone says, "Riots, routs and unlawful assemblies must have three persons at least to constitute them. An unlawful assembly is when three, or more, do assemble themselves together to do an unlawful act, as to pull down inclosures, to destroy a warren or the game therein, and part without doing it, or making any motion toward it. A rout is where three or more meet to do an unlawful act upon a common quarrel, as forcibly breaking down fences upon a right claimed of common or of way; and make some advances toward it. A riot is where three or more actually do an unlawful act of violence, either with or without a common cause or quarrel: as if they beat a man; or hunt and kill game in another's park, chase, warren, or liberty; or do any other unlawful act with force and violence; or even do a lawful act, as removing a nuisance in a violent and tumultuous manner."[1]

§ 683. Unlawful assembly.—Unlawful assembly consists in three or more persons assembling together with intent to commit a crime by open force, or with intent to carry out a common purpose, either lawful or unlawful, in a manner that will give firm and courageous persons reasonable grounds to apprehend a breach of the peace.[2] Hawkins de-

[1] 4 Bl. Comm. 146.

[2] State v. Stalcup, 23 N. Car. 30, 35 Am. Dec. 732.

fines it as "any meeting whatsoever of great numbers of people, with such circumstances of terror as can not but endanger the public peace and raise fears and jealousies among the king's subjects."[3] It has been held, however, that it is not unlawful assembly for members of the Salvation Army to assemble and march through the streets quietly and peaceably, although tumultuous and riotous proceedings, with stone throwing and fighting causing a disturbance of the public peace and terror to the inhabitants of the city is likely to result solely because of unlawful and unjustifiable interference and molestation by a body of persons opposed to them.[4]

§ 684. Rout.—Rout consists in "an unlawful assembly which has made a motion toward the execution of the common purpose of the persons assembled."[5]

§ 685. Riot.—Riot consists in a tumultuous disturbance of the peace by three or more persons, who have assembled lawfully or unlawfully, and who have begun to execute an unlawful purpose to the terror of the people.[6] Thus, where a crowd of persons, engaged in charivariing a newly married couple, marched back and forth in the highway before a public house, at night until two o'clock in the morning, blowing horns, singing songs and shouting, although they carried no weapons nor offered violence, they were held guilty of riot.[7]

[3] 1 Hawk. P. C. 297, § 9.

[4] Beatty v. Gillbanks, 15 Cox Cr. C. 138. See also, Casteel v. State, 13 Okla. Cr. 19, 161 Pac. 330; Cole v. State (Tex. Cr.), 194 S. W. 830.

[5] Stephen's Dig. Crim. L., art. 71.

[6] Fisher v. State, 78 Ga. 258; State v. Brown, 69 Ind. 95, 35 Am. Rep. 210; Commonwealth v. Runnels, 10 Mass. 518, 6 Am. Dec. 148; Reg. v. Cunninghame, 16 Cox Cr. C. 420. See also, Casteel v. State, 13 Okla. Cr. 19, 161 Pac. 330; Commonwealth v. Merrick, 65 Pa. Super. Ct. 482, 499; Commonwealth v. Blum, 65 Pa. Super Ct. 493, 498; Commonwealth v. Tepsick, 65 Pa. Super. Ct. 493; Commonwealth v. Detwiler, 65 Pa. Super. Ct. 494; Commonwealth v. Weston, 65 Pa. Super Ct. 497; Commonwealth v. Zeber, 65 Pa. Super Ct. 497; Commonwealth v. Esick, 65 Pa. Super. Ct. 498; Commonwealth v. Goldberg, 65 Pa. Super. Ct. 494.

[7] Bankus v. State, 4 Ind. 114.

If three or more persons, pursuant to agreement, unlawfully assemble at a designated place, and go thence in a body to another place with the avowed purpose of assaulting another person and upon reaching this place commit the assault to the terror of the people, they are guilty of criminal conspiracy, unlawful assembly, rout and riot.

These four offenses at common law are only misdemeanors, but in many of the states riot is made a felony by statute.

TITLE SEVEN.

Crimes Against Public Welfare, Health, Safety, Morals and Religion.

Article I. Nuisance and Like Offenses Against Morals and Public Welfare.

Section
690. Generally.

§ 690. **Generally.**—This subdivision is concerned with various crimes which may be considered crimes against the community and community rights. By most of them the rights of no single person are invaded more than those of another, the habitation is not affected, property rights are only incidentally affected, they are not concerned with the obstruction of justice and the workings of the courts, nor do they affect the public peace. Many of the crimes in this division are statutory, most of them grow out of an extension of the common-law doctrine of nuisance, and are a violation of the old maxim, sic utere tuo ut alienum non laedas. Some of them are offenses against morals and religion, but most of these also come under the general classification of nuisances, and were indictable at common law. Then there is a large body of statutory crimes concerned with the violation of statutory regulations prescribed for businesses, factories, mines, workshops, etc., all regulations enacted with the object to promote the public welfare. These will all be touched upon briefly under this subdivision.

CHAPTER LI

NUISANCE.

§ 691. Definition.—Whatever tends to endanger life, or health, to outrage decency, or otherwise injure public morals, comfort, or safety, is a misdemeanor at common law and indictable as a nuisance.[1] A public nuisance must affect the community in general. A private nuisance which affects one or a few individuals is not indictable.[2] But it is not necessary that all members of the community be affected. It is enough that there is a condition of things, which, to escape risk, the members of the community must avoid.[3] A nuisance may be caused by the doing of something unlawful, or the failure to perform some legal duty.

Very many things which would be indictable generally as nuisances, have been made specific offenses by statute.

§ 692. Acts and conditions indictable.—Among acts and conditions which have been held indictable as a public nui-

[1] Whart. Crim. L. (11th ed.), § 1676; Kensy Outlines Crim. L. (Am. ed.) 309.

[2] State v. Wolfe, 112 N. Car. 889, 17 S. E. 528; note to 107 Am. St. 199-252.

[3] Hackney v. State, 8 Ind. 494; Commonwealth v. Rush. 11 Lans. L. Rev. (Pa.) 97; People v. Weeks, 158 N. Y. S. 39, 172 App. Div. 117; People v. Wabash Ry. Co., 197 Mich. 404, 163 N. W. 996.

sance are the following: Setting a spring gun so as to put in danger persons passing on a highway,[4] habitually making loud noises in a public place,[5] keeping a swine yard or pigsty in a city,[6] contaminating water in a spring or well,[7] selling provisions so spoiled as to be unfit for food,[8] slaughter houses in cities,[9] a tannery in a city,[10] a petroleum factory in a city,[11] a tallow chandlery in a city,[12] storage of explosives in such a manner as to endanger the safety of the community,[13] continuous production of smoke,[14] or noxious vapors affecting the air in the neighborhood,[15] burning soft coal in locomotives, when declared a nuisance by statute,[16] a mill-dam causing the accumulation of decaying matter and noxious vapors,[17] projecting buildings which endanger passersby,[18] exposure of a person, corpse or animal infected with a conta-

[4] State v. Moore, 31 Conn. 479, 83 Am. Dec. 159.

[5] Bankus v. State, 4 Ind. 114; Rex v. Smith, 1 Strange 704.

[6] State v. Holcomb, 68 Iowa 107, 26 N. W. 33, 56 Am. Rep. 853; Commonwealth v. Alden, 143 Mass. 113, 9 N. E. 15.

[7] State v. Taylor, 29 Ind. 517; State v. Buckman, 8 N. H. 203, 29 Am. Dec. 646.

[8] State v. Smith, 3 Hawks. (N. Car.) 378, 14 Am. Dec. 594.

[9] Commonwealth v. Upton, 6 Gray (Mass.) 473; Taylor v. People, 6 Park. Cr. (N. Y.) 347; State v. Woodbury, 67 Vt. 602, 32 Atl. 495.

[10] State v. Cadwalader, 36 N. J. L. 283.

[11] Commonwealth v. Kidder, 107 Mass. 188.

[12] Bliss v. Hall, 4 Bing. N. Cas. 183.

[13] Hazard Powder Co. v. Volger, 58 Fed. 152; State v. Excelsior Powder Mfg. Co., 259 Mo. 254, 169 S. W. 267, L. R. A. 1915A, 615n; People v. Sands, 1 Johns. (N. Y.) 78, 3 Am. Dec. 296; State v. Paggett, 8 Wash. 579, 36 Pac. 487; Webley v. Wooley, L. R. 7 Q. B. 61.

[14] Bates v. Holbrook, 171 N. Y. 460, 64 N. E. 181; Cooper v. Woolley, 36 L. J. M. C. 27, L. R. 2 Exch. 88, 15 L. T. 539, 15 W. R. 450.

[15] Waters-Pierce Oil Co. v. Cook, 6 Tex. Civ. App. 573, 26 S. W. 96; Crump v. Lambert, L. R. 3 Eq. Cas. 409; Rex v. Pappineau, 1 Strange 686.

[16] State v. Chicago &c. R. Co., 114 Minn. 122, 130 N. W. 545, Ann. Cas. 1912B, 1030.

[17] State v. Holman, 104 N. Car. 861, 10 S. E. 758; Stacy v. State, 54 Tex. Cr. 610, 114 S. W. 807, 22 L. R. A. (N. S.) 1259; Douglass v. State, 4 Wis. 387.

[18] Grove v. Ft. Wayne, 45 Ind 429, 15 Am. Rep. 262.

gious disease,[19] keeping dogs which frighten travelers or horses,[20] a fertilizer factory.[21] Stables are not a nuisance when kept orderly,[22] but may be conducted with such offensiveness as to become nuisances.[23] A gas plant, as a necessary utility of a city, properly conducted, is not a nuisance,[24] neither are brick kilns, unless negligently conducted.[25]

§ 693. Locality determining a nuisance.—Most of the acts mentioned in the previous section are nuisances only because the places where they exist are populous. The offensive trades and buildings would not be such were they in a thinly populated place. However, it may be that a building or factory, when erected was in a thinly settled district, but the advance of population has caused the community to become populous, and that which was not a nuisance when the district was thinly settled becomes indictable.[26]

§ 694. When public benefit prevents a thing from being a nuisance.—Works of public improvement authorized by the legislature which necessarily cause incidental annoyance are not indictable as nuisances,[27] nor acts are for the common

19 Rex v. Vantandillo, 4 Maule & S. 73; Rex v. Burnett, 4 Maule & S. 272.

20 Brill v. Flagler, 23 Wend. (N. Y.) 354; King v. Kline, 6 Pa. St. 318.

21 Acme Fertilizer Co. v. State, 34 Ind. App. 346, 72 N. E. 1037, 107 Am. St. 190.

22 Phillips v. Denver, 19 Colo. 179, 34 Pac. 902, 41 Am. St. 230; Shiras v. Olinger, 50 Iowa 571, 32 Am. Rep. 138.

23 Dargan v. Waddill, 31 N. Car. 244, 49 Am. Dec. 421.

24 Beatrice Gas Co. v. Thomas, 41 Nebr. 662, 59 N. W. 925, 43 Am. St. 711; People v. New York Gas Light Co., 64 Barb. (N. Y.) 55.

25 Huckenstine's Appeal, 70 Pa. St. 102, 10 Am. Rep. 669; Bamford v. Turnley, 3 Best. & S. 62; Wanstead Bd. Health v. Hill, 13 C. B. (N. S.) 479, 32 L. J. M. C. 135, 9 Jur. (N. S.) 972, 11 W. R. 368, 7 L. T. (N. S.) 744, Rev. Rep. 613.

26 Seacord v. People, 121 Ill. 623, 13 N. E. 194; Board of Health v. Lederer, 52 N. J. Eq. 675, 29 Atl. 444; Commonwealth v. Vansickle, 4 Clark (Pa.) 104, 7 Pa. L. J. 82.

27 Toledo Disposal Co. v. State, 89 Ohio St. 230, 106 N. E. 6, L. R. A. 1915B, 1207; Commonwealth v. Reed, 34 Pa. St. 275, 75 Am. Dec. 661.

health such as those of officers in burning infected bedding.[28] But courts will not weigh public benefits against the annoyance caused, in order to determine which is greater, since the effect of so doing might be to impose a servitude on part of the community, for the benefit of other localities.[29]

Further, there must be a reasonable degree of annoyance before anything can be declared a nuisance; and for a slight annoyance to others, in the exercise of a constitutional right, for instance, the use of gas, or of steam or electric railways, or the annoyances from smoke, dust, and noise incident to city life, there can be no indictment.[30]

The length of time a nuisance has been established is no defense, for there can be no prescriptive right to maintain a nuisance.[31]

§ 695. Abatement.—Where a continuing nuisance is charged and proved, the court may order an abatement of the nuisance, independently of punishment by fine or imprisonment.[32] A private person has the right at common law to abate a nuisance which specially affects him, if he can do so without a breach of the peace.[33] Usually a judgment of

[28] State v. Knoxville, 12 Lea. (Tenn.) 146, 47 Am. Rep. 331.

[29] Seacord v. People, 121 Ill. 623, 13 N. E. 194; Board of Health v. Lederer, 52 N .J. Eq. 675, 29 Atl. 444; Commonwealth v. Vansickle, 4 Clark (Pa.) 104, 7 Pa. L. J. 82.

[30] Powell v. Macon & I. S. R. Co., 92 Ga. 209, 17 S. E. 1027; State v. Board of Health, 54 N. J. L. 325, 23 Atl. 949; People v. Rosenberg, 138 N. Y. 410, 34 N. E. 285; Commonwealth v. Miller, 139 Pa. St. 77, 21 Atl. 138, 23 Am. St. 170; Whart. Crim. L. (11th ed.), §§ 1680, 1694.

[31] Wright v. Moore, 38 Ala. 593, 82 Am. Dec. 731; Kissel v. Lewis, 156 Ind. 233, 59 N. E. 478; Stoughton v. Baker, 4 Mass. 522, 3 Am. Dec. 236; State v. Vandalia, 119 Mo. App. 406, 94 S. W. 1009; note to 26 Am. Dec. 102; note to 24 Am. Dec. 162; note to 107 Am. St. 218; note to 53 L. R. A. 894; Weld v. Hornby, 7 East 195.

[32] Campbell v. State, 16 Ala. 144; State v. Marshall, 100 Miss. 626, 56 So. 792, Ann. Cas. 1914A, 434; Meigs v. Lister, 25 N. J. Eq. 489; People v. Vanderbilt, 28 N. Y. 396, 25 How. Pr. 139, 84 Am. Dec. 351; Smith v. State, 22 Ohio St. 539.

[33] Commonwealth v. Ruddle, 142 Pa. St. 144, 21 Atl. 814; Colchester v. Brooke, 7 Q. B. 339, 15 L. J. Q. B. 173, 10 Jur. 610; 3 Bl. Comm. 5, 220; Cooley on Torts (3d ed.),

abatement will direct the person causing the nuisance to discontinue or abate it, and if he refuses to do so, the order will be enforced by public authority.[34] In abating a nuisance, there is no right to injure property any more than is necessary to stop the nuisance.[35]

§ 696. Nuisance caused by personal conduct.—At common law and under some statutes persons may be indicted for certain nuisances caused by different phases of personal conduct, such as being a common barrator,[36] that is, one who habitually stirs up litigation among persons whether or not he is personally interested, a common brawler,[37] that is, one who is habitually brawling and quarreling in public, a common drunkard,[38] a common profane swearer,[39] an habitual eavesdropper,[40] one who surreptitiously listens and divulges what he hears, a common scold,[41] one who repeatedly scolds so that she disturbs the community, a false news monger, one who spreads broadcast false and alarming information,[42] a street walker,[43] one who parades the streets

57; Whart. Crim. L. (11th ed.), §§ 128, 129. See also, note to 124 Am. St. 595 et seq.

34 Schultz v. State, 32 Ohio St. 276; Commonwealth v. Erie & N. E. R. Co., 27 Pa. St. 339, 67 Am. Dec. 471; Barclay v. Commonwealth, 25 Pa. St. 503, 64 Am. Dec. 715.

35 Barclay v. Commonwealth, 25 Pa. St. 503, 64 Am. Dec. 715; Lancaster Tpk. Co. v. Rogers, 2 Pa. St. 114, 44 Am. Dec. 179; Roberts v. Rose, 4 Hurlst. & C. 103.

36 State v. Chitty, 1 Baily L. (S. Car.) 379; 4 Bl. Comm. 134; Reg. v. Hardwicke, 1 Sid. 282

37 Commonwealth v. Foley, 99 Mass. 497; Pollock v. State, 32 Tex. Cr. 29, 22 S. W. 19; Reg. v. Taylor, 2 Ld. Raym. 879.

38 State v. Welch, 88 Ind. 308; Commonwealth v. Boon, 2 Gray (Mass.) 74; State v. Pratt, 34 Vt. 323.

39 Newton v. State, 94 Ga. 593, 19 S. E. 895; Foreman v. State, 31 Tex. Cr. 477, 20 S. W. 1109.

40 Commonwealth v. Foley, 99 Mass. 499; Commonwealth v. McHale, 97 Pa. St. 397, 39 Am. Rep. 808; Rex v. Foxby, 6 Mod. 11.

41 United States v. Royall, Fed. Cas. No. 16201, 3 Cranch (U. S.) 618; 4 Bl. Comm. 168.

42 Koppersmith v. State, 51 Ala. 6; 4 Bl. Comm. 149; In re Harris' Trial, 7 How. St. Tr. 925.

43 Stokes v. State, 92 Ala. 73, 9 So. 400, 25 Am. St. 22; Ex parte McCarthy, 72 Cal. 384, 14 Pac. 96.

for immoral purposes, and any one guilty of repeated and open lewdness.[44]

§ 697. Nuisances made specific offenses by statute.— There remains to be considered certain offenses, many of them made specific crimes or misdemeanors. These will be discussed in succeeding chapters and include among other offenses obstructing highways, wanton driving, vagrancy, indecent conduct and obscenity, keeping a disorderly house, adulteration of food, violation of factory, shop and mine regulations, and selling intoxicating liquors contrary to statute.

[44] Crouse v. State, 16 Ark. 566; Commonwealth v. Wardell, 128 Mass. 52, 35 Am. Rep. 357; Delany v. People, 10 Mich. 241.

CHAPTER LII

CRUELTY TO ANIMALS.

§ 700. A statutory offense.—At common law animals, as such, had no right to protection from abuse or brutal treatment by man.[1] One who mistreated an animal in such a manner as to impair its property value to its owner, might be liable to an action of trespass.[2] Under some authorities one who maltreated an animal because of malice toward its owner is liable at common law for malicious mischief,[3] other authorities hold the contrary,[4] while statutes in many states make malicious mischief perpetrated on animals a crime, in which case the malicious intent must exist toward the owner, and not toward the animal.[5]

At the present time in most American states and in England, there are statutes which render it a criminal offense to cruelly and wantonly beat, wound, mutilate, or kill an animal. Other statutes punish cruel driving or overloading animals, or unnecessary cruelty in not providing food and water.

1 Waters v. People, 23 Colo. 33, 46 Pac. 112, 33 L. R. A. 836, 58 Am. St. 215.

2 Note to 72 Am. Dec. 357.

3 Commonwealth v. Sowle, 9 Gray (Mass.) 304, 69 Am. Dec. 289; Snap v. People, 19 Ill. 80, 68 Am. Dec. 582; State v. Manuel, 72 N. Car. 201, 21 Am. Rep. 455.

4 State v. Beekman, 27 N. J. L. 124, 72 Am. Dec. 352; State v. Wheeler, 3 Vt. 344, 23 Am. Dec. 212.

5 State v. Churchill, 15 Idaho 645, 98 Pac. 853, 19 L. R. A. (N. S.) 835, 16 Ann. Cas. 947; People v. Jones, 241 Ill. 482, 89 N. E. 752, 16 Ann. Cas. 332.

These are crimes without regard to the ownership of the animal, and may be committed by the one who owns it.[6] An acquittal of killing an animal with malice toward its owner does not bar prosecution for cruelly killing it.[7]

There are two theories advanced by the courts as the basis for these laws, one that the offenses are punishable under the police powers to prevent corruption of public morals by cruelty to living creatures;[8] the other, that animals have rights like human beings subject to protection.[9] Some of the statutes apply to all animals,[10] others specify domestic animals, cattle, or the like.[11] A mule is held to be a "domestic animal,"[12] a horse to be included among "cattle,"[13] but a tame buffalo is not among "cattle."[14] A dog is "a dumb animal"[15] and pet birds raised in captivity are included among domestic animals.[16]

§ 701. **Malice or intent as essential to offense.**—Malice toward the owner of the animal is not an element of the offense.[17] It seems to be sufficient if the provisions of the statute were violated and the accused was actually guilty of a cruel or forbidden act toward an animal, even though he did

6 Commonwealth v. Lufkin, 7 Allen (Mass.) 579; State v. Hambleton, 22 Mo. 452; State v. Avery, 44 N. H. 392; Ex parte Phillips, 33 Tex. Cr. 126, 25 S. W. 629.

7 Irwin v. State, 7 Tex. App. 78.

8 Jenks v. Stump, 41 Colo. 281 93 Pac. 20, 14 Ann. Cas. 914; Bland v. People, 32 Colo. 319, 76 Pac. 359, 65 L. R. A. 424, 105 Am. St. 80; Waters v. People, 23 Colo. 33, 46 Pac. 112, 33 L. R. A. 836, 58 Am. St. 215.

9 State v. Karstendick, 49 La. Ann. 1621, 22 So. 845, 39 L. R. A. 520; Hodge v. State, 11 Lea (Tenn.) 528, 47 Am. Rep. 307.

10 Waters v. People, 23 Colo. 33, 46 Pac. 112, 33 L. R. A. 836, 58 Am. St. 215; Hodge v. State, 11 Lea (Tenn.) 528, 47 Am. Rep. 307.

11 Wilcox v. State, 101 Ga. 563, 28 S. E. 981, 39 L. R. A. 709.

12 State v. Gould, 26 W. Va. 258.

13 State v. Hambleton, 22 Mo. 452.

14 State v. Crenshaw, 22 Mo. 457.

15 McDaniel v. State, 5 Tex. App. 475.

16 Colam v. Pagett, 12 Q. B. Div. 66.

17 People v. Tessmer, 171 Mich. 522, 137 N. W. 214, 41 L. R. A. (N. S.) 433n; Irvin v. State, 7 Tex. App. 78.

not intend to mistreat it.[18] Where the charge was knowingly and intentionally overdriving a horse, no specific intent to injure the animal was necessary, it was enough that the driver acted in wanton disregard of its suffering.[19]

It may be a defense that the animal was killed or wounded to prevent injury to one's property by it, if no other means of protection were available.[20] Punishing an animal for discipline, done in good faith with proper motives, may also be a defense.[21]

§ 702. **What acts indictable.**—It is said that any unjustifiable, wilful or needless killing, even if done without torture, when the slayer was angry, is punishable under the statutes.[22] Loosing a fox to be hunted with dogs,[23] cock-fighting,[24] dog-fighting,[25] docking a horse's tail,[26] shooting at live pigeons during a shooting match as a test of skill in marksmanship,[27] have been held punishable. Other courts hold the shooting at live pigeons not a crime.[28]

Under a federal statute it is a crime for an interstate carrier to confine animals in transit between states for more than twenty-eight hours without unloading for food, rest and water.

18 Commonwealth v. Edmands, 162 Mass. 517, 39 N. E. 183; Commonwealth v. Curry, 150 Mass. 509, 23 N. E. 212; Commonwealth v. Whitman, 118 Mass. 458.

19 Commonwealth v. Wood, 111 Mass. 408.

20 Stephens v. State, 65 Miss. 329, 3 So. 458, 8 Am. Cr. 157; Farmer v. State, 21 Tex. App. 423, 2 S. W. 767; Thomas v. State, 14 Tex. App. 200.

21 State v. Avery, 44 N. H. 392.

22 State v. Neal, 120 N. Car. 613, 27 S. E. 81, 58 Am. St. 810.

23 Commonwealth v. Turner, 145 Mass. 296, 14 N. E. 130; note to 11 L. R. A. 522; note to 3 Eng. Rul. Cas. 149.

24 Commonwealth v. Tilton, 8 Metc. (Mass.) 232; Murphy v. Manning, 2 Ex. D. 307, 3 Eng. Rul. Cas. 143, 46 L. J. M. C. 211-214, 36 L. T. 592.

25 Commonwealth v. Thornton, 113 Mass. 457.

26 Bland v. People, 32 Colo. 319, 76 Pac. 359, 65 L. R. A. 424, 105 Am. St. 80.

27 Waters v. People, 23 Colo. 33, 46 Pac. 112, 33 L. R. A. 836, 58 Am. St. 215.

28 Commonwealth v. Lewis, 140 Pa. St. 261, 21 Atl. 396, 11 L. R. A. 522.

CHAPTER LIII

DISORDERLY HOUSE.

§ 705. Definition.—The keeping of a disorderly house, that is, one kept so as to disturb, scandalize or annoy the community, or persons passing in its vicinity, is indictable at common law.[1] If the building is open to the public, as an inn, there may be an indictment for disorder which affects only those of the public who go inside, and does not annoy any one outside.[2] However, the disorder must affect the public in some manner, and offend persons other than the dwellers in the house.[3]

A disorderly house has also been defined as a house in which illegal practices are carried on habitually, or to which people resort promiscuously for immoral purposes.[4]

This latter definition embraces not only disorderly houses proper, but what were known at common law as bawdy-houses, indictable as such, that is, houses kept to receive

1 Hackney v. State, 8 Ind. 494; Commonwealth v. Cobb, 120 Mass. 356; State v. Bailey, 21 N. H. 343.

2 State v. Mathews, 19 N. Car. 424; Chicago v. Doe, 195 Ill. App. 582; Guthrie v. State, 80 Tex. Cr. 126, 189 S. W. 256; People v. Claffy, 160 N. Y. S. 760, 95 Misc. 400; State v. Clough (Iowa), 165 N. W. 59.

3 Overman v. State, 88 Ind. 6; Cheek v. Commonwealth, 79 Ky. 359.

4 Smith v. Commonwealth, 6 B. Mon. (Ky.) 21; State v. Bailey, 21 N. H. 343; McClain Crim. L. § 1137.

persons who choose to go to it for illicit sexual intercourse;[5] and also tippling houses, kept for promiscuous noisy tippling, or where unlawful sales of liquor are made to all who desire it.[6]

A licensed drinking-place may become a nuisance because of the disorderly manner in which it is conducted, thus annoying others, though the acts done are not themselves unlawful.[7] So a house may be disorderly, merely because disorderly characters resort there, although the public is not affected.[8] Conduct on Sunday which would not be disorderly on a week-day may render a house disorderly.[9] It has been held that the keeper of a place where the law against usury is habitually violated, is guilty of keeping a disorderly house,[10] but this holding is contrary to the best authority.[11]

§ 706. Bawdy houses, or houses of ill-fame.—To constistitute a bawdy house, other women than its keeper must resort to it for immoral purposes;[12] but it makes no difference whether the disorderly conduct is perceptible from the outside.[13] It is not necessary that the reputation of the house

5 Ex. parte Birchfield, 52 Ala. 377; State v. Lee, 80 Iowa 75, 45 N. W. 545, 20 Am. St. 401; Commonwealth v. Kimball, 7 Gray (Mass.) 328; 4 Bl. Comm. 168; Reg. v. Williams, 10 Mod. 63.

6 Mains v. State, 42 Ind. 327, 13 Am. Rep. 364; Meyer v. State, 41 N. J. L. 6.

7 State v. Sopher, 157 Ind. 360, 61 N. E. 785; State v. Mulliken, 8 Blackf. (Ind.) 260; Commonwealth v. McDonough, 13 Allen (Mass.) 581.

8 United States v. Elder, Fed. Cas. No. 15039, 4 Cranch (U. S.) 507; Commonwealth v. Cobb, 120 Mass. 356; Lord v. State, 16 N. H. 325, 41 Am. Dec. 729.

9 United States v. Columbus, Fed. Cas. No. 14841, 5 Cranch (U. S.) 304; Brown v. State, 49 N. J. L. 61, 7 Atl. 340.

10 State v. Martin, 77 N. J. L. 652, 73 Atl. 548, 24 L. R. A. (N. S.) 507n, 134 Am. St. 814n, 18 Am. Cas. 986.

11 Note to 134 Am. St. 819.

12 State v. Main, 31 Conn. 572; State v. Lee, 80 Iowa 75, 45 N. W. 545, 20 Am. St. 401; State v. Calley, 104 N. Car. 858, 10 S. E. 455, 17 Am. St. 704. But see People v. Mallette, 79 Mich. 600, 44 N. W. 962.

13 King v. People, 83 N. Y. 587; Reg. v. Rice, L. R. 1 C. C. 21; Steph. Dig. Cr. L. art. 180.

be bad,[14] neither can one be convicted merely because the house has a bad reputation.[15] The essential element is the keeping of the house as a bawdy house; and neither its reputation, nor general annoyance to the public.

There must be evidence of more than one act of illicit intercourse in the house.[16] It has been held that one may be convicted of keeping a bawdy house because his wife and daughter engage in lewd conduct without his dissent,[17] although the contrary is also held.[18] A house of assignation, where parties meet for illicit intercourse, though none of them live there, is held a bawdy house.[19] One distinction to be remembered is that no disorder perceptible from without need be shown to convict of keeping a bawdy house, and no acts of public prostitution are necessary to convict one of keeping a disorderly house.[20]

§ 707. What is a house and who a keeper.—It is sufficient to show the use of a single room in a house for illegal purposes under the charge of keeping a disorderly house;[21] and a woman lodger having one room may be convicted of keeping a house of ill-fame.[22] The term house implies any building kept for immoral purposes;[23] even a boat,[24] or tent,[25] have been held to fall within the definition.

14 State v. Boardman, 64 Maine 523; King v. People, 83 N. Y. 587. See also, Davis v. State, 79 Tex. Cr. 321, 184 S. W. 510; State v. Levich, 174 Iowa 688, 156 N. W. 824.

15 Botts v. United States, 155 Fed. 50, 12 Ann. Cas. 271; Putnam v. State, 9 Okla. Cr. 535, 131 Pac. 916, 46 L. R. A. (N. S.) 593; State v. Brunell, 29 Wis. 435; McGary v. State (Tex. Cr.), 198 S. W. 574.

16 State v. Garing, 74 Maine 152; People v. Gastro, 75 Mich. 127, 42 N. W. 937; State v. Evans, 27 N. Car. 603; State v. Flick (Mo.), 198 S. W. 1134.

17 Scarborough v. State, 46 Ga. 26.

18 State v. Calley, 104 N. Car. 858, 10 S. E. 455, 17 Am. St. 704.

19 People v. Hulett, 61 Hun 620, 15 N. Y. S. 630, 39 N. Y. St. 646.

20 Brooks v. State, 4 Tex. App. 567. See also, King v. People, 83 N. Y. 587; Reg. v. Rice, L. R. 1 C. C. 21.

21 People v. Buchanan, 1 Idaho 681.

22 People v. Buchanan, 1 Idaho 681.

23 State v. Powers, 36 Conn. 77.

24 State v. Mullen, 35 Iowa 199.

25 Killman v. State, 2 Tex. App. 222, 28 Am. Rep. 432.

All who take part in carrying on and directing the business of a disorderly house are indictable as keepers.[26] One who merely resides in the house is not so indictable,[27] nor, it is generally held, one who merely lets it;[28] but if the owner who lets it has knowledge of the intent to use it for immoral purposes, convictions of keeping have been upheld against him.[29]

§ 708. Letting house of ill-fame, or procuring or encouraging its keeping.—Letting or hiring a house knowing it is to be used for prostitution is indictable at common law,[30] as well as under various statutes. But a landlord without control who was ignorant when letting of the use purposed, is not liable.[31]

Any one procuring, encouraging, aiding or abetting the keeping of a disorderly house is guilty as a principal.[32]

26 Commonwealth v. Gannett, 1 Allen (Mass.) 7, 79 Am. Dec. 693; People v. Wright, 90 Mich. 362, 51 N. W. 517; Johnson v. State, 32 Tex. Cr. 504, 24 S. W. 411.

27 Toney v. State, 60 Ala. 97; Moore v. State, 4 Tex. App. 127.

28 State v. Pearsall, 43 Iowa 630.

29 State v. Wells, 46 Iowa 662; State v. Stafford, 67 Maine 125; State v. Smith, 15 R. I. 24, 22 Atl. 1119; Commonwealth v. La Pointe, 228 Mass. 266, 117 N. E. 345.

30 United States v. Gray, Fed. Cas. No. 15251, 2 Cranch (U. S.) 675; Smith v. State, 6 Gill. (Md.) 425; Commonwealth v. Harrington, 3 Pick. (Mass.) 26; People v. Saunders, 29 Mich. 269; People v. Erwin, 4 Denio (N. Y.) 129; People v. O'Melia, 67 Hun 653, 22 N. Y. S. 465, 51 N. Y. St. 333, 10 N. Y. Cr. 350.

31 Blocker v. Commonwealth, 153 Ky. 304, 155 S. W. 723, 44 L. R. A. (N. S.) 859n; State v. Williams, 30 N. J. L. 102; Reg. v. Barrett, Leigh. & C. 263; Commonwealth v. Berney, 66 Pa. Super. Ct. 440.

32 Clifton v. State, 53 Ga. 241; Commonwealth v. Gannett, 1 Allen (Mass.) 7, 79 Am. Dec. 693; Commonwealth v. Harrington, 3 Pick. (Mass.) 26; State v. Engeman, 54 N. J. L. 247, 23 Atl. 676.

CHAPTER LIV

GAME.

§ 710. Definition.—Fish and game are wild animals, and whatever property there is in them is in the state for the benefit of all its people. Therefore the preservation of game and fish is a proper subiect for the exercise of the state's police powers.[1]

§ 711. Regulations.—It is usual to enact statutes regulating the time and method of taking fish and game, and prescribing a penalty for violation of such regulations.

Among common regulations are those which prescribe a closed season for hunting or fishing during which time game or fish or certain designated kinds of game or fish, may not be taken, or limit the number which may be taken by one person in a day or season; forbid hunting on lands which are posted; forbid fishing in certain manners, or prescribe certain methods for fishing; forbid or limit the sale of killed

[1] Lawton v. Steele, 152 U. S. 133, 38 L. ed. 385; State v. Mallory, 73 Ark. 236, 83 S. W. 955, 67 L. R. A. 773; Ex parte Maier, 103 Cal. 476, 37 Pac. 402, 42 Am. St. 129; Gentile v. State, 29 Ind. 409; Commonwealth v. Manchester, 152 Mass. 230, 25 N. E. 113, 23 Am. St. 820; State v. Shagren, 91 Wash. 48, 157 Pac. 31; State v. Carey (S. Dak.), 165 N. W. 539 (wild ducks); Barrett v. State, 220 N. Y. 423, 116 N. E. 99 (wild beaver); People v. Clair, 221 N. Y. 108, 116 N. E. 868, L. R. A. 1917F, 766n, reversing judgment in 160 N. Y. S. 1140, 175 App. Div. 912 (game birds, "pot hunting"); Ex parte Cencinino, 31 Cal. App. 238, 160 Pac. 167.

game; forbid its export; require a license for fishing or hunting; violations of all of which are punishable criminally.

Game is so much the property of the state that a discrimination as to the right of hunting or fishing may be made between residents and non-residents of a state or county, and such laws do not interfere with the privileges and immunities of citizens of other states;[2] but a game law discriminating between residents of the state living in different counties is unconstitutional.[3] Nor does the restriction on the transportation of game affect interstate commerce.[4]

Statutes are valid which make criminal the having in possession of game during the closed season without regard to the killing[5] even if taken in another state.[6] An exception to the game law made in favor of the owner of the land is not a transferable right.[7] An act establishing a closed season for fishing does not apply to fishing in private ponds.[8] Statutes protecting game protect game birds raised in captivity.[9]

Prosecutions for violations of game laws are similar to those for violation of other statutory police regulations.

[2] Manchester v. Massachusetts, 139 U. S. 240, 35 L. ed. 159; McCready v. Virginia, 94 U. S. 391, 24 L. ed. 248; State v.. Medbury, 3 R. I. 138.

[3] Harper v. Galloway, 58 Fla. 255, 19 Ann. Cas. 235.

[4] Geer v. Connecticut, 161 U. S. 519, 40 L. ed. 793; Organ v. State, 56 Ark. 267, 19 S. W. 840; State v. Geer, 61 Conn. 144, 22 Atl. 1012, 13 L. R. A. 804; People v. Hesterberg, 184 N. Y. 126, 76 N. E. 1032, 3 L. R. A. (N. S.) 163, 128 Am. St. 528.

[5] Ex parte Maier, 103 Cal. 476, 37 Pac. 402, 42 Am. St. 129; Phelps v. Racey, 60 N. Y. 10, 19 Am. Rep. 140; Roth v. State, 51 Ohio St. 209, 37 N. E. 259.

[6] People v. Hesterberg, 184 N. Y. 126, 76 N. E. 1032, 3 L. R. A. (N. S.) 163, 128 Am. St. 528.

[7] Hart v. State, 29 Ohio St. 666.

[8] Territory v. Hoy Chong, 21 Hawaii 39, Ann. Cas. 1915A, 1155.

[9] Cook v. Trevener, L. R. (1911), 1 K. B. 9, 20 Ann. Cas. 619.

CHAPTER LV

GAMES AND GAMING.

§ 713. **Games.**—Ordinary games are rather encouraged by the law than discouraged. But if public sentiment is scandalized, games may be indictable as nuisances.[1] So disorderly bowling alleys which draw crowds of idlers,[2] or disorderly billiard rooms, or noisy baseball playing on Sunday[3] or public spectacles which collect needless crowds,[4] have been held nuisances, and indictable as such.

§ 714. **Gaming.**—At common law gaming in a public place, whereby persons inexperienced lose their money on games of chance, is indictable as a nuisance.[5] In this sense

[1] Whart. Crim. L. (11th ed.), § 1733.

[2] State v. Records, 4 Har. (Del.) 554; State v. Haines, 30 Maine 65; State v. Hall, 32 N. J. L. 158; Tanner v. Albion, 5 Hill (N. Y.) 121, 40 Am. Dec. 337.

[3] Gilbough v. West Side Amusement Co., 64 N. J. Eq. 27, 53 Atl. 289.

[4] Rex. v. Carlile, 6 Car. & P. 636; Reg. v. Grey, 4 Fost. & F. 73.

[5] United States v. Dixon, Fed. Cas. No. 14970, 4 Cranch (U. S.) 107; Vanderworker v. State, 13 Ark. 700; Bloomhuff v. State, 8 Blackf. (Ind.) 205; Commonwealth v. Stahl, 7 Allen (Mass.) 304; Barada v. State, 13 Mo. 94; State v. Saunders, 66 N. H. 39, 25 Atl. 588, 18 L. R. A. 646; Lord v. State, 16 N. H. 325, 41 Am. Dec. 729; People v. Jackson, 3 Denio (N. Y.) 101, 45 Am. Dec. 449; Rex. v. Medlor, 2 Show. 36.

gaming means the staking of something of value upon the result of a game of chance, that is, games which depend more largely on chance than skill.[6] Private gaming was not indictable at common law.[7]

§ 715. **Public place.**—To sustain a common-law indictment for gaming the place must be public, but it does not matter if it be secluded, when the fact that gaming is there carried on is publicly known.[8] The following, among others, have been held to be public places, either under common law, or statutes similar to the common law; any place where there is an assemblage of people,[9] a barber shop and room above,[10] a bedroom kept locked, but opened to all who wished to gamble,[11] an infirmary,[12] inclosed grounds to which an entrance fee is charged,[13] a ferry-boat,[14] a dismantled jail,[15] a jury room,[16] the office of a justice of the peace,[17] an outhouse,[18] a place near enough to a public road to be seen by passers,[19] a

[6] Allen v. Commonwealth, 178 Ky. 250, 198 S. W. 896; Almy Mfg. Co. v. Chicago, 202 Ill. App. 240; People v. McDonald, 165 N. Y. S. 41, 177 App. Div. 806.

[7] Hanrahan v. State, 57 Ind. 527; State v. Currier, 23 Maine 43; Commonwealth v. Emmons, 98 Mass. 6; Needham v. State, 1 Tex. 139.

[8] United States v. Dixon, Fed. Cas. No. 14970, 4 Cranch (U. S.) 107; Vanderworker v. State, 13 Ark. 700; Bloomhuff v. State, 8 Blackf. (Ind.) 205; Commonwealth v. Stahl, 7 Allen (Mass.) 304; Barada v. State, 13 Mo. 94; State v. Saunders, 66 N. H. 39, 25 Atl. 588, 18 L. R. A. 646; Lord v. State, 16 N. H. 325, 41 Am. Dec. 729; People v. Jackson, 3 Denio (N. Y.) 101, 45 Am. Dec. 449; Rex v. Medlor, 2 Show. 36. See also, Dickey v. State, 68 Ala. 508, 4 Am. Cr. 249; State v. Book, 41 Iowa 550, 20 Am. Rep. 609, 1 Am. Cr. 234; State v. Barns, 25 Tex. 654; note to 7 Ann. Cas. 240.

[9] Campbell v. State, 17 Ala. 369.

[10] Cochran v. State, 30 Ala. 542.

[11] Smith v. State, 52 Ala. 384.

[12] Flake v. State, 19 Ala. 551.

[13] Eastwood v. Millar, L. R. 9, Q. B. 440.

[14] Dickey v. State, 68 Ala. 508.

[15] Walker v. Commonwealth, 2 Va. Cas. 515.

[16] Wilcox v. State, 26 Tex. 145.

[17] Burnett v. State, 30 Ala. 19.

[18] Downey v. State, 90 Ala. 644, 8 So. 869; State v. Norton, 19 Tex. 102.

[19] Bledsoe v. State, 21 Tex. 223.

railway coach,[20] a room in an inn,[21] a school house,[22] a steamboat,[23] a path near a school house used by children,[24] a shoemaker's shop,[25] a toll house,[26] an umbrella tent at a race course,[27] or a movable booth used to sell chances.[28]

Among others, the following have been held not to be public places: a club room open to members only,[29] the office of a lawyer,[30] or a physician, also used for sleeping quarters,[31] to which friends are invited, a private house,[32] a livery-stable,[33] a bedroom back of an office,[34] a secluded place on the top of a mountain.[35]

§ 716. What have been held games of chance.—It has been held in England that racing between trained dogs is not a game of chance,[36] nor horse racing for improvement of stock, also dependent on training,[37] unless the element of chance preponderates.[38] Cock fighting is gaming, being dependent on chance.[39] The decisions have been upheld that games of

20 Langrish v. Archer, L. R. 10 Q. B. Div. 44, 15 Cox Cr. C. 194.

21 McCalman v. State, 96 Ala. 98, 11 So. 408; State v. Mosby, 53 Mo. App. 571.

22 Cole v. State, 28 Tex. App. 536, 13 S. W. 859, 19 Am. St. 856.

23 Coleman v. State, 13 Ala. 602.

24 Henderson v. State, 59 Ala. 89.

25 Campbell v. State, 17 Ala. 369.

26 Arnold v. State, 29 Ala. 46.

27 Bows v. Fenwick, L. R. 9 C. P. 339.

28 Rex v. Saunders, 12 Ont. L. Rep. 615, 7 Ann. Cas. 232.

29 Koenig v. State, 33 Tex. Cr. 367, 26 S. W. 835, 47 Am. St. 35; Grant v. State, 33 Tex. Cr. 527, 27 S. W. 127.

30 Burdine v. State, 25 Ala. 60.

31 Clarke v. State, 12 Ala. 492.

32 Coleman v. State, 20 Ala. 51.

33 Metzer v. State, 31 Tex. Cr. 11, 19 S. W. 254.

34 Wilson v. State, 31 Ala. 371.

35 Gerrels v. State, (Tex. Cr.) 26 S. W. 394.

36 Hirst v. Molesbury, L. R. 6 Q. B. 130. Generally, as to what is a gambling device, see note 121 Am. St. 693.

37 Delier v. Plymouth County Agr. Soc., 57 Iowa 481, 10 N. W. 872. See also, State v. Hayden, 31 Mo. 35; Coombes v. Dibble, L. R. 1 Exch. 248; Oliphant, Horses, 412.

38 Tollet v. Thomas, L. R. 6 Q. B. 514. See also, Morgan v. Beaumont, 121 Mass. 7.

39 Commonwealth v. Tilton, 8 Metc. (Mass.) 232.

chance include: "rondo,"[40] draw poker,[41] monte,[42] craps,[43] tan,[44] baccarat,[45] keno,[46] faro,[47] roulette,[48] thimble and balls,[49] the selling of Paris mutual or French pools on horse races,[50] pool selling on base ball,[51] or pool selling generally;[52] and under some decisions betting on horse races.[53]

Ninepins, fairly conducted,[54] football and base ball,[55] wrestling matches, [56] rowing matches,[57] cricket,[58] bowls,[59] foot racing,[60] billiards,[61] backgammon,[62] dominoes,[63] and shuffle-

[40] Glascock v. State, 10 Mo. 508.

[41] Wren v. State, 70 Ala. 1; Lyle v. State, 30 Tex. App. 118, 16 S. W. 765, 28 Am. St. 893.

[42] Wardlow v. State, 18 Tex. App. 356.

[43] Bell v. State, 32 Tex. Cr. 187, 22 S. W. 687; State v. Wade, 267 Mo. 249, 183 S. W. 598.

[44] People v. Ah Own, 85 Cal. 580, 24 Pac. 780.

[45] Jenks v. Turpin, L. R. 13 Q. B. Div. 505, 15 Cox Cr. C. 486.

[46] United States v. Hornibrook, Fed. Cas. No. 15390, 2 Dill. (U. S.) 229; Schuster v. State, 48 Ala. 199; Hazen v. State, 18 Fla. 184; Brown v. State, 40 Ga. 689.

[47] Wren v. State, 70 Ala. 1; Waddell v. Commonwealth, 84 Ky. 276, 1 S. W. 480; State v. Andrews, 43 Mo. 470.

[48] Mims v. State, 88 Ga. 48, 14 S. E. 712; Ritte v. Commonwealth, 18 B. Mon. (Ky.) 35.

[49] State v. Red, 7 Rich. L. (S. Car.) 8.

[50] Rogers v. State, 26 Ala. 76; Commonwealth v. Simonds, 79 Ky. 618; Brown v. State, 88 Tenn. 566, 13 S. W. 236. But see Rice v. State, 63 Md. XIV.

[51] People v. Weithoff, 51 Mich. 203, 16 N. W. 442, 47 Am. Rep. 557.

[52] Scollans v. Flynn, 120 Mass. 270; People v. Reilly, 50 Mich. 384, 15 N. W. 520, 45 Am. Rep. 47; Jones v. State, 38 Okla. 218, 132 Pac. 319, 44 L. R. A. (N. S.) 161; People v. McDonald, 165 N. Y. S. 41, 177 App. Div. 806; State v. Bird, 29 Idaho 47, 156 Pac. 1140; State v. Pelham, 29 Idaho 52, 156 Pac. 1141; People v. Solomon, 160 N. Y. S. 942, 174 App. Div. 144.

[53] James v. State, 40 Okla. Cr. 103, 113 Pac. 226, 33 L. R. A. (N. S.) 827; State v. Vaughan, 81 Ark. 117, 98 S. W. 685, 7 L. R. A. (N. S.) 899, 11 Ann. Cas. 277.

[54] State v. King, 113 N. Car. 631, 18 S. E. 169.

[55] Maca v. State, 58 Ark. 79, 22 S. W. 1108.

[56] People v. Taylor, 96 Mich. 576, 56 N. W. 27, 21 L. R. A. 287.

[57] Bostock v. R. R., 3 M. Dig. 274.

[58] Hodson v. Terrill, 1 Cromp. & M. 797, 2 L. J. Exch. (N. S.) 282.

[59] Sigel v. Jebb, 3 Stark. 1.

[60] Batty v. Marriott, 5 C. B. 818.

[61] People v. Forbes, 52 Hun 30, 4 N. Y. 757; Parsons v. Alexander, 1 Jur. (N. S.) 660, 5 El. & Bl. 263.

[62] Wetmore v. State, 55 Ala. 198.

[63] Whitney v. State, 10 Tex. App. 377; Reg. v. Ashton, 1 El. & Bl. 286, 17 Jur. 501. But see Harris v. State, 31 Ala. 362, 33 Ala. 373.

board,[64] have been held to be lawful even though played for a stake; but under some statutes a wager on such games would be indictable.

§ 717. **Statutes against gaming.**—Gaming as indictable by statute is gambling, that is, the staking of money on a game involving chance.[65] As at common law neither gaming or betting was indictable of itself.[66] The statutes are strictly construed.[67] However, immaterial variances will be disregarded.[68] Any contest for a wager, more or less dependent on chance is said to be gambling,[69] as is the staking of money on the result of a game either of chance or skill,[70] or even determining by throwing cards who shall pay the expenses of a party.[71] Playing a single prohibited game may be sufficient to support the indictment.[72] All who have anything to do with the management of the game or table are principals, whether or not they take part in the game;[73] for

[64] State v. Bishop, 30 N. Car. 266.

[65] McInnis v. State, 51 Ala. 23; Williams v. Warsaw, 60 Ind. 457; Carr v. State, 50 Ind. 178; Commonwealth v. Taylor, 14 Gray (Mass.) 26; Carper v. State, 27 Ohio St. 572; Harrison v. State, 4 Coldw. (Tenn.), 195; Bachellor v. State, 10 Tex. 258.

[66] Hanrahan v. State, 57 Ind. 527; State v. Currier, 23 Maine 43; Commonwealth v. Emmons, 98 Mass. 6; Needham v. State, 1 Tex. 139.

[67] Gibbons v. People, 33 Ill. 442; Commonwealth v. Kammerer, 13 S. W. 108, 11 Ky. L. 777; State v. Bryant, 90 Mo. 534, 2 S. W. 836.

[68] Ballentine v. State, 48 Ark. 45, 2 S. W. 340; Commonwealth v. Hogarty, 141 Mass. 106, 4 N. E. 831; State v. Marchant, 15 R. I. 539, 9 Atl. 902, 7 Am. Cr. 217.

[69] State v. Smith, Meigs (Tenn.) 99, 33 Am. Dec. 132.

[70] Commonwealth v. Taylor, 14 Gray (Mass.) 26; State v. Bryant, 90 Mo. 534, 2 S. W. 836.

[71] McDaniel v. Commonwealth, 6 Bush (Ky.) 326; State v. Leighton, 23 N. H. 167.

[72] Swallow v. State, 20 Ala. 30; Bell v. State, 92 Ga. 49, 18 S. E. 186; Hankins v. People, 106 Ill. 628; Torney v. State, 13 Mo. 455; State v. Melville, 11 R. I. 417, 3 Am. Cr. 158.

[73] Poteete v. State, 72 Ala. 558; People v. Sam Lung, 70 Cal. 515, 11 Pac. 673; State v. Haines, 30 Maine 65; State v. Crummey, 17 Minn. 72.

instance, one who watches to guard against the detection of those gambling.[74]

§ 718. **Gaming, acts constituting statutory offense.**—If the statute punishes the playing of a specific game, it is enough to show the playing of this game.[75] No wager need be shown, if merely the playing is punishable;[76] but if the statute is against gaming, a wager must be alleged and proved.[77] If the statute prohibits generally playing games of chance for money, it must be shown that the game played was one of chance.[78] Some statutes require proof that the game was in a public place[79] and some except private residences.[80]

§ 719. **Wager.**—So that the wager has some value[81] its amount is immaterial.[82] Beers, cigars or treats,[83] the use of the table on which the game is played,[84] to be paid for by

[74] Ransom v. State, 26 Fla. 364, 7 So. 860; Soly v. People, 134 Ill. 66, 25 N. E. 109; Commonwealth v. Watson, 154 Mass. 135, 27 N. E. 1003; Earp v. State (Tex.), 13 S. W. 888.

[75] State v. Jeffrey, 33 Ark. 136; State v. Kaufman, 59 Iowa 273, 13 N. W. 292; Commonwealth v. Monarch, 6 Bush (Ky.) 301; State v. Mann, 13 Tex. 61; State v. Lewis, 12 Wis. 434; Reg v. Ashton, 1 El. & Bl. 286, 17 Jur. 501.

[76] Stockden v. State, 18 Ark. 186.

[77] Rosson v. State, 92 Ala. 76, 9 So. 357; State v. Stillwell, 16 Kans. 24.

[78] Bryan v. State, 26 Ala. 65; People v. Carroll, 80 Cal. 153, 22 Pac. 129; State v. Dole, 3 Blackf. (Ind.) 294; Commonwealth v. Ferry, 146 Mass. 203, 15 N. E. 484; Campbell v. State, 2 Tex. App. 187.

[79] Flake v. State, 19 Ala. 551; State v. Norton, 19 Tex. 102; Linkous v. Commonwealth, 9 Leigh (Va.) 608.

[80] Purvis v. State, 62 Tex. Cr. 302, 137 S. W. 701, Ann. Cas. 1913C, 536.

[81] Carr v. State, 50 Ind. 178.

[82] Long v. State, 22 Tex. App. 194, 2 S. W. 541, 58 Am. Rep. 633; Commonwealth v. Garland, 5 Rand. (Va.) 652.

[83] State v. Wade, 43 Ark. 77, 51 Am. Rep. 560; State v. Bishel, 39 Iowa 42; Brown v. State, 49 N. J. L. 61, 7 Atl. 340; Hitchins v. People, 39 N. Y. 454; Bachellor v. State, 10 Tex. 258.

[84] State v. Sanders, 86 Ark. 353, 111 S. W. 454, 19 L. R. A. (N. S.) 913; Hopkins v. State, 122 Ga. 583, 50 So. 351, 69 L. R. A. 117, 2 Ann. Cas. 617; Alexander v. State, 99

the losers, are within the prohibition. If the stake itself has no value, as chips or checks, but is convertible into value, this is enough.[85] It is not even necessary for the stakes to be put up,[86] or an agreement made definitely to pay it, if it is understood the loser shall pay if he wishes.[87] One who bets chips which cost nothing, has nothing at stake, and is not guilty of gaming.[88] The offense is complete when the wager is made and accepted and the game begun.[89] If the statutes punish playing at a game of cards at which money was bet, it is immaterial whether the defendant bet or knew that money was wagered on the game.[90]

§ 720. **Betting.**—Betting on certain games is incidentally punishable as part of the offense of gaming, as has been seen. Betting itself is made an offense by statute in some jurisdictions. The offense is defined as an agreement that one of two parties will pay the other a specific sum, if a contingent future happening occurs.[91]

Betting is criminal only by statute[92] and in some jurisdictions is held not to be punishable as gaming.[93] Betting on horse races is made a specific offense by statute in some jurisdictions.[94] The giving of a premium to the owner of a win-

Ind. 450; State v. Book, 41 Iowa 550, 20 Am. Rep. 609; Commonwealth v. Taylor, 14 Gray (Mass.) 26; State v. Leighton, 23 N. H. 167. But see Clark v. State, 49 Ala. 37; Blewett v. State, 34 Miss. 606; State v. Hall, 32 N. J. L. 158.

85 Porter v. State, 51 Ga. 300; Gibbons v. People, 33 Ill. 442.

86 Alexander v. State, 99 Ind. 450.

87 Walker v. State, 2 Swan (Tenn.) 287.

88 Fagan v. State, 21 Ark. 390.

89 Sikes v. State, 67 Ala. 77; State v. Welch, 7 Port. (Ala.) 463.

90 Reeves v. State, 9 Tex. 447.

91 Ansley v. State, 36 Ark. 67, 38 Am. Rep. 29; People v. Weithoff, 51 Mich. 215, 16 N. W. 442, 47 Am. Rep. 557; State v. Shaw, 39 Minn. 153, 39 N. W. 305, 8 Am. Cr. 321; People v. Todd, 51 Hun 446, 4 N. Y. S. 25, 6 N. Y. Cr. 203, 21 N. Y. St. 399; State v. Smith, Meigs (Tenn.) 99, 33 Am. Dec. 132; Long v. State, 22 Tex. App. 194, 2 S. W. 541, 58 Am. Rep. 633.

92 Smoot v. State, 18 Ind. 18.

93 State v. Rorie, 23 Ark. 726; Harless v. United States, Morris (Iowa) 169; Commonwealth v. Shelton, 8 Grat. (Va.) 592.

94 State v. Lovell, 39 N. J. L. 458, 463; Williams v. State, 92 Tenn. 275, 21 S. W. 662.

ning horse in a race is not betting;[95] nor is it gambling to race horses for a prize offered by a third party.[96] Betting on a race outside the state is indictable under the statute.[97] All parties concerned in a bet are principals.[98] A conspiracy to cheat by betting is a common-law offense.[99]

Betting on elections will be treated later.[1]

Pool selling is made an offense in many states. Persons forming the pool pay in money, which according to the agreement goes to certain ones of them when some contingency happens[2] and the seller is the one in control of the scheme who sells chances or records bets.[3]

§ 721. Keeping gaming house.—At common law keeping a gaming house may be indictable as a nuisance, since it brings together disorderly persons, and promotes immorality and breach of the peace.[4] The hazard on the games may be anything with value, as was seen in the discussion of the wager.[5] Any place fitted up for gaming and intended to be

[95] Delier v. Plymouth Co. Ag. Soc., 57 Iowa 481, 10 N. W. 872.

[96] Alvord v. Smith, 63 Ind. 58; Harris v. White, 81 N. Y. 532; Misner v. Knapp, 13 Ore. 135, 9 Pac. 65, 57 Am. Rep. 6; Porter v. Day, 71 Wis. 296, 37 N. W. 259. But see Bronson Ag. &c. Assn. v. Ramsdell, 24 Mich. 441; Comly v. Hillegass, 94 Pa. St. 132, 39 Am. Rep. 774.

[97] Stearns v. State, 81 Md. 341, 32 Atl. 282; State v. Lovell, 39 N. J. L. 463; Williams v. State, 92 Tenn. 275, 21 S. W. 662.

[98] State v. Welch, 7 Port. (Ala.) 463; Parmer v. State, 91 Ga. 152, 16 S. E. 937; Stone v. State, 3 Tex. App. 675.

[99] Reg. v. Bailey, 4 Cox Cr. C. 390; Reg. v. Hudson, 8 Cox Cr. C. 305.

[1] See Chap. LXVII, § 812.

[2] Commonwealth v. Watsen, 154 Mass. 135, 27 N. E. 1003; People v. McDonald, 165 N. Y. S. 41, 177 App. Div. 806; State v. Bird, 29 Idaho 47, 156 Pac. 1140; State v. Pelham, 29 Idaho 52, 156 Pac. 1141.

[3] State v. Howard, 9 Ind. App. 635, 37 N. E. 27; Commonwealth v. Clancy, 154 Mass. 128, 27 N. E. 1001.

[4] United States v. Ismenard, Fed. Cas. No. 15450, 1 Cranch (U. S.) 150; State v. Layman, 5 Harr. (Del.) 510; State v. Savannah, T. U. P. Charlt. (Ga.) 235, 4 Am. Dec. 708; Lord v. State, 16 N. H. 325, 41 Am. Dec. 729; People v. Jackson, 3 Denio (N. Y.) 101, 45 Am. Dec. 449; State v. Baker, 69 W. Va. 263, 71 S. E. 186, 33 L. R. A. (N. S.) 549; Rex v. Rogier, 1 Barn. & C. 272.

[5] State v. Markham, 15 La. Ann. 498; People v. Sergeant, 8 Cow.

so used is a gambling house.[6] The offense is not a continuing one, and keeping for a day or allowing play once, is enough.[7] The keeping of a house used for betting on horse races may be indictable,[8] and the keeper of a bucket shop may be convicted.[9]

§ 722. Keeping gaming tables or devices.—Some statutes create the offense of keeping and exhibiting gaming tables and devices, as distinct from gaming. They often provide for the seizure and destruction of the gambling devices.[10] These statutes are often worded to prohibit expressly keeping devices for playing specific games, such as faro,[11] keno,[12] poker[13] "and games of like nature."[14] These general words include only devices similar to those enumerated.[15] Slot machines are included under the general prohibition.[16] Ordi-

(N. Y.) 139; State v. Black, 94 N. Car. 809.

6 State v. Carpenter, 60 Conn. 97, 22 Atl. 497; Robbins v. People, 95 Ill. 175; Commonwealth v. Stahl, 7 Allen (Mass.) 304; State v. Hicks, 101 Kans. 782, 168 Pac. 861 (evidence held insufficient to sustain the conviction).

7 State v. Pancake, 74 Ind. 15; State v. Crogan, 8 Iowa 523; State v. Markham, 15 La. Ann. 498; Hitchins v. People, 39 N. Y. 454.

8 State v. Vaughan, 81 Ark. 117, 98 S. W. 685, 7 L. R. A. (N. S.) 899.

9 Wade v. United States, 33 App. D. C. 29, 20 L. R. A. (N. S.) 347, 17 Ann. Cas. 707. See also ante § 716, note 53.

10 Mullen v. Moseley, 13 Idaho 457, 90 Pac. 986, 13 Ann. Cas. 450; Woods v. Cottrell, 55 W. Va. 476, 47 S. E. 275, 65 L. R. A. 616, 104 Am. St. 1004, 2 Ann. Cas. 933.

11 State v. Holland, 22 Ark. 242; Commonwealth v. Monarch, 6 Bush (Ky.) 301.

12 Miller v. State, 48 Ala. 122; Portis v. State, 27 Ark. 360; Hazen v. State, 18 Fla. 184.

13 State v. Mathis, 206 Mo. 604, 105 S. W. 604, 121 Am. St. 687.

14 Euper v. State, 35 Ark. 629; Commonwealth v. Kinsley, 133 Mass. 578; State v. Grimes, 49 Minn. 443, 52 N. W. 42; State v. Flack, 24 Mo. 378; State v. Howery, 41 Tex. 506.

15 Pemberton v. State, 85 Ind. 507; State v. Bryant, 90 Mo. 534, 2 S. W. 836.

16 Ferguson v. State, 178 Ind. 568, 99 N. E. 806, 42 L. R. A. (N. S.) 720; Territory v. Jones, 14 N. Mex. 579, 99 Pac. 338, 20 L. R. A. (N. S.) 239, 20 Ann. Cas. 128; Mueller v. Stoecker Cigar Co., 89 Nebr. 438, 131 N. W. 923, 34 L. R. A. (N. S. 573; Allen v. Commonwealth, 178 Ky. 250, 198 S. W. 896; Almy Mfg. Co. v. Chicago, 202 Ill. App. 240.

nary tables on which poker[17] or dice[18] are played, or playing cards,[19] are not gambling devices, under these statutes. Under some statutes the tables must be kept for hire or gain.[20] Under some the keeping of such devices for the members of a social club constitutes the offense.[21] The wires, blackboard and ticker of a bucket shop are not gambling devices.[22]

§ 723. Allowing gaming on premises.—Other statutes punish one who allows or permits gaming on his premises.[23] This is an offense distinct from keeping a gaming house.[24] Guilty knowledge is essential to the crime,[25] but such knowledge may be presumed from occupancy.[26]

The prohibition applies to all games embraced in the gaming statute.[27]

The offense may be committed in a private house,[28] and need not be in a public place.

17 Lyle v. State, 30 Tex. App. 118, 16 S. W. 765, 28 Am. St. 893.

18 Chappell v. State, 27 Tex. App. 310, 11 S. W. 411; Hanks v. State, 54 Tex. Cr. 1, 111 S. W. 402, 17 L. R. A. (N. S.) 1210n.

19 State v. Gilmore, 98 Mo. 206, 11 S. W. 620, 8 Am. Cr. 312; Furlow v. State, 123 Ark. 471, 185 S. W. 788. But see Eubanks v. State, 5 Mo. 450.

20 People v. Weithoff, 100 Mich. 393, 58 N. W. 1115.

21 State v. Chauvin, 231 Mo. 31, 132 S. W. 243, Ann. Cas. 1912A, 992.

22 Jacobi v. State, 59 Ala. 71; Ives v. Boyce, 85 Nebr. 324, 123 N. W. 318, 25 L. R. A. (N. S.) 157. But see Harris v. State (Tex. Cr.), 198 S. W. 956 (tent held a private residence and not within the statute).

23 Stoltz v. People, 5 Ill. 168; Commonwealth v. Lampton, 4 Bibb (Ky.) 261.

24 State v. Currier, 23 Maine 43. But it has been held indictable as gaming. Fugate v. State, 2 Humph (Tenn.) 397.

25 State v. Mathis, 3 Ark. 84; State v. Middleton, 11 Iowa 246; Marston v. Commonwealth, 18 B. Mon. (Ky.) 485; Commonwealth v. Watson, 2 Duv. (Ky.) 408.

26 Mount v. State, 7 Smedes & M. (Miss.) 277; Robinson v. State, 24 Tex. 152.

27 Commonwealth v. Goding, 3 Metc. (Mass.) 130; Wortham v. State, 59 Miss. 179; Ward v. State, 17 Ohio St. 32; State v. Lewis, 12 Wis. 434.

28 State v. Brice, 2 Brev. (S. Car.) 66.

The one in control of the place is the one responsible, so a lessor having control,[29] or club manager[30] may be guilty.

§ 724. Permitting minors to gamble.—Some statutes prohibit persons who keep billiard, pool or gaming tables, from allowing minors to play on them or resort to the place where such gaming takes place.[31] Some statutes prohibit the allowing of minors to bet in such places;[32] others prohibit the allowing of minors to resort there without the consent of parents or guardians.[33] Some authorities hold lack of knowledge of the minor's age is a defense.[34] Others hold the contrary.[35] If the statute punishes the congregation of minors, it must appear that two or more minors were together at the place.[36]

[29] Diebel v. State, 68 Miss. 725, 9 So. 354; Kimbrough v. State, 25 Tex. App. 397, 8 S. W. 476.

[30] Jacobi v. State, 59 Ala. 71.

[31] Snow v. State, 50 Ark. 557, 9 S. W. 306; Bird v. State, 104 Ind. 384, 3 N. E. 827; State v. Probasco, 62 Iowa 400, 17 N. W. 607.

[32] Ready v. State, 62 Ind. 1; Green v. Commonwealth, 5 Bush (Ky.) 327.

[33] Kiley v. State, 120 Ind. 63, 22 N. E. 99; Commonwealth v. Emmons, 98 Mass. 6.

[34] Stern v. State, 53 Ga. 229, 21 Am. Rep. 266.

[35] State v. Probasco, 62 Iowa 400, 17 N. W. 607; Commonwealth v. Emmons, 98 Mass. 6.

[36] Powell v. State, 62 Ind. 531.

CHAPTER LVI

LOTTERIES.

§ 726. Definition.—The conducting of lotteries or selling lottery tickets is indictable under varying statutes in many states. It is not a common-law offense unless a nuisance.[1] A lottery is defined as a scheme for distributing property by lot or chance, among persons who have paid to participate in such scheme.[2]

It is a species of gaming,[3] and the reason for punishing the offense is the same, since lotteries create an inordinate desire for gain with small expenditure, and tend to arouse passions, create mendicancy and idleness.[4] The sale of tickets in a lottery carried on without the state is indictable.[5]

1 Ex parte Blanchard, 9 Nev. 101.

2 State v. Nebraska Home Co., 66 Nebr. 349, 92 N. W. 763, 60 L. R. A. 448, 103 Am. St. 706, 1 Ann. Cas. 88. See also United States v. Olney, Fed Cas. No. 15918, 1 Abb. (U. S.) 275, Deady 461; Russell v. Equitable Loan &c. Co., 129 Ga. 154, 12 Ann. Cas. 129; State v. Kansas Mercantile Assn., 45 Kans. 351, 25 Pac. 984, 11 L. R. A. 430, 23 Am. St. 727; Ballock v. State, 73 Md. 1, 20 Atl. 184, 8 L. R. A. 671, 25 Am. St. 559; Commonwealth v. Sullivan, 146 Mass. 142, 15 N. E. 491; People v. Elliott, 74 Mich. 264, 41 N. W. 916, 3 L. R. A. 403n, 16 Am. St. 640; State v. Moren, 48 Minn. 555, 51 N. W. 618; People v. American Art Union, 7 N. Y. 240.

3 Thomas v. People, 59 Ill. 160; Eubanks v. State, 3 Heisk. (Tenn.) 488.

4 Yellow-Stone Kit v. State, 88 Ala. 196, 7 So. 338, 7 L. R. A. 599, 16 Am. St. 38; Ehrgott v. New York, 96 N. Y. 264, 48 Am. Rep. 622.

5 State v. Sykes, 28 Conn. 225; State v. Moore, 63 N. H. 9, 56 Am. Rep. 478; People v. Warner, 4 Barb. (N. Y.) 314. See also, McDaniels v. State, 185 Ind. 245, 113 N. E. 1004 (evidence held insufficient to convict).

§ 727. What schemes punishable.—A private arrangement between individuals to dispose of property by lot, does not fall within the statutory prohibition, which is aimed at public lotteries, since the latter are open to the public and corrupt an appreciable portion thereof.[6] But any scheme open to all who choose to buy tickets is punishable.[7] Wharton says, "A gift 'enterprise' or a 'raffle,' in which the public is invited to take shares in the distribution of prizes by chance, is a lottery, no matter how artfully the object may be disguised."[8] Many schemes in which purchasers of certain kinds of goods are given tickets with the chance to secure something more valuable by lot, have been considered lotteries and are indictable.[9]

Even if the purpose of the lottery is to raise funds for charity, this is immaterial, if the scheme itself is of the character prohibited.[10]

Nor does it matter that every purchaser receives something, if there are larger prizes to be distributed by chance.[11]

[6] Yellow-Stone Kit v. State, 88 Ala. 196, 7 So. 338, 7 L. R. A. 599, 16 Am. St. 38; Commonwealth v. Manderfield, 8 Phila. (Pa.) 457; Whart. Crim. L. (11th ed.) § 1776.

[7] Buckalew v. State, 62 Ala. 334, 34 Am. Rep. 22; Cross v. People, 18 Colo. 321, 32 Pac. 821, 36 Am. St. 292; Long v. State, 74 Md. 565, 22 Atl. 4, 12 L. R. A. 425, 28 Am. St. 268; State v. Clarke, 33 N. H. 329, 66 Am. Dec. 723; Kohn v. Koehler, 96 N. Y. 362, 48 Am. Rep. 628.

[8] Whart. Crim. L. (11th ed.) § 1776. See also Horner v. United States, 147 U. S. 449, 37 L. ed. 237; State v. Stripling, 113 Ala. 120, 21 So. 409, 36 L. R. A. 81; Meyer v. State, 112 Ga. 20, 37 S. E. 96, 51 L. R. A. 496, 81 Am. St. 17; Hudelson v. State, 94 Ind. 426, 48 Am. Rep. 171; State v. Boneil, 42 La. Ann. 1110, 8 So. 298, 10 L. R. A. 60, 21 Am. St. 413; State v. Willis, 78 Maine 70, 2 Atl. 848, 6 Am. Cr. 284; Commonwealth v. Thacher, 97 Mass. 583, 93 Am. Dec. 125; People v. Elliott, 74 Mich. 264, 41 N. W. 916, 3 L. R. A. 403, 16 Am. St. 640; State v. Shorts, 32 N. J. L. 398, 90 Am. Dec. 668; People v. Noelke, 94 N. Y. 137, 1 N. Y. Cr. 495, 46 Am. Rep. 128.

[9] United States v. Olney, Fed. Cas. No. 15918, 1 Abb. (U. S.) 275, Deady 461; Dunn v. People, 40 Ill. 465; State v. Mumford, 73 Mo. 647, 39 Am. Rep. 532.

[10] Thomas v. People, 59 Ill. 160.

[11] Den v. Shotwell, 23 N. J. L. 465; Seidenbender v. Charles, 4 Serg. & R. (Pa.) 151, 8 Am. Dec. 682.

Among schemes which have been held within the statutory ban are the following: the sale of keys, one of which opens a box containing a prize,[12] the sale of tickets to an entertainment where those who attend share in a distribution of prizes by lot,[13] trade premiums or prizes given by lot,[14] the sale of prize candy packages for more than their value, some of them containing tickets entitling the holder to a piece of silverware,[15] an agreement by which persons pay a dollar a week each into a common fund and a suit of clothes was purchased each week for one, determined by lot, until all were supplied,[16] the giving of a prize to all purchasers of goods who guess the correct number of beans in a jar,[17] or to the one who correctly guesses the popular vote for president in a state,[18] baseball pools,[19] the sale of books for more than their value, the purchaser to be entitled to gifts, if there was a correspondence between certain numbers placed on the books, and numbers on the prize packages,[20] the sale of envelopes, some of which contained tickets whereby the holder could buy valuable property for a small price,[21] a sale of public bonds, at which a bonus is given to certain purchasers, depending on the turn of a wheel of fortune,[22] or the sale of

[12] Davenport v. Ottawa, 54 Kans. 711, 39 Pac. 708, 45 Am. St. 303.

[13] Thomas v. People, 59 Ill. 160; State v. Overton, 16 Nev. 136; State v. Shorts, 32 N. J. L. 398, 90 Am. Dec. 668.

[14] Meyer v. State, 112 Ga. 20, 37 S. E. 96, 51 L. R. A. 496, 81 Am. St. 17.

[15] Hull v. Ruggles, 56 N. Y. 424.

[16] State v. Moren, 48 Minn. 555, 51 N. W. 618; Grant v. State, 54 Tex. Cr. 403, 112 S. W. 1068, 21 L. R. A. (N. S.) 876, 16 Ann. Cas. 844. See also People v. McPhee, 139 Mich. 687, 103 N. W. 174, 69 L. R. A. 505, 5 Ann. Cas. 835.

[17] Hudelson v. State, 94 Ind. 426, 48 Am. Rep. 171.

[18] Waite v. Press Pub. Assn., 155 Fed. 58, 11 L. R. A. (N. S.) 609, 12 Ann. Cas. 319.

[19] State v. Sedgwick, 25 Del. 453, 81 Atl. 472.

[20] State v. Clarke, 33 N. H. 329, 66 Am. Dec. 723.

[21] Dunn v. People, 40 Ill. 465; State v. Lumsden, 89 N. Car. 572.

[22] Horner v. United States, 147 U. S. 449, 37 L. ed. 237; Ballock v. State, 73 Md. 1, 20 Atl. 184, 8 L. R. A. 671, 25 Am. St. 559.

lots of land of different values, the purchasers getting the more valuable ones being selected by lot.[23]

The essential elements of a lottery are said to be (1) consideration, (2) prize, (3) chance.[24]

§ 728. What is not lottery.—Gratuitous distribution of cards as advertisement, entitling holder to a chance on a piano, is not a lottery,[25] nor are gifts to persons receiving the most votes in a "popularity" contest,[26] nor the giving of trading stamps to a customer by a retail merchant.[27]

[23] Whitley v. McConnell, 133 Ga. 738, 66 S. E. 933, 27 L. R. A. (N. S.) 287.

[24] Burks v. Harriss, 91 Ark. 205, 120 S. W. 979, 18 Ann. Cas. 566; Equitable Loan &c. Co. v. Waring, 117 Ga. 599, 44 S. E. 320, 62 L. R. A. 93, 97 Am. St. 177.

[25] Cross v. People, 18 Colo. 321, 32 Pac. 821, 36 Am. St. 292.

[26] Commonwealth v. Jenkins, 159 Ky. 80, 166 S. W. 794, Ann. Cas. 1915B, 170; Quatsoe v. Eggleston, 42 Ore. 315, 71 Pac. 66.

[27] State v. Caspare, 115 Md. 7, 80 Atl. 606.

CHAPTER LVII

OFFENSES AS TO HIGHWAYS.

§ 730. Obstructing highways.—Obstructing a public highway is indictable as a nuisance.[1] The way obstructed must be public.[2] It is not necessary that the road should have been accepted by the authorities if the public have a right to pass,[3] but it must appear that the highway was acquired by the authorities in a legal manner, or was dedicated by the owner, or that the public had a prescriptive right by user.[4] It does not make the offense less that the public must pay toll to pass over the way.[5] The same rule applies to the obstruction of bridges,[6] harbors[7] and navigable rivers.[8]

[1] State v. Berdetta, 73 Ind. 185, 38 Am. Rep. 117; State v. Miskimmons, 2 Ind. 440.

[2] Root v. Commonwealth, 98 Pa. St. 170, 42 Am. Rep. 614; State v. Randall, 1 Strob. (S. Car.) 110, 47 Am. Dec. 548.

[3] Mills v. State, 20 Ala. 86; Commonwealth v. Wilkinson, 16 Pick. (Mass.) 175, 26 Am. Dec. 654, 1 Hawk. P. C. ch. 76; Co. Litt. 56a.

[4] Mauck v. State, 66 Ind. 177; People v. Jones, 6 Mich. 176.

[5] Commonwealth v. Wilkinson, 16 Pick. (Mass.) 175, 26 Am. Dec. 654; State v. McIver, 88 N. Car. 686.

[6] In re Clinton Bridge, 10 Wall. (U. S.) 454, 19 L. ed. 969; Commonwealth v. Newburyport Bridge 9 Pick. (Mass.) 142.

[7] State v. Wilson, 42 Maine 9; Rex v. Tindell, 6 Ad. & El. 143.

[8] Thompson v. Androscoggin R. Imp. Co., 54 N. H. 545; State v. Narrows Island Club, 100 N. Car. 477, 5 S. E. 411, 6 Am. St. 618; Reg. v. Betts, 16 Q. B. 1022, 4 Cox Cr. C. 211.

It is not necessary that the obstruction be over the traveled part of the way, if passage is made less convenient.[9] The owner of the way may be guilty of the offense, provided the public right is established.[10]

§ 731. **What is an obstruction.**—The placing on a highway and keeping thereon for a considerable space of time anything which obstructs or diminishes the public use is indictable.[11] The following have been held obstructions: Digging a ditch or plowing across the way,[12] allowing wagons to stand before a warehouse for an unreasonable time,[13] keeping a boarding before a house for repair purposes an unreasonable time,[14] erecting posts or fences appreciably within the limits of the way,[15] blasting in such a manner that passers are endangered,[16] making excavations close to the way,[17] placing goods for sale in the street,[18] causing crowds to collect therein, by shows, exhibitions, etc.,[19] setting up near the highway objects calculated to frighten

9 State v. Merrit, 35 Conn. 314; Commonwealth v. King, 13 Metc. (Mass.) 115.

10 State v. Sweeney, 33 Minn. 23, 21 N. W. 847; Mercer v. Woodgate, L. R. 5 Q. B. 26, 12 Eng. Rul. Cas. 573.

11 State v. Chicago, M. &c. R. Co., 77 Iowa 442, 42 N. W. 365, 4 L. R. A. 298 and note; Commonwealth v. Blaisdell, 107 Mass. 234; Reg. v. United Kingdom Elec. Tel. Co., 9 Cox Cr. C. 137, 12 Eng. Rul. Cas. 562.

12 Henline v. People, 81 Ill. 269; Kelley v. Commonwealth, 11 Serg. & R. (Pa.) 345; 1 Russ. on Crimes (9th Am. ed.) 485.

13 Rex v. Russell, 6 East 427, 2 Smith 424, 8 Rev. Rep. 506.

14 Rex v. Jones, 3 Campb. 230, 13 Rev. Rep. 797.

15 Zimmerman v. State, 4 Ind. App. 583, 31 N. E. 550; Sanders v. State (Tex.) 26 S. W. 62; Reg. v. Lepine, 15 L. T. (N. S.) 158; Reg. v. Lepille, 15 W. R. 45.

16 Booth v. Rome &c. R. Co., 140 N. Y. 267, 35 N. E. 592, 24 L. R. A. 105, 37 Am. St. 552; Reg. v. Mutters, 1 Leigh &. C. 491, 10 Cox Cr. C. 6.

17 Fisher v. Prowse, 2 Best & S. 770, 6 L. T. (N. S.) 711.

18 State v. Berdetta, 73 Ind. 185, 38 Am. Rep. 117; Davis v. New York, 14 N. Y. 524, 67 Am. Dec. 186.

19 People v. Cunningham, 1 Denio (N. Y.) 524, 43 Am. Dec. 709; State v. Hughes, 72 N. Car. 25; Rex v. Sarmon, 1 Burr. 516.

horses,[20] setting spring guns near it,[21] extending the steps of a house into the highway,[22] or erecting things overhanging it which endanger passers.[23]

§ 732. **Intent and defenses.**—Intent is immaterial in the offense of obstructing a highway,[24] unless the indictment is under a statute for wilfully or knowingly obstructing a highway, when scienter must be alleged and proved.[25]

License may be a defense, as where telegraph posts are authorized by the proper authorities.[26]

Prescription because of the length of time the nuisance has been maintained is not a defense, for prescription does not run against the public.[27]

§ 733. **Maintaining nuisance in highway by municipality.**—A municipality may be criminally liable for permitting a street to become so out of repair as to constitute a public nuisance.[28]

§ 734. **Obstructing highway by railroad.**—Unless authorized by a statute, it is a criminal nuisance for a railroad company to lay its tracks across a highway.[29] If authority has been granted, a failure to put the highway back in good con-

20 Commonwealth v. Allen, 148 Pa. 358, 23 Atl. 1115, 16 L. R. A. 148, 33 Am. St. 830.

21 State v. Moore, 31 Conn. 479, 83 Am. Dec. 159.

22 Commonwealth v. Blaisdell, 107 Mass. 234.

23 Commonwealth v. Goodman, 117 Mass. 114; Callanan v. Gilman, 107 N. Y. 360, 14 N. E. 264, 1 Am. St. 831; Reg. v. Watts, 1 Salk. 357.

24 State v. Gould, 40 Iowa 372.

25 Brinkoeter v. State, 14 Tex. App. 67; Bailey v. Commonwealth, 78 Va. 19; Wyman v. State, 13 Wis. 742.

26 Commonwealth v. Boston, 97 Mass. 555.

27 Commonwealth v. Tucker, 2 Pick. (Mass.) 44.

28 Ludlow v. Commonwealth, 147 Ky. 706, 145 S. W. 406, 39 L. R. A. (N. S.) 410; Elkins v. State, 2 Humph. (Tenn.) 543.

29 St. Louis, A. & T. R. Co. v. State, 52 Ark. 51, 11 S. W. 1035; Commonwealth v. Erie & N. E. R. Co., 27 Pa. St. 339, 67 Am. Dec. 471.

dition,[30] or keeping rails above the level of the crossing,[31] habitually failing to give signals of passing trains,[32] or unnecessarily obstructing a highway crossing by cars may be indicted.[33] Statutory authority must be strictly pursued, but a certain degree of license may be allowed to a railroad company, because of public benefit.

§ 735. Obstructing or polluting waters.—Unless authorized by statute, the obstruction of navigable rivers by bridges or similarly is a criminal nuisance.[34] It is also indictable at common law to obstruct the passage of fish in a non-navigable stream.[35] Diverting so much of the water of a stream as to hinder navigation is indictable.[36] A wharf may be a nuisance,[37] or the obstruction of public docks.[38]

A vessel sunk by accident so as to obstruct navigation is not a nuisance such as to render the owner indictable[39] nor is a ferry wire stretched across a stream necessary which is for crossing of travelers and does not greatly obstruct the stream,[40] and the owner of adjoining lands may erect such structures as he pleases between high and low water mark, if he does not hinder navigation.[41]

[30] State v. Portland, S. & P. R. Co., 58 Maine 46.

[31] Paducah & E. R. Co. v. Commonwealth, 80 Ky. 147.

[32] Louisville & N. R. Co. v. Commonwealth, 13 Bush (Ky.) 388, 26 Am. Rep. 205.

[33] State v. Louisville &c. R. Co., 86 Ind. 114; Cincinnati R. Co. v. Commonwealth, 80 Ky. 137; State v. Norfolk &c. R. Co., 168 N. Car. 103, 82 S. E. 963, L. R. A. 1915B, 329.

[34] State v. Narrows Island Club, 100 N. Car. 477, 5 S. E. 411, 6 Am. St. 618; Rex v. Stanton, 2 Show. 30. See also note to 59 L. R. A. 33 et seq.

[35] Commonwealth v. Chapin, 5 Pick. (Mass.) 199, 16 Am. Dec. 386.

[36] 1 Hawk. P. C. ch. 75, § 11.

[37] Rex v. Grosvenor, 2 Stark. 448, 20 Rev. Rep. 732.

[38] Reg. v. Leech, 6 Mod. 145.

[39] McLean v. Mathews, 7 Ill. App. 599; Rex v. Watts, 2 Esp. 675, 5 Rev. Rep. 766.

[40] The Vancouver, Fed. Cas. No. 16838, 2 Sawy. (U. S.) 381; State v. Wilson, 42 Maine 9.

[41] Zug v. Commonwealth, 70 Pa. St. 138.

§ 736. **Other highway offenses.**—One responsible for the repair of roads may be indicted for neglect to do so.[42]

Obstruction or interference with the operation of railroads is made criminal by statute in some states.[43]

It may be an offense when meeting another person on a highway to fail tc drive to the right sufficiently to allow him to pass in safety, each being entitled to the portion of the road to the right of the center of the traveled portion.[44]

Statutes also frequently punish riding or driving on a sidewalk.

Racing on the highway, that is, engaging in a trial of speed of animals, is indictable, being dangerous to public safety.[45]

Wanton and furious driving which injures others is indictable under some statutes. There are many statutes and ordinances which set a speed limit for trains, vehicles, and automobiles in passing through towns and cities, or even anywhere on the highways, violation being punishable as a misdemeanor.

42 State v. Hogg, 5 Ind. 515; People v. Albany, 11 Wend. (N. Y.) 539, 27 Am. Dec. 95; State v. King, 25 N. Car. 411.

43 Mitchell v. State, 94 Ala. 68, 10 So. 518; Hodge v. State, 82 Ga. 643, 9 S. E. 676; State v. Hessenkamp, 17 Iowa 25; Weinecke v. State, 34 Nebr. 14, 51 N. W. 307.

44 Commonwealth v. Allen, 11 Metc. (Mass.) 403; Clark v. Commonwealth, 4 Pick. (Mass.) 125; State v. Collins, 16 R. I. 371, 17 Atl. 131, 3 L. R. A. 394.

45 Robb v. State, 52 Ind. 216; State v. Ellis, 6 Baxt. (Tenn.) 549; State v. Catchings, 43 Tex. 654.

CHAPTER LVIII

OFFENSES AGAINST RELIGION.

§ 740. Blasphemy.—The common law recognizes Christianity as the prevailing religion and punishes offenses which wantonly violate the religious feelings of the community. Blasphemy is said to consist in maliciously reviling God or religion.[1] It is also defined as using language concerning the Deity calculated to impair reverence, with an impious purpose to derogate from the divine majesty, and alienate others from the reverence of God.[2] Statutes against blasphemy are constitutional.[3] Formerly such laws were very rigidly enforced, and convictions were even upheld for selling Paine's "Age of Reason."[4] But under the modern rule a mere denial in controversy or as a statement of belief of the truth of Christianity or even of the existence of the Deity, is not blasphemy, unless made in an indecent and scandalous manner, with a blasphemous intent.[5]

§ 741. Profanity.—Profanity is the uttering of words importing an imprecation for divine vengeance or implying di-

[1] People v. Ruggles, 8 Johns. (N. Y.) 290, 5 Am. Dec. 335, Ann. Cas. 1914 A, 812 and note.

[2] Commonwealth v. Kneeland, 20 Pick. (Mass.) 206; Updegraff v. Commonwealth, 11 Serg. & R. (Pa.) 394.

[3] Commonwealth v. Kneeland, 20 Pick. (Mass.) 206, Ann. Cas. 1914A, 812n.

[4] Rex v. Williams, 26 How. St. Tr. 654.

[5] People v. Ruggles, 8 Johns. (N. Y.) 290, 5 Am. Dec. 335, Ann. Cas. 1914 A, 814 and note.

vine condemnation, used so grossly and scandalously in public as to constitute a nuisance.[6]

Profanity is indictable only when a nuisance, therefore it must have been in the hearing of various persons[7] and there must have been more than a single oath,[8] although continuous swearing profanely for five minutes before others in a public place has been held indictable.[9] Statutes in many jurisdictions punish public profanity.[10]

§ 742. **Working on Sunday.**—In most states there are statutes prohibiting secular, worldly, or common labor or the following of one's usual avocation, on Sunday. Such statutes are constitutional.[11] If no exceptions are made, such statutes are even enforcible against Jews, Seventh Day Adventists, and other persons who keep the seventh day as the Sabbath.[12] It is probable that a common-law prosecution for

6 State v. Chrisp, 85 N. Car. 528, 39 Am. Rep. 713; Gaines v. State, 7 Lea (Tenn.) 410, 40 Am. Rep. 64.

7 Carr v. Conyers, 84 Ga. 287, 10 S. E. 630, 20 Am. St. 357; State v. Pepper, 68 N. Car. 259, 12 Am. Rep. 637; Morrison v. State, 56 Tex. Cr. 20, 118 S. W. 541, Ann Cas. 1914 A, 811.

8 Goree v. State, 71 Ala. 7; Gaines v. State, 7 Lee (Tenn.) 410, 40 Am. Rep. 64.

9 State v. Chrisp, 85 N. Car. 528, 39 Am. Rep. 713.

10 Note to 22 L. R. A. 353 et seq.; note to Ann. Cas. 1914 A, 817. See also, Ogletree v. State, 18 Ga. App. 41, 88 S. E. 751; People v. Whitman, 157 N. Y. S. 1107; Chicago v. Noonan, 204 Ill. App. 195; Commonwealth v. Kane, 65 Pa. Super. Ct. 258.

11 District of Columbia v. Robinson, 30 App. Cas. (D. C.) 283, 12 Ann. Cas. 1094; Scoles v. State, 47 Ark. 476, 1 S. W. 769, 58 Am. Rep. 768; Ex parte Jentzsch, 112 Cal. 468, 44 Pac. 803, 32 L. R. A. 664; Judefind v. State, 78 Md. 510, 28 Atl. 405, 22 L. R. A. 721; People v. Havnor, 149 N. Y. 195, 43 N. E. 541, 31 L. R. A. 689, 52 Am. St. 707; State v. Barnes, 22 N. Dak. 18, 132 N. W. 215, Ann. Cas. 1913 E, 930; Specht v. Commonwealth, 8 Pa. St. 312, 49 Am. Dec. 518; State v. Sopher, 25 Utah, 318, 71 Pac. 482, 60 L. R. A. 468, 95 Am. St. 845; Rosenbaum v. State, 131 Ark. 251, 199 S. W. 388; Krieger v. State, 12 Okla. Cr. 566, 160 Pac. 36; Graham v. State, 134 Tenn. 285, 183 S. W. 983; State v. Davis, 171 N. Car. 809, 89 S. E. 40, Ann. Cas. 1918 E, 1168; People ex rel. Bender v. Joyce, 161 N. Y. S. 771, 174 App. Div. 574.

12 Commonwealth v. Starr, 144 Mass. 359, 11 N. E. 533; Commonwealth v. Has, 122 Mass. 40; State v. Weiss, 97 Minn. 125, 105 N. W.

misdemeanor would lie for breach of the Sabbath.[13] However, the best authorities uphold these statutes, not upon religious grounds, but as a civil regulation of a sanitary nature under the police powers on the ground of necessity for periodical rest from toil for the general good.[14] Such laws do not prevent the transaction of business by religious and philanthropic associations,[15] but are held to prohibit all secular businesses which disturb rest.[16] Also, in addition to the general Sunday laws, often there have been enacted special statutes which single out certain occupations or acts, such as theatrical exhibitions,[17] or playing baseball,[18] or amusements generally,[19] or barbering,[20] and enforce a greater penalty than the ordinary penalty under the general laws, for their transaction on Sunday and such statutes are not unconstitutional as class legislation if the classification is reasonable.

§ 743. Work excepted from operation of Sunday laws.—

1127, 7 Ann. Cas. 932; Specht v. Commonwealth, 8 Pa. St. 312, 49 Am. Dec. 518.

13 Commonwealth v. Eyre, 1 Serg. & R. (Pa.) 347.

14 Hennington v. Georgia, 163 U. S. 299, 41 L. ed. 166; Carr v. State, 175 Ind. 241, 93 N. E. 1071, 32 L. R. A. (N. S.) 1190; Freund, Police Power, § 185; Cooley, Const. Lim. (7th ed.) 675; Krieger v. State, 12 Okla. Cr. 566, 160 Pac. 36; Gray v. Commonwealth, 171 Ky. 269, 188 S. W. 354, L. R. A. 1917 B, 93n.

15 Feital v. Middlesex R. Co., 109 Mass. 398, 12 Am. Rep. 720; People v. Young Men's, Father Matthew Benev. Soc., 65 Barb. (N. Y.) 357.

16 Quarles v. State, 55 Ark. 10, 17 S. W. 269, 14 L. R. A. 192; Smith v. Wilcox, 25 Barb. (N. Y.) 341; Cincinnati v. Rice. 15 Ohio St. 225; Ex parte Axsome, 63 Tex. Cr. 627, 141 S. W. 793, Ann. Cas. 1913 D, 794n; Koelble v. Woods, 159 N. Y. S. 704, 96 Misc. 63; People v. Adler, 160 N. Y. S. 539, 174 App. Div. 301.

17 Lindenmuller v. People, 33 Barb. (N. Y.) 548; Ex parte Lingenfelter, 64 Tex. Cr. 30, 142 S. W. 555, Ann. Cas. 1914 C, 765; note to 16 Ann. Cas. 407; note to 21 Ann. Cas. 682; Zucarro v. State (Tex. Cr.), 197 S. W. 982.

18 State v. Hogreiver, 152 Ind. 652, 53 N. E. 921, 45 L. R. A. 504.

19 In re Hull, 18 Idaho 475, 110 Pac. 256, 30 L. R. A. (N. S.) 465n.

20 Stratman v. Commonwealth, 137 Ky. 500, 125 S. W. 1094, 136 Am. St. 299; Stanfeal v. State, 78 Ohio St. 24, 84 N. E. 419, 14 Ann. Cas. 138. See also, Adams v. Cook, 91 Vt. 281, 100 Atl. 42 (the return and receipt of a verdict on Sunday held a ministerial act, and one of "necessity and charity").

Most statutes exempt works of charity or necessity from the prohibition. In other cases it has been held such exceptions are implied.[21] By various courts the following have been held work of necessity: Feeding stock,[22] driving to worship,[23] mending a railroad switch,[24] harvesting crops which would probably be lost,[25] boiling down maple sap which would have spoiled,[26] hauling ripe melons,[27] carrying mail,[28] or shoeing horses for a mail coach which under contract must leave early Monday,[29] operating an ice factory when it would mean a day's additional loss to close,[30] selling medicines,[31] and undoubtedly, furnishing water or milk to customers.

It is not a work of necessity to sell cigars,[32] or newspapers,[33] or liquor, even to one requiring stimulus,[34] or bread, meat, ice, or groceries,[35] or for a barber to shave persons in his shop,[36] or to pilot a canal boat,[37] drive an omnibus,[38] or

21 Whart. Crim. L. (11th ed.) § 1700.

22 Edgerton v. State, 67 Ind. 588, 33 Am. Rep. 110.

23 Commonwealth v. Nesbit, 34 Pa. St. 398.

24 Yonaski v. State, 79 Ind. 393, 41 Am. Rep. 614.

25 State v. Goff, 20 Ark. 289; Turner v. State, 67 Ind. 595.

26 Morris v. State, 31 Ind. 189.

27 Wilkinson v. State, 59 Ind. 416, 26 Am. Rep. 184, 2 Am. Cr. 596.

28 Commonwealth v. Knox, 6 Mass. 76.

29 Nelson v. State, 25 Tex. App. 599, 8 S. W. 927.

30 Hennersdorf v. State, 25 Tex. App. 597, 8 S. W. 926, 8 Am. St. 448.

31 Commonwealth v. Marzynski, 149 Mass. 68, 21 N. E. 228; Elkin v. State, 63 Miss. 129.

32 Friedeborn v. Commonwealth, 113 Pa. St. 242, 6 Atl. 160, 57 Am. Rep. 464.

33 Commonwealth v. Matthews, 152 Pa. St. 166, 25 Atl. 548, 18 L. R. A. 761.

34 State v. Ambs, 20 Mo. 214. But see Hall v. State, 4 Har. (Del.) 132.

35 Commonwealth v. Crowley, 145 Mass. 430, 14 N. E. 459; State v. James, 81 S. Car. 197, 62 S. E. 214, 18 L. R. A. (N. S.) 617, 16 Ann. Cas. 277.

36 State v. Frederick, 45 Ark. 347, 55 Am. Rep. 555; Ungericht v. State, 119 Ind. 379, 21 N. E. 1082, 12 Am. St. 419; Commonwealth v. Waldman, 140 Pa. St. 89, 21 Atl. 248, 11 L. R. A. 563. But see Paizer v. Commonwealth, 4 Kulp. (Pa.) 286; Hunt v. State, 19 Ga. App. 448, 91 S. E. 879.

37 Scully v. Commonwealth, 35 Pa. St. 511.

38 Johnston v. Commonwealth, 22 Pa. St. 102.

run horse cars to carry passengers,[39] or carry pleasure seekers to a picnic,[40] or gathering crops merely for convenience,[41] or collecting clothes for a laundry.[41a]

Generally travelling on Sunday on business other than charity or necessity is indictable.[42] The general rule now is that it is not unlawful to operate railroad trains for passengers, or freight which would be injured by delay.[43] The publishing of a newspaper has been held worldly employment.[44]

Many of the statutes exempt the operation of trains and persons engaged in collecting and publishing news, also exempt from punishment those who observe another day as the Sabbath. And, whereas, specific prohibitions of Sunday labor have been upheld, so specific exceptions have been upheld; as for instance, baseball playing for hire[45] or the sale of confectionery or tobacco.[46]

§ 744. **Disturbing religious meeting.**—The disturbance of an orderly conducted assembly of the people for a lawful purpose is indictable at common law.[47] Under this rule disturbance of public worship is indictable at common law.[48]

39 Commonwealth v. Jeandell, 2 Grant Cas. (Pa.) 506, 3 Phila. (Pa.) 509.

40 Dugan v. State, 125 Ind. 130, 25 N. E. 171, 9 L. R. A. 321.

41 Commonwealth v. White, 190 Mass. 578, 77 N. E. 636, 5 L. R. A. (N. S.) 320.

41a. State v. Lavoie (N. H.), 97 Atl. 566. See also, Wilson v. State (Ark.), 187 S. W. 937 (collecting logs for saw mill); Rosenbaum v. State, 131 Ark. 251, 199 S. W. 388 (operating a moving picture machine).

42 Connolly v. Boston, 117 Mass. 64, 19 Am. Rep. 396; Holcomb v. Danby, 51 Vt. 428.

43 Augusta & S. R. Co. v. Renz, 55 Ga. 126; Commonwealth v. Louisville & N. R. Co., 80 Ky. 891, 44 Am. Rep. 475; Philadelphia, W. &c. R. Co. v. Lehman, 56 Md. 209, 40 Am. Rep. 415.

44 Commonwealth v. Matthews, 152 Pa. St. 166, 25 Atl. 548, 18 L. R. A. 761.

45 Carr v. State, 175 Ind. 241, 93 N. E. 1071, 32 L. R. A. (N. S.) 1190n.

46 State v. Justus, 91 Minn. 447, 98 N. W. 325, 64 L. R. A. 510, 103 Am. St. 521, 1 Ann. Cas. 91.

47 Campbell v. Commonwealth, 59 Pa. St. 266.

48 United States v. Brooks, Fed. Cas. No. 14655, 4 Cranch (U. S.) 427; State v. Jasper, 15 N. Car. 323.

There are also statutes punishing disturbing a public meeting, and others which specifically punish the disturbance of religious meetings. The statutes seem to cover an offense committed only when the meeting is in a regular place of worship, and do not embrace an assembly in a public street,[49] or a private house,[50] but any method or mode of worship is protected, without regard to creed.[51] There must be a considerable number of persons collected about the place for worship and at about the time for worship to constitute an assembly.[52] The protection is in effect until the congregation has dispersed.[53] Irreverent conduct annoying the minister,[54] such as cracking and eating nuts,[55] loud and profane talking,[56] engaging in a fight,[57] speaking insultingly upon leave,[58] or refusal to desist speaking when so directed by the minister,[59] may constitute a disturbance. Singing by one conscientiously taking part in worship, though of a nature to excite mirth and indignation, is not punishable.[60] It is not necessary to constitute the offense that the whole congregation be disturbed, if a few members or even one be disturbed.[61]

[49] State v. Schieneman, 64 Mo. 386.

[50] State v. Starnes, 151 N. Car. 724, 66 S. E. 347, 19 Ann. Cas. 448.

[51] Hull v. State, 120 Ind. 153, 22 N. E. 117; Cline v. State, 9 Okla. Cr. 40, 130 Pac. 510, 45 L. R. A. (N. S.) 108n; note to 30 L. R. A. (N. S.) 829.

[52] State v. Bryson, 82 N. Car. 576.

[53] Lancaster v. State, 53 Ala. 398, 25 Am. Rep. 625; State v. Lusk, 68 Ind. 264; State v. Jones, 53 Mo. 486; State v. Ramsay, 78 N. Car. 448; Commonwealth v. Jennings, 3 Grat. (Va.) 624.

[54] Friedlander v. State, 7 Tex. App. 204.

[55] Hunt v. State, 3 Tex. App. 116, 30 Am. Rep. 126.

[56] McElroy v. State, 25 Tex. 507.

[57] Wright v. State, 8 Lea (Tenn.) 563.

[58] Lancaster v. State, 53 Ala. 398, 25 Am. Rep. 625.

[59] State v. Ramsay, 78 N. Car. 448.

[60] State v. Linkhaw, 69 N. Car. 214, 12 Am. Rep. 645.

[61] Cockreham v. State, 7 Humph. (Tenn.) 11; McElroy v. State, 25 Tex. 507.

A specific intent to disturb the congregation is not necessary to constitute the offense,[62] though under some statutes the disturbance must be "willful."[63]

[62] Walker v. State, 103 Ark. 336, 146 S. W. 862, Ann. Cas. 1914 B, 739n.

[63] State v. Stroud, 99 Iowa 16, 68 N. W. 450.

CHAPTER LIX

VIOLATION OF LIQUOR LAWS

§ 746. Generally.—At common law a tippling house was indictable as a nuisance[1] and there are some statutes which make the same an offense. This offense was sufficiently discussed in the chapter on Disorderly House.[2]

From early English times the sale of intoxicating liquor has been regulated by statute.[3] There is no other business or occupation which is so much regulated by statute today as the selling of intoxicating liquor, and the statutes are so various in form that no attempt will be made here to treat the subject more than generally. The statutes regulating such sale are an exercise of the police power of the state on the theory that the free sale and use of intoxicants is detri-

1 Stephens v. Watson, 1 Salk, 45.

2 See ch. 53, § 705.

3 2 Hen. VII, ch. 2, (1494) permitting the denial of the right to keep an ale house; 5 & 6 Edw. VI, ch. 25, (1552) restricting keeping of ale and drinking houses to persons licensed.

mental to the public.[4] There is also the fact that the licensing of the sale of liquors forms a considerable source of revenue to the state, and for this reason also the state is interested in protecting its revenues, and the rights of those who have purchased a license to sell liquors.

§ 747. Liquor statutes and Federal Constitution.—Statutes regulating the sale of liquor when tested have been held not to violate the Federal constitution, for they do not impair the privileges and immunities of citizens of the United States by regulating or taking away the right to sell liquor[5] nor deny to citizens of another state privileges and immunities granted to its own citizens when the issue of licenses is restricted to citizens of a state;[6] and the diminution in value of property devoted to the manufacture and sale of liquor is neither de-

[4] Giozza v. Tiernan, 148 U. S. 657, 37 L. ed. 599; Crowley v. Christensen, 137 U. S. 86, 34 L. ed. 620; Bostick v. State, 47 Ark. 126; State v. Hodgson, 66 Vt. 134, 28 Atl. 1089; State v. Hampton, 106 S. Car. 275, 91 S. E. 314; State v. Stoughton Club, 163 Wis. 362, 158 N. W. 93; People v. Johnson, 200 Ill. App. 603; Pine v. Commonwealth, 121 Va. 652, 93 S. E. 652; State v. Hemrich, 93 Wash. 439, 161 Pac. 79, L. R. A. 1917 B, 962n; State v. Theodore (Mo.), 191 S. W. 422; Stratford, Inc. v. Seattle Brewing & Malting Co., 94 Wash. 125, 162 Pac. 31, L. R. A. 1917 C, 931n.

[5] Foster v. Kansas, 112 U. S. 201, 28 L. ed. 629; Beer Co. v. Massachusetts, 97 U. S. 25, 24 L. ed. 989; Bartemeyer v. Iowa, 18 Wall. (U. S.) 129, 21 L. ed. 929; In re Hoover, 30 Fed. 51; Prohibitory Amendment Cases, 24 Kans. 700; State v. Brennan, 2 S. Dak. 384, 50 N. W. 685; Bell v. State, 28 Tex. App. 96, 12 S. W. 410. See also note to 15 L. R. A. (N. S.) 908; State v. Fabbri, 98 Wash. 207, 167 Pac. 133; State v. Wilbur, 85 Ore. 565, 166 Pac. 51, 167 Pac. 569; Crane v. Campbell, 245 U. S. 304, 38 Sup. Ct. 98, 62 L. ed. 304; People v. Jones, 280 Ill. 259, 117 N. E. 417 (prohibiting intoxication on railroad premises is not violative of Fourteenth Amendment); People ex rel. Doscher v. Sisson, 167 N. Y. S. 801, 180 App. Div. 464 (law authorizing excise commissioner to prohibit sales of intoxicants in proximity to army camps, etc., held constitutional as proper exercise of state police power), affirmed 222 N. Y. 387, 118 N. E. 789.

[6] Kohn v. Melcher, 29 Fed. 433; Christian Moerlein Brewing Co. v. Roser, 169 Ky. 198, 183 S. W. 479; State v. Little, 171 N. Car. 805, 88 S. E. 723; Kansas City v. Jordan, 99 Kans. 814, 163 Pac. 188, Ann. Cas. 1918 B, 273.

priving persons of property without due process of law, nor taking property for public use without compensation, since property rights are subject to the police power, and there is nothing taken for public use.[7] Nor do statutes providing for the abating in an equity trial of keeping liquor for unlawful sale, or selling it unlawfully, deny due process of law.[8]

However, it seems that statutes discriminating in favor of liquor made in the state, are unconstitutional.[9] So is a state statute restricting transportation into a state,[10] and regulations as to the sale of liquor do not apply to their sale in the state as articles of interstate commerce in the original package in which they were shipped.[11]

After the decision as to sales in the original package was made, the Wilson Act was passed by congress. This act made liquors brought into the state subject to the state regulations to the same extent as if produced in the state, even if sold in the original package.[12]

Even under this act a state could not prohibit importation of liquor into the state.[13]

§ 748. Liquor statutes and state constitutions.—Usually the liquor statutes have been held valid under state consti-

[7] Kidd v. Pearson, 128 U. S. 1, 32 L. ed. 346; Mugler v. Kansas, 123 U. S. 623, 31 L. ed. 205; Kaufman v. Dostal, 73 Iowa 691, 36 N. W. 643.

[8] Eilenbecker v. District Court, 134 U. S. 31, 33 L. ed. 801; Kidd v. Pearson, 128 U. S. 1, 32 L. ed. 346; Mugler v. Kansas, 123 U. S. 623, 31 L. ed. 205; Kaufman v. Dostal, 73 Iowa 691, 36 N. W. 643.

[9] Walling v. Michigan, 116 U. S. 446, 29 L. ed. 691; Tiernan v. Rinker, 102 U. S. 123, 26 L. ed. 103; Ex parte Edgerton, 59 Fed. 115; McCreary v. State, 73 Ala. 480; State v. Deschamp, 53 Ark. 490, 14 S. W. 653.

[10] Bowman v. Chicago &c. R. Co., 125 U. S. 465, 31 L. ed. 700; Ex parte Loeb, 72 Fed. 657.

[11] Leisy v. Hardin, 135 U. S. 100, 34 L. ed. 128.

[12] U. S. Comp. Stat. (1916), § 8738. See also, Brown v. Maryland, 12 Wheat. (U. S.) 419, 6 L. ed. 678.

[13] Ex parte Jervey, 66 Fed. 957; Ex parte Edgerton, 59 Fed. 115.

tutions, as not violating any rights secured thereunder;[14] and it is held that they do not take property without due process of law or without compensation,[15] and that equitable abatement does not deny the right to jury trial;[16] that, as a license is not a contract, the imposing of additional restrictions on, or prohibition of the sale, does not impair the obligation of contracts as to sellers already licensed;[17] that laws prohibiting sales within a certain distance from a church or city are not invalid as being local laws,[18] and local option laws are valid;[19] that the imposition of licenses is not taxa-

14 Lodano v. State, 25 Ala. 64; Dennehy v. Chicago, 120 Ill. 627, 12 N. E. 227; Streeter v. People, 69 Ill. 595; State v. Durein, 70 Kans. 1, 78 Pac. 152, 15 L. R. A. (N. S.) 908n; Commonwealth v. Blackington, 24 Pick. (Mass.) 352; People v. Gallagher, 4 Mich. 244.

15 Dickinson v. Heeb Brewing Co., 73 Iowa 705, 36 N. W. 651; People v. Hawley, 3 Mich. 330; Heck v. State, 44 Ohio St. 536, 9 N. E. 305; State v. Snow, 3 R. I. 64; Ex parte Lynn, 19 Tex. App. 293.

16 Martin v. Blattner, 68 Iowa 286, 25 N. W. 131, 27 N. W. 244, 6 Am. Cr. 148; Littleton v. Fritz, 65 Iowa 488, 22 N. W. 641, 54 Am. Rep. 19; Carleton v. Rugg, 149 Mass. 550, 22 N. E. 55, 5 L. R. A. 193, 14 Am. St. 446; State v. Aiken, 42 S. Car. 222, 20 S. E. 221, 26 L. R. A. 345.

17 Cooper v. State (Ariz.), 172 Pac. 276; Cartz v. State (Ark.), 204 S. W. 207; People v. Pera (Cal. App.), 171 Pac. 1091; Columbus City v. Cutcomp, 61 Iowa 672, 17 N. W. 47; State v. Durein, 70 Kans. 1, 78 Pac. 152, 15 L. R. A. (N. S.) 908-946n; Prohibitory Amendment Cases, 24 Kans. 700; State v. Isabel, 40 La. Ann. 340, 4 So. 1; Commonwealth v. Brennan, 103 Mass. 70; State v. Barringer, 110 N. Car. 525, 14 S. E. 781; Commonwealth v. Donahue, 149 Pa. St. 104, 24 Atl. 188; State v. Holland, 99 Wash. 645, 170 Pac. 332. See further note to State v. Durein, 15 L. R. A. (N. S.) 908-946.

18 Streeter v. People, 69 Ill. 595; Toledo v. Edens, 59 Iowa 352, 13 N. W. 313; State v. Rauscher, 1 Lea (Tenn.), 96.

19 State v. Wilcox, 42 Conn. 364, 19 Am. Rep. 536; Commonwealth v. Bennett, 108 Mass. 27; Feek v. Bloomingdale, 82 Mich. 393, 47 N. W. 37, 10 L. R. A. 69; State v. Cooke, 24 Minn. 247, 31 Am. Rep. 344; Fouts v. Hood River, 46 Ore. 492, 81 Pac. 370, 1 L. R. A. (N. S.) 483. See also note to 114 Am. St. 324; Ingram v. Commonwealth, 176 Ky. 706, 197 S. W. 411; Ex parte Deats, 22 N. Mex. 536, 166 Pac. 913; People v. Henderson, 201 Ill. App. 247; People v. Knoll, 200 Ill. App. 595, 276 Ill. 58, 114 N. E. 525; State v. McCue, 141 La. 417, 75 So. 100; Poisel v. Cash, 130 Md. 373, 100 Atl. 364; State v. Theodore (Mo.), 191 S. W. 422.

tion in such a sense that it must be uniform in all localities, or at the same rate as other businesses are licensed;[20] that the requirement that the seller shall be of good moral character, etc., is constitutional;[21] that a prohibitory law is valid,[22] also a law vesting the sale in a public agent and forbidding sales by private parties.[23]

Statutes relative to evidence, and procedure which place burdens on the defendant heavier than in other prosecutions are valid if they leave fair opportunity for defense.[24]

§ 749. Construction of liquor statutes.—Various questions of construction arise when by a subsequent statute a method of dealing with intoxicating liquor is adopted which conflicts with the former method. Conflicts also exist between the power of the state and of cities to regulate. Generally, it may be said that regulations not inconsistent with each other will be enforced though not part of the same system;[25] but if the systems are distinct and exclusive there can be prosecution under only one.[26] If the statute granting power to cities to regulate gives the city exclusive power then the state laws will not be enforced in the city, if the city ordinance authorizes sales;[27] but a sale not authorized

20 Ex parte Hurl, 49 Cal. 557; Dennehy v. Chicago, 120 Ill. 627, 12 N. E. 227; State v. Hudson, 78 Mo. 302; Fahey v. State, 27 Tex. App. 146, 11 S. W. 108, 11 Am. St. 182.

21 Commonwealth v. Blackington, 24 Pick. (Mass.) 352; People v. Brown, 85 Mich. 119, 48 N. W. 158; Rohrbacher v. Jackson, 51 Miss. 735.

22 State v. Kane, 15 R. I. 395, 6 Atl. 783; State v. Becker, 3 S. Dak. 29, 51 N. W. 1018.

23 Lauten v. Rowan, 59 N. H. 215; State v. Aiken, 42 S. Car. 222, 20 S. E. 221, 26 L. R. A. 345; Atkins v. Randolph, 31 Vt. 226; State v. Parks, 29 Vt. 70.

24 Santo v. State, 2 Iowa 165, 63 Am. Dec. 487; State v. Hurley, 54 Maine 562; Commonwealth v. Williams, 6 Gray (Mass.) 1.

25 State v. Deaton, 101 N. Car. 728, 7 S. E. 895; New v. State, 34 Tex. 100; State v. Cain, 8 W. Va. 720.

26 Butler v. State, 25 Fla. 347, 6 So. 67.

27 State v. Wheeler, 27 Minn. 76, 6 N. W. 423; Craddock v. State, 18 Tex. App. 567.

by ordinance may be punishable under the state law.[28] Provisions of an ordinance in violation of authority are void.[29] If the systems are changed, as by the adoption of local option, there may be prosecutions after the taking effect of the new law for violations of the general statute committed prior thereto if the general statute is merely suspended in operation, and not repealed;[30] but if the new law repeals the old by implication and there is no saving clause there can be no prosecution for former violations.[31]

Generally speaking, the power granted to a city is not considered exclusive, but subordinate to the general laws of the state,[32] although a city may make additional restrictions.[33] In such a case the seller must comply with both state and city laws.[34]

The same act may be prosecuted under both the state law and the ordinances of a city.[35]

§ 750. License.—The most common regulation of the sale of intoxicating liquor is probably the license system. "A license is permission granted by some competent authority to do an act which, without such permission, would be illegal."[36] Under the license system liquor can only be sold by those

[28] State v. Langdon, 31 Minn. 316, 17 N. W. 859; State v. Pfeifer, 26 Minn. 175, 2 N. W. 474.

[29] Adams v. Albany, 29 Ga. 56; State v. Winkelmeier, 35 Mo. 103.

[30] People v. Wade, 101 Mich. 89, 59 N. W. 438; Winterton v. State, 65 Miss. 238, 3 So. 735; Sanders v. Commonwealth, 117 Pa. St. 293, 11 Atl. 63.

[31] Dawson v. State, 25 Tex. App. 670, 8 S. W. 820; Halfin v. State, 5 Tex. App. 212.

[32] Sweet v. Wabash, 41 Ind. 7; State v. Chase, 33 La. Ann. 287; State v. Peterson, 38 Minn. 143, 36 N. W. 443; State v. Harper, 58 Mo. 530; Ex parte Ginnochio, 30 Tex. App. 584, 18 S. W. 82.

[33] Morris v. Rome, 10 Ga. 532; Dennehy v. Chicago, 120 Ill. 627, 12 N. E. 227; People v. Townsey, 5 Denio (N. Y.) 70.

[34] Ex parte Lawrence, 69 Cal. 608; Paton v. People, 1 Colo. 77; Elk Point v. Vaughn, 1 Dak. 113, 46 N. W. 577; State v. Sherman, 50 Mo. 265; State v. Propst, 87 N. Car. 560.

[35] Elk Point v. Vaughn, 1 Dak. 113, 46 N. W. 577; State v. Stevens, 114 N. Car. 873, 19 S. E. 861.

[36] State v. Hipp, 38 Ohio St. 199, 226.

having legal license. Such license must be issued by proper authority,[37] contain all items required by statute,[38] and the proper preliminaries must have been complied with.[39] If the requirements of the statute are not substantially complied with, the sales under the license will be illegal.[40] Usually a bond conditioned that the licensee will not violate the provisions of the statute is required.[41] Sales can not be made under the license until it is in fact issued, although an order for the license has been issued.[42] Conditions annexed to the license privilege must be complied with strictly.[43] A license to sell for certain specified purposes impliedly prohibits sales for any other purpose.[44] The issuance of a license can not validate previous sales,[45] even if it is dated back.[46] License granted by a tribunal having authority can be attacked only by appeal; and if the issuing tribunal is reversed sales made under the license before that time are unlawful,[47] but the jurisdiction of the issuing tribunal may be inquired into collaterally, and the license is void if it is shown that the

[37] Cronin v. Stoddard, 97 N. Y. 271.

[38] Commonwealth v. McCormick, 150 Mass. 270, 22 N. E. 211; Commonwealth v. Merriam, 136 Mass. 433.

[39] Ex parte Cox, 19 Ark. 688; Crutz v. State, 4 Ind. 385; State v. Shaw, 32 Maine 570; Commonwealth v. Welch, 144 Mass. 356, 11 N. E. 423; Commonwealth v. Heaganey, 137 Mass. 574.

[40] State v. Mullenhoff, 74 Iowa 271, 37 N. W. 329; State v. Fisher, 33 Wis. 154; State v. Riesen, 165 Wis. 258, 161 N. W. 747.

[41] Lightner v. Commonwealth, 31 Pa. St. 341; Providence v. Bligh, 10 R. I. 208.

[42] Wiles v. State, 33 Ind. 306; Commonwealth v. Spring, 19 Pick. (Mass.) 396; State v. Bach, 36 Minn. 234, 30 N. W. 764. See also Padgett v. State, 93 Ind. 396.

[43] Barnard v. Houghton, 34 Vt. 264; Boerner v. Thompson, 278 Ill. 153, 115 N. E. 866 (a municipal ordinance providing that an applicant for a liquor license shall agree to abide by all regulations, and mayor authorized to forfeit license for failure, is valid, and the mayor may declare such forfeiture and this will not amount to denial of due process).

[44] State v. Perkins, 26 N. H. 9.

[45] Wilson v. State, 35 Ark. 414; Bolduc v. Randall, 107 Mass. 121; State v. Hughes, 24 Mo. 147.

[46] Reese v. Atlanta, 63 Ga. 344; Dudley v. State, 91 Ind. 312; Commonwealth v. Welch, 144 Mass. 356, 11 N. E. 423.

[47] Padgett v. State, 93 Ind. 396.

necessary preliminary steps were omitted.[48] A license granted contrary to state law by a city will not bar criminal prosecution but may estop the city from recovering the penalty.[49] Statutes often provide for the revocation of licenses for illegal sales.[50]

Privilege conferred by a license is personal and not assignable.[51] So the executor or administrator of a deceased licensee can not carry on the business under the license.[52] And one who purchases a saloon keeper's business can not sell under the license of the former owner.[53] But the licensee may sell through an agent and the principal's license protects the agent,[54] although the agent is liable if he makes sales exceeding his principal's authority.[55] If the principal removes from the state the agent is not protected by the license,[56] an exception being made to this rule where the principal was

[48] Commonwealth v. Welch, 144 Mass. 356, 11 N. E. 423; Commonwealth v. Whelan, 134 Mass. 206; People v. Davis, 36 N. Y. 77, 33 How. Pr. 442; State v. Fisher, 33 Wis. 154.

[49] Genoa v. Van Alstine, 108 Ill. 555.

[50] State v. Lamos, 26 Maine 258; Commonwealth v. Moylan, 119 Mass. 109; State v. Tomah, 80 Wis. 198, 49 N. W. 753.

[51] Godfrey v. State, 5 Blackf. (Ind.) 151; Lewis v. United States 1 Morris (Iowa) 199; State v. Hadlock, 43 Maine 282; Citizens' Brewing Corp. v. Lighthall, 221 N. Y. 71, 116 N. E. 791. But see Appeal of Cordano, 91 Conn. 718, 101 Atl. 85 (property in a license to sell liquor recognized to the fullest extent as property having a recognized pecuniary value and subject of sale, attachment, levy, or replevy).

[52] United States v. Overton, Fed. Cas. No. 15979, 2 Cranch (U. S.) 42; People v. Sykes, 96 Mich. 452, 56 N. W. 12; In re Blumenthal, 125 Pa. St. 412, 18 Atl. 395.

[53] Heath v. State, 105 Ind. 342, 4 N. E. 901; State v. Lydick, 11 Nebr. 366, 9 N. W. 560.

[54] Runyon v. State, 52 Ind. 320; Barnes v. Commonwealth, 2 Dana (Ky.) 388; Commonwealth v. Mahoney, 152 Mass. 493, 25 N. E. 833; State v. Hart, 107 N. Car. 796, 12 S. E. 378. See also Duncan v. Commonwealth, 2 B. Mon. (Ky.) 281, 38 Am. Dec. 152.

[55] People v. Metzger, 95 Mich. 121, 54 N. W. 639; Commonwealth v. Holstein, 132 Pa. St. 357, 19 Atl. 273; Peitz v. State, 68 Wis. 538, 32 N. W. 763.

[56] Keiser v. State, 58 Ind. 379; Krant v. State, 47 Ind. 519.

absent in the war.[57] License to one member of a partnership gives no right to the other members to sell liquor.[58]

Usually the issuing tribunal is given some discretion in issuing licenses from which discretion there is no appeal;[59] but an arbitrary refusal, without a reason, to grant a license may be ground for the issuance of a writ of mandamus to compel its granting.[60] If a license is issued without authority quo warranto will lie.[61] But a wrongful refusal to grant license is not a defense for selling without a license.[62] Neither is impossibility to obtain a license a defense.[63]

Sale without license is punishable as such.[64] License to sell for certain purposes is no defense to sales made for other purposes.[65] Usually a license describes the place where the liquor shall be sold under it, and sales elsewhere are criminal.[66] Two buildings are considered not the same place even though on the same lot or connected,[67] neither are two

57 Pickens v. State, 20 Ind. 116.

58 Long v. State, 27 Ala. 32; Shaw v. State, 56 Ind. 188. But see Barnes v. Commonwealth, 2 Dana (Ky.) 388.

59 Ex parte Levy, 43 Ark. 42, 51 Am. Rep. 550; State v. Tippecanoe, 45 Ind. 501; Pierce v. Commonwealth, 10 Bush (Ky.) 6; Toole's Appeal, 90 Pa. St. 376; Ailstock v. Page, 77 Va. 386; French v. Noel, 22 Grat. (Va.) 454.

60 Zanone v. Mound City, 103 Ill. 552; Sparrow's Petition, 138 Pa. St. 116, 20 Atl. 711; Rosenoff v. Cross, 95 Wash. 525; 164 Pac. 236 (held that county auditor could not be compelled to issue a liquor permit to a druggist who had been convicted as violating a prior local option law, two years earlier).

61 Swarth v. People, 109 Ill. 621.

62 Deitz v. Central, 1 Colo. 323; Roberts v. State. 26 Fla. 360, 7 So. 861; Brock v. State, 65 Ga. 437; Commonwealth v. Blackington, 24 Pick. (Mass.) 352; State v. Jamison, 23 Mo. 330.

63 State v. Tucker, 45 Ark. 55; Reese v. Atlanta, 63 Ga. 344; Welsh v. State, 126 Ind. 71, 25 N. E. 883, 9 L. R. A. 664; State v. Brown, 41 La. Ann. 771, 6 So. 638.

64 Keller v. State, 11 Md. 525, 69 Am. Dec. 226; State v. Thornburg, 16 S. Car. 482.

65 State v. Keen, 34 Maine 500; Commonwealth v. Chadwick, 142 Mass. 595, 8 N. E. 589.

66 State v. Prettyman, 3 Har. (Del.) 570; State v. Walker, 16 Maine 241; State v. Hughes, 24 Mo. 147; State v. Moody, 95 N. Car. 656.

67 Commonwealth v. Estabrook, 10 Pick. (Mass.) 293; State v. Fredericks, 16 Mo. 382.

rooms in the same building one place,[68] but sales may be made under one license in two rooms in the same building connected by doors or arch ways.[69]

Some courts hold that the prosecution must prove that the sale was made without license.[70] It is more commonly held that the defendant should prove that he is licensed.[71] The indictment should negative the license.[72]

§ 751. What are intoxicating liquors.—Some statutes specify intoxicating liquors by name. The only question then is one of fact, as to whether a named kind of liquor was sold.[73] Others define intoxicating liquors as those containing a certain per cent. of alcohol.[74] In both these it is immaterial whether the liquor is actually intoxicating. But when the liquor which was sold is not particularly named in the statute, which uses general terms such as, "intoxicating," "spirituous," "vinous," "malt," "fermented" and so on, some decisions hold that it is a question of fact for the jury whether the liquor sold is within the statute.[75] Other cases hold that

[68] Malkan v. Chicago, 217 Ill. 471, 75 N. E. 548, 2 L. R. A. (N. S.) 488.

[69] Hockstadler v. State, 73 Ala. 24; Brown v. State. 27 Ala. 47; Gray v. Commonwealth, 9 Dana (Ky.) 300, 35 Am. Dec. 136; St. Louis v. Gerardi, 90 Mo. 640, 3 S. W. 408.

[70] Berning v. State, 51 Ark. 550, 11 S. W. 882.

[71] Williams v. State, 35 Ark. 430; Shearer v. State, 7 Blackf. (Ind.) 99; State v. Whittier, 21 Maine, 341, 38 Am. Dec. 272; Commonwealth v. Kennedy, 108 Mass. 292; People v. Curtis, 95 Mich. 212, 54 N. W. 767; State v. Taylor, 73 Mo. 52; State v. Emery, 98 N. Car. 668, 3 S. E. 636; Bell v. State, 62 Tex. Cr. 242, 137 S. W. 670, 36 L. R. A. (N. S.) 98n, Ann. Cas. 1913 C, 617n.

[72] Higgins v. People, 69 Ill. 11; Frankfort v. Aughe, 114 Ind. 77, 15 N. E. 802; State v. Burkett, 51 Kans. 175, 32 Pac. 925; Commonwealth v. Thurlow, 24 Pick. (Mass.) 374; State v. Nerbovig, 33 Minn. 480, 24 N. W. 321; White v. State, 11 Tex. App. 476.

[73] State v. Curley, 33 Iowa 359; Commonwealth v. Curran, 119 Mass. 206; State v. Spaulding, 61 Vt. 505, 17 Atl. 844.

[74] Commonwealth v. Brelsford, 161 Mass. 61, 36 N. E. 677; People v. Ingraham, 100 Mich. 530, 59 N. W. 234.

[75] State v. Starr, 67 Maine 242, 2 Am. Cr. 390; Commonwealth v. Blos, 116 Mass. 56; State v. Biddle, 54 N. H. 379, 1 Am. Cr. 490.

the court takes judicial notice that whiskey, ale, wine, lager beer and similar liquors are intoxicating and the only question for the jury is whether the liquor is one of these kinds.[76]

A liquor commonly used as a beverage which contains enough alcohol to intoxicate if used in large quantities is an "intoxicating liquor."[77] It has been held unnecessary to give specific proof to the jury that the following liquors were intoxicating: whisky,[78] alcohol,[79] gin,[80] beer,[81] cordial[82] and whisky or brandy mixed with water;[83] also mixed liquors of these classes.[84] It is generally held that there must be proof of the intoxicating qualities of wine,[85] cider,[86] or bitter.[87] If the sale of a certain kind of liquor, as malt liquor, is prohibited, the sale of non-intoxicating malt liquor falls within the prohibition.[88]

§ 752. **What is a sale.**—The charge and proof of the illegal sale must, of course, vary with the provisions of the statute

76 Adler v. State, 55 Ala. 16; Fenton v. State, 100 Ind. 598; State v. Schaefer, 44 Kans. 90, 24 Pac. 92; State v. Tisdale, 54 Minn. 105, 55 N. W. 903; State v. Packer, 80 N. Car. 439; Briffitt v. State, 58 Wis. 39, 16 N. W. 39, 46 Am. Rep. 621.

77 Commissioners v. Taylor, 21 N. Y. 173; State v. Giersch, 98 N. Car. 720, 4 S. E. 193; Pearce v. State, 48 Tex. Cr. 352, 88 S. W. 234, 13 Ann. Cas. 637. Generally, see note to 20 L. R. A. 645, et seq.

78 Schlicht v. State, 56 Ind. 173; State v. Munger, 15 Vt. 290.

79 Snider v. State, 81 Ga. 753, 7 S. E. 631, 12 Am. St. 350.

80 Commonwealth v. Peckham, 2 Gray (Mass.) 514.

81 Adler v. State, 55 Ala. 16; Rau v. People, 63 N. Y. 277; State v. Goyette, 11 R. I. 592, 3 Am. Cr. 282; Moreno v. State, 64 Tex. Cr. 660, 143 S. W. 156, Ann. Cas. 1914 C, 863.

82 State v. Bennet, 3 Harr. (Del.) 565.

83 Commonwealth v. Odlin, 23 Pick. (Mass.) 275.

84 Carl v. State, 87 Ala. 17, 6 So. 118, 4 L. R. A. 380, 8 Am. Cr. 404; State v. Pigg, 78 Kans. 618, 97 Pac. 859, 19 L. R. A. (N. S.) 848, 130 Am. St. 387. "Manhattan Cocktail."

85 Jackson v. State, 19 Ind. 312; State v. Packer, 80 N. Car. 439.

86 Feldman v. Morrison, 1 Ill. App. 460; Commonwealth v. Chappel, 116 Mass. 7; State v. Williams, 172 N. Car. 973, 90 S. E. 905.

87 Carl v. State, 89 Ala. 93, 8 So. 156; Davis v. State, 50 Ark. 17, 6 S. W. 388.

88 In re Lockman, 18 Idaho 465, 110 Pac. 253, 46 L. R. A. (N. S.) 759n; State v. Billups, 63 Ore. 277, 127 Pac. 686, 48 L. R. A. (N. S.) 308n.

under which the indictment is laid. Some statutes prohibit selling to a minor or a drunkard, in which case the chief element of proof is as to the vendee; others prohibit sales in quantities smaller than a quart, sales to be drunk on the premises, sales before or after certain hours, sales on holidays, in each of which cases the essential elements to be proved are different. There is also the general offense of selling without license.

Sales on credit fall within the statutory prohibition.[89] A mere agreement to sell, not completed by delivery, is not punishable.[90] It is a sale where the liquor is left for purchasers to find it and the money left in the same place,[91] or where a drink is given with a meal,[92] or with the admission fee to an amusement place,[93] and a valuable consideration is paid.

Barter or exchange is not considered a sale;[94] nor is the distributing of drinks by clubs to members so considered by some courts[95] though others hold the contrary.[96] The giving

[89] Perkins v. State, 92 Ala. 66, 9 So. 536; Ihrig v. State, 40 Ind. 422; Ex parte Aki, 32 Cal. App. 483, 163 Pac. 338 (a single illegal sale sufficient).

[90] Archer v. State, 45 Md. 33, 2 Am. Cr. 404; People v. Schlick, 200 Ill. App. 605 (act done by means of shifts and devices held a sale).

[91] Stultz v. State, 96 Ind. 456; State v. Sullivan, 97 Wash. 639, 166 Pac. 1123 (a sale where defendant told alleged purchaser where liquor might be found and he found it and took possession); State v. Elmore, 195 Mo. App. 15, 189 S. W. 612.

[92] Feldman v. Morrison, 1 Ill. App. 460; Seelbach Hotel Co. v. Commonwealth, 135 Ky. 376, 122 S. W. 190, 25 L. R. A. (N. S.) 943; Commonwealth v. Worcester, 126 Mass. 256; Commonwealth v. Chappel, 116 Mass. 7.

[93] Stockwell v. State, 85 Ind. 522; Richardson v. Commonwealth, 76 Va. 1007, 4 Am. Cr. 479.

[94] Coker v. State, 91 Ala. 92, 8 So. 874; Stevenson v. State, 65 Ind. 409.

[95] Commonwealth v. Pomphret, 137 Mass. 564, 50 Am. Rep. 340; Barden v. Montana Club, 10 Mont. 330, 25 Pac. 1042, 11 L. R. A. 293, 34 Am. St. 27n; People v. Adelphi Club, 149 N. Y. 5, 43 N. E. 410, 31 L. R. A. 510, 52 Am. St. 700; State v. Colonial Club, 155 N. Car. 177, 69 S. E. 771, Ann. Cas. 1912A, 1079.

[96] South Shore Country Club v. People, 228 Ill. 75, 81 N. E. 805, 10 Ann. Cas. 383, 119 Am. St. 417; State v. Minnesota Club, 106 Minn.

away of liquor is not a sale,[97] though in some states the giving or furnishing liquor to another is prohibited and some decisions hold a loan of liquor punishable,[98] while others hold that it is not.[99]

§ 753. Sale or purchase by agent or servant.—The keeper of any place is liable for an unlawful sale of liquor made by his employé in the course of his business.[1] It is so held by many courts even where the sale is made without the master's knowledge or in violation of his order.[2] Other courts, though the sale was made in the scope of the servant's employment, do not hold the master unless he expressly authorized the sale.[3]

The one set of decisions holds the illegal sale a police wrong, punishable regardless of intent; the others apply the

515, 119 N. W. 494, 20 L. R. A. (N. S.) 1101; State v. Missouri Athletic Club, 260 Mo. 576, 170 S. W. 904, L. R. A. 1915C, 876; Albrecht v. People, 78 Ill. 510, 2 Am. Cr. 401; People v. Bird, 138 Mich. 31, 100 N. W. 1003, 67 L. R. A. 424, 110 Am. St. 299, 4 Ann. Cas. 1062.

97 Williams v. State, 91 Ala. 14, 8 So. 668.

98 State v. Mitchell, 156 N. Car. 659, 72 S. E. 632, Ann. Cas. 1913A, 469; Tombeaugh v. State, 50 Tex. Cr. 286, 98 S. W. 1054, 8 L. R. A. (N. S.) 937, 14 Ann. Cas. 275; Turner v. State, 18 Ga. App. 393, 89 S. E. 538.

99 Jones v. State, 108 Miss. 530, 66 So. 987, L. R. A. 1915C, 648.

1 Carey v. State, 83 Ind. 597; State v. Wentworth, 65 Maine 234, 20 Am. Rep. 688; Commonwealth v. Lynch, 160 Mass. 298, 35 N. E. 854; Commonwealth v. Nichols, 10 Metc. (Mass.) 259, 43 Am. Dec. 432; State v. Scoggins, 107 N. Car. 959, 12 S. E. 59, 10 L. R. A. 542; 2 Whart. Crim. L. (11th ed.), § 1794. Generally, see note to 41 L. R. A. 661-676; Hoskins v. Commonwealth, 171 Ky. 204, 188 S. W. 348; Cashin v. State, 18 Ga. App. 87, 88 S. E. 996.

2 Loeb v. State, 75 Ga. 258; Commonwealth v. Joslin, 158 Mass. 482, 33 N. E. 653, 21 L. R. A. 449; State v. Kittelle, 110 N. Car. 560, 15 S. E. 103, 15 L. R. A. 694, 28 Am. St. 698; State v. Gilmore, 80 Vt. 514, 13 Ann. Cas. 321; State v. Wilbur, 85 Ore. 565, 166 Pac. 51, rehearing denied, 85 Ore. 565, 167 Pac. 569.

3 Lathrope v. State, 51 Ind. 192, 1 Am. Cr. 468; Commonwealth v. Wachtendorf, 141 Mass. 270, 4 N. E. 817; People v. Hughes, 86 Mich. 180, 48 N. W. 945; Elliott v. State (Ariz.), 164 Pac. 1179; Steinkuhler v. State, 100 Nebr. 95, 158 N. W. 437.

general principle of criminal law, that one is not criminally liable for unauthorized acts of a servant or agent. In any case a principal who neither expressly nor impliedly authorized the sale can not be convicted.[4]

One may be convicted because of sales made by his partner,[5] or his wife.[6] The agent or servant who makes the unlawful sale is usually held liable, whether his principal is liable or not.[7]

One who has no interest in the sale but merely procures it for another, as an agent, servant or friend is not liable as a seller.[8] However, one who secures whisky for another on a prescription which he procured for his own use is guilty of a sale,[9] and a sale to a minor who does not disclose that he is buying as another's agent, is a violation of law by the seller.[10]

§ 754. Sale for medical use.—The greater number of liquor statutes except from penalty sales by a druggist for medical use upon a physician's prescription, or sales by a phy-

[4] Perkins v. State, 92 Ala. 66, 9 So. 536; Hipp v. State, 5 Blackf. (Ind.) 149, 33 Am. Dec. 463; State v. Hayes, 67 Iowa 27, 24 N. W. 575, 6 Am. Cr. 335.

[5] Segars v. State, 88 Ala. 144; Mathre v. Story City Drug Co., 130 Iowa 111, 106 N. W. 368, 8 Ann. Cas. 275; Whitton v. State, 37 Miss. 379.

[6] Hensly v. State, 52 Ala. 10; Pennybaker v. State, 2 Blackf. (Ind.) 484; Commonwealth v. McDaniel, 148 Mass. 130.

[7] Zeller v. State, 46 Ind. 304; Lochnar v. State, 111 Md. 660, 19 Ann. Cas. 579; Mo Yaen, 18 Ariz. 491, 163 Pac. 135, L. R. A. 1917 D, 1014 (waiter held liable); State v. Lane (Mo. App.), 193 S. W. 948. Contra: Hamilton v. State, 80 Tex. Cr. 516, 191 S. W. 1160.

[8] Campbell v. State, 79 Ala. 271; Anderson v. South Chicago Brewing Co., 173 Ill. 213, 50 N. E. 655; Martin v. Commonwealth, 153 Ky. 784, 156 S. W. 870, 45 L. R. A. (N. S.) 957; State v. Ito, 114 Minn. 426, 131 N. W. 469, Ann. Cas. 1912C, 631; Reed v. State, 3 Okla. Cr. 16, 103 Pac. 1070, 24 L. R. A. (N. S.) 268; Pitts v. State, 17 Ga. App. 836, 88 S. E. 712 (ownership of the liquor by defendant not essential).

[9] Hawkins v. State, 55 Tex. Cr. 75, 114 S. W. 813, 21 L. R. A. (N. S.) 1008.

[10] Tony v. State, 144 Ala. 87, 40 So. 388, 3 L. R. A. (N. S.) 1196, 113 Am. St. 20, 6 Ann. Cas. 865.

sician for such use. The requirements of the statutory exception must be complied with, in order to assert it as a defense.[11] If the statute makes no such exception, sale for medical use is no defense,[12] unless, perhaps, in case of necessity.[13]

Where a physician's prescription is used as a mere subterfuge in order to obtain intoxicating liquor it is no defense.[14] The furnishing of liquor by a physician to a patient for medical use is not a sale.[15] A sale to a minor for medical use upon a prescription is not an illegal sale to a minor.[16]

§ 755. Intent and knowledge.—The general rule is, that lack of knowledge by the seller that the liquor is of a kind the sale of which is prohibited, or that the vendee was one of a class to whom sales are prohibited, as a minor or drunkard, is not a defense to the illegal sale. Criminal intent or guilty knowledge is not an essential element of the offense. It is not the sale, not the intention which accompanies it, which constitutes the offense. This rule obtains also where the prosecution is for violating a local option law. But the question of good faith enters into every sale of alcohol by a druggist, notwithstanding the formal sufficiency of his record.[17]

11 United States v. Smith, 45 Fed. 115; Carson v. State, 69 Ala. 235; Ryan v. State, 174 Ind. 468, 92 N. E. 340, Ann. Cas. 1912D, 1341n; Barton v. State, 99 Ind. 89; State v. Tetrick, 34 W. Va. 137, 11 S. E. 1002; State v. McCaskey, 97 Wash. 401, 166 Pac. 1163 (druggist not guilty in sale of alcohol to person who makes a false statement to procure it).

12 Woods v. State, 36 Ark. 36, 38 Am. Rep. 22; State v. Shank, 79 Iowa 47, 44 N. W. 241; Commonwealth v. Kimball, 24 Pick. (Mass.) 366; State v. Gummer, 22 Wis. 441.

13 Thomasson v. State, 15 Ind. 449; 2 Whart. Crim. (11th ed.), § 1799.

14 Davis v. State, 93 Ga. 45, 18 S. E. 998; State v. Oeder, 80 Iowa 72, 45 N. W. 543; State v. Morton, 38 S. Dak. 504, 162 N. W. 155, Ann. Cas. 1918 E, 913.

15 Schaffner v. State, 8 Ohio St. 642.

16 State v. Larrimore, 19 Mo. 391; Atkinson v. State, 46 Tex. Cr. 229, 79 S. W. 31, 3 Ann. Cas. 838.

17 United States v. Dodge, Fed. Cas. No. 14974, Deady (U. S.) 186 Harper v. State, 91 Ark. 422, 121 S. W. 737, 25 L. R. A. (N. S.) 801, 18 Ann. Cas. 435; Crampton v.

There are some cases which take the contrary view and hold that an honest mistake of fact where due care was used, is a defense.[18]

§ 756. Keeping intoxicating liquor for sale.—Some statutes provide a penalty for keeping intoxicating liquor for sale.

This offense is strictly statutory and the principal element is the intent to sell, so that without evidence from which such intent can be inferred, a conviction would be improper.[19]

§ 757. The Wilson Act—The Webb-Kenyon Act—The Reed Amendment.—The Wilson Act of 1890 (26 Stat. 313), ch. 728, provides that intoxicating liquors transported into any state or territory, or remaining therein for use, consumption, sale or storage, shall be subject on the arrival therein to the operation of the laws of the state or territory enacted in the exercise of the police power.

The Webb-Kenyon Act of 1913 (37 Stat. 699), ch. 90, prohibits the shipment and transportation of intoxicating liquor from one state into another state when such liquor is intended to be received, possessed, sold or used in violation of the laws of such state.

The Reed Amendment, which is a part of § 5 of the Post-Office Appropriation Act of 1917, ch. 162 (39 Stat. 1058, 1069), goes farther than either of the two preceding acts. It

State, 37 Ark. 108; Woods v. State, 36 Ark. 36, 38 Am. Rep. 22; McCutcheon v. People, 69 Ill. 601, 1 Am. Cr. 471; Ryan v. State, 174 Ind. 468, 92 N. E. 340, Ann. Cas. 1912D, 1341; Commonwealth v. Julius, 143 Mass. 132, 8 N. E. 898; Bacot v. State, 94 Miss. 225, 48 So. 228. 20 L. R. A. (N. S.) 524; State v. Hartfiel, 24 Wis. 60; State v. Moser, 98 Wash. 481, 167 Pac. 1101; Mitchell v. State, 20 Ga. App. 778, 93 S. E. 709; Nies v. District Court, 179 Iowa 326, 161 N. W. 316.

18 Robinius v. State, 67 Ind. 94; Crabtree v. State, 30 Ohio St. 382.

19 Eidge v. Bessemer, 164 Ala. 599, 51 So. 246, 26 L. R. A. (N. S.) 394; Wakeman v. Chambers, 69 Iowa 169, 28 N. W. 498, 58 Am. Rep. 218; Commonwealth v. Kane, 150 Mass. 294, 22 N. E. 903; 2 Whart. Crim. L. (11th ed.), § 1834.

provides, among other things, that "whoever shall order, purchase, or cause intoxicating liquors to be transported in interstate commerce, except for scientific, sacramental, medicinal and mechanical purposes, into any State or Territory the laws of which State or Territory prohibit the manufacture or sale therein of intoxicating liquors for beverage purposes shall be punished as aforesaid: Provided, That nothing herein shall authorize the shipment of liquor into any State contrary to the laws of such State."

While the Wilson Act of 1890 permits state laws to operate on interstate shipments of intoxicating liquors after termination of transportation to the consignee, and the Webb-Kenyon Act of 1913 prohibits interstate transportation of intoxicating liquors into a state to be dealt with therein in violation of the laws of that state, it should not be forgotten that the interstate transportation of intoxicating liquors still remains within the sole jurisdiction of congress.[20] By virtue of the Wilson Act and the remedial authority thereby conferred by congress upon the states to regulate sales of liquor after arrival in the state and before sale in the original packages, a state has power to prevent solicitation of orders for intoxicating liquors to be shipped from other states.[21] Speaking generally, however, the states are without power to directly burden an interstate shipment until after its arrival and delivery and sale in the original package; and this rule applies to the transportation of intoxicating liquors as well as to other commodities. The Wilson Act, however, modifies this rule as to shipments of intoxicating liquors so as to bring them under state control after delivery, but before sale, in the original package.[22] The Wilson Act expressly provides that intoxicating liquors coming into a state shall be as completely under the control of the state

[20] Adams Express Co. v. Commonwealth, 238 U. S. 190, 35 Sup. Ct. 824.

[21] Delamater v. South Dakota, 205 U. S. 93, 27 Sup. Ct. 447, 51 L. ed. 724.

[22] Rosenberger v. Pacific Express Co., 241 U. S. 48, 36 Sup. Ct. 510.

as though manufactured therein. Hence the owner of intoxicating liquors in one state may not, under the commerce clause of the Federal Constitution, go himself or send his agent into another state and, in defiance of its laws, carry on the business of soliciting proposals for the purchase of such liquors.[23] But a state may not forbid a resident therein from ordering for his own use intoxicating liquors from another state.[24] The power to make interstate commerce shipments C. O. D. is incidental to the right to make the shipment, and an attempt by a state to prohibit contracts to that effect or prevent fulfillment thereof is, as a burden upon, and an interference with, interstate commerce, repugnant to the Federal Constitution. Hence a state statute which imposes special licenses on express companies maintaining offices for C. O. D. shipments of intoxicating liquors is an unconstitutional burden on, and interference with, interstate commerce.[25] The Webb-Kenyon Act is a legitimate exertion of the power of congress to regulate commerce, and is not repugnant to the due process clause of the Fifth Amendment.[26] This act, which is entitled "An Act divesting intoxicating liquors of their interstate character in certain cases," subjects interstate shipments of intoxicating liquors to state legislation. Hence a state law which requires carriers to keep records of such shipments, open for the inspection of any officer or citizen, is valid, notwithstanding the prohibition of § 15 of the Act to Regulate Commerce, as amended, June 18, 1910, against the divulging of information by interstate carriers.[27] And the

[23] Delameter v. South Dakota, 205 U. S. 93, 27 Sup. Ct. 447, 51 L. ed. 724; Pabst Brewing Co. v. Crenshaw, 198 U. S. 17, 25 Sup. Ct. 552, 49 L. ed. 925.

[24] Vance v. W. A. Vandercook Co., 170 U. S. 438, 18 Sup. Ct. 674, 42 L. ed. 1100.

[25] Rosenberger v. Pacific Express Co., 241 U. S. 48, 36 Sup. Ct. 510, and cases therein cited.

[26] Clark Distilling Co. v. Western Maryland Ry. Co., 242 U. S. 310, 37 Sup. Ct. 180; Leisy v. Hardin, 135 U. S. 100, 10 Sup. Ct. 681, 34 L. ed. 128.

[27] Seaboard Air Line Ry. Co. v. State of North Carolina, 245 U. S. 298, 38 Sup. Ct. 96.

power of a state under the Webb-Kenyon Act to forbid shipment into its territory of intoxicating liquors from other states includes the lesser power to prescribe by law the conditions under which such shipments may be allowed.[28] The purpose of congress in enacting this statute was not to prohibit all interstate shipments or transportation of intoxicating liquors into so-called dry territory, but to render the prohibitory provisions of the statute operative whenever, and only when, the liquors are to be dealt with in violation of the law of the state into which it is shipped.[29] The test of interstate commerce is importation into one state from another.[30] The transportation of one's goods from state to state is interstate commerce, and, as such, subject to the regulatory power of congress.[31] The transportation of prohibited articles upon the person of one being carried in interstate commerce is within the well-established meaning of the words "interstate commerce."[32]

§ 758. Case of United States v. Hill, decided Jan. 13, 1919. —In this case the indictment charged that the defendant, Dan Hill, on Nov. 20, 1917, being in the state of Kentucky, there intended to go and be carried by means of a common carrier, engaged in interstate commerce, from the state of Kentucky into the state of West Virginia, and intended to carry upon his person, as a beverage for his personal use, a quantity of intoxicating liquor, to-wit: one quart thereof, into the state of West Virginia, and did in the state of Kentucky purchase and procure a quantity of intoxicating liquor, to-wit: one quart thereof, contained in bottles, and

28 Seaboard Air Line Ry. Co. v. State of North Carolina, 245 U. S. 298, 38 Sup. Ct. 96.

29 Adams Express Co. v. Commonwealth, 238 U. S. 190, 35 Sup. Ct. 824.

30 International Textbook Co. v. Pigg, 217 U. S. 91, 107, 30 Sup. Ct. 481; Lottery Case, 188 U. S. 321, 325, 23 Sup. Ct. 321, 47 L. ed. 492.

31 Pipe Line Cases, 234 U. S. 548, 560, 34 Sup. Ct. 956.

32 United States v. Chavez, 228 U. S. 525, 532, 33 Sup. Ct. 595.

did then and there board a certain trolley car, being operated by a common carrier corporation engaged in interstate commerce, and by means thereof, did cause himself and the said intoxicating liquor, then upon his person, to be carried and transported in interstate commerce into the state of West Virginia. It also charged that said Hill violated the Act of congress approved March 3d, 1917, commonly known as the Reed Amendment, by thus carrying in interstate commerce from Kentucky into West Virginia a quantity of intoxicating liquor as a beverage for his personal use, the manufacture and sale of intoxicating liquors for beverage purposes being then prohibited by the laws of the state of West Virginia. And further, that the intoxicating liquor was not ordered, purchased, or caused to be transported for scientific, sacramental, medicinal or mechanical purposes.

The indictment was filed in the District Court of the United States for the Southern District of West Virginia, and the court sustained a demurrer and motion to quash the indictment on the ground that the phrase "transported in interstate commerce," as used in the act, was intended to mean and apply only to liquor transported for commercial purposes. This conclusion was reached from a construction of the act when read in the light of other legislation, especially the Wilson Act of 1890 and the Webb-Kenyon Act of 1913.

Under the Criminal Appeals Act, by writ of error the case was brought before the United States Supreme Court to be reviewed, and this court decided that the United States District Court gave to the Reed Amendment too narrow a construction, and reversed the judgment of the latter court.[88] In the opinion in this case the United States Su-

[88] United States v. Hill, 248 U. S. 420, 39 Sup. Ct. 143. See also Minnesota Rate Cases, 230 U. S. 352, 399, 33 Sup. Ct. 729; St. Louis, San Francisco & Tex. Ry. Co. v. Seale, 229 U. S. 156, 33 Sup. Ct. 651; St. Louis, Iron Mountain & Southern Ry. Co. v. Hesterly, 228 U. S. 702, 33 Sup. Ct. 703; Seaboard Air Line Ry. Co. v. Horton, 233 U. S. 492, 34 Sup. Ct. 635.

preme Court says: "In view of the authority of congress over the subject-matter, and the enactment of previous legislation embodied in the Wilson and Webb-Kenyon Laws, we have no question that congress enacted this statute (the Reed Amendment) because of its belief that in states prohibiting the sale and manufacture of intoxicating liquors for beverage purposes the facilities of interstate commerce should be denied to the introduction of intoxicants by means of interstate commerce, except for the limited purposes permitted in the statute which have nothing to do with liquor when used as a beverage. That the state saw fit to permit the introduction of liquor for personal use in limited quantity in no wise interferes with the authority of congress, acting under its plenary power over interstate commerce, to make the prohibition against interstate shipment contained in this act. It may exert its authority, as in the Wilson and Webb-Kenyon Acts, having in view the laws of the state, but it has a power of its own, which in this instance it has exerted in accordance with its view of public policy."

"When congress exerts its authority in a matter within its control, state laws must give way in view of the regulation of the subject-matter by the superior power conferred by the Constitution."

§ 759. The Eighteenth Amendment to the Federal Constitution.—In December, 1917, congress passed a resolution submitting the text of the proposed Eighteenth Amendment to the Federal Constitution to the state legislatures for their approval; and on January 16th, 1919, the necessary three-fourths of the states had ratified the Amendment. It reads as follows: "After one year from the ratification of this article the manufacture, sale, or transportation of intoxicating liquors within, the importation thereof into, or the exportation thereof from the United States and all territory subject to the jurisdiction thereof, for beverage purposes, is hereby prohibited.

"The congress and the several states shall have concurrent power to enforce this article by appropriate legislation.

"This article shall be inoperative unless it shall have been ratified as an amendment to the Constitution by the legislatures of the several states as provided in the Constitution within seven years from the date of the submission hereof to the states by the congress."[84]

§ 760. The "Bone-Dry" Law of the State of Kansas.— The most drastic prohibitory intoxicating liquor law in force in the United States at present (May 1, 1919), is what is known as the "Bone-Dry" Law of the State of Kansas. This statute, which became effective February 14, 1917, provides, among other things, as follows: "It shall be unlawful for any person to keep or have in his possession for personal use or otherwise, any intoxicating liquors, or permit another to have or keep or use intoxicating liquors on any premises owned or controlled by him, or to give away or furnish intoxicating liquors to another, except druggists or registered pharmacists as hereinafter provided. . . . It shall be unlawful for any common carrier, firm or corporation or any other person for hire or without hire to bring or carry into this state, or carry from one place to another within this state, intoxicating liquors for another or for itself or himself, even when intended for personal use; and it shall be unlawful for any common carrier, its agent or employee to deliver any intoxicating liquors that may be in its possession to any person for any purpose whatsoever. . . . It shall be unlawful for any person in this

[84] The movement which had its culmination in the prohibition amendment to the federal constitution and the drastic war legislation may be said to have had its inception in a resolution of the continental congress, adopted in 1777, which reads: "Resolved, that it be recommended to the several legislatures of the United States immediately to pass laws the most effectual for putting an immediate stop to the pernicious practice of distilling grain, by which the most extensive evils are likely to be derived."

state to receive, directly or indirectly intoxicating liquor from a common carrier or other carrier or person, and it shall also be unlawful for any person in this state to possess intoxicating liquors received directly or indirectly from a common carrier, other carrier or person. This section will apply to such liquors intended for personal use as well otherwise and to interstate as well as intrastate carriage." Penalties are expressly provided for violations of any of the aforesaid provisions. The act also expressly excepts from its operation certain transactions by certain persons under certain circumstances. Thus the act does not prevent any regularly ordained minister or regular priest of any church from receiving or possessing wine for communion purposes; nor prohibit and common carrier from receiving such wine for shipment and delivery to such regularly ordained minister or priest for such communion purposes. Nor does the act, under certain circumstances, apply to druggists, or regularly established hospitals, or manufacturers whose products require a certain amount of alcohol for medicinal, mechanical or scientific purposes.

The act also provides that it shall be considered as supplemental to laws in force relating to intoxicating liquors, and furthermore, if for any reason any part of the act shall be held void such holding shall not invalidate any other portion of the act.[85]

[85] Laws of Kansas 1917, c. 215 (House bill No. 432).

Article II. Sexual Crimes Against Decency and Morality.

CHAPTER LX

ADULTERY.

§ 761. Definitions.—At common law adultery was merely a civil wrong and consisted in sexual intercourse by a man with another man's wife.[1] At Roman law this was a crime, both man and woman being principals.[2] The crime was

[1] Commonwealth v. Call, 21 Pick. (Mass.) 509, 32 Am. Dec. 284; State v. Lash, 16 N. J. L. 380, 32 Am. Dec. 397; Anderson v. Commonwealth, 5 Rand. (Va.) 627, 16 Am. Dec. 776; 3 Bl. Comm. 139; 4 Bl. Comm. 65.

[2] State v. Weatherby, 43 Maine 258, 69 Am. Dec. 59; Whart. Crim. L. (11th ed.) § 2063.

against the rights of the husband, and the tendency to adulterate his issue. Neither at common law, nor under the Roman civil law, was it an offense for a married man to have intercourse with a single woman, since this neither violated a husband's rights to his wife's person, nor could force spurious issue on another.

Under the Ecclesiastical law adultery is sexual intercourse by a married person with anyone other than the lawful husband or wife.[3] The crime is statutory in this country, its elements varying with the different wording of the statutes. Some statutes follow the Ecclesiastical law, and both man and woman are guilty,[4] others follow the ecclesiastical definition, but make only the married party guilty,[5] others adhere strictly to the Roman rule.[6] If the statute merely defines the crime as adultery, then, Wharton says, it means sexual connection between a man and a woman, one of whom is lawfully married to a third person, and both are principals.[7]

§ 762. Elements of offense—What must be proved.—There must be evidence of a valid marriage of one party, the requirements and proof of the existence or termination of which are the same as in bigamy.[8]

[3] Bashford v. Wells, 78 Kans. 295, 98 Pac. 663, 18 L. R. A. (N. S.) 580, 16 Ann. Cas. 310; State v. Lash, 16 N. J. L. 380, 32 Am. Dec. 397; Whart. Crim. L. (11th ed.) § 2063.

[4] State v. Hinton, 6 Ala. 864; State v. Wilson, 22 Iowa 364.

[5] Buchanan v. State, 55 Ala. 154; Cook v. State, 11 Ga. 53, 56 Am. Dec. 410; Miner v. People, 58 Ill. 59; State v. Hutchinson, 36 Maine 261; Commonwealth v. Call, 21 Pick. (Mass.) 509, 32 Am. Dec. 284; Helfrich v. Commonwealth, 33 Pa. St. 68, 75 Am. Dec. 579; Swancoat v. State, 4 Tex. App. 105; State v. Fellows, 50 Wis. 65, 6 N. W. 239.

[6] State v. Pearce, 2 Blackf. (Ind.) 318; State v. Armstrong, 4 Minn. 335; State v. Taylor, 58 N. H. 331; State v. Lash, 16 N. J. L. 380, 32 Am. Dec. 397. See also Commonwealth v. Elwell, 2 Met. (Mass.) 190, 35 Am. Dec. 398.

[7] Whart. Crim. L. (11th ed.) § 2066. See also Bashford v. Wells, 78 Kans. 295, 98 Pac. 663, 18 L. R. C. (N. S.) 580, 16 Ann. Cas. 310n.

[8] See Ch. LXI.

It is unnecessary to prove emission in adultery, the rule being the same as in rape.[9]

Intercourse should be proved, but this may be done by circumstantial evidence; as occupying the same bed,[10] living together in the same room for some time,[11] or evidence of cohabitation and birth of children.[12] Evidence of previous improper familiarities is generally held admissible,[13] and sometimes evidence of subsequent familiarities or intercourse.[14] Admissions and confessions may be used in evidence, both as to adultery, or as to prior marriage, for what they are worth.[15]

Intent is an element, but may be inferred from the act.[16] Insanity or a mistake of fact, on the part of one party, may render that one innocent, though the other is guilty.[17] So where a woman supposes herself legally married, she is not guilty of adultery because the marriage is void, on account of a prior existing marriage of the man.[18]

9 Commonwealth v. Hussey, 157 Mass. 415, 32 N. E. 362; Noble v. State, 22 Ohio St. 541; State v. Wheeler, 93 Wash. 538, 161 Pac. 373; Anderson v. State (Tex. Cr.), 193 S. W. 301; State v. McGlammery, 173 N. Car. 148, 91 S. E. 371.

10 Blackman v. State, 36 Ala. 295; Commonwealth v. Mosier, 135 Pa. St. 221, 19 Atl. 934.

11 Richardson v. State, 34 Tex. 142.

12 State v. Chancy, 110 N. Car. 507, 14 S. E. 780.

13 Lawson v. State, 20 Ala. 65, 56 Am. Dec. 182; State v. Bridgman, 49 Vt. 202, 24 Am. Rep. 124.

14 Lawson v. State, 20 Ala. 65, 56 Am. Dec. 182; State v. Bridgman, 49 Vt. 202, 24 Am. Rep. 124. See also Commonwealth v. Nichols, 114 Mass. 285, 19 Am. Rep. 346. In a prosecution for adultery by habitual carnal intercourse, evidence of nine specific acts of sexual intercourse, only three of which were corroborated, was not sufficient to sustain a conviction. Cordill v. State (Tex. Cr.), 201 S. W. 181.

15 State v. Moore, 36 Utah 521, 105 Pac. 293, Ann. Cas. 1912 A, 284n; Whart. Crim. L. (11th ed.) § 2080.

16 Hood v. State, 56 Ind. 263, 26 Am. Rep. 21, 2 Am. Cr. 165; Commonwealth v. Elwell, 2 Met. (Mass.) 190, 35 Am. Dec. 398; State v. Westmoreland, 76 S. Car. 145, 56 S. E. 673, 8 L. R. A. (N. S.) 842; State v. Audette, 81 Vt. 400, 70 Atl. 833, 18 L. R. A. (N. S.) 527, 130 Am. St. 1061.

17 State v. Cutshall, 109 N. Car. 764, 14 S. E. 107, 26 Am. St. 599; Alonzo v. State, 15 Tex. App. 378, 49 Am. Rep. 207.

18 Banks v. State, 96 Ala. 41, 11 So. 469.

§ 763. **Defenses.**—Divorce is a defense, as in bigamy.[19] A divorce which does not give the right to marry again is a defense in adultery.[20] An honest though erroneous belief of the defendant that he had been divorced is no defense.[21] Also it is held that ignorance by the man that the woman is married is no defense if the intercourse was illicit.[22] Nor is a morganatic marriage a defense.[23] Acquittal of one defendant is not a bar to the prosecution of the other.[24] But where one person marries another believing on reasonable ground that such other is unmarried or that a prior spouse of the other is dead, a prosecution for adultery is barred.[25] Acquittal of one party is not a bar to a prosecution of the other.[26]

§ 764. **Witnesses.**—The one with whom the defendant is alleged to have committed the offense is a competent witness for either prosecution or defense,[27] but as an accomplice such testimony must be corroborated.[28] At common law

19 State v. Weatherby, 43 Maine 258, 69 Am. Dec. 59.

20 Haddock v. Haddock, 201 U. S. 562, 50 L. ed. 867, 5 Ann. Cas. 1; Watkins v. Watkins, 125 Ind. 163, 25 N. E. 175, 21 Am. St. 217; In re Ellis Estate, 55 Minn. 401, 56 N. W. 1056, 23 L. R. A. 287n, 43 Am. St. 514; Vanfossen v. State, 37 Ohio St. 317, 41 Am. Rep. 507.

21 Hood v. State, 56 Ind. 263, 26 Am. Rep. 21, 2 Am. Cr. 165; State v. Whitcomb, 52 Iowa 85, 2 N. W. 970, 35 Am. Rep. 258.

22 Commonwealth v. Elwell, 2 Metc. (Mass.) 190, 35 Am. Dec. 398.

23 Reynolds v. United States, 98 U. S. 145, 25 L. ed. 244; United States v. Benner, Fed. Cas. No. 14568, Baldw. (U. S.) 234.

24 Commonwealth v. Bakeman, 131 Mass. 577, 41 Am. Rep. 248.

25 State v. Cutshall, 109 N. Car. 764, 14 S. E. 107, 26 Am. St. 599; Commonwealth v. Thompson, 11 Allen (Mass.) 23, 87 Am. Dec. 685; State v. Audette, 81 Vt. 400, 70 Atl. 833, 18 L. R. A. (N. S.) 527, 130 Am. St. 1061.

26 Woody v. State, 10 Okla. Cr. 322, 136 Pac. 430, 49 L. R. A. (N. S.) 479n.

27 State v. Crowley, 13 Ala. 172; People v. Knapp, 42 Mich. 267, 3 N. W. 927, 36 Am. Rep. 438; State v. Stubbs, 108 N. Car. 774, 13 S. E. 90; United States v. Bredemeyer, 6 Utah 143, 22 Pac. 110.

28 Williams v. State, 86 Ga. 548, 12 S. E. 743; State v. Henderson, 84 Iowa 161, 50 N. W. 758; Merritt v. State, 10 Tex. App. 402; United States v. Bredemeyer, 6 Utah 143, 22 Pac. 110.

neither husband nor wife could be a witness for or against the other in a prosecution for adultery.[29]

§ 765. Complaint of husband or wife.—Under some statutes the prosecution may be had only at the instance of the spouse of the married participant, the offense being considered as primarily against the husband or wife;[30] and the fact that the prosecution was begun by the injured spouse must be proved by the state.[31] Such party may withdraw the proceedings and the prosecution may go no further.[32] But once begun by the spouse, it is unnecessary that such spouse cooperate further, and the court may carry on the proceeding.[33] If such spouse has been divorced before the proceedings, there is no right to prosecute;[34] but a divorce after the proceedings are begun can not affect them.[35]

§ 766. Conviction of other offense.—It has sometimes been held that if there is a failure of proof of marriage of one party, there may be a conviction for fornication.[36]

If the evidence shows a lack of consent of the woman, it is sometimes said the crime is merged into rape,[37] while in other cases it is held the state may elect as to the offense.[38]

29 State v. Burlingham, 15 Maine 104; State v. Armstrong, 4 Minn. 335; State v. Berlin, 42 Mo. 572.

30 State v. Bennett, 31 Iowa 24; State v. Wesie, 17 N. Dak. 567, 118 N. W. 20, 19 L. R. A. (N. S.) 786n; Stone v. State, 12 Okla. Cr. 313, 155 Pac. 701; State v. Ledford, 177 Iowa 528, 159 N. W. 187.

31 State v. Briggs, 68 Iowa 416, 27 N. W. 358.

32 People v. Dalrymple, 55 Mich. 519, 22 N. W. 20.

33 State v. Russell, 90 Iowa 569, 58 N. W. 915, 28 L. R. A. 195n.

34 State v. Bennett, 31 Iowa 24; State v. Wesie, 17 N. Dak. 567, 118 N. W. 20, 19 L. R. A. (N. S.) 786n.

35 State v. Russell, 90 Iowa 569, 58 N. W. 915, 28 L. R. A. 195n.

36 State v. Cowell, 26 N. Car. 231; Respublica v. Roberts, 2 Dall. (Pa.) 124, 1 Yeates 6, 1 L. ed. 316. But see State v. Hinton, 6 Ala. 864; State v. Pearce, 2 Blackf. (Ind.) 318.

37 Commonwealth v. Parr, 5 Watts & S. (Pa.) 345.

38 Commonwealth v. Bakeman, 131 Mass. 577, 41 Am. Rep. 248.

§ 767. Living in adultery—Illicit cohabitation.—The foregoing discussion has been confined to cases in which proof of a single act of intercourse is sufficient to sustain an indictment.

There are some statutes which punish the offense of living in adultery; that is, where a man and woman, not married to each other, live together openly and notoriously as if husband and wife.[39] The theory of such statutes is that there is no offense to the public in illicit intercourse until the element of indecency and public immorality enters. It is usually held that living in the same habitation together is necessary to a conviction under such statutes.[40] The contrary is also held.[41] A single act of illicit intercourse does not constitute this offense, there must be continuous living together.[42] But a single act may be sufficient if there is also cohabitation.[43] And living together adulterously a single day may be enough.[44] Clandestine, though continuous, acts of intercourse do not make the crime, for it is open and notorious living together which constitutes the offense.[45]

Under some statutes, however, it is no defense that the intercourse is secret, or mere habitual illicit intercourse is made adultery. Under these statutes it is not necessary to the offense that either party be married.

39 Richey v. State, 172 Ind. 134, 87 N. E. 1032, 139 Am. St. 362n, 19 Ann. Cas. 654; Carotti v. State, 42 Miss. 334, 97 Am. Dec. 465. See generally note to 113 Am. St. 271.

40 Richey v. State, 172 Ind. 134, 87 N. E. 1032, 139 Am. St. 362n, 19 Ann. Cas. 654n; Bird v. State, 27 Tex. App. 635, 11 S. W. 641, 11 Am. St. 214.

41 Bodiford v. State, 86 Ala. 67, 5 So. 559, 11 Am. St. 20; Winkles v. State, 4 Ga. App. 559, 61 S. E. 1128.

42 Hall v. State, 88 Ala. 236, 7 So. 340, 16 Am. St. 51; Wright v. State, 5 Blackf. (Ind.) 358, 35 Am. Div. 126; Carotti v. State, 42 Miss. 334, 97 Am. Dec. 465; Swancoat v. State, 4 Tex. App. 105.

43 Bird v. State, 27 Tex. App. 635, 11 S. W. 641, 11 Am. St. 214.

44 Hall v. State, 53 Ala. 463.

45 People v. Salmon, 148 Cal. 303, 83 Pac. 42, 2 L. R. A. (N. S.) 1186n, 113 Am. St. 268n; Richey v. State, 172 Ind. 134, 87 N. E. 1032, 139 Am. St. 362n, 19 Ann. Cas. 654; State v. Chandler, 132 Mo. 155, 33 S. W. 797, 53 Am. St. 483; Boswell v. State, 48 Tex. Cr. 47, 85 S. W. 1076, 122 Am. St. 731.

§ 768. Attempt to commit adultery.—In some states where both parties may be convicted for an adulterous act solicitation to commit adultery is punishable as an attempt.[46] The better rule seems to be that it is not an attempt, not an overt act leading to the crime and is not indictable.[47] Especially is this true where the one who solicits is unmarried and under the statute incapable of committing the offense.[48]

§ 769. Presumptions—Burden of proof—Weight and sufficiency.—It is not essential that the state prove that the alleged adulterer's spouse was living at the time of the offense charged; proof that he was alive within one year prior thereto sustains the rebuttable presumption that he still lived.[49] The fact of commencement of the prosecution for adultery by the wife of the defendant is not such an element of the crime charged as to require proof thereof beyond a reasonable doubt.[50] A preponderance of the evidence will suffice.[51] Where there is evidence that at the time of the offense accused was married to one other than his alleged paramour, a variance between the allegation and evidence as to the name of the wife of the accused is not material.[52] The act of adultery may be established by circumstantial evidence.[53] Evidence of illicit conduct prior to the two years has been competent in corroboration.[54] Evidence merely of

[46] State v. Avery, 7 Conn. 266, 18 Am. Dec. 105.

[47] Smith v. Commonwealth, 54 Pa. St. 209, 93 Am. Dec. 686; State v. Butler, 8 Wash. 194, 35 Pac. 1093, 25 L. R. A. 434, 40 Am. St. 900; Cole v. State (Okla. Cr.), 166 Pac. 1115.

[48] State v. Goodrich, 84 Wis. 359, 54 N. W. 577.

[49] Simmons v. State, 79 Tex. Cr. 341, 184 S. W. 226.

[50] State v. Ledford, 177 Iowa 528, 159 N. W. 187.

[51] O'Hern v. State, 12 Okla. Cr. 505, 159 Pac. 938.

[52] Wong Goon Let v. United States, 245 Fed. 745, 158 C. C. A. 147.

[53] Reinhardt v. State, 101 Nebr. 667, 164 N. W. 654.

[54] State v. McGlammery, 173 N. Car. 148, 91 S. E. 371.

the disposition of the accused to indulge in the act of sexual intercourse and opportunity to do so are not sufficient to sustain a conviction.[55] The indictment need not allege the name of the spouse of the accused. Even if the name is alleged it may be treated as surplusage.[56]

[55] State v. Riley, 177 Iowa 313, 158 N. W. 570.

[56] Simmons v. State, 79 Tex. Cr. 341, 184 S. W. 226.

CHAPTER LXI

BIGAMY OR POLYGAMY.

§ 770. Definition and history.—The crime of bigamy or polygamy consists in marrying one person when already legally married to another.[1] In earliest times bigamy was an ecclesiastical offense, but by statute, 1 James I, chapter 11, it was made a felony. In our states the offense is statutory, though one early decision holds it a common-law misdemeanor.[2]

§ 771. Elements of offense.—The gist of the offense is a marriage, while there is in existence a valid prior marriage undissolved by death of the other spouse, presumption of death or divorce, with criminal intent.

Each of these elements, the second marriage, the valid prior marriage, and the intent to do an act prohibited by law,

1 Cannon v. United States, 116 U. S. 55, 29 L. ed. 561; Murphy v. Ramsey, 114 U. S. 15, 29 L. ed. 47; Nelms v. State, 84 Ga. 466, 10 S. E. 1087, 20 Am. St. 377; State v. Stewart, 194 Mo. 345, 92 S. W. 878, 112 Am. St. 529, 5 Ann. Cas. 963. See generally note to 126 Am. St. 201-219.

2 State v. Darrah, Houst. Cr. C. (Del.) 321; State v. Burns, 90 N. Car. 707.

must concur to support conviction. Bigamous cohabitation is not an element of the crime but statutes frequently punish this as a separate offense, and cohabitation under the second marriage may be punished as adultery.[3]

§ 772. **Jurisdiction.**—The prosecution must be where the crime, that is, the second marriage, was committed; and one can not be prosecuted in one state for a bigamous marriage entered into in another.[4] But under a statute which punishes bigamous cohabitation, it does not matter whether the second marriage was contracted in the state;[5] and there are also statutes punishing the leaving of the state with intent to contract a bigamous marriage, which intent is carried out.[6]

§ 773. **Valid prior marriage.**—A valid prior marriage is an essential element of the crime, a part of the corpus delicti,[7] and usually the part with which the evidence is most concerned and over which questions of law most frequently arise. It is necessary, unless common-law marriages are recognized, to show that the parties declared before some authorized person, that they took each other for man and wife, and it is immaterial whether they afterward cohabited,[8] or had sexual intercourse.[9] The law of the place where the marriage took place determines its validity.[10]

[3] Owens v. State, 94 Ala. 97, 10 So. 669; Hildreth v. State, 19 Tex. App. 195.

[4] Johnson v. Commonwealth, 86 Ky. 122, 5 S. W. 365, 9 Am. St. 269; State v. Ray, 151 N. Car. 710, 66 S. E. 204, 134 Am. St. 1005, 19 Ann. Cas. 566.

[5] State v. Stewart, 194 Mo. 345, 92 S. W. 878, 112 Am. St. 529, 5 Ann. Cas. 963. But see State v. Ray, 151 N. Car. 710, 66 S. E. 204, 134 Am. St. 1005, 19 Ann. Cas. 566.

[6] Rex v. Brinkley, 14 Ont. L. R. 434, 10 Ann. Cas. 407.

[7] Dumas v. State, 14 Tex. App. 464, 46 Am. Rep. 241.

[8] State v. Patterson, 24 N. Car. 346, 38 Am. Dec. 699.

[9] Commonwealth v. Lucas, 158 Mass. 81, 32 N. E. 1033; Gise v. Commonwealth, 81 Pa. St. 428.

[10] Scoggins v. State, 32 Ark. 205; State v. Johnson, 12 Minn. 476, 93 Am. Dec. 241.

Proof that the parties lived together and held themselves out as husband and wife and had children born to them is sufficient in some states,[11] and insufficient in others. It is usually sufficient to show a marriage prima facie valid.[12] Where residents of a state whose marriage would there be illegal, are married in another state, that fact alone does not render the marriage illegal in the state of their residence, so that a subsequent marriage there is not bigamous.[13] Where statutes prescribing the form of marriage merely impose punishment for noncompliance with the form and do not make the marriage illegal, a second marriage by one of the parties is bigamy.[14]

The prior marriage must be proved beyond a reasonable doubt in a prosecution for bigamy, and the presumption in favor of marriage and the legitimacy of children, which arises when the question concerns the distribution of an estate, is very much weakened and overcome by conflicting presumptions, among them that of innocence, and of the validity of the second marriage.[15]

§ 774. Voidable prior marriage.—It is no defense that the prior marriage was voidable, if it had not been avoided prior to the second marriage, for a voidable marriage subsists until avoided.[16] So if one of the parties was under the age of consent and has not avoided the marriage, a subsequent mar-

[11] State v. Gonce, 79 Mo. 600, 4 Am. Cr. 68. But see Hiler v. People, 156 Ill. 511, 41 N. E. 181, 47 Am. St. 221.

[12] Murphy v. State, 50 Ga. 150; Taylor v. State, 52 Miss. 84, 2 Am. Cr. 13; State v. Abbey, 29 Vt. 60, 67 Am. Dec. 754; Rex v. Hind, Russ. & Ry. 253.

[13] Commonwealth v. Lane, 113 Mass. 458, 18 Am. Rep. 509.

[14] Robinson v. Commonwealth, 6 Bush (Ky.) 309; State v. Parker, 106 N. Car. 711, 11 S. E. 517; Carmichael v. State, 12 Ohio St. 553.

[15] Whart. Crim. L. (11th ed.) § 2028. See also State v. McClelland, 152 Iowa 704, 133 N. W. 111; Morville v. State, 63 Tex. Cr. 553, 141 S. W. 102; Bryan v. State, 63 Tex. Cr. 200, 139 S. W. 981.

[16] Cooley v. State, 55 Ala. 162; People v. Baker, 76 N. Y. 78, 32 Am. Rep. 274; State v. Cone, 86 Wis. 498, 87 N. W. 50; 1 East P. C. 466.

riage by the other party is bigamous.[17] If the party under age subsequently marries before the former marriage became binding, such subsequent marriage annuls the former and is not bigamous.[18] And where a marriage by parties under age of consent is made valid only when they cohabit after becoming of age, a second marriage is not bigamous unless such cohabitation is shown.[19] If a marriage ceremony performed without license or with a void license is followed by cohabitation, it is so far validated, as to form a foundation for a bigamy prosecution.[20] Nor is fraud in the previous marriage a good defense to the charge of bigamy, if the parties later lived together as husband and wife.[21]

§ 775. Void previous marriage.—It is a complete defense to a charge of bigamy that the prior marriage was absolutely void.[22] So where a statute makes void a marriage with a deceased wife's sister, a subsequent marriage is not bigamous.[23] If the ceremony is performed without license or proper ceremonies and is not followed by cohabitation, then a subsequent marriage by one of the parties is not bigamous.[24] So where one contracts a bigamous second marriage, and subsequently the first marriage is dissolved by death or divorce, and he marries a third time, the third marriage is not bigamous, since the second one was void.[25] If the second wife was recognized after the termination of the first marriage, then

[17] Cooley v. State, 55 Ala. 162; Walls v. State, 32 Ark. 565; People v. Beevers, 99 Cal. 286, 33 Pac. 844; People v. Slack, 15 Mich. 193.

[18] Shafher v. State, 20 Ohio 1.

[19] People v. Bennett, 39 Mich. 208.

[20] People v. McQuaid, 85 Mich. 123, 48 N. W. 161. See also note to 126 Am. St. 215, 216, 217.

[21] Hayes v. People, 25 N. Y. 390, 24 How. Pr. 452, 5 Park Cr. 325, 82 Am. Dec. 364.

[22] People v. McQuaid, 85 Mich. 123, 48 N. W. 161; Shafher v. State, 20 Ohio 1; Sunderland's Case, 2 Lewin 111.

[23] Reg. v. Chadwick, 11 Q. B. 205, 2 Cox Cr. C. 381.

[24] People v. McQuaid, 85 Mich. 123, 48 N. W. 161; Weinberg v. State, 25 Wis. 370.

[25] Halbrook v. State, 34 Ark. 511, 36 Am. Rep. 17; People v. Chase, 27 Hun (N. Y.) 256.

in some jurisdictions he could be convicted of bigamy in the third marriage.[26] In many jurisdictions a consensual marriage is held invalid, and proof of such marriage will not support a conviction of bigamy.[27] Mistake in believing a prior marriage invalid is a mistake of law and not a defense.[28]

§ 776. Divorce from first marriage.—If the prior marriage was terminated prior to the date of the second by a divorce which in the state of the former would entitle the defendant to remarry, the second marriage is not bigamous.[29] Generally speaking, a divorce valid as to one of the parties terminates the marriage as to the other and should be recognized everywhere.[30] But if one is indicted in one state for marrying a second time in that state and his first wife is alive, it is not a defense that he was divorced from her in another state unless such divorce is valid in the state of the former.[31] Where a statute prohibits the party for whose fault the divorce was granted from marrying again, his second marriage in that state will not be bigamous unless so declared by statute.[32] Nor is it bigamy for him to remarry in another state unless he does so merely to avoid the laws of the state in which he resides.[33] If a divorce decree is invalid for want of jurisdiction of the court which rendered it, it is no defense to a charge of bigamy.[34] According to the weight of author-

[26] Hayes v. People, 25 N. Y. 390, 24 How. Pr. 452, 5 Park Cr. 325, 82 Am. Dec. 364.

[27] Denison v. Denison, 35 Md. 361.

[28] Staley v. State, 89 Nebr. 701, 131 N. W. 1028, 34 L. R. A. (N. S.) 613.

[29] State v. Weatherby, 43 Maine 258, 69 Am. Dec. 59; Baker v. People, 2 Hill (N. Y.) 325; Lolley's Case, 2 Clark & F. 567.

[30] People v. Baker, 76 N. Y. 78, 32 Am. Rep. 274.

[31] Whart. Confl. L., § 224; Whart. Crim. L. (11th ed.), § 2026. See also People v. Faber, 92 N. Y. 146, 1 N. Y. Cr. 115, 44 Am. Rep. 357.

[32] Commonwealth v. Richardson, 126 Mass. 34, 30 Am. Rep. 647; Crawford v. State, 73 Miss. 172, 18 So. 848, 35 L. R. A. 224.

[33] Commonwealth v. Lane, 113 Mass. 458, 18 Am. Rep. 509.

[34] Tucker v. People, 122 Ill. 583, 13 N. E. 809; Davis v. Commonwealth, 13 Bush (Ky.) 318; Van Fossen v. State, 37 Ohio St. 317.

ity the fact that one believed in good faith he had been lawfully divorced from his first wife, when in fact he had not, is no defense.[85] The statute requires persons who have been married to know that the first marriage has been terminated before entering into another. A divorce from the first marriage obtained after the second marriage, is no defense.[86]

§ 777. Death of former spouse—Proof and presumptions. —Most statutes exempt from prosecution for bigamy a marriage where the first spouse has been absent seven years and the other has no knowledge of the absent one being alive during that time. This exception is a part of the common law.[87] The prosecution must therefore prove that the first spouse was alive at the time of the second marriage. If the proof shows such spouse alive within less than seven years before the second marriage, then the question becomes one of fact for the jury and there may be presumptions of fact which will overcome that of continuance of life, as where when last heard of the spouse was mortally ill, and the intervening time has been such that the presumption of innocence may prevail.[88] After seven years' absence the prosecution must prove not only that the first spouse was alive within that period, but that the defendant had knowledge of that fact.[89]

85 Russell v. State, 66 Ark. 185, 49 S. W. 821, 74 Am. St. 78; People v. Spoor, 235 Ill. 230, 85 N. E. 207, 126 Am. St. 197, 14 Ann. Cas. 638; Hood v. State, 56 Ind. 263, 26 Am. Rep. 21, 2 Am. Cr. 165; Rex v. Brinkley, 14 Ont. L. R. 434, 10 Ann. Cas. 407, note.

86 Baker v. People, 2 Hill (N. Y.) 325.

87 Eubanks v. Banks, 34 Ga. 407; Barber v. State, 50 Md. 161.

88 Whart. Crim. L. (11th ed.), § 2048. See also People v. Fellen, 58 Cal. 218, 41 Am. Rep. 258; Squire v. State, 46 Ind. 459; Commonwealth v. McGrath, 140 Mass. 296, 6 N. E. 515; Dunlap v. State, 126 Tenn. 415, 150 S. W. 86, 41 L. R. A. (N. S.) 1061, Ann. Cas. 1913E, 264n; Reg. v. Lumley, L. R. 1 C. C. 196, 11 Cox Cr. C. 274.

89 Reg. v. Dane, 1 Fost. & F. 323; Reg. v. Curgenwen, L. R. 1 C. C. 1, 10 Cox Cr. C. 152.

Continuous absence for the statutory period without knowledge on the part of the other spouse, is a complete defense.[40] An honest belief in the death of the other party has often been held not a defense,[41] but some cases hold that it is, if based on reasonable grounds.[42]

§ 778. **Proof of marriage or divorce.**—We have stated that in a bigamy prosecution marriage must be proved beyond a reasonable doubt. In many jurisdictions this must be done by direct evidence.[43] In some jurisdictions proof of cohabitation and a holding out as husband and wife is sufficient.[44] An official certificate of the record is usually sufficient evidence,[45] with identification of the parties.[46] Marriage may also be proved by the testimony of a witness present at the ceremony,[47] and the one who performed the ceremony or the party to the bigamous marriage may testify.[48]

It seems to be the present controlling rule that proof of a marriage in fact in another state, followed by cohabitation, is sufficient, without further proof as to its validity.[49]

[40] People v. Spoor, 235 Ill. 230, 85 N. E. 207, 126 Am. St. 197, 14 Ann. Cas. 638.

[41] Dotson v. State, 62 Ala. 141, 34 Am. Rep. 2; Reynolds v. State, 58 Nebr. 49, 78 N. W. 483, 11 Am. Cr. 159; State v. Ackerly, 79 Vt. 69, 64 Atl. 450, 118 Am. St. 940, 8 Ann. Cas. 1103; Reg. v. Bennett, 14 Cox Cr. C. 45.

[42] Reg. v. Tolson, L. R. 23 Q. B. Div. 168, 16 Cox Cr. C. 629, 8 Am. Cr. 59, 8 Eng. Rul. Cas. 16.

[43] Green v. State, 21 Fla. 403, 58 Am. Rep. 670; Lowery v. People, 172 Ill. 466, 50 N. E. 165, 64 Am. St. 50; Rogers v. State Tex. Cr.), 204 S. W. 222.

[44] Bynon v. State, 117 Ala. 80, 23 So. 640, 67 Am. St. 163; Halbrook v. State, 34 Ark. 511, 36 Am. Rep. 17; State v. Gonce, 79 Mo. 600, 4 Am. Cr. 68; Dumas v. State, 14 Tex. App. 464, 46 Am. Rep. 241.

[45] Commonwealth v. Hayden, 163 Mass. 453, 40 N. E. 846, 28 L. R. A. 318, 47 Am. St. 468; Dumas v. State, 14 Tex. App. 464, 46 Am. Rep. 241; Whart. Crim. Ev., §§ 169 et seq.; Whart. Crim. L. (11th ed.), §§ 2038-2041.

[46] Reg. v. Hawes, 1 Den. 270; Reg. v. Tolson, 4 Fost. & F. 103.

[47] State v. Williams, 20 Iowa 98; Commonwealth v. Dill, 156 Mass. 226, 30 N. E. 1016.

[48] Commonwealth v. Hayden, 163 Mass. 453, 40 N. E. 846, 28 L. R. A. 318, 47 Am. St. 468.

[49] Miles v. United States, 103 U. S. 304, 26 L. ed. 481; Dale v. State, 88 Ga. 552, 15 S. E. 287; Whart. Crim. L. (11th ed.), §§ 2028-2038.

Admissions of the defendant as to the prior marriage, made during cohabitation under such marriage, have been held sufficient evidence of its validity.[50] Registry is the best evidence of a foreign marriage,[51] but testimony of witnesses may be enough,[52] or even proof by cohabitation and recognition, by admissions and conduct, where consensual marriages are recognized,[53] but some courts do not recognize this as sufficient proof.[54]

Divorce should be proved by the record.[55]

§ 779. Second marriage.—The attempted second marriage may be in any form or by any words which would constitute a good marriage, except for the bar of the first marriage. A common-law agreement followed by cohabitation may be sufficient in some states.[56] Since the offense consists in appearing to contract a second marriage and thus bringing the other party into marital intercourse, it is not a defense that the second marriage would have been void or voidable on other grounds than bigamy, as where it was fraudulently

[50] Williams v. State, 54 Ala. 131, 25 Am. Rep. 665; State v. Seals, 16 Ind. 352; Commonwealth v. Jackson, 11 Bush (Ky.) 679, 21 Am. Rep. 225, 1 Am. Cr. 74; State v. Libby, 44 Maine 469, 69 Am. Dec. 115; Wolverton v. State, 16 Ohio 173, 47 Am. Dec. 373; State v. Moore, 36 Utah 521, 105 Pac. 293, Ann. Cas. 1912A, 284. But see State v. Roswell, 6 Conn. 446.

[51] State v. Dooris, 40 Conn. 145; Whart. Crim. L. (11th ed.), § 2042.

[52] State v. Kean, 10 N. H. 347, 34 Am. Dec. 162; Wolverton v. State, 16 Ohio 173, 47 Am. Dec. 373; Reg. v. Mainwaring, 7 Cox Cr. C. 192.

[53] Miles v. United States, 103 U. S. 304, 26 L. ed. 481; Lowery v. People, 172 Ill. 466, 50 N. E. 165, 64 Am. St. 50, 11 Am. Cr. 169; State v. Wylde, 110 N. Car. 500, 15 S. E. 5; Lee v. State, 44 Tex. Cr. 354, 72 S. W. 1005, 61 L. R. A. 904.

[54] Hiler v. People, 156 Ill. 511, 41 N. E. 181, 47 Am. St. 221.

[55] State v. Barrow, 31 La. Ann. 691; Commonwealth v. Boyer, 7 Allen (Mass.) 306; State v. Herren, 173 N. Car. 801, 92 S. E. 596 (mere offering by the accused of a decree of divorce from his first wife in another state is not sufficient to establish, ipso facto, the validity of the divorce. The question as to its validity is one of fact for the jury).

[56] People v. Mendenhall, 119 Mich. 404, 78 N. W. 325, 75 Am. St. 408; Draughn v. State, 12 Okla. Cr. 479, 158 Pac. 890.

performed,[57] or the parties were within prohibited degrees of kin,[58] or that the marriage was one between a negro and a white, prohibited by law,[59] or it would have been voidable for a technical defect.[60] But the ceremony may be so imperfect, that if not followed by cohabitation, it will not sustain a conviction.[61]

§ 780. Intent.—A guilty intent is an element of the crime, but an intent to do an act prohibited by law is sufficient, and a religious belief that polygamy is proper is not a defense.[62]

A mistake of law is not a defense, as we have seen, since an honest belief in the invalidity of a former marriage,[63] or in the validity of a divorce,[64] does not avail a defendant. It has been held that a bona fide belief that the other party procured a divorce in another state, is a mistake of fact and a defense.[65]

English courts hold that a mistaken belief in the death of the first spouse, based on reasonable grounds, is a defense, as this is a mistake of fact.[66] Most United States courts are inclined to hold one guilty in such a case, and intent immaterial as in police wrongs.[67] It is said that the consequences

[57] Hayes v. People, 25 N. Y. 390, 24 How. Pr. 452, 5 Park Cr. 325, 82 Am. Dec. 364.

[58] Reg. v. Allen, L. R. 1 C. C. 367, 12 Cox Cr. C. 193.

[59] People v. Brown, 34 Mich. 339, 22 Am. Rep. 531.

[60] Robinson v. Commonwealth, 6 Bush (Ky.) 309; Carmichael v. State, 12 Ohio St. 553.

[61] Kopke v. People, 43 Mich. 41, 4 N. W. 551.

[62] Church of Jesus Christ v. United States, 136 U. S. 1, 3 L. ed. 478; Reynolds v. United States, 98 U. S. 145, 25 L. ed. 244.

[63] Staley v. State, 89 Nebr. 701, 131 N. W. 1028, 34 L. R. A. (N. S.) 613.

[64] People v. Spoor, 235 Ill. 230, 85 N. E. 207, 126 Am. St. 197, 14 Ann. Cas. 638.

[65] Squire v. State, 46 Ind. 459.

[66] Reg. v. Tolson, L. R. 23 Q. B. Div. 168, 16 Cox Cr. C. 629, 8 Am. Cr. 59, 8 Eng. Rul. Cas. 16.

[67] Cornett v. Commonwealth, 134 Ky. 613, 121 S. W. 424, 21 Ann. Cas. 399; Commonwealth v. Hayden, 163 Mass. 453, 40 N. E. 846, 28 L. R. A. 318, 47 Am. St. 468; State v. Zichfeld, 23 Nev. 304, 46 Pac. 802, 34 L. R. A. 784, 62 Am. St. 800; State v. Ackerly, 79 Vt. 69, 64 Atl. 450, 118 Am. St. 940, 8 Ann. Cas. 1103. See also Reg. v. Bennett, 14 Cox Cr. C. 45.

to society and the innocent party are so injurious that the law requires positive evidence of death before one contracts a second marriage. Mistaken belief, however, may mitigate the punishment.[68]

§ 781. Other defenses.—Actual duress is a defense, but it is not duress that one who seduced a girl married her to escape prosecution.[69]

The statute of limitations begins to run from the date of the second marriage unless bigamous cohabitation is made a crime.[70] Insanity may be a defense.[71]

§ 782. Polygamy.—At common law the offense now called bigamy was first known as polygamy. Today the terms are practically interchangeable. Congress passed in 1882 the Edmunds Act, which punishes not only marrying more than one woman, but also cohabiting with more than one woman, and holding them out as wives, creating a continuous offense.[72]

68 Russell v. State, 66 Ark. 185, 49 S. W. 821, 74 Am. St. 78.

69 Medrano v. State, 32 Tex. Cr. 214, 22 S. W. 684, 40 Am. St. 775.

70 State v. Sloan, 55 Iowa 217, 7 N. W. 516; Gise v. Commonwealth, 81 Pa. St. 428. See also note to 93 Am. Dec. 256.

71 Martin v. State, 100 Ark. 189, 139 S. W. 1122.

72 Ex parte Snow, 120 U. S. 274, 30 L. ed. 658; Cannon v. United State, 116 U. S. 55, 29 L. ed. 561.

CHAPTER LXII

FORNICATION.

§ 785. Definition.—At common law fornication is illict sexual intercourse between a man and an unmarried woman, and was not indictable.[1] By the ecclesiastical law any illicit sexual intercourse on the part of an unmarried person was fornication and punishable by ecclesiastical courts.[2] By statute in many states fornication is a misdemeanor, in most states the offense being distinguished from adultery because committed by an unmarried person.[3] In Georgia all illicit intercourse is made criminal, it being adultery if both parties are married, adultery and fornication if one only is married, fornication if both are single.[4] The punishable common-law offense was that of the habitual living together of a man and woman, neither of whom was married.[5] It is thus seen

[1] Richey v. State, 172 Ind. 134, 87 N. E. 1032, 139 Am. St. 362n, 19 Ann. Cas. 654; State v. Lash, 16 N. J. L. 380, 32 Am. Dec. 397; Anderson v. Commonwealth, 5 Rand. (Va.) 627, 16 Am. Dec. 776; Reg. v. Pierson, 1 Salk. 382, 2 Ld. Raym. 1197.

[2] Richey v. State, 172 Ind. 134, 87 N. E. 1032, 139 Am. St. 362n, 19 Ann. Cas. 654; Territory v. Whitcomb, 1 Mont. 359, 25 Am. Rep. 740; State v. Lash, 16 N. J. L. 380, 32 Am. Dec. 397; Reg. v. Pierson, 1 Salk. 382, 2 Ld. Raym 1197.

[3] Richey v. State, 172 Ind. 134, 87 N. E. 1032, 139 Am. St. 362n, 19 Ann. Cas. 654.

[4] Bennett v. State, 103 Ga. 66, 29 S. E. 919, 68 Am. St. 77.

[5] Cosgrove v. State, 37 Tex. Cr. 249, 39 S. W. 367, 66 Am. St. 802.

that the common-law distinction between fornication and adultery is that the former is intercourse by a man with an unmarried woman, the latter intercourse by a man with a married woman.

§ 786. **What must be shown to convict.**—The prosecution must show the parties are not married to each other.[6] Illicit intercourse must be shown in the same manner as in adultery. The proof must make a case under the particular statute.

§ 787. **Bastardy.**—Under statutes in most states, there is a proceeding in the name of the state, instituted by the mother of a bastard child to compel the putative father to support it. These proceedings are in their nature more civil than criminal.[7] In some states bastardy is punishable together with fornication,[8] and it has been said that bastardy is a misdemeanor at common law,[9] the offense being complete when a child is begotten.[10] The prosecuting witness in bastardy proceedings is a party to the proceedings.[11] The mother of a bastard child may compromise and settle with the reputed father her claim for damages against him, but to preclude the prosecution of a bastardy proceeding the contract must be fair, free from fraud, and founded upon a sufficient consideration.[12] In a bastardy proceeding the

6 Territory v. Whitcomb, 1 Mont. 359, 25 Am. Rep. 740.

7 State v. Addington, 143 N. Car. 683, 57 S. E. 398, 11 Ann. Cas. 314n; People v. Wunsch, 198 Ill. App. 437 (a bastardy proceeding is criminal in form but civil in effect). See also, Cogburn v. State (Ala. App.), 76 So. 473; State v. Waltermath, 162 Wis. 602, 156 N. W. 946.

8 Gorman v. Commonwealth, 124 Pa. St. 536, 17 Atl. 26. In Alabama, upon a conviction of bastardy, the court may sentence the defendant to 12 months imprisonment at hard labor for the county. Grace v. State (Ala. App.), 77 So. 978.

9 Coleman v. Frum, 8 Scam. (Ill.) 378; State v. Phelps, 9 Md. 21.

10 Sheay v. State, 74 Md. 52, 21 Atl. 607; State v. Wynne, 116 N. Car. 981, 21 S. E. 35.

11 People v. Kirby, 199 Ill. App. 91.

12 Burr v. Phares (W. Va.), 94 S. E. 30.

prosecutrix is a competent witness as to the paternity of the child.[13] Moreover, the statement of the prosecutrix herself that she continued to accuse the defendant during her travail has been held admissible.[14] Evidence of the mother's previous unchastity is admissible, but it must be restricted to her credibility and to the question of the paternity of the child.[15]

§ 788. Presumption of legitimacy—Burden of proof.—The law presumes a child born in wedlock to be legitimate; but such presumption may be rebutted by facts and circumstances showing that the husband could not have been the father, as that he was impotent or could not have had access.[16] Where access is either admitted or opportunity for it is reasonably certain from the evidence, the presumption of legitimacy will prevail, unless the jury are convinced that it was impossible for the husband to have been the father of the child.[17] The presumption that a child born of a married woman is legitimate is not to be rebutted by circumstances which only create suspicion, but it may be wholly removed by evidence of incompetency.[18] It has been held, however, that where the evidence shows that the plaintiff's mother was legally married to a man, and that there was opportunity for procreation within the period of gestation, a conclusive presumption is raised that the plaintiff is his legitimate son.[19] On the other hand it has been held that the presumption of legitimacy may be overcome by sufficient evidence of incompetence, entire absence, absence during the

13 State v. Chambers, 37 S. Dak. 555, 159 N. W. 113.

14 Akeson v. Doidge, 225 Mass. 574, 114 N. E. 726.

15 State v. Chambers, 37 S. Dak. 555, 159 N. W. 113.

16 West v. Redmond, 171 N. Car. 742, 88 S. E. 341; State v. Woods, 102 Kans. 499, 170 Pac. 986, L. R. A. 1918 C, 889.

17 Wilson v. Wilson, 174 Ky. 771, 193 S. W. 7.

18 People v. Woodson, 29 Cal. App. 531, 156 Pac. 378; Craig v. Shea (Nebr.), 168 N. W. 135.

19 Vanover v. Steele, 173 Ky. 114, 190 S. W. 667.

period of begetting, or presence with proof of no sexual intercourse.[20] Declarations of the wife that her child, born in lawful wedlock, is not the child of her husband are inadmissible.[21] But where the mother is a feme sole, evidence is admissible which shows intercourse between her and other men about the time the child was conceived.[22]

20 In re Walker's Estate (Cal.), 168 Pac. 689.

21 Croom v. Whitehead, 174 N. Car. 305, 93 S. E. 854.

22 Samples v. State (Ala. App.), 74 So. 758.

CHAPTER LXIII

INCEST.

§ 790. **Definition.**—Incest is carnal connection between a man and woman lineally related to each other, or collaterally related in such a degree that marriage between them is prohibited by law.[1] It is said that this, like adultery, was an offense punishable only by the ecclesiastical law, not by the common law.[2] Since the degrees within which marriage is permitted are regulated by statute, and vary in different jurisdictions, it has been held necessary to show that the parties are not married, for if contracted out of the state, the marriage might be valid.[3]

The statutory relationship includes illegitimate kinship,[4]

[1] Taylor v. State, 110 Ga. 150, 35 S. E. 161; State v. Hertges, 55 Minn. 464, 57 N. W. 205; Dinkey v. Commonwealth, 17 Pa. St. 126, 55 Am. Dec. 542. See also Daniels v. People, 6 Mich. 381; note to 111 Am. St. 19-31.

[2] 4 Bl. Comm. 604. See also, State v. Smith, 30 La. Ann. 846; State v. Keesler, 78 N. Car. 469, 2 Am. Cr. 331.

[3] State v. Fritts, 48 Ark. 66, 2 S. W. 256. But see State v. Nakashima, 62 Wash. 686, 114 Pac. 894, Ann. Cas. 1912D, 220.

[4] Baker v. State, 30 Ala. 521; Lipham v. State, 125 Ga. 52, 53 S. E. 817, 114 Am. St. 181, 5 Ann. Cas. 67; State v. Schaunhurst, 34 Iowa 547; Cecil v. Commonwealth, 140 Ky. 717, 131 S. W. 781, Ann. Cas. 1912B, 501; People v. Jenness, 5 Mich. 305; People v. Lake, 110 N. Y. 61, 17 N. E. 146, 6 Am. St. 344.

and kinship by the halfblood,[5] or relationship by affinity, so as to make intercourse with a sister-in-law criminal.[6] In other jurisdictions relationship by affinity is not included.[7]

But a relationship dependent on marriage, exists only while the marriage endures, thus it is held there can not be incest with a step-daughter unless her mother is the living wife of the defendant,[8] although other courts hold relationship by affinity continues so long as there are living issue of the marriage.[9] Relation by marriage extends only to the spouse's blood relations, thus, one is not related by affinity to his wife's brother's wife.[10]

The reasons for punishing incest are said to be that proper propagation of the race demands parents of different families, and that the practice is contrary to natural feeling.[11]

§ 791. **Elements of offense.**—It is as unnecessary to prove emission as in case of rape.[12] It is usually held that mere proof of marriage is sufficient without showing carnal intercourse;[13] and in no jurisdiction is more than one act of intercourse essential.[14]

It is usually held that the crime involves mutual consent, that both parties are guilty of the offense, and that both

[5] State v. Reedy, 44 Kans. 190, 24 Pac. 66; People v. Jenness, 5 Mich. 305; Shelley v. State, 95 Tenn. 152, 31 S. W. 492, 49 Am. St. 926; Simon v. State, 31 Tex. Cr. 186, 20 S. W. 399, 716, 37 Am. St. 802.

[6] Stewart v. State, 39 Ohio St. 152.

[7] State v. Tucker, 174 Ind. 715, 93 N. E. 3, Ann. Cas. 1913A, 100.

[8] Noble v. State, 22 Ohio St. 541; McGrew v. State, 13 Tex. App. 340.

[9] Tagert v. State, 143 Ala. 88, 39 So. 293, 111 Am. St. 17.

[10] Chinn v. State, 47 Ohio St. 575, 26 N. E. 986, 11 L. R. A. 630.

[11] Whart. Crim. L. (11th ed.), § 2096n.

[12] State v. Judd, 132 Iowa 296, 109 N. W. 892, 11 Ann. Cas. 91. But see Noble v. State, 22 Ohio St. 541, later modified by statute.

[13] State v. Schaunhurst, 34 Iowa 547; Simon v. State, 31 Tex. Cr. 186, 20 S. W. 399, 716, 37 Am. St. 802.

[14] Barnhouse v. State, 31 Ohio St. 39; Hollingsworth v. State, 80 Tex. Cr. 299, 189 S. W. 488.

must be proved guilty to sustain the indictment,[15] although both need not be jointly indicted.[16] If the statute is so worded, the prosecution must prove that the offense was committed, knowing the relationship.[17] Consent of the woman is not a defense,[18] nor the fact that she is a prostitute.[19]

§ 792. **Incest and rape.**—It is generally held that consent is necessary to incest, and that if force was used by the man, the act was rape, and there can be no conviction for incest.[20] But there are other cases holding consent of both parties not necessary.[21] And it is held that under an indictment for rape, where force was not shown, a conviction of incest may be sustained.[22] If the woman be under age of consent, the offense is rape, not incest.[23]

§ 793. **Corroboration of evidence of female.**—By corroboration is meant evidence other than that of the prosecutrix which, in itself and without the aid of her evidence, tends

15 People v. Patterson, 102 Cal. 239, 36 Pac. 436; People v. Turner, 260 Ill. 84, 102 N. E. 1036, Ann. Cas. 1914D, 144; Baumer v. State, 49 Ind. 544, 19 Am. Rep. 691, 1 Am. Cr. 354; State v. Thomas, 53 Iowa 214, 4 N. W. 908; Delany v. People, 10 Mich. 241; State v. Jarvis, 20 Ore. 437, 26 Pac. 302, 23 Am. St. 341. See also note to 21 Ann. Cas. 1257.

16 People v. Patterson, 102 Cal. 239, 36 Pac. 436; Yeoman v. State, 21 Nebr. 171, 31 N. W. 669.

17 Baumer v. State, 49 Ind. 544, 19 Am. Rep. 691, 1 Am. Cr. 354; State v. Rennick, 127 Iowa 294, 103 N. W. 159, 4 Ann. Cas. 568; Simon v. State, 31 Tex. Cr. 186, 20 S. W. 399, 716, 37 Am. St. 802.

18 Schoenfeldt v. State, 30 Tex. App. 695, 18 S. W. 640,

19 State v. Winningham, 124 Mo. 423, 27 S. W. 1107.

20 Raiford v. State, 68 Ga. 672; State v. Thomas, 53 Iowa 214, 4 N. W. 908; People v. Rouse, 2 Mich. N. P. 209; People v. Harriden, 1 Park. Cr. (N. Y.) 344; Noble v. State, 22 Ohio St. 541; State v. Winslow, 30 Utah 403, 85 Pac. 433, 8 Ann. Cas. 908.

21 People v. Barnes, 2 Idaho 161, 9 Pac. 532; State v. Nugent, 20 Wash. 522, 56 Pac. 25, 72 Am. St. 133.

22 Commonwealth v. Goodhue, 2 Metc. (Mass.) 193. See also State v. Rennick, 127 Iowa 294, 103 N. W. 159, 4 Ann. Cas. 568; People v. Rouse, 2 Mich. N. P. 209.

23 DeGroat v. People, 39 Mich. 124.

to connect the accused with the commission of the offense.[24] In some states, it is not required that the evidence of the injured party be corroborated.[25] In other states corroborating evidence is essential.[26] Where the evidence of the prosecutrix is contradictory, or her general reputation for truth, honesty and integrity in the community is bad, and the accused denies the accusation against him and is corroborated, evidence of the prosecutrix will not warrant conviction of incest without corroboration.[27]

§ 794. Weight and sufficiency of evidence.—Where the evidence of the female is corroborated, and there is positive evidence of the defendant's guilt, a new trial for insufficiency of evidence will not be granted although it is conceded that the prosecutrix is an accomplice.[28] In the prosecution of a father for incest with his daughter, evidence of her mental attitude toward him and conduct goes only to the weight and credibility of her evidence as tending to show a motive to falsify and does not destroy its probative force.[29]

[24] State v. Andrus, 29 Idaho 1, 156 Pac. 421.

[25] State v. Dunn (Iowa), 160 N. W. 302; State v. Pelser (Iowa), 163 N. W. 600, female was under the age of consent).

[26] Bradshaw v. State (Tex. Cr.), 198 S. W. 942 (held that the evidence of a stepdaughter, 19 years of age, who consents to intercourse, being an accomplice in a prosecution for incest, must be corroborated).

[29] State v. Dunn (Iowa), 110 N. 156 Pac. 421.

[28] Brown v. State, 18 Ga. App. 30, 88 S. E. 710.

[29] State v. Dunn (Iowa), 110 N. W. 302.

CHAPTER LXIV

INDECENT CONDUCT AND OBSCENITY.

§ 795. **Public indecency.**—Any grossly indecent conduct in public is indictable as a nuisance, such as open, notorious lewdness,[1] openly frequenting houses of ill-fame,[2] habitually using profane or indecent language in public,[3] habitual public notorious drunkenness,[4] or permitting the copulation of animals in public.[5]

§ 796. **Indecent exhibitions.**—The exhibition of an indecent picture is indictable as a nuisance,[6] and is also prohibited by many statutes, not as a nuisance, but as an offense against morals.[7] Generally, a lewd picture is such not from the fact of representing a nude body, but when it is one tending to debauch, corrupt and inflame the minds of those who see it with inordinate lustful desires.[8]

1 Crouse v. State, 16 Ark. 566, 23 So. 1005; Delany v. People, 10 Mich. 241.

2 State v. Brunson, 2 Bailey L. (S. Car.) 149.

3 Goree v. State, 71 Ala. 7; State v. Appling, 25 Mo. 315, 69 Am. Dec. 469.

4 State v. Sowers, 52 Ind. 311; Smith v. State, 1 Humph. (Tenn.) 396.

5 Nolin v. Franklin, 4 Yerg. (Tenn.) 163.

6 Reg. v. Grey, 4 Fost. & F. 73.

7 Commonwealth v. Sharpless, 2 Serg. & R. (Pa.) 91, 7 Am. Dec. 632.

8 People v. Muller, 96 N. Y. 408, 2 N. Y. Cr. 375, 48 Am. Rep. 685; Commonwealth v. Sharpless, 2 Serg. & R. (Pa.) 91, 7 Am. Dec. 632.

If the picture is in itself indecent and offensive, it is held that an innocent motive is no defense.[9] The same rules apply to scandalous and indecent exhibitions other than pictures.[10]

§ 797. Obscene language.—The utterance of obscene words in public, is indictable at common law as a violation of decency and morals.[11] The publication of an obscene book, photograph or picture is also indictable as a libel.[12] Some statutes make the sending of obscene letters through the mails,[13] or use of obscene language in public or in presence of a woman,[14] indictable.

It has been said that it is for the court to determine whether the language used is obscene, and for the jury to determine the intention of the person using it;[15] but other courts have held that the entire question of obscenity is for the jury.[16]

If the question is of libel, it is held that, where publications necessary to medical instruction are generally disseminated, so as to corrupt the public, the publishers are indictable and philanthropic or scientific intent is no defense.[17]

[9] Reg. v. Grey, 4 Fost. & F. 73; Steele v. Brannan, L. R. 7 C. P. 261.

[10] Jacks v. State, 22 Ala. 73; Commonwealth v. Dejardin, 126 Mass. 46, 30 Am. Rep. 652, 3 Am. Cr. 290; People v. Doris, 14 App. Div. (N. Y.) 117, 43 N. Y. S. 571, 12 N. Y. Cr. 100; State v. Andrews, 35 Ore. 388, 58 Pac. 765; Reg. v. Saunders, L. R. 1 Q. B. Div. 15, 13 Cox Cr. C. 116.

[11] State v. Appling, 25 Mo. 315, 69 Am. Dec. 469; State v. Toole, 106 N. Car. 736, 11 S. E. 168; Bell v. State, 1 Swan (Tenn.) 42.

[12] People v. Eastman, 188 N. Y. 478, 81 N. E. 459, 11 Ann. Cas. 302; In re Worthington Co., 30 N. Y. S. 361, 62 N. Y. St. 115, 24 L. R. A. 110n. See also, ante, § 815.

[13] Larison v. State, 49 N. J. L. 256, 9 Atl. 700, 60 Am. Rep. 606; note to Ann. Cas. 1912A, 434.

[14] Thomas v. State, 92 Ala. 85, 9 So. 398; St. Louis v. Slupsky, 254 Mo. 309, 162 S. W. 155, 49 L. R. A. (N. S.) 919n.

[15] Smith v. State, 24 Tex. App. 1, 5 S. W. 510.

[16] People v. Muller, 96 N. Y. 408, 2 N. Y. Cr. 375, 48 Am. Rep. 635, 4 Am. Cr. 453.

[17] Commonwealth v. Landis, 8 Phila. (Pa.) 453; Reg. v. Hicklin, L. R. 3 Q. B. 360.

If certain filthy details of court proceedings are published in a newspaper, this may transgress the privilege allowed of printing court news, and may constitute an indictable offense.[18]

§ 798. Indecent exposure of person.—An intentional or negligent indecent exposure of the private parts of the person to public view is indictable at common law as a nuisance.[19] There must be more than an exposure merely to the waist, at least a portion of the private parts must actually be shown,[20] and the exposure must be in a public place in view of others,[21] and of more than one person,[22] though it is enough that the exposure was where people were in view, even if they did not see the exposure.[23] This is also in many jurisdictions a statutory offense.

§ 799. Indecent treatment of the dead—Sepulture—Cemeteries.—At common law indecent treatment of the dead is indictable. Among acts so indictable are the exposure of a dead body or its disposal without proper burial rites,[24] this offense sometimes being called sepulture; to wantonly disturb a dead body;[25] to sell it for dissection, without authority of the deceased, in his life, or his relatives, or direction

18 Commonwealth v. Herald Pub. Co., 128 Ky. 424, 108 S. W. 892, 16 Ann. Cas. 761.

19 State v. Rose, 32 Mo. 560; Britain v. State, 3 Humph. (Tenn.) 203; Rex v. Crunden, 2 Campb. 89, 11 Rev. Rep. 671; In re Sedley's Case, 17 How. St. Tr. 155.

20 Ardery v. State, 56 Ind. 328; Tucker v. State, 28 Tex. App. 541, 13 S. W. 1004; Rex v. Gallard, 1 Sess. Cas. 231.

21 Lorimer v. State, 76 Ind. 495; State v. Pepper, 68 N. Car. 259, 12 Am. Rep. 637; State v. Griffin, 43 Tex. 538.

22 Reg. v. Webb, 1 Den. 338, 2 Car. & K. 933.

23 Van Houten v. State, 46 N. J. L. 16, 50 Am. Rep. 397, 4 Am. Cr. 272; Reg. v. Farrell, 9 Cox Cr. C. 446.

24 Kanavan's Case, 1 Greenl. (Maine) 226; Reg. v. Stewart, 12 Ad. & El. 773.

25 Reg. v. Sharpe, 7 Cox Cr. C. 214.

of public authorities;[26] to remove a body after burial;[27] to dispose without inquest of a body on which an inquest should have been held.[28]

It is also indictable at common law to deface a monument to the dead, or a tombstone;[29] and many statutes make the desecration of a cemetery by cutting trees, removing fences, and similar acts criminal;[30] and if a place has once been legally established as a cemetery, the mere passage of time does not remove it from the law's protection.[31]

26 State v. McClure, 4 Blackf. (Ind.) 328; Rex v. Cundick, Dowl. & R. (N. P.) 13; Rex v. Lynn, 2 Term. Rep 733.

27 State v. Pugsley, 75 Iowa 742, 38 N. W. 498, 8 Am. Cr. 100; Commonwealth v. Cooley, 10 Pick. (Mass.) 37.

28 Reg. v. Clerk, 1 Salk. 377; Stephen Dig. Crim. L., art. 175.

29 Commonwealth v. Viall, 2 Allen (Mass.) 512; Phillips v. State, 29 Tex. 226.

30 Lay v. State, 12 Ind. App. 362, 39 N. E. 768; Phillips v. State, 29 Tex. 226.

31 Commonwealth v. Wellington, 7 Allen (Mass.) 299.

Section
802. Definition.

§ 802. Definition.—Miscegenation is a statutory crime and is the marriage or sexual union of a negro and a white person. Statutes making miscegenation a crime are constitutional.[1] Where citizens resident of one state go to another for the purpose of evading the marriage laws and contract a marriage forbidden by the miscegenation statutes, it is invalid in the state where they reside.[2] Ignorance of the statute is no defense.[3] The reason for such statutes is to prevent the mixing of races, and crossing of blood. One with less than one-fourth negro blood is not a negro under the statute.[4]

1 Pace v. Alabama, 106 U. S. 583, 27 L. ed. 207; Ex parte Francois, Fed. Cas. No. 5047, 3 Woods (U. S.) 367; Green v. State, 58 Ala. 190, 29 Am. Rep. 739; Lonas v. State, 2 Heisk. (Tenn.) 287; Frasher v. State, 3 Tex. App. 263, 30 Am. Rep. 131; State v. Daniel, 141 La. 900, 75 So. 836; Metcalf v. State (Ala. App.), 78 So. 305; Neuberger v. Gueldner, 139 La. 758, 72 So. 220.

2 Ex parte Kinney, Fed. Cas. No. 7825, 3 Hughes (U. S.) 9; Kinney v. Commonwealth, 30 Grat. (Va.) 858, 32 Am. Rep. 690.

3 Hoover v. State, 59 Ala. 57.

4 State v. Threadaway, 126 La. 300, 52 So. 500, 20 Ann. Cas. 1297; Heirn v. Bridault, 37 Miss. 209; McPherson v. Commonwealth, 28 Grat. (Va.) 939.

CHAPTER LXVI

SODOMY.

§ 805. **Definition.**—Sodomy is the "crime against nature" or "infamous" or "abominable crime against nature." It consists of unnatural carnal copulation and is said to have received its name from the city of Sodom, whose people were addicted to this practice.[1] It is said these practices were originally religious rites in honor of the goddess Ashtaroth or Astarte.[2] The crime is variously classified as one against the person or against decency, the latter seemingly the better one. Sodomy includes sodomy proper, bestiality and buggery.

Sodomy proper at common law is the copulation of human beings against nature per anum.[3] It may be between either man and man,[4] or man and woman,[5] even man and wife,[6] or one or both parties may be children.[7] There is a conflict

[1] Ausman v. Veal, 10 Ind. 355, 71 Am. Dec. 331; Commonwealth v. Poindexter, 133 Ky. 720, 118 S. W. 943; 6 Bacon Abr. title Sodomy; 1 Russ. Crimes (9th Am. ed.), 936-939.

[2] Whart. Crim. L. (11th ed.), § 753.

[3] Lewis v. State, 36 Tex. Cr. 37, 35 S. W. 372, 61 Am. St. 831; Reg. v. Allen, 1 Den. Cr. C. 364, 3 Cox Cr. C. 270; Whart. Crim. L. (11th ed.), § 754.

[4] Ausman v. Veal, 10 Ind. 355, 71 Am. Dec. 331.

[5] Adams v. State, 48 Tex. Cr. 90, 86 S. W. 334, 122 Am. St. 733; Lewis v. State, 36 Tex. Cr. 37, 35 S. W. 372, 61 Am. St. 831.

[6] Reg. v. Jellyman, 8 Car. & P. 604.

[7] Mascolo v. Montesanto, 61 Conn. 50, 23 Atl. 714, 29 Am. St. 170; Lewis v. State, 36 Tex. Cr. 37, 35 S. W. 372, 61 Am. St. 831.

as to whether in the absence of a specific provision in the statute, the general crime of sodomy includes unnatural copulation other than per anum. Many authorities hold that it does not include copulation per os;[8] others, equally weighty, hold that copulation per os,[9] or other unnatural copulation,[10] is sodomy.

§ 806. Buggery.—Buggery is that species of sodomy which is carnal copulation of a human being with an animal.[11]

§ 807. Bestiality.—According to Wharton this should include sodomy proper, buggery, and other beastly and revolting acts not involving penetration.[12] Some definitions con-

8 People v. Boyle, 116 Cal. 658, 48 Pac. 800; Commonwealth v. Poindexter, 133 Ky. 720, 118 S. W. 943; People v. Hodgkin, 94 Mich. 27, 53 N. W. 794, 34 Am. St. 321, 9 Am. Cr. 658; Kinnan v. State, 86 Nebr. 234, 125 N. W. 594, 27 L. R. A. (N. S.) 478, 21 Ann. Cas. 335; Mitchell v. State, 49 Tex. Cr. 535, 95 S. W. 500; Prindle v. State, 31 Tex. Cr. 551, 21 S. W. 360, 37 Am. St. 833; Rex v. Jacobs, 1 Russ. & Ry. 331.

9 Glover v. State, 179 Ind. 459, 101 N. E. 629, 45 L. R. A. (N. S.) 473.

10 White v. State, 136 Ga. 158, 71 S. E. 135; Herring v. State, 119 Ga. 709, 46 S. E. 876; Kelly v. People, 192 Ill. 119, 61 N. E. 425, 85 Am. St. 323; Honselman v. People, 168 Ill. 172, 48 N. E. 304; State v. Whitmarsh, 26 S. Dak. 426, 128 N. W. 580; State v. Nelson, 36 N. Dak. 564, 163 N. W. 278 (mouth). See also, Dewberry v. State, 80 Tex. Cr. App. 514, 191 S. W. 1164; Jones v. State, 17 Ga. App. 825, 88 S. E. 712 (by mouth or otherwise). See also, State v. Altwater, 29 Idaho 107, 157 Pac. 256; Comer v. State (Ga. App.), 94 S. E. 314; State v. Griffin, 175 N. Car. 767, 94 S. E. 678; Ex parte DeFord (Okla. Cr.), 168 Pac. 58.

11 Bradford v. State, 104 Ala. 68, 16 So. 107, 53 Am. St. 24 (cow); People v. Williams, 59 Cal. 397; Shigley v. Snyder, 45 Ind. 541 (sow); Ausman v. Veal, 10 Ind. 355, 71 Am. Dec. 331 (dog); Haynes v. Ritchey, 30 Iowa 76, 6 Am. Rep. 642; State v. Campbell, 29 Tex. 44, 94 Am. Dec. 251 (mare); Almendaris v. State (Tex. Cr.), 73 S. W. 1055 (jennet); Reg. v. Allen, 1 Car. & K. 496 (bitch); Rex v. Cozins, 6 Car. & P. 351 (ewe); Reg. v. Brown, L. R. 24 Q. B. Div. 357, 16 Cox Cr. C. 715 (duck); 6 Bacon Abr. "Sodomy"; 4 Bl. Comm. 215; 3 Co. Inst. 58, 59.

12 Whart. Crim. L. (11th ed.), § 756.

sider it synonymous with buggery,[13] while others use it as a synonym for sodomy in general.[14]

§ 808. Elements of offense.—In most states the crime of sodomy is defined by statute, in various words.

The essential elements are much the same as the elements of rape and include assault,[15] where the subject or pathic is a human, and penetration of the body of the pathic to some extent.[16] Emission, however, is unnecessary.[17]

Attempts to commit sodomy or assaults with such intent may be indicted at common law.[18]

§ 809. Defenses.—Consent of the pathic is no defense.[19] A consenting pathic is an accomplice.[20] Infancy may be a defense, the presumption being that a child under fourteen is incapable of committing the act.[21] Insanity is a defense, where the defendant acted from an uncontrollable insane motive, or was incapable of understanding the purpose and significance of the act.[22]

[13] Commonwealth v. J—, 21 Pa. Co. Ct. 625.

[14] Ausman v. Veal, 10 Ind. 355, 71 Am. Dec. 331.

[15] People v. Oates, 142 Cal. 12, 75 Pac. 337; Darling v. State (Tex. Cr.) 47 S. W. 1005.

[16] State v. Gage, 139 Iowa 401, 116 N. W. 596; State v. McGruder, 125 Iowa 741, 101 N. W. 646; Moody v. State, 57 Tex. Cr. 76, 121 S. W. 1117; Rex v. Jacobs, Russ. & Ry. 331; Steph. Dig. Crim. L., art. 168; 2 Russ. Crimes (9th Am. ed.) 936-939.

[17] White v. Commonwealth, 115 Ky. 473, 73 S. W. 1120; Williams v. State, 14 Ohio 222, 45 Am. Dec. 536; Rex v. Cozins, 6 Car. & P. 351.

[18] People v. Williams, 59 Cal. 397; State v. Frank, 103 Mo. 120, 15 S. W. 330; Reg. v. Eaton, 8 Car. & P. 417; Reg. v. Lock, L. R. 2 C. C. 12, 12 Cox Cr. C. 244.

[19] Reg. v. Allen, 2 Car. & K. 869, 3 Cox Cr. C. 270; Reg. v. Jellyman, 8 Car. & P. 604.

[20] Commonwealth v. Poindexter, 133 Ky. 720, 118 S. W. 943; State v. Vicknair, 52 La. Ann. 1921, 28 So. 273.

[21] Reg. v. Hartlen, 30 N. S. 317.

[22] State v. McGruder, 125 Iowa 741, 101 N. W. 646.

ARTICLE III. VIOLATION OF THE ELECTIVE FRANCHISE.

CHAPTER LXVII

OFFENSES AGAINST THE ELECTIVE FRANCHISE.

§ 812. A common-law crime.—Where a government derives its authority from popular elections, a forceful or fraudulent disturbance or fraudulent abuse, of the right to the elective franchise is punishable as an offense against the government, under the common law.[1] But in this country prosecutions for such offenses are usually brought under specific statutes. The offenses more commonly punishable by statute are illegal voting,[2] fraud or breach of duty by elective officers,[3] interference with elections by other parties,[4] bribing voters,[5] betting at elections,[6] failure to disclose expenditures by candidates,[7] and similar acts.

1 Mason v. State, 55 Ark. 529, 18 S. W. 827; Commonwealth v. McHale, 97 Pa. St. 397, 39 Am. Rep. 808.

2 Whart. Crim. L. (11th ed.), §§ 2185-2190; note to Ann. Cas. 1912 A, 436.

3 State v. Vause, 84 Ohio St. 207, 95 N. E. 742, Ann. Cas. 1912C, 513.

4 United States v. Souders, Fed. Cas. No. 16358, 2 Abb. (U. S.) 456; Whart. Crim. L. (11th ed.), § 2206.

5 State v. Bunnell, 131 Wis. 198, 110 N. W. 177, 11 Ann. Cas. 560n.

6 Parsons v. State, 2 Ind. 499; Commonwealth v. Shouse, 16 B. Mon. (Ky.) 325, 63 Am. Dec. 551.

7 Commonwealth v. Schrotnick, 240 Pa. St. 57, 87 Atl. 280, Ann. Cas. 1915A, 365n.

ARTICLE IV. POSTAL OFFENSES AND OTHER FEDERAL CRIMES.

CHAPTER LXVIII

OTHER FEDERAL CRIMES—POSTAL OFFENSES.

§ 815. Postal crimes under Federal statutes.—There are various Federal statutes which make criminal certain acts relative to the carrying and delivery of mail.

Obstructing or retarding the transmission of mail is criminal, whether done intentionally or negligently.[1] Examples of this offense are, where a tollgate keeper hinders a mail wagon to obtain payment of toll,[2] or the holder of a lien on horses used to draw a mailcoach enforces the lien in a manner to prevent the mail being carried,[3] or where obstructions are placed on a railroad track over which mails are carried

[1] United States v. Thomas, 55 Fed. 380; United States v. Claypool, 14 Fed. 127.

[2] United States v. Sears, 55 Fed. 268.

[3] United States v. Barney, Fed. Cas. No. 14525, 3 Hughes (U. S.) 545, 2 Wheeler Cr. C. 513.

and delay ensues.[4] It seems, therefore, that intent is immaterial in this offense.

Robbery of a carrier of mail is a felony under federal statutes.[5]

The opening or detaining mail matter is indictable.[6]

The secreting, embezzlement, or destruction of any mail matter by postal servants and the embezzlement by such servants of any mail containing an article of value are punishable.[7] To constitute this offense, the letter or package must be taken from the custody of the government service, before delivery to a third person.[8] A decoy letter which is sent out for the purpose of detecting one who takes articles from the mail may be the subject of embezzlement.[9]

It is also criminal by statute to use the mails for fraudulent purposes.[10] Sending out circulars to induce persons to send back money or stamps for which no returns were to be made,[11] or circulars offering for sale counterfeit money,[12] come under this classification.

It is immaterial whether or not the fraud was actually perpetrated,[13] but the intent to defraud must have existed.[14]

[4] United States v. Cassidy, 67 Fed. 698; United States v. Thomas, 55 Fed. 380; United States v. Kane, 19 Fed. 42, 9 Sawy. (U. S.) 614; United States v. Clark, 23 Int. Rev. Rec. (N. Y.) 306.

[5] Harrison v. United States, 163 U. S. 140, 41 L. ed. 104.

[6] United States v. Parsons, Fed. Cas. No. 16000, 2 Blatchf. (U. S.) 104; United States v. Nutt, Fed. Cas. No. 15904; United States v. Holmes, 40 Fed. 750; United States v. McCready, 11 Fed. 225; Russ. Crimes (9th Am. ed.) 493.

[7] United States v. Lacher, 134 U. S. 624, 33 L. ed. 1080; United States v. Davis, 33 Fed. 865.

[8] United States v. Parsons, Fed. Cas. No. 16000, 2 Blatchf. (U. S.) 104.

[9] United States v. Dorsey, 40 Fed. 752; United States v. Wight, 38 Fed. 106.

[10] U. S. Comp. Stat. (1916), § 10385 et seq. See also, Stokes v. United States, 60 Fed. 597.

[11] United States v. Whittier, Fed. Cas. No. 16688, 5 Dill. (U. S.) 35; United States v. Stickle, 15 Fed. 798.

[12] United States v. Jones, 10 Fed. 469, 20 Blatchf. (U. S.) 235.

[13] Weeber v. United States, 62 Fed. 740; United States v. Mitchell, 36 Fed. 492, 1 L. R. A. 796.

[14] United States v. Beach, 71 Fed. 160; United States v. Harris, 68 Fed. 347.

Use of the mails to perpetrate a single isolated fraud is not indictable under this statute.[15]

The mailing or posting of obscene or indecent matter is indictable, under statutes,[16] and they include the mailing of sealed private letters as well as matter not sealed or books or papers intended for public circulation.[17] Obscene matter is such that it tends to deprave and corrupt the minds of those open to immoral influences by exciting lustful and sensual desires.[18]

The mailing of defamatory or threatening matter is indictable by statute,[19] also the mailing of lottery advertisements.[20]

[15] United States v. Owens, 17 Fed. 72, 5 McCrary (U. S.) 307.

[16] United States v. Bott, Fed. Cas. No. 14626, 11 Blatchf. (U. S.) 346; United States v. Chase, 27 Fed. 807.

[17] Andrews v. United States, 162 U. S. 420, 40 L. ed. 1023; United States v. Warner, 59 Fed. 355; United States v. Wilson, 58 Fed. 768; United States v. Gaylord, 50 Fed. 410.

[18] United States v. Bennett, Fed. Cas. No. 14571, 16 Blatchf. (U. S.) 338, 2 N. Y. Cr. 284; United States v. Martin, 50 Fed. 918; United States v. Clarke, 38 Fed. 732; United States v. Harman, 38 Fed. 827.

[19] Act of September 26, 1888, ch. 1039, 25 Stat. at Large, 496. See also, United States v. Gee, 45 Fed. 194; United States v. Clark, 43 Fed. 574; United States v. Bayle, 40 Fed. 664, 6 L. R. A. 742; United States v. Pratt, Fed. Cas. No. 16082.

[20] In re Jackson, Fed. Cas. No. 7124, 14 Blatchf. (U. S.) 245; United States v. Moore, 19 Fed. 39; United States v. Duff, 6 Fed. 45, 19 Blatchf. (U. S.) 9.

CHAPTER LXIX

COUNTERFEITING AND UTTERING COUNTERFEIT MONEY.

§ 818. **Definition.**—Counterfeiting is making false money in the semblance of that which is genuine.[1] Coining or uttering false money is a crime at common law, indictable on the same principles as cheating or forgery. In addition, Federal statutes provide for the punishment of counterfeiting United States money. The principles applicable are very similar to those laid down in the chapter on forgery.[2]

§ 819. **Distinction between Federal and common-law crimes.**—The constitution gives to congress power to punish the counterfeiting of the securities and coin of the United States.[3] Under this provision statutes have been enacted, and the crime of counterfeiting, under the Federal statutes, bears a somewhat different aspect from the common-law crime. The Federal courts have complete jurisdiction of the crime under the Federal statutes,[4] but the offense is indict-

1 2 Bish. New Crim. L., § 289; Whart. Crim. L. 11th ed.), § 956.

2 See ante, ch. XXIX.

3 U. S. Const., art. I, § 8.

4 Ex parte Geisler, 50 Fed. 411; Commonwealth v. Fuller, 8 Metc. (Mass.) 313, 41 Am. Dec. 509; Whart. Crim. L. (11th ed.), §§ 307, 955. See also, Linningen v. Morgan, 241 Fed. 645, 154 C. C. A. 403; York v. United States, 241 Fed. 656, 154 C. C. A. 414; Leib v. Halligan, 236 Fed. 82, 149 C. C. A. 292.

able in the state courts as a common-law crime, or under state statutes, as an offense in the nature of a fraud.[5]

Under the Federal statutes, the crime is the making of something in the similitude of the coin or securities of the United States, and it is essential to the crime that the imitation exists,[6] though it is sufficient if the imitation be calculated to deceive a person using ordinary care.[7] Under some state statutes it is unnecessary to show similitude to genuine coin.[8]

§ 820. What acts have been held to be counterfeiting.— There is much variation in the language of the different statutes against counterfeiting. Under a statute making it a crime to make an instrument in the similitude of a bill issued by a bank established by law, a note not like that of any known bank, but purely fictitious, is not included;[9] but if the note purports to be issued by a bank having authority, it is not necessary that it imitate any bill which the bank has actually issued.[10] Generally, it is held that a token which does not purport to imitate any known coin is not a counterfeit.[11] It is usually held that the offense of making a counterfeit coin is not indictable if anything remains to be done to complete the coin.[12] To file off the edges of a true coin, and fraudulently make a new milling, is counterfeiting.[13]

5 United States v. Hargrave, Fed. Cas. No. 15306; People v. McDonnell, 80 Cal. 285, 22 Pac. 190, 13 Am. St. 159; Dashing v. State, 78 Ind. 357; Whart. Am. L., § 524.

6 United States v. Stevens, 52 Fed. 120; United States v. Williams, 14 Fed. 550.

7 United States v. Sprague, 48 Fed. 828.

8 State v. Williams, 8 Iowa 533.

9 State v. McKenzie, 42 Maine 392; Commonwealth v. Morse, 2 Mass. 138.

10 Commonwealth v. Smith, 7 Pick. (Mass.) 137; Trice v. State, 2 Head (Tenn.) 591.

11 United States v. Bogart, Fed. Cas. No. 14617, 9 Ben. (U. S.) 314.

12 United States v. Burns, Fed. Cas. No. 14691, 5 McLean 22, 23; Rex v. Varley, 1 East. P. C. 164; Rex v. Elliott, 1 Leach 175. But see United States v. Abrams, 18 Fed. 823, 21 Blatchf. (U. S.) 553.

13 Reg. v. Hermann, 14 Cox Cr. C. 279, 4 Q. B. Div. 284.

All persons taking part in the making are principals.[14] Under statutes which forbid the making of counterfeit coin, intent is immaterial.[15]

§ 821. **Uttering counterfeit coin.**—The uttering of counterfeit coin, that is, offering counterfeit coin with intent to defraud, is also a crime.[16] Staking such coin in gambling is an attempt to utter or pass it, and losing it in gambling is held indictable.[17] Also, it has been held an uttering to pay it to a woman for sexual intercourse,[18] to take a true coin offered in payment for a sale, substitute a false one, and claim that the coin offered in payment was bad, this being known as ringing the changes,[19] to give it to a confederate to pass,[20] to offer it in payment though it be refused,[21] or even to give it to charity,[22] though it was formerly held that the latter was not uttering.[23]

Selling counterfeit coin is an offense distinct and different from uttering it.[24] Under some statutes, it is an offense to have counterfeit coin in one's possession, with intent to pass it as true,[25] or intent to put it in circulation,[26] the two offenses being different, and the latter including the selling of it. Where the indictment is for selling counterfeit coin, it is immaterial that the purchaser believed he was buying counterfeit money.[27] Where the coin is found in one's pos-

14 Whart. Crim. L. (11th ed.), § 957.

15 United States v. Russell, 22 Fed. 390.

16 United States v. Nelson, Fed. Cas. No. 15861, 1 Abb. (U. S.) 135.

17 State v. Beeler, 1 Brev. (S. Car.) 482.

18 Reg. v. ——, 1 Cox Cr. C. 250.

19 Rex v. Franks, 2 Leach 644.

20 Rex v. Palmer, Russ. & Ry. 72.

21 Reg. v. Welch, 2 Den. 78.

22 Reg. v. Ion, 2 Den. 475.

23 Reg. v. Page, 8 Car. & P. 122.

24 Van Valkenburg v. State, 11 Ohio 404.

25 Gabe v. State, 6 Ark. 519; People v. Stewart, 4 Mich. 655.

26 People v. Stewart, 4 Mich. 655; Bevington v. State, 2 Ohio St. 160.

27 Leonard v. State, 29 Ohio St. 408.

session, guilty knowledge may be inferred from continued possession,[28] and intent from circumstances.[29]

§ 822. Possession of counterfeiting tools.—It is a misdemeanor at common law to have tools for counterfeiting with intent to use them.[30] There are also statutes declaratory of the same crime. Under the common law, or the statutes, the following have been held to be tools for counterfeiting: a mold with the stamp of one side of a coin, though useless without the reverse,[31] a press for coining,[32] or an iron collar to mark the edges of the coins.[33] But the having of an instrument which is not fit for use, as a mold with no opening for the metal to run,[34] or an instrument which may also be used lawfully, as a crucible,[35] is not a crime. It is essential that the tools should be had for the purpose of making counterfeit coin, and that there is an intent to use them,[36] but such intent may be inferred from possession[37] and it is enough that another is to use them.[38]

28 Harrison's Case, 2 Lew. 118.

29 State v. Vincent, 91 Mo. 662, 4 S. W. 430; Reg. v. Jarvis, Dears. 552.

30 Rex v. Sutton, 1 East. P. C. 172.

31 Commonwealth v. Kent, 6 Metc. (Mass.) 221; Rex v. Lennard, 1 East. P. C. 170.

32 Rex v. Bell, 1 East. P. C. 169.

33 Rex v. Moore, 2 Car. & P. 235.

34 Reg. v. MacMillan, 1 Cox Cr. C. 41.

35 State v. Bowman, 6 Vt. 594.

36 People v. White, 34 Cal. 183; Commonwealth v. Morse, 2 Mass. 128; State v. Collins, 10 N. Car. 191.

37 Reg. v. Harvey, L. R. 1 C. C. 284; Reg. v. Weeks, Leigh. & C. 18.

38 Sasser v. State, 13 Ohio 453.

CHAPTER LXX

MISCELLANEOUS FEDERAL OFFENSES.

§ 825. Generally.—There are many other Federal statutes creating offenses as to matters within the power of Congress to regulate, which will be briefly noted here. The principles concerning the prosecution of these offenses are the same as in most other statutory crimes, consisting merely in showing that the accused committed an act within the purview of the statutory definition.

§ 826. Commerce regulations.—The statutes regulating interstate commerce provide for penalties for giving preferences to one shipper over another, and discriminating between shippers.[1] There are also statutes providing for the punishment of unlawful combinations in restraint of trade.[2] There are also penalties against interstate carriers which confine stock in transportation more than twenty-eight hours without unloading for water, feed and rest. There are certain regulations concerning trading with Indians without license. The transportation of women from one state to another for immoral purposes is indictable under these statutes.

§ 827. Banking regulations.—The statutes relating to the organization and regulation of national banks make it crim-

[1] U. S. Comp. Stat. (1916), § 8565.

[2] U. S. Comp. Stat. (1916), § 8820.

inal for an officer to make false entries in books, reports or statements of a national bank with the intent to mislead the officers of the bank or of the government concerning the bank's condition. Under these statutes the entries must be wilfully and intentionally false and not merely erroneous.[8] The banking acts also make punishable the embezzlement or wilful misapplication of the moneys of a national bank.

§ 828. **Revenue laws—Smuggling.**—The importation of goods subject to the payment of an import duty without the payment of such duty, is punishable by Federal statutes. Federal license is required for carrying on of certain kinds of business, such as the retail of spirituous liquors under certain circumstances and the sale without such license is punishable. It is criminal to change or alter revenue stamps or their cancellation marks, to present false claims against the government for payment, to cut timber from government land for private purposes, to make false certificate, a false affidavit in support of an application for a pension is criminal. There are various other offenses connected with the obtaining of pensions.

§ 829. **Navigation laws.**—Some offenses against the navigation laws are punishable criminally. Among other criminal offenses are the making of a false affidavit to obtain naturalization papers; bringing persons into this country in defiance of immigration laws; aiding other nations in the violation of neutrality statutes; assaulting or offering violence to the person of a foreign minister.

[8] United States v. Graves, 53 Fed. 634; United States v. Allen, 47 Fed. 696.

ARTICLE V. ADMIRALTY CRIMES.

CHAPTER LXXI

PARTICULAR CRIMES.

§ 832. Generally.—This chapter treats of crimes committed on the high seas punishable under admiralty jurisdiction. Most of the crimes treated are violations of Federal statutes.

§ 833. Piracy.—Piracy is an offense committed on the high seas, equivalent to robbery on land.[1] It is a crime against the English common law and the law of nations, punishable by any sovereignty which may seize the guilty party.[2]

Under Federal statute piracy as an offense against the United States may include acts which are not piracy by the

1 United States v. Baker, Fed. Cas. No. 14501, 5 Blatchf. (U. S.) 6; United States v. Smith, 5 Wheat. (U. S.) 153, 5 L. ed. 57; Attorney-General v. Kwok-a-Sing, L. R. 5 P. C. 180; 2 Whart. Crim. L. (11th ed.), §§ 2218, 2219; Bl. Comm. 72.

2 United States v. Tully, Fed. Cas. No. 16545, 1 Gall. (U. S.) 247; The Marianna Flora, 11 Wheat. (U. S.) 1, 6 L. ed. 405. See also, United States v. Baker, Fed. Cas. No. 14501, 5 Blatchf. (U. S.) 6; United States v. Smith, 5 Wheat. (U. S.) 153, 5 L. ed. 57; Attorney-General v. Kwok-a-Sing, L. R. 5 P. C. 180.

common law.[3] There have been English statutes against piracy from earliest times.

The United States has jurisdiction to punish the offense if committed on the high seas on an American ship,[4] even if committed by a foreign citizen or subject,[5] or if committed by an American citizen on a foreign vessel,[6] and also takes jurisdiction over piratical acts committed by those owing allegiance to no country or on a ship not lawfully under the flag of any nation, or a piratical vessel.[7]

All who aid are principals.[8] Privateers[9] and belligerents[10] are not pirates.

§ 834. Maltreatment of crew.—The master of a ship has the authority to punish summarily and corporally any misconduct of the members of the crew,[11] but the lower officers have no similar right, except in the master's absence,[12] or in case of necessity.[13] If the master beat or wound one of the

[3] U. S. Comp. Stat. (1916), §§ 10463-10483. See also United States v. Jones, Fed Cas. No. 15496, 3 Wash. C. C. 228.

[4] U. S. Comp. Stat. (1916) §§ 10463-10483.

[5] United States v. Peterson, Fed. Cas. No. 16037, 1 Woodb. & M. 305.

[6] United States v. Peterson, Fed. Cas. No. 16037, 1 Woodb. & M. 305.

[7] United States v. Pirates, 5 Wheat. (U. S.) 184, 5 L. ed. 64; United States v. Klintock, 5 Wheat. (U. S.) 144, 5 L. ed. 55; The Ambrose Light, 25 Fed. 408.

[8] United States v. Howard, Fed. Cas. No. 15404, 3 Wash. C. C. 340; Whart. Crim. L. (11th ed.), § 2221.

[9] Whart. Crim. L. (11th ed.), § 2222.

[10] United States v. Baker, Fed. Cas. No. 14501, 5 Blatchf. (U. S.) 6; Whart. Crim. L. (11th ed.), § 2224. See also Bangs v. Little, Fed. Cas. No. 839, 1 Ware (506) 520; Turner's Case, Fed Cas. No. 14248, 1 Ware (83) 77, 2 Wheeler Cr. C. 615.

[11] Bangs v. Little, Fed Cas. No. 839, 1 Ware (506) 520; Turner's Case, Fed. Cas. No. 14248, 1 Ware (83) 77, 2 Wheeler Cr. C. 615; United States v. Hunt, Fed Cas. No. 15423, 2 Story (U. S.) 120; Carleton v. Davis, Fed. Cas. No. 2408, 2 Ware 225.

[12] United States v. Taylor, Fed. Cas. No. 16442, 2 Sumn. (U. S.) 584.

[13] United States v. Hunt, Fed. Cas. No. 15423, 2 Story (U. S.) 120.

crew he is liable to penalty under Federal statute,[14] except in case of necessity.[15]

§ 835. **Revolt.**—Revolt is the usurpation of the authority and command of the ship overthrowing that of the master, and is punishable by statute.[16] An endeavor to revolt, that is, a conspiracy among the members of the crew to bring about a revolt or to resist the master, is also punishable.[17] An overt act is necessary to constitute the offense of endeavor to revolt.[18]

Any deprivation of access by the master to any part of the ship or deprivation of personal freedom, or restraint, from performing his duties, maliciously done, constitutes the offense of confining the master.[19]

§ 836. **Leaving seaman on shore.**—To leave maliciously and without justifiable cause an officer or seaman on shore in a foreign country, or to force maliciously and without justifiable cause a seaman or officer ashore in a foreign country, or to refuse maliciously and without justifiable cause to bring home again all the officers and seamen who are willing and able to return, is punishable under Federal statute.[20]

14 U. S. Comp. Stat. (1916), § 10464.

15 Carleton v. Davis, Fed. Cas. No. 2408, 2 Ware (U. S.) 225; United States v. Freeman, Fed. Cas. No. 15162, 4 Mason (U. S.) 505.

16 U. S. Comp. Stat. (1916), §§ 10466, 10467.

17 United States v. Seagrist, Fed. Cas. No. 16245, 4 Blatchf. (U. S.) 420; United States v. Kelly, 11 Wheat. (U. S.) 417, 6 L. ed. 508.

18 United States v. Savage, Fed. Cas. No. 16226, 5 Mason (U. S.) 460; United States v. Kelly, 11 Wheat. (U. S.) 417, 6 L. ed. 508.

19 United States v. Hemmer, Fed. Cas. No. 15345, 4 Mason (U. S.) 105; United States v. Bladen, Fed. Cas. No. 14606, Pet. C. C. 213; United States v. Sharp, Fed. Cas. No. 16264, 1 Pet. C. C. 118; United States v. Stevens, Fed. Cas. No. 16394, 4 Wash. C. C. 547; United States v. Henry, Fed. Cas. No. 15351, 4 Wash. C. C. 428.

20 U. S. Comp. Stat. (1916), § 10468. See also United States v. Netcher, Fed. Cas. No. 15866, 1 Story (U. S.) 307; United States v. Coffin, Fed. Cas. No. 14824, Sumn. (U. S.) 394

Engaging a vessel in the slave trade is a Federal crime.[21] So is destroying a vessel with intent to defraud the underwriters.[22]

[21] U. S. Comp. Stat. (1916), § 10419 et seq. See also United States v. Battiste, Fed Cas. No. 14545, 2 Sumn. (U. S.) 240; United States v. Gooding, 12 Wheat. (U. S.) 460, 6 L. ed. 693; United States v. Andrews, Brunner Col. Cas. 422.

[22] U. S. Comp. Stat. (1916), § 10469. See also, United States v. Cole, Fed. Cas. No. 14832, 5 McLean (U. S.) 513; United States v. Amedy, 11 Wheat. (U. S.) 392, 6 L. ed. 502; United States v. Johns, Fed. Cas. No. 15481, 1 Wash. C. C. 363, 4 Dall. (U. S.) 412, 1 L. ed. 888.

ARTICLE VI. MISCELLANEOUS STATUTORY OFFENSES UNDER POLICE REGULATIONS.

CHAPTER LXXII

PARTICULAR OFFENSES.

§ 840. Generally.—The difference between police wrongs and other crimes has been previously considered. Perhaps the greatest difference is that the acts punishable by the statutes as police wrongs, are not usually considered to involve moral turpitude, but are acts which the growth of public opinion has recognized as inimical to the public good, and which the legislature has rendered punishable.[1] In most crimes of this class a specific act is punishable, and intent is not an essential element of the offense.

In considering illegal sales of liquor and some other offenses, some specific crimes of this class have been treated. In this chapter little more will be done than to name other

[1] See note to 78 Am. St. 236.

offenses made such by statute in most American jurisdictions, repeating that the only essential difference in prosecutions for these offenses is that a specific intent to violate the statute or do an unlawful act is usually immaterial. It is sufficient if an act is done which the law prohibits.

§ 841. Sale of adulterated and unwholesome food.—The sale of unwholesome food, or that which is unfit for consumption, is punishable by statute.

There are many state and Federal statutes which provide penalties for the sale of adulterated foods and drinks. These statutes are intended both to protect the public health and to prevent fraud of the purchasers. It is often made punishable, for instance, to sell milk which falls below a certain legal standard in the percentage of its constituent elements; to sell certain foods colored with certain dyes; to sell foods containing ingredients other than those claimed; to sell imitations of butter as butter; and many other specific adulterations of food and drink are punishable. The Federal Food and Drugs Act of 1906 defines and punishes the adulteration of food and the misbranding of packages in which food and drugs are sold.[2]

§ 842. Housing laws—Regulation of conditions of employment.—Statutes may specify certain conditions under which houses may be erected, and certain specifications as to their character, in the interests of health and public welfare, which must be complied with, and render violation of these conditions indictable.

There may be penalties fixed for employing persons for a time longer than a certain number of hours in a day or week,

[2] United States v. Lexington Mill &c. Co., 232 U. S. 399, 58 L. ed. 658, L. R. A. 1915 B, 774n; McDermott v. Wisconsin, 228 U. S. 115, 57 L. ed. 754, 48 L. R. A. (N. S.) 984n, Ann. Cas. 1915 A, 39n; In re Afnew, 89 Nebr. 306, 131 N. W. 817, 35 L. R. A. (N. S.) 836, Ann. Cas. 1912 C, 676; McDermott v. State, 143 Wis. 18, 126 N. W. 888, 21 Ann. Cas. 1315n.

for failure to maintain working places in accordance with statutory specifications.

The employment of children may be forbidden under penalty. It is usual to regulate by statute to some degree working conditions in mines, factories and workshops.

§ 843. Regulation of professions and occupations.—Many professions and occupations require such a degree of skill in those practicing them, that the legislature may prescribe certain qualifications which one must have to follow them, usually ascertained by examination, and may punish those who follow these professions or occupations without license. The reason for this is to protect the public from incompetent persons following these callings. So it is well recognized that the practice of medicine, dentistry and pharmacy should be licensed by the state, in order to protect public health.

Locomotive and steamboat engineers, and captains of vessels are required to have licenses to show their competency. The practice of law may be regulated both on the ground of protecting the public, and because attorneys are officers of the court, and for that reason the practice of law is subject to regulation.

In most of the occupations in which license is required it is a misdemeanor to follow them without license.

The conducting of public markets, public warehouses, carriers and other kinds of businesses are regulated because of their public nature, and violations of these regulations are sometimes indictable.

§ 844. Other police regulations.—Vagrancy is punishable under some statutes. There are many regulations as to conduct of business, some of which render a violation indictable.

The use of false weights and measures may be punishable criminally, the taking of usury, the using of certain classes of vehicles on streets, peddling without license, driving vehicles at certain rates of speed, or without license. Many of such acts are punishable by municipal ordinances.

TITLE EIGHT.

CRIMES AGAINST THE SOVEREIGNTY.

CHAPTER LXXIII.

CRIMES AGAINST THE SOVEREIGNTY.

§ 847. Subdivisions of crimes against sovereignty.—Crimes against sovereignty are subdivided as follows: (1) Treason. (2) Misprision of treason. (3) Sedition.

§ 848. Treason.—Treason is the highest crime known to the law. It consists, as heretofore stated, in a criminal renunciation of one's allegiance to the sovereign power.[1] This renunciation may consist in levying war against one's country, or in aiding or adhering to her enemies.

§ 849. Allegiance—Two grades.—The term allegiance is applicable both to citizens and to alien friends. That due

[1] United States v. Werner, 247 Fed. 708. See also, ante, § 196 and notes.

from the former, however, is more pronounced than that due from the latter. "Allegiance is of two kinds; that due from citizens, and that due from aliens resident within the United States. Every sojourner who enjoys our protection is bound to good faith toward our government, and although an alien, he may be guilty of treason by co-operation either with rebels or foreign enemies. The allegiance of aliens is local, and terminates when they leave our country. That of citizens is not so limited."[2]

§ 850. **Levying war—Requisites.**—Levying war includes two things. The offender must entertain a warlike intent, and he must perform an overt act which pertains to warlike operations. A mere conspiring to levy war is not a sufficient overt act to constitute treason. There must be an "act of war."[3] But, at common law, a mere conspiring to compass the death or deposition of the sovereign is a sufficient act to constitute treason.[4]

§ 851. **Adhering to enemies—Giving them aid and comfort—Requisites.**—To constitute an adherence to the enemies of one's country there must be, on the part of the offender, an overt act; but written words may be sufficient. Thus, an intercepted document intended for an enemy may be adequate.[5]

Chief Justice Marshall says, "If war be actually levied, that is, if a body of men be actually assembled, for the purpose of effecting by force a treasonable purpose, all those who perform any part, however minute, or however remote from the scene of action, and who are actually leagued in the gen-

[2] 23 Law Reporter 705, 7010. See also, United States v. Wiltberger, 5 Wheat. (U. S.) 76, 5 L. ed. 37.

[3] Ex parte Bollman, 4 Cranch (U. S.) 75, 2 L. ed. 554; Reg. v. Frost, 9 Car. & P. 129.

[4] 1 Bish. New Crim. L., § 432; 2 Bish. New Crim. L., § 1231.

[5] Rex v. Jackson, 1 Craw. & D. 149.

eral conspiracy, are to be considered as traitors."[6] "What amounts to adhering to and giving aid and comfort to our enemies, it is somewhat difficult in all cases to define; but certain it is that furnishing them with arms, or munitions of war, vessels, or other means of transportation, or any materials which will aid the traitors in carrying out their traitorous purposes, with a knowledge that they are intended for such purposes, or inciting and encouraging others to engage in or aid the traitors in any way, does come within the provisions of the act. And it is immaterial whether such acts are induced by sympathy with the rebellion, hostility to the government, or a desire for gain."[7]

§ 852. Misprision of treason.—Misprision of treason consists in possessing knowledge that treason has been committed and not making it known. In other words, it is the concealment of treason by being merely passive.[8]

It is the duty of every good citizen, who possesses knowledge that a treason has been committed, to inform a magistrate. The same duty exists where one has knowledge that a felony has been committed. Where a person stands by and sees a felony committed, and conceals it, he is guilty of a misprision.[9]

§ 853. Sedition.—Sedition consists in verbal or written statements which tend to excite the public against the sovereign. In this country sedition is not recognized as a crime.

[6] Ex parte Bollman, 4 Cranch (U. S.) 75, 2 L. ed. 554; United States v. Wursterbarth, 249 Fed. 908.

[7] Charge of Judge Smalley to Grand Jury, 23 Law Reporter, 597, 601. See also Whart. Crim. L. (11th ed.), 2304 et seq.

[8] United States Comp. Stat. (1916), § 10167; 1 East P. C. 139.

[9] 4 Bl. Comm. 119; 1 Bish. New Crim. L., § 720; 1 Russ. Crimes (9th Am. ed.), 79, 194. See also, Carpenter v. State, 62 Ark. 286, 36 S. W. 900; State v. Hildreth, 31 N. Car. 429, 51 Am. Dec. 369.

§ 854. Cancellation of certificate of naturalization.—A certificate of naturalization issued to an alien may, under the Naturalization Act, under certain circumstances, be cancelled.[10] In such proceeding, where the good faith of the respondent is highly questionable as to any of the essentials the burden is upon him to dispel the doubt.[11] Where a state circuit court issued a certificate to an alien, after war had been declared by the United States against the government of which he was a subject, the federal district court has jurisdiction to cancel the certificate.[12]

10 United States v. Morena, 247 Fed. 484, 159 C. C. A. 538.

11 United States v. Wursterbarth, 249 Fed. 908.

12 United States v. Kamm, 247 Fed. 968.

PART THREE

CRIMINAL PROCEDURE

PART THREE

CRIMINAL PROCEDURE

CHAPTER LXXIV

PRELIMINARY.

§ 860. Generally.—Criminal procedure is the prescribed method of enforcing criminal law, and embraces all the steps for the apprehension and trial, and if guilty, conviction and punishment of persons believed to have committed crimes. It is the adjective branch of criminal law, which regulates its enforcement, as distinguished from the substantive branch treated in the preceding chapters, which prescribes rules for conduct.

Procedure includes pleading, which is the science or system of rules and principles applied to the written allegations called pleadings, in a criminal prosecution, the object of which is to produce a proper issue for trial; evidence, the rules of law which determine the admissibility and weight of evidence to support the issues made by the pleadings; and practice, the steps taken to bring accused persons into court and the methods and course pursued in trials and enforcing judgments. In a broader sense practice includes something of pleading and evidence. Evidence is also used in reference to the actual testimony, pleading in reference to the arguments of counsel, but the subdivisions of the law known as evidence and pleading have no reference to such meanings. The law of procedure, like substantive law, comes largely from usage, partly from statute, in many instances usage being crystallized in form by statute.

§ 861. Jurisdiction.—By jurisdiction is meant the right to authority by which judicial officers investigate and decide cases. A criminal prosecution is not valid unless the court is legally created and constituted, and unless it has jurisdiction to try the offense[1] and the person charged with the offense.[2] Acts by the court outside of its jurisdiction are void.[3] The defendant can not confer upon the court jurisdiction of an offense by his mere consent to be tried before it.[4] However, merely the fact that the accused was illegally arrested or illegally brought within the court's jurisdiction will not affect the legality of the trial.[5] And if the court has jurisdiction of the offense charged, but the proof establishes a less offense, one of which the court would not originally have had jurisdiction, yet it can render a legal judgment of

1 Commonwealth v. Knowlton, 2 Mass. 580; State v. Cooper, 104 N. Car. 890, 10 S. E. 510.

2 Ledgerwood v. State, 134 Ind. 81, 33 N. E. 631.

3 Jackson v. Commonwealth, 13 Grat. (Va.) 795; State v. Bloom, 17 Wis. 521.

4 People v. Granice, 50 Cal. 447; People v. Campbell, 4 Parker Cr. (N. Y.) 386.

5 Cabell v. Arnold, 86 Tex. 102, 23 S. W. 645, 22 L. R. A. 87.

conviction for the lesser offense. For instance, if the indictment is for grand larceny, and the court has jurisdiction of grand larceny but not of petit larceny, the defendant may be convicted of petit larceny.[6] But a court which has jurisdiction only for petit larceny can not render judgment in cases of grand larceny. Where by statute the place and time for the court to sit are prescribed, such requirements must be observed or the proceedings will be void.[7]

§ 862. **State courts.**—State courts are created by the statutes or constitutions of the several states, and their jurisdiction is fixed and defined in the same manner. In every county of each state there is a court of general jurisdiction, which has authority to try cases in general except some minor offenses of which justices of the peace have exclusive jurisdiction. The names given to this court in the different states vary; such as circuit court, district court, superior court, court of common pleas, etc. In some instances there are other courts between the court of general jurisdiction and the justice of the peace court. There are in all the states higher courts which have jurisdiction to review the judgment of the trial court on appeal or writ of error.

Justices of the peace have jurisdiction to hold preliminary examinations of persons charged with crime and either to discharge them, admit them to bail, or commit them for trial. They also have jurisdiction to bind over persons to keep the peace; and are given exclusive jurisdiction of certain petty offenses such as vagrancy or disorderly conduct, and concurrent jurisdiction with the higher courts in some other cases. In certain cases the accused has the right to appeal to the court of general jurisdiction, where he is tried again. Police courts in cities have practically the same jurisdiction as justices of the peace.

6 State v. Lesperman, 108 N. Car. 770, 14 S. E. 14.

7 In re Terrill, 52 Kans. 29, 34 Pac. 457, 39 Am. St. 327; Jackson v. Commonwealth, 13 Grat. (Va.) 795.

Also in every county there is a coroner, who calls a coroner's court or inquest to inquire into the causes of sudden death where violence is indicted.

§ 863. **Federal courts.**—The Federal courts are created by the Federal constitution and Federal statutes. They are the Supreme Court, the circuit courts of appeals, the district courts, and the commissioners' courts.

The Supreme Court has original jurisdiction in a few classes of cases expressly stated in the constitution. By various Federal statutes it is given appellate jurisdiction to review convictions of capital or otherwise infamous crimes by the circuit and district courts;[8] to review decisions made by the circuit courts of appeal;[9] to review the decisions made state courts of last resort in certain cases;[10] and has power by writ of habeas corpus to investigate cases where persons are held in custody under color of Federal authority.[11]

The circuit courts of appeals have appellate jurisdiction over decisions of the district courts.[12]

United States Commissioners have jurisdiction similar in the Federal government to that of the justices of the peace in state governments.[13]

[8] U. S. Comp. Stat. (1916), §§ 1210, 1213. See also, Marbury v. Madison, 1 Cranch (U. S.) 137, 2 L. ed. 60; Osborn v. United States Bank, 9 Wheat. (U. S.) 738, 6 L. ed. 204

[9] U. S. Comp. Stat. (1916), § 1216. See also, Dickinson v. United States, 174 Fed. 808; Cella v. Brown, 144 Fed. 742; Louisville, N. A. & C. R. Co. v. Pope, 74 Fed. 1.

[10] U. S. Comp. Stat. (1916), § 1214. See also, Murdock v. Memphis, 20 Wall. (U. S.) 590, 22 L. ed. 429; Caperton v. Ballard, 14 Wall (U. S.) 238, 20 L. ed. 885.

[11] U. S. Comp. Stat. (1916), § 1291. See also, Caper v. Fitzgerald, 121 U. S. 87, 30 L. ed. 882; Ex parte Parks, 93 U. S. 18, 23 L. ed. 987; In re Yerger, 8 Wall (U. S.) 85, 19 L. ed. 332.

[12] U. S. Comp. Stat. (1916), § 1120. See also, Lau Ow Bew v. United States, 144 U. S. 47, 36 L. ed. 340; McLish v. Roff, 144 U. S. 661, 35 L. ed. 893.

[13] U. S. Comp. Stat. (1916), § 1333. See also, United States v. Allred, 155 U. S. 591, 39 L. ed. 273; United States v. Hom Hing, 48 Fed. 635.

All Federal courts are confined in their jurisdiction expressly to that which is given them by statute and the constitution, and none of them has general jurisdiction.

§ 864. Venue.—The county in which an offense is committed and must be tried is called the venue of the crime. The general rule is that a person charged with a crime must be tried in the county where it was committed. There are some exceptions to this rule at common law, and others have been created by statute. The principal reason for the rule is that the accused is entitled to be tried by a jury of his peers, selected from the county where the offense was committed.

An interesting question as to venue arises when the agency of the crime is set in motion in one county, and the result is accomplished in another; as where a mortal blow is struck in one county, and the person struck dies in another county. The general rule in such cases is that the crime is committed where the blow is struck.[14] It was held at a very early date that the accused could not be tried in either county, for a jury of one county could only take cognizance of the blow, and of the other only of the death and not of the blow.[15] To set the matter at rest the statute of 2 & 3 Edw. VI. ch. 24 was passed, providing that in such case the prosecution might be held in the county where the victim died. The result of this statute was to allow trial in either county. Similar statutes are found in some of the states of this country.

Where one sets in motion an agency in one county, the impact of which causes death in another, the venue is in the latter county; as where one feloniously shoots across the boundary line of a county, and kills a person in another, the

[14] Green v. State, 66 Ala. 40, 41 Am. Rep. 744; 1 Hale C. P. 426; 1 East P. C. 361.

[15] 1 Hale C. P. 426; 1 East P. C. 361; 2 Hawk. P. C. C. 25, § 36.

murder is committed in the latter county.[16] One who while in one county commits a crime in another county through an innocent agent is held to have committed the crime in the latter county and must be tried there.[17] The venue of larceny is where the property is taken. But at common law the thief may be prosecuted in any county, even of another state, into which he takes the property.[18] The legal possession of the goods remains in the owner, and therefore there is a continuing trespass, and felony. In cases of false pretenses the venue may be laid in the county in which the property was obtained by the pretense, though it may have been sent from another county.[19] The same rule also holds in forgery,[20] or libel.[21] It is also held that if these offenses are committed by letter, the offender may be tried in the county where the letter is prepared, though the former would seem the better rule.[22] The venue of embezzlement is the county where the property is appropriated, unless the transaction extends beyond that county.[23] The venue of robbery is in the county where the property is taken;[24] the venue of libel the county of publication.[25] At common law prosecutions for bigamy must be in the county where the bigamous marriage took place,[26] but by statute in some jurisdictions the offense

16 People v. Adams, 3 Denio (N. Y.) 207, 45 Am. Dec. 468; 1 Hale P. C. 475; 1 East P. C. 367.

17 People v. Rathbun, 21 Wend. (N. Y.) 509; Anonymous, J. Kelyng 53; 1 Hale P. C. 430, 431, 615, 617.

18 Commonwealth v. De Witt, 10 Mass. 154; 4 Bl. Comm. 305; 2 Hale P. C. 163; 1 Chit. Crim. L. 178; 2 East P. C. 771, 772.

19 Norris v. State, 25 Ohio St. 217, 18 Am. Rep. 291.

20 People v. Rathbun, 21 Wend. (N. Y.) 509.

21 Commonwealth v. Blanding, 3 Pick. (Mass.) 304, 15 Am. Dec. 214.

22 Landa v. State, 26 Tex. App. 580, 10 S. W. 218.

23 People v. Murphy, 51 Cal. 376; State v. Bailey, 50 Ohio St. 636, 36 N. E. 233.

24 Sweat v. State, 90 Ga. 315, 17 S. E. 273.

25 Commonwealth v. Blanding, 3 Pick. (Mass.) 304, 15 Am. Dec. 214; Rex v. Johnson, 7 East 65.

26 Brewer v. State, 59 Ala. 101; 1 Hale P. C. 692, 693.

is made a continuous one, and the prosecution may be wherever the parties are found living in bigamy.[27]

A person who takes such a part in a misdemeanor that if the offense were a felony he would be an accessory, but as it is a misdemeanor, is punishable as a principal, may be prosecuted where the crime is committed, even if acting in another county.[28] But there is some doubt as to whether one who is accessory in one county to a felony perpetrated by a guilty agent in another, may be tried as an accessory in the county where the crime is committed,[29] though such is the general provision of statutes.

One who creates a nuisance in one county, which affects residents in another county, may be tried in either county.[30]

One who on shore kills another upon the high seas by firing a gun is triable by the admiralty courts, which have jurisdiction of the high seas.[31] There is more uncertainty where a gun fired on the high seas kills one on land.[32]

Crimes against the United States committed within the territory of a state must be tried in the state and district of commission; those committed in territory not that of a state at such a place as congress may direct.[33] Crimes committed outside of the jurisdiction of any particular state or district are tried in the district in which the offender is first brought into custody.[34]

In addition to the instances already mentioned, the common law rules of venue have been largely changed by statute. It is provided in many jurisdictions that when a crime is com-

[27] Commonwealth v. Bradley, 2 Cush. (Mass.) 553; State v. Johnson, 12 Minn. 476, 93 Am. Dec. 241.

[28] Commonwealth v. Gillespie, 7 Serg. & R. (Pa.) 469, 10 Am. Dec. 475; Rex v. Brisac, 4 East 164; 1 Bish. New Crim. Prac., § 57, 4.

[29] 1 Bish. New Crim. Prac., § 58.

[30] State v. Lord, 16 N. H. 357; 2 Hawk, P. C., ch. 25, § 37.

[31] Rex v. Coombes, 1 Leach 888; 1 East P. C. 367.

[32] United States v. Magill, Fed. Cas. No. 15676, 4 Dall. (U. S.) 426, 1 Wash. C. C. 463, 1 L. ed. 894.

[33] U. S. Const., art. 3, § 2.

[34] U. S. Comp. Stat. (1916), § 1023.

mitted on or near the boundaries of counties, the venue may be laid in either of the counties. There is also a common statutory provision to the effect that where a crime is committed partly in one county and partly in another, the offender may be tried and punished in either. Other statutes provide that where a crime is committed in a moving vehicle, such as a railway car, automobile, or vessel, and there is doubt as to the county in which it occurred, the venue may be laid in any county through which the offender passes in the vehicle.

§ 865. **Change of venue.**—A change of venue is the removal by order of court of a cause from one county to an adjoining county for trial. In most states the grounds for such a change are fixed by statute, and are usually, either such prejudice against the defendant in the community that he can not have a fair trial,[35] or prejudice or unfitness of the judge.[36] In some states proof must be given of the facts alleged in the motion for change of venue,[37] in others affidavits are sufficient.[38] In some states the court must grant a change of venue upon proper application;[39] in others the granting of the application is within judicial discretion.[40] In most jurisdictions the change can be made only upon motion of the de-

[35] Smith v. State, 145 Ind. 176, 42 N. E. 1019; State v. Furbeck, 29 Kans. 532.

[36] State v. King, 20 Fla. 19; State v. Gates, 20 Mo. 400; State v. Wills (Fla.), 78 So. 693; People v. St. Louis Merchants' Bridge Co., 282 Ill. 408, 118 N. E. 733; City of Leavenworth v. Green River Asphalt Co., 101 Kan. 82, 165 Pac. 824 (judge disqualified because he had been counsel in the case); Callaghan v. Callaghan, 30 Idaho 431, 165 Pac. 1122.

[37] Howard v. State, 165 Ala. 18, 50 So. 954; Emporia v. Volmer, 12 Kans. 622.

[38] Mershon v. State, 44 Ind. 598. See also, People v. May, 276 Ill. 332, 114 N. E. 685; People v. Samuel, 199 Ill. App. 294; Huffman v. State (Ind. App.), 117 N. E. 874.

[39] Rafferty v. People, 66 Ill. 118; Johnson v. Commonwealth, 82 Ky. 116.

[40] Hubbard v. State, 7 Ind. 160; State v. Turlington, 102 Mo. 642, 15 S. W. 141; Gallaher v. State, 40 Tex. Cr. 296, 50 S. W. 388.

fendant;[41] in some the prosecution may take a change.[42] The motion for change of venue must be made before the jury is sworn.[43]

§ 866. Steps in trial—The various steps in the apprehension of an offender and trial of his case will be discussed here largely in the order of their natural sequence, beginning with the arrest, and preliminary examination, and followed by a discussion of the grand jury and the indictment or presentment, the defendant's pleadings, the conduct of the trial, sentence and execution of the sentence and appeal or review of the trial proceedings.

[41] Ex parte Rivers, 40 Ala. 712; In re Nelson, 19 S. Dak. 214, 102 N. W. 885.

[42] Smith v. Commonwealth, 108 Ky. 53, 55 S. W. 718; People v. Webb, 1 Hill (N. Y.) 179.

[43] Hunnel v. State, 86 Ind. 431; State v. Kent, 5 N. Dak. 516, 67 N. W. 1052, 35 L. R. A. 518.

CHAPTER LXXV.

ARREST AND EXTRADITION.

§ 870. **Arrest.**—An arrest is the act of taking a person into custody under lawful authority.[1] It may be made by virtue of a warrant, or in some cases without a warrant.

Some physical act is necessary to constitute arrest. Spoken words are not enough; but a mere touching of the finger upon the person of the accused, or the act of locking a room in which he is, is sufficient.[2] The purpose to arrest must be made known.[3]

§ 871. **Resisting arrest—Liabilities.**—To resist an attempted legal arrest is a criminal act.[4] If the offender kills the one who seeks to arrest him lawfully, it is murder.[5] An

[1] Hogan v. Strophlet, 179 Ill. 150, 53 N. E. 604, 44 L. R. A. 809; Bish. New Crim. Prac., § 156.

[2] Hill v. Taylor, 50 Mich. 549, 15 N. W. 899; Genner v. Sparks, 6 Mod. 173, 1 Salk. 79.

[3] Brooks v. Commonwealth, 61 Pa. St. 352, 100 Am. Dec. 645.

[4] People v. Haley, 48 Mich. 495, 12 N. W. 671; Gross v. State (Ind.), 117 N. E. 562.

[5] Mockabee v. Commonwealth, 78 Ky. 380.

unlawful escape from a legal arrest is at least a misdemeanor.[6] A third person who assists to resist arrest to escape therefrom, commits a criminal act.[7]

But if an attempted arrest is illegal, it may be resisted by any necessary force short of taking life or inflicting serious bodily harm;[8] and if life is taken in resisting illegal arrest, the homicide is not deemed murder, but manslaughter.[9]

If an arrest is authorized and is not made in an improper manner, there is no liability on the part of the one making it;[10] but one attempting or making an unlawful arrest is guilty of assault and battery or false imprisonment and is liable both civilly and criminally.[11] One illegally arrested or illegally held in custody may obtain release by a writ of habeas corpus.[12] An officer may be liable in damages for the use of unnecessary force in making an arrest,[13] but this does not entitle the prisoner to release from custody.

§ 872. Warrant.—A warrant is a written command issued in the name of the state by a magistrate having authority addressed to some competent officer or person, to take a particular individual and dispose of him for a specified crime

6 State v. Leach, 7 Conn. 452, 18 Am. Dec. 113; Commonwealth v. Filburn, 119 Mass. 297.

7 Clark's Crim. Law, 325.

8 Creighton v. Commonwealth, 83 Ky. 142, 4 Am. St. 143.

9 People v. Burt, 51 Mich. 199, 16 N. W. 378.

10 State v. Pugh, 101 N. Car. 737, 7 S. E. 757, 9 Am. St. 44.

11 Burns v. State, 80 Ga. 544, 7 S. E. 88.

12 In re Keeler, Fed. Cas. No. 7637, 1 Hempst. (U. S.) 306; In re Moyer, 35 Colo. 159, 85 Pac. 190, 117 Am. St. 189; Randall v. Bridge, 2 Mass. 549; Commonwealth v. Brickett, 8 Pick. (Mass.) 138; Commonwealth v. Lecky, 1 Watts (Pa.) 66, 26 Am. Dec. 37; Lacey v. Palmer, 93 Va. 159, 24 S. E. 930, 31 L. R. A. 822, 57 Am. St. 795.

13 Rhodes v. King, 52 Ala. 272; State v. Phillips, 119 Iowa 652, 94 N. W. 229, 67 L. R. A. 292; Petrie v. Cartwright, 114 Ky. 103, 70 S. W. 297, 59 L. R. A. 720, 102 Am. St. 274; People v. McCord, 76 Mich. 200, 42 N. W. 1106; Firestone v. Rice, 71 Mich. 377, 38 N. W. 885, 15 Am. St. 266; Jackson v. State, 66 Miss. 89, 5 So. 690, 14 Am. St. 542; State v. Hancock, 73 Mo. App. 19.

according to law.[14] In order to render a warrant legal it must conform to certain formalities. It must issue from a magistrate having jurisdiction of the subject matter, or at least with power to hold the accused to the grand jury.[15] In some jurisdictions it must be under seal.[16] It must show when it was issued.[17] It must be directed to a person authorized to make arrests and command him to bring the accused before the magistrate who issued it or some other magistrate, who has jurisdiction.[18] It must give the correct name of the accused if known; if not, he must be so described as to identify him. Description as unknown, or by a fictitious name, is insufficient.[19] If a blank is left for the name, the officer to whom it is addressed has no power to fill it in, and the warrant is void.[20] A warrant may be issued at any time of day or night or on Sunday.[21] It must show on its face that there is authority to issue it and that it is issued on a proper complaint.[22] Clerical errors or defects in form are immaterial.[23] But material alterations by anyone save the issuing magistrate make it void.[24] It must state the offense, and such an offense that an arrest may be made.[25] After service a warrant should be returned by the officer.[26] A warrant is in force until returned.[27]

14 1 Bish. New Crim. Prac., § 187; 4 Bl. Com. 290-292.

15 State v. Shelton, 79 N. Car. 605; Pierce v. State, 17 Tex. App. 232.

16 Beekman v. Traver, 20 Wend. (N. Y.) 67; 4 Bl. Comm. 290.

17 Donahoe v. Shed, 8 Metc. (Mass.) 326.

18 Bookhout v. State, 66 Wis. 415, 28 N. W. 179.

19 People v. Gosch, 82 Mich. 22, 46 N. W. 101; Scott v. Ely, 4 Wend. (N. Y.) 555.

20 Rafferty v. People, 69 Ill. 111, 18 Am. Rep. 601.

21 Pearce v. Atwood, 13 Mass. 327.

22 Gold v. Bissell, 1 Wend. (N. Y.) 210, 19 Am. Dec. 480.

23 Commonwealth v. Martin, 98 Mass. 4.

24 Haskins v. Young, 19 N. Car. 527, 31 Am. Dec. 426.

25 People v. Belcher, 58 Mich. 325, 25 N. W. 303.

26 Dehm v. Hinman, 56 Conn. 320, 15 Atl. 741, 1 L. R. A. 374.

27 Cooper v. Adams, 2 Blackf. (Ind.) 294.

§ 873. **Arrest by warrant.**—Known and sworn officers within their precincts need not show their warrants before arrest to the accused,[28] though he should state its substance if demanded; but private persons and officers out of their precincts, to whom warrants are specially directed, must show them before arrest if demanded except that when one resists arrest the officer need not show the warrant before making the arrest.[29] Where arrest is made by warrant, the person executing it must be authorized to do so, or the arrest will be illegal.[30]

In the absence of statutory enactments, the warrant must be executed within the jurisdiction of the issuing magistrate.[31] If directed to an officer by the description of his office, and not by his name, he may execute it only in his own precinct.[32] However, in many states, statutes allow warrants to be executed anywhere in the state.[33]

§ 874. **Liability of officer executing warrant.**—An officer is liable for executing a warrant which is void on its face.[34] But if a warrant is regular and valid on its face, and has been issued by a magistrate having jurisdiction of the subject matter, the officer is protected, although the warrant is voidable, or even void.[35] An officer is not compelled to examine into the circumstances under which a warrant, regular and valid on its face, is issued, but is bound to execute such a warrant, so far as he has jurisdiction.[36] An officer may justify acts done by him under a process that is void, unless it appears on its face to be void, as well as acts done under a

28 Commonwealth v. West (Ky.), 113 S. W. 76.

29 Commonwealth v. Field, 13 Mass. 321; Frost v. Thomas, 24 Wend. (N. Y.) 418.

30 Wood v. Ross, 11 Mass. 271.

31 Little v. Rich (Tex. Civ. App.), 118 S. W. 1077; 4 Bl. Comm. 291; 2 Hale P. C. 115.

32 Krug v. Ward, 77 Ill. 603.

33 1 Bish. New Crim. Proc., § 189.

34 Parker v. Walrod, 16 Wend. (N. Y.) 514, 30 Am. Dec. 124.

35 Nichols v. Thomas, 4 Mass. 232.

36 Stoddard v. Tarbell, 20 Vt. 321.

process that is voidable and has been avoided.[37] But where the face of the warrant shows it was insufficient, the officer is not bound to execute it, and will be liable civilly and criminally for the consequences of an illegal arrest or attempted arrest, should he execute or attempt to execute the warrant.[38] This rule applies where the warrant fails to charge the accused with the commission of a specific crime,[39] or fails to name him or properly identify him,[40] or lacks a seal where the law requires it,[41] or, if it is patent that the issuing magistrate had no jurisdiction of the subject matter.[42] But if the warrant is valid on its face, mere knowledge by the officer of facts making it void for lack of jurisdiction does not make him liable for its execution. Nor does the insufficiency of the complaint upon which the warrant is based, if it does not appear upon the face of the warrant, render the officer liable.[43]

§ 875. Arrest without warrant by private persons.—The rule of the common law is that any private person who witnesses the commission of a treason or a felony must arrest the offender though he has no warrant. Failure to do so is to commit the misdemeanor of misprision of treason or felony.[44] It is also the rule that when a treason or felony has in fact been committed, and a private person on reasonable grounds suspects a particular person, he may arrest him and if he acts in good faith will incur neither civil or criminal liability if this suspicion is proven to be unfounded in fact.[45] But to

37 Kennedy v. Duncklee, 1 Gray (Mass.) 65; People v. Warren, 5 Hill (N. Y.) 440.

38 Sandford v. Nichols, 13 Mass. 286, 7 Am. Dec. 151.

39 People v. Phillips, 1 Edm. Sel. Cas. 386, 1 Parker Cr. (N. Y.) 104.

40 Gurnsey v. Lovell, 9 Wend. (N. Y.) 319.

41 Beekman v. Traver, 20 Wend. (N. Y.) 67.

42 Tracy v. Williams, 4 Conn. 107, 10 Am. Dec. 102.

43 Donahoe v. Shed, 8 Metc. (Mass.) 326.

44 Holley v. Mix, 3 Wend. (N. Y.) 350, 20 Am. Dec. 702; 4 Bl. Comm. 293.

45 Kennedy v. State, 107 Ind. 144, 6 N. E. 305, 57 Am. Rep. 99.

excuse him from liability there must be proved not only reasonable cause for his suspicion, but also that a crime was actually committed.[46] A private person may also arrest one engaged in riot, affrays, or the like.[47] He also it seems has the right to retake one who has broken from prison or escaped from lawful custody.[48] At common law a private person has not the right to arrest one for committing an ordinary misdemeanor, unless it amounts to a breach of the peace.[49] Any private person must inform the one whom he attempts to arrest of his purpose.[50]

§ 876. **Arrest without warrant by officer.**—Any peace officer may arrest without a warrant not only when any private person may arrest but also under the following additional circumstances: First, by verbal direction of a judge or justice of the peace for a felony or breach of the peace committed in the presence of the judge or justice, or for any offense committed in the presence of the judge or justice in court.[51] Without either warrant or verbal order he may arrest for a felony or breach of the peace committed in his own presence or view, provided that in the latter case he makes the arrest during the commission of the misdemeanor, or immediately after.[52] In many states statutes give him the right to arrest without warrant for any misdemeanor committed in his presence or view.[53] He may also arrest without

[46] Holley v. Mix, 3 Wend. (N. Y.) 350, 20 Am. Dec. 702; Brooks v. Commonwealth, 61 Pa. St. 352, 100 Am. Dec. 645.

[47] Timothy v. Simpson, 1 Cromp. M. & R. 757.

[48] State v. Holmes, 48 N. H. 377.

[49] Phillips v. Trull, 11 Johns. (N. Y.) 486.

[50] State v. Bryant, 65 N. Car. 327; Tarwater v. State (Ala. App.), 75 So. 816 (officer too in some cases).

[51] Lancaster v. Lane, 19 Ill. 242.

[52] People v. Bartz, 53 Mich. 493, 19 N. W. 161; State v. Mancini, 91 Vt. 507, 101 Atl. 581; DeSilva v. New York Cent. Ry. Co., 169 N. Y. S. 924, 182 App. Div. 497; People v. Ostrosky, 160 N. Y. S. 493, 95 Misc. 104; Samino v. State (Tex. Cr.), 204 S. W. 233.

[53] State v. Brown, 5 Har. (Del.) 505; People v. Wilson, 55 Mich. 506, 21 N. W. 905. See also, Hudley v. State (Tex. Cr.), 194 S. W. 160; Larson v. Feeney, 196 Mich. 1, 162 N. W. 275, L. R. A. 1917 D, 694.

warrant upon his own reasonable suspicion that a felony has been committed and that he is arresting the guilty person, and in such case he is not liable even though no felony has been committed,[54] his liability in this respect differing from that of a private person. Or if a third person makes an accusation based on reasonable grounds that a felony has been committed, and that a certain person is guilty of its commission, he may arrest without warrant.[55] He also may recapture a prisoner, who has escaped from lawful custody, either before or after conviction.[56]

§ 877. **Assisting officer.**—Any justice of the peace for just cause may raise what is known as a posse comitatus of the citizens of the county in any number he thinks proper, in order to pursue and arrest law breakers.[57] A sheriff may raise a posse comitatus whether he is acting under a warrant or without a warrant.[58] Any peace officer who is making an arrest may call upon a person present to aid in the arrest, or may even summon all bystanders.[59] The command of a proper officer in a case in which he has apparent authority is a justification to one who in his presence comes to his assistance.[60] A refusal to assist may be indictable;[61] and one who obstructs an officer making an arrest, may himself be arrested. The hue and cry, an old common-law method of pursuing, with horns and voice, a felon or one who had dangerously wounded another, might be raised by

[54] Doering v. State, 49 Ind. 56, 19 Am. Rep. 669; Holley v. Mix, 3 Wend. (N. Y.) 350, 20 Am. Dec. 702; Zucker v. Zarembowitz, 168 N. Y. S. 805, 181 App. Div. 288; Allen v. Lopinsky (W. Va.), 94 S. E. 369; Davis v. Carroll, 159 N. Y. S. 568, 172 App. Div. 729; State v. Bradshaw (Mont.), 161 Pac. 710 (bona fide belief of officer not sufficient).

[55] People v. McLean, 68 Mich. 480, 36 N. W. 231.

[56] Simpson v. State, 56 Ark. 8, 19 S. W. 99.

[57] 4 Bl. Comm. 293.

[58] 4 Bl. Comm. 293.

[59] Commonwealth v. Field, 13 Mass. 321.

[60] Firestone v. Rice, 71 Mich. 377, 38 N. W. 885, 15 Am. St. 266.

[61] Commonwealth v. Field, 13 Mass. 321.

either officers or private persons, with the same rights and protection as under a warrant; and if an officer had a warrant, and the felon fled into another county, he might be followed by hue and cry into the other county.[62] Private persons joining in the hue and cry are not liable, even though no felony was committed.[63]

§ 878. Amount of force which may be used—Breaking doors.—To effect an arrest or prevent an escape in the case of a felony all necessary force may be used even to the extent of taking life.[64] All unnecessary force, however, is illegal.[65] To justify the killing of the accused a reasonable necessity for so doing is essential.[66] One who has committed a misdemeanor may not be killed to effect his arrest, or prevent his escape, but if he resists arrest all necessary force, even to taking life, is justifiable.[67] An officer may take life in self defense.[68] The same rules as to force used also apply to lawful arrests by private persons.

A peace officer, provided he has given notice of his authority and purpose to do so, and has been refused admittance, may break a door or window of a house in order to execute a warrant or make a lawful arrest without warrant.[69] Where a person has escaped from lawful custody and taken refuge in a house, an officer or private person either with or without a warrant may break into the house to retake if admittance has been refused upon demand.[70] The officer breaking doors is not liable for trespass if the house is that of the

62 4 Bl. Comm. 293; Clark Crim. Proc. 48.

63 4 Bl. Comm. 293; Clark Crim. Proc. 48.

64 Clements v. State, 50 Ala. 117.

65 Skidmore v. State, 43 Tex. 93.

66 State v. Dierberger, 96 Mo. 666, 10 S. W. 168, 9 Am. St. 380.

67 Clements v. State, 50 Ala. 117; State v. Dierberger, 96 Mo. 666, 10 S. W. 168, 9 Am. St. 380.

68 State v. Dierberger, 96 Mo. 666, 10 S. W. 168, 9 Am. St. 380; Brooks v. Commonwealth, 61 Pa St. 352, 100 Am. Dec. 645.

69 Commonwealth v. Reynolds, 120 Mass. 190, 21 Am. Rep. 510.

70 Allen v. Martin, 10 Wend. (N. Y.) 300, 25 Am. Dec. 564.

accused and there was probable cause to believe he was there, although he may not be found within;[71] and the same rule is probably true if the house is that of a third person.[72] A private person may not break into a house to arrest a suspected felon,[73] but he may break into it to arrest a person for a felony actually committed by him, or to prevent the commission of a felony.[74] He also may break into a house to arrest a person who has escaped from lawful custody, provided he has made a proper demand to be admitted and his demand has been refused.[75]

§ 879. **Disposal after arrest.**—A private person, who without a warrant has arrested another for treason or felony, may either take him immediately before a magistrate or deliver him to a police officer or jailor.[76] He must not retain him in his custody an unreasonable time, but if he has arrested him for affray he may keep him until the heat is over.[77] An officer, after making an arrest, must without unnecessary delay take the prisoner before some proper magistrate for examination.[78]

§ 880. **Search warrants**—The United States Constitution and the state constitutions prohibit unreasonable searches and seizures. Reasonable searches are allowed both by statute and at common law, both to recover stolen property or discover evidence of a crime. A magistrate may issue a warrant directing the party to whom it is addressed to search

71 Commonwealth v. Reynolds, 120 Mass. 190, 21 Am. Rep. 510.

72 Commonwealth v. Irwin, 1 Allen (Mass.) 587.

73 Brooks v. Commonwealth, 61 Pa. St. 352, 100 Am. Dec. 645.

74 Handcock v. Baker, 2 Bos. & P. 260; 1 Chitty Crim. L. 53.

75 Genner v. Sparks, 6 Mod. 173, 1 Salk. 79.

76 Commonwealth v. Tobin, 108 Mass. 426, 11 Am. Rep. 375.

77 1 Chitty Crim. L. 20; 2 Hawk. P. C., ch. 13, § 8.

78 Commonwealth v. Wilcox, 1 Cush. (Mass.) 503; Davis v. Carroll, 159 N. Y. S. 568, 172 App. Div. 729; Haglund v. Burdick State Bank, 100 Kans. 279, 164 Pac. 167.

and seize the property therein described. The warrant must be based upon proper complaint and this must appear upon the face of the warrant.[79]

The warrant must describe accurately the place to be searched, the person whose place is to be searched, and the property to be seized. Only the place described may be searched.[80] Generally speaking, the warrant must direct search to be made in daytime, but in special cases may direct a search at night.[81] It must command that the property be brought before the magistrate.[82] The premises may be broken into if necessary, but where there is a person at hand, upon whom demand may be made, admittance must be demanded and refused before breaking.[83] General search warrants are void.[84] Statutory requirements must be strictly complied with.

§ 881. Extradition and fugitives—Generally.—The authority of a warrant extends only to the territory within which the issuing court sits. One who commits a crime in one state or country, and flees to another, is a fugitive from justice, and usually may be arrested and sent back to the state or country where he committed the crime, there to be tried. This is accomplished by the process called extradition. Extradition from one state to another of the same nation is interstate extradition; and from one nation to another international extradition.

[79] Commonwealth v. Phillips, 16 Pick. (Mass.) 211; Allen v. Colby, 47 N. H. 544.

[80] Commonwealth v. Intoxicating Liquors, 140 Mass. 287, 3 N. E. 4.

[81] 2 Hale P. C. 150.

[82] White v. Wagar, 185 Ill. 195, 57 N. E. 26, 50 L. R. A. 60; Early v. People, 117 Ill. App. 608; Hibbard v. People, 4 Mich. 125; Bell v. Clapp, 10 Johns. (N. Y.) 263, 6 Am. Dec. 339; Cooley Const. Lim. 369.

[83] Androscoggin R. Co. v. Richards, 41 Maine 233.

[84] 2 Hawk. P. C., ch. 13, § 17.

§ 882. Interstate extradition.—Interstate extradition is based upon provisions of the United States Constitution and acts of Congress. In most of the states there are statutes providing the mode of extradition; but where they conflict with the mode provided by Congress the latter governs. The acts of Congress, following the constitutional authorization, provide for extradition in the case of treason, felony, or other crimes.[85] This has been said to include misdemeanors.[86] However, a governor will not usually issue a warrant of extradition for a fugitive whose crime is a misdemeanor where committed. Where the crime was a felony where committed, but only a misdemeanor in the state to which the fugitive has fled, an extradition requisition will be issued.[87] Extradition warrants will issue only where the accused is a "fugitive from justice." Actual flight is not essential to make one a fugitive from justice, but if the accused personally committed the crime in one state, and then went into another, with or without the intention of avoiding justice, for any purpose, even to his own home, he is subject to extradition by the authorities of the state where the crime was committed.[88] But one who as a principal commits a crime in one state through an agent, himself being in another state, may not be extradited, for he has never been in the state where the crime was committed.[89] In cases of interstate extradition, a fugitive from justice who has been surrendered for one crime

[85] United States Const., art. 4, § 2.

[86] In re Clark, 9 Wend. (N. Y.) 212; State v. Stewart, 60 Wis. 587, 19 N. W. 429, 50 Am. Rep. 488.

[87] Johnston v. Riley, 13 Ga. 97; Wilcox v. Nolze, 34 Ohio St. 520.

[88] Roberts v. Reilly, 116 U. S. 80, 29 L. ed. 544; Kingsbury v. United States, 106 Mass. 223; Taft v. Lord, 92 Conn. 539, 103 Atl. 644; People ex rel. Goldfarb v. Gargan, 168 N. Y. S. 1027, 181 App. Div. 410, 36 N. Y. Crim. Rep, 233.

[89] In re Mohr, 73 Ala. 503, 49 Am. Rep. 63; 1 Bish. New Crim. Proc., § 53; State v. Wellman, 103 Kans. 503, 170 Pac. 1052, L. R. A. 1918 D, 949; Ex parte Montgomery, 244 Fed. 967; Taft v. Lord, 92 Conn. 539, 103 Atl. 644; Innes v. Tobin, 240 U. S. 127, 36 Sup. Ct. 290, 60 L. ed. 562.

may be tried for any other for which he may not have been extradited.[90] This rule does not apply to a case of foreign extradition, which is governed entirely by treaty agreements between different countries; and in such cases, usually, if extradited for one crime, he may not be tried for another until he has returned to the foreign country and has been again extradited for another offense, or has been given a reasonable time in which to return to the foreign country.[91]

If the accused is kidnapped from one state to another, the fact that he has not been legally extradited is no defense to the charge of crime against him.[92] He has a right of action for damages against the person who kidnapped him. This principle applies in a case where he has been kidnapped from a foreign country, and in such case the country from which he has been kidnapped may have an action against the kidnapper, or may demand reparation from the country into which he is taken. Though the language of the constitutional provision which requires governors to deliver up fugitives from justice is mandatory, it is in fact not obligatory, for there is no means of compelling a governor to issue a warrant of requisition if he refuses. The governor is not presumed to base his decision on the merits of the case, but if he believes that the object in seeking requisition of a fugitive is private gain instead of public interest, or in some cases in which the crime with which the fugitive is charged bears a political aspect, he will refuse to issue a warrant.[93]

[90] Lascelles v. Georgia, 148 U. S. 537, 37 L. ed. 549; Commonwealth v. Wright, 158 Mass. 149, 33 N. E. 82, 19 L. R. A. 206, 35 Am. St. 475.

[91] United States v. Rauscher, 119 U. S. 407, 30 L. ed. 425; State v. Vanderpool, 39 Ohio St. 273, 48 Am. Rep. 431.

[92] State v. Ross, 21 Iowa 467; Brookin v. State, 26 Tex. App. 121, 9 S. W. 735; State v. Wellman, 102 Kans. 503, 170 Pac. 1052.

[93] Kentucky v. Dennison, 24 How. (U. S.) 66, 16 L. ed. 717; Ex parte Manchester, 5 Cal. 237.

The first step in the procedure of obtaining an interstate extradition warrant is for the state's attorney in the county in which the crime was committed to make a complaint against the accused, and have a warrant issued for his arrest. A formal indictment is not essential. The substance of the charge must appear, but need not be alleged with the formality required in an indictment.[94] After obtaining the warrant, the state's attorney should file with the secretary of state certified copies of the complaint and warrant, together with affidavits of good faith and of the flight of the accused to the other state.[95] These papers are presented by the secretary of state to the governor who examines them, and if satisfactory, issues his requisition to the governor of the state to which the accused has fled. This requisition, together with copies of papers filed in the case is taken by the agent of the governor of the demanding state and filed by him with the secretary of state of the other state. This secretary of state, in whose office they are filed, submits them to the governor, who, after examining them, either issues or refuses to issue his warrant of extradition.[96] After the warrant of extradition is issued, the accused may sue out a writ of habeas corpus, and this will entitle him to be heard by the court,[97] as to the regularity of the extradition proceedings. The court, however, will not consider whether the object of the extradition is private gain or not, but as said before, the governor will consider this matter.

[94] People v. Stockwell, 135 Mich. 341, 97 N. W. 765; Hard v. Splain (D. C.), 45 App. D. C. 1; Hart v. Mangum, 146 Ga. 497, 91 S. E. 543.

[95] Kingsbury v. United States, 106 Mass. 223; State v. Clough, 71 N. H. 594, 53 Atl. 1086, 67 L. R. A. 946; Ex parte Jones (Tex. Cr.), 199 S. W. 1110; Pool v. State (Ala. App.), 79 So. 311.

[96] People v. Brady, 56 N. Y. 182; In re Clark, 9 Wend. (N. Y.) 212.

[97] Roberts v. Reilly, 116 U. S. 80, 29 L. ed. 544; Work v. Corrington, 34 Ohio St. 64, 32 Am. Rep. 345.

If in conveying a prisoner from one state to another he is taken through a foreign country, and sues out a habeas corpus in the foreign country, he is entitled to his freedom, for interstate requisitions will afford in the foreign country no justification to the persons having him in charge.

§ 883. **International extradition.**—International or foreign extradition is based entirely on treaties. A fugitive from justice can not be extradited except for a crime enumerated in a treaty.[98] When extradited for a crime therein enumerated he can not be tried for any other until after reasonable time and opportunity have been afforded him to return to his own country.[99] He can not be extradited unless a fugitive from justice, but as in the case of interstate extradition, this does not mean that he must actually have gone to the foreign country to escape the consequences of his acts. It is sufficient that he has been in the foreign country at all after the commission of the crime.

In extraditing from this country a person charged with an extraditable crime, first the foreign sovereign requests of the president the delivery of the accused. The president then appoints an examiner to investigate the case, who may be a Federal or state judge, or a United States Commissioner. Such examiner issues a warrant for the arrest of the fugitive, and receives whatever evidence is offered in the case. He certifies this evidence to the secretary of state who examines it, and reports his conclusions to the president, who then either issues or refuses to issue a warrant of extradition. The president has discretion, as a governor has, and can not be compelled to issue a warrant where he refuses. Nor will

98 Ex parte McCabe, 46 Fed. 363, 12 L. R. A. 589.

99 State v. Vanderpool, 39 Ohio St. 273, 48 Am. Rep. 431; Blandford v. State, 10 Tex. App. 627.

the courts review his action in issuing a warrant, if there is material evidence of the fugitive's guilt, and the proceedings are regular. But the accused may sue out a writ of habeas corpus to try a question of law even after the president has issued his warrant.

CHAPTER LXXVI.

PRELIMINARY PROCEEDINGS AND BAIL.

§ 885. Preliminary proceedings.—Ordinarily a person arrested can not be tried immediately, and must therefore be held for trial. So a person arrested, charged with crime, has a right to a preliminary examination, before a proper magistrate as soon as the circumstances will permit, in order to ascertain whether in fact a crime has been committed, and if it is so found, whether there is probable cause to believe him guilty.[1] If an indictment against the accused has already been found by the grand jury, it is not necessary to hold an examination before a magistrate, for he can be held under the indictment; nor is examination necessary if the accused was a fugitive from justice when arrested.[2] A coroner's inquest is a preliminary inquiry, and at common law is equivalent to an examination before a magistrate.[3] The right of examination may be waived by the accused.[4]

[1] Simmons v. Vandyke, 138 Ind. 380, 37 N. E. 973, 26 L. R. A. 33, 46 Am. St. 411; Papineau v. Bacon, 110 Mass. 319.

[2] People v. Kuhn, 67 Mich. 463, 35 N. W. 88.

[3] Commonwealth v. Lafferty, 11 Pa. Co. Ct. 513; Wormeley v. Commonwealth, 10 Grat. (Va.) 658.

[4] Stuart v. People, 42 Mich. 255, 3 N. W. 863.

If preliminary examination is delayed an unreasonable and unnecessary length of time, the holding of the accused becomes false imprisonment.[5]

§ 886. **Procedure in examination.**—At common law the officer may take his prisoner before either the magistrate issuing the warrant or any other magistrate having jurisdiction of the offense.[6] In some staes, by statute, it must be taken before the issuing magistrate.[7] Justices of the peace have authority to commit accused persons for their trials,[8] and this power may also be exercised by United States Commissioners or Federal judges and in some states by higher judicial officers of mayors of cities.[9] The procedure in a preliminary examination must follow the rules prescribed by statute.[10] There should be a complaint whether the arrest has been made with or without a warrant,[11] but in most cases the complaint upon which the warrant is issued will serve as the complaint for the examination.[12] The complaint should be verified by oath or evidence under oath should be given as to the crime.[13] The complaint, need not be in the technically correct form of an indictment.[14] In most instances the accused person may be held if the evidence shows him guilty of a crime different from that alleged in the complaint.[15] An insufficient complaint may usually be amended.[16]

[5] Tubbs v. Tukey, 3 Cush. (Mass.) 438, 50 Am. Dec. 744; Arnold v. Steeves, 10 Wend. (N. Y.) 515.

[6] Wiggins v. Norton, 83 Ga. 148, 9 S. E. 607.

[7] People v. Fuller, 17 Wend. (N. Y.) 211.

[8] Ormond v. Ball, 120 Ga. 916, 48 S. E. 383.

[9] United States v. Hughes, 70 Fed. 972; United States v. Rundlett, Fed. Cas. No. 16208, 2 Curt. C. C. 41; Cluggish v. Rogers, 13 Ind. 538.

[10] Papineau v. Bacon, 110 Mass. 319.

[11] Tracy v. Williams, 4 Conn. 107, 10 Am. Dec. 102.

[12] Tracy v. Williams, 4 Conn. 107, 10 Am. Dec. 102.

[13] Allen v. Staples, 6 Gray (Mass.) 491.

[14] Field v. Ireland, 21 Ala. 240.

[15] People v. Wheeler, 73 Cal. 252, 14 Pac. 796.

[16] State v. Shaw, 4 Ind. 428.

At common law the accused had no right to be represented by counsel, but is given this right by statute in most states,[17] and also it is provided by statute that the examination shall be in the presence of the accused.[18] Probably at common law the accused could not insist upon the right to examine witnesses, but by statute in most states he has this right.[19] The accused can not be compelled to testify, but in most jurisdictions is permitted by statute to testify in his own defense which he could not do at common law.[20] The issue to be tried before the magistrate is not whether the prisoner is guilty, but whether there is probable cause to believe him guilty. Therefore the same degree of proof is not required to hold a man for trial as is necessary to convict him on trial.[21] The magistrate at common law in cases of felony has the power to bind over the witnesses for the prosecution to appear at the trial of the cause either by commitment or recognizance.[22] If the magistrate determines that he should hold the accused to trial, he should make an order to that effect, and fix the amount of bail, if the offense is bailable.[23] If he thinks the evidence insufficient to show probable cause for believing the accused committed the crime he must discharge him.[24] But a discharge by a magistrate on preliminary examination is not a bar to any new proceedings.[25]

Irregularities at preliminary hearing can not affect the right of the grand jury to investigate a case and return an indictment,[26] but in states where trial may be had upon infor-

17 Cox v. Coleridge, 1 Barn. & C. 37.

18 Harris v. People, 130 Ill. 457, 22 N. E. 826.

19 United States v. White, Fed. Cas. No. 16685, 2 Wash. C. C. 29; Whart. Crim. Pl. & Prac., § 72.

20 Commonwealth v. Nichols, 114 Mass. 285, 19 Am. Rep. 346; State v. Kinder, 96 Mo. 548, 10 S. W. 77; Black on Const. Law 497.

21 Bostick v. Rutherford, 11 N. Car. 83; 4 Bl. Comm. 296.

22 2 Hawk. P. C., ch. 16, § 2.

23 Goodwin v. Dodge, 14 Conn. 206.

24 Templeton v. People, 27 Mich. 501.

25 State v. Ritty, 23 Ohio St. 562.

26 Osborn v. Commonwealth, (Ky), 20 S. W. 223.

mation, in lieu of indictment, the proper preliminary examination is essential to the validity of the information.[27] Proceedings before a magistrate are presumed to have been regular.[28] The accused may waive any irregularity in the examination.[29] In some states if the evidence shows that the magistrate has complete jurisdiction over the offence concurrent with the higher court he may in his discretion either bind over the prisoner or enter a conviction.[30] In other states the accused may if he wishes demand the full trial.[31]

§ 887. Bail.—An arrested person in many cases may obtain his liberty temporarily by giving bail, that is, by entering into a recognizance upon his own part and that of others, that he will appear for trial or further examination or forfeit a certain amount of money. Theoretically the arrested person is delivered to the surety who becomes entitled to his custody, and becomes responsible for his appearance at the time and place agreed. The power to admit to bail is judicial and not ministerial and may not be delegated.[32] The magistrate may become liable criminally for wrongfully refusing bail or for wrongfully allowing it.

§ 888. Right to bail.—In most of our states constitutional or statutory provisions give the accused an absolute right to give bail where the punishment is not death, and even in those cases unless the presumption and evidence against the

27 State v. Wise, 83 Iowa 596, 50 N. W. 59.

28 Boynton v. State, 77 Ala. 29.

29 Cunningham v. State, 116 Ind. 433, 17 N. E. 904; State v. Woods, 49 Kans. 237, 30 Pac. 520.

30 Commonwealth v. Sullivan, 156 Mass. 487, 31 N. E. 647.

31 Commonwealth v. Harris, 8 Gray (Mass.) 470.

32 State v. Winninger, 81 Ind. 51.

accused are strong.[33] The right to admit to bail at common law was discretionary with the magistrate, and bail was usually denied in cases of felony. The amount of bail required depends upon the circumstances of the case, and should be only such as is reasonably sufficient to assure the appearance of the accused.[34] Even by this rule, in cases where the punishment is only by a fine, the amount of bail should exceed the maximum penalty.[35] The United States Constitution forbids the taking of excessive bail. The sufficiency of the sureties is in the discretion of the magistrate.[36] In most states they must answer by oath or affidavit as to their financial responsibility.[37] At common law, infants, married women, persons convicted of infamous crimes and insane persons were incompetent to become bail.[38] Now the disabilities of married women have been removed generally by statute, and unless, expressly precluded by statute, any person capable of contracting may become bail. An infant may be bound as principal by a bail bond or recognizance.[39]

Where an accused person has been improperly denied bail, his remedy is by writ of habeas corpus.[40]

[33] Ex parte McAnally, 53 Ala. 495, 25 Am. Rep. 646; Commonwealth v. Keeper of Prison, 2 Ashm. (Pa.) 227; Ex parte Weinberg (Cal.), 171 Pac. 937; Ex parte Haley (Tex. Cr.), 204 S. W. 330; Ex parte Holden (Okla. Cr.), 171 Pac. 925; Ex parte Nagel (Nev.), 167 Pac. 689; People v. Mott, 162 N. Y. S. 272, 97 Misc. 86.

[34] State v. Hopson, 10 La. Ann. 550; Commonwealth v. Rutherford, 5 Rand. (Va.) 646; Ex parte Glass (W. Va.), 93 S. E. 1036; Ex parte Bowman (Tex. Cr.), 204 S. W. 329.

[35] State v. Martinez, 11 La. Ann. 23.

[36] 2 Hale P. C. 125.

[37] People v. Vermilyea, 7 Cow. (N. Y.) 108.

[38] Bennet v. Watson, 3 Maule & S. 1.

[39] McCall v. Parker, 13 Metc. (Mass.) 372, 46 Am. Dec. 735; Patchin v. Cromach, 13 Vt. 330; Bish. Cont., § 148.

[40] Farrel v. Hawley, 78 Conn. 150, 61 Atl. 502, 70 L. R. A. 686, 112 Am. St. 98; Evans v. Foster, 1 N. H. 374.

§ 889. Forms and requisites of bail.—The common form of bail is either by bond or recognizance, obliging the principal and sureties to pay to the state a sum of money should the accused fail to appear at the time and place specified, and must be executed in the manner prescribed by law in order to be valid. By statute a deposit of money may be given in lieu of either.[41] A bail bond is a contract under seal between the accused and his sureties on one part, and the state on the other, and must be signed and delivered.[42] A recognizance is a contract of record containing a similar obligation, and it is not essential that it be signed or sealed, unless statute requires.[43] The recognizance must be acknowledged before the magistrate, who certifies to the acknowledgment, and files the instrument for record.[44] Often, however, the magistrate merely repeats to the recognizors the obligation into which they are to enter, and the condition attached, and asks them if they are content, makes a memorandum of the proceedings, and subsequently draws up the recognizance in full and certifies it to the court.[45]

Either a bail bond or a recognizance "must contain and express in the body of it, the material parts of the obligation and condition."[46] It should state the offense accurately and with reasonable certainty,[47] but need not state all the circumstances or facts.[48] If an indictable offense is not stat-

41 People v. Laidlaw, 102 N. Y. 588, 7 N. E. 910.

42 Clark on Cont. 73.

43 Slaten v. People, 21 Ill. 28; State v. Weatherwax, 12 Kans. 463; Commonwealth v. Mason, 3 A. K. Marsh (Ky.) 456.

44 Bridge v. Ford, 4 Mass. 641; People v. Kane, 4 Denio (N. Y.) 530.

45 Commonwealth v. Emery, 2 Bin (Pa.) 431; State v. Smoot (W. Va.), 95 S. E. 526.

46 State v. Crippen, 1 Ohio St. 399; Buzan v. State (Tex. Civ. App.), 127 S. W. 1030.

47 Nicholson v. State, 2 Ga. 363.

48 Patterson v. State, 12 Ind. 86.

ed, the recognizance is void.[49] The time and place at which the accused is to appear must be manifest,[50] and the court should be described, unless fixed by statute.[51]

§ 890. Release of sureties.—The sureties occupy the position of private jailers of their principal, may take him into custody at any time,[52] may use reasonable force for this purpose,[53] and may even upon occasion break doors to take him.[54] Their obligation is released when they produce the principal in court and surrender him, or surrender him to the sheriff by order of the court,[55] or when because of an act of God, an act of the state, or of law, it becomes impossible to produce him. So the death of the accused before the time fixed for his appearance releases the sureties,[56] or a great degree of sickness,[57] or a change in the law preventing performance,[58] or a material change in the contract of recognizance by the state, as an agreement of the state with the accused to postpone his trial without consent of the sureties.[59] Imprisonment by the state will usually excuse the sureties,[60] or surrender as a fugitive from justice,[61] but not arrest in another state where the sureties have voluntarily permitted him to go.[62] Where the indictment is for a

49 Badger v. State, 5 Ala. 21; Dailey v. State, 4 Tex. 417.

50 State v. Allen, 33 Ala. 422; Mooney v. People, 81 Ill. 134.

51 People v. Carpenter, 7 Cal. 402.

52 Commonwealth v. Brickett, 8 Pick. (Mass.) 138; Nicolls v. Ingersoll, 7 Johns (N. Y.) 145.

53 Pease v. Burt, 3 Day (Conn.) 485; Commonwealth v. Brickett, 8 Pick. (Mass.) 138; Nicolls v. Ingersoll, 7 Johns. (N. Y.) 185.

54 Commonwealth v. Brickett, 8 Pick. (Mass.) 138; Nicolls v. Ingersoll, 7 Johns. (N. Y.) 185.

55 Bean v. Parker, 17 Mass. 591; Harp v. Osgood, 2 Hill (N. Y.) 216.

56 Merritt v. Thompson, 1 Hilt. (N. Y.) 550.

57 People v. Tubbs, 37 N. Y. 586.

58 Ringeman v. State, 136 Ala. 131, 34 So. 351; Bish. Cont., § 594.

59 Reese v. United States, 9 Wall. (U. S.) 13, 19 L. ed. 541; Vincent v. People, 25 Ill. 500.

60 Buffington v. Smith, 58 Ga. 341; State v. Orsler, 48 Iowa 343.

61 State v. Allen, 2 Humph. (Tenn.) 258.

62 Yarbrough v. Commonwealth, 89 Ky. 151, 12 S. W. 143, 25 Am. St. 524; Devine v. State, 5 Sneed (Tenn.) 623.

misdemeanor, usually the accused may appear and plead by attorney, and be tried in his absence, and his bond will not be forfeited.[63]

§ 891. Forfeiture of bail.—The sureties become bound on their obligation, when the condition of the bond or recognizance is broken. Thus, where the principal fails to appear at the time and place agreed on, the sureties then become liable for the amount of the penalty.[64] But the court may remit the forfeiture, upon good cause shown,[65] and in many states the governor has the power to remit the forfeiture of a bail bond or recognizance.[66] The mere fact of appearance does not discharge the sureties, the principal must be taken into custody by the proper officer,[67] but if he escapes after having been taken into custody, the sureties are no longer liable.[68] The forfeiture of bail does not affect the right of the state afterwards to arrest and prosecute the accused.[69] The mode of enforcing a forfeiture of bail is usually prescribed by statute, and may be by an action on the obligation in the name of the state, or in other cases, by making an entry of the forfeiture and judgment and scire facias thereon.

§ 892. Commitment.—Where the offense is not bailable, or bail is refused, or is not offered, and there is sufficient evidence to require that the accused be held for trial, he must be committed to jail. To do this, a mittimus or warrant to the jailer is necessary, and to be valid this warrant must be in writing under the seal of the magistrate who

[63] People v. Ebner, 23 Cal. 158; State v. Couneham, 57 Iowa 351, 10 N. W. 677.

[64] Commonwealth v. Johnson, 3 Cush. (Mass.) 454.

[65] Commonwealth v. Dana, 14 Mass. 65.

[66] Harbin v. State, 78 Iowa 263, 43 N. W. 210.

[67] Commonwealth v. Coleman, 2 Met. (Ky.) 382.

[68] Lyons v. State, 1 Blackf. (Ind.) 309.

[69] State v. Rollins, 52 Ind. 168; State v. Meyers, 61 Mo. 414.

issues it,[70] must show his authority,[71] where and when made,[72] must issue in the name of the proper authority,[73] and be directed to the proper jailer,[74] must sufficiently describe the accused to identify him, giving his Christian name if known,[75] must state the nature of his offense,[76] and the time and place of his imprisonment.[77] Errors in commitment do not affect the validity of subsequent proper proceedings.[78] The remedy for illegal commitment is by habeas corpus.

70 State v. Caswell, Charlt. (Ga.) 280; 4 Bl. Comm. 300.

71 State v. Manley, 1 Overt. (Tenn.) 428; 1 Chitty Crim. L. 109.

72 2 Hale P. C. 122.

73 1 Chitty Crim. L. 109.

74 Rex v. Smith, 2 Strange 934.

75 1 Hale P. C. 577.

76 Commonwealth v. Ward, 4 Mass. 497; 4 Bl. Comm. 300.

77 Rex v. Fell, 1 Ld. Raym. 424; 1 Chitty Crim. L. 111.

78 In re Schurman, 40 Kans. 533, 20 Pac. 277.

CHAPTER LXXVII.

MODES OF ACCUSATION AND INDICTMENT.

§ 895. Modes of accusation—Indictment—Information.—Before a person can be put on trial for a crime a formal accusation must be made against him, otherwise the court has no jurisdiction, even by consent of the accused.[1] The chief modes of accusation are indictment by a grand jury, and information by the proper prosecuting officer, without intervention of a grand jury. Accusation may be by coroner's inquisition in cases of homicide, or by complaint and information upon oath of a private person.

Originally the indictment was an informal, oral statement made by the foreman of the grand jury and taken down in writing by the clerk of the court, who later recorded it. In the reign of Edward I a statute was passed requiring the grand jury to make its presentments in writing, and by the year 1500 the present rigid form of indictment, with its many technicalities, had been established.

There is a certain distinction between an indictment and a presentment, in that a presentment was drawn up by the grand jury, from information possessed or obtained by them, upon which an indictment was afterwards drawn up by the proper officer, while an indictment was drawn up by the prosecuting officer, submitted by him to the grand jury, and by them found as true. This distinction is of little practical value today.

An information lies at common law for all misdemeanors, but not for felonies. The information is merely the allegation of the prosecuting officer, that he believes that there is sufficient evidence for instituting a criminal action against a certain person. The procedure is regulated in most states by statutes, some of which require verification;[2] others that

[1] People v. Campbell, 4 Park Cr. (N. Y.) 386; State v. Duhon, 142 La. 919, 77 So. 791; Reynolds v. State (Tex. Cr.), 198 S. W. 958; State v. LaFlamme, 116 Maine 41, 99 Atl. 772; Sherrod v. State, 197 Ala. 286, 72 So. 540; Merchant v. State, 12 Okla. Cr. 360, 157 Pac. 272; United States v. Rintelen, 233 Fed. 793; Turman v. State (Tex. Cr.), 196 S. W. 181; 1 Bish. Crim. Proc., §§ 79, 95 et seq.

[2] State v. Hayward, 83 Mo. 299.

there shall have been a preliminary examination before a magistrate, and a finding of probable cause.[3] At common law the information need not be verified.

Where a death occurs under circumstances requiring investigation, the coroner summons a jury, who are sworn, view the body, and take evidence, and if the jury finds that the deceased was killed by some person, under circumstances amounting to murder or manslaughter, the record of their finding, or inquisition, which is similar to the finding of a grand jury, is sufficient for the foundation of a prosecution.[4] The formal rules applying to indictments also apply to inquisitions.

In case of certain petty misdemeanors only, statutes permit in some states that prosecution may be had in an inferior court upon an information made under oath by a private person, similar to the complaint made for the purpose of arrest.

§ 896. The grand jury.—The grand jury dates from early English times, even as early as the reign of Henry II and came to this country with the early colonists as a part of our heritage of English law. As we have seen, at common law, prosecution for a felony must be upon indictment returned by a grand jury. The institution has been regarded as an essential to liberty, and is required by some constitutions, though in other states it is held that the grand jury system is not essential to the trial by due process of law which is guaranteed by constitutions, if some other formal and sufficient mode of accusation is provided.[5]

The grand jury is a body of men summoned from all parts of the county to determine whether sufficient evidence exists against persons charged with crime within the county

[3] O'Hara v. People, 41 Mich. 623, 3 N. W. 161.

[4] Reg. v. Ingham, 9 Cox Cr. C. 508.

[5] Ex parte Bain, 121 U. S. 1, 30 L. ed. 849; Hurtado v. People, 110 U. S. 516, L. ed. 232; Alt v. State (Tex. Cr.), 203 S. W. 53.

to put them on trial. At common law a full panel consists of twenty-three men, twelve of whom must concur in order to return an indictment.[6] In some states the number has been changed by statute. In Indiana, for instance, a grand jury consists of six men, five of whom must concur in a finding.[7]

§ 897. **Qualifications of grand jurors.**—The qualifications of grand and petit jurors are not the same. Unless statutes provide otherwise, grand jurors should be free holders of the county. But as grand jurors may find an indictment from their personal knowledge, and are not confined, as a petit jury is, to a finding based upon evidence offered before them, the fact that a grand juror has formed or expressed an opinion as to the guilt of the accused,[8] or the fact that he is related to the injured party,[9] or that he has a personal interest in his prosecution,[10] does not disqualify him.

§ 898. **Procedure of grand jury.**—After impaneling, a foreman is chosen, and the jurors are sworn, the usual oath binding them to diligently inquire into the matters given them in charge, to keep secret their proceedings, to present no one from envy, hatred or malice, to leave no one unpresented from fear, favor, affection, hope of reward, or gain, but to present all things truly, as they come to their knowledge, to the best of their understanding.[11] As a rule the oath is given to the foreman in the presence of the others,

6 State v. Barker, 107 N. Car. 913, 12 S. E. 115, 10 L. R. A. 50; 2 Hale P. C. 121.

7 Burns' Rev. Stat. (1914), §§ 1955, 1981. See also, State v. Wood, 175 N. Car. 809, 95 S. E. 1050; State v. Bachman (Nev.), 168 Pac. 733.

8 State v. Clarissa, 11 Ala. 57.

9 In re Tucker, 8 Mass. 286; State v. Sharp, 110 N. Car. 604, 14 S. E. 504; State v. Easter, 30 Ohio St. 542, 27 Am. Rep. 478.

10 In re Tucker, 8 Mass. 286. See also, Christopoulo v. United States, 230 Fed. 788, 145 C. C. A. 98.

11 2 Bish. New Crim. Proc., § 856, (2).

who swear to abide by its provisions, without repeating it.[12] The court then instructs them as to their duties and the law applicable to the cases which may come before them, whereupon they withdraw to the room where they sit, and there hear testimony against persons charged with offenses, and pass upon the accusations. Usually bills of indictments, or formal written accusations prepared in advance are sent with them, by the prosecutor, to become indictments if found to be true bills by the jury. The prosecutor may summon or send witnesses into the room, and in some states the jury may themselves summon witnesses.

§ 899. **Powers of grand jury.**—There are differing views as to the powers of grand juries. In England the grand jury may institute on its own motion, any prosecution it sees fit, and summon witnesses.[13] A few American states follow this view. Another holding is that the grand jury can not act until after a preliminary examination of the accused before a magistrate.[14] The general rule in this country is that the grand jury may inquire into offenses of which it has personal knowledge or which are of public notoriety, and such other offenses as it is called upon by the court or prosecuting officer to investigate, but can not inquire into other offenses unless the accused has been examined before a magistrate.[15] The grand jury may examine witnesses, but should hear only legal evidence, and an indictment must be founded upon at least some legal evidence.[16]

The general rule is, however, that if the evidence is legal, its sufficiency and the competency of the witnesses can not

12 Roe v. State (Ala.), 2 So. 459.

13 United States v. Tompkins, Fed. Cas. No. 16483, 2 Cranch C. C. 46.

14 Whart. Crim. Pl. & Pr., § 339.

15 People v. Horton, 4 Parker Cr. (N. Y.) 222; McCullough v. Commonwealth, 67 Pa. St. 30.

16 Sparrenberger v. State, 53 Ala. 481, 25 Am. Rep. 643; People v. Lauder, 82 Mich. 109, 46 N. W. 956.

be elsewhere inquired into.[17] The accused has no right to be present himself or by counsel, or to send witnesses.[18] Witnesses refusing to testify are punishable for contempt of court.[19] Generally speaking, the prosecuting attorney not only may, but should attend the sessions of the grand jury, at which evidence is taken, and assist them, and may bring his assistants, or his stenographer.[20] But no one can be present during their deliberations, not even the prosecuting attorney,[21] and no one else has a right to be present at the taking of evidence.[22] As we have seen, the grand jurors are sworn to secrecy, and can not ordinarily testify as to what took place in the grand jury room, nor state how any member voted.[23] But in certain cases, such as in a prosecution for perjury before them, grand jurors may testify,[24] and by statute they are relieved from secrecy in other cases.

The doctrine of former jeopardy is not applicable to the finding of a grand jury. Thus, one grand jury may ignore a bill, and a subsequent one find a true bill.[25] The same grand jury after ignoring a bill, may reconsider its action

17 State v. Randolph, 139 Mo. App. 314, 123 S. W. 61; Hope v. People, 83 N. Y. 418, 38 Am. Rep. 460.

18 State v. Wolcott, 21 Conn. 272.

19 State v. Orleans Crim. Judge, 32 La. Ann. 1222; People v. Kelly, 24 N. Y. 74.

20 Courtney v. State, 5 Ind. App. 356, 32 N. E. 335; McCullough v. Commonwealth, 67 Pa. St. 30. See also, Badders v. United States, 240 U. S. 391, 36 Sup. Ct. 367, 60 L. ed. 706 (absence of judge from the district during part of the deliberations of the grand jury does not invalidate the indictment).

21 Wilson v. State, 70 Miss. 595, 13 So. 225, 35 Am. St. 664.

22 Shattuck v. State, 11 Ind. 473.

23 State v. Fassett, 16 Conn. 457; Commonwealth v. Hill, 11 Cush. (Mass.) 137; 3 Russ. Crimes (9th Am. ed.) 520.

24 Pilgrim v. State, 3 Okla. Cr. 49, 104 Pac. 383; Reg. v. Hughes, 1 Car. & K. 519; United States v. Perlman, 247 Fed. 158.

25 State v. Harris, 91 N. Car. 656; State v. Cox, 6 Ired. L. (N. Car.) 444.

and find a true bill.[26] The authorities do not agree as to whether, where an indictment is quashed for invalidity, another may be found by the same jury without hearing evidence again.[27]

If the required majority of the grand jurors vote in favor of sustaining the bill the foreman indorses it "a true bill" and signs it under the indorsement, and returns it in open court. This presentment in open court renders it an indictment.[28] If less than the required number vote for the bill, the foreman indorses it "not a true bill," and thus it is thrown out or ignored. A bill may be sustained as to some of the counts and rejected as to others.[29] It may be sustained as to one or more defendants and rejected as to others.[30] At common law the prosecuting attorney need not countersign the indictment,[31] but this is required by statute in some jurisdictions. In many states it is required that the names of the witnesses shall be indorsed on the indictment.[32] Objections to the organization of the grand jury may be taken by challenge to the array, before indictment, by the person whose case is before them, if discovered in time; objections to the competency of a juror, by challenge to the polls.[33] If the objection be not thus taken it may be raised by plea in abatement, or if the defect appears on the face[34] of the record, by motion to quash.[35] Objections to individual jurors may be taken by challenge to the polls, or by plea in abatement

26 United States v. Simmons, 46 Fed. 65.

27 McIntire v. Commonwealth, 4 S. W. 1, 26 Ky. L. 469; State v. Ivey, 100 N. Car. 539, 5 S. E. 407.

28 Mose v. State, 35 Ala. 421; Strange v. State, 110 Ind. 354, 11 N. E. 357.

29 Clark's Crim. Proc. 114.

30 Clark's Crim. Proc. 114.

31 Vanderkarr v. State, 51 Ind. 91; Commonwealth v. Beaman, 8 Gray (Mass.) 497.

32 2 Bish. New Crim. Proc., § 869a (2).

33 People v. Jewett, 3 Wend. (N. Y.) 314; Moore v. Navassa Guano Co., 130 N. Car. 229, 41 S. E. 293, 294.

34 Bellair v. State, 6 Blackf. (Ind.) 104; Vanhook v. State, 12 Tex. 252.

35 Avirett v. State, 76 Md. 510, 25 Atl. 676; State v. Ward, 60 Vt. 142, 14 Atl. 189.

or motion to quash.[36] In some jurisdictions personal disqualifications of the grand jurors can not be raised by objections to the indictment.[37]

A grand jury has no power to dissolve itself, but it is dissolved either by the court discharging it or by the final adjournment of court.[38]

§ 900. Record and caption of indictment.—The caption is not a part of the indictment. It is merely a formal statement of the court before which the indictment was found, where and when it was found, and the jurors by whom it was found.[39] The name of the county must appear, and the fact that the jurors are of that county.[40] All of these must be set forth with sufficient certainty.[41] The indictment must be shown to have been found upon oath, or oath and affirmation, or the caption will be bad.[42] An indictment may be quashed because of material defect in the caption.[43] But as the caption is no part of the indictment, being merely a ministerial record, it may be amended at any time, even after conviction, to conform with other records.[44]

§ 901. Parts of indictment.—An indictment consists of three parts, the commencement, the statement and the conclusion. The commencement states the venue, that is the name of the county from which the grand jurors have come,

[36] Conkey v. People, 1 Abb. (N. Y.) 418, 5 Parke Cr. (N. Y.) 31; Commonwealth v. Williams, 5 Grat. (Va.) 702.

[37] Lienburger v. State (Tex.), 21 S. W. 603; State v. Henderson, 29 W. Va. 147, 1 S. E. 225.

[38] Clem v. State, 33 Ind. 418.

[39] Noles v. State, 24 Ala. 672; State v. Gary, 36 N. H. 359; 2 Hale P. C. 165.

[40] 2 Hale P. C. 166. See also, Reed v. State (Ga.), 95 S. E. 692; Fussell v. State (Nebr.), 166 N. W. 197.

[41] State v. Conley, 39 Maine 78; 2 Hawk. P. C., ch. 25, §§ 16, 17, 118-120.

[42] Roe v. State (Ala.), 2 So. 459; 2 Hale P. C. 167.

[43] 2 Hawk. P. C., ch. 25, § 146.

[44] Commonwealth v. James, 1 Pick. (Mass.) 375; 1 Chitty Crim. L. 335.

in which the offense was committed, and in which the trial is to take place. The venue is stated usually in the margin of the indictment, but may be stated in the body of the caption or in the body of the commencement, and if it appears in the body of the caption is referred to in the commencement as the "county aforesaid."[45] The commencement must also set forth the fact of presentment by the grand juror under oath, or under oath and affirmation. The word present or some equivalent word in the present tense showing that the grand jury charge the defendant must appear.[46] The fact of presentment under oath or oath and affirmation must appear in every count of the indictment, either directly or by appropriate reference to the preceding count.[47] The fact of presentment is ordinarily made to appear by a statement similar to the following: "The jurors of the (state, commonwealth, or people of the state, as the practice may be) of -------------------- in and for the county of -------------------- upon their oath present."[48]

The statement is the portion of the indictment which describes the defendant, and the offense with which he is charged.

§ 902. **Description of defendant.**—If the name of the accused is known, his Christian name and surname should be given in full.[49] Usually a middle name need not be included,[50] but some courts hold a middle name or initial essential.[51] The omission of the words junior or senior,

[45] Commonwealth v. Quin, 5 Gray (Mass.) 478; 2 Hale P. C. 165 et seq.

[46] Vanvickle v. State, 22 Tex. App. 625, 2 S. W. 642.

[47] Curtis v. People, Breese (Ill.) 256; State v. McAllister, 26 Maine 374.

[48] 1 Bish. New Crim. Proc., § 668.

[49] Commonwealth v. Perkins, 1 Pick. (Mass.) 388; Pancho v. State, 25 Tex. App. 402, 8 S. W. 476.

[50] Erskine v. Davis, 25 Ill. 251; Choen v. State, 52 Ind. 347, 21 Am. Rep. 179.

[51] Commonwealth v. Shearman, 11 Cush. (Mass.) 546.

which are no part of a man's name, ordinarily makes no difference.[52] If a man is known by two names, he may be indicted by either,[53] or if he holds himself out as having a certain name, that may be used.[54] It is sufficient if the name given in the indictment is idem sonans (has the same sound) with the defendant's real name.[55] Corporations should be indicted by their full corporate names.[56] Misnomer can only be taken advantage of by a plea in abatement before pleading to the merits which states the true name of the defendant, and the effect of such plea can be no more than to delay matters, since a new indictment may then be presented.[57] At common law it was necessary to state the estate or degree or mystery of the defendant in addition to his name, and also the place of his residence. By estate or degree is meant title, rank or condition; by mystery is meant the trade, calling or profession of the defendant. This rule as to addition, though abrogated in most states, still holds good in some states.[58]

[52] Commonwealth v. Parmenter, 101 Mass. 211; Cobb v. Lucas, 15 Pick. (Mass.) 7.

[53] Commonwealth v. Gale, 11 Gray (Mass.) 320.

[54] City Council v. King, 4 McCord (S. Car.) 487.

[55] Rex v. Shakespeare, 10 East 84; Clark Crim. Proc. 341, note 75; 2 Bish. Crim. Proc., § 688. See also, Woods v. State, 123 Ark. 111, 184 S. W. 409 ("Wood" and "Woods" are not idem sonans); Culliver v. State (Ala. App.), 73 So. 556 ("Culliver" and "Cullifer" held idem sonans); Watkins v. State, 18 Ga. App. 500, 89 S. E. 624 ("Maria" and "Maree" held idem sonans); Lunsford v. State, 807 Tex. Cr. 41, 190 S. W. 157 ("McKeg" and "McCaig" held idem sonans); Taylor v. State (Ala. App.), 72 So. 557 ("McClure" and "McLure" held idem sonans); Golson v. State (Ala. App.), 73 So. 753 ("Golson" and "Gholdston" held idem sonans).

[56] Commonwealth v. Demuth, 12 Serg. & R. (Pa.) 389.

[57] State v. Hughes, 1 Swan (Tenn.) 261; 1 Chitty Crim. L. 203; James v. State (Ala. App.), 78 So. 316; Putnam v. State (Ala. App.), 76 So. 408; State v. Kelly, 113 Miss. 461, 74 So. 325; Ah Poo v. Stevenson, 83 Ore. 340, 163 Pac. 822.

[58] State v. Bishop, 15 Maine 122; State v. Hughes, 2 Har. & McH. (Md.) 479.

§ 903. **Certainty.**—There are three degrees of certainty recognized in pleading, viz: Certainty to a common intent, certainty to a certain intent in general, and certainty to a common intent in every particular. Clark says: "A pleading is certain to a common intent when it is clear enough according to reasonable intendment or construction, though not worded with absolute precision. Certainty to a certain intent in general means what upon a fair and reasonable construction may be called certain without recurring to possible facts which do not appear except by inference or argument. Certainty to a certain intent in every particular requirės the 'utmost fullness and particularity of statement, as well as the highest attainable accuracy and precision, leaving nothing to be supplied by argument, inference or presumption, and no supposable answer wanting. The pleader must not only state the facts of his own case in the most precise way, but must add to them such facts as will anticipate the case of his adversary.' The first is the lowest degree of pleading allowed, and is allowed only in pleas in bar, and in certain parts of the indictment other than the charge. * * * The second degree is required in that part of the indictment which charges the offense. The third degree is required in pleas in abatement and other dilatory pleas."[59] Every fact or circumstance which to any extent in law affects or enhances the punishment must be pleaded, specifically.[60] So where an act is not inherently unlawful, but is made so by circumstances surrounding it, they must be alleged. The certainty should be sufficient to enable the court to say that if the facts pleaded are true, an offense has been committed, to know what punishment to impose, and to confine the proof to the offense charged; to give the defendant reasonable notice of the charge he must defend; to make a record of

[59] Clark's Crim. Proc. 151.

[60] Commonwealth v. Newburyport Bridge, 9 Pick. (Mass.) 142; Commonwealth v. Whitney, 5 Gray (Mass.) 85; State v. Perry, 2 Bailey (S. Car.) 17.

what offense is charged, for purposes of review, and in order that acquittal or conviction may be pleaded in bar of a subsequent prosecution for the same offense.[61]

Facts which are particularly within the knowledge of the defendant need only be alleged with certainty to a common intent.[62] The certainty required as to particulars is only such as the circumstances will permit, and unknown particulars need not be alleged, provided all the essentials of the offense are shown.[63]

§ 904. **Particularity of description.**—Merely to charge the accused generally with the commission of a certain kind of crime is not sufficient. The particular act or acts constituting the offense must be alleged, and not merely the conclusion that a crime was committed. Thus if a forgery is charged, the writing must be set forth,[64] if a burglary, the house must be specifically described,[65] if a larceny, the articles taken must be particularly described.[66] For instance, in case of a theft of money it is not sufficient to set forth the total amount, but the particular bills or coins must be described. "Where the definition of an offense, whether it be at common law or by statute, 'includes generic terms, it is not sufficient that the indictment shall charge the offense

[61] Commonwealth v. Dean, 109 Mass. 349; Commonwealth v. Phillips, 16 Pick. (Mass.) 211; Davis v. State, 131 Ark. 542, 199 S. W. 902; State v. Atkins, 142 La. 862, 77 So. 771; City of Astoria v. Malone, 87 Ore. 88, 169 Pac. 749.

[62] Rex v. Holland, 5 Term. Rep. 607; 2 Hawk. P. C., ch. 25, § 112; Allen v. Commonwealth, 178 Ky. 250, 198 S. W. 896; Davis v. State, 131 Ark. 542, 199 S. W. 902.

[63] Commonwealth v. Webster, 5 Cush. (Mass.) 295, 52 Am. Dec. 711; Cox v. People, 80 N. Y. 500.

[64] Crossland v. State, 77 Ark. 537, 92 S. W. 776; Rooker v. State, 65 Ind. 86; State v. Cook, 52 Ind. 574; Davis v. State, 58 Nebr. 465, 78 N. W. 930; Rex v. Gilchrist, 2 Leach 753.

[65] Thomas v. State, 97 Ala. 3, 12 So. 409; McElreath v. State, 55 Ga. 562; State v. Evans, 18 S. Car. 137.

[66] People v. Machado, 130 Cal. xviii, 63 Pac. 66; Walthour v. State, 114 Ga. 75, 39 S. W. 872; Harrington v. State, 76 Ind. 112.

in the same generic terms as in the definition; but it must state the species,—it must descend to particulars.' "[67] The nature of certain offenses, however, is such that they may be alleged generally, such as being a common scold,[68] or a common prostitute,[69] or a common seller of intoxicating liquors,[70] since these indictments include a habitual succession of acts, and not particular instances. The act of a person by his agent may be averred to have been done by the principal.[71] Only the facts should be alleged, and it is unnecessary to allege their legal effect. Generally speaking the facts may be pleaded either according to their legal import or their outward form, for example, what one does by his agent may be alleged to have been done by the principal himself, as in legal import it was, or according to the outward form of the transaction may be alleged as having been done by the agent for the principal.[72] The charge must be stated positively, and if there is an attempt made to allege an essential element of the offense argumentatively, or by way of recital, the indictment is bad.[73] This is merely another expression of the rule of certainty to every intent. Where the averment of one fact necessarily implies the exist-

[67] United States v. Cruikshank, 92 U. S. 542, 23 L. ed. 588. See also, United States v. Rintelen, 233 Fed. 793; State v. Duhon, 142 La. 919, 77 So. 791; Merchant v. State, 12 Okla. Cr. 360, 157 Pac. 272; State v. LaFlamme, 116 Maine 41, 99 Atl. 772; State v. Atkins, 142 La. 862, 77 So. 771; United States v. Bopp, 230 Fed. 723; 1 Arch. Crim. Pr. & Pl. 291.

[68] Commonwealth v. Davis, 11 Pick. (Mass.) 432; 2 Hawk. P. C., ch. 25, § 59.

[69] State v. Dowers, 45 N. H. 543; State v. Russell, 14 R. I. 506.

[70] State v. Collins, 48 Maine 217; Commonwealth v. Odlin, 23 Pick. (Mass.) 275.

[71] State v. Brown, 31 Maine 520; Commonwealth v. Bagley, 7 Pick. (Mass.) 279.

[72] State v. Wentworth, 35 N. H. 442.

[73] Comonwealth v. Shaw, 7 Metc. (Mass.) 52; Rex v. Knight, 1 Salk. 375; 2 Hawk. P. C., ch. 25, § 60; United States v. Welch, 243 Fed. 996; People v. Stoyan, 280 Ill. 300, 117 N. E. 464; Ah Poo v. Stevenson, 83 Ore. 340, 163 Pac. 822; United States v. United States Brewers' Assn., 239 Fed. 163.

ence of another fact, the direct averment of the latter is not essential.[74] It is not essential to aver that of which the court will take judicial notice,[75] as for instance, to expressly state the statute upon which the indictment is based. Mere matters of evidence should not be alleged.[76]

Any averment which is essential, however, to a proper description of the crime, must be contained in the indictment. Thus, in an indictment for conspiracy, the object of the unlawful agreement must be set forth specifically.[77] And in an indictment for perjury, all the requisites of the crime must be averred.[78]

§ 905. Technical words.—Certain crimes can be properly described only by the use of technical words. For instance, any indictment for common law felony must allege that the act was committed feloniously.[79] An indictment for burglary must allege that the act was committed "feloniously" and "burglariously."[80] All indictments for treason must contain the word "traitorously."[81] The term "forcibly" and "against the will" must appear in indictments for robbery.[82] Nothing will take the place of the words "malice aforethought" and "murder" in murder indictments,[83] and perhaps

[74] State v. Smith, 106 N. Car. 653, 11 S. E. 166; Rex v. Tilley, 2 Leach 759.

[75] Gady v. State, 83 Ala. 51, 3 So. 429; Damron v. State (Tex. Cr.), 27 S. W. 7; United States v. Scott, 248 Fed. 361; Meredith v. State, 79 Tex. Cr. 277, 184 S. W. 204; McLain v. State (Ala. App.) 72 So. 511.

[76] Mead v. State, 53 N. J. L. 601, 23 Atl. 264; Rex v. Turner, 1 Strange 139.

[77] United States v. Patterson, 55 Fed. 605; Lambert v. People, 9 Cow. (N. Y.) 578.

[78] State v. Ammons, 3 Murph. (N. Car.) 123; Stedman's Case, 1 Cro. (Eliz.) 137.

[79] Commonwealth v. Scannel, 11 Cush. (Mass.) 547; State v. Muir (Mo.), 186 S. W. 1047; 2 Hawk. P. C., ch. 26, § 55.

[80] State v. McDonald, 9 W. Va. 456; Vaux v. Brooke, 2 Coke, pt. IV, 39, 40; 2 Hale P. C. 172, 184.

[81] 4 Bl. Comm. 307.

[82] Collins v. People, 39 Ill. 233; Commonwealth v. Humphries, 7 Mass. 242.

[83] McElroy v. State, 14 Tex. App. 235; Commonwealth v. Gibson, 2 Va. Cas. 70.

the word "ravish" is essential in an indictment for rape.[84] If a statute in describing an offense which it creates uses the word "unlawfully" an indictment based on the statute is bad unless the word is used.[85]

In general, an indictment on a statute should use the word in the statute in defining the crime. Not all the above common law rules apply to indictments on statutes.

§ 906. **Matters of defense.**—Matters of defense need not be anticipated or negatived in the indictment.[86] An indictment is adequate when the facts charged in it, if true, make out a prima facie crime.[87] In an indictment for rape it is not essential to aver that the accused was more than fourteen years of age, [88] or in an indictment for disobeying an order of the court to aver that the order was not revoked.[89] But where a statute creating an offense contains exceptions, and the exceptions are a part of the definition of the crime, these exceptions must be negatived.[90]

§ 907. **Averment in the disjunctive.**—An averment of an offense in the disjunctive makes the indictment bad for uncertainty,[91] for example, that the defendant "burned or caused to be burned" a house,[92] or "forged or caused to

[84] Christian v. Commonwealth, 23 Grat. (Va.) 954; Howel v. Commonwealth, 5 Grat. (Va.) 664.

[85] Commonwealth v. Twitchell, 4 Cush. (Mass.) 74; Rex v. Ryan, 2 Moody 15. But see State v. Briggs, 142 La. 785, 77 So. 599; City of Astoria v. Malone, 87 Ore. 88, 169 Pac. 749; Holsman v. United States, 248 Fed. 193, 160 C. C. A. 271; State v. Kerr, 117 Maine 254, 103 Atl. 585.

[86] Commonwealth v. Hart, 11 Cush. (Mass.) 130; Rex v. Baxter, 5 Term Rep. 83, 2 Leach 660.

[87] Commonwealth v. Hart, 11 Cush. (Mass.) 130.

[88] People v. Wessel, 98 Cal. 352, 33 Pac. 216.

[89] 1 East P. C. 19, 20.

[90] Commonwealth v. Jennings, 121 Mass. 47, 23 Am. Rep. 249; Gee Wo v. State, 36 Nebr. 241, 54 N. W. 513; 2 Hawk. P. C., ch. 25, § 112.

[91] State v. Stephenson, 83 Ind. 246; Commonwealth v. Perrigo, 3 Met. (Ky.) 5.

[92] People v. Hood, 6 Cal. 236.

be forged an instrument,"[93] or "administered a drug or poison,"[94] or that he "sold spirituous or intoxicating liquors."[95] All spirituous liquors are intoxicating, but all intoxicating liquors are not spirituous. But if the terms used in the disjunctive are equivalent to or explanatory of each other the indictment is good.[96] So where an indictment upon a statute charged the defendant with having "bank bills or promissory notes" payable to the bearer signed by the president of the bank, the term promissory note being used in the statute to explain the term "bank bill," meaning the same thing, the indictment was good.[97] If a disjunctive statement is superfluous or immaterial, it will be rejected as mere surplusage.[98]

§ 908. Repugnancy.—If there is repugnancy in the material part of an indictment, the whole indictment is bad.[99] But if the repugnancy is as to expressions, not stating essential elements of the crime, and the indictment is good without them, they are rejected as surplusage.[1] An indictment for manslaughter which avers that the accused "wilfully" and with "culpable negligence" killed the deceased, is bad for repugnancy.[2] Where terms can have more than one meaning, the meaning will be taken which will support the

[93] People v. Tomlinson, 35 Cal. 503; Rex v. Stocker, 5 Mod. 137, 1 Salk. 342, 371.

[94] State v. Drake, 30 N. J. L. 422; State v. Greene, 3 Heisk. (Tenn.) 131.

[95] Commonwealth v. Grey, 2 Gray (Mass.) 501, 61 Am. Dec. 476; Morgan v. Commonwealth, 7 Grat. (Va.) 592.

[96] Brown v. Commonwealth, 8 Mass. 59; Commonwealth v. Grey, 2 Gray (Mass.) 501, 61 Am. Dec. 476; State v. Gilbert, 13 Vt. 647.

[97] Russell v. State, 71 Ala. 348; State v. Ellis, 4 Mo. 474.

[98] 1 Hale P. C. 535.

[99] Commonwealth v. Lawless, 101 Mass. 32; State v. Haven, 59 Vt. 399, 9 Atl. 841; 2 Hawk. P. C., ch. 25, § 62.

[1] State v. Kendall, 38 Nebr. 817, 57 N. W. 525; People v. Laurence, 137 N. Y. 517, 33 N. E. 547.

[2] State v. Lockwood, 119 Mo. 463, 24 S. W. 1015.

indictment, and not that which would render it bad.[3] If from the context it can be determined in what sense the words were intended to be used, ambiguity or repugnancy can not be said to exist.[4]

§ 909. **Language used—Abbreviations.**—The rule in this country and in England is that the indictment should be in the English language.[5] In earlier times in England indictments and all legal proceedings were in the Latin language. English words of foreign origin are proper, such as alias, or Anno Domini.[6]

But where the indictment was for the forgery of a note in the German language, and the note was set out without translating it, the indictment was bad.[7] Likewise the indictment was bad where a Chinese lottery ticket was set out by means of a photograph of the original, and no translation was made.[8]

In England indictments are required by statute to be in words at length, and neither abbreviations or figures may be used in the indictment proper.[9] There the only exception to the rule is where a fac simile of a document must be set out in the indictment, as in case of forgery.[10] In this country the rule is not so strict, and it is held that the

[3] Commonwealth v. Butler, 1 Allen (Mass.) 4; Rex v. Wright, 1 Ad. & El. 434.

[4] Commonwealth v. Kelly, 123 Mass. 417; Jeffries v. Commonwealth, 12 Allen (Mass.) 145.

[5] 1 Bish. New Crim. Proc., §§ 341, 342.

[6] Kennedy v. People, 39 N. Y. 245, 5 Abb. Pr. (N. S.) 147; State v. Gilbert, 13 Vt. 647.

[7] See Beyerline v. State, 147 Ind. 25, 45 N. E. 772.

[8] People v. Ah Sum, 92 Cal. 648, 28 Pac. 680.

[9] 1 Chitty Crim. L. 176.

[10] Rex v. Goldstein, 7 Moore 1, 3 Brod. & B. 201, Russ. & Ry. 473.

ordinary abbreviations may be used for dates,[11] and, perhaps in some other cases, if the abbreviations used are those of which there is common knowledge as & for and.[12]

If abbreviations peculiar to the arts or sciences or to certain businesses are used, they must be fully explained in words.[13]

§ 910. **Clerical errors.**—Mere clerical[14] or grammatical errors,[15] incorrect spelling,[16] or wrong punctuation[17] do not render an indictment bad, if the meaning intended is plain. The rule is otherwise if the meaning is changed or destroyed, or an essential word is omitted.[18] Some decisions on this point would be considered today as very technical.

§ 911. **Videlicet — Inducement — Innuendo.** — Often in framing indictments, allegations of time, place, number, etc., are set forth by means of a videlicet or scilicet, usually following the words "to-wit" or "namely," explaining and making certain that which was before alleged generally. If the averment under a scilicet is immaterial, it may be rejected as surplusage, but if material, the proof must correspond to the

11 State v. Reed, 35 Maine 489, 58 Am. Dec. 727; Commonwealth v. Clark, 4 Cush. (Mass.) 596.

12 Pickens v. State, 58 Ala. 364; State v. McPherson, 114 Iowa 492, 87 N. W. 421.

13 State v. Brown, 51 Conn. 1; Stukeley v. Butler, Hob. 172.

14 State v. Raymond, 20 Iowa 582; Ewing v. State, 1 Tex. App. 362; Dupree v. State, 80 Tex. Cr. 211, 190 S. W. 181; Lopez v. State (Ariz.), 161 Pac. 874.

15 State v. Hedge, 6 Ind. 330; State v. Raymond, 20 Iowa 582; Perdue v. Commonwealth, 96 Pa. St. 311; Ewing v. State, 1 Tex. App. 362; State v. Kruppa (Iowa), 158 N. W. 401.

16 Peacock v. State, 174 Ind. 185, 91 N. E. 597; Johns v. State, 88 Nebr. 145, 129 N. W. 247.

17 Fuller v. State, 117 Ala. 200, 23 So. 688; Ward v. State, 50 Ala. 120.

18 People v. St. Clair, 55 Cal. 524; State v. Chicago, B. & P. R. Co., 63 Iowa 508, 19 N. W. 299; State v. Atkins, 142 La. 862, 77 So. 771 (an allegation charging that defendant did feloniously "shoow" A with intent to kill is not sufficient to authorize a conviction of shooting with intent to kill).

allegation under the scilicet.[19] An inducement is a statement of preliminary facts not a part of the description of the offense, but which are necessary to show that the offense charged is criminal, and need be stated only with certainty to a common intent,[20] for instance, in an indictment for libel where the writing is not necessarily libelous, the facts must be stated which make it libelous.[21]

If in cases of libel the matter alleged is not obviously libelous, or plainly applicable to the party alleged to have been libeled, its real meaning must be explained by what is called an innuendo, for the facts must be stated with legal precision in order to be brought before the jury.[22] An innuendo is merely matter explanatory of what has already been alleged, in order to relieve it from ambiguity, but the innuendo can not change or alter the sense of the other averments.[23]

§ 912. **Written instruments.**—Where, as in cases of accusations of libel, forgery, or writing threatening letters, a written instrument is a part of the gist of the crime charged, it should be set out in its exact words,[24] or the indictment will be bad. This is important for the court to see whether or not an offense has been committed, and merely to set forth its substance, or the legal conclusion of the pleader as to its effect is not sufficient.

19 Paine v. Fox, 16 Mass. 129; Hastings v. Lovering, 2 Pick. (Mass.) 214, 13 Am. Dec. 420; State v. Heck, 23 Minn. 549; State v. Haney, 1 Hawks. (N. Car.) 460.

20 Commonwealth v. Reynolds, 14 Gray (Mass.) 87, 74 Am. Dec. 665; Reg. v. Wyatt, 2 Ld. Raym. 1189.

21 People v. Collins, 102 Cal. 345, 36 Pac. 669; Rogers v. State, 30 Tex. App. 462, 17 S. W. 548.

22 People v. Collins, 102 Cal. 345, 36 Pac. 669; Rogers v. State, 30 Tex. App. 462, 17 S. W. 548; 3 Chitty Crim. L. 875.

23 Goodrich v. Hooper, 97 Mass. 1, 93 Am. Dec. 49; Commonwealth v. Keenan, 67 Pa. St. 203.

24 Rooker v. State, 65 Ind. 86; Commonwealth v. Wright, 1 Cush. (Mass.) 46; State v. Wheeler, 19 Minn. 98; Wood v. Brown, 1 Marsh. 522, 6 Taunt. 169.

If the written instrument does not form part of the gist of the crime, but it is mentioned in the description of the offense, it is not necessary to set it out verbatim, but a statement of its purport is sufficient.[25] Where it is necessary to set forth a writing verbatim and according to its tenor, the indictment should state that this is done, and it is not sufficient to state that such is the effect, substance or purpose of the writing.[26]

The rules regarding spoken words are substantially the same as those stated in the case of written words.[27]

§ 913. Description of property.—If the offense charged is one of which real property is the subject, the premises must be described with enough particularity to identify them, and if ownership, occupancy or character is material, the averments must show it,[28] for example, in an indictment for burglary at common-law, the building must be described as a dwelling house, with certainty to a common intent, and the proof must conform to the description.[29] And an indictment for burglary or arson must show the ownership or occupancy of the property, for one can not be guilty of these offenses if he owns or occupies the property.[30] It is said however, that in an indictment for maintaining a disorderly house, it is sufficient to describe the premises as a certain house located in a certain city and county.[31]

[25] Commonwealth v. Coe, 115 Mass. 481; People v. Taylor, 3 Denio (N. Y.) 99; State v. Dunn, 109 N. Car. 839, 13 S. E. 881.

[26] McDonnell v. State, 58 Ark. 242, 24 S. W. 105; State v. Twitty, 9 N. Car. 441, 11 Am. Dec. 779; Wood v. Brown, 1 Marsh. 522, 6 Taunt. 169.

[27] Commonwealth v. Moulton, 108 Mass. 307; Robinson v. Commonwealth, 101 Mass. 27.

[28] Thomas v. State, 97 Ala. 3, 12 So. 409; State v. Keena, 63 Conn. 329, 28 Atl. 522; Commonwealth v. Brown, 15 Gray (Mass.) 189.

[29] Thomas v. State, 97 Ala. 3, 12 So. 409; Commonwealth v. Brown, 15 Gray (Mass.) 189.

[30] State v. Keena, 63 Conn. 329, 28 Atl. 522.

[31] Commonwealth v. Skelley, 10 Gray (Mass.) 464; State v. Nixon, 18 Vt. 70, 46 Am. Dec. 135.

Personal property also, if the subject of the offense, must be described with certainty to a common intent.[32]

In an indictment for larceny, it is not sufficient to charge generally that a certain person's goods and chattels were taken away.[33] As some things can not be the subject of larceny, the indictment must show that the things taken were such as could be subject to larceny, for instance, an indictment for stealing animals once ferae naturae, it must be averred that they had been killed or tamed. An indictment for stealing minerals must show that they had been severed from the ground.[34] An indictment naming the articles stolen "and a hundred other articles of household furniture" is bad for uncertainty.[35] However, minute details are not necessary. So to describe an animal as "a certain hog, the property and chattel of one L" is sufficient without giving the color, kind, size, weight, or mark.[36] In the case of a chemical mixture[37] it should be described by the name of the mixture; and in the case of a mechanical mixture, where the articles comprising it are changed in character and given a different name, as where cloth, buttons, thread, etc., are made into a suit of clothes, or where wood, iron, etc., are made into a buggy, the finished article should be described by its name.[38] The number or quantity of the property taken must be stated, and if there are several different kinds the number or quantity of each kind.[39] If value is ma-

32 People v. Williams, 35 Cal. 671; Commonwealth v. Gavin, 121 Mass. 54, 23 Am. Rep. 255; State v. Burt, 64 N. Car. 619; Robinson v. Commonwealth, 32 Grat. (Va.) 866.

33 Commonwealth v. Gavin, 121 Mass. 54, 23 Am. Rep. 255; Robinson v. Commonwealth, 32 Grat. (Va.) 866.

34 People v. Williams, 35 Cal. 671; State v. Burt, 64 N. Car. 619.

35 Rex v. Forsyth, Russ. & Ry. 274.

36 People v. Stanford, 64 Cal. 27, 28 Pac. 106; State v. Friend, 47 Minn. 449, 50 N. W. 692.

37 Reg. v. Bond, 1 Den. 517.

38 Commonwealth v. Clair, 7 Allen (Mass.) 525.

39 Commonwealth v. Maxwell, 2 Pick. (Mass.) 139; Leftwich v. Commonwealth, 20 Grat. (Va.) 716

terial, it should be stated, and if several different kinds of property are stated the value of each must be shown.[40] Value is always material in indictments for larceny, since that which has no value can not be the subject of larceny.[41] And upon the value of the articles taken, it is determined whether the offense is grand or petit larceny.[42]

§ 914. Descriptions of third persons.—In order to identify some offenses with sufficient certainty, the name of a third person must be stated. If it is necessary to mention the name of a third person, the name should be stated fully and accurately, and the proof should correspond with the allegation.[43] If the offense is murder, manslaughter, rape or other offense against a person, the name of the person against whom the offense is committed must appear.[44] An indictment for larceny should state the name of the owner of the goods stolen, if he is known.[45] The same rule holds in the case of embezzlement where the name of the person defrauded must be shown.[46] The name of the owner of the premises must be stated in indictments for burglary or arson.[47] If

[40] 1 Hale P. C. 531; 2 Hale, P. C. 185; People v. Dempsey, 283 Ill. 342, 119 N. E. 333 (variance not fatal).

[41] Wilson v. State, 1 Port. (Ala.) 118; People v. Willey, 3 Hill (N. Y.) 194.

[42] State v. Tillery, 1 Nott. & McC. (S. Car.) 9. See also, Wilson v. State, 1 Port. (Ala.) 118.

[43] Commonwealth v. Shearman, 11 Cush. (Mass.) 546; 2 Hawk. P. C., ch. 25, § 72; 1 Chitty Crim. L. 213.

[44] State v. Stucky, 2 Blackf. (Ind.) 289; 1 Chitty Crim. L. 211.

[45] Commonwealth v. Morse, 14 Mass. 217; Long v. State (Tex.), 20 S. W. 576; Kahanek v. State (Tex. Cr.), 201 S. W. 994; Wool v. State (Tex. Cr.), 201 S. W. 1002; Allen v. Commonwealth (Va.), 94 S. E. 783; Parker v. State (Fla.), 78 So. 980.

[46] Commonwealth v. Morse, 14 Mass. 217; Long v. State (Tex.), 20 S. W. 576.

[47] People v. Parker, 91 Cal. 91, 27 Pac. 537; Commonwealth v. Perris, 108 Mass. 1; Commonwealth v. Hartnett, 3 Gray (Mass.) 450; Winslow v. State, 26 Nebr. 308, 41 N. W. 1116; People v. Gates, 15 Wend. (N. Y.) 159.

the names of the third persons in the above cases are unknown, they should be described as persons unknown.[48] In naming a third person only certainty to a common intent is required.[49] His full Christian and surname should be used if known.[50] Where the accused is charged with making an illegal sale, it is usually sufficient to describe the goods sold. Thus, in an indictment for illegal sale of intoxicating liquor, it is not essential to describe the purchaser.[51] In a few jurisdictions, however, the contrary is held.[52] And it has been held that where the accused is charged with illegal sale of a lottery ticket that the name of the purchaser, if known, must be stated.[53]

§ 915. Intent.—In certain crimes or misdemeanors a particular intention is an essential element of the offense, and in such cases the intent must be expressly and specifically alleged.[54] This is especially true where a crime is attempted but not accomplished, and the only thing which can be punished is the attempt to carry out a criminal intention.[55] There are many acts which are criminal in themselves, the doing of which is held to include a criminal intent, and in such cases intent need not be alleged. This is true in an indictment for murder, committed by means of a deadly

[48] Holford v. State, 2 Blackf. (Ind.) 103; Commonwealth v. Tompson, 2 Cush. (Mass.) 551; 1 Chitty Crim. L. 212.

[49] State v. Crank, 2 Bailey (S. Car.) 66, 43 Am. Dec. 117, 1 Chitty Crim. L. 215.

[50] Commonwealth v. Perkins, 1 Pick. (Mass.) 388; State v. Martin, 10 Mo. 391; Walden v. Holman, 6 Mod. 115.

[51] Rice v. People, 38 Ill. 435.

[52] McLaughlin v. State, 45 Ind. 338.

[53] Commonwealth v. Sheedy, 159 Mass. 55, 34 N. E. 84.

[54] Commonwealth v. Hersey, 2 Allen (Mass.) 173; State v. McCarter, 98 N. Car. 637, 4 S. E. 553; Jones v. State, 101 Nebr. 847, 166 N. W. 252; Savage v. State (Ala. App.), 72 So. 694; State v. Authement, 139 La. 1070, 72 So. 739.

[55] People v. Congleton, 44 Cal. 92; Commonwealth v. Merrill, 14 Gray (Mass.) 415, 77 Am. Dec. 336; People v. Pettit, 3 Johns. (N. Y.) 511.

weapon,[56] or for rape.[57] But in burglary the intent to commit a felony in the house broken into is essential to the crime and must be alleged.[58] The same rule holds in forgery or false pretenses, in which intent to defraud is essential to the crime, and must be alleged.[59] The same is true of attempt to murder, or assault with intent to rape.[60]

§ 916. **Notice, request or knowledge.**—Particular knowledge is an essential element of some offenses, and must be alleged. Thus, where there is a penalty for knowingly selling unwholesome provisions, it must not alone be alleged that the defendant "did knowingly sell" unwholesome provisions, but that he knew at the time that they were unwholesome, for, it is said, a person may knowingly seil an unwholesome article without knowing it to be unwholesome.[61] An indictment for receiving stolen goods must allege that the defendant knew they were stolen. To allege that he "knowingly received" them is insufficient.[62] In indictments for uttering forged instruments or counterfeit coin,[63] knowingly voting illegally,[64] selling an obscene

56 Commonwealth v. Hersey, 2 Allen (Mass.) 173.

57 Commonwealth v. Hersey, 2 Allen (Mass.) 173.

58 State v. Tyrrell, 98 Mo. 354, 11 S. W. 734; Portwood v. State, 29 Tex. 47, 94 Am. Dec. 258.

59 Commonwealth v. Dean, 110 Mass. 64; State v. Jackson, 89 Mo. 561, 1 S. W. 760.

60 Commonwealth v. Merrill, 14 Gray (Mass.) 415, 77 Am. Dec. 336; State v. Patrick, 3 Wis. 812.

61 Commonwealth v. Boynton, 12 Cush. (Mass.) 499. See also, Stein v. State, 37 Ala. 123. But see United States v. Clark, 37 Fed. 106.

62 Commonwealth v. Cohen, 120 Mass. 198; Commonwealth v. Merriam, 7 Allen (Mass.) 356.

63 Powers v. State, 87 Ind. 97; Gates v. State, 71 Miss. 874, 16 So. 342.

64 United States v. Watkinds, 6 Fed. 152, 7 Sawy. (U. S.) 85.

book,[65] resisting an officer,[66] or any other case where knowledge is an essential element of the offense, it must be averred. But where knowledge must be presumed, as common to all men, it is unnecessary to allege or probe it.[67] Also where an act is unlawful without regard to the defendant's ignorance or knowledge of the facts, it cannot be necessary to allege knowledge. For instance, an indictment under statute against an unmarried man for adultery with a married woman, need not allege the defendant knew she was a married woman,[68] and under a statute prohibiting the sale of intoxicating liquor or adulterated food, it is held that knowledge is not essential, therefore it need not be alleged.[69]

§ 917. Place.—The place where the offense was committed must be alleged in order to show jurisdiction of the grand jury to present the indictment and of the court over the offense.[70] The venue should not only appear in the caption, but also in the statement of the offense.[71] In indictments for certain offenses, such as burglary, arson, or larceny from a building, the particular place is a part of the local description of the crime.[72] In other cases it is not essential to prove that the offense was committed at the

65 United States v. Clark, 37 Fed. 106.

66 Commonwealth v. Kirby, 2 Cush. (Mass.) 577.

67 State v. Freeman, 6 Blackf. (Ind.) 248; Turner v. State, 1 Ohio St. 422.

68 Commonwealth v. Elwell, 2 Metc. (Mass.) 190, 35 Am. Dec. 398.

69 Commonwealth v. Raymond, 97 Mass. 567; Commonwealth v. Boynton, 2 Allen (Mass.) 160.

70 Robinson v. State, 20 Fla. 804; People v. Schultz, 85 Mich. 114, 48 N. W. 293; Cross v. State, 11 Tex. App. 84; State v. Mahoney, 115 Maine 251, 98 Atl. 750; United States v. Baker, 243 Fed. 741; People v. Speedy, 198 Ill. App. 427; State v. Kelly, 138 Tenn. 84, 195 S. W. 1125 (name of county sufficient).

71 Commonwealth v. Elwell, 2 Metc. (Mass.) 190, 35 Am. Dec. 398. See also, Fussell v. State (Nebr.), 166 N. W. 197; State v. Hayden (Mo.), 190 S. W. 311.

72 People v. Slater, 5 Hill (N. Y.) 401.

place alleged, but it may be shown that it was committed at any other place within the jurisdiction of the court.[73] An allegation that the offense was committed within the jurisdiction of the court, however, is never sufficient, because it is a mere conclusion of law. In many cases such as murder, robbery, assaults, gaming or affray, the name of the county is a sufficient location of the place.[74] As a rule, the name of the county should appear, but if the offense is stated to have been committed in a certain city or town which the court judicially knows is in the county, this is sufficient.[75] Where the county is named in the caption, an allegation that the offense was committed in said "county," or "then and there" is sufficient.[76] Where the charge is burglary,[77] selling intoxicating liquor in a certain place,[78] maintaining a house of ill-fame,[79] etc., or where the restitution of property is sought,[80] or the abatement of a nuisance is asked,[81] the place must be particularly alleged, and the proof must conform to the allegation. It is also the rule that where the place of the commission of the offense is described with greater particularity than necessary, it must be proved as

[73] State v. Smith, 5 Har. (Del.) 490; Wingard v. State, 13 Ga. 396; Carlisle v. State, 32 Ind. 55; Commonwealth v. Lavery, 101 Mass. 207; Commonwealth v. Tolliver, 8 Gray (Mass.) 386, 69 Am. Dec. 252; Rex v. Wardle, Russ. & Ry. 9.

[74] Covy v. State, 4 Port. (Ala.) 186; State v. Smith, 5 Har. (Del.) 490; Commonwealth v. Springfield, 7 Mass. 19; Commonwealth v. Tolliver, 8 Gray (Mass.) 386, 69 Am. Dec. 252; Haskins v. People, 16 N. Y. 344; Rex v. Wardle, Russ. & Ry. 9.

[75] Territory v. Doe, 1 Ariz. 507, 25 Pac. 472; Rex v. Journeyman Tailors, 8 Mod. 10.

[76] State v. Slocum, 8 Blackf. (Ind.) 315; Turns v. Commonwealth, 6 Metc. (Mass.) 224.

[77] Rex v. Woodward, Moody 323; Reg. v. St. John, 9 Car. & P. 40.

[78] Hagan v. State, 4 Kans. 89; Grimme v. Commonwealth, 5 B. Mon. (Ky.) 263; Botto v. State, 26 Miss. 108.

[79] Commonwealth v. Logan, 12 Gray (Mass.) 136; State v. Nixon, 18 Vt. 70, 46 Am. Dec. 135.

[80] 2 Russ. Crimes (9th Am. ed.) 354.

[81] Commonwealth v. Heffron, 102 Mass. 148; Rex v. White, 1 Burr. 333.

described thus, where an indictment averred that arson was committed on a house in the sixth ward of the city of New York, it is a fatal variance if the proof shows that the house was in the fifth ward.[82] The place of the offense should not only be alleged at the beginning of the indictment, but should be repeated as to each issuable fact, and the same is true of the time, but when once the time and place have been alleged, other facts which occurred at the same time and place may be alleged to have been committed then and there.[83]

§ 918. Time of the offense.—The rule is that the indictment should state specifically the time of the offense, but, unless time is of the essence of the offense, it is not necessary to prove that it was committed on the day alleged, provided it was committed on a day prior to the bringing of the indictment, and within the statute of limitations.[84] The day, month and year should be alleged.[85] If a single act is charged as having been done on two days, the indictment is void either for uncertainty, or repugnancy.[86] If an offense could have been committed only at a certain time, as violation of a Sunday ordinance,[87] or hunting or fishing at certain seasons of the year, the act must be charged as having

[82] State v. Crogan, 8 Iowa 523; Moore v. State, 12 Ohio St. 387.

[83] State v. Williams, 4 Ind. 234, 58 Am. Dec. 627; State v. Welker, 14 Mo. 398; State v. Bacon, 7 Vt. 219.

[84] Commonwealth v. Harrington, 3 Pick. (Mass.) 26; Williams v. State, 12 Tex. App. 226; Loftus v. Commonwealth, 3 Grat. (Va.) 631; Adams v. United States, 246 Fed. 830, 159 C. C. A. 132; People v. Van Every, 222 N. Y. 74, 118 N. E. 244; Goldberg v. State (Ga. App.), 95 S. E. 541; State v. Wilson (S. Dak.), 167 N. W. 396; State v. Ivy (Mo.), 192 S. W. 733; Morgan v. Commonwealth, 172 Ky. 684, 189 S. W. 943; United States v. Gaag, 237 Fed. 728 (an excellent case); 1 Chitty Crim. L. 224.

[85] State v. Offutt, 4 Blackf. (Ind.) 355; State v. McCarthy, 44 La. Ann. 323, 10 So. 673, 4 Bl. Comm. 306.

[86] Commonwealth v. Adams, 1 Gray (Mass.) 481; State v. Temple, 38 Vt. 37.

[87] Megowan v. Commonwealth, 2 Metc. (Ky.) 3; State v. Drake, 64 N. Car. 589.

been committed at a time when it would constitute an offense.[88] Ordinarily where an offense may be a continuing one, as the keeping of a disorderly house, it may be alleged to have taken place on one day and thence continually until another specified day, this form of allegation being known as a continuando.[89] If a continuance of acts is necessary in order to constitute an offense, as in the case of being a common seller of intoxicating liquors, the cumulative acts must be charged.[90]

§ 919. **Surplusage.**—Superfluous matter does not render an indictment bad, because such matter may be rejected.[91] If a misdemeanor is alleged to have been done feloniously, the averment may be rejected as surplusage.[92] If an allegation is defective, and the remainder of the indictment states the offense, the indictment is not impaired.[93] It is surplusage to allege that a robbery was committed "in or near a certain highway" for the place is immaterial, and the indictment is not bad because the allegation is in the disjunctive.[94] So to allege that defendant did "embezzle, take, steal and carry away" certain property does not make the indictment bad for duplicity, since the word embezzle may be stricken out as surplusage.[95]

88 State v. Dodge, 81 Maine 391, 17 Atl. 313.

89 1 Bish. New Crim. Proc., § 394.

90 Wells v. Commonwealth, 12 Gray (Mass.) 326; Commonwealth v. Adams, 4 Gray (Mass.) 27.

91 Feigel v. State, 83 Ind. 580; Commonwealth v. Jeffries, 7 Allen (Mass.) 548, 83 Am. Dec. 712; State v. Kendall, 38 Nebr. 817, 57 N. W. 525; People v. White, 22 Wend. (N. Y.) 167.

92 Commonwealth v. Philpot, 130 Mass. 59.

93 State v. Freeman, 8 Iowa 428, 74 Am. Dec. 317; State v. Wilson, 106 N. Car. 718, 11 S. E. 254.

94 Moyer v. Commonwealth, 7 Pa. St. 439; State v. Gilbert, 13 Vt. 647.

95 Commonwealth v. Brown, 14 Gray (Mass.) 419; Commonwealth v. Simpson, 9 Metc. (Mass.) 138.

But averment, which is descriptive of that which is essential to the charge in the indictment, may not be rejected as surplusage, for instance, in an indictment for stealing a horse, it is not necessary in describing it to mention the color, but if it is alleged to have been a black horse, the proof must conform to the allegation, this being an exemplification of the rule that if too great particularity is alleged, it must be proved.[96] So in an indictment for bigamy, alleging that the woman the defendant married is a widow, when the proof shows she is a spinster, there is a fatal variance.[97]

Thus an indictment for receiving stolen goods need not state the name of the thief, but if it does, the proof must conform.[98]

The rule as stated by Story is, "No allegation, whether it be necessary or unnecessary, whether it be more or less particular, which is descriptive of the identity of that which is legally essential to the charge in the indictment can ever be rejected as surplusage." If the whole of the statement can be stricken out without destroying the accusation and charge, it is not necessary to prove the particular allegation; but if the whole can not be stricken out without getting rid of a part essential to the accusation then, though the averment be more particular than it need have been, the whole must be proved, or the indictment can not be maintained.[99]

§ 920. Duplicity and misjoinder.—Duplicity is charging two or more independent crimes in the same count. Misjoinder is charging two or more independent crimes in dif-

96 State v. Gilbert, 13 Vt. 647; 3 Greenl. Ev. (16th ed.), § 10.

97 Rex v. Deeley, 1 Moody 303.

98 Semon v. State, 158 Ind. 55, 62 N. E. 625; Commonwealth v. King, 9 Cush. (Mass.) 284.

99 United States v. Howard, Fed. Cas. No. 15403, 3 Sumn. (U. S.) 12.

ferent counts of the same indictment. Each renders the indictment bad. But the same offense may be stated, however, in two or more ways. In an indictment for murder, the killing may be charged in several ways.[1] But if more acts than one are charged, or acts with respect to more than one person, the count is not double if such acts were all part of the transaction constituting the offense. Thus, a battery and murder of two or more persons may be alleged in one count.[2] And in burglary, a breaking and entering with intent to commit a felony, and the commission of the felony after entering, may be charged in one count.[3] The rule is that a crime within a crime may be charged in the same count, that is where the charge of a crime in its largest form includes one or more crimes of lesser degree, there is no duplicity. An indictment for rape may include an assault with intent to rape,[4] or an indictment under a statute for assault with a deadly weapon with intent to kill, may include the elements of three crimes.[5] Two or more averments having substantially the same meaning, made with the same purpose may be used, as

1 People v. Casey, 72 N. Y. 393; People v. Schlessel, 22 N. Y. Cr. 543, 112 N. Y. S. 45; Thomas v. State (Tex.), 26 S. W. 724. See also, People v. Crawford, 278 Ill. 134, 115 N. E. 901.

2 People v. Ellsworth, 90 Mich. 442, 51 N. W. 531; Wilkinson v. State, 77 Miss. 705, 27 So. 639; Rucker v. State, 7 Tex. App. 549; People v. Goodman, 283 Ill. 414, 119 N. E. 429; State v. Thornton, 142 La. 797, 77 So. 634; People v. Warriner (Cal. App.), 173 Pac. 489; McNeil v. United States, 246 Fed. 827, 159 C. C. A. 129; People v. Stine, 199 Ill. App. 422.

3 Reed v. State, 147 Ind. 41, 46 N. E. 135; 1 Bish. New Crim. L. (8th ed.), § 1062.

4 Farrell v. State, 54 N. J. L. 416, 24 Atl. 723; State v. Fleeman, 102 Kans. 670, 171 Pac. 618 (prosecution under White Slave Law); State v. Kerr, 117 Maine 254, 103 Atl. 585; Ruthenberg v. United States, 245 U. S. 480, 38 Sup. Ct. 168, 62 L. ed. 414; United States v. Casey, 247 Fed. 362 (conspiracy to set up or keep house of ill fame, brothel, or bawdy house within prohibited zone of military post in violation of the Selective Service Act, May 18, 1917); Rodgers v. State (Ark.), 201 S. W. 845 (charge that accused received for storage, distribution, or on consignment for another, alcoholic liquors, not bad for duplicity).

5 People v. Beam, 66 Cal. 394, 5 Pac. 677; State v. Bednar, 18 N.

the accused may be charged with keeping a disorderly house to which lewd persons did resort.[6] It is held where one count charges larceny and another receiving stolen goods, or where one count charges burglary and another receiving stolen goods, there is no misjoinder.[6a] This holding, however, is anomalous. It has been held that where one count charges burglary, another larceny, and a third receiving stolen goods, that the indictment is demurrable for misjoinder.[6b] Upon principle this view is correct, as the indictment in such case charges more than one crime.

A count is not double which charges in addition to the specific offense, merely aggravating circumstances, such as a previous conviction, which affect only the penalty.[7] If two offenses are charged and one insufficiently alleged, it may be rejected as surplusage, and whenever allegations may be rejected as surplusage, the count is not double.[8] An indictment which charges conspiracy to commit a certain crime and also the commission of the crime is not bad for duplicity. For this there are two reasons assigned: First, that the averment of the commission of the crime is a mere averment of an overt act, which is evidence of the conspiracy; second, that where the completed act is a felony, the conspiracy merges in it, hence the averments as to conspiracy may be treated as surplusage.[9] But where conspiracy is by statute made a felony, or where the act done in pursuance of the conspiracy is only a misdemeanor, the second reason fails. The same rule applies to the indictment for

Dak. 484, 121 N. W. 614, 20 Ann. Cas. 458.

6 State v. Toombs, 79 Iowa 741, 45 N. W. 300; People v. Carey, 4 Park. Cr. (N. Y.) 238, Sheld. 573; State v. Gipson, 92 Wash. 646, 159 Pac. 792 (desertion and nonsupport).

6a State v. Thornton, 142 La. 797, 77 So. 634; People v. Goodman, 283 Ill. 414, 119 N. E. 429.

6b People v. May, 166 N. Y. S. 351, 179 App. Div. 290.

7 State v. Moore, 121 Mo. 514, 26 S. W. 345, 42 Ann. St. 542.

8 State v. Palmer, 35 Maine 9; State v. Henn, 39 Minn. 464, 40 N. W. 564.

9 Hoyt v. People, 140 Ill. 588, 30 N. E. 315, 16 L. R. A. 239.

burglary, which avers a breaking with intent to commit a felony, and also the commission of the felony.[10] A single criminal act may constitute two separate crimes. It does not follow that both crimes may be averred in the same indictment.[11] A single criminal act may injure two or more persons, thus the property of several different owners can be stolen at the same time by one act, and in this case the value of all the property may be considered to make the offense grand larceny, and in the same indictment the ownership of the property may be laid in the several owners, the criminal act constituting but a single offense.[12] Some authorities, however, hold the contrary.[13]

Duplicity in the indictment may be waived by the defendant.[14] It may be taken advantage of by motion to quash,[15] demurrer,[16] or compelling the prosecutor to elect as to the charge.[17] It may be cured by pleading over, since it is merely a formal defect. In some states where two distinct offenses are charged, which require distinct punishments, it is held that advantage may be taken of such fact by motion in arrest of judgment, or perhaps appeal;[18] but the general rule is that a failure to object before verdict is a waiver. A conviction as to one of the offenses and an acquittal as to the other effects a cure.[19]

10 Bailey v. State, 116 Ala. 437, 22 So. 918; Reed v. State, 147 Ind. 41, 46 N. E. 135.

11 See Commonwealth v. Igo, 158 Mass. 199, 33 N. E. 339; State v. Dorsett, 21 Tex. 656.

12 Bushman v. Commonwealth, 138 Mass. 507; Hudson v. State, 9 Tex. App. 151, 35 Am. Rep. 732.

13 Martin v. State, 1 Lea (Tenn.) 498.

14 State v. Jarvis, 18 Ore. 360, 23 Pac. 251; State v. McCormick, 56 Wash. 469, 105 Pac. 1037.

15 Kotter v. People, 150 Ill. 441, 37 N. E. 932; State v. Sherman, 137 Mo. App. 70, 119 S. W. 479.

16 People v. Weaver, 47 Cal. 106; State v. Rees, 76 Miss. 435, 22 So. 829.

17 People v. Shotwell, 27 Cal. 394; State v. Miller, 24 Conn. 522.

18 State v. Sherman, 137 Mo. App. 70, 119 S. W. 479; People v. Wright, 9 Wend. (N. Y.) 193.

19 State v. Miller, 24 Conn. 522; State v. Merrill, 44 N. H. 624.

§ 921. **Variance.**—In order to convict one under an indictment so much of the charge must be proved as to show the commission of an offense, and the proof must correspond with the charge, for a person can not be tried and convicted without an accusation. Therefore variance between the proof and the charge as to any of the essential elements of the offense is fatal to a conviction, and entitles the defendant to be acquitted of the charge.[20] If an allegation of the indictment can be rejected as surplusage, a failure to prove it will not be a fatal variance.[21] As we have seen, if a necessary allegation is made unnecessarily particular in description, the proof must correspond with the description, even to the particulars which were in the first instance not necessary.[22] In preceding sections the essential principles of conformity of the proof to the allegations are treated.

§ 922. **Joinder of counts and offenses.**—An indictment may contain any number of counts charging the same crime in different ways. The word count is a synonym of declaration, and means a complete statement of a cause of action.[23] For instance, in an indictment for murder, the accused may be charged in one count with killing the deceased by shooting, in another by poison, in another by striking with a club, etc.[24] In an indictment for burglary, in one count the owner-

[20] Walker v. State, 96 Ala. 53, 11 So. 401; State v. Kye, 46 La. Ann. 424, 14 So. 883; Commonwealth v. Richardson, 126 Mass. 34, 30 Am. Rep. 647; Commonwealth v. Dejardin, 126 Mass. 46, 30 Am. Rep. 652; Reynolds v. State (Tex. Cr.), 198 S. W. 958; Kelly v. State (Tex. Cr.), 195 S. W. 853.

[21] Commonwealth v. Adams, 127 Mass. 15; Commonwealth v. Randall, 4 Gray (Mass.) 36. See also, State v. Wisdom, 99 Kans. 802, 162 Pac. 1174.

[22] Commonwealth v. Luscomb, 130 Mass. 42; Commonwealth v. Gavin, 121 Mass. 54, 23 Am. Rep. 255; Kahanek v. State (Tex. Cr.), 201 S. W. 994. See also, Semon v. State, 158 Ind. 55, 62 N. E. 625; Commonwealth v. King, 9 Cush. (Mass.) 284.

[23] Watson v. People, 134 Ill. 374, 25 N. E. 567; 3 Bl. Comm. 293; Gould Pl. (5th ed.), ch. 4, §§ 2, 3.

[24] Merrick v. State, 63 Ind. 327; Smith v. Commonwealth, 21 Grat. (Va.) 809.

ship of the premises may be alleged in one person, and in another count in another person.[25] One count may allege that the breaking and entry were with intent to steal, another that the intent was to murder, another to commit rape, etc.[26] In cases such as this the prosecuting attorney can not be compelled to elect upon which count the trial will be had, but the accused may be convicted upon those counts which are proved against him.[27]

The rule against duplicity merely forbids the joining of two or more offenses in one count, and it is not duplicity to charge different offenses growing out of the same transaction in separate counts, provided they are of the same nature, and the mode of prosecution is the same.[28] So, in one count burglary may be charged, and in another larceny; in one forgery, and in another uttering of a forged paper; one may charge embezzlement, one larceny, and another false pretenses; one may charge the accused as accessory before the fact and another as accessory after the fact, etc.[29] Nor is the prosecuting attorney compelled to elect in such cases. Also, where several offenses are substantially parts of the same transaction, a motion made at the beginning of the trial, either to quash the indictment or compel an election, will ordinarily be denied, as where the accused was charged with burning several houses, and it appeared that one of them had been set on fire and the first had communicated to the

25 Commonwealth v. Dobbins, 2 Pars. Eq. Cas. (Pa.) 380; Newman v. State, 14 Wis. 393.

26 2 East. P. C. 515.

27 Thompson v. State, 32 Tex. Cr. 265, 22 S. W. 979; Vaden v. State, (Tex.) 25 S. W. 777.

28 Kane v. People, 8 Wend. (N. Y.) 203; Dowdy v. Commonwealth, 9 Grat. (Va.) 727, 60 Am. Dec. 314.

29 Welch v. State, 156 Ala. 112, 46 So. 856; Tompkins v. State, 17 Ga. 356; McCullough v. State, 132 Ind. 427, 31 N. E. 1116; Griffith v. State, 36 Ind. 406; State v. Porter, 26 Mo. 201; State v. Lincoln, 49

others.[30] In no case, however, may the accused be tried on the same indictment for more than one distinct felony. But there are instances in which the prosecuting attorney will not be required to make his election until after the evidence is all in, as where the accused is indicted for robbing two persons at the same time as a part of the same transaction;[31] or for commiting two burglaries on the same night in the same locality;[32] or even for two murders committed at about the same time, where the proof as to one would be substantially the same as the proof of the other, and it would be practically impossible to separate them.[33]

At common law a felony and a misdemeanor might not be joined in the same indictment under any circumstances, for the reason that a person charged with a misdemeanor was entitled to be defended by counsel, to have a copy of the indictment and a special jury to try him, while one charged with a felony was entitled to none of these.[34] But in this country the English rule has been generally repudiated. In most jurisdictions here, felonies and misdemeanors which are kindred offenses, growing out of the same transaction, may be joined in the same indictment at the discretion of the court,[35] such as the felony of rape and the misdemeanor of assault to commit rape.[36] If the offenses charged

N. H. 464; People v. Adler, 140 N. Y. 331, 35 N. E. 644; Commonwealth v. Birdsall, 69 Pa. St. 842, 8 Am. Rep. 283; Barnwell v. State, 1 Tex. App. 745; Anthony v. Commonwealth, 88 Va. 847, 14 S. E. 834; 2 Bish. New Cr. L. (8th ed.), § 609 (1).

30 Reg. v. Truman, 8 Car. & P. 727.

31 Rex v. Giddins, Car. & M. 634.

32 Martin v. State, 79 Wis. 165, 48 N. W. 119.

33 Pointer v. United States, 151 U. S. 396, 38 L. ed. 208.

34 State v. Smalley, 50 Vt. 736; Scott v. Commonwealth, 14 Grat. (Va.) 687.

35 Herman v. People, 131 Ill. 594, 22 N. E. 471, 9 L. R. A. 182; Commonwealth v. McLaughlin, 12 Cush. (Mass.) 612.

36 People v. Jailles, 146 Cal. 301, 79 Pac. 965; Wadkins v. State, 58 Tex. Cr. 110, 124 S. W. 959, 137 Am. St. 922, 21 Ann Cas. 556.

are repugnant in their nature and legal bearing, and the trial and judgment so incongruous that the accused is deprived of some legal advantage, the joinder is not permitted.[37] The general rule is that several different felonies growing out of the same transaction may be joined in one indictment.[38] In most American jurisdictions, the prosecutor may join in one indictment as many misdemeanors of a kindred nature growing out of the same transaction as he wishes, and can not be compelled to elect.[39] However, the rule is that wherever the accused may be prejudiced by the joinder, the prosecutor should be required to elect,[40] and in some cases convenience or the administration of justice may require election.

§ 923. **Joinder of parties.**—Where several persons join in the commission of a crime, since they are severally liable to the same extent as if each had committed the whole offense alone, they may be all or any part of them joined in the same count, and all or any number of them convicted.[41] The parties need not act jointly if all commit one and the same offense, as in case of a nuisance occasioned by the acts

[37] Herman v. People, 131 Ill. 594; 22 N. E. 471, 9 L. R. A. 182; State v. Fitzsimon (R. I.), 27 Atl. 446.

[38] Bailey v. State, 116 Ala. 437, 22 So. 918; State v. Toombs, 79 Iowa 741, 45 N. W. 300; State v. Palmer, 35 Maine 9; State v. Henn, 39 Minn. 464, 40 N. W. 564; State v. Moore, 121 Mo. 514, 26 S. W. 345, 142 Am. St. 542; People v. Carey, 4 Park. Cr. (N. Y.) 238; McKenzie v. State, 32 Tex. Cr. 568, 25 S. W. 426, 40 Am. St. 795.

[39] Commonwealth v. Tuttle, 12 Cush. (Mass.) 505; People v. Budd, 117 N. Y. 1, 22 N. E. 670, 682, 5 L. R. A. 559, 15 Am. St. 460; Kane v. People, 8 Wend. (N. Y.) 203. See also, People v. Warner, 201 Mich. 547, 167 N. W. 878; People v. Hartenbower, 283 Ill. 591, 119 N. E. 605; State v. Owen, 97 Wash. 466, 166 Pac. 793.

[40] Hamilton v. People, 29 Mich. 173; Allen v. Commonwealth (Va.), 94 S. E. 783; 1 Bish. New Crim. Proc. (2d ed.), § 425.

[41] State v. Winstandley, 151 Ind. 316, 51 N. E. 92; State v. Brown, 49 Vt. 437.

of several persons.[42] However, they must all commit the same crime, not merely the same kind of crime.[43] Two persons gaming at cards together may be indicted together, but if neither is present when the other plays in the same game, they can not be jointly indicted.[44]

Some offenses by their peculiar nature can not be committed by one person, such as conspiracy,[45] or riot,[46] and an indictment for either must charge more than one with guilt, whether or not more are made defendants. Principals and accessories, whether before or after the fact, may be joined in the same indictment. The offense committed by the principal should first be charged, and then the acts constituting the others accessories.[47] It must be averred that an accessory after the fact had knowledge of the crime.[48] If the innocence of the principal is shown, the accessory can not be convicted.[49] If indicted after the conviction of the principal, the indictment should set out the record of the conviction and follow it by the statement of the acts which made the accused accessories.[50] A principal of the second degree may be indicted as either principal or accessory.[51]

42 Rex v. Trafford, 1 Barn. & Ad. 874.

43 Elliott v. State, 26 Ala. 78; Stephens v. State, 14 Ohio 386; Durston v. State (Tex. Cr.), 200 S. W. 524 (unlawfully practicing medicine without a license. License personal to individual); State v. Hendricks, 193 Mo. App. 660, 187 S. W. 272 (same).

44 Fowler v. State, 3 Heisk. (Tenn.) 154; Galbreath v. State, 36 Tex. 200.

45 Grunberg v. United States, 145 Fed. 81; Rex v. Heaps, 2 Salk. 593.

46 1 Bish. New Crim. L., § 534 (4); 2 Bish. New Crim. L., § 1143 (1).

47 People v. Lucas, 244 Ill. 603, 91 N. E. 659; Commonwealth v. Darling, 129 Mass. 112; 1 Chitty Crim. L. 272.

48 Rex v. Thompson, 2 Lev. 208; 1 Hale P. C. 622; 2 Hawk. P. C. chap. 29, § 33.

49 Commonwealth v. Knapp, 10 Pick. (Mass.) 477, 20 Am. Dec. 4 Bl. Comm. 324.

50 Commonwealth v. Knapp, 10 Pick. (Mass.) 477, 20 Am. Dec. 534; Holmes v. Walsh, 7 Term. Rep. 454; 1 Chitty Crim. L. 273.

51 Rex v. Towle, Russ. & Ry. 314; 2 Hawk. P. C., ch. 25, § 64.

Where more than one are charged with a joint offense, one or more may be found guilty, and the others acquitted.[52] But in offenses which require more than one to convict, such as conspiracy or riot, enough must be found guilty to constitute the number required to commit the crime—three in riot, two in conspiracy—or a conviction will be set aside.[53]

There are some crimes the nature of which is such that one only can commit them, and even though several commit them at the same time, indictments must be several,[54] such as for being jointly drunk,[55] or for the same perjury,[56] or for being common scolds,[57] or for publishing the same libel at different times.[58]

§ 924. **Remedy in case of misjoinder.**—Misjoinder of counts does not make an indictment bad as a matter of law. Hence it can not be raised by demurrer.[59] A motion to quash, or to compel an election, is the proper remedy.[60] Motion in arrest of judgment is not proper unless either motion to quash or compel an election has been made.[61] It would seem that a demurrer should lie if the punishment for

[52] Commonwealth v. Brown, 12 Gray (Mass.) 135; Commonwealth v. Slate, 11 Gray (Mass.) 60.

[53] Clark's Crim. L., 117, 342.

[54] Elliott v. State, 26 Ala. 78; 2 Hawk. P. C., ch. 25, § 89.

[55] State v. Deaton, 92 N. Car. 788.

[56] Rex v. Philips, 2 Strange 921; Rex v. Benfield, 2 Burr. 980; Young v. Rex, 3 Term. Rep. 98.

[57] Rex v. Philips, 2 Strange 921.

[58] Cox v. State, 76 Ala. 66; State v. Roulstone, 3 Sneed (Tenn.) 107.

[59] Johnson v. State, 29 Ala. 62, 65 Am. Dec. 383; Wreidt v. State, 48 Ind. 579; State v. Hodges, 45 Kans. 389, 26 Pac. 676; Commonwealth v. Hills, 10 Cush. (Mass.) 530; Carlton v. Commonwealth, 5 Metc. (Mass.) 532; People v. Rynders, 12 Wend. (N. Y.) 425; State v. Smalley, 50 Vt. 736; Dowdy v. Commonwealth, 9 Grat. (Va.) 727, 60 Am. Dec. 314.

[60] Dowdy v. Commonwealth, 9 Grat. (Va.) 727, 60 Am. Dec. 314; People v. Miller, 278 Ill. 490, 116 N. E. 131, L. R. A. 1917 E, 797n; People v. Crawford, 278 Ill. 134, 115 N. E. 901.

[61] State v. Armstrong, 106 Mo. 395, 16 S. W. 604, 13 L. R. A. 419, 27 Am. St. 361; State v. Brown, 8 Humph. (Tenn.) 89; State v. Owen, 97 Wash. 466, 166 Pac. 793; Pine v. Commonwealth, 121 Va. 812, 93 S. E. 652.

the offense is different, for in such case, if the verdict is general, the court would not know what punishment to impose; and after a general verdict of guilty in such case, a motion in arrest of judgment will lie, if more than one count is good; but if only one count is good, the verdict will then be held to have been based on the good count.[62] If a misjoinder of parties appears on the face of the indictment, objection may be taken either by demurrer, motion in arrest, motion to quash, or writ of error.[63] If no misjoinder appears on the face of the indictment, objection should be raised by plea in abatement, or the defendant may ask acquittal after the evidence is in.[64] If several persons are charged in the same indictment with different offenses of a kindred nature, the court, in its discretion, may sustain a motion to quash.[65] But the indictment is not bad as a matter of law, and neither demurrer, motion in arrest of judgment, or writ of error will lie.[66]

§ 925. **The overt act.**—Every act necessary to be proved must be alleged in the indictment. Also, every fact which the proof must negative must be expressly negatived in the indictment.[67] Greater particularity must be used in a description of some crimes than in others. In some instances the means of accomplishing the crime must be alleged with great particularity, as an indictment for forgery, false pretense or murder.[68] In other cases, as in an indictment for arson, larceny, assault, or assault with intent to kill, it is

62 Adams v. State, 55 Ala. 143; Davis v. State, 57 Ga. 66.

63 People v. Hawkins, 34 Cal. 181; Rex v. Weston, 1 Strange 623.

64 Elliott v. State, 26 Ala. 78; Stephens v. State, 14 Ohio 386.

65 Rex v. Kingston, 8 East. 41.

66 Rex v. Kingston, 8 East. 41.

67 Commonwealth v. Jennings, 121 Mass. 47, 23 Am. Rep. 249; Commonwealth v. Hart, 11 Cush. (Mass.) 130; Commonwealth v. Maxwell, 2 Pick. (Mass.) 139; State v. Abbey, 29 Vt. 60, 67 Am. Dec. 754.

68 Rex v. Perrott, 2 Maule & S. 379; Rex v. Gilchrist, 2 Leach 753.

not necessary to allege the means of accomplishment.[69] In the class of crimes where the offense consists in the character acquired by the accused because of continuance in wrong doing, as in an indictment for being a common barrator or a common night-walker or a common scold, the particular acts committed need not be stated.[70] Where the charge is false pretense, the particular acts must be stated.[71] Where the offense charged includes an intent to commit another crime, it is not essential to state the particulars of the latter offense.[72] Thus in an indictment for conspiracy to cheat and defraud, it is sufficient to describe the latter offense merely as "to cheat and defraud of his goods and chattels."[73]

§ 926. **Indictments on statutes.**—Generally the rules applicable to indictments at common law apply to the indictments on statutes. An indictment on a statute must purport to be based upon the statute, which is usually done by the use in the conclusion of the indictment of the words "contrary to the form of the statute in such cases made and provided." The statute itself need not be recited,[74] nor is it necessary to indicate in the indictment the particular statute or section of the statute on which it is founded.[75] What is essential is to state all the facts and circumstances which go to make up the offense as defined in the statute, and in doing so it is better to use the technical term employed in

[69] See People v. Myers, 20 Cal. 76; State v. Bowles, 146 Mo. 6, 47 S. W. 892, 69 Am. St. 598; Lee v. State, 44 Tex. Cr. 460, 72 S. W. 195.

[70] Commonwealth v. Pray, 13 Pick. (Mass.) 359; Commonwealth v. Davis, 11 Pick. (Mass.) 432; Lambert v. People, 9 Cow. (N. Y.) 578; State v. Russell, 14 R. I. 506; 1 Chitty Crim. L. 230.

[71] Rex v. Perrott, 2 Maule & S. 379.

[72] Rex v. Perrott, 2 Maule & S. 379.

[73] Rex v. Gill, 2 B. & Ald. 204; 2 Bish. New Crim. L., § 200.

[74] Commonwealth v. Griffin, 21 Pick. (Mass.) 523; People v. Walbridge, 6 Cow. (N. Y.) 512.

[75] Commonwealth v. Thompson, 108 Mass. 461; Commonwealth v. Griffin, 21 Pick. (Mass.) 523.

the statute and follow its language.[76] But if the statute in defining an offense uses general terms, the indictment must enumerate the essential particulars;[77] as where a statute punishes a person "who shall act as the agent of any other person, or persons, for the sale of intoxicating liquors," the indictment must name the person for whom the defendant acted;[78] an indictment for obtaining money by false tokens or pretenses must state the particular false tokens or pretenses used.[79] An indictment under a statute for rape, it is held, must use the word "ravished" used in the statute, and if the statute uses the term "unlawfully" in defining the defense it must be used in the indictment.[80] If the word used in the indictment means all that is meant by the word in the statute, and more, as "malicious" used where the statute uses "willful,"[81] or "unlawfully" or "feloniously" where the statute uses "falsely,"[82] or "feloniously" where the statute uses "unlawfully,"[83] the indictment is good. If a statute merely creates a crime without defining it, as if it forbids something by its common law name, resort must be had to the common law for the description of the crime.[84] Generally speaking, the indictment must employ enough of the substantial words of the statute to enable the court to ascertain on what statute it is founded; it must also have such other statutory words as are, alone, or in conjunction with other words, necessary

[76] United States v. Cook, 17 Wall. (U. S.) 168, 21 L. ed. 538; State v. Cady, 47 Conn. 44; Brown v. Commonwealth, 8 Mass. 59; Commonwealth v. Twitchell, 4 Cush. (Mass.) 74.

[77] United States v. Cruikshank, 92 U. S. 542, 23 L. ed. 588; Commonwealth v. Chase, 125 Mass. 202.

[78] State v. Higgins, 53 Vt. 191.

[79] Rex v. Munoz, 2 Strange 1127; 2 East P. C. 837.

[80] 2 Hawk. P. C., ch. 23, §§ 77, 79.

[81] State v. Brown, 41 La. Ann. 345, 6 So. 541; State v. Robbins, 66 Maine 324.

[82] State v. Dark, 8 Blackf. (Ind.) 526.

[83] Elliott, J., in Franklin v. State, 108 Ind. 47, 8 N. E. 695.

[84] Bates v. State, 31 Ind. 72; Tully v. Commonwealth, 4 Metc. (Mass.) 357.

to completely describe the offense; or the pleader may use words equivalent to the statutory words or words more than their equivalents, if they include the full meaning of the words used in the statute.[85] As regards statutory crimes, a particular description of the acts constituting the offense is not essential. An averment that the acts prohibited were committed is usually sufficient.[86] Thus, in an indictment for unlawfully practicing a certain profession without a license, or for participating in a prize fight, an averment of the doing of the thing prohibited, without stating the particular acts, is sufficient, because the word indicates clearly enough the character of the act. There are a few crimes, however, including false pretenses, bribery, and malicious mischief, which constitute exceptions to the foregoing rule. In an indictment for either of them the particular acts committed must be alleged. It also has been held that in an indictment for distributing obscene literature, the mode of doing the act must be alleged.

§ 927. What statutory exceptions must be negatived.— In some cases it is necessary to negative exceptions or provisos in statutes and in other cases it is not. As a general rule, where the exception forms a part of the description of the offense, or material qualification of the language used in defining or creating the offense, it must be negatived; otherwise, not.[87] Matters of defense need not be nega-

[85] Commonwealth v. Parker, 117 Mass. 112; Tully v. People, 67 N. Y. 15.

[86] Commonwealth v. Ashley, 2 Gray (Mass.) 356; 2 Hawk. P. C., ch. 25, § 111.

[87] Commonwealth v. Jennings, 121 Mass. 47, 23 Am. Rep. 249; Commonwealth v. Maxwell, 2 Pick. (Mass.) 139; Commonwealth v. Hart, 11 Cush. (Mass.) 130; State v. Abbey, 29 Vt. 60, 67 Am. Dec. 754; People v. Kenyon, 201 Mich. 647, 167 N. W. 997; State v. Perello, 102 Kans. 695, 171 Pac. 630; State v. Burns (Iowa), 165 N. W. 346; Cochran v. Commonwealth (Va.), 94 S. E. 329.

tived.[88] It also has been stated frequently that where the exception is in the enacting clause of the statute it should be negatived and not otherwise.[89] According to this rule, if the exception is contained in a subsequent clause of the statute, or in a subsequent statute, it is not essential to negative it.[90] This rule, however, is misleading. Thus, a proviso in a subsequent clause may be referred to in such a way as to make it descriptive of the offense charged; and in such case the proviso must be negatived.[91] It is to be observed, therefore, that the other rule stated above is the safer one to follow. A negative not required by law may be rejected as surplusage, and a negative averment need not be so minute, or so nearly in the statutory words, as must an affirmative one; but any negation in general terms, covering the entire substance of the matter will suffice.[92]

§ 928. **Conclusion.**—The third part of the indictment is the conclusion. Without a formal conclusion, unless statute provides otherwise, an indictment is bad.[93] In most states a form of conclusion is prescribed by constitution or statute and must be followed.[94] The form usually used is, "against

[88] United States v. Cook, 17 Wall. (U. S.) 168, 21 L. ed. 538; Thompson v. State, 54 Miss. 740; State v. Fuller, 33 N. H. 259; Fleming v. People, 27 N. Y. 329; Grisson v. Commonwealth, 181 Ky. 189, 203 S. W. 1075; Quaternick v. State (Tex. Cr.), 204 S. W. 328; State v. Evertz (Mo. App.), 202 S. W. 614; State v. Wild (Mo. App.), 202 S. W. 613; United States v. Scott, 248 Fed. 361; People v. Kesseling (Cal. App.), 170 Pac. 627; Commonwealth v. Gallatta, 228 Mass. 308, 117 N. E. 343; United States v. O'Hara, 242 Fed. 749; State v. Hopkins, 54 Mont. 52, 166 Pac. 304.

[89] Barber v. State, 50 Md. 161; State v. Lanier, 88 N. Car. 658.

[90] United States v. Nelson, 29 Fed. 202; Bell v. State, 104 Ala. 79, 15 So. 557.

[91] United States v. Nelson, 29 Fed. 202; State v. Abbey, 29 Vt. 60, 67 Am. Dec. 754.

[92] State v. Watson, 5 Blackf. (Ind.) 155; Commonwealth v. Chisholm, 103 Mass. 213.

[93] State v. Washington, 1 Bay (S. Car.) 120, 1 Am. Dec. 601; Reg. v. Wyat, 1 Salk. 380.

[94] People v. Enoch, 13 Wend. (N. Y.) 159, 27 Am. Dec. 197; Commonwealth v. Carney, 4 Grat. (Va.) 546.

the peace and dignity of the state," or in some jurisdictions "the people of the state," or "common law" is used instead of the word "state." In England the form is "against the peace of the King." The words "and dignity" are not necessary.[95] If the indictment is upon a statute, the conclusion must contain the words "against the form of the statute," where the statute creates an offense which did not exist at common law or enlarges a common-law offense;[96] but the conclusion "contra formam statuti" is not essential where the statute merely declares the common law, fixes the punishment of a common-law crime, or deprives the defendant of some benefit to which he was entitled at common law or changes the rule of evidence.[97] In England and some of the American states it is provided by statute that no indictment shall be insufficient because of the omission of the conclusion.[98] In other states, it has been provided that indictments shall not be invalidated by formal defects, and it has been held that the conclusion of an indictment is "a mere rhetorical flourish adding nothing to the substance of the indictment."[99] When an indictment contains more than one count, each must have an appropriate conclusion.[1] Surplusage may be rejected to make a conclusion good,[2] and generally a substantial compliance with the formula is sufficient.[3]

95 Commonwealth v. Caldwell, 14 Mass. 330; 2 Hale P. C. 188.

96 Commonwealth v. Dennis, 105 Mass. 162; Commonwealth v. Northampton, 21 Mass. 116; State v. Johnson, 1 Walk. (Miss.) 392; 2 Hawk. P. C., ch. 25, § 116.

97 People v. Enoch, 13 Wend. (N. Y.) 159, 27 Am. Dec. 197; Chiles v. Commonwealth, 2 Va. Cas. 260; 2 Hale, P. C. 190; 2 Hawk. P. C., ch. 46, § 43.

98 Commonwealth v. Kennedy, 15 B. Mon. (Ky.) 531; State v. Dorr, 82 Maine 341, 19 Atl. 861.

99 Nichols v. State, 35 Wis. 308.

1 McGuire v. State, 37 Ala. 161; State v. Johnson, 1 Walk (Miss.) 392; Brown v. Commonwealth, 86 Va. 466, 10 S. E. 745.

2 State v. Allen, 8 W. Va. 680.

3 State v. Waters, 1 Mo. App. 7; State v. Mason, 54 S. Car. 240, 32 S. E. 357.

§ 929. Amendment.—The rule at common law is that an indictment is not subject to amendment by either prosecuting attorney or court whether the offense be a felony or a misdemeanor, in manner of form or matter of substance.[4] It may not even be amended with the consent of the defendant.[5] The reason is that the indictment is found upon the oath of the grand jury and should only be amended by them.[6] However, informations, which were framed originally by the prosecuting attorney, may, therefore, by him be amended.[7] The caption may be amended as it is no part of the indictment.[8] Statutes in England and in most of our states allow in the discretion of the court amendments in the matter of form.[9] The courts do not agree as to what is matter of form and what is matter of substance. The name of the defendant, being a mere matter of form, may be amended.[10] Some courts allow the indictment to be amended as to the name of third persons; for instance the name of the owner of the premises in an indictment for arson or burglary,[11] the name of the owner of the goods in an indictment for

4 Commonwealth v. Phillipsburg, 10 Mass. 78; Commonwealth v. Mahar, 16 Pick. (Mass.) 120; 2 Hawk. ch. 25, § 98.

5 Commonwealth v. Adams, 92 Ky. 134, 17 S. W. 276; People v. Campbell, 4 Park. Cr. (N. Y.) 386.

6 People v. VanEvery, 222 N. Y. 74, 118 N. E. 244; State v. Kiefer (Iowa), 163 N. W. 698; State v. Davis (R. I.), 97 Atl. 818, 98 Atl. 57; 2 Hawk. P. C. ch. 25, § 98; 2 Bish. New Crim. Proc., § 709.

7 State v. Rowley, 12 Conn. 101; State v. Terrebonne, 45 La. Ann. 25, 12 So. 315; State v. Fleeman, 102 Kans. 670, 171 Pac. 618; State v. Hay (Utah), 172 Pac. 721; People v. Thompson, 203 Ill. App. 296; State v. Sieff, 54 Mont. 165, 168 Pac. 524; State v. McCullough, 101 Kans. 52, 165 Pac. 644.

8 State v. Paine, 1 Ind. 163, Smith 73; State v. McCarty, 2 Chand. (Wis.) 199; 54 Am. Dec. 150; State v. Pelser (Iowa), 163 N. W. 600.

9 People v. Campbell, 4 Park. Cr. (N. Y.) 386.

10 Miller v. State, 68 Miss. 221, 8 So. 273; Shifflett v. Commonwealth, 90 Va. 386, 18 S. E. 838; State v. Grimms (La.), 78 So. 661.

11 People v. Hagan, 60 Hun (N. Y.) 577, 14 N. Y. 233, 37 N. Y. St. 660.

larceny,[12] the name of the victim in an indictment for assault and battery,[13] the name of the purchasers in an indictment for selling intoxicating liquor without a license.[14] There can be no amendment which changes the identity of the offense.[15]

§ 930. Defects cured by statute.—In some jurisdictions, objections are not allowed to merely formal defects in an indictment.[16] Other statutes, similar to the old Statutes of eofails, provided that objections to formal defects shall be unavailing if not taken before a particular time or step in the cause.[17] We have already mentioned the statutes which permit amendment. These statutes are constitutional, but statutes prohibiting objections to defects in matters of substance would be unconstitutional,[18] so where an indictment fails to describe the offense with sufficient certainty to give the accused notice of the charge, the defect can not be cured by statute.[19] However, it is held that there may be cured by statute such defects as an omission of the day or month where time is not of the essence of the crime,[20] or failure of an information for receiving stolen goods to allege when, where and by whom they were stolen.[21]

12 State v. Christian, 30 La. Ann. 367; Baker v. State, 88 Wis. 140, 59 N. W. 570.

13 Rasmussen v. State, 63 Wis. 1, 22 N. W. 835.

14 Rough v. Commonwealth, 78 Pa. St. 495.

15 Blumenberg v. State, 55 Miss. 528.

16 Eakin v. Burger, 1 Sneed (Tenn.) 417; Rex v. Landorff, 2 Strange 1006.

17 2 Bish. New Crim. Proc., § 705; 3 Bl. Comm. 407.

18 State v. Sullivan, 35 La. Ann. 844; People v. Scanlon, 23 N. Y. Cr. 426, 117 N. Y. S. 57.

19 Pattee v. State, 109 Ind. 545, 10 N. E. 421; Newcomb v. State, 37 Miss. 383.

20 Phillips v. State, 86 Ga. 427, 12 S. E. 650; State v. Peters, 107 N. Car. 876, 12 S. E. 74.

21 People v. Smith, 94 Mich. 644, 54 N. W. 487.

§ 931. Aider by verdict.—Under the common law, a defective statement in the indictment may be cured by verdict of guilty, provided the crime charged is sufficiently described to show the commission of an offense, and to apprise the accused of the charge against him, whether the defect is in form or substance.[22] It was said in an early case, "where there is any defect, imperfection, or omission in any pleading, whether in substance or form, which would have been a fatal objection upon demurrer, yet, if the issue joined by it was such as necessarily required on the trial proof of the facts so defectively or imperfectly stated or omitted, and without which it is not to be presumed that either the judge would direct the jury to give, or the jury would have given the verdict, such defect, imperfection, or omission is cured by the verdict of the common law."[23] When an indictment wholly fails to state an essential element of the crime the verdict will not aid the omission. Where the crime charged was the publishing of an obscene book, which was described by its title and its contents not set forth, the court held the omission fatal and said, "The rule is very simple, and it applies equally to civil and criminal cases; it is, that the verdict only cures defective statements. In the present case the objection is not that there is a defective statement, but an absolute and total want in stating that which constitutes the criminal act, namely, the words complained of."[24]

22 Black, Law Dict. "Aides by Verdict." See also, People v. Costello, 170 N. Y. S. 341, 182 App. Div. 341, 36 N. Y. Cr. R. 369; Guigton v. State (Nebr.), 163 N. W. 858; People v. Stine, 199 Ill. App. 422; Gargan v. Harris, 90 Conn. 188, 96 Atl. 940; Bridger v. State, 122 Ark. 491, 183 S. W. 962 (error in name of accused).

23 Smith v. Cleveland, 6 Metc. (Mass.) 332; Stennel v. Hogg, 1 Wms. Saund. 226.

24 Bradlaugh v. Reg., 3 Q. B. Div. 607. See also, Reyes v. State, 34 Fla. 181, 15 So. 875; Mahaffey v. State (Ala. App.), 75 So. 647; State v. Seymour (Utah), 163 Pac. 789; People v. Holtzman, 272 Ill. 447, 112 N. E. 370.

§ 932. **Certain special indictments—Indictment for murder.**—The common law indictment for murder is complex and cumbersome, due, in large extent, to the fact that numerous details connected with the means and mode of killing, nature, size and location of the wound, etc., are necessary. There are many allegations used in the old form of indictment which are not essential, but are retained merely as a matter of form. The indictment must expressly charge the defendant with causing the death of the deceased.[25] Where the death was caused by a violent act on the part of the defendant, it must be alleged that he did the violent act, and that death resulted therefrom. In the case of death resulting from the neglect of the accused to perform a legal duty, the duty, the negligence and the fact that death resulted from the neglect, must be alleged. When the means of causing death is known it must be stated,[26] also the manner of using the means to produce the death must be alleged.[27] An allegation that the accused "with a rifle did kill," or "with poison did kill" or "with a knife did strike, of which mortal wound deceased died," is not sufficient because it does not show the manner in which the means employed produced the death. If the means of causing the death is unknown, this fact must be alleged. In the case of several means of killing contributing to the death,[28] all of them may be alleged.[29] A substantial variance between the allegation, and the proof, relative to the means

25 West v. State, 48 Ind. 483; State v. Borders (Mo.), 199 S. W. 180.

26 Commonwealth v. Martin, 125 Mass. 394.

27 Edwards v. State, 27 Ark. 493; Meiers v. State, 56 Ind. 336; 1 East P. C. 341; Barranetine v. State 72 Fla. 1, 72 So. 280; Carr v. State (Tex. Cr.), 190 S. W. 727. See also, Green v. Commonwealth (Va.), 94 S. E. 940; Azbill v. State (Ariz.), 172 Pac. 658; Knight v. State (Ga.), 95 S. E. 679; People v. Falkovitch, 280 Ill. 321, 117 N. E. 398; McDonald v. Commonwealth, 177 Ky. 224, 197 S. W. 665; Howard v. State (Fla.), 74 So. 882 (held variance not fatal where instrument used produces or may produce same kind of wound).

28 Willey v. State, 46 Ind. 363.

29 State v. Baldwin, 79 Iowa 714, 45 N. W. 297; State v. Jones, 86 S. Car. 17.

of killing makes the indictment bad, but if it is an unconsequential point, and is immaterial it is not necessarily fatal.[30] Blackstone says: "If a person be indicted for one species of killing, as by poisoning, he can not be convicted by evidence of a totally different species of death, as by shooting with a pistol, or by starving. But where they only differ in circumstance, as if a wound be alleged to be given with a sword, and it proves to have arisen from a staff, an ax, or a hatchet, this difference is immaterial."[31]

Where the means alleged is a spade and the proof shows it was a shovel, or where the means alleged is strychnine, and it is proved that it was some other kind of poison, the variance is not fatal because immaterial; but where the means of killing is alleged to be a club, and proof shows it to have been a revolver, or it is alleged to be a knife and proof shows it to have been a club, the variance is fatal. If it is alleged that death was caused by a wound, the wound must be properly described, though at present there is not as great particularity as formerly existed. Thus, an erroneous allegation as to the location of a wound used to be fatal; but according to the better opinion today it is considered immaterial. Even though the allegation locates the wound on the right side of the head, in a case where the proof shows it to be on the left side, the variance is not fatal.[32] However, repugnancy in the allegation itself, with respect to the location of a wound, may be fatal, as where it is described as "on the head and body,"[33] or where the allegation states the blow was struck on the

30 Dukes v. State, 11 Ind. 557, 71 Am. Dec. 370; State v. Lauteuschlager, 22 Minn. 514; State v. Barnhart (La.), 78 So. 975; Watson v. State (Ga. App.), 94 S. E. 857.

31 4 Bl. Comm. 196. See also, State v. Spahr (Ind.), 117 N. E. 648 (indictment charged that killing was with a shovel, held that proof of killing with a brick or rock not a fatal variance).

32 Curtis v. Commonwealth, 87 Va. 589, 13 S. E. 73.

33 State v. Anderson, 98 Mo. 461, 11 S. W. 981.

left temple, causing a mortal wound on the right temple.[84] In some states an error of this nature is cured by statute.

An averment that the act was done with malice aforethought must be incorporated in an indictment for murder.[85] As a rule the averment is made that the act was done wilfully, or with intent to kill; but omission to so allege is not fatal to the indictment.[86]

In some states murder is divided by statute into two or three degrees, and in a few of these states an indictment for murder in the first degree must allege all facts necessary to constitute this degree of the offense. But usually the old form of indictment for murder is sufficient.

The following is a typical form of indictment for murder by violence:

"That John Doe, on ------, at ------, with force and arms, in and upon one Richard Roe, in the peace of the state then and there being, did make an assault, and that the said John Doe, with a certain club, of large size and weight, to wit, two feet long and weighing four pounds, which he, the said John Doe, in both his hands then and there had and held, the said Richard Roe, in and upon the left side of the head of him, the said Richard Roe, then and there feloniously, wilfully, and of his malice aforethought, did strike and bruise, giving the said Richard Roe, then and there, with the club aforesaid, in and upon the said left side of the head of him the said Richard Roe, one mortal wound, of which said mortal wound the said Richard Roe then and there instantly died. And so the jurors aforesaid, upon their oath aforesaid;

[84] Dias v. State, 7 Blackf. (Ind.) 20, 139 Am. Dec. 448; State v. Robinson (La.), 78 So. 933; State v. Allen, 98 Kans. 778, 99 Kans. 187, 160 Pac. 795.

[85] State v. Scott, 38 La. Ann. 387; McElroy v. State, 14 Tex. App. 235.

[86] State v. Harris, 27 La. Ann. 572; 1 Hale P. C. 466; State v. Robinson (La.), 78 So. 933; People v. Falkovitch, 280 Ill. 321, 117 N. E. 398; McDonald v. Commonwealth, 177 Ky. 224, 197 S. W. 655; Burnett v. Commonwealth, 172 Ky. 397, 189 S. W. 460.

do say that the said John Doe, the said Richard Roe, then and there, in manner and form aforesaid, feloniously, wilfully and of his malice aforethought, did kill and murder; against the peace of the said state, and the form of the statute in such case made and provided.

§ 933. Indictment for larceny.—The correct form of the indictment for larceny is very simple. The following is typical of the form used at common law:

That John Doe, on ------, at ------, one cow, of the value of more than forty dollars, of the property of Richard Roe, feloniously did steal, take, and carry away. And so the jurors aforesaid, upon their oath aforesaid, do say, etc.

§ 934. Indictment for embezzlement.—The accused can not be convicted of embezzlement on an indictment for larceny unless it is so authorized by statute.[37] The statutes provide for this, in some states, and they have been held constitutional. While it is not necessary to state particulars in alleging the offense, and an averment only that the accused "embezzled" certain property is enough,[38] it is essential to state the exact nature of the fiduciary relation existing between the victim and the person accused, and it is necessary to allege that the property was received by him by virtue of this relationship.[39] The particulars of the employment, however, are not necessary in the indictment.[40]

The following is a typical form of indictment for embezzlement:

37 Kibs v. People, 81 Ill. 599; Commonwealth v. King, 9 Cush (Mass.) 284.

38 Nelson v. State, 50 Fla. 137; Mills v. State, 53 Nebr. 263, 73 N. W. 761; State v. Marx, 139 Minn. 448, 166 N. W. 1082; State v. Campbell, 99 Wash. 502, 169 Pac. 968; State v. Chaplain, 101 Kans. 413, 166 Pac. 238; State v. Greco (Del.), 102 Atl. 62 ("stick pin").

39 Flenner v. State, 58 Ark 98, 23 S. W. 1; People v. Tryon, 4 Mich. 665.

40 State v. Poland, 33 La. Ann. 1161.

"That John Doe, on ------, at ------, being then and there the agent of Richard Roe, did by virtue of his said employment receive and take into his possession ten silver dollars, of the value of ten dollars, for and in the name and on the account of the said Richard Roe, and afterward did then and there fraudulently embezzle the same; and so the said John Doe did then and there, in the manner and form aforesaid, the said ten silver dollars, the property of the said Richard Roe, his principal, from the said Richard Roe, feloniously steal, take, and carry away. And so the jurors do say all of which the said John Doe then and there knew."

§ 935. Indictment for false pretenses.—An indictment for false pretenses is of a very complex character, and it is necessary to set out the pretense with great particularity. It is not sufficient to allege in the words of the statute that the property was obtained by false pretenses; the nature of the pretense must be substantially alleged, though not necessarily according to its tenor.[41] In the indictment it must be clearly shown that the pretense related to a past or existing fact or circumstance and was not merely an expression of opinion or a promise;[42] that it was knowingly false, and was made with the intention to deceive;[43] that it was calculated to defraud, and actually did defraud.[44] The indictment for false pretenses has been simplified to some extent in some states. In Massachusetts, the statute provides that the crime of false pretenses may be incorporated into one crime together with larceny and embezzlement, and that proof of either of the three offenses is sufficient to support the indictment.

[41] State v. Tatum, 96 Miss. 430; State v. Switzer, 63 Vt. 604; 22 Atl. 724; 25 Am. St. 789; People v. Butler (Cal. App.), 169 Pac. 918.

[42] Reg. v. Henshaw, Leigh & C. 444.

[43] Maranda v. State, 44 Tex. 442.

[44] Clifford v. State, 56 Ind. 245; Enders v. People, 20 Mich. 233.

The following typical form of indictment for false pretenses, at common law, is sufficient:

"That John Doe, on ------, at ------, feloniously devising to cheat and defraud Richard Roe, did then and there falsely and feloniously pretend to the said Richard Roe that (set forth the pretense), by means of which false pretenses he, the said John Doe, did then and there fraudulently and feloniously obtain of the said Richard Roe, of the property of the said Richard Roe (describing said property), of the value of ------, whereas in truth and fact (specifically denying the truth of the pretenses alleged) all of which the said John Doe then and there knew.

§ 936. Analogous offenses.—Larceny, embezzlement and false pretenses are analogous crimes. In the former two, however, the defendant does not acquire title to the property appropriated. In an indictment for the larceny of a check, ownership may be alleged in different persons.[45] While in an indictment for larceny it is essential to allege the value of the property stolen, it is not necessary to prove the amount as charged.[46] Where ownership of the property stolen is alleged in A and the proof shows that A was in possession of the property on consignment there is no variance.[47] An indictment for larceny must sufficiently describe the property stolen.[48] An indictment for the larceny of a branded cow need not allege or describe the brand, but where it is alleged as descriptive of the stolen animal a material variance between the allegation and proof is fatal.[49] In an indictment for larceny ownership of the stolen property may be laid in

[45] Allen v. Commonwealth (Va.), 94 S. E. 783.

[46] State v. Curry, 103 S. Car. 338, 88 S. E. 27 (alleged value $65, value proved $20); People v. Demsey, 283 Ill. 342, 119 N. E. 333.

[47] Smith v. State (Ind.), 118 N. E. 954, L. R. A. 1918 D, 688.

[48] Adams v. State (Ga. App.), 94 S. E. 82.

[49] Smith v. State (Fla.), 76 So. 774.

an agent, but not in a mere servant.[50] The conviction of an agent for larceny by embezzlement is not dependent upon the scope or duration of the agency.[51] Repayment of the money embezzled or an attempt to do so, does not bar or impede the prosecution.[52] In an indictment for embezzlement the property appropriated should be described with the same degree of particularity as in the case of larceny.[53] But the term "shotgun" constitutes a sufficient description of the property embezzled.[54] The crime of false pretenses must be alleged with sufficient definiteness and clearness.[55] To sustain an indictment for obtaining money by a confidence game the proof must show that the money was obtained by reason of the confidence reposed in the defendant by his victim.[56]

50 Jackson v. State (Ga. App.), 94 S. E. 55.

51 State v. Campbell, 99 Wash. 502, 169 Pac. 968.

52 State v. Campbell, 99 Wash. 502, 169 Pac. 968.

53 Henderson v. State (Fla.), 78 So. 427.

54 Henderson v. State (Fla.), 78 So. 427.

55 Blanck v. State (Okla. Cr.), 169 Pac. 1130.

56 People v. Gallowich, 283 Ill. 360, 119 N. E. 283. See also, People v. Dempsey, 283 Ill. 342, 119 N. E. 333; People v. Koelling, 284 Ill. 118, 119 N. E. 993.

CHAPTER LXXVIII

ARRAIGNMENT AND DEFENDANT'S PLEAS.

§ 940. Arraignment.—Before the accused can be tried he must first be arraigned, that is, in open court the indictment must be read to him and he must be asked whether he is guilty of the crime.[1] He may, instead of answering, plead in abatement or demur to the indictment or plead specially.[2] His right to any of these pleadings is waived by a pleading of "guilty" or "not guilty."[3] In some states a formal arraignment may be expressly or impliedly waived by the defendant.[4] If the defendant's demurrer or dilatory plea be overruled the arraignment proceeds and he is again asked to

1 4 Bl. Comm. 322, 332.

2 2 Hale P. C. 219. See also, Whitehead v. Commonwealth, 19 Grat. (Va.) 640.

3 Foster v. State, 1 Tex. App. 531; 2 Hale, P. C. 175.

4 Hicks v. State, 111 Ind. 402, 12 N. E. 522; Goodin v. State, 16 Ohio St. 344.

plead guilty or not guilty.[5] At a new trial a second arraignment is not necessary.[6] There must be a plea before there can be a valid trial,[7] even if the defendant voluntarily goes to trial without a plea. The plea must precede the impaneling and swearing of the jury.[8] The rule is that if the prisoner tenders no plea the plea of "not guilty" is entered for him.[9]

§ 941. Various kinds of defendant's pleas.—In addition to a motion to quash the indictment, the defendant may plead to the jurisdiction, plead in abatement of the indictment, demur to the indictment, specially plead in bar, or generally plead "not guilty." The principal special pleas in bar are those of "former jeopardy," that is "autrefois acquit" or "autrefois convict." The plea of pardon, or, in some states, an agreement to turn state's evidence, may be pleaded in bar. Or the defendant may confess his guilt either expressly by a plea of guilty or impliedly by the plea of nolo contendere. Generally speaking a plea of guilty may be retracted any time before sentence, and a plea of not guilty entered.[10] After either the plea of guilty or nolo contendere evidence may be heard in mitigation of the sentence. Either plea is equivalent to a conviction.[11]

§ 942. Plea to the jurisdiction.—By this plea a defendant denies that the court has authority to try him either because of the nature of the crime or because it was not committed within the territorial jurisdiction of the court, or because the court has no jurisdiction of the defendant's person.[12] Such

[5] Rex v. Delamere, 11 How. St. Tr. 509.

[6] People v. McElvaine, 125 N. Y. 596, 26 N. E. 929.

[7] Lacefield v. State, 34 Ark. 275, 36 Am. Rep. 8; State v. Cunningham, 94 N. Car. 824.

[8] State v. Hughes, 1 Ala. 655; State v. Chenier, 32 La. Ann. 103; State v. Montgomery, 63 Mo. 296.

[9] Commonwealth v. McKenna, 125 Mass. 397; Connon v. State, 5 Tex. App. 34.

[10] Krolage v. People, 224 Ill. 456, 79 N. E. 570; Pattee v. State, 109 Ind. 545, 10 N. E. 421; People v. Richmond, 57 Mich. 399, 24 N. W. 124.

[11] Commonwealth v. Horton, 9 Pick. (Mass.) 206.

[12] Rex v. Johnson, 6 East 583; 4 Bl. Comm. 333; 2 Hale P. C. 256.

a plea must be certain to the highest degree. The objection presented by such a plea may usually be raised under the plea of not guilty,[13] or may be raised by demurrer, motion in arrest of judgment, or on appeal or writ of error.[14]

§ 943. Plea in abatement.—A plea in abatement is merely dilatory and does not go into the merits of the case, serving only to procure delay. This plea is available for defects either apparent on the record, or not apparent on the record.[15] If the defect is apparent on the record, the court might direct the grand jury to send in a new bill or hold the prisoner until the next session.[16] This kind of plea must be certain to every intent and verified by affidavit.[17] It must be filed before any plea in bar.[18] A plea in abatement is available for certain defects not appearing in the record, among them, if the defendant be indicted by a wrong name.[19] The pendency of another indictment for the same cause is not ground for plea in abatement.[20] The prosecutor may demur to this plea thus forming an issue of law, or file a replication thus creating an issue of fact.[21] Motion to quash is not proper.[22]

13 Parker v. Elding, 1 East. 352; Rex v. Johnson, 6 East. 583.

14 Rex v. Fearnley, 1 Term. Rep. 316, 2 Leach 475.

15 Day v. Commonwealth, 2 Grat. (Va.) 562; Commonwealth v. Long, 2 Va. Cas. 318; 2 Bish. New Crim. Proc. §§ 738, 739, 740; Goodman v. Rutchik, Inc., 171 N. Y. S. 152 (test of a valid plea in abatement).

16 2 Hawk. P. C. ch. 34, § 2.

17 Hardin v. State, 22 Ind. 347; Commonwealth v. Sayers, 8 Leigh (Va.) 722; Feather v. Husted, 254 Pa. St. 357, 98 Atl. 971; Scheeline v. Moshier, 172 Cal. 565, 158 Pac. 222 (pleas in abatement are not favored and are strictly construed).

18 Martin v. Commonwealth, 1 Mass. 347.

19 2 Hale P. C. 175; 2 Hawk. P. C. ch. 25, § 70; 2 Bish. New Crim. Proc. § 740.

20 Commonwealth v. Drew, 3 Cush. (Mass.) 279; Commonwealth v. Churchill, 5 Mass. 175.

21 1 Chitty Crim. L. 460. See also Hite v. State, 9 Yerg. (Tenn.) 357; State v. Locklin, 59 Vt. 654, 10 Atl. 464; Rex v. Vandercom, 2 Leach 715; Rex v. Wildey, 1 Maule & S. 183.

22 Rex v. Cooke, 2 Barn. & C. 618.

§ 944. **Demurrer.**—"By demurrer, the defendant refers it to the court to pronounce whether admitting the matters of fact alleged against him to be true they do in point of law constitute him guilty of an offense sufficiently charged against."[23] It puts the legality of the whole proceedings in issue, and compels the court to examine the whole record; thus raising objection, not only to the subject-matter of the charge, but also the jurisdiction of the court.[24] It should be made after arraignment, but before plea in bar.[25] If he pleads in bar, the court may in its discretion allow the defendant to withdraw his plea and file a demurrer.[26] If the demurrer is overruled at common law, the court may, and usually does, allow him to plead over.[27] In some states statutes provide that as a matter of right, where his demurrer is overruled, the judgment shall be respondeat ouster which gives the right to .plead over. When he demurs to the indictment on the ground that he is not charged by it with any crime, he should be discharged from custody if his demurrer is sustained.[28] If the objection is merely to the form of the indictment, he is not entitled to a discharge but may be detained until a new indictment is filed.[29] At common law, a defendant on motion in arrest of judgment could obtain all the advantage possible by a demurrer;[30] but under the

[23] 2 Bish. New Crim. Proc. § 741. See also Rex v. Fearnley, 1 Tenn. Rep. 316.

[24] Commonwealth v. Trimmer, 84 Pa. St. 65; 1 Chitty. Crim. L. 440.

[25] People v. Villarino, 66 Cal. 228, 5 Pac. 154; Commonwealth v. Chapman, 11 Cush. (Mass.) 422.

[26] People v. Villarino, 66 Cal. 228, 5 Pac. 154; Reg. v. Purchase, Car. & M. 617.

[27] Commonwealth v. Goddard, 13 Mass. 455; Wilson v. Laws, 1 Salk. 50; 1 Chitty. Crim. L. 439.

[28] Rex v. Burder, 4 Term. Rep. 778; Rex v. Haddock, Andrews, 137.

[29] Rex v. Haddock, Andrews 137; 1 Chitty Crim. L. 443.

[30] 1 Chitty Crim. L. 442.

statutes of most of our states certain defects must be raised by motions to quash or demurrer if raised at all. Demurrer will also lie by the prosecutor to any plea of the defense.[31]

§ 945. Motion to quash.—The judge in his discretion may quash an indictment; that is, may cause it to abate, whenever it can not be proceeded with advantageously to public justice, or without doing a wrong to the defendant.[32] He may either enter an order quashing it, or merely refuse to try the indictment.[33] This motion should be made ordinarily before arraignment and plea; but in the absence of statute may be heard, in the discretion of the court, any time before verdict.[34] A motion to quash will lie when there is a defect on the face of the indictment or for duplicity or misjoinder.[35] In some states the motion will lie where the defect is not apparent upon the face of the record as where the grand jury is defectively constituted or hears illegal evidence.[36] Indictments may be quashed for want of jurisdiction,[37] where the statute of limitations has run against the offense charged,[38] for repugnancy,[39] for failure to state an offense,[40] for failure to state the crime, or stating the time at a future date,[41] for

[31] Rooks v. State, 83 Ala. 79, 3 So. 720; State v. Roberts, 166 Ind. 585, 77 N. E. 1093; State v. McNay, 100 Md. 622, 60 Atl. 273; State v. Laughlin, 180 Mo. 342, 79 S. W. 401.

[32] Reg. v. Wilson, 6 Q. B. 620; 6 Ad. & El. 619, 51 E. C. L. 619.

[33] United States v. Kuhl, 85 Fed. 624; State v. Brown, 47 Ohio St. 102, 23 N. E. 747, 21 Am. St. 790.

[34] State v. Oliver, 42 La. Ann. 943, 8 So. 471; State v. Summerlin, 116 La. 449, 40 So. 792; State v. Reeves, 97 Mo. 668, 10 S. W. 841, 10 Am. St. 349; State v. Prater, 59 S. Car. 271, 37 S. E. 933.

[35] Wickwire v. State, 19 Conn. 477; Lewellen v. State, 18 Tex. 538.

[36] United States v. Kilpatrick, 16 Fed. 765; State v. Richard, 50 La. Ann. 210, 23 So. 331; State v. Batchelor, 15 Mo. 207; State v. Grady, 12 Mo. App. 361.

[37] Justice v. State, 17 Ind. 56; Bell v. Commonwealth, 8 Grat. (Va.) 600.

[38] State v. J. P., 1 Tyler (Vt.) 283.

[39] State v. Johnson, 5 Jones L. (N. Car.) 221.

[40] People v. Eckford, 7 Cow. (N. Y.) 535; Williams v. State, 42 Tex. 392.

[41] State v. Roach, 2 Hayw. (N. Car.) 352; State v. Sexton, 3 Hawk. (N. Car.) 184.

omission in material averment,[42] for misjoinder of parties,[43] or misjoinder of offenses,[44] or defects in the caption.[45] The motion, however, being addressed to the court's discretion should be overruled in a doubtful case wherever the insufficiency is not clearly palpable.[46] If there is a motion to quash, the court, by the better rule, may quash bad counts without affecting the good counts.[47] After quashing an indictment a new one may be brought against the defendant.[48] At common law, all objections which could be presented by motion to quash could be raised after verdict by motion in arrest of judgment;[49] but by statutes in certain of our states certain objections must be raised by motion to quash or forever be waived.

§ 946. **Plea of not guilty.**—The plea of not guilty, usually spoken of as the general issue, the only general plea in bar. This plea puts in question the entire issue of guilt, and denies all facts necessary to render the accused guilty of the offense charged.[50] Under such a plea special defenses may be proved such as, if the indictment be for murder, justification, insanity or self-defense;[51] or under an indictment for unlawfully selling liquor, that the sale was by license.[52] The statute of limitations may be offered under the general plea.[53]

42 Rex v. Lease, Andrews, 226; Rex v. Trevilian, 2 Strange, 1268.

43 Rex v. Weston, 1 Strange 623.

44 Clarks' Crim. L. 365.

45 State v. Hickman, 8 N. J. L. 299; Rex v. Brown, 1 Salk. 376.

46 Commonwealth v. Eastman, 1 Cush. (Mass.) 189; 48 Am. Dec. 596; People v. Davis, 56 N. Y. 95; Commonwealth v. Litton, 6 Grat. (Va.) 691.

47 Commonwealth v. Lapham, 156 Mass. 480, 31 N. E. 638; Scott v. Commonwealth, 14 Grat. (Va.) 687.

48 Perkins v. State, 66 Ala. 457.

49 Rex v. Wheatley, 2 Burr. 1125; 1 Chitty Crim. L. 304.

50 Madisonville, etc. Co. v. Commonwealth, 140 Ky. 255, 130 S. W. 1084; 4 Bl. Comm. 338.

51 People v. Carlin, 194 N. Y. 448, 87 N. E. 805; 4 Bl. Comm. 338.

52 Peters v. State, 3 Greene (Iowa) 74.

53 United States v. Brown, Fed. Cas. No. 14665, 2 Lowell (U. S.) 267; Thompson v. State, 54 Miss. 740.

Should the accused stand mute, the plea of not guilty is entered for him by the court.[54]

The plea of not guilty may at any time be withdrawn to permit a plea of guilty or a confession.[55]

§ 947. Plea of guilty or nolo contendere.—The plea of guilty is a record admission of the truth of whatever is well alleged in the indictment, and if the indictment is good, the court may proceed to sentence.[56]

The plea of nolo contendere is a declaration of record by the defendant that he does not wish to contend with the prosecution. The same judgment and sentence may be rendered as upon a plea or verdict of guilty.[57] A plea of nolo contendere does not bind the defendant in civil action for the same injury, as a plea of guilty does.[58]

§ 948. Plea of former jeopardy.—Under a rule of the common law, incorporated in the Constitution of the United States and the constitutions of the states, no person may be placed twice in jeopardy for the same offense. The plea of autrefois acquit is sustained by showing either that a verdict of not guilty was returned or that the prosecution was discontinued after jeopardy had attached. That of autrefois convict can only be sustained by showing a conviction and verdict of guilty.

A prosecution by one of two or more sovereignties for an act which is a separate offense against each, is not a bar to a prosecution by the other.[59] For instance where one em-

54 Commonwealth v. Quirk, 155 Mass. 296, 29 N. E. 514; Commonwealth v. Harvey, 103 Mass. 451; Ellenwood v. Commonwealth, 10 Metc. (Mass.) 222.

55 Epps v. State, 102 Ind. 539, 1 N. E. 491; State v. Abrahams, 6 Iowa 117, 71 Am. Dec. 399.

56 State v. Branner, 149 N. Car. 559, 63 S. E. 169.

57 Commonwealth v. Holstine, 132 Pa. St. 357, 19 Atl. 273; 1 Chitty Crim. L. 431.

58 Commonwealth v. Horton, 9 Pick. (Mass.) 206; 1 Chitty Crim. L. 431.

59 United States v. Barnhart, 22 Fed. 285; 10 Sawy. (U. S.) 491; Bloomer v. State, 48 Md. 521.

bezzles funds of a national bank, he commits a crime against the United States and one against the state and may be prosecuted by both. It has been held the same rule applies where the same act violates both a city ordinance and a state statute,[60] but there are contrary decisions.[61] Nor does the fact that one has been compelled in a civil action to pay damages to an injured person prevent his being criminally punished for the same act, or criminal conviction prevent civil liability for the same act. Both person and property may be required to pay the penalty.

§ 949. **When jeopardy begins.**—Jeopardy begins as soon as the jury has been fully empanelled and sworn, provided the accusation is sufficient, and the accused has been previously arraigned and has pleaded not guilty. Before this time the prosecution may be dismissed without prejudice to the right to institute another prosecution.[62] After the jury is sworn and charged with the deliverance of the accused, the entering of a nolle prosequi, or its unnecessary discharge without the defendant's consent, amounts to an acquittal.[63]

§ 950. **Jurisdiction of former court.**—In order for a previous acquittal or conviction to bar a subsequent prosecution, the court before which the trial was had must have had jurisdiction of the person and the offense.[64]

[60] Robbins v. People, 95 Ill. 175; People v. Stevens, 13 Wend. (N. Y.) 341.

[61] Preston v. People, 45 Mich. 486, 8 N. W. 96; State v. Thornton, 37 Mo. 360.

[62] Patterson v. State, 70 Ind. 341; Commonwealth v. Tuck, 20 Pick. (Mass.) 356.

[63] State v. Walker, 26 Ind. 346; Commonwealth v. Hart, 149 Mass. 7, 20 N. E. 310.

[64] Barber v. State, 151 Ala. 56, 43 So. 808; People v. Connor, 65 Hun. (N. Y.) 392, 8 N. Y. Cr. 439. 48 N. Y. St. 25, 20 N. Y. S. 209.

If the defendant procures the cessation of the trial,[65] or there is a mistrial through his fault, as when he absents himself when the verdict is rendered, or fails to object before judgment to a defective verdict, or he consents to a discharge of the jury, he is not entitled to claim jeopardy.[66] If the jury is discharged through necessity on account of death, sickness or misconduct of a juror, or for illness of a judge or of the prisoner, or other cause of necessity, it is not equivalent to an acquittal.[67] Nor is a discharge because of disagreement after due deliberation a bar to subsequent prosecution for the same offense.[68]

§ 951. **Identity of party and offense.**—To constitute the plea of jeopardy a good defense the two offenses must have been the same in law and fact. The general rule is that the offenses are not the same if the defendant could not have been convicted under the first indictment upon proof of the facts alleged in the second.[69] Whether the offenses are identical or not is a question for the court.[70]

§ 952. **Former jeopardy for lesser or greater offense.**—If the accused has been in jeopardy for a lesser offense growing out of the same transaction, it is the better view that the plea of former jeopardy is a good defense, provided the lesser offense is a necessary and integral part of the greater.

65 Veatch v. State, 60 Ind. 291; Commonwealth v. Green, 17 Mass. 515; Sutcliffe v. State, 18 Ohio 469, 51 Am. Dec. 459.

66 People v. Higgins, 59 Cal. 357; Wright v. State, 5 Ind. 527; Commonwealth v. Sholes, 13 Allen (Mass.) 554; Reg. v. Deane, 5 Cox Cr. C. 501.

67 Simmons v. United States, 142 U. S. 148, 35 L. ed. 968; People v. Ross, 85 Cal. 383, 24 Pac. 789.

68 United States v. Perez, 9 Wheat (U. S.) 579, 6 L. ed. 165; People v. Pline, 61 Mich, 247, 28 N. W. 83.

69 Burk v. State, 81 Ind. 128; State v. Price, 127 Iowa 301, 103 N. W. 195.

70 Reynolds v. People, 83 Ill. 479; 25 Am. Rep. 410; State v. Cross, 101 N. Car. 770, 7 S. E. 715, 9 Am. St. 53.

Thus one who has been in jeopardy for an assault with intent to rape, to rob, or to murder, may not be again prosecuted for a consummated rape, robbery, or murder arising out of the same transactions, if under the indictment for the greater offense he could be convicted of the lesser.[71] Or if on trial for rape former jeopardy for fornication is a good defense.[72] And where the accused has been in jeopardy for a greater offense growing out of the same transaction the plea of former jeopardy is a good defense, provided he might have been convicted of the less offense under the first indictment.[73] Thus in a trial for murder a former jeopardy for manslaughter is a defense. Where both indictments charge a less crime in common, former jeopardy for such less crime is a good defense to the later indictment; as where the accused is on trial for robbery, former jeopardy for assault with intent to kill growing out of the same transaction,[74] or where the trial is for rape, former jeopardy for assault and battery.[75]

§ 953. Where one indictment is for felony, the other for misdemeanor.—As we have seen, under the English common law, one indicted for a felony might not, because of the difference in the incidents of trial be convicted of a misdemeanor.[76] But under the modern rule, one indicted for a felony may be convicted of any misdemeanor which is an essential element of it.[77] The contrary is sometimes held.[78]

71 Franklin v. State, 85 Ga. 570, 11 S. E. 876; State v. Smith, 43 Vt. 324.

72 Commonwealth v. Arner, 149 Pa. St. 35, 24 Atl. 83.

73 Hamilton v. State, 36 Ind. 280, 10 Am. Rep. 22; Commonwealth v. Roby, 12 Pick. (Mass.) 496.

74 Herera v. State, 35 Tex. Cr. 607, 34 S. W. 943.

75 Bell v. State, 103 Ga. 397, 30 S. E. 394, 68 Am. St. 102.

76 See §922.

77 State v. Brechbill, 10 Kans. App. 575, 62 Pac. 251; Commonwealth v. Crowley, 167 Mass. 434, 45 N. E. 766; Hanna v. People, 19 Mich. 316; State v. Musick, 101 Mo. 260, 14 S. W. 212; State v. Rambo, 95 Mo. 462, 8 S. W. 365.

78 Commonwealth v. Newell, 7 Mass. 245; Commonwealth v.

In such states, where one indicted for a felony may not be convicted of a misdemeanor, upon a subsequent indictment for a misdemeanor growing out of the same transaction, the former trial for the felony is no defense. Conversely, if one is indicted for the felony, a plea of former jeopardy for a misdemeanor growing out of the same transaction is no defense. For instance, where assault with intent to rape is merely a misdemeanor, former jeopardy for such offense is not a defense to an indictment for rape.[79]

Conviction of a minor offense included in the charge of the indictment is acquittal of the higher offense and may be pleaded in a bar of a subsequent prosecution for the higher offense.[80]

§ 954. Injury affecting more than one person.—Where one act similarly injures more than one person, there is but one crime. Therefore acquittal or conviction for injuring one is a good defense to a prosecution for injuring the others. Where one by a single blow kills two persons, conviction for the killing of one is a defense to an indictment for killing the other.[81] But there are some contrary holdings; among them that where one assaults two with a pistol and obtains their property, he commits an assault and robbery on each and may be prosecuted for two offenses.[82]

§ 955. Plea of pardon.—If one has been pardoned, this is a bar to trial and punishment for the offense; but in order to take advantage of the pardon, it must be brought to the court's notice. The courts take judicial notice of a pardon,

Roby, 12 Pick. (Mass.) 496; State v. Huffman, 136 Mo. 58, 37 S. W. 797.

79 Severin v. People, 37 Ill. 414; State v. Hattabough, 66 Ind. 223; Commonwealth v. Roby, 12 Pick. (Mass.) 496.

80 People v. Knapp, 26 Mich. 112; State v. Belden, 33 Wis. 120, 14 Am. Rep. 748; 2 Hale P. C. 246.

81 Gunter v. State, 111 Ala. 23, 20 So. 632, 56 Am. St. 17.

82 Keeten v. Commonwealth, 92 Ky. 522, 18 S. W. 350. But see State v. Damon, 2 Tyler (Vt.) 387.

however, when contained in a public statute.[83] If the pardon is executive, it must be pleaded.[84] A pardon may be waived and it is said that the defendant is estopped from taking advantage of the pardon at the trial unless his plea of pardon is made before he has pleaded not guilty.[85] However, advantage of it may be taken to prevent punishment even after trial and judgment.[86]

§ 956. Agreement to turn state's evidence.—It was held by the Texas court that an agreement by the accused with the state's attorney to turn state's evidence against his accomplice may be pleaded in bar, the entire question including the sufficiency of the evidence to sustain the plea, being a matter for the court.[87]

[83] 2 Hawk. P. C. ch. 37, § 58 et seq.

[84] United States v. Wilson, 7 Pet. (U. S.) 150, 8 L. ed. 640; 2 Hawk. P. C. ch. 37, § 64.

[85] United States v. Wilson, 7 Pet. (U. S.) 150, 8 L. ed. 640; 2 Hawk. P. C. ch. 37, § 57.

[86] Commonwealth v. Lockwood, 109 Mass. 323, 12 Am. Rep. 699; 4 Bl. Comm. 337; 2 Hawk. P. C. ch. 37, § 59.

[87] Cameron v. State, 32 Tex. Cr. 180, 22 S. W. 682, 40 Am. St. 763; Cameron v. State (Tex. Cr.) 25 S. W. 288.

§ 960. Time for trial.—The first step in a trial is getting control of the defendant by arrest, or otherwise.

The time of trial is largely in the discretion of the court. The order in which cases must be tried on the docket is usually in the discretion of the prosecuting officer.[1] Theoretically, the cause is ready for trial when the indictment is found and returned into court, the defendant is in its possession and arraigned and issue is joined. In most of our states a constitutional or statutory provision gives the accused the

[1] Shay v. Commonwealth, 36 Pa. St. 305.

right to a speedy trial, or discharge by habeas corpus.[2] The Habeas Corpus Act, upon which these provisions are founded, provides that the accused shall be indicted the next term of court or bailed, and that he be tried the second term or discharged.

§ 961. **Continuance.**—Though a cause is ready for trial, either party may, if the circumstance justify, be granted a continuance, in the court's discretion, or sometimes as a matter of right. It is only in case of a gross abuse of discretion that a new trial will be allowed for a failure to grant a continuance.[3] In order to obtain a continuance a motion stating the grounds, must be addressed to the court. This motion should usually be accompanied by affidavits showing the grounds.[4] Among the grounds for which a continuance may be granted are the absence of witnesses who will give material testimony, where due diligence has been used to obtain their presence at the trial;[5] public excitement or unfair prejudice against the accused;[6] lack of time to make necessary preparation for the trial;[7] and sometimes illness of the accused[8] or absence or illness of his counsel.[9] In order to obtain a continuance because of the absence of witnesses, testimony is not considered material which is irrelevant,[10] or is merely cumulative or could be proved by other wit-

[2] United States v. Fox, 3 Mont. 512; Ex parte Stanley, 4 Nev. 113.

[3] Alexander v. State, 97 Ark. 643, 134 S. W. 953; Commonwealth v. Donovan, 99 Mass. 425, 96 Am. Dec. 765; Commonwealth v. Fenecz, 226 Pa. 114, 75 Atl. 19.

[4] Mitchell v. State, 92 Tenn. 668, 23 S. W. 68; 1 Chitty Crim. L. 492.

[5] State v. Brown (Iowa), 121 N. W. 513; State v. Woodward, 182 Mo. 391; 81 S. W. 857, 103 Am. St. 646; State v. Thompson, 141 Mo. 408, 42 S. W. 949; Hart v. State, 61 Tex. Cr. 509, 134 S. W. 1178.

[6] Woolfolk v. State, 85 Ga. 69; 11 S. E. 814; Maddox v. State, 32 Ga. 581, 79 Am. Dec. 307.

[7] State v. Nash, 7 Iowa 347; State v. Deschamps, 41 La. Ann. 1051, 7 So. 133.

[8] Hays v. Hamilton, 68 Ga. 833.

[9] Loyd v. State, 45 Ga. 57; State v. Rainsbarger, 74 Iowa 196, 37 N. W. 153.

[10] People v. Anderson, 53 Mich. 60, 18 N. W. 561.

nesses present,[11] or is merely impeaching,[12] or is as to character,[13] or if due diligence has not been used to obtain it.[14] There must also appear a reasonable prospect of attendance at the time to which the continuance is asked.[15] Inability of the accused to attend because of his voluntary intoxication is not a ground for a continuance.[16]

§ 962. Presence of the accused at trial.—As a general rule one charged with a felony must be present at his trial;[17] during the time when the jury is called and sworn, while witnesses are being examined, when the jury is charged, arguments of counsel are made, verdict returned, and sentence pronounced. His right to be present at these times is such that it is held that a trial without such presence is without due process of law.[18] Some courts hold that the defendant may waive his right to be present.[19] It, however, is not essential that he be present during certain formal matters, such as making motions to quash or for a continuance, for arrest of judgment, or for a new trial, etc.[20] Nor is it necessary that he be present during the consideration of his appeal by a higher court.[21] Where the accused is on trial for a mis-

11 State v. Hillstock, 45 La. Ann. 298, 12 So. 352; Higginbotham v. State (Tex. Cr.), 20 S. W. 360.

12 State v. Howell, 117 Mo. 307, 23 S. W. 263.

13 Rhea v. State, 10 Yerg. (Tenn.) 258.

14 People v. Lewis, 64 Cal. 401, 1 Pac. 490; McDermott v. State, 89 Ind. 187.

15 Commonwealth v. Millard, 1 Mass 6.

16 State v. Ellvin, 51 Kans. 784, 33 Pac. 547.

17 Hopt v. Utah, 110 U. S. 574, 28 L. ed. 262; Dunn v. Commonwealth, 6 Pa. St. 384; Smith v. State, 51 Wis. 615, 8 N. W. 410, 37 Am. Rep. 845.

18 Harris v. People, 130 Ill. 457, 22 N. E. 826.

19 State v. Peacock, 50 N. J. L. 34, 11 Atl. 270; State v. Kelly, 97 N. Car. 404, 2 S. E. 185, 2 Am. St. 299.

20 Commonwealth v. Andrews, 97 Mass. 543.

21 Schwab v. Berggren, 143 U. S. 442, 36 L. ed. 218.

demeanor his presence at the trial may be waived.[22] The defendant should not be unnecessarily manacled or restrained at the trial, or if so, he will be entitled to a new trial for this cause.[23]

§ 963. **Change of venue.**—As a rule the accused must be tried in the county in which the offense is alleged to have taken place. At common law, and by statute in most states, if the accused can show by sufficient proof supported by affidavits that he can not have a fair and impartial trial in the county of the offense, he is entitled to a change of venue; that is, to have his trial in an adjoining county.[24] The state may usually file counter affidavits,[25] but it is held sometimes that this may not be done where the ground of change is prejudice of the judge.[26] It is usually held that where the motion is made on this ground the change should be granted as a matter of course.[27] One only of several defendants may be granted a change of venue.[28]

§ 964. **Publicity of trial.**—The Constitution of the United States and the state constitutions grant to persons accused of crime the right to a public trial. Such a provision is for the benefit of the accused, in order to insure to him a fair trial. It is not necessary, however, that more than a reason-

22 Bloomington v. Heiland, 67 Ill. 278; State v. Dry, 152 N. Car. 813, 67 S. E. 1000.

23 Faire v. State, 58 Ala. 74; People v. Harrington, 42 Cal. 165, 10 Am. Rep. 296; State v. Kring, 1 Mo. App. 438.

24 State v. Albee, 61 N. H. 423, 60 Am. Rep. 325; State v. Sullivan, 39 S. Car. 400, 17 S. E. 865.

25 Pierson v. State, 21 Tex. App. 14, 17 S. W. 468; Perrin v. State, 81 Wis. 135, 50 N. W. 516.

26 Cantwell v. People, 138 Ill. 602, 28 N. E. 964.

27 Cantwell v. People, 138 Ill. 602, 28 N. E. 964; Manley v. State, 52 Ind. 215.

28 State v. Martin, 2 Ired. L. (N. Car.) 101.

able proportion of the public be allowed to attend; and those who attend merely from idle curiosity may under certain circumstances be excluded.[29]

§ 965. **Counsel for defendant.**—The defendant is entitled to be represented at the trial by counsel and in most states the court must assign counsel to a defendant who is unable to employ counsel.[30] The old rule under the common law was that one indicted for treason or felony was not entitled to be represented by counsel at the trial, but might have their advice, or have them to argue a question of law.[31] A defendant is not required to accept the services of the counsel assigned; and if he refuses to accept them, the trial may proceed without his representation by counsel.[32]

§ 966. **Counsel for the prosecution.**—In this country criminal prosecutions before courts of a higher degree than a justice of the peace court, are carried on by a public prosecuting officer, a professional lawyer, elected by the people or appointed by executive authority. The duties of this attorney are usually to draw indictments, present cases to the grand jury, and prepare them for trial and try them before the petit jury. It many times is within his discretion to determine whether a prosecution should be instituted, as in case of technical violations of the law. Private persons may employ counsel to aid in the prosecution,[33] or the court may appoint attorneys to assist in the prosecution or act in the case of the illness of the regular attorney, or his inability

29 People v. Murray, 89 Mich. 276, 50 N. W. 995, 14 L. R. A. 809, 28 Am. St. 294; Cooley Const. Lim. (6th ed.) 379.

30 Hendryx v. State, 130 Ind. 265, 29 N. E. 1131.

31 1 Chitty Crim. L. 407; 2 Hawk. P. C. ch. 39, §§ 1, 4.

32 State v. Moore, 121 Mo. 514, 26 S. W. 345, 42 Am. St. 542; Reg. v. Yscuado, 6 Cox Cr. C. 386.

33 People v. Powell, 87 Cal. 348, 25 Pac. 481, 11 L. R. A. 75; Keyes v. State, 122 Ind. 527, 23 N. E. 1097.

to conduct the case.[34] The prosecuting attorney represents the public interests, which, while they require the conviction of the guilty, are opposed to the conviction of the innocent, and should compel the use of none but fair methods in the trial.[35] He should not tamper with witnesses,[36] declare his personal belief of the guilt of the accused,[37] state anything as a fact not in evidence,[38] or use any tricks or deceptions at the trial.[39]

§ 967. Defendant's right to copy of indictment—Names of jurors or witnesses and bill of particulars.—The defendant is entitled under statutes in most of our states, to be furnished with a copy of the indictment before trial.[40] In many states he is entitled to a list of witnesses who are to appear against him[41] and the names of those who have been summoned to act as jurors.[42] In cases where the offense is such that from the indictment the defendant can not ascertain the exact nature of the crime charged, as where there is a general charge of being a common scold, common prostitute or common seller of intoxicating liquors, the court, upon the accused's request, may require the prosecuting attorney to furnish the accused a bill of particulars;[43] and also where there is a general charge of adultery or embezzlement.[44]

[34] Dukes v. State, 11 Ind. 557, 71 Am. Dec. 370; State v. Johnson, 12 Tex. 231.

[35] Engle v. Chipman, 51 Mich. 524, 16 N. W. 886.

[36] Gandy v. State, 24 Nebr. 716, 40 N. W. 302.

[37] State v. Phillips, 233 Mo. 299, 135 S. W. 4.

[38] Cheatham v. State, 67 Miss. 335, 7 So. 204, 19 Am. St. 310; State v. Kent, 5 N. Dak. 516, 67 N. W. 1052, 35 L. R. A. 518.

[39] People v. McCann, 247 Ill. 130, 93 N. E. 100, 20 Ann. Cas. 496; People v. Dane, 59 Mich. 550, 26 N. W. 781; State v. Hagan, 164 Mo. 654, 65 S. W. 249.

[40] Robertson v. State, 43 Ala. 325; Woodall v. State, 25 Tex. App. 617, 8 S. W. 802.

[41] Logan v. United States, 144 U. S. 263, 36 L. ed. 429; Scott v. People, 63 Ill. 508.

[42] Bain v. State, 70 Ala. 4.

[43] Commonwealth v. Davis, 11 Pick. (Mass.) 432; Williams v. Commonwealth, 91 Pa. St. 493.

[44] People v. Davis, 52 Mich. 569, 18 N. W. 362.

§ 968. Presence and conduct of judge at trial.—The judge must be present during the whole trial and his absence at any essential part of the proceedings is fatal.[45] If there should be misconduct of the judge prejudicial to the defendant, a conviction should be set aside.

§ 969. Joint defendants tried separately.—Where several defendants are jointly indicted it rests in the court's discretion to determine whether under all the circumstances, they should be tried separately.[46] If a joint trial would prejudice either defendant, separate trials should be ordered.[47] If there are separate indictments against one defendant charging offenses which might have been joined in different counts of the same indictment, the court may order a trial for both offenses at the same time;[48] but separate trials must be had if the offenses are not such as might have been joined in a single count.[49]

§ 970. Right to jury trial.—Any person charged with a criminal offense is entitled to a jury trial. This right was given by the English common law, and is one of the guarantees of the Magna Charta of 1215. This right is secured to the people of this country by both the federal and the state constitutions.

However, if a statute so provides, city ordinances may be enforced without jury trials,[50] contempt of court may be punishable without a jury,[51] and whatever may have been

[45] Thompson v. People, 144 Ill. 378, 32 N. E. 968; Palin v. State, 38 Nebr. 862, 57 N. W. 743.

[46] Doyle v. People, 147 Ill. 394, 35 N. E. 372; Commonwealth v. Bingham, 158 Mass. 169, 33 N. E. 341.

[47] Commonwealth v. James, 99 Mass. 438.

[48] Cummins v. People, 4 Colo. App. 71, 34 Pac. 734; State v. Lee, 114 N. Car. 844, 19 S. E. 375.

[49] State v. Devlin, 25 Mo. 174.

[50] In re Kinsel, 64 Kans. 1, 67 Pac. 634, 56 L. R. A. 475.

[51] People v. Tool, 35 Colo. 225, 86 Pac. 224, 6 L. R. A. (N. S.) 822, 117 Am. St. 198; People v. Kipley, 171 Ill. 44, 49 N. E. 229, 41 L. R. A. 775.

under former usage tried without a jury;[52] but, one's life, liberty or property can not be taken without a jury trial.[53] A statute is constitutional which provides for trial of a criminal offense without a jury, if it allows an unrestricted right of appeal and trial by jury before the appellate tribunal.[54]

The authorities do not agree as to whether the right to a jury trial may be waived by the defendant. Some hold that he may not do so in cases of felony;[55] others that a jury may be waived in all cases, where there is a statute permitting the case to be tried by the court without a jury.[56] But the right to a jury trial may not be waived by mere consent, and there must be statutory authority permitting it;[57] and where constitution or statute expressly requires a jury trial it can not be waived.[58] Where a statute permits the waiver of a jury trial, the defendant may consent to a trial by more or less than twelve men;[59] but otherwise the constitutional guarantee of a jury trial prevents the waiver of a trial by twelve men.[60]

§ 971. **Right of challenge.**—The accused is entitled to be tried by an impartial jury, of men who have been summoned, chosen and impaneled according to the method laid down by law, and who are individually qualified to serve. Therefore

[52] State v. Churchill, 48 Ark. 426, 3 S. W. 352.

[53] Atchison, &c. R. Co. v. Baty, 6 Nebr. 37, 29 Am. Rep. 356.

[54] Beers v. Beers, 4 Conn. 535, 10 Am. Dec. 186; Flint R. Steamboat v. Foster, 5 Ga. 194, 48 Am. Dec. 248.

[55] Williams v. State, 12 Ohio St. 622.

[56] United States v. Rathbone, Fed. Cas. No. 16121, 2 Paine (U. S.) 578; Commonwealth v. Whitney, 108 Mass. 5; Dillingham v. State, 5 Ohio St. 280.

[57] State v. Maine, 27 Conn. 281; Neales v. State, 10 Mo. 498.

[58] Arnold v. State, 38 Nebr. 752, 57 N. W. 378.

[59] Commonwealth v. Dailey, 12 Cush. (Mass.) 80.

[60] Cancemi v. People, 18 N. Y. 128, 7 Abb. Prac. 271; Oborn v. State, 143 Wis. 249, 31 L. R. A. (N. S.) 966, 126 N. W. 737; 1 Chitty Crim. L. 505; 2 Hale P. C. 161.

the defendant has a right to challenge jurors, which can not be defeated by legislative enactment, though the legislature may prescribe the time and manner of making objections.[61]

There are challenges to the array, and challenges to the polls, and of each of these there are principal challenges and challenges to the favor.

Challenges to the array are challenges to the panel as a whole, and if sustained the entire panel is quashed and a new one summoned.[62] Challenges to the polls are objections to individual jurors.

Where a juror is not free from certain conditions which might cause him to have a bias against the defendant or in his favor, he is subject to challenge. Among the grounds of challenge are near relationship;[63] other civil and social relationships, such as a witness summoned by the prisoner,[64] or one in his employment,[65] or one with whom he has a pending lawsuit;[66] a general bias for or against a party, which is ground for challenge to the favor, not for principal challenge;[67] a pecuniary interest in the result of the trial;[68] formed or expressed opinion as to the prisoner's guilt,[69] although an inclination from mere rumor to believe the prisoner guilty of the facts heard about him are true, does not usually disqualify;[70] a previous passing upon the question in some capacity, such as being a member of the grand jury

61 Palmore v. State, 29 Ark. 248; Black Const. Law (2 ed.) 572.

62 Co. Litt. 156, 158; 3 Bl. Comm. 359.

63 State v. Andrews, 29 Conn. 100, 76 Am. Dec. 593; O'Neal v. State, 47 Ga. 229; 1 Chitty Crim. L. 541.

64 Commonwealth v. Jolliffe, 7 Watts (Pa.) 585.

65 Block v. State, 100 Ind. 357.

66 Co. Litt. 157.

67 1 Chitty Crim. L. 544; Co. Litt. 157b.

68 Brazleton v. State, 66 Ala. 96; Cluverius v. Commonwealth, 81 Va. 787.

69 State v. Meaux, 127 La. 259, 53 So. 557; 1 Bish. New Crim. Proc. §§ 908-910; 2 Hawk. P. C. ch. 43, § 28.

70 Thompson v. People, 24 Ill. 60, 76 Am. Dec. 733; Rice v. State, 7 Ind. 332; Commonwealth v. Webster, 5 Cush. (Mass.) 295, 52 Am. Dec. 711; Holt v. People, 13 Mich. 224; Stokes v. People, 53 N. Y. 164, 13 Am. Rep. 492.

which found the indictment;[71] a biased view of the law, as where one is opposed to capital punishment;[72] active connection with the prosecution or defense;[73] lack of freehold qualifications in some states;[74] non-residence in the county in some states;[75] alienage;[76] infamy;[77] want of mental capacity.[78] Certain persons by statute are exempted from jury service in most states, but if they consent to serve, and are otherwise qualified, they can not be challenged for cause.[79]

Among the grounds for principal challenge to the array are irregularities in summoning the jurors,[80] relationship of the officer who summoned them to one of the parties,[81] or the fact that one or more jurors were summoned at the instance of the prosecutor or defendant.[82] The chief ground for challenges to the array for favor is bias on the part of the officer who summoned the jury.[83]

Challenges are also divided into challenges for cause, which must state specifically the ground of objection, and peremptory challenges. All challenges to the array must be for

[71] Rice v. State, 16 Ind. 298; Stewart v. State, 15 Ohio St. 155.

[72] Stephenson v. State, 110 Ind. 358, 11 N. E. 360, 59 Am. Rep. 216; State v. Wooley, 215 Mo. 620, 115 S. W. 417; Hyde v. State, 16 Tex. 445, 67 Am. Dec. 630.

[73] Boyle v. People, 4 Colo. 176, 34 Am. Rep. 76; Johnson v. Hazlehurst, 8 Ga. App. 841, 70 S. E. 258; Pierson v. State, 11 Ind. 341.

[74] Nelson v. State, 57 Miss. 286, 34 Am. Rep. 444; Dowdy v. Commonwealth, 9 Grat. (Va.) 727, 60 Am. Dec. 314.

[75] Nordan v. State, 143 Ala. 13, 39 So. 406; People v. Powell, 87 Cal. 348, 25 Pac. 481, 11 L. R. A. 75.

[76] Queenan v. Oklahoma, 190 U. S. 548, 47 L. ed. 1175; Queenan v. Oklahoma, 11 Okla. 261, 71 Pac. 218, 61 L. R A. 324.

[77] Queenan v. Oklahoma, 11 Okla. 261, 71 Pac. 218, 61 L. R. A. 324; 2 Hawk. P. C. ch. 43, § 25.

[78] Thomas v. State, 27 Ga. 287; State v. Casey, 44 La. Ann. 969, 11 So. 583; State v. Eloi, 34 La. Ann. 1195; State v. Scott, 1 Hawk (N. Car.) 24.

[79] State v. Noland, 36 S. Car. 515, 15 S. E. 599, 2 Hawk. P. C. ch. 43, § 26.

[80] Reid v. State, 50 Ga. 556; Morgan v. State, 31 Ind. 193.

[81] Vanauken v. Beemer, 4 N. J. L. 364; Baylis v. Lucas, 1 Cowp. 112.

[82] Co. Litt. 156.

[83] People v. Coyodo, 40 Cal. 586; Co. Litt. 156.

cause. Peremptory challenges are those to which the party objecting is entitled as a matter of right, without showing any cause or ground. The number allowed is regulated by statute.[84] The time for making a challenge and the mode of making it, and also of trying objections to a juror, are regulated by statute.

Generally, no objection can be taken to a juror or to the panel, after acceptance and swearing, because of any fact then known to a party and not properly brought to the court's notice; or even because of such fact, unless the objection was thereby prejudiced.[85] An objection unknown at the time of the paneling should be taken as soon after its discovery as practicable.[86]

§ 972. **Swearing the jury.**—At common law, every juror must be sworn and this must appear of record.[87] Statutes usually permit a juror to affirm who is conscientiously opposed to taking an oath.

§ 973. **Opening statement.**—After the jury is sworn, the prosecuting attorney makes a statement of the case to the jury, stating briefly the facts which he expects to prove, the evidence by which he expects to prove them and the accusation and law governing the offense.[88] The statement should be such as to show to the jury in what way the evidence will support the accusation. The evidence for the prosecution is introduced after the opening statement, and then the defense makes a statement as to the nature of the defense to the charge, and introduces his evidence.

[84] See statutes of various states. See also 1 Bish. New Crim. Proc. §§ 935-945.

[85] State v. Powers, 10 Ore. 145, 45 Am. Rep. 138; Yanez v. State, 6 Tex. App. 429, 32 Am. Rep. 591.

[86] Lampkin v. State, 87 Ga. 516, 13 S. E. 523.

[87] Commonwealth v. Knapp, 9 Pick. (Mass.) 496, 20 Am. Dec. 491; Rex v. Morris, 2 Strange, 901.

[88] People v. Lewis, 124 Cal. 551, 57 Pac. 470, 45 L. R. A. 753; Morales v. State, 1 Tex. App. 494, 28 Am. Rep. 419; 1 Bish. New Crim. Proc., §§ 967-971.

§ 974. **Functions of the court and jury.**—In some of our states the court, in criminal cases, is the judge of the law, and the jury is judge of the facts. In such states the jury must follow the court's instructions, and a conviction contrary to such instructions will be set aside.[89] However, an acquittal in disregard of such instructions does not entitle the state to a new trial. In other states the jury, in criminal cases, is the judge both of the law and the facts; but in such states it is the duty of the judge to instruct the jury as to the law.[90] And here the jury has only the power, not the right, to disregard such instructions; so that if the accused is convicted on incompetent evidence, or the jury refuses to consider competent evidence, the conviction will be set aside.[91] It is also the court's function to pass on the competency of witnesses,[92] the admissibility of testimony and the sufficiency of the evidence to make a prima facie case.[93] The jury passes upon the weight and effect of the evidence, and upon the credibility of witnesses.[94]

§ 975. **Examination of witnesses.**—The next step in the trial after the opening statement by the prosecuting attorney is the examination of witnesses. The prosecuting attorney announces the name of his first witness, and he is called to the stand by the clerk of the court and sworn. The prosecution then examines him in chief, and turns him over to the defendant for cross-examination. At the close of the cross-examination the prosecutor may re-examine the witness if desired. Both examination and cross-exami-

89 Sparf v. United States, 156 U. S. 51, 39 L. ed. 343.

90 Sparf v. United States, 156 U. S. 51, 39 L. ed. 343 (dissenting opinion); 4 Bl. Comm. 361; Co. Litt. 228.

91 Commonwealth v. Knapp, 10 Pick. (Mass.) 477, 20 Am. Dec. 534.

92 State v. McDonnell, 32 Vt. 491.

93 Commonwealth v. Packard, 5 Gray (Mass.) 101.

94 People v. O'Brien, 96 Cal. 171, 31 Pac. 45; Lefler v. State, 122 Ind. 206, 23 N. E. 154.

nation must relate only to facts relevant to the issues and cross-examinations must be confined to the facts, to which the witness testified in his examination in chief.[95] Re-examination must be confined to the explanation of statements made in cross-examination.[96] Any witness may be recalled for further examination in chief or cross-examination and in such case the opposing party has the right of further cross-examination or further re-examination as the case may be.[97] The general rules as to the examination and impeachment are the same in criminal as in civil cases. Leading questions should not be asked, in examination in chief or re-examination, unless the witness appears hostile to the party introducing, or where they are necessary to bring items, dates, or details to memory; but upon cross-examination leading questions may usually be asked.[98] Also in cross-examination the witness may be asked questions which tend to test accuracy or credibility or to affect his credit by showing his bad character.[99] Statements of the witness relative to the subject-matter of the action and inconsistent with his present testimony may be proved.[1] A witness also may be impeached by showing that his general reputation for truth and veracity is bad.[2] One may not impeach his own witness unless adverse, but may introduce witnesses who will testify to the contrary.[3] After all of the witnesses for the prosecution have been examined in the same manner as the first, and the last one has completed his testimony, the state rests its case. The witnesses for the defense are then similarly examined.

[95] State v. Smith, 49 Conn. 376; People v. Beach, 87 N. Y. 508.

[96] Schaser v. State, 36 Wis. 429.

[97] Commonwealth v. McGorty, 114 Mass. 299.

[98] People v. Mather, 4 Wend. (N. Y.) 229, 21 Am. Dec. 122.

[99] Commonwealth v. Mason, 105 Mass. 163, 7 Am. Rep. 507; People v. Irving, 95 N. Y. 541, 2 N. Y. Cr. 171.

[1] People v. Mather, 4 Wend. (N. Y.) 229, 21 Am. Dec. 122; Steph. Digest Ev. (Chase's ed.) 227.

[2] Laclede Bank v. Keeler, 109 Ill. 385; Lenox v. Fuller, 39 Mich. 268.

[3] State v. Knight, 43 Maine 11.

§ 976. **Arguments of counsel.**—After the evidence has all been heard the counsel in the case make their arguments to the jury. The prosecuting attorney makes the first argument and in some states he is entitled to a reply to the arguments of the counsel for the defendant.[4] The summing up must be confined to the facts which have been proved, or which it is contended the evidence tends to show.[5] Matters of common knowledge, such as historical facts, may be referred to.[6] Even this is not allowed if done in such a manner as to inflame the passions of the jury and cause them to lay aside reason.[7] Only legitimate arguments should be used.[8] Abuse of the defendant is improper.[9] Full comment may be made on the evidence and its probative effect,[10] but the prosecutor should not argue from his own special knowledge,[11] or argue from what is not probative.[12] The counsel should not express his personal opinion as to guilt or innocence of the accused.[13] Objection should promptly be taken to improper argument on the part of the counsel.[14] The court may also interfere of its own motion.[15] Usually, if the court admonishes the offending counsel and instructs the

[4] Doss v. Commonwealth, 1 Grat. (Va.) 557.

[5] Ferguson v. State, 49 Ind. 33; State v. Ferrell, 233 Mo. 542, 136 S. W. 709.

[6] Siebert v. People, 143 Ill. 571, 32 N. E. 431; Northington v. State, 14 Lea. (Tenn.) 424.

[7] People v. McCann, 247 Ill. 130, 93 N. E. 100, 20 Ann. Cas. 496; Tillery v. State, 24 Tex. App. 251, 5 S. W. 842, 5 Am. St. 882.

[8] People v. Lemperle, 94 Cal. 45, 29 Pac. 709; State v. Romeo, 117 La. 1003, 42 So. 482.

[9] Rhodes v. Commonwealth, 107 Ky. 354, 54 S. W. 170, 92 Am. St. 360; Coble v. Coble, 79 N. Car. 589, 28 Am. Rep. 338.

[10] Wilson v. State, 175 Ind. 458, 93 N. E. 609; People v. Hovey, 92 N. Y. 554, 1 N. Y. Cr. 283.

[11] People v. Lieska, 161 Mich. 630, 126 N. W. 636.

[12] Bessette v. State, 101 Ind. 85; Cartwright v. State, 16 Tex. App. 473; 49 Am. Rep. 826.

[13] Keesier v. State, 154 Ind. 242, 56 N. E. 232; State v. Church, 199 Mo. 605, 98 S. W. 16.

[14] Holmes v. State, 82 Nebr. 406, 118 N. W. 99; Gilmore v. State, 37 Tex. Cr. 81, 38 S. W. 787.

[15] Coleman v. Commonwealth, 25 Grat. (Va.) 865, 18 Am. Rep. 711.

jury to disregard the improper remarks, a verdict of conviction will not be reversed.[16] However, if the court refuses to interfere when it should, or the harm is such that the court's instruction can not remove it, a new trial may be granted.[17]

§ 977. **Charge of the court to the jury.**—Upon the completion of the arguments of the counsel the court instructs the jury. In charging the jury the court should instruct it fully as to the law bearing upon the case, stating the issues, the law as to each issue, their duties to each issue and their duties to the final conclusion, and as to the punishment where the punishment is fixed by the jury. The judge, unless there be a plea of guilty, can not direct a verdict upon the evidence however conclusive it may be.[18] All extraneous matter, such as irrelevant testimony, should be excluded.[19] The court should not refer to any facts not in evidence nor allegations not in the record.[20] The law should not be laid down abstractly but as applied to all the facts in controversy.[21] It is usually error to read from a law book.[22] It is error to state the law incorrectly.[23] Ordinarily a mere omission to instruct the jury as to the law relative to some point in the case, is not a sufficient ground for a new trial unless such instruction is requested.[24] The language of the charge must

16 Cheatham v. State. 67 Miss. 335, 7 So. 204, 19 Am. St. 310; Wilson v. State, 175 Ind. 458, 93 N. E. 609.

17 State v. Balch, 31 Kans. 465, 2 Pac. 609; State v. Moxley, 102 Mo. 374, 14 S. W. 969, 15 S. W. 556.

18 Tucker v. State, 57 Ga. 503; 1 Bish. New Crim. Proc., § 977, 2.

19 Gibson v. State, 89 Ala. 121, 8 So. 98, 18 Am. St. 96; Commonwealth v. Gilson, 128 Mass. 425.

20 Willis v. State, 134 Ala. 429, 33 So. 226; People v. Zachello, 168 N. Y. 35. 60 N. E. 1051.

21 Anthony v. State, 6 Ga. App. 784, 65 S. E. 816; Spears v. State, 220 Ill. 72, 77 N. E. 112, 4 L. R. A. (N. S.) 402n; Hudson v. State, 40 Tex. 12.

22 Mitchell v. State, 73 Ark. 291, 83 S. W. 1050.

23 Beaudien v. State, 8 Ohio St. 634; Marie v State, 28 Tex. 698.

24 State v. Johnson, 8 Iowa 525, 74 Am. Dec. 321; State v. Rash, 12 Ired. L. (N. Car.) 382, 55 Am. Rep. 420.

be unambiguous and direct and such that the persons to whom it is directed will understand.[25]

§ 978. Custody and conduct of the jury.—In most states in cases of felonies, especially those that are capital, the jury at all times when not in the actual presence of the court should not be allowed to separate, and must be kept in charge of a sworn officer of the court.[26] In cases of misdemeanor, however, it is within the discretion of the court to allow a separation during the trial;[27] and in some states this rule applies in felonies.[28] If these rules are violated and the defendant has been harmed he is entitled to a new trial; otherwise not.[29] In some cases, if necessity or comfort requires it, the court may allow the jury to separate, or to walk abroad, the officer going with them and they communicating with no one.[30] The jury, after they have retired, should not be allowed to hold any communication with outsiders,[31] even with the judge of the court,[32] or with the officer in charge of them, other than is necessary.[33] Material misconduct on the part of the jury which affects the verdict is a sufficient ground for a new trial.[34] Even the reading of newspapers by one or

[25] Sumner v. State, 5 Blackf. (Ind.) 579, 36 Am. Dec. 561; State v. Sebastian, 215 Mo. 58, 114 S. W. 522.

[26] Berry v. State, 10 Ga. 511; Jumpertz v. People, 21 Ill. 375; Quinn v. State, 14 Ind. 589.

[27] Prewitt v. State, 65 Miss. 437, 4 So. 346; Rex v. Woolf, 1 Chit. 401.

[28] Davis v. State, 15 Ohio 72, 45 Am. Dec. 559; Armstrong v. State, 2 Okla. Cr. 567, 103 Pac. 658.

[29] Roberts v. State, 14 Ga. 8, 58 Am. Dec. 528; State v. Brown, 45 Iowa 418; Rowan v. State, 30 Wis. 129, 11 Am. Rep. 559.

[30] State v. Griffin, 71 Iowa 372, 32 N. W. 447; Commonwealth v. Gearhardt, 205 Pa. 387, 54 Atl. 1029; Crockett v. State, 52 Wis. 211, 8 N. W. 603, 38 Am. Rep. 733.

[31] Hoberg v. State, 3 Minn. 262 (Gil. 181).

[32] Hoberg v. State, 3 Minn. 262 (Gil. 181); State v. Patterson, 45 Vt. 308, 12 Am. Rep. 200.

[33] State v. Langford, 45 La. Ann. 1177, 14 So. 181, 40 Am. St. 277; Brown v. State, 69 Miss. 398, 10 So. 579.

[34] People v. Mitchell, 100 Cal. 328, 34 Pac. 698.

more of the jurors during the trial is a sufficient ground for a new trial, unless the prosecution shows that the defendant has not been prejudiced thereby.[35] Determining the verdict by casting lots is clearly such misconduct as will invalidate the verdict.[36] The use of intoxicants by any of the jury may be grounds for setting the verdict aside.[37]

§ 979. What the jury may take to their room.—With the permission of the court the jury may take the records into the jury room of the case,[38] the instructions of the judge,[39] real evidence used as exhibits at the trial,[40] the entire written evidence,[41] and in some states, where the jury are judges of the law, books of statutes.[42]

§ 980. Verdict based on the evidence.—A juror must not be influenced by facts within his own knowledge. His verdict must be wholly based upon evidence regularly given in open court. In case he has personal knowledge of material facts in the case he should go upon the stand and testify. If he fails to do so, and communicates such private information to the other members of the jury, the verdict should be set aside.[43]

§ 981. The verdict.—After the jury have deliberated and agreed upon a verdict they return to the court room, and report their verdict in open court. This verdict, unless a

[35] State v. Walton, 92 Iowa 455, 61 N. W. 179.

[36] State v. Woods, 49 Kans. 237, 30 Pac. 520.

[37] Davis v. State, 35 Ind. 496, 9 Am. Rep. 760.

[38] Sanders v. State, 131 Ala. 1, 31 So. 564; Cooke v. People, 231 Ill. 9, 82 N. E. 863.

[39] Ragland v. State, 125 Ala. 12, 27 So. 983; People v. Monat, 200 N. Y. 308, 93 N. E. 982.

[40] Jackson v. State, 76 Ga. 551; Yates v. People, 38 Ill. 527.

[41] Davis v. State, 91 Ga. 167, 17 S. E. 292; Masterson v. State, 144 Ind. 240, 43 N. E. 138.

[42] People v. Cochran, 61 Cal. 548; Jack v. Territory, 2 Wash. Ter. 101, 3 Pac. 832.

[43] State v. Woods, 49 Kans. 237, 30 Pac. 520.

statute provides otherwise, may be either general or special. A general verdict is the finding of guilty or not guilty on the whole charge.[44] A special verdict, which is rare in criminal cases, finds the facts of the case only, leaving the law to be applied by the court.[45] Partial verdict is one which convicts as to a part of the charge and acquits or is silent as to the residue.[46] The verdict must be the unanimous decision of the jury. It must be rendered in open court in the presence of the defendant,[47] unless he has waived the right to be present. It is delivered orally,[48] unless a statute requires it to be delivered in writing,[49] and all the jurors must be present when it is received.[50] The verdict may be returned on Sunday or a legal holiday.[51] In most states a party may demand a poll of the jury; that is, each juror is asked, "Is this your verdict?"[52] At any time before the jury is polled and the verdict recorded it may change the verdict, or one juror may defeat it by dissent.[53] The verdict should be certain and complete and responsive to the issues,[54] but merely technical errors will not render it bad if upon a reasonable construction what is intended can be clearly seen.[55] However, if an essential element is omitted the verdict is bad; as where the statute requires the jury to find the degree of the crime and

[44] 4 Bl. Comm. 361; Co. Litt. 228.

[45] Commonwealth v. Chathams, 50 Pa. St. 181, 88 Am. Dec. 539.

[46] Blackshare v. State, 94 Ark. 548, 128 S. W. 549, 140 Am. St. 144.

[47] State v. Mills, 19 Ark. 476. See also § 923, supra.

[48] Lord v. State, 16 N. H. 325.

[49] Morton v. State, 3 Tex. App. 510.

[50] Patterson v. State, 122 Ga. 587, 50 S. E. 489; Commonwealth v. Gibson, 2 Va. Cas. 70.

[51] Reid v. State, 53 Ala. 402, 25 Am. Rep. 627, 4 Cent. L. J. 154n; Dunlap v. State, 9 Tex. App. 179, 35 Am. Rep. 736.

[52] Harris v. State, 31 Ark. 196; Mitchell v. State, 22 Ga. 211, 68 Am. Dec. 493.

[53] Sledd v. Commonwealth, 19 Grat. (Va.) 813; Rothbauer v. State, 22 Wis. 468.

[54] State v. Coon, 18 Minn. 518; Westbrook v. State, 52 Miss. 777.

[55] Polson v. State, 137 Ind. 519, 35 N. E. 907; State v. Lee, 80 Iowa 75, 45 N. W. 545, 20 Am. St. 401.

cases.[72] Among these exceptions are, dying declarations, made by the deceased in a homicide case as to the cause of his death if it is shown that they were made when the deceased was in extremis, and had no hope of recovery;[73] evidence given in a former trial, under certain circumstances, such as when the witness who there testified is dead, insane, or can not be produced at the trial.[74] In prosecutions for rape the woman's conduct, especially the fact that she made complaint after the commission of the crime, may be shown in evidence.[75] Evidence of another crime, other than that charged, is admissible when it falls under any of the rules above stated. The acts or declarations of any one of two or more persons who conspire to commit an offense, said or done in the presence of the others in the furtherance of their common design are admissible against any of them.[76] Voluntary confessions by the defendant that he committed the crime with which he is charged are admissible in evidence.[77] Involuntary confessions are not admissible. An involuntary confession is one induced by hope of reward or fear of punishment with reference to the particular charge held out by some person in authority.[78] Persons in authority, as the term is here used, includes the prosecuting witness, the prosecuting

72 United States v. Wilson, 60 Fed. 890; Bedford v. State, 36 Nebr. 702, 55 N. W. 263; Davis v. State, 32 Tex. Cr. 377, 23 S. W. 794.

73 Simons v. People, 150 Ill. 66, 36 N. E. 1019; Jones v. State, 71 Ind. 66; State v. Johnson, 118 Mo. 491, 24 S. W. 229, 40 Am. St. 405.

74 Reynolds v. United States, 98 U. S. 145, 25 L. ed. 244; Bass v. State, 136 Ind. 165, 36 N. E. 124; Brown v. Commonwealth, 73 Pa. St. 321, 13 Am. Rep. 740.

75 Richards v. State, 36 Nebr. 17, 53 N. W. 1027; Baccio v. People, 41 N. Y. 265; Proper v. State, 85 Wis. 615, 55 N. W. 1035.

76 Williams v. State, 47 Ind. 568; Commonwealth v. Scott, 123 Mass. 222, 25 Am. Rep. 81; People v. Arnold, 46 Mich. 268, 9 N. W. 406; People v. Davis, 56 N. Y. 95.

77 Walker v. State, 136 Ind. 663, 36 N. E. 356; Commonwealth v. Johnson, 162 Pa. St. 63, 29 Atl. 280.

78 Commonwealth v. Myers, 160 Mass. 530, 36 N. E. 481; State v. Drake, 113 N. Car. 624, 18 S. E. 166.

attorney, the magistrate or judge, and the officer who has the accused in custody.[79] A witness must only state facts and not opinions, as a general rule.[80] When some question of science or art is involved the opinion of a person specially skilled in such matters may be given in evidence.[81] The defendant always may show that he has a good character,[82] but the prosecutor may not show that he has a bad character until the accused has introduced evidence of good character, unless the character of the accused is itself in issue.[83] Also in homicide cases where the defendant claims that he acted in self defense, he may show that the deceased was a violent and dangerous man.[84]

§ 983. Presumptions and burden of proof.—A person charged with crime is presumed to be innocent and the state must prove every element of his offense and convince the jury of his guilt beyond a reasonable doubt.[85] This requires a much higher degree of proof than in civil cases where the plaintiff is only required to prove his case by a preponderance of the evidence. When there is a defense of insanity to a criminal charge, the correct rule is, after the defendant has introduced evidence tending to show insanity, the burden is then upon the state to show beyond a reasonable doubt that the defendant is sane.[86] An insane person

79 State v. Staley, 14 Minn. 105; People v. Phillips, 42 N. Y. 200.

80 Jones v. State, 58 Ark. 390, 24 S. W. 1073; State v. Coella, 8 Wash. 512, 36 Pac. 474.

81 State v. Ginger, 80 Iowa 574, 46 N. W. 657; Coyle v. Commonwealth, 104 Pa. St. 117.

82 Hall v. State, 132 Ind. 317, 31 N. E. 536; Stover v. People, 56 N. Y. 315.

83 People v. White, 14 Wend. (N. Y.) 111.

84 Garner v. State, 28 Fla. 113, 9 So. 835, 29 Am. St. 232; Cannon v. People, 141 Ill. 270, 30 N. E. 1027.

85 Spies v. People, 122 Ill. 1, 12 N. E. 865, 17 N. E. 898, 3 Am. St. 320; Fanton v. State, 50 Nebr. 351, 69 N. W. 953, 36 L. R. A. 158.

86 United States v. Foulkner, 35 Fed. 730; Grubb v. State, 117 Ind. 297, 20 N. E. 257, 725.

can not commit a crime. Some courts erroneously hold that the burden of proof is upon the defendant to establish his insanity by a preponderance of the evidence.[87]

[87] Commonwealth v. Rogers, 7 Metc. (Mass.) 500, 41 Am. Dec. 458; State v. Davis, 109 N. Car. 780, 14 S. E. 55.

CHAPTER LXXX.

PROCEEDINGS AFTER VERDICT.

§ 990. Motion in arrest of judgment.—After verdict of conviction a motion in arrest of judgment will lie for any fatal error which appears upon the record.[1] The most common ground for such a motion is insufficiency of the indictment to sustain the judgment.[2] In some states this motion will lie only for grounds which are specified in the statutes. Since misconduct on the part of the jury does not appear on the face of the record, motion in arrest will not lie for such ground,[3] nor will it lie for any defects which are cured by the verdict, such as a formal defect in the indictment.[4] The court, on its own motion, may arrest the judgment.[5]

[1] Commonwealth v. Donahue, 126 Mass. 51; Hall v. Commonwealth, 80 Va. 555.

[2] Commonwealth v. Hinds, 101 Mass. 209; State v. Gove, 34 N. H. 510.

[3] Commonwealth v. Donahue, 126 Mass. 51; Hall v. Commonwealth, 80 Va. 555; State v. Martin, 38 W. Va. 568, 18 S. E. 748; Bellasis v. Hester, 1 Ld. Raym. 280.

[4] People v. Smith, 94 Mich. 644, 54 N. W. 487.

[5] United States v. Plummer, Fed. Cas. No. 16056, 3 Cliff. (U. S.) 28.

§ 991. Motion for new trial, and to set aside the verdict.—The defendant in all criminal cases is entitled to make a motion for new trial in the court where the cause was tried.[6] The general rule is that where an error does not injure the party or influence the result a new trial will not be granted.[7] It is also the general rule that if error is shown there is a presumption of injury.[8] The granting of a new trial is to a certain extent within the discretion of the court.[9] A motion for new trial should be made before judgment, or during the judgment term.[10] Among the grounds for motion for new trial is insufficiency of the evidence to support the verdict. This, more than some other grounds, is an appeal to the judicial discretion,[11] and a new trial is not usually granted if the evidence is conflicting or there is any evidence to sustain the verdict.[12] A verdict contrary to law will be set aside as a matter of course.[13] Newly discovered evidence is a common ground for a new trial.[14] A motion upon this ground must be supported by sufficient affidavits showing that the evidence was discovered since the trial,[15] that the

[6] Turner v. State, 175 Ind. 1, 93 N. E. 225; Gray v. Commonwealth, 101 Pa. St. 380, 47 Am. Rep. 733; 1 Bish. New Crim. L. (8th ed.), §§ 992, 1009, 1026.

[7] Ballew v. State, 36 Tex. 98; Cremeans v. Commonwealth, 104 Va. 860, 52 S. E. 362, 2 L. R. A. (N. S.) 721.

[8] State v. Coleman, 186 Mo. 151, 84 S. W. 978, 69 L. R. A. 381; Tyson v. State, 14 Tex. App. 338.

[9] Smith v. State, 165 Ala. 50, 51 So. 610; Rex v. Edmonds, 4 B. & Ald. 471.

[10] Palatka, etc., R. Co. v. State, 23 Fla. 546, 3 So. 158, 11 Am. St. 395; Keefer v. State, 174 Ind. 588, 92 N. E. 656; Burke v. State, 72 Ind. 392.

[11] People v. Chun Heong, 86 Cal. 329, 24 Pac. 1021; Williams v. State, 85 Ga. 535, 11 S. E. 859.

[12] United States v. Ducournau, 54 Fed. 138; People v. Chun Heong, 86 Cal. 329, 24 Pac. 1021; Williams v. State, 85 Ga. 535, 11 S. E. 859.

[13] State v. Ingold, 4 Jones L. (N. Car.) 216, 67 Am. Dec. 283; Sutton v. State, 41 Tex. 513.

[14] Andersen v. State, 43 Conn. 514, 21 Am. Rep. 669; Smith v. State, 60 Tex. Cr. 81, 131 S. W. 313.

[15] Holeman v. State, 13 Ark. 105; Stalcup v. State, 129 Ind. 519, 28 N. E. 1116.

failure to discover it earlier was not from lack of diligence,[16] that it can probably be obtained at the new trial,[17] and that it is material and such as will probably change the result.[18] Ordinarily a new trial will not be granted for evidence that is merely cumulative,[19] or impeaches a witness,[20] but it is necessary that the evidence should fall clearly within the will and be cumulative [20a] or impeaching evidence.[21] Surprise at the testimony of a witness may also be a ground for a new trial.[23] A new trial also may be granted for misconduct of the jury,[24] or for prejudicial errors in the court's charge,[25] or occasionally for the erroneous admission or exclusion of evidence;[26] and it has been granted because of the misconduct or gross ignorance of the defendant's counsel.[27] Motion for new trial does not lie for defects in pleading.[28]

§ 992. Sentencing the prisoner.—It is the court's duty to render judgment and pronounce sentence. After plea or verdict of guilty sentence should be given in open court[29] on a judicial day,[30] in the presence of the accused,[31] unless merely a fine is imposed. If he is convicted of a capital crime the practice is to ask the prisoner whether he has any-

[16] Reagan v. State, 28 Tex. App. 227, 12 S. W. 601, 19 Am. St. 833; State v. Sargood, 80 Vt. 412, 68 Atl. 51, 130 Am. St. 992.

[17] Friar v. State, 3 How. (Miss.) 422.

[18] Young v. State, 56 Ga. 403; Rainey v. State, 53 Ind. 278.

[19] Andersen v. State, 43 Conn. 514, 21 Am. Rep. 669; State v. Stumbo, 26 Mo. 306.

[20] Walsh v. People, 65 Ill. 58, 16 Am. Rep. 569; Hauck v. State, 1 Tex. App. 357.

[20a] Fletcher v. People, 117 Ill. 184, 7 N. E. 80.

[21] State v. Townsend, 7 Wash. 462, 35 Pac. 367.

[23] Thomas v. State, 52 Ga. 509; State v. Williams, 27 Vt. 724.

[24] Dooley v. State, 28 Ind. 239.

[25] Anonymous, 2 Salk. 649; Howe v. Strode, 2 Wils. 269.

[26] Rex v. Ball, Russ. & R. 132.

[27] State v. Jones, 12 Mo. App. 93; Augustine v. State, 20 Tex. 450.

[28] White v. State, 93 Ga. 47, 19 S. E. 49.

[29] See also, Reed v. State, 147 Ind. 41, 46 N. E. 135.

[30] Blood v. Bates, 31 Vt. 147.

[31] Young v. State, 39 Ala. 357; Harris v. People, 130 Ill. 457, 22 N. E. 826.

thing to say why sentence should not be pronounced against him.[32] It is held in some states, however, that it is not essential to ask this question[33] in other than capital felonies, and it has been held that it is not necessary in capital cases.[34] It is not necessary to render judgment or pronounce sentence immediately after conviction.[35]

§ 993. The sentence.—An illegal sentence does not entitle the prisoner to be discharged or even to be granted a new trial.[36]

The severity of the sentence is in the sound discretion of the court, within the limits prescribed by law. It is only in very exceptional cases that the appellate court will disturb it. It has been held that a sentence of imprisonment for ninety-nine years will not be disturbed where the law allows an imprisonment for life or for any term of years.[37] The Constitution of the United States and the state constitutions prohibit cruel and unusual punishments; this prevents such punishments as burning, branding, mutilating, the pillory or the ducking stool, but the ordinary modes of punishment, such as hanging, imprisonment and fines, are not prohibited.[38]

§ 994. Cumulative sentences.—Where the accused is convicted on two or more counts of the same indictment, and the different counts are descriptive of the same offense, he can be sentenced on only one count.[39] But where the counts are not descriptive of the same offense, he may be sentenced

[32] Ball v. United States, 140 U. S. 118, 35 L. ed. 377; Dougherty v. Commonwealth, 69 Pa. 286.

[33] Bressler v. People, 117 Ill. 422, 8 N. E. 63.

[34] Gannon v. People, 127 Ill. 507, 21 N. E. 525, 11 Am. St. 147.

[35] 1 Chitty Crim. L. 699.

[36] In re Bonner, 151 U. S. 242.

[37] Hickan v. People, 137 Ill. 75, 27 N. E. 88.

[38] Black Const. Law, 510; Cooley Const. Lim. (7th ed.), 471.

[39] Claassen v. United States, 142 U. S. 140, 35 L. ed. 966; 2 Bish. New Crim. Proc., § 1327.

on each count.[40] Also, where two sentences to imprisonment are imposed upon the same person at the same time, they should be made cumulative.[41] It has been held that where this is not done they shall be so regarded.[42] There are, however, some decisions to the contrary.[43] Sentences are cumulative where one begins upon the expiration of the other.

§ 995. **Execution of the sentence.**—If the sentence is imprisonment, it begins at once. At common law, if an imprisonment is to commence on the expiration of another, it must be so stated in the sentence, or the terms of the two punishments will run simultaneously.[44] If the sentence is death, the time is not usually set in the sentence, but is afterwards fixed by the court or the officer in charge of the execution,[45] or in some states by the governor.[46] If a prisoner escapes and is retaken, the time during which he was out of prison is not counted in the term of his sentence.[47] The execution of a capital sentence upon a pregnant woman will be delayed until after the birth of her child.[48]

40 United States v. Peeke, 153 Fed. 166, 9 L. R. A. (N. S.) 1043; Ex parte Peeke, 144 Fed. 1016; Commonwealth v. Birdsall, 69 Pa. 482, 8 Am. Rep. 283.

41 Martin v. People, 76 Ill. 499; Ex parte Roberts, 9 Nev. 44, 16 Am. Rep. 1.

42 Mullinx v. People, 76 Ill. 211; Booth v. Commonwealth, 5 Metc. (Mass.) 535; 3 South. Law. Rev. (N. S.) 50.

43 People v. Liscomb (Tweed's Case), 60 N. Y. 559, 19 Am. Rep. 211.

44 State v. Smith, 5 Day. (Conn.) 175, 5 Am. Dec. 132; Martin v. People, 76 Ill. 499.

45 In re Storti, 178 Mass. 549, 60 N. E. 210, 52 L. R. A. 520.

46 In re Dyer, 56 Kans. 489, 43 Pac. 783; Webster v. Commonwealth, 5 Cush. (Mass.) 386.

47 Neal v. State, 104 Ga. 509, 517, 30 S. E. 858, 69 Am. St. 175, 42 L. R. A. 190; In re Edwards, 43 N. J. L. 555, 39 Am. Rep. 610; Sartain v. State, 10 Tex. App. 651, 38 Am. Rep. 653n.

48 1 Chitty Crim. L. 760; 2 Hale P. C. 413. See also, Holeman v. State, 13 Ark. 105; State v. Arden, 1 Bay (S. Car.) 487.

§ 996. **Review of the proceedings.**—The method at common law of reviewing a criminal case was by a writ of error issuing upon application from the appellate court to the trial court and commanding the entire record to be sent up for review. Such a writ would lie only for errors of record and could issue only to a court of record.[49] If the court was not a court of record or the proceeding summary, the proper remedy was certiorari.[50] The writ of error will issue only to review a final judgment.[51] The only remedy for review of errors of fact was the writ of error coram nobis where the rehearing was in the court of trial.[52]

The procedure for review of a criminal case in many states is by appeal, not writ of error; in others by a bill of exceptions. Among grounds for reversal on appeal are insufficiency of the evidence to sustain a conviction, error in admitting or excluding testimony, or erroneous instructions to the jury prejudicial to the defendant. In order to take advantage of such errors by appeal, proper and seasonable objection must have been made in the trial court. It is the general rule that a writ of error or appeal by the state from a verdict of acquittal will not lie,[53] though in some jurisdictions the state may appeal to settle questions of law for future guidance.

[49] White v. Wagar, 185 Ill. 195, 57 N. E. 26, 50 L. R. A. 60, 2 Bish. New Crim. Proc., § 1364.

[50] White v. Wagar, 185 Ill. 195, 57 N. E. 26, 50 L. R. A. 60; 2 Bish. New Crim. Proc., § 1364.

[51] Patten v. People, 18 Mich. 314, 100 Am. Dec. 173; Kinsley v. State, 3 Ohio St. 508.

[52] State v. Stanley, 225 Mo. 525, 125 S. W. 475; Irwin v. Grey, L. R. 2, H. L. 20; Stephen Pl. (4th ed.), 117, 118, 119.

[53] United States v. Sanges, 144 U. S. 310, 36 L. ed. 445; Commonwealth v. Cummings, 3 Cush. (Mass.) 212, 50 Am. Dec. 732; Commonwealth v. Steimling, 156 Pa. St. 400, 27 Atl. 297; 2 Bish. New Crim. Proc., § 1272.

§ 997. **Habeas corpus.**—When a person is illegally deprived of his liberty, the law provides a remedy for him by means of the writ of habeas corpus.[54] Through this writ he may obtain his speedy release.

In early periods the common law provided that any one imprisoned had the right by the writ of habeas corpus to bring his case before the king's bench, which would set him at liberty if no specific offense was charged against him, or admit him to bail if his offense was bailable. There were many contests between the people and the crown over this right, but the Habeas Corpus Act of 31 Car. II. finally secured the right for all time.[55]

The United States Constitution and most of the state constitutions recognize and secure this right to the people of this country. However, it may be suspended when in cases of rebellion or invasion the public safety demands it.[56]

All courts of general jurisdiction, or the judges thereof when the courts are not in session, have the power to issue writs of habeas corpus. Judges of the Supreme or higher courts may issue the writ anywhere in their jurisdictions.[57] Application should be made to the nearest court.[58]

Upon a hearing secured by this writ, the court will release one who is privileged from arrest,[59] discharge one arrested on a void warrant,[60] admit one to bail if wrongfully denied,[61]

[54] Ex parte Watkins, 3 Pet. (U. S.) 193, 7 L. ed. 650; Ex parte Madison (Wyo.), 169 Pac. 336; Myers v. Halligan, 244 Fed. 420, 157 C. C. A. 46; Ex parte McKay (Tex. Cr.), 199 S. W. 637.

[55] Ex parte Merryman, Fed. Cas. No. 9487, Taney (U. S.) 246.

[56] U. S. Const., Art. 1, § 9. See also, Ex parte Milligan, 4 Wall. (U. S.) 2, 18 L. ed. 281; In re Kemp's case, 16 Wis. 382.

[57] Ex parte Clarke, 100 U. S. 399, 25 L. ed. 715.

[58] Thompson v. Oglesby, 42 Iowa 598; Ex parte Lynn, 19 Tex. App. 120.

[59] Ex parte Dakins, 16 C. B. 77.

[60] O'Malia v. Wentworth, 65 Maine 129; Ex parte Smith, 5 Cow. (N. Y.) 273. See also, People v. Green, 281 Ill. 52, 117 N. E. 764; Stoneberg v. Morgan, 246 Fed. 98, 158 C. C. A. 324; Ex parte Kostriken (Cal. App.), 168 Pac. 150.

[61] United States v. Hamilton, 3 Dall. (U. S.) 17, 1 L. ed. 490; In re Troia, 64 Cal. 152, 28 Pac. 231.

or an excessive amount asked,[62] or test the regularity of extradition proceedings.[63] After judgment the only questions which can be reviewed are the jurisdiction of the court[64] and its power to render the sentence imposed.[65]

One who is entitled to release because of the running of the statute of limitations against his offense,[66] or who is retained in prison after pardon, may secure his liberty by habeas corpus.[67]

The federal courts on habeas corpus will release one who is imprisoned by state authorities in violation of the Constitution, laws or treaties of the United States, but will not interfere with the ordinary administration of justice in the state by its courts.[68] A state court can not issue the writ for the release of one held under United States authority.[69]

A petition for habeas corpus should be verified [70] and should show fully the facts entitling the prisoner to release.[71] If the prisoner is unable himself to make the application for the writ, a relative or friend may do so for him.[72]

The writ issues in the name of the President of the United States or in the name of the state,[73] must be signed by the judge granting it;[74] and is directed to the one who detains the prisoner[75] commanding him to bring the body of the

62 Lynch v. People, 38 Ill. 494.

63 United States v. Rauscher, 119 U. S. 407, 30 L. ed. 425; Ex parte Smith, Fed. Cas. No. 12968, 3 McLean (U. S.) 121.

64 Ex parte Sam, 51 Ala. 34.

65 Ex parte Watkins, 7 Pet. (U. S.) 568, 8 L. ed. 786.

66 State v. Maurignos, T. U. P. Charlt. (Ga.) 24.

67 People v. Cavanagh, 2 Abb. Pr. (N. Y.) 84, 2 Park. A. 650.

68 Ex parte Royall, 117 U. S. 241, 29 L. ed. 868.

69 Ableman v. Booth, 21 How. (U. S.) 506, 16 L. ed. 169.

70 Ex parte Walpole, 84 Cal. 584, 24 Pac. 308.

71 Ex parte Walpole, 84 Cal. 584, 24 Pac. 308; Sim's Case, 7 Cush. (Mass.) 285.

72 Ferguson v. Ferguson, 36 Mo. 197; People v. Mercein, 3 Hill (N. Y.) 399.

73 Church Hab. Corp., § 110.

74 Stat. 31 Car. II.

75 Nicols v. Cornelius, 7 Ind. 611.

prisoner before the court or judge and show why he detains him. The prosecuting officer should have notice of the writ's issuance.[76]

The person to whom the writ is directed must make a return in writing,[77] either denying the detention[78] or showing cause for it,[79] and must produce the prisoner in court or show cause.[80] After return and hearing of evidence the prisoner will be discharged unless cause appears for his detention.[81]

If one court fails to discharge on the writ, application may be made to another court having jurisdiction.[82] One who has been released on habeas corpus and rearrested should be discharged on a new writ.[83]

76 Ex parte Smith, Fed. Cas. No. 12968, 3 McLean (U. S.) 121.

77 Seavey v. Seymour, Fed. Cas. No. 12596, 3 Cliff. (U. S.) 439.

78 United States v. Green, Fed. Cas. No. 15256, 3 Mason (U. S.) 482.

79 State ex rel. Neider v. Reuff, 29 W. Va. 751.

80 Rex v. Bethuen, And. 281.

81 In re Doo Woon, 18 Fed. 898, 9 Sawy. (U. S.) 417.

82 Ex parte Pattison, 56 Miss. 161.

83 In re Da Costa, 1 Park. Cr. (N. Y.) 129.

INDEX

[*References are to Sections*]

[*References are to Sections*]

[*References are to Sections*]

[*References are to Sections*]

[*References are to Sections*]

[*References are to Sections*]

[*References are to Sections*]

[*References are to Sections*]

C

[*References are to Sections*]

[*References are to Sections*]

[*References are to Sections*]

[*References are to Sections*]

[*References are to Sections*]

[*References are to Sections*]

[*References are to Sections*]

[*References are to Sections*]

[*References are to Sections*]

5

[*References are to Sections*]

[*References are to Sections*]

[References are to Sections]

[*References are to Sections*]

[*References are to Sections*]

I

[*References are to Sections*]

[*References are to Sections*]

[*References are to Sections*]

[*References are to Sections*]

[*References are to Sections*]

[*References are to Sections*]

M

[*References are to Sections*]

[*References are to Sections*]

[*References are to Sections*]

[*References are to Sections*]

[References are to Sections]

O

[*References are to Sections*]

[*References are to Sections*]

[*References are to Sections*]

[*References are to Sections*]

[*References are to Sections*]

[*References are to Sections*]

[*References are to Sections*]

[References are to Sections]

S

[*References are to Sections*]

[*References are to Sections*]

[*References are to Sections*]

[References are to Sections]

[*References are to Sections*]

Total number of pages
in this volume, 798

Lightning Source UK Ltd.
Milton Keynes UK
UKHW050247190119
335792UK00018B/687/P